UNDERSTANDING TEXTILES

FIFTH EDITION

PHYLLIS G. TORTORA
Queens College

BILLIE J. COLLIER
Louisiana State University

Merrill,
an imprint of Prentice Hall
Upper Saddle River, New Jersey   Columbus, Ohio

Library of Congress Cataloging-in-Publication Data

Tortora, Phyllis G.
      Understanding textiles / Phyllis G. Tortora, Billie J. Collier. —
5th ed.
      p. cm.
      Includes bibliographical references and index.
      ISBN 0-13-439225-6 (hardcover)
      1. Textile industry. 2. Textile fibers. 3. Textile fabrics.
I. Collier, Billie J. II. Title
TS1445.T55 1997   95-47801
677—dc20   CIP

Cover photo: ©Michael Agliolo/International Stock
Editor: Bradley J. Potthoff
Production Editor: Patricia S. Kelly
Design Coordinator: Jill E. Bonar
Text Designer: Proof Positive/Farrowlyne Assoc., Inc.
Cover Designer: Brian Deep
Production Manager: Laura Messerly

This book was set in AGaramond by The Clarinda Company and was printed and bound by Courier/Kendallville, Inc. The cover was printed by Phoenix Color Corp.

© 1997 by Prentice-Hall, Inc.
Simon & Schuster/A Viacom Company
Upper Saddle River, New Jersey 07458

Earlier editions © 1978, 1982, 1987, and 1992 by Macmillan Publishing Company.

Printed in the United States of America

10 9 8 7 6 5 4 3 2 1

ISBN: 0-13-439225-6

Prentice-Hall International (UK) Limited, *London*
Prentice-Hall of Australia Pty. Limited, *Sydney*
Prentice-Hall of Canada, Inc., *Toronto*
Prentice-Hall Hispanoamericana, S. A., *Mexico*
Prentice-Hall of India Private Limited, *New Delhi*
Prentice-Hall of Japan, Inc., *Tokyo*
Simon & Schuster Asia Pte. Ltd., *Singapore*
Editora Prentice-Hall do Brasil, Ltda., *Rio de Janeiro*

PREFACE

The purpose of this book is to provide a common background for students who are making a study of textiles. Some students may be planning to enter one of the many career areas that require some knowledge about textiles. Others may be interested in becoming better informed consumers. Whatever may motivate students to enter an introductory course in textiles, certain basic concepts are essential to their understanding of the subject. It is our hope that these concepts are presented in a clear, logically developed format.

The text begins with an overview of the textile industry. The majority of students are likely to begin their study of textiles without any prior knowledge of the origin, manufacture, and distribution of the wide variety of textile products they use daily. The first chapter presents an overview of the journey of textile products that begins with fiber production and goes on to manufacture of yarns or other components, to fabric production, to design, and to manufacture of the final product. It is our intention to set a context for the chapters that follow, in which basic processes, rooted in science and technology, are explored in depth, beginning with the basic building blocks of fabrics: fibers. In subsequent chapters emphasis is placed on the interrelationships of fibers, yarns, fabric constructions, and finishes. What is known about each of these components is applied to the understanding of textile behavior and performance.

To this end, diagrams and photographs have been selected with care to illustrate the concepts and processes described in the text. Many students study in parts of the country where they have no access to field trips to textile manufacturing sites; therefore, photographs of various types of machinery are included.

Each chapter includes review questions that invite students to summarize and apply the concepts presented in the text.

The recommended readings at the end of each chapter have been selected to complement the subject matter of the chapters. We have made a conscious effort to include both relatively elementary and highly technical material so as to introduce students to the variety of resources in the field. We have also tried to include readings from the most widely used periodicals in the field. An extensive bibliography, broken down under special subject headings, is appended to the book.

After chapter 1 introduces the reader to the various elements from which textiles are made, their historical development, and the present-day organization of the textile industry, chapters 2 and 3 establish the relationship of fiber properties to fiber behavior. Chapter 2 focuses on physical properties of fibers, and chapter 3 deals with the chemical and physical concepts basic to understanding the behavior of textile fibers. Chapter 3 is written for the reader who has had no previous chemistry training. The students should be able to gain some understanding of these elementary concepts and to appreciate not only the integral role that chemistry plays in the manufacture and finishing of textile products but also the role of chemistry in the use and care of textiles by consumers. Often this kind of material is integrated into varying parts of a text. We have not done so here because a separate chapter on the subjects offers a better opportunity to explain elementary chemical terminology and concepts and to relate these concepts to the science of textiles. Some teachers may prefer to emphasize this chapter a great deal, whereas others may wish to discuss it briefly. Either approach may be taken.

The chapters on textile fibers (chapters 4 to 14) have been reordered in this fifth edition. This material begins with the natural fibers (chapters 4 and 5). Cellulosic fibers are discussed first because they are simpler in structure than the protein fibers and because cotton is so widely used. Protein fibers, with emphasis on wool and silk, follow. Chapter 6, new to this edition, introduces important concepts about manufactured fibers, after which chapter 7 reviews manufactured cellulosic fibers. Chapters 8 to 14 each cover related groups of manufactured fibers.

Chapters about fibers are all organized in the same way, with many of the topic headings being repeated in each chapter. These topic headings are also used in chapter 2, "Textile Fibers and Their Properties," in order to facilitate comparisons between fibers. For those manufactured fibers that are produced under a number of trademarks, a table of trademarks is included. This feature is new in this edition. Each chapter ends with a table summarizing some of the more important characteristics of the major fiber groups discussed in that chapter.

From fibers the text moves to yarns and their production (chapter 15), and from yarns the text goes on to fabric structures. Those who have used previous editions of this text will note that chapters dealing with fabric manufacture have been reorganized, with separate chapters dealing with woven fabrics (chapter 16), knitted fabrics (chapter 17), nonwoven fabrics (chapter 18), and multicomponent fabrics (chapter 19). These chapters deal with processes ranging from traditional methods of manufacture to innovations in the production of materials such as high technology composites.

The various methods of finishing fabrics and adding color and design are discussed in chapters 20 to 23. Chapter 24, "The Care of Textile Products," is included as a separate chapter, even though some material about the care of textiles is also included in preceding chapters, because of the importance of care in relation to consumer satisfaction with textiles. Chapter 25 explores the important topic of "Textiles and the Environment, Health, and Safety."

Throughout the text, the authors have incorporated material about textile testing and evaluation as it relates to specific topics. Also integrated into the text at various places are Consumer Boxes that explore in depth topics of particular interest to consumers. These boxes include such diverse topics as how to select carpet, T-shirts, developments in manufacture of recycled polyester, and washable silk apparel.

The final chapter has been much expanded. It helps the reader to see how fiber, yarn, fabric construction, and finishes contribute to the total structure of the fabric and how the structure of the fabric is, in turn, related to its performance. This is further illustrated by a number of case studies of fabrics for specific uses, such as sail cloth, bathing suits, and automotive textiles.

Special reference tools within the text are provided in appendices. These include the aforementioned bibliography, a glossary of terms (many from the *Annual Book of ASTM Standards*), and a summary of textile legislation.

A Basic Textiles Swatch Kit is available for use in conjunction with this edition of *Understanding Textiles*. The swatch kit consists of 120 fabric swatches, mounting sheets, a master list with fabric name/description/fiber content, and a 3-ring binder. It is available through Textile Fabric Consultants, Inc., P.O. Box 111431, Nashville, TN 37222/615-459-7510.

Acknowledgments

We have received assistance in the preparation of this revision from many individuals and organizations. They range from the encouragement and support provided by our families, especially our respective husbands, Vincent Tortora and Dr. John R. Collier, to the assistance of Melissa Phillips and Julia Thames, graduate students in the School of Human Ecology, Louisiana State University.

We extend our thanks to the librarians and staff of the libraries at Fashion Institute of Technology, N.Y.; Louisiana State University; Queens College; and the Port Washington, N.Y., and New York City Public libraries.

A number of readers from academic institutions provided invaluable input. These included Dr. Robert S. Merkel, Florida International University, whose reviews not only of this but of previous editions have been exceptionally helpful; Mary Ann Moore, Florida State University; Theresa Perenich, University of Georgia; Mary W. Warnock, University of Arkansas; and Yiqi Yang, Institute of Textile Technology.

Finally, we want to thank the many individuals and trade and professional associations from the textile industry who provided both information and illustrations. Individuals or organizations who provided illustrative materials are acknowledged in the captions of the figures. Among the trade associations that provided useful information were the American Textile Manufacturers Institute (ATMI); American Society for Testing and Materials (ASTM); Crafted with Pride in the U.S.A. Council, Inc.; INDA, the Association of the Nonwovens Industry; and the International Fabricare Institute (IFI).

Some individuals, however, should be singled out for special mention: Jess Barr, National Cotton Council of America, for cotton data; Pauline Delli Carpini, International Linen Promotion Council, for data and illustrations; Bob Frei, Mayer Textile Machine Corporation, for information and illustrations related to knitting and stitchbonding; Bill Hummelsine of Wellman, Inc.; Christie Ingrassia, Mohair Council of America, for mohair data and illustrations; Lewis Rabbage of Monarch Knitting Machinery Company, for help obtaining knitting machinery photographs; Glyn Raven of Courtaulds, for data about and illustrations of Tencel®; and Mike Ravnitzky of Industrial Fabrics Association International (IFAI), for his willingness to read and critique sections of the text.

Space does not permit the specific listing of many others who also assisted, but readers should know that without the help of representatives of the textile industry we could not have completed this revision.

Brief Contents

CONTENTS

CHAPTER 5
Protein Fibers   **93**

CHAPTER 15
Making Fibers into Yarns   219

CHAPTER 16
Woven Fabrics   253

CHAPTER 22
Adding Color to Textiles   409

CHAPTER 23
Textile Printing and Design   427

INTRODUCTION

Each day each of us makes decisions about textiles. From the simplest choice of what clothes to wear to the commitment of a major portion of the family budget to buy a new carpet, judgments about the performance, durability, attractiveness, and care of textiles are consciously or unconsciously made. The economic implications of decisions about fibers, yarns, and fabrics obviously increase if someone is involved professionally with textiles. But whether or not understanding textiles is required for personal or for professional purposes, the key to informed decision making is knowledge about fibers, yarns, fabrics, and finishes and the ways in which these are interrelated.

Textiles fulfill so many purposes in our lives that their study can be approached in a number of ways. Textiles may be seen as being purely utilitarian, in relationship to the numerous purposes they serve. On awaking in the morning, for example, we climb out from under sheets and blankets and step into slippers and a robe. We wash our faces with washcloths, dry them with towels, and put on clothing for the day. Even the bristles of our toothbrushes are made from textile fibers. If we get into a car or bus, we sit on upholstered seats; the machine moves on tires reinforced with strong textile cords. We stand on carpets, sit on upholstered furniture, and look out of curtained windows. The insulation of our houses may be glass textile fiber. Not only are golf clubs, tennis rackets, and ski poles reinforced with textile fibers, but so are roads, bridges, and buildings. Strong, heat-resistant textile fibers in the nose cones of spaceships travel to distant planets. Physicians implant artificial arteries made of textiles or use fibers for surgery that gradually dissolve as wounds heal. Few of our manufactured products could be made without textile conveyor belts. Even our processed foods have been filtered through textile filter paper. There is truly no aspect of modern life that is untouched by some area of textiles. (See Figure 1.1.)

Some individual or some group of persons will be the ultimate consumer of each textile product. The ultimate consumer selects the product for a particular end use, whether that use be a fashionable garment or a fabric used to reinforce high technology building materials. In all cases, consumers want to select products that will perform well in the projected end uses. Most also seek to minimize cost. The ways in which textiles are produced affect their costs. Some steps in manufacturing are more expensive than others. Manufacturers may be able to choose one procedure instead of another. When alternatives are available, manufacturers are likely to select processes that will maximize their profits while making products that will sell at competitive prices and also fulfill the customers' desire for satisfactory performance. Many products must also meet the demands of current fashion.

Even though we all personally experience textiles at home, at work, and at play, we usually encounter only the complete product; rarely do we deal with the individual components. But each finished product makes a long journey from its beginnings in the laboratory or on the farm to the place where it is acquired by the ultimate consumer. An introductory course in textile study can be a sort of road map or itinerary of that journey; therefore, this text is organized to begin with the first steps in the long progression from fiber to completed fabric and goes on to examine subsequent steps in a generally chronological sequence.

If you were to take the shirt or sweater that you are wearing at this moment and break it down into its components, you would have to work backward, taking apart the fabric structure. Most likely your garment is woven or knitted. Weaving and knitting are the two most common means of creating fabrics for apparel, although other methods do exist. Both weaving and knitting are subject to a great many possible variations, and these differences contribute to the enormous variability in appearance, drapability, texture, crease recovery, handle, and the many other qualities of fabrics.

To take a woven or knitted structure apart requires that the fabric be unraveled into the yarns from which it was constructed. The yarns (with some few exceptions) are likely to have been made from short or long continuous fibers that are twisted together. By untwisting the yarns, it should be possible to separate the yarn into a number of small, fine, hairlike fibers. These fibers are the basic units that make up the majority of textile products encountered in apparel and home furnishings. (See Figure 1.2.)

Fibers

Textile fibers exist in nature or are created through technology. Technical definitions of the term *textile fiber* such as that of the American Society for Testing Materials (ASTM) tend to stress their dimensions: "a generic term for any one of the various types of matter that form the basic elements of a textile and that is characterized by having a length at least 100 times its diameter" (ASTM 1986)[1]

Although this may explain how a fiber looks, some materials that do fit this definition are not suitable for use in textiles. The fibrous structure of an overcooked pot roast, for example, is obviously not suitable for use in a textile. Fibers appropriate for

---

1. A glossary of technical terms is provided in Appendix B.

Figure 1.1

Fibers are used in applications that range from apparel to high technology. (a) Mountain climber in active wear made from polypropylene fiber. Photograph courtesy of Helly-Hansen, Inc. (b) Sofa upholstered in fabric made from olefin fiber. Photograph courtesy of Amoco Fabrics and Fibers/West Point Pepperell. (c) Automobile airbags usually made from nylon or polyester fiber. Photograph courtesy of Industrial Fabrics Association International. (d) Nonwoven textile fabric used to stabilize the banks of a river. Photograph courtesy of Industrial Fabrics Association International. (e) Protective clothing made from high temperature–resistant high technology fibers. Photograph courtesy of Industrial Fabrics Association International.

a

b

c

d

e

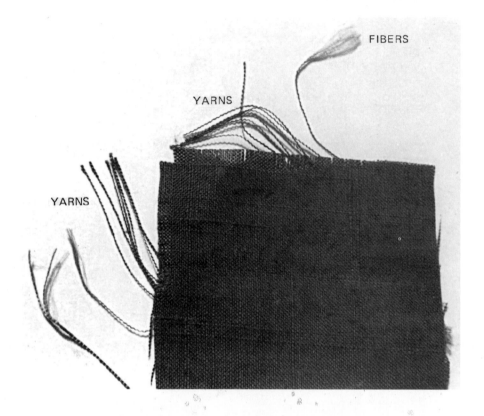

Figure 1.2

Fabric unravels into separate yarns. Yarns untwist into individual fibers.

use in textiles must have not only fineness and flexibility but also sufficient strength and durability to withstand conditions encountered in use.

To understand and evaluate suitability of different fibers for particular products, professionals in the textile field and consumers need to understand the physical and chemical properties of fibers. Particular fibers may be suitable for use in some textile applications but not in others. Carbon fiber, excellent for use in high technology products and sports equipment, is not useful for wearing apparel. Even among those fibers used in many apparel and home furnishing items, some are preferred for particular applications. Nylon has become synonymous with sheer women's hosiery—women may refer to their stockings as "nylons"—although in fact, in the past, fibers such as silk or rayon were used to make women's dress hosiery. On reflection, then, it is obvious that we tend to prefer some kinds of fibers for certain uses because those particular fibers offer some special advantages. For example, a particular fabric may seem to be more comfortable in warm or cool weather, may soil less easily, may dry more quickly, or may have an appearance that is best suited to a particular kind of occasion. The reasons for these differences among fibers reside in the specific properties of each fiber. If we are to have a clear understanding of the finished products and what qualities are to be expected of them, we need to know the fibers from which the product is made—and the characteristics of those fibers.

Yarns

Fibers alone cannot make a textile. Although it is possible to entangle groups of fibers or to bond them together in some way to create a textile (as is done with felt, for example), most of the cloth that is made into wearing apparel is formed from yarns. Yarns

Figure 1.3 Fabrics made from the same fiber and in the same (plain) weave look different because different kinds of yarns were used.

a

b

c

are assemblies of fibers twisted or otherwise held together in a continuous strand. An almost endless variety of yarns can be created by using different fibers, by twisting fibers more or less tightly, by combining two or more individual yarns to form a more complex yarn, or by giving yarns a wide range of other special treatments.

Just as different fibers will vary in their individual properties, different kinds of yarns have varying characteristics (Figure 1.3). And to complicate matters still further, two yarns of the same structure will have different properties if they are made from markedly different kinds of fibers.

Fabric Structures

Yarns must be united in some way if they are to form a cohesive structure. The transformation of individual yarns into textile fabrics can be accomplished by an individual with a pair of knitting needles, a crochet hook, or a hand loom or through the use of powerful machines that combine yarns by weaving, knitting, or stitch bonding to produce thousands of yards of completed fabrics. As with fibers and yarns, the

Figure 1.4

Fabrics made from the same fiber and from similar types of yarns look different because different types of weaves were used in their construction.

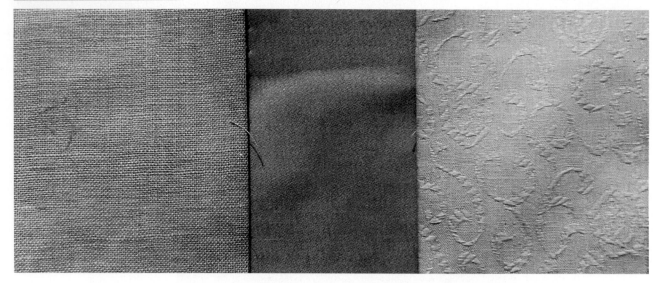

potential for variations in the structure is enormous, and a walk through any department store will reveal to even the most casual observer the almost endless variety of textile structures produced and consumed by the public in the form of apparel or household textiles.

And, once again, if the construction being used is varied, the resulting properties will differ. Furthermore, even when the same weave or knit construction is used, the end product will be distinctive if the fiber or yarn type is varied (Figure 1.4).

Finishing and Coloring

As the reader will learn, certain properties are inherent to each fiber, yarn, or fabric structure. Consumers find some of these properties desirable, while others are not valued. For example, fabrics of synthetic fibers dry quickly after laundering. Most consumers value this quality. But the same fabrics may tend to build up static electric charges, producing small electrical shocks or "static cling." Consumers do not like this quality. When a fiber, yarn, or fabric has unacceptable properties, special treatments called *finishes* may be applied to the fiber, yarn, or fabric to overcome undesirable properties. Finishes may be used to give to the fibers, yarns, or fabrics some properties that they do not normally possess but that will enhance performance. Static cling can thus be decreased or overcome. Most people are familiar with durable press finishes, for example, or may have purchased upholstered furniture with soil-resistant finishes. Other examples are discussed in the chapters dealing with finishes.

Appearance—color, pattern, or texture—is one of the major factors that leads consumers to purchase one product over another. Most textile fabrics intended for personal, household, or architectural use have been decorated in some way, by dyeing the fabric, printing designs on it, or weaving with varicolored yarns. Large segments of the textile industry are devoted to dyeing and/or printing fabrics, yarns, or fibers.

Textile History

The place of textiles in the world economy is enormously complex. How the production of textiles moved out of the home to become the business of huge, multinational corporations is a part of the evolution of modern society. The origin of textile production is lost in prehistory. No one knows exactly when the spinning and weaving of textiles began. Recent archeological discoveries of the imprint of woven material on clay pots dating from some 27,000 years ago indicate that people knew how to weave even before they domesticated plants and animals (Fowler 1995).

The oldest actual fragment of cloth found thus far is from archeological excavations at a site in southern Turkey called Cayonu. This piece of white fabric, probably linen, has been dated at about 7000 B.C. (Wilford 1993b). For most of the time that people have made fabrics, the only fibers available for use were found in nature, and the processes used to make these fibers into cloth were carried out by hand.

In spite of limited technology, people created a wide variety of fabrics for themselves and for use in their homes. Some of these fabrics, such as the simple, plain homespun cloth used daily, were strictly utilitarian. Others were elaborately patterned, printed, or dyed in order to satisfy the universal human need for beauty.

As the complex social and political organizations of people evolved, some of the small hunting villages were replaced by larger towns and eventually by cities and urban centers. Along with the growth of cities, nations, and empires, there were improvements in technology and the development of international trade, both of which involved textiles.

Textiles were sought-after items of commerce, with Chinese silk among the most prized items. Historians have long thought that silk from China first reached ancient Greece and Rome along a trade route called "the silk road" in the latter part of the second century B.C., but recent archeological evidence indicates that silk may have reached ancient Egypt as early as 1000 B.C. (Wilford 1993a).

The Romans imported not only Chinese silk but also cotton from nearby Egypt. Close to storehouses in Roman settlements excavated in India, archeologists have found facilities for dyeing and finishing cotton fabrics. The remains of many Roman towns contain evidence of installations for finishing and dyeing fabrics.

During the Middle Ages the production and trading of the plant called *woad,* an important source of dye, was a highly developed industry. Returning Crusaders brought luxurious silk and cotton fabrics from the Middle East to their homes in Europe, and these "foreign novelties" became an important item in trade. During the fifteenth century, the trade fairs of southern France provided a place for the active exchange of wools from England and silks from the Middle East. The economic activities surrounding these events gave rise to the first international banking arrangements.

Even the discovery of America was a result of the desire of Europeans to find a faster route not only to the spices but also to the textiles of the Orient. Once the American colonies had been established, the colonists sold native dyes such as indigo and cochineal to Europe and bought cottons from India. At the time when textiles were assuming an increasingly important role in international trade, advances were being made in the technology of textile production. Even so, the manufacture of cloth was still essentially a hand process. In Western Europe in 1700, spinning was still being done on a spinning wheel. Fabrics were woven by hand on looms for which the power was provided by the weaver.

The production of textiles was the first area to undergo industrialization during the Industrial Revolution, which occurred during the latter half of the 1700s in Western Europe, especially in Great Britain, France, and the Low Countries. The vast changes that took place during this period, not only technological but also sociological, economic, and cultural, included a major reorganization of manufacturing of a variety of goods. This came about during the seventeenth and eighteenth centuries when good-quality textile products, produced inexpensively in India and the Far East, were gradually replacing European goods in the international market. In England this competition produced a severe economic crisis within the textile field, and it became imperative that some means be found to increase domestic production, to lower costs, and to improve the quality of textiles. The solution was found in the substitution of machine or nonhuman power for hand processes and human power.

Many important inventions were made during this period that improved the output and quality of fabrics. The most important of these were spinning machines, automatic looms, and the cotton gin. These inventions provided the technological base for the industrialization of the textile industry. Each invention that improved one step of textile manufacture also had an effect on other parts of the process. For example, an improvement that increased the speed of spinning meant that looms were needed that consumed yarn more rapidly. More rapid yarn production required greater quantities of fiber. The growth of the textile industry was further hastened by the use of machines that were driven first by water power, then by steam, and finally by electricity.

The textile industry was fully mechanized by the early part of the nineteenth century. The next major developments in the field were to take place in the chemist's laboratory. Experimentation with the synthesis of dyestuffs in the laboratory rather than from natural plant materials led to the development and use of synthetic dyestuffs in the latter half of the nineteenth century. Other experiments proved that certain natural materials could be dissolved in chemical solvents and re-formed into fibrous form. This principle was used to produce "artificial silk" (now called rayon) from cellulosic materials such as mulberry leaves, wood chips, or cotton linters. By 1910 the first plant for manufacturing rayon had been established in the United States.

The manufacture of rayon marked the beginning of the manufactured textile fibers industry. Since that time, enormous advances have been made in the technology for making fibers, spinning them into yarns, constructing fabrics, and coloring and finishing them. Today, the textile industry utilizes a complex technology based on scientific processes and a vast economic organization. With the application of advanced technology to the textile field, textile use has expanded from the traditional areas of clothing and home furnishings into the fields of construction, medicine, aerospace, sporting goods, and industry. These applications have been made possible by the ability of textile scientists to "engineer" textile fibers, yarns, and fabrics for specific uses. At the same time that textile technology is making strides in new directions, the fabrics that consumers buy for clothing and household use also benefit from the development of new fibers, new methods of yarn and fabric construction, and new finishes for existing fibers and fabrics.

The Modern Textile Industry

Today, a huge international industrial complex encompasses the production of fiber, spinning of yarns, fabrication of cloth, dyeing, finishing, printing, and manufacture of goods for purchase. Consumers purchase products made of textiles. The story of the journey that these products make as they progress from fiber to yarn to fabric to finished product is not just the story of spinning yarns, weaving or knitting fabric, or constructing the end product. It is also the story of a complex network of interrelated industries.

The Fiber Producer

Natural Fibers

The producer of natural fibers and the producer of manufactured fibers are engaged in two very different businesses. The farmer who raises cotton, the rancher who herds sheep, or the grower of silkworms is trying to produce a maximum quantity of fiber from animal or vegetable sources. The grower may attempt to improve the quality of the seeds or breeding stock but is limited in production by natural factors. If the demand for the product increases or decreases, the grower cannot, like the manufactured fiber producer, simply increase or decrease the short-term supply of fiber.

The natural fiber producer sells fibers to mills or to wholesalers for resale. Except for cotton, which is produced in large quantities domestically, much of the supply of natural fibers such as wool, flax, and other vegetable fibers is produced abroad and imported into the United States. Natural fiber producers have little direct involvement in what happens to their products after they have been sold. The fabrication and finishing of the textiles are undertaken by other segments of the industry.

There is, of course, economic self-interest on the part of the fiber producer in the promotion of the fiber. To stimulate interest in or demand for products made of wool, cotton, linen, or silk fibers, fiber producers and others involved in their manufacture, processing, and sale have formed trade associations. The purpose of such trade associations is to stimulate interest in fabrics made from natural fibers through advertising, educational materials, and other promotional campaigns.

Some trade organizations maintained by natural fibers groups include the American Wool Council, the National Cotton Council of America, Cotton Inc., the Mohair Council, and the International Linen Promotion Association. These organizations produce educational materials for use in schools and by consumer groups, provide publicity photographs and information to the press, and sponsor a variety of advertising and public relations campaigns designed to keep the name of the fiber constantly before the public. Such publicity emphasizes the name of the fiber, not the fiber producer. (See Figure 1.5.)

Manufactured Fibers

The term *manufactured fiber* describes a fiber produced commercially through regeneration from natural materials or synthesized from chemicals.[2]

Trade associations in the manufactured fibers industry may be industrywide or specific to particular fibers. The American Fiber Manufacturers Association, Inc. (AFMA) is the trade organization for the manufactured fibers industry, conducting many of the same kinds of promotional activities as described for the natural fibers associations. AFMA always uses generic fiber names—such as polyester, nylon, rayon, and so on—in printed materials, while its individual fiber producing members con-

---

2. The term *manufactured fiber* has superceded the older term *man-made fiber* in most segments of the textile industry.

Examples of some trade association logos for both natural and manufactured fibers.

centrate on their trademarked fiber names, such as DuPont's Dacron® (polyester) or Hoechst Celanese's Trevira® (polyester).

Producers of particular fibers may also join together to form fiber-specific trade associations. The Acrylic Council, the American Polyolefin Association, and the Polyester Council of America are examples of fiber-focused trade associations.

Production in the manufactured fibers industry differs from the production of natural fibers in a number of ways. While the manufactured fibers industry must depend on available supplies of the raw materials from which fibers are made, this industry is not dependent on natural forces that regulate the supply of fiber. A great many manufactured fibers are made from materials derived from petroleum, and therefore supplies and costs of raw materials may be affected by changes in the price of oil. Manufacturers can regulate production according to supply and demand. Manufacturers can also help to create demand for increased quantities of fiber products through advertising and other publicity.

Many manufactured fiber producers and firms are, or were originally, chemical companies. The fiber manufacturer generally sells the fibers produced to a firm that will make yarns and/or fabrics. These fibers may be sold as unbranded products or commodities. When fibers are sold in this way, the purchaser has no obligation to the fiber manufacturer to produce a product of any specific quality. Products must meet no minimum standards. In short, the buyers can do whatever they wish with the fibers they have purchased.

Other fibers may be sold as *trademarked fibers.* The manufacturer owns the trademark, which is denoted by placing either the symbol ® or ™ after the trademarked name. Trademarked names are always capitalized—for example, Fortrel® polyester. The owner of a trademark can bring court action to prevent unauthorized use of the trademark. When the fiber manufacturer's trademarked name is carried by the finished product, the fiber manufacturer has some control over the quality of the fabric, although it is still possible that a poorly made garment could be constructed from the fabric. One advantage to the fabric and garment manufacturers of buying a trademarked fiber is that they can capitalize on the publicity and promotional materials distributed by the fiber manufacturer.

Licensed trademarked fibers are sold only to those manufacturers whose fabrics meet the standards established by the fiber manufacturer. Standards may be set in regard to the construction of fabrics, the manufacture of garments, and, in blends or combinations of two or more fibers, the appropriate proportion of fibers to be combined.

As an alternative to trademarking, some fiber companies assign *certification mark* names to yarns or fabrics made from their fibers. Such designations require that the items identified with the certification mark meet criteria established by the fiber manufacturer.

Not only do the fabric and garment manufacturers benefit from customer familiarity with the brand name of the fiber, but the fiber manufacturer often shares the costs of advertising or mounts intensive publicity campaigns to promote the fabric, the garment, and even retail outlets where the products are sold.

The interest of manufactured fiber producers in their products does not end when the fiber is sold. Because techniques for spinning and fabricating manufactured fibers may not be uniform for all fibers, the fiber producer provides technical assistance to the fabric manufacturer. Technical bulletins are published that recommend the most effective ways of processing fibers. Consultants from the fiber companies provide information about new developments in textile machinery and finishing. Research and development in fiber-producing companies is often focused on more effective ways of handling manufactured fibers during fabrication.

Fiber producers assist manufacturers of fabrics, garments, or other products to locate sources of yarns and fabrics. The marketing department of a fiber-producing company also maintains a library of fabrics that can be used by garment manufacturers and their designers.

A wide variety of other services is offered to the direct customers of the fiber companies and to the general public. Exhibits of current products are presented, often at trade and professional meetings. Educational materials for schools, retailers, and consumers are prepared and distributed. Retail stores may be assisted in promoting trademarked products through fashion shows, publicity materials, or cooperative advertising in which the fiber producer pays some part of the advertising costs. Fashion consultants may be available to assist the designers of fabrics and clothes.

Many of these activities are part of an organized advertising and public relations program. In addition to the services offered that result indirectly in publicity and goodwill for the company, direct advertising is also utilized. Besides advertising cooperatively with manufacturers of retail products and retail stores, fiber companies also advertise in publications ranging from those for the trade to general magazines.

Research and development (often abbreviated as R & D) is an important function in most large textile fiber companies. Researchers are constantly looking for new fibers, fiber modifications, and improvements in processing at all steps of manufacture. The whole synthetic fibers industry might be said to have grown out of the research and development program at the chemical company DuPont, for it was in this program that W. H. Carothers first synthesized nylon.

From the Fiber Manufacturer to the Fabric Producer

Fiber must be converted into yarn, except in some specialized "nonwoven" products where the fibers themselves are bonded into a cohesive structure. The production of yarns from short, staple fibers is done by *spinners*. When continuous filament yarns are given special treatments such as texturing, this is done by *throwsters*. *Yarn converters,* who may also be throwsters, dye yarns or add special protective finishes that facilitate knitting or weaving. Textile mills produce knitted, woven, or nonwoven goods. Completed cloth that has not been given any special finishes or coloration is known as *greige goods.*

The organization of the textile manufacturing industry differs from company to company and also exhibits some differences from one type of textile to another. Cotton fabrics, for example, may be made in a series of steps. One mill may take the raw fiber and turn it into yarn. Then the yarn may be sold to another mill that, in turn, weaves it into cloth. The cloth may be sold to yet another plant where it is dyed or finished. The wool industry, by contrast, has traditionally processed the fiber from beginning to end. The same mill buys the fiber, spins the yarn, weaves or knits the goods, and finishes the cloth.

Since World War II there has been an increased tendency for all segments of the fabric manufacturing industry to follow the pattern of the wool mills. Although all the operations may not necessarily be carried out in the same location, one company performs all these operations as part of the overall production of the fabric. This form of business organization is known as *vertical integration.*

Vertically integrated companies produce their own yarn, make that yarn into fabric, and finish the fabrics. Some textile firms, especially those making knits, may also manufacture the final product.

The mills sell their products to garment or home furnishings manufacturers. Some yard goods are sold to retail stores for resale to the home sewer. The mill may also sell unfinished fabric to jobbers and converters.

Since the number of vertically integrated companies has expanded, converters no longer play quite as important a role in the textile business as they once did. In these large integrated companies, the conversion of unfinished (greige) goods is done within the framework of the company. The traditional role of the converter has been to buy greige goods from mills, to arrange for dyeing and finishing companies to dye or finish the fabric, and then to resell the finished goods.

Converters serve a useful purpose in the textile industry: because they do not have a large commitment of money to machinery and buildings, they have great flexibility. They can, for example, produce smaller runs of high-fashion dress fabric for a manufacturer without having to be concerned about keeping their machines working over the long term. Converters can be more responsive to fashion trends, as they enter into only the very last stages of production.

Mills and converters may have excess fabrics to dispose of. These are often sold to a *jobber,* who buys lots of fabrics for resale to garment manufacturers or retail stores. The jobber sells in smaller quantities, as a rule, than does the mill or the converter. Manufacturers of garments who want to buy small yardages or specialty fabrics may be able to obtain these more easily from a jobber than from a mill or a converter.

In addition to becoming vertically integrated some fabric-producing companies have moved as well into *horizontal integration* of functions. Here, a parent company joins with other companies that produce related kinds of goods. For example, one company may manufacture apparel fabrics, upholstery fabrics, and carpet fabrics.

The advertising and publicity functions of fabric manufacturers are similar to those of the fiber producers. As noted before, the fiber producers and fabric manufacturers may cooperate in publicity campaigns. Fabric producers provide fashion consultants to work with apparel designers and manufacturers, participate in trade and professional shows, produce educational materials, and assist retailers in promoting retail items made from their fabrics.

From the Fabric Manufacturer to the Retailer

After the fabric manufacturer has sold its cloth to the garment manufacturer or to the manufacturer of household goods, the fabrics are converted into the products found on the racks and shelves of the retail store. The garment and household textile industries must be involved in the identification of current fashion trends.

The usual practice in the garment industry has been to work four to five months in advance of the time at which a garment will be sold. This requires that the textiles for these garments be prepared twelve to eighteen months before the garments are sold. With the introduction of computer-based, automated procedures for textile manufacture and management of apparel production, some firms have instituted more rapid production and delivery systems. Called *Quick Response* or *Just-in-Time* production, these procedures can cut delivery time from months to weeks. Industry leaders see Quick Response as one advantage of American manufacturers in the competition with foreign producers. (Computerization and Quick Response are discussed more fully later in this chapter.)

Textile manufacturers must keep up with current trends in design in general and with fashion trends in particular. They must anticipate the direction in which fashion will move, not only for apparel but also for household textiles.

Designs for garments come from fashion designers. Some fashion designers have attained sufficient prominence that they own their own manufacturing companies. Others work for specific manufacturing houses; still others may work on a freelance basis, selling individual designs to smaller fashion houses. The fashion designer often works closely with the textile company. The fabric company provides the fashion designer with swatches of fabrics from its new lines, or in some instances, the company may make an "exclusive" fabric that will be sold only to a particular fashion house. It is rare for fabric manufacturers to grant exclusive rights to a fabric to one apparel producer. When this is done, the fashion house is generally a very good customer, and the exclusive rights to the fabric usually last for only a limited time before the fabric becomes available more widely.

After the designs for a particular season have been prepared, the garment manufacturer shows the line to retail buyers and to the press. Retail store buyers place orders for the items shown in the line. If sufficient orders are placed, the garment is manufactured, and the orders are delivered to the store for sale.

Because the garment manufacturer does not sell directly, but through retail outlets, advertising and promotional campaigns of manufacturers are most often tied directly or indirectly to retail store promotions. Some garments are selected by manufacturers for national or regional advertisements. Knowing that a particular garment is slated for advertisement in *Vogue, Bazaar,* or *Seventeen* magazine may encourage a buyer to place orders for the item. The additional press exposure may enhance the salability of the garment. Retail stores that are especially good customers may be singled out for cooperative advertising in which the names of several stores at which the item is available are specifically mentioned in the advertisement. Other cooperative promotional efforts between retail store and manufacturer include fashion shows, provision of counter cards and other display materials for the retailer, and training programs for sales personnel. (See Figure 1.6 for an overview of the flow of goods in the apparel industries.)

In addition to apparel, which accounts for about 38 percent of the textile market, consumers purchase a wide variety of household textiles. Household textiles account for 35 percent of the textile market.[3] Many household textile products, such as sheets, towels, tablecloths, curtains, bed coverings, and area carpets, are constructed in the appropriate dimensions and require only some simple finishing such as hemming before they are sold to wholesalers or to retailers.

---

3. Statistics provided by American Textile Manufacturers Institute, October 1994.

Figure 1.6

Overview of the textile business flow in the apparel industries.

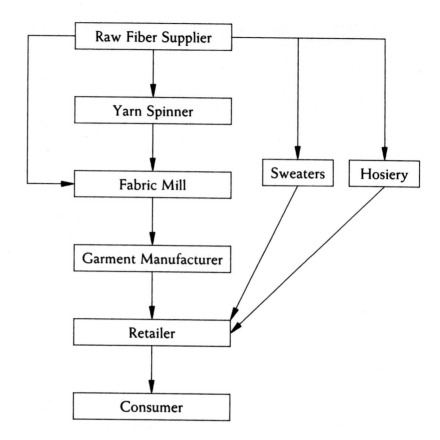

Wall-to-wall carpet and wall covering materials are usually installed by skilled technicians who work for the retailer. Vertically integrated manufacturers will sell materials directly to the retailer. Other firms may sell to wholesalers who, in turn, supply retailers.

Fabric used for coverings of mattresses and upholstery for furniture is sold to the manufacturer where it is cut and applied to the mattress or furniture body.

Fashion is an important consideration in household textiles as well as in apparel. Designers' names may play an important role in merchandising products such as bedcovers, sheets, and towels.

Industrial Textiles

Most consumers are not aware of the segment of the textile industry known as *industrial textiles,* even though they encounter these products every day. Industrial textiles is the most commonly used name for textile applications in agriculture, air and water filtration, architecture, automobiles, banners and flags, casual furniture, environmental protection, earth stabilization, medical products, recreational products, and transportation vehicles. Apparel items in this category are those in which performance is paramount: cleanroom garments, protective gloves and clothing for industry and farming, industry garments that don't develop electrostatic charges *(World of Industrial Fabrics)*.

Other descriptive terms applied to this segment of the industry are *industrial fabrics, technical textiles, engineered fabrics,* and *technical fabrics.* The industrial fabric

Figure 1.7

Flexible geotextile channel with 100 percent coconut fiber matrix sewn between two heavyweight, ultraviolet light stabilized nets. Channel is placed on roadsides and in ditches to prevent erosion of soil after construction. Product of North American Green. Photograph by Julia Thames.

segment of the textile field has grown rapidly. Estimates of the industrial textile market share of textile products in 1994 range from 23 percent to 35 percent, depending on which products are included in the data.[4]

Industrial textiles may be woven, knitted, or nonwoven, often of manufactured fibers. Fashion is not a factor in industrial textiles, but instead such functional characteristics as strength, stability, chemical resistance, and weight are likely to be important. Examples of industrial textiles range from small products such as filters and auto safety belts to enormous structures such as roofs, tents, and storage tanks. Consumers of industrial products include the construction, mining, sanitation, and transportation industries; medicine; and the military. Some of the more dramatic examples of progress in textile technology have come in the area of industrial textiles, particularly fiber-reinforced composites for the aerospace industry and *geotextiles*. Geotextiles are those used in soil and soil-based structures such as roads, dams, and erosion-control products. (See Figure 1.7.)

Automation and Computer Use

Electronic technology has become an important part of textile production. Managers of textile firms may use computers for planning and tracking operations, forecasting product demand, projecting manufacturing capacities, and following item lots through the various phases of manufacture. Where possible, production has been automated. Research serves as a foundation for these advances.

$(TC)^2$

The textile and apparel industries have formed an organization called the Textile/Clothing Technology Corporation or $(TC)^2$. The purpose of $(TC)^2$ is to conduct

---

4. Statistics provided by Industrial Fabrics Association International, April 1995.

research about applications of electronic technology in the textile and apparel industries and to educate executives, engineers, technologists, and educators about automated systems, their potential, and their use. $(TC)^2$ is funded jointly, largely by matching grants, by the industry and the federal government.

CAD

Computer-aided design (CAD) in textiles is applied to the design of yarns and fabrics and to coloration. In those firms that are vertically integrated, CAD may also be applied to apparel design and manufacture. Programs allow the textile designer to develop and modify ideas on the screen of the computer monitor. The advantages cited for this capability are: (1) because it is faster, it speeds up productivity; (2) the computer-generated designs allow for faster transfer of the designs to engraved screens, which are used for printing (see pages 431–434); and (3) some designers find it helps to stimulate design ideas. In addition, (4) new techniques in three-dimensional (3-D) imaging enable simulation of the actual fabric structure and texture on screen, and (5) advances in color printing allow better reproduction of the design on paper or other media. Designs can be scanned into the system and then modified or redesigned. CAD applications for knitted fabrics and garments have advanced quite rapidly. A variety of CAD systems that interface design and construction in the production of woven fabrics and knitted goods are currently available and in use.

Some disadvantages have also been noted. Managers complain that by relying too much on computer programs, some designers no longer understand technology, especially for knitted fabrics.

Current research is focusing on predicting the drape of fabric on 3-D moving figures. This involves mathematical modeling using fabric behavioral properties. The fabric's physical characteristics are separated from the surface design so that different types of motion can be applied to any design (Gray 1994; see Figure 1.8.)

Computer figures are also used in *3-D scanning*, one of the more recent developments in CAD, although it has more importance to the apparel manufacturing industry than to the textile industry. Under study by $(TC)^2$ for some time, the process uses computers to produce patterns for custom-fitted clothing.

Women's jeans produced through such a process were first marketed in November 1994 (Rifkin 1994). Custom Clothing Technology, Inc., developed the specific process used by Levi Strauss & Company. Software transmits customer body measurements electronically to a factory where a robot cuts a pattern to the correct individualized measurements. The garment is assembled and shipped to the retailer or to the customer in about three weeks.

CAD systems have uses other than for designing yarn, fabric, or garments. They can also help to plan factory layouts and structures to maximize efficiency of operations.

CAM

Computer-aided manufacturing (CAM) helps with the production of fabrics. Specific areas of application include electronic equipment for monitoring operations, equipment that controls specific operations, and equipment that diagnoses and corrects problems. Looms, knitting machines, and dyeing processes can now be controlled by computer. Sometimes CAM systems can eliminate some steps or processes.

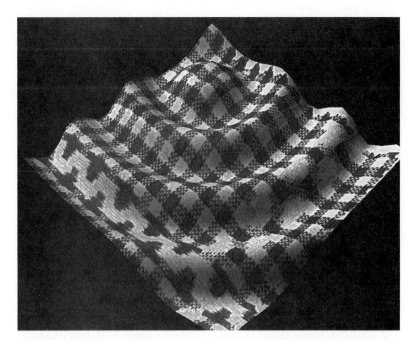

a

Figure 1.8

Images from a computer screen of the predictions of the three-dimensional draping qualities of textiles. Photographs courtesy of Stephen Gray and Anthony Rosella, researchers, Nottingham Trent University.

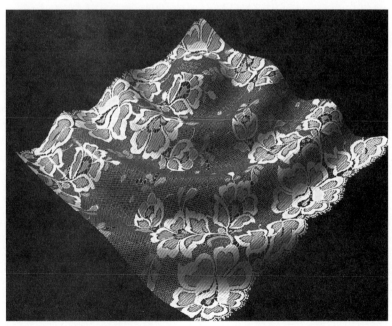

b

Electronic robots perform tasks that range from transport of materials within the plant to storing and retrieving products. Electronic controls perform on-line inspection of fabrics and map the location of defects.

CIM

Especially important to the success of Quick Response is the ability of computers to monitor inventories and store and retrieve data about raw materials, the progress of orders during manufacturing, and linkages with customers. Systems that permit intersystem communication are called computer-integrated manufacturing (CIM). A number of spokespersons for the textile industry have expressed concerns about the lack of standardization among the various types of computer systems installed within the industry. Incompatible systems inhibit electronic communication between the varying segments of the industry. Unless CIM systems can link all elements from manufacturing through to retailing, the maximum advantages of electronic capability cannot be realized.

International Textile Concerns

No discussion of the textile industry can be complete without mention of the international nature of the production, distribution, and consumption of textiles. All the operations mentioned thus far—namely, fiber production, yarn manufacture, spinning, weaving or knitting, coloration and finishing of textiles, and fabrication of garments can be and are carried out in many different parts of the world.

Many factors ranging from the wages paid to laborers to the exchange rate paid for American dollars tend to make textiles and textile products manufactured abroad cheaper than those produced in the United States. As a result, retailers have tended to increase the quantity of imported apparel and household textiles. The domestic textile production industry has suffered severe economic losses as penetration of imports into the U.S. market has continued to increase each year. (See Figure 1.9.)

The next decade will see still more changes in the international textile trade as the new General Agreement on Tariffs and Trade (GATT) takes effect. Renegotiation of the GATT, which covers international trade not only in textiles but in a wide variety of goods, began with a series of talks in 1986 known as the Uruguay Round. The U.S. Senate approved the new agreement in December 1994.

Before renegotiation the GATT had included a special Multifiber Arrangement (MFA) that had established quotas and other procedures that were intended to protect both the importer and exporter of textile goods. The new GATT will phase out the MFA so that by the end of a ten-year transition period, all quotas will be terminated, not only in the developed countries of the world but also in the developing countries. The agreement also provides for reductions in tariffs on textile products. (For a detailed description of the provisions of the new GATT agreement, see Khanna 1994.)

Precisely what will happen when the agreement is implemented is not clear. Its full effects are not likely to be felt for several years as the agreement will be phased in gradually. Some segments of the industry will experience even greater competition from imports, while others will find increased opportunities to export goods. Spokespersons for the U.S. textile and apparel industries predict that the net impact of the Uruguay Round will result in increased imports and a decline of 50 to 60 percent in domestic textile and apparel production, with the greatest impact being felt in apparel production (Manzella 1994.)

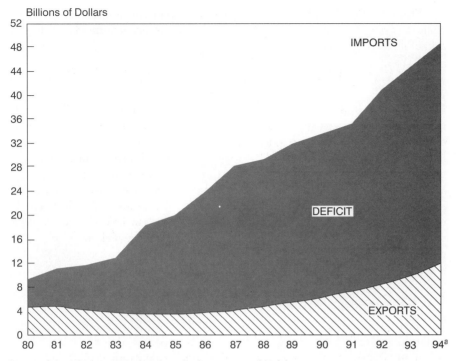

Billions of Dollars

Figure 1.9

Graph showing the growth of U.S. textile and apparel imports as compared with exports between 1980 and 1994. Courtesy of the American Textile Manufacturers Institute.

aFigures for 1994 are estimates based on the first nine months of the year.

As imports have made increasing inroads into the U.S. textile and apparel markets, these industries have tried to increase the awareness of consumers about imports and their effect on the American industry. Congress has acted in support of American textiles by passing legislation requiring that all textile products carry labels indicating the country of origin, including a designation showing that the product was produced in the United States. A "Crafted with Pride in the U.S.A." campaign sponsored by a number of trade organizations and textile- and apparel-producing companies has been initiated with print and other media publicity designed to tell the consuming public about American products and the importance of purchasing "Made in America" textiles (Figure 1.10).

Many experts in the textile field believe that the most important advantage the American textile industry has over foreign competition in the long run is its technological sophistication and, particularly, its potential for automation. These persons believe that increased automation can cut costs and make American products more competitive. They also point out the need of the retail industry for a "fast turnaround." For example, if a particular item of fashionable apparel sells exceptionally well and fast, the retailer cannot reorder the item from Hong Kong and expect to have it for the same season. If American manufacturers can supply products quickly and dependably, some retailers have indicated that they are willing to pay slightly more for products.

Given the increase in imports that is expected as a result of the new GATT agreement, U.S. textile firms will seek to expand their exports. Products with greatest export potential are industrial fabrics, finished apparel fabrics, warp knits, specialty yarns, and home furnishings textiles. Manufacturers and trade associations are likely to accelerate their efforts to educate the public about domestically made products. They will intensify research to improve manufacturing technology, especially empha-

Figure 1.10

Informational and promotional materials, hang tags, and labels of the Crafted with Pride in U.S.A. Council, Inc.

sizing increased automation, and seek to improve their ability to meet customers' needs for merchandise quickly.

The Responsibility for Quality

All segments of the textile products industry—the fiber producer, the fabric manufacturer, the product manufacturer, and the retailer—are responsible to some extent for maintaining quality and for complying with legal requirements for labeling. Unless product labeling or promotion makes specific claims about performance, no standard of performance is required by law for most products purchased by consumers. Nevertheless, many companies in the textile and apparel industries accept the maintenance of quality as an ethical responsibility.

Most purchased textile products are from retail or mail-order merchants. If these merchants value their reputations, they respond to justified customer complaints by promptly exchanging goods or refunding purchase price. Retailers can usually obtain refunds for defective products from manufacturers.

Labeling

Some labeling information, however, is required by law. Provisions of the Textile Fiber Products Identification Act mandate labeling of fabrics for fiber content and country of origin. Care labeling regulations require that permanent labels giving care instructions be affixed to apparel. (See Appendix C for a summary of regulatory legislation applied to textiles.) The textile manufacturer must supply information for the labels to the product manufacturer. The product manufacturer must attach any required labels to the product. In two instances the retailer is responsible for label contents: when the retailer is also the importer and when the retailer affixes a private label.

Textile Standards

Manufacturers of textile products are sometimes required to conform to *standard specifications,* defined levels of performance that products must achieve to be considered acceptable for use. The shortened term *standards* refers to established standard specifications. Products must conform to textile product standards when mandated by legislation such as the Flammable Fabrics Act. Some retailers direct the manufacturers from whom they buy to meet certain standards for products. The Department of Defense establishes minimum specifications for textiles used by the military and some federal agencies. Funding regulations for federally financed construction products require that carpets, draperies, and the like conform to stated specifications. Standard specifications also provide a basis for comparing the results of textile studies by different researchers.

Organizations That Establish Standards

The organization most actively involved in establishing textile standards is the American Society for Testing and Materials (ASTM). ASTM is an organization of industrial and academic professionals that establishes standard test methods and specifications through a system of technical committees. One of these committees, D–13, deals with textile materials and products. The American National Standards Institute (ANSI) is a nonprofit federation whose membership is composed of trade, labor, technical, and consumer organizations and governmental agencies. ANSI does not originate standards but serves as a clearinghouse and coordinator for standards in many fields. Textile fabric performance standards developed by ASTM Committee D–13 are accepted by ANSI.

Activities related to the setting of standards are not limited to the United States. International standardized systems of measurement and standard specifications have been developed by the International Organization for Standardization (ISO). Development of international standards facilitates the exchange of goods as global trade increases. A new system of measurement, *Systéme international d'unités* (SI), or the International System of Units, is gradually being adopted. Its details are published and controlled by an international treaty organization called the International Bureau of Weights and Measures.

ISO 9000

A series of quality management standards for industry (called ISO 9000) has been established by the ISO and adopted by ANSI. ISO 9000 does not mandate specific standards for a manufacturer or product but seeks to ensure that a product is what the customer expects. Under the program a company can apply for ISO 9000 registration to ensure quality in the design, production, inspection, and installation of its products. Most fiber manufacturers in the United States are registered under ISO 9000.

Textile Testing

Products must be tested to determine whether they meet established standards. Two groups in the United States have been closely involved in developing testing methods. The American Association of Textile Chemists and Colorists (AATCC) is composed of persons from the textile wet processing industry, textile chemists, others working in varying segments of the textile industry, and educators. The association establishes testing methods, largely in the area of chemical testing, and maintains an active educational program implemented through national and regional meetings and a monthly journal, the *Textile Chemist and Colorist,* The *Technical Manual* describes specific test methodologies.

Tests established by ASTM are focused more specifically on physical testing and the testing of fabric construction. ASTM publishes *ASTM Standards,* a compilation of test methods, and *ASTM Standard Performance Specifications for Textile Fabrics,* a group of voluntary fabric performance standards that serves as a guide to manufacturers and consumers.

Career Opportunities in the Textile Field

From the preceding discussion of the organization of the textile industry, it is evident that a wide variety of employment opportunities exists in this field and its related areas. The following brief, and very general, list provides not only a view of the breadth of the field but also an appropriate summary for this chapter.

Textile careers include the areas of:

Business Management
   In textile fiber, fabric, finishing, apparel, and retail segments of the industry.
Textile Chemistry
   In manufacturing fibers, research and development, finishing, and coloration.
Textile Technology
   In manufacturing fibers, yarns, and fabrics.
   In research and development of new techniques for manufacturing fibers, yarns, and fabrics and other textile products.
   In developing new machinery for apparel manufacture.
   In the application of dyes and finishes.
Marketing
   Of fibers, yarns, fabrics, textile auxiliaries, and finished products.
   Market research.
   Retail sales.
   Of textile machinery and equipment.
Advertising and Public Relations
   For fiber, fabric, apparel, and retail segments of the industry.
Design
   Of yarns, fabrics, apparel, household and industrial textile products.
Buying
   Of fibers, fabrics, or textile items for the fabric, apparel, or retail industries.
Care, Preservation, and Restoration
   In laundering and dry-cleaning industries.

For historic textiles in museums, historic buildings, public and private collections.

Education

Through industry, trade organizations, technical schools, colleges, and universities, continuing education, and cooperative extension.

References

ASTM. 1986. *Compilation of ASTM standard definitions.* Philadelphia: American Society for Testing and Materials.

Fowler, B. 1995. Find suggests weaving preceded settled life. *New York Times,* May 9, C1.

Gray, S. 1994. Formula for a fashion show. *Bobbin* 34 (January): 54.

Khanna, S. R. 1994. The new GATT agreement: Implications for the world's textile and clothing industries. *Textile Outlook International* 52(March): 10–37.

Manzella, J. 1994. Uruguay Round will benefit some—and hurt others. *America's Textiles International* 23 (October): 53.

Rifkin, G. 1994. Digital blue jeans pour data and legs into customized fit. *New York Times,* November 8, A1.

Wilford, J. N. 1993a. New finds suggest even earlier trade on fabled silk road. *New York Times,* March 16, C1, C8.

Wilford, J. N. 1993b. Site in Turkey yields oldest cloth ever found. *New York Times,* July 13, C1, C8.

World of industrial fabrics. St. Paul: Industrial Textiles International.

Review Questions

1. Explain the difference between fibers, yarns, and fabrics.
2. Identify at least three specific instances of trade in textiles before the Industrial Revolution.
3. Describe the role of trade associations in the natural fibers industry. Describe their role in the manufactured fibers industry.
4. What is the difference between a trademark and a certification mark?
5. Describe the flow of textile products in the apparel industry from the procuring of the fiber until the product reaches the ultimate consumer.
6. Explain the differences between CAD, 3-D CAD, CAM, and CIM.
7. What is the GATT? What is the importance of the Uruguay Round to the American textile industry?
8. Give the full name of the organization represented by each of the following acronyms and explain the functions of the organization: AATCC, ASTM, ANSI, ISO.

Recommended Readings

Barber, E. J. W. 1991. *Prehistoric textiles.* Princeton, N.J.: Princeton Univ. Press.

Berkstresser, G. A., and D. R. Buchanan. 1986. *Automation and robotics in the textile and apparel industries.* Park Ridge, N.J.: Noyes.

Black, S. S. 1994. Big guns get serious about QR. *Bobbin* 35 (May): 19–21.

Dickerson, K. G. 1995. *Textiles and apparel in the international economy.* 2d ed. Englewood Cliffs, N.J.: Prentice Hall.

Ellis, K. 1993. Think Quick. *New York Apparel News,* March, 34ff.

Hall, A. J. 1994. Developing international and European standards. *Textile Chemist and Colorist* 26 (May):17.

Kalogerdis, C. 1994. Whatever happened to Quick Response? *America's Textiles International* 23 (October): 43.

Kincade, D. H., et al. 1993. The quick response management system: Structure and components for the apparel industry. *Journal of the Textile Institute* 84 (2): 147.

Moore, L. 1994. Protection and competition in the U.S. market for textiles and clothing. *Journal of the Textile Institute* 85 (2): 244.

Novina, T. 1993. Home textiles market evolves. *America's Textiles International* 22 (November): K/A 11.

Roberts, M. 1993. Computerization in textiles. *Textile Horizons* (December): 59.

Textile World 140, October 1990. Special issue devoted to U.S. textile industry bicentennial.

TEXTILE FIBERS AND THEIR PROPERTIES

Textile fibers may be obtained from natural materials or created through technology. Natural fibers are taken from animal, vegetable, or mineral sources. The most important animal fibers are wool and silk. Cotton and flax (from which linen is made) are the most important vegetable fibers. Asbestos, a mineral fiber, had been used for special products where non-flammable materials were important, but it proved to be carcinogenic and has been replaced in most applications by manufactured fibers.

Manufactured fibers are created through technology. They can be made from natural materials that cannot be used for textiles in their original form but that can be *regenerated* (re-formed) into usable fibers by chemical treatment and processing. These *regenerated fibers* can be made from such diverse substances as wood, corn protein, milk protein, small cotton bits (called *linters*), and seaweed. The first commercially successful manufactured fiber was a forerunner of modern rayon, a regenerated cellulose fiber, production of which began around the beginning of the twentieth century. The second, also regenerated, was cellulose acetate, first used after World War I. Synthetic fibers, those synthesized from chemical substances, represent another type of manufactured fiber, the first of which was developed by W. H. Carothers for DuPont.

Nylon, the generic name given to this fiber by DuPont, was first marketed in 1938, and its commercial distribution was beginning when the outbreak of World War II required the diversion of nylon and its constituent materials into wartime use.

It was not until after the war that commercial nylon production for the civilian market was initiated on a large scale.

The invention of nylon, and its successful marketing after the war, stimulated the synthesis of additional fibers. Gradually, a wide variety of manufactured fibers were introduced: vinyon, 1939; saran, 1941; olefin and modacrylic, 1949; acrylic, 1950; polyester, 1953; triacetate[1], 1954; spandex, 1959; aramid, 1961[2]; anidex,[3] 1970; novoloid,[3] 1972; sulfar, 1986; P.B.I., 1986.

Generic Fiber Classification

Groups of fibers that are related in their chemical structure may be compared with large, extended families. Each fiber family group is made up of smaller family units. These smaller family units are, in turn, composed of a number of individual units. For example, some fibers have a structure made of protein (the large extended family). Subunits of the "protein" family include silk, which has no other close relatives; animal hair fibers, including wool, mohair, cashmere, camel's hair, and the like; and regenerated protein fibers that can be made from corn, soybean, peanut, or milk protein.

Within the family are certain "family resemblances," or ways in which the members of each group are alike. Most protein fibers, for example, show these similarities: they are harmed by the same chemicals, are fairly resilient, are harmed by dry heat, and are weaker wet than dry. Like human family members, however, each fiber has its own talents or eccentricities: silk has high luster, wool does not; vicuña and cashmere are exceptionally soft and luxurious to the touch; and the color of camel's hair cannot be removed easily.

As a result of legislation known as the Textile Fiber Products Identification Act, the Federal Trade Commission (FTC) has established names and definitions for each of the families of manufactured fibers. The "family" name is the *generic* name or generic classification of the fiber.

Generic classifications are based on chemical repeat units present in fibers. Read several of the generic fiber definitions included in chapters dealing with manufactured fibers to see how the chemical composition serves as the basis for the definition. Fibers that are members of the same generic group have similar chemical and physical properties. (See Figure 2.1.) Producers of manufactured fibers also give each of their fibers a name that is known as the *trademark*. Mary Smith, John Smith, and George Smith may be members of the same human family, each with the same family name, but each has a different given name. In the same way, Dacron® polyester, Fortrel® polyester, and Trevira® polyester are all members of the generic group of polyesters, but each has a different trademark. These trademarked variations in structure, usually about 15 percent by weight, are not sufficient to produce significant changes in the chemical or physical properties of the different members of the generic family.

By law, all manufactured items must (at the point of purchase) carry the generic name of the fiber on the label. Most producers of manufactured fibers use the generic

---

1. No longer manufactured in the United States.

2. Although the generic category of aramid fibers was established in 1974, these fibers had been produced from 1961 to 1974 under the generic classification of nylon.

3. No longer produced.

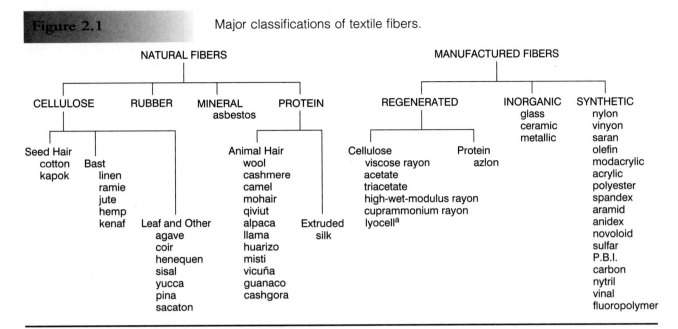

Figure 2.1   Major classifications of textile fibers.

[a]Lyocell is a generic name used in Europe. Application for U.S. generic fiber designation is being reviewed by the FTC, and a final decision is pending.

term along with their own trademark, so that the consumer will find such terms as Dacron® (trademark of E. I. du Pont de Nemours & Company) polyester (generic name) or Trevira® (trademark of Hoechst Celanese) polyester on labels of textile products. Trademarks protect the exclusive rights of one manufacturer to a particular product, in this case a generic fiber.

Textile Fiber Products Identification Act

Fiber manufacturers introduced ever-increasing varieties of new fibers to the public after World War II. No regulation was made of the use of manufactured fiber names, so that each manufacturer that made its own version of a fiber gave it its own trademark. The consumer was confronted with a variety of fiber names and had no ability to distinguish one from the other. Furthermore, two or more fibers might be blended together without the consumer's knowledge. The purchaser of a man's shirt had no way of knowing whether it was made of cotton, rayon, or a cotton and polyester blend.

The consumer confusion resulting from this situation led to enactment of the Textile Fiber Products Identification Act (often abbreviated TFPIA), which requires fiber content labeling of all textile products. An earlier law, the Wool Products Labeling Act of 1939, had set a precedent in textile labeling and served as a model for the TFPIA. The TFPIA became effective March 3, 1960, and has been amended several times since that date. The legislation assigned responsibility for the enforcement and drafting of rules and regulations under the act to the FTC.

Under the provisions of the TFPIA, all fibers, either natural or manufactured, all yarns, fabrics, household textile articles and wearing apparel are subject to this law. One of the first tasks assigned to the FTC was the establishment of generic names or classifications for manufactured fibers. (See Figure 2.1.)

A natural fiber is defined in the act as "any fiber that exists as such in the natural state." The common English names of natural fibers, *cotton, linen, silk,* and *wool,* appear on labels as generic names. A manufactured fiber is defined as "any fiber derived by a process of manufacture from any substance which, at any point in the manufacturing process, is not a fiber." These categories or generic classifications established by the FTC were based on similarities in chemical composition. Along with similarities in chemical composition, fibers in these groupings had many common physical properties, care requirements, and performance characteristics. New generic classes may be added when manufacturers are able to demonstrate that fibers are sufficiently unique to warrant a separate classification from those already in existence, so that it is possible that further generic classes may be established in the future as new fibers are synthesized.

In May 1985, for example, the FTC issued a call for public comment on the request of two companies for the establishment of new generic names for fibers that they believed met the commission's criteria for granting new generic names. These criteria are "that the fiber must have a chemical composition 'radically different' from other fibers and that chemical composition must give it significantly different physical properties; the fiber must currently be, or soon be, in active commercial use; and the granting of the generic name must be of importance to the consuming public 'at large,' rather than to a small group of knowledgeable professionals."[4] The evidence collected by the FTC led to the conclusion that these criteria had been satisfied, and two new generic names, sulfar and P.B.I., became effective July 9, 1986.

The TFPIA requires that all textile products have a label attached that lists the names of the fibers from which they are made.[5] Fiber listing must be done in order of the percentage of fiber by weight that is present in the product. The largest amount must be listed first, the next largest second, and so on. Thus, for example, a fabric might be labeled

60% polyester

30% cotton

10% spandex

The manufacturer must list the generic name of the fiber but may also list the trademark. So, for example, the same label could also read as follows:

60% Dacron® polyester

30% cotton

10% Lycra® spandex

Note that the trademark is capitalized but that the generic term is not.

Fiber quantities of less than 5 percent must be labeled as "other fiber," unless the fibers serve a specific purpose in the product. If the fibers are listed, the function of these minor components must be stated. For example, a manufacturer could say, "96 percent nylon, 4 percent spandex for stretch," because spandex is an elastic fiber and does perform a specific function. The intent of this provision is to prevent manufac-

---

4. Federal Trade Commission information sheet requesting public comment, May 28, 1985.

5. With these exceptions: upholstery stuffing; outer coverings of furniture, mattresses, and box springs; linings, interlinings, stiffenings, or paddings incorporated for structural purposes and not for warmth; sewing and handicraft threads; and bandages and surgical dressings.

turers from implying that 5 percent or less of a fiber will produce some positive benefit. Quantities of less than 5 percent of most fibers normally have little or no effect on fabric performance. Examples of exceptions are in the use of elastomeric fibers such as spandex or metallic fibers that control static.

Where products are made from fibers that have not been identified, for instance, from mixed reused fiber, the label may indicate that such a product is "composed of miscellaneous scraps, rags, odd lots, textile by-products, secondhand materials, or waste materials." Such a label might read, for example,

45% rayon

35% acetate

20% miscellaneous scraps of undetermined fiber content

No trademarks or other terms may be used that imply the presence of a fiber that is not actually a part of the product. For example, it would be illegal to use the following labels:

SILK-SHEEN Blouses   or   Wooly Warm Blankets
100% nylon   100% acrylic

(Also see Figure 2.2.)

The law also requires that either the name of the manufacturer of the product, a registered trademark, or a registered identification number appear on the label. All the mandated information must appear on the same side of the label, and all fiber content information must appear in type or lettering of equal size or conspicuousness, except for the manufacturer's name or identification number. This information may be placed on the reverse side of the label or on a separate label close to the fiber content label.

Amendment to the TFPIA in 1984 sought to clarify and improve country-of-origin labeling requirements and to increase consumer awareness of origin. (A parallel amendment was added to the aforementioned Wool Products Labeling Act at the same time. See chapter 5.)

The specific requirements under the amendment are as follows. The country of origin, whether foreign or domestic, must be disclosed in a label placed in the neck of any garment having a neck; for those without necks, it must be placed on a conspicuous spot on the inside or outside of the product. All products are to be separately labeled except when several pairs of hosiery are enclosed in one retail package that will not be opened before its sale. Not only the product itself but also packages

Figure 2.2

Label that violates the TFPIA. Not only is the fabric labeled both as "washable silk" and 100 percent polyester, but the print identifying the fabric as polyester is partially obscured by the overprinting of an American flag.

must be labeled unless the individual product label can be seen clearly through the package. Mail-order catalogs and mail promotional materials such as department store advertising flyers must disclose whether a product advertised was made in the United States or imported or both, if the products are intended for customer purchase by mail or by phone without prior examination.

Once the law had been passed, major questions surfaced as to how to identify the point of origin of an item that, for example, was made from fiber produced in one country, spun and woven into cloth in another, and constructed into apparel in yet another. The rules promulgated following the law were hotly debated by individuals in the textile industry during a period when comments were invited. The report in the *Federal Register,* April 17, 1985 (pp. 15101–15107), makes fascinating reading, as the debate over the implementation of the provisions of the law is summarized. After considering the comments offered, the following rules went into effect in May 1985. Products made entirely in the United States must carry a label that says "Made in the U.S.A." or some other "clear and equivalent" term. (Acceptable examples include "Crafted with Pride in the U.S.A." or "Made in New York, U.S.A.")

Products made in the United States using foreign materials are required to carry a label such as "Made in the U.S.A. of imported fabric" or equivalent terms. The FTC requires only that the manufacturer go back one manufacturing step to determine origin. For example, the manufacturer of knitting yarn sold at retail needs to identify the origin of the fiber; the manufacturer of retail piece goods needs to identify the origin of the yarn but need not identify the origin of the fiber; and the apparel manufacturer must identify the origin of the cloth. The specific country of origin need not be identified, although it may be given. Therefore, for example, a knitting yarn spun in the United States of Australian wool would need to be labeled as "Made in U.S.A. of imported wool fibers." However, if the manufacturer wished, it could say "Made in U.S.A. of Australian wool fiber."

Properties of Textile Fibers

Fibers are the primary materials from which most textile products are made. Many substances found in nature can be classified as fibers according to this definition; however, only a limited number of these materials are useful in the production of yarns or fabrics.

Whether a fiber can be used in the creation of a yarn or fabric depends upon the physical, mechanical, and chemical properties of the fiber. Many fibrous substances lack one or more essential qualities required of textile fibers. They may not, for example, be sufficiently long to be spun into a yarn. Or they may be too weak to use, too inflexible, too thick in diameter, or too easily damaged in spinning and weaving.

Comparison of fiber qualities and characteristics requires the use of certain basic terms and a technical vocabulary. Definition of these terms and of their meanings as they relate to textile performance and/or behavior is important for communication and understanding.

Determination of Textile Properties and Performance

A number of specific textile properties are defined and discussed in the following pages. The determination of the properties of specific fibers is made through one or more of a variety of different fiber-, yarn-, or fabric-testing methods. Test methods are standardized by organizations such as the American Society for Testing and Materials, the American Association of Textile Chemists and Colorists; or by the government through federal test method standards.

Testing of textile materials requires standardized procedures and controlled testing conditions. Even the temperature or the quantity of moisture present in a room may affect the results of tests. For this reason, testing is done only under conditions of controlled humidity and temperature, and before testing samples are "conditioned" for a specific period of time at a temperature of 70°F and 65 percent relative humidity. The conditioning time is usually at least 24 hours, temperature may be plus or minus 2°F, and humidity may be plus or minus 2 percent.

A precise technical vocabulary is used in describing textile properties and reporting the results of textile testing. These terms are explained in the sections of this text that discuss various textile properties. Textile measurement terminology that was unique to different countries or regions developed over a number of centuries. As a result, methods of measurement have, in the past, been difficult to compare from country to country. As textile trade has become more global, the industry has attempted to develop worldwide, standard terminology.

Part of this effort involves adopting the metric measurements of the International System of Units (SI). Its details are controlled by the International Bureau of Weights and Measures. The textile industry tends to be quite traditional, and not all segments of the textile industry use the SI system consistently. However, researchers and those writing technical literature do prefer the SI system.

Physical Properties

Some qualities of textile fibers are related to their physical characteristics. Since most single fibers are so small that they cannot be examined adequately with the naked eye, the physical appearance of these fibers is best observed under a microscope. With a microscope, it is possible to observe such properties as length, diameter, surface contour, and color. The physical characteristics of each individual fiber affect the appearance and behavior of the yarns and fabrics into which the fibers are manufactured.

Color

The color of natural fibers varies. Some, like linen, have just enough pigment to make them yellow or off-white; others, like wool, may range from white to black. If their color interferes with dyeing or printing, the color may be removed by bleaching. Manufactured fibers are usually white or "bright."

Shape

The shape of a fiber can be examined both in *cross section* and in its *longitudinal* form. Since cross section is a practical way in which to view the three-dimensional form of a fiber, cross sections are often used as a means of comparisons. Cross sections vary from fiber to fiber, ranging from circular to oval, triangular, dog-bone shaped, U-shaped, trilobal to multilobal, and hollow. (See Figure 2.3.) Differences in cross section contribute to differences in fiber characteristics such as appearance, hand or feel, surface texture, body, covering power, and luster.

Luster

Luster is the amount of light reflected by the fiber. Luster may be desirable in some products and undesirable in others. Current fashion trends may increase or decrease consumer acceptance of bright or dull fabrics. Manufactured fibers may have bright

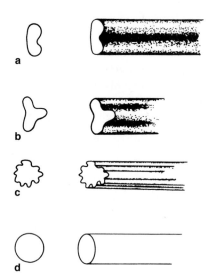

Figure 2.3

Typical variations in manufactured fiber cross-sectional shape together with the resulting longitudinal appearance: (a) dog bone, (b) trilobal, (c) serrated, and (d) round. Notice how the shape of the cross section forms visual lines and/or shadows in the appearance of the longitudinal view.

luster. If it is desirable to decrease the luster, the chemical titanium oxide is added to the material from which the fiber is made. The small particles of the chemical break up the reflected light, giving the fiber a lower luster. They are said to *deluster* the fiber. Untreated fibers may be known as *bright* fibers; delustered fibers may be called *dull* or *semidull* fibers.

Covering Power

Fabrics are often used to conceal what is placed beneath them. The ability of a fabric to obscure an object is known as its *covering power*. The covering power of fibers and fabrics has two aspects: the visual and the geometric. Visual covering power is related to the ability of the fiber to hide what is placed beneath it. The more transparent the fiber, the less covering power it has. The second aspect, that of geometric covering power, might be described as the quantity of fiber required to make a fabric that will cover a specific area. The better the geometric covering power, the less expensive it will be to manufacture a yarn or fabric, because a smaller quantity of fiber will be required.

Relationships Between Shape and Appearance

One property of a fiber may have a strong influence on other properties. While fiber luster depends on a number of factors such as the polymer from which the fiber is made and the size of the fiber, the shape and surface contours of fibers are among the most important determinants of the character of fiber luster.

The cross-sectional shapes of manufactured fibers are uniform. Some irregularities appear in natural fibers, and although the range of differences is slight enough that fabric appearance is not much affected, these slight irregularities produce a more subtle luster than that of most manufactured fibers.

Fibers with round cross-sections have a soft, smooth, sometimes slippery feel. Unless a special treatment has been given to the fiber to decrease its luster, the luster of round fibers is high. Covering power is, however, poor. This is because the surface area of round fibers is less than that of any other shape. Also being both round and smooth, the fiber will pack closely together into a yarn.

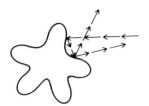 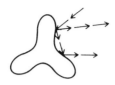 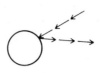

Figure 2.4

Diagrams showing differences in reflection of light in round, trilobal, and pentalobal fibers.

Dog-bone–shaped and flat cross-section fibers have a harsher, less smooth handle. The covering power of these fibers is excellent. Completely flat cross sections have a high luster, and some manufacturers have produced flat fibers with a glittering luster. But those with less regular surface, such as cotton, which has a somewhat flat but irregular cross section, do not have high luster.

Fibers with three- and five-lobed shapes have been manufactured. Three-lobed fibers are known as trilobal fibers; those with five lobes are known as pentalobal. The term *multilobal* is used to refer to all fibers with a number of lobes in the cross section. Trilobal fibers with triangular-shaped cross sections have increased covering power, a more silklike feel, and an increased luster. The luster results from the reflection of light not only from the surface of the fiber but also from the light being reflected from one lobe to another. (See Figure 2.4.) Pentalobal fibers also have this tendency to reflect light from one lobe to another, but because there are more lobes among which the light can be reflected, the fibers have a soft, subdued sheen.

When the lobes of the fiber are increased still further, light rays are broken up and the luster decreases. Octolobal fibers have been made to decrease luster or glitter.

Surface Contour

Some fibers have smooth, even contours when examined longitudinally; others are rough and uneven. Wool, for example, is covered with many small scales that cause wool fibers to cling closely together. Cotton is twisted, making it reflect light unevenly and giving it a dull appearance. Horizontal lines or other markings may appear in the length of some manufactured fibers as a result of irregularities in the cross-sectional shape of the fiber. The valleys between the lobes of multilobal fibers cause shadows that (under the microscope) appear as dark lines and are known as *striations*. (See Figure 2.5.)

Smooth, round filaments with little variation in surface contour show soiling more readily than do striated or multilobal fibers. W. J. Morris (1989) has compared

Figure 2.5

A longitudinal view of rayon showing striations. Photograph courtesy of the DuPont Company.

smooth, round fibers to smooth surfaces such as a polished mirror or silver plate on which finger marks and smears are very visible. When the smoothness of these surfaces has been altered by frosting or a matte finish, these smudges are less obvious. In the same way, altering the surface of the fiber helps to decrease obvious soiling. The ability to hide soil is especially important in some products, such as carpets, for which a variety of special multilobal fibers have been developed.

Crimp

Some fibers possess a wavy, undulating physical structure. This characteristic is called *crimp*. Wool has a natural three-dimensional crimp. A number of texturing processes can be used to add crimp to manufactured fibers or yarns. Fabrics made from crimped fibers and/or yarns tend to be more resilient and have increased bulk, cohesiveness, and warmth. *Cohesiveness* is the ability of fibers to cling together.

Length

By microscopic examination of textile fibers, one can readily observe the ratio (or comparison) of the length of the fiber in relation to its width. Although fibers are, by definition, always long and narrow, the length of the fiber is one basis for division or classification. Fibers of relatively short length, measured in centimeters or inches, are called *staple* fibers. Indefinitely long fibers, those measured in yards or meters, are known as *filaments*.

All natural fibers except silk are staple fibers. Manufactured fibers are usually extruded in filament form, but the filaments can be cut into shorter, staple lengths. Therefore, manufactured fibers may be found in either staple or filament form.

The length of the fiber will have an effect on the appearance of the yarn into which it is made. Filaments can be made into yarns with little or no twisting. These will look smooth and lustrous. Staple fibers, being short, must be twisted together or otherwise assembled to make them into a long, continuous yarn. Shorter fibers will produce more fiber ends on the surface of a yarn, thus creating a duller appearance.

The *hand* or *texture* of the fabric is affected by the use of either filament or staple fibers. If an untextured filament form is selected, there are fewer fiber ends on the surface of a fabric, creating a smooth, even surface. If staple fibers are used, the short fiber ends on the surface of a fabric can create a fabric that feels soft and fluffy to the touch. Judicious selection of short staple, longer staple, or textured or untextured filament yarns enables the manufacturer to vary the appearance, the texture, and other properties of fabrics.

Diameter or Fineness

The diameter of the fiber is the distance across its cross section. In natural fibers the diameter usually varies from one part of the fiber to another because of irregularities in fiber size. Unless specifically made to have an uneven diameter, manufactured fibers usually have a uniform diameter throughout.

Fiber diameter is measured in millimeters or in microns. One micron (called a micrometer in the SI system) is 1/1000th of a millimeter or 0.000039th of an inch. Cotton fiber diameter is usually from 12 to 20 microns in width, for example.

Fiber diameter is an aspect of *fineness*. Fineness is a relative measure of size, diameter, linear density, or weight per unit length. Instead of measuring the distance across the fiber, a calculation is made of the weight of a specified length of fiber. Measurements used in the textile industry can be reported either in *denier,* which is the weight in grams of 9,000 meters of fiber or yarn, or in *tex*. Tex, the SI measurement, is the weight in grams of 1,000 meters of fiber or yarn. (To convert from denier to tex measurements, divide denier by 9 or multiply it by .11.) Fibers with lower denier or tex numbers are finer; those with higher denier or tex numbers are less fine.

Manufactured fibers can have any diameter that the manufacturer chooses, and the selection of diameter is generally related to the projected end use of the fiber. Clothing fibers are made in relatively small diameters, whereas heavy-duty fibers for household items or industrial uses are made with larger diameters. Fineness of fibers is related to softness, pliability, and handle, characteristics that consumers often take into account when choosing products. Fine manufactured fibers are more costly to produce than are coarser sizes, and finer natural fibers generally command higher prices as well.

Among the recent technological advances in the production of manufactured fibers has been the development of very fine fibers called *microfibers* or *microdenier fibers*. This term is generally applied to fibers that are less than one denier. The term *ultrafine fibers* is usually applied to fibers of 0.01 denier per filament or less. (For purposes of comparison, consider that hosiery fibers are generally about 15 denier.)

Microfibers are being promoted for use in lightweight, soft fabrics. They can be fabricated into cloth with very fine pores and a dense surface. In addition to their use in apparel fabrics with attractive handle and draping qualities, microfibers are being used in specialized applications such as surgical masks, filtration materials, ski jacket insulation, and surgical wrapping materials. (See Figure 2.6.)

Density and Specific Gravity

Density and *specific gravity* are terms that are used in relation to the weight of fibers. Both terms show a relationship, but each has a somewhat different technical definition.

Density is the ratio of a mass of a substance to a unit of volume. In the case of a fiber, density is expressed as grams of fiber per cubic centimeter of fiber.

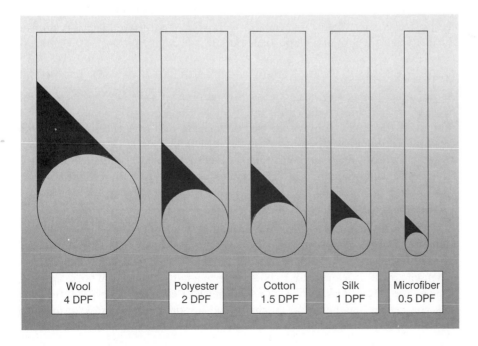

| Wool 4 DPF | Polyester 2 DPF | Cotton 1.5 DPF | Silk 1 DPF | Microfiber 0.5 DPF |

Figure 2.6

Relative fiber diameters. Reprinted by permission from A. J. Sabia, "Use of Silicones to Enhance the Aesthetic and Functional Properties of Microfibers," *Textile Chemist and Colorist* (August 1994): 13.

The concept of specific gravity is an alternative and more common and convenient means of expressing density and is defined as the density of the fiber in relation to the density of an equal volume of water at a temperature of 4°C. The specific gravity of water is 1. If a fiber has a specific gravity of more than 1, it is heavier than water; if it has a specific gravity that is less than 1, it is lighter than water. Only a few textile fibers have a specific gravity that is less than that of water, so that the specific gravity of most fibers will fall in a range of from 1.0 to 2.0 or slightly above. (See Table 2.1.) Since specific gravity is a relative value, it cannot be reported in units such as grams or centimeters.

Density has significance for the consumer in a number of ways. Olefins, with a specific gravity less than water, will float on top of water during laundering. The low density of olefin fibers makes possible the manufacture of fibers from smaller weights of raw materials. This results in lower costs for the fiber. Cotton has a moderate specific gravity, and glass fiber has a high specific gravity. Therefore, if a cotton fabric and a glass fabric are made of yarns of comparable size and of similar weave, the glass fabric will be much heavier than the cotton.

Strength

The mechanical properties of textiles are those that describe the textile material's behavior under applied forces and deformation. Deformation is a change of shape or size, usually as a result of application of some type of force. The applied force may cause the textile to stretch, to compress, or to twist. The most important of these behaviors for fibers is their resistance to stretching, that is, to forces applied parallel to the fiber axis. The tensile force required to break a fiber is called *tensile strength*. Tenacity of fibers is strength relative to linear density and is measured in *grams per tex* or *grams per denier (g/d)*.

Although measuring the tenacity of a fiber will provide some guide to potential strength in a fabric, many other factors will also affect the durability of the fabric into which the fiber is made. The structure of the yarn into which fibers are made and the fabric construction are important. The strength of filaments is more comparable to the strength of yarns and fabrics than is the strength of staple fibers. Such factors as the twist of a staple fiber yarn will also be important in determining the ultimate durability and strength of a fabric made from it.

Modulus

An important property related to tensile strength is fiber *modulus*. This refers to the fiber's initial resistance to the tensile force, before it breaks, and is a measure of fiber stiffness. If this initial resistance is low, the material will stretch considerably with very little force applied. Examples of materials with low modulus are rubber bands and spandex fibers. High modulus materials exhibit much lower stretch under tensile force. A steel wire would have a high modulus, as would glass and flax fibers.

Elongation and Elastic Recovery

Elongation is the amount of stretching or lengthening of a fiber under a tensile force. Elongation does not imply that the fiber will return to its original form but merely that the fiber length can be elongated or extended. Measurement of elongation is commonly made as "elongation to break," the amount of stretch the fiber can withstand before it will break. A fiber that will stretch or elongate more before breaking will show greater "toughness," or durability, than a stiffer fiber that breaks at the same load but at lower elongation.

If recovery after a stress is removed occurs instantaneously, like a rubber band, it is *elastic recovery*. A slow return to original length is called *creep recovery*. Elastic recovery can be quantified or measured and is calculated in numerical terms as the percentage of elastic recovery. A measured fiber (or fabric) is elongated or stretched to a specific degree, for a specified period of time. The stress is then removed, and the fiber is allowed to recover for a short period of time. After recovery the fiber is remeasured, and the percentage of recovery is calculated. A fiber with 100 percent recovery has returned to its original length. A fiber with 80 percent recovery is 20 percent longer after stretching.

Elongation and elastic recovery are separate qualities. One fiber (fiber A) may stretch (elongate) but not return to its original length, while another (fiber B) may stretch to the same extent and return to (recover) its original size. Both fibers show similar qualities of elongation, but they differ in their elastic recovery. For the manufacturer who wishes to produce a serviceable product that has some "give" but will not stretch out of shape, use of fiber B will produce the better product. For example, good elastic recovery is highly desirable in a product such as pantyhose. Without it, wearers would notice bags of stretched fabric at the knees.

Resiliency

Resiliency refers to the ability of a fiber to spring back to its natural position after folding, creasing, or other deformations. Fibers differ in their natural resiliency, and those that are resilient are likely to recover from creasing or wrinkling more quickly. Although resiliency and elasticity are not the same, high elastic recovery is associated with good resilience. (Wool is an exception.)

The term *loft* is related to resiliency. Sometimes known as *compressional resiliency*, loft is the ability of fiber assemblies to return to their original thickness after being flattened or compressed. A fabric with loft is one that is springy and resists flattening.

Flexibility

Flexibility of fibers refers to their ability to be bent or folded and is an essential quality of textile fibers. The consumer perceives fiber flexibility in terms of stiffness. Not only is it difficult to spin inflexible fibers into yarns, but fabrics made from such fibers feel stiff, do not drape well, and are not comfortable to wear. Except for special uses for household or industry, fabrics that lack flexibility have poor consumer acceptance. Furthermore, the fiber must bend or flex often without breaking or splitting; the textiles in many end products are subject to manipulation that causes fibers to bend or fold. Glass fiber, for example, can be made into woven textiles, but its uses are limited because the fibers are relatively inflexible. Fabrics made from glass fiber tend to break where they are folded and are rather stiff.

Dimensional Stability

Fibers that neither stretch nor shrink when exposed to moisture or heat are dimensionally stable. Shrinkage is a decrease in the length of fibers and may be accompanied by an increase in the width of the fiber. Fibers that absorb moisture readily will exhibit this behavior.

Many fibers are described as being inherently dimensionally stable, yet the fabrics into which they are made may shrink. This fabric shrinkage results from the stretching of fabrics during their construction and/or finishing. Fabrics that are distorted during processing tend to relax to their natural dimensions after the first few

Table 2.1   Selected Properties of Some Manufactured and Natural Fibers

Fiber	Breaking Tenacity[a] (grams per denier)		Specific Gravity[b]	Standard Moisture Regain (%)[c]	Effects of Heat
	Standard	Wet			
Acetate (filament and staple)	1.2–1.5	0.8–1.2	1.32	6.0	Sticks at 350°F (177°C) to 375°F (191°C). Softens at 400°F (205°C) to 445°F (230°C). Melts at 500°F (260°C). Burns relatively slowly.
Acrylic (filament and staple)	2.0–3.5	1.8–3.3	1.14–1.19	1.3–2.5	Sticks at 450°F (232°C) to 497°F (258°C), depending on type.
Aramid					
Regular-tenacity filament	4.8	4.8	1.38	5.0	Decomposes above 800°F (427°C).
High-tenacity filament	22.0	22.0	1.44	2.7–7.0	Decomposes above 900°F (482°C).
Staple	3.0–4.5	3.0–4.5	1.38	5.0	Decomposes above 800°F (427°C).
Cotton	3.0–5.0	3.3–6.4	1.54	7–11	Burns, does not melt.
Linen	5.5–6.5	6.0–7.2	1.54	8–12	Burns, does not melt.
Modacrylic (filament and staple)	2.0–3.5	2.0–3.5	1.30–1.37	0.4–4.0	Will not support combustion. Shrinks at 250°F (121°C). Stiffens at temperatures over 300°F (149°C).
Nylon					
Nylon 66 (regular-tenacity filament	3.0–6.0	2.6–5.4	1.14	4.0–4.5	Sticks at 445°F (229°C). Melts at about 500°F (260°C).
Nylon 66 (high-tenacity) filament	6.0–9.5	5.0–8.0	1.14	4.0–4.5	Same as above.
Nylon 66 (staple)	3.5–7.2	3.2–6.5	1.14	4.0–4.5	Same as above.
Nylon 6 (filament)	6.0–9.5	5.0–8.0	1.14	4.5	Melts at 414°F (212°C) to 428°F (220°C).
Nylon 6 (staple)	2.5	2.0	1.14	4.5	Melts at 414°F (212°C) to 428°F (220°C).
Olefin (polypropylene; filament and staple)	4.8–7.0	4.8–7.0	0.91	—	Melts at 325°F (163°C) to 335°F (168°C).

launderings. This type of fabric shrinkage is called *relaxation shrinkage*. If fabrics continue to shrink each time they are washed, even after many launderings, then they are displaying *progressive shrinkage*.

Manufactured fibers that are thermoplastic or heat sensitive may shrink when subjected to heat. Special treatment with heat called *heat setting* can, however, be used to set the fiber and make it dimensionally stable. The manufactured fibers or

Table 2.1					Continued

Fiber	Breaking Tenacity[a] (grams per denier)		Specific Gravity[b]	Standard Moisture Regain (%)[c]	Effects of Heat
	Standard	Wet			
Polyester					
Regular-tenacity filament	4.0–5.0	4.0–5.0	1.22, 1.38[d]	0.4, 0.8[d]	Melts at 480°F (249°C) to 550°F (288°C).
High-tenacity filament	6.3–9.5	6.2–9.4	1.22, 1.38[d]	0.4, 0.8[d]	Melts at 480°F (249°C) to 550°F (288°C).
Regular-tenacity staple	2.5–5.0	2.5–5.0	1.22, 1.38[d]	0.4, 0.8[d]	Melts at 480°F (249°C) to 550°F (288°C).
High-tenacity staple	5.0–6.5	5.0–6.4	1.22, 1.38[d]	0.4, 0.8[d]	Melts at 480°F (249°C) to 550°F (288°C).
Rayon (filament and staple)					
Regular tenacity	0.73–2.6	0.7–1.8	1.50–1.53	13.0	Does not melt. Decomposes at 350°F (177°C) to 464°F (240°C).
Medium tenacity	2.4–3.2	1.2–1.9	1.50–1.53	13.0	Burns readily.
High tenacity	3.0–6.0	1.9–4.6	1.50–1.53	13.0	
High wet modulus	2.5–5.5	1.8–4.0	1.50–1.53	13.0	
Silk	2.4–5.1	1.8–4.2	1.25 (boiled off)	10–11%	Burns slowly, sometimes self-extinguishing when flame is removed.
Spandex (filament)	0.6–0.9	0.6–0.9	1.20–1.21	.75–1.3	Degrades slowly at temperatures over 300°F (149°C). Melts at 446°F (230°C) to 518°F (270°C).
Wool	1.0–1.7	0.8–1.6	1.32	about 15%	Burns slowly, sometimes self-extinguishing when flame is removed.

Note: Standard laboratory conditions for fiber tests were 70°F and 65% relative humidity. Data given in ranges may fluctuate according to introduction of fiber modifications or additions and deletions of fiber types.

Source: Manufactured fiber data from the American Fiber Manufacturers' Association, Inc.

[a]Breaking tenacity: the stress at which a fiber breaks, expressed in terms of grams per denier.

[b]Specific gravity: the ratio of the weight of a given volume of fiber to an equal volume of water.

[c]Standard moisture regain: the moisture regain of a fiber (expressed as a percentage of the moisture-free weight) at 70°F and 65% relative humidity.

[d]Depending on type.

fabrics that have been heat-set do not shrink unless the heat-setting temperature is exceeded.

Abrasion Resistance

One of the most important physical properties of a fiber in relation to durability is its ability to withstand abrasion. *Abrasion* is the rubbing or friction of fiber against fiber or fiber against other materials. Fibers with poor abrasion resistance break and splinter, which produces worn or broken areas in fabrics.

Abrasion of fabrics may take place when they are flat, folded, or curved, so that fibers can be subjected to three types of abrasion: flat, flex, and edge abrasion. For example, flat abrasion may be seen on carpets as the feet of passersby constantly rub against the surface; flex abrasion takes place at the back of the knee in trousers or with the folding and unfolding of linens as they are stored; and edge abrasion occurs at the permanently folded edges of collars and cuffs. Color change in dyed textiles as a result of abrasive wear is known as *frosting*.

Prediction of durability in relation to abrasion is considered to be difficult (see chapter 16 for a discussion of the methods of evaluating abrasion) as many factors influence abrasion.

Price and Cohen (1994) list five variables that must be considered in evaluating abrasion resistance. They are

1. Type of abradant.
2. Amount of pressure between fabric and abradant.
3. Position of the fabric while being abraded.
4. Frequency and time duration of the abrading sequence.
5. Tension exerted on the fabric while it is being abraded. (p. 438)

Morton and Hearle (1975), who note that abrasion depends largely on construction of yarn and fabric, state that no way has been found to eliminate the influences of these factors and calculate a basic fiber property. For this reason, fiber abrasion properties are not discussed in the following chapters as a separate category. Table 2.2 does, however, present a summary of general evaluations of abrasion resistance for a number of widely used fibers.

Pilling takes place when a fabric has been subject to abrasion that causes fiber ends to break, migrate to the surface, and form into a small ball that clings to the surface of the fabric. Pilling is a more serious problem in strong fibers, as weaker fibers tend to break and fall off the surface of the fabric when pills are formed, whereas the stronger fibers do not break away and the pills stay on the surface of the cloth.

Table 2.2	A Comparison of Abrasion Resistance in Selected Fibers
Fiber	**Abrasion Resistance**
Nylon	Good to excellent abrasion resistance.
Polyester	Ratings range from good to excellent depending on variety.
Acrylic	Good abrasion resistance.
Viscose rayon	Fair abrasion resistance.
Acetate and triacetate	Rated as low to fair abrasion resistance.
Cotton	More resistant to abrasion than other natural fibers; sometimes rated lower than wool, sometimes higher.
Wool	More resistant to abrasion than other natural fibers; sometimes rated lower than cotton, sometimes higher.
Linen	Good resistance to abrasion but damaged by repeated flexing.
Silk	Poor abrasion resistance, lower than cotton and wool.

Sources: H. M. Taylor, "Abrasion in Fabrics," *Textiles* 7 (June 1978), 36ff; *Textile World Man-made Fiber Chart* 13 (August 1980); W. E. Morton and J. W. S. Hearle, *Physical Properties of Textile Fibers* (New York: Wiley, 1975), 437.

Chemical Properties

Absorbency

The ability of a fiber to absorb or take water into itself affects many aspects of its use. The ability of a bone-dry fiber to absorb moisture is called *moisture regain*. In calculating the properties of textiles, textile technologists will take a sample of fibers or fabric, dry it thoroughly, and return the sample to a controlled atmosphere in which temperature and humidity are accurately maintained at a temperature of 70°F and 65 percent relative humidity. The amount of moisture that is taken up by the sample is then measured to determine the *standard regain*. This figure is reported in percentage and is calculated using this formula:

$$\text{regain} = \frac{(\text{moist weight} - \text{dry weight}) \times 100}{\text{dry weight}}$$

See Table 2.1 for reporting of standard regain data. *Saturation regain,* measured at 95 to 100 percent relative humidity, is numerically higher.

A fiber that permits some moisture absorption is comfortable to wear, especially in hot weather. Absorbent fibers accept water-borne dyes and special finishes readily and are easy to launder. On the other hand, fibers that absorb moisture readily dry slowly and may be stained by water-borne soil.

Some fibers *adsorb* moisture rather than absorb it. When water is adsorbed, it is held on the surface of the fiber rather than being taken into the fiber itself. If such fibers have a low moisture regain, they dry more quickly than do absorbent fibers and stain less readily. *Wicking* takes place when liquid moisture travels along the surface of the fiber but is not absorbed into the fiber. Some fibers both absorb moisture and also have wicking ability. Most synthetics have low absorbency, but some also have excellent wicking properties that make them more comfortable to wear, since perspiration can travel to the surface of the fabric where it can evaporate.

The strength of some fibers is affected by the moisture that they contain. Cotton, for example, is stronger when wet than when dry, whereas rayon and wool are weaker wet than dry. For the consumer this means that handling some fabrics during laundering may require greater care. For the manufacturer, it means that processing of fibers during dyeing or finishing must be modified.

Electrical Conductivity

Electrical conductivity is the ability of a fiber to carry or transfer electrical charges. Fabrics with low or poor conductivity build up electrical charges with the result that these fabrics cling or produce electrical shocks. The mechanical action of automatic dryers also serves to build up static electricity on fabrics of low conductivity, thereby producing static cling. Many synthetic fibers have low conductivity, and when several layers of clothing of low electrical conductivity are worn, the problem of charge buildup is aggravated.

Poor conductivity is related to low moisture regain. Water is an excellent conductor of electricity, and fibers with good absorbency are not as likely to build up static electricity as are those that are nonabsorbent. Furthermore, some fibers with fairly good moisture absorbency but poor conductivity display static buildup, and fabrics cling only when weather conditions are dry. Treatments given to fabrics to decrease static accumulation involve finishes that enable fibers to hold moisture on the surface or to absorb more moisture. Some manufactured fibers are modified in chemical structure during manufacture so as to increase electrical conductivity.

Effect of Heat

Textile products may be subjected to heat not only during manufacture and processing but also in use. In home care, for example, fabrics may be pressed or dried in a hot dryer. The way in which various fibers respond to the application of heat depends on their chemical composition. Many synthetic fibers soften or melt at various temperatures. Cellulosic and protein fibers scorch or turn brown. The specific behavior exhibited by each fiber will, of course, determine the way in which the fiber must be handled during manufacture and use.

Some manufactured fibers are said to be thermoplastic because they soften or melt on exposure to heat. This characteristic is used to advantage in the manufacturing of some textile products because the application of the right amount of heat will permanently set pleats or shape into the fabric. Careful control of heat causes physical changes to take place within the fiber that alters its form, thereby establishing a permanent shape. In fabrics made from thermoplastic fibers, heat may be used to fuse seams and make buttonholes. (See Table 2.1 for descriptions of the effect of heat on fibers.)

Flammability

Some fibers ignite and burn, some smoulder, and others are noncombustible. Fibers that burn when they are held in a direct flame and stop burning when the flame is removed are designated *self-extinguishing*.

Burning of small quantities of textile fibers may be used as a means of differentiating one fiber group from another. Although precise identification of individual fibers cannot be made by burning, burning can help to establish the general fiber group to which the fiber belongs. Cellulosic fibers, for example, exhibit flammability characteristics much like that of paper, protein fibers burn in a manner similar to hair, and some synthetics melt when they burn. The odor produced when a fiber burns and the kind of ash that remains after burning aid in the identification of the fiber.

The flammability of textile fibers may be related to their selection for use in particular products. Certain fibers are inherently noncombustible, whereas others exhibit flame-retardant or flame-resistant properties. Special finishes are applied to fabrics to retard flammability. Children's sleepwear and certain household products, such as carpets and mattresses, must, by law, be tested to determine whether they pass established test standards relating to flammability.

Chemical Reactivity and Resistance

The chemical reactivity and resistance of textile fibers are discussed at length in chapter 3. Many of the substances used in the manufacture of fibers, in their finishing, and in the care of fabrics in the home are common household chemicals. Therefore, the behavior of textiles when they are exposed to these chemical substances is important to the consumer as well as to the textile technologist.

Environmental Properties

Sensitivity to Microorganisms and Insects

Some fibers support the growth of microorganisms (such as molds or mildew) that will deteriorate the fibers. Others may permit such bacterial growth without damage to the fabric. Still other fibers do not support bacterial growth at all. Fiber characteristics in this respect will affect the choice of fibers for certain uses. Boat sails are subject to the conditions favorable to the development of mildew when they become wet. Synthetics, which resist mildew, thus compete favorably with cotton in making sails for boats. Mildew will develop on most fabrics if they are stored in warm, dark, damp areas.

Carpet beetles, clothes moths, and silverfish are the most common insect pests that attack certain textile fibers. Special finishes may be given to vulnerable fabrics to make them resistant to insects. Proper care and storage of susceptible fabrics, notably wool, can prevent insect damage.

Sensitivity to Environmental Conditions

A number of general environmental conditions may have an adverse effect on textile fibers. These include exposure to sunlight and air pollution. For example, many fabrics lose strength after long exposure to sunlight, whereas others may be discolored. Certain dyes used on acetate fibers may be discolored by air pollution, and some fibers lose strength or degrade as they age.

Interrelatedness of Fiber Characteristics

The particular qualities that distinguish one textile fiber from another result from the combination of the characteristics that have been discussed. No one single fiber characteristic stands alone, but each property contributes to, and modifies, fiber behavior. (Fabric properties are further changed or modified by methods of yarn and fabric construction.) For example, a fiber might have good tensile strength but poor abrasion resistance. This fiber would, therefore, be less serviceable than a fiber of moderate strength with better abrasion resistance. Another fiber might possess excellent abrasion resistance but have poor resiliency or poor elastic recovery. *In short, it is the sum of its qualities or characteristics that determines the usefulness of a fiber.*

Some of the negative qualities of fibers can be overcome through special finishes or processing. A finish is a treatment given to a fiber, yarn, or fabric to enhance or alter some of its qualities. It is possible to treat wool fabrics so that they become mothproof, or to treat cotton so that it gains in luster and in strength. Some finishes increase absorbency and/or resilience, whereas others decrease flammability. Special texturing processes for manufactured yarns can increase the stretch, bulk, and covering power of the yarn or decrease pilling.

Relation of Care Procedures to Properties

Care procedures that are appropriate for fabrics are determined by an evaluation of the behavior of the fiber in relation to many of the factors discussed earlier in this chapter. Laundering or dry cleaning and ironing procedures must be determined by taking into account the reaction of the fiber to the chemical substances used in home and professional cleaning and the fiber's sensitivity to heat. Resistance to microorganisms, insects, and environmental conditions affects the type of care that is necessary in the storage of textiles.

Care procedures are not determined by fiber content alone. In ready-to-wear garments, the care requirements for all components from trimmings to interfacings must be taken into account. Chapter 24 gives a more complete discussion of the care of textile products.

References

Morris, W. J. 1989. Fiber shape and fabric properties. *Textiles* 18(1): 6.

Morton, W. E., and J. W. S. Hearle. 1975. *Physical properties of textile fibers.* New York: Wiley.

Price, A., and A. C. Cohen. 1994. *Fabric science.* New York: Fairchild.

Review Questions

1. What is the difference between a generic fiber and a fiber trademark? Which must be included on labels under the TFPIA and why?
2. To what kind of products is the TFPIA applicable? Summarize its requirements.
3. Why are standardized procedures, measurements, and conditions required for textile testing and research?
4. List and define those properties that describe how a textile fiber looks either to the naked eye or under the microscope.
5. Differentiate between:
   - fiber strength, fiber modulus, and abrasion resistance
   - elongation, elastic recovery, and resiliency
   - electrical conductivity, the effect of heat, and flammability
6. Explain what is meant by the statement, "It is the sum of its qualities or characteristics that determines the usefulness of a fiber."

Recommended Readings

Cook, J. G. 1984. *Handbook of textile fibers.* 2 vols. Watford, England: Merrow Textile Books.

Ford, J. E. 1985. Textile units for fibers and yarns. *Textiles* 14 (Spring): 17.

Gohl, E. P. H., and D. Vilensky. 1981. *Textile science: An explanation of fiber properties.* London: Longman.

Morton, W. E., and J. W. S. Hearle. 1975. *Physical properties of textile fibers.* New York: Wiley.

Quantifying yarn abrasion. 1994. *High performance textiles* (September): 3.

Wada, O. 1992. Control of fiber form and yarn and fabric structure. *Journal of the Textile Institute* 83(3): 322.

Xu, B., B. Pourdeyhimi, and J. Sobus. 1993. Fiber cross-sectional shape analysis using image processing techniques. *Textile Research Journal* 63 (December): 717.

CHEMICAL AND PHYSICAL CONCEPTS BASIC TO TEXTILES

CHAPTER

3

Fundamental Concepts of Chemistry

Chemistry deals with the composition, properties, and reactions of the material, or matter, that make up physical objects. All such objects, whether solids, liquids, or gases, whether fibers, trees, water, or air, are comprised of matter. Matter is anything that has mass and occupies space. It is made up of combinations of one or more of the over one hundred different chemical elements. An *element* is a substance that cannot be broken down any further by chemical means and so is considered the simplest form of matter.

Atoms: Basic Building Blocks

The basic building block of an element is the *atom,* which is the smallest amount of an element that can exist. The atom is made up of *electrons, protons,* and *neutrons.* The atom contains a nucleus of protons, particles that carry one positive electrical charge each, and neutrons, which are uncharged particles. Electrons orbit the nucleus in energy levels called shells. Electrons are much lighter than protons and neutrons, but each one carries a negative electrical charge equal in strength to that on a proton. The opposite charges on protons and electrons create a mutual attraction that keeps them together in the atoms; the attraction is much like that between the North and South poles of magnets. In an isolated atom the numbers of electrons and protons are the same, giving the atom no net electrical charge.

45

Atoms can combine into *molecules* by sharing or giving up electrons in their outermost, or *valence*, shell. The number of electrons in this valence shell helps chemists predict which elements will combine easily. For example, sodium and potassium both have one electron in their outer shell and would exhibit similar combining capacities.

The most stable form of the valence shell is to have a full complement of electrons, and atoms will seek this stable form in combining with other atoms. For most atoms a complete shell contains eight electrons. Sodium chloride, common table salt, is a compound of one sodium atom and one chlorine atom. Sodium has one electron in its valence shell; chlorine has seven. If sodium gives up one electron, its next lower shell is complete with eight electrons, and chlorine, by gaining an electron, will have eight in its outer shell. Since sodium lost an electron, it now has a net positive charge, and likewise chlorine has a net negative charge. The opposite charges attract each other and hold the two atoms of the molecule together. This is an *ionic* bond because the now charged atoms, sodium with a positive charge and chlorine with a negative charge, are called *ions*. The number of electrons transferred is the combining capacity of an atom.

In a different type of bonding, *covalent* bonding, atoms fill up their outer shells by sharing pairs of electrons, rather than donating or accepting them. The orbits, usually called *orbitals,* of the electrons overlap. Orbitals from two atoms, each with only one electron, merge to form a *molecular orbital* with two electrons, thus binding the atoms together. It is also possible for a molecular orbital to form with two electrons contributed by only one of the atoms; this is called a *coordinate covalent bond.*

Carbon has four electrons in its valence shell and can complete this shell by sharing its electrons to form four covalent bonds. These bonds can be with four different atoms or more than one bond with the same atom. If two carbon atoms share two pairs of electrons in two covalent bonds, a double bond is formed. If they share three pairs of electrons, a triple bond is formed.

Many times when two unlike atoms form a covalent bond, the electrons are not shared equally but are shifted toward one of the atoms that has a greater attraction for them. The bond is then said to be *polar;* one atom will have a slightly negative charge, and one atom will have a slightly positive charge. Water is a molecule that exhibits this polar bonding. Water has one oxygen atom that shares electrons with two hydrogen atoms. The oxygen attracts the two shared electron pairs quite strongly and becomes negatively charged. The hydrogen atoms become positively charged.

Table 3.1 lists some of the more common elements and the number of valence electrons needed to achieve a stable configuration. Oxygen and sulfur both have six electrons in their valence shells and exhibit similar bonding behavior.

Chemical Formulas

In the language of chemistry, signs and symbols represent atoms of elements and the ways in which they connect. Each of the elements has an abbreviation, or symbol, usually the first letter or a combination of two letters found in the name of the element. The symbol for carbon is *C;* oxygen, *O;* hydrogen, *H;* chlorine, *Cl;* and so on. Some of the abbreviations are based on the Latin name of an element: *Fe,* from *ferrum,* for iron; *Pb,* from *plumbum,* for lead; *Ag,* from argentum, for silver. (See Table 3.1 for the symbols of other common elements.)

Not only the atoms that make up the molecule but also the way in which the atoms are arranged determine the behavior of a specific compound. These arrangements are so important to chemists that they make diagrammatic representations, or

Element	Symbol	Protons	Valence Electrons	Electrons Need for Stable Configuration
Hydrogen	H	1	1	Needs 1 or gives up 1
Carbon	C	6	4	Needs 4
Nitrogen	N	7	5	Needs 3[a]
Oxygen	O	8	6	Needs 2
Fluorine	F	9	7	Needs 1
Sodium (*natrium*)	Na	11	1	Gives up 1
Magnesium	Mg	12	2	Gives up 2
Aluminum	Al	13	3	Gives up 3 or needs 5
Silicon	Si	14	4	Needs 4
Phosphorus	P	15	5	Needs 3[a]
Sulfur	S	16	6	Needs 2[a]
Chlorine	Cl	17	7	Needs 1
Potassium (*kalium*)	K	19	1	Gives up 1
Calcium	Ca	20	2	Gives up 2

Table 3.1

Selected Chemical Elements and Their Structural Features

[a]These elements have a tendency to form coordinate covalent bonds by sharing one or more pairs of electrons with other atoms.

formulas, to show the structure of molecules. These formulas, a kind of chemical shorthand, show the positions occupied by all the atoms. A subscript follows the element symbol when more than one atom of an element is required for a compound. The chemical formula for water, H_2O, shows that water consists of two hydrogen atoms and one oxygen atom. Sulfuric acid (H_2SO_4) contains two atoms of hydrogen, one of sulfur, and four of oxygen.

Chemical Reactions

The combination of substances to form new substances is a chemical reaction. The formation of ionic or covalent bonds is a reaction. A common type of reaction in which either ionic or covalent bonds can be formed is an oxidation-reduction reaction. In *oxidation* an atom loses an electron or partly loses an electron in a shared bond; in *reduction* electrons are gained. The reactions are usually coupled because what one substance loses, another gains. Fire, or combustion, is very rapid oxidation of the material that is burning.

Perhaps the simplest oxidation-reduction reaction is that between hydrogen (the reducing agent) and oxygen (the oxidizing agent). Hydrogen is the simplest element, with one proton in the nucleus and one electron orbiting the proton. Hydrogen gas consists of hydrogen molecules, pairs of atoms each held together by a molecular orbital containing two electrons. An oxygen atom has six electrons in the valence shell and, in the chemical reaction forming water, shares an electron from each of two hydrogen atoms to reach the stable configuration of eight electrons:

$$2H_2 + O_2 \rightarrow 2H_2O$$

An example of an oxidation-reduction reaction in textiles is dyeing with indigo dye. Because the colored form of the dye is not soluble in water and is hard to apply, it is reduced by reacting it with a substance that donates electrons. The dye is reduced, gaining electrons, while the reducing agent is oxidized. This reduced dye, which now dissolves in water, is applied to, and absorbed by, the fabric. Because the reducing agent changes the color of the dye, the dye must be oxidized back to its original blue color by reaction with a compound that gains electrons.

Acids and Bases

Two other classes of compounds whose reactions are important are acids and bases. In the simplest sense, an *acid* is a compound that releases hydrogen ions. When added to water, hydrochloric acid (HCl) dissociates into hydrogen ions (which are really just protons without electrons) and chloride ions, each of which keeps an electron from the hydrogen:

$$HCl \rightarrow H^+ + Cl^-$$

Acids are characterized by a sour or tart taste and the ability to turn a special indicator paper, litmus paper, from blue to red. They can be strong or weak, organic (containing carbon) or inorganic. Among the better known strong inorganic acids are sulfuric acid and hydrochloric acid. Acetic acid is a weak organic acid (vinegar is a dilute solution of acetic acid). Other organic acids include lactic acid, present in sour milk, and ascorbic acid (vitamin C). These few examples may serve to illustrate the diversity of acid types.

The strength of an acid in water is an important property influencing the effect of acids on other substances, including textiles. The more hydrogen ions in the solution, the stronger the acid. A standard way to measure strength is *pH,* a scale of 0 through 14 representing the hydrogen ion concentration. The scale is the negative logarithm of the concentration, so the lower the pH, the more hydrogen ions there are in the solution and the stronger the acid. As the pH goes up or down one value on the scale, the concentration of hydrogen ions increases or decreases tenfold.

A *base* is a substance that yields hydroxyl ions in water. A hydroxyl ion is an oxygen atom joined to a hydrogen atom with an overall negative charge (OH^-). Bases, also called alkalis, react with acids to form *salts* and water. When dissolved in water, bases are slippery to the touch, have an acrid taste, and change litmus paper from red to blue.

The most important strong base is sodium hydroxide (NaOH), also called caustic soda. In water the compound dissociates into Na^+ ions and OH^- ions. Sodium hydroxide is used extensively by textile and related industries in making soap, in special treatments given to cotton, and in manufacturing rayon fiber. Borax, baking soda, household ammonia, and drain cleaner are also bases.

There is a relationship between hydrogen ion and hydroxide concentrations in water; as the hydrogen ion concentration goes down, the hydroxide concentration goes up, yielding a higher pH. Solutions with a high hydroxide concentration—high pH—are *alkaline;* solutions with a low pH are *acidic.* A solution that is neutral, neither acidic or basic, has a pH of 7; a pH of less than 7 is acidic, while more than 7 is basic.

Acids and bases often catalyze a reaction known as *hydrolysis.* In hydrolysis a molecule is split; H^+ bonds with one fragment of the split molecule, and OH^- bonds with the other fragment. As molecules in fibers are broken up by hydrolysis, the fibers are considerably weakened.

Some compounds that are classed as acids may not immediately release hydrogen ions but may react in water to bring about the formation of hydrogen ions. The latent acid catalysts, such as magnesium chloride, that are used in durable press finishing of cotton fabrics, act this way (see chapter 21 for discussion of durable press finishes.)

Organic Chemistry

As mentioned previously, almost all fibers are organic, and all organic compounds contain carbon together with a few other elements such as hydrogen, oxygen, nitrogen, the halogens (fluorine, chlorine, bromine, and iodine), and sulfur. Carbon atoms frequently combine with each other in a linear, chainlike arrangement as in the following:

Carbon to carbon to carbon to carbon
→   →   →   →

The connections between atoms may be shown by drawing lines to indicate the bonds:

C—C—C—C—   and so on

If a double bond is formed between two atoms, a double line may be drawn: C=C.
Carbon atoms can combine not only in a linear fashion but also to form a ring:

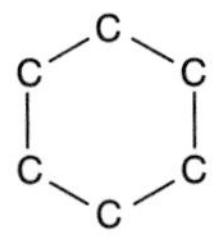

This ring structure is usually drawn without showing all the carbon atoms:

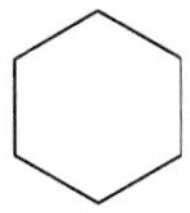

A common structure in organic chemistry is the benzene ring, which occurs in the molecules of a number of different textile fibers and dyes. Benzene consists of six carbon atoms in a ring structure with six hydrogen atoms, one on each carbon, and bonded in alternating, or *conjugated,* single and double bonds:

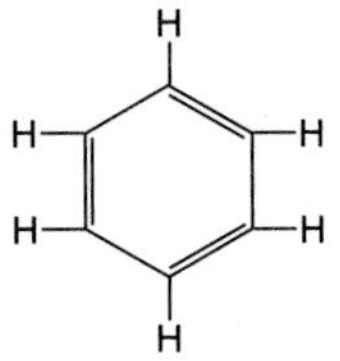

The electrons in the double bonds do not remain at specific bonds but are spread over the ring, or delocalized. Consequently, benzene is more commonly represented as:

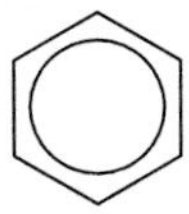

Compounds containing one or more benzene rings or more complex fused rings are called *aromatic* compounds. The name derives from the fact that these rings are often part of the structure of substances with strong, and usually pleasant, odors.

The formulas included thus far to illustrate the shorthand of chemistry have been fairly simple. Formulas of organic compounds, however, are rarely simple. The formula for the repeating unit of cellulose, the basic material of which cotton, rayon, linen, and other vegetable fibers are composed, is shown as the chemist would write it:

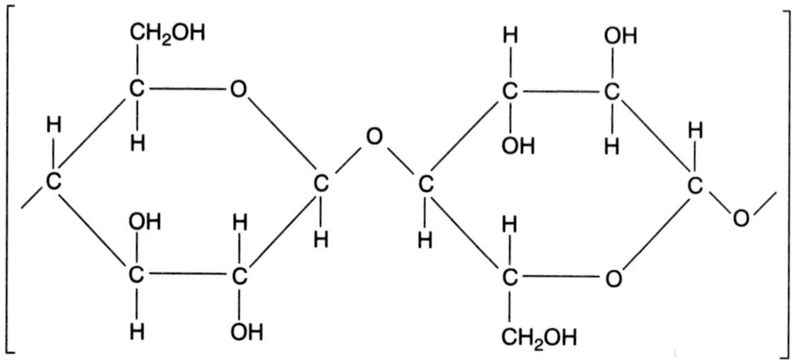

The generic definitions of textile fibers (provided in the chapters about fibers) identify the major repeating units that make up the fiber. In most of these definitions, the unit is named and its formula shown. For example, acrylic fibers are defined as "a manufactured fiber in which the fiber-forming substance is any long-chain synthetic polymer composed of at least 85 percent by weight of acrylonitrile units ($-CH_2-CH-$)."

$$-CH_2-CH-$$
$$|$$
$$CN$$

Chemistry of Color

Light, or electromagnetic energy, exists in a wide number of wavelengths, the range of wavelengths constituting a *spectrum*. The spectrum spans from very short wavelengths such as gamma rays (0.01 nanometers, where one nanometer is one billionth of a meter) to very long wavelengths such as radio waves (10 meters). The human eye, however, is able to see light in the range of only 380–760 nanometers.

Molecules with the right number of conjugated double and single bonds absorb light in the visible range. Different structures will selectively absorb particular wavelengths and reflect other wavelengths. The particular color of a dye or pigment (see chapter 22) is determined by which wavelengths are absorbed and which are reflected. For example, a dye that absorbs all light except that between 430 and 490 nm will reflect the light of those wavelengths. The dye will appear blue when that light enters our eyes and excites sensitive cells in the retina that send the appropriate signals to our brain. (See Figure 3.1.)

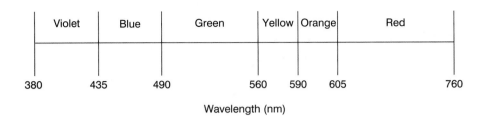

Violet	Blue	Green	Yellow	Orange	Red

380   435   490   560 590 605   760

Wavelength (nm)

Figure 3.1

Color spectrum.

Objects that appear a pure white reflect all the visible wavelengths while absorbing none. Black objects absorb all visible light.

The structures of dye molecules are usually complex. The molecules will have a series of conjugated double bonds for color and will often have functional groups that aid in absorption and retention of the dye by the fiber. An example of a dye structure (C. I. Direct Red 81) is seen here:

Polymers and Polymerization

The definition of acrylic given earlier used the term *polymer.* The word *polymer* means "many parts," and these molecules, also known as *macromolecules,* contain hundreds or thousands of atoms bonded together. Analysis of these large molecules shows that they are composed of molecular subunits containing perhaps three to twenty or more atoms and that the polymers were built up from many of these smaller units, or *monomers,* joined together. In cellulose, for instance, the subunit is glucose. Interestingly, glucose is also the subunit of another well-known polymer, starch. Starch and cellulose have completely different properties, however, because the monomers are bonded to each other differently; starch is not fibrous and can be digested by humans, whereas the opposite is true for cellulose.

The formation of polymers, or *polymerization,* is accomplished through the joining of monomers, one to the other. In the formation of polymers, several intermediate steps take place. Two monomers may join to form a *dimer* (two-monomer molecule), a dimer and a monomer join to form a *trimer* (three-monomer molecule), two dimers join to form a *tetramer* (four-monomer structure), and so on.

Monomers may be combined and can be arranged in a variety of ways to make polymers. *Homopolymers* are polymers composed of identical units of the same monomer substance. *Copolymers* contain two or more different units. Copolymerization is likely to be used to create textile fibers with desirable properties not present in the homopolymer. These compounds are usually classified as *oligomers.*

As oligomers grow into large polymer molecules, the number of repeating units in the molecule becomes important. This number is the degree of polymerization (DP). Longer polymers, with high DPs, contribute strength to fibers.

The arrangement of repeating units in polymers can vary. Imagine that M below represents identical units of the same monomer in a homopolymer.

$$—M—M—M—M—M—M—M—M—M—$$

Copolymer structures may have any of several different arrangements. Imagine that M represents one monomer unit and m represents a second monomer unit. Copolymer structures may have:

1. random arrangement with no clear pattern in the alternating of monomers:

$$—M—M—m—m—M—m—M—M—m—m—M—m—M—$$

2. alternating copolymer arrangement:

$$—M—m—M—m—M—m—M—m—M—m—M—m—M—$$

3. block copolymer arrangement, with individual monomers grouped together and these groups alternating:

$$—MMMM—mmmm—MMMM—mmmm—$$

Sometimes a small amount of a third monomer may be added to impart some desired quality otherwise lacking in the polymer. For example, the polymer may benefit from having some sites that would react with certain types of dyes or to form cross-links. Imagine that x represents the third monomer added to a random polymer arrangement:

$$—M—M—m—x—m—M—m—m—x—M—M—m—$$

Yet another structure can also be formed, that of graft polymers that are made by attaching monomers onto long-chain polymers. The long chain forms the base structure, rather like the trunk of a tree, with the side chains branching off. Grafting makes possible the addition of qualities not present in the "mother" fiber. Grafting of monomers can reduce static electricity buildup, improve dyeability, improve soil resistance, increase strength, or decrease shrinkage.

A graft of a monomer to a homopolymer might be represented as follows:

Linear polymers are formed either by *condensation polymerization* or by *addition polymerization*. In condensation polymerization, as a small molecule (usually water, ammonia, or hydrogen chloride) is eliminated, monomers join other molecules:

monomer + monomer → dimer + water (eliminated)

dimer + dimer → tetramer + water (eliminated)

Monomers may link up with monomers, monomers with polymers, polymers with polymers, and so on to form a growing chain, with the elimination of water or another compound during the process. Examples of this process are, among the natural fibers, cellulose from glucose and, among the manufactured fibers, nylon from its components. (See Figure 3.2.)

Figure 3.2

Schematic representation of condensation reaction. (a) Unreacted monomer units with chemically reactive groups shown as shaded area at each end of the molecule. (b) Collisions between moving monomer units; collisions 1, 2, and 3 occur at reactive sites on each unit, leading to bond formation and release of by-product molecules. The molecules bounce off each other in collision 4. (c) New dimer units have formed, each with reactive site at both ends. (d) Larger fragments have formed by further reaction with monomer units. (e) End of reaction; fragments have joined together to form part of molecular chains. The by-product is removed at the end of the reaction or preferably as it is liberated on bond formation. Reprinted by permission from *Textiles Magazine,* a publication of The Textile Institute, UK.

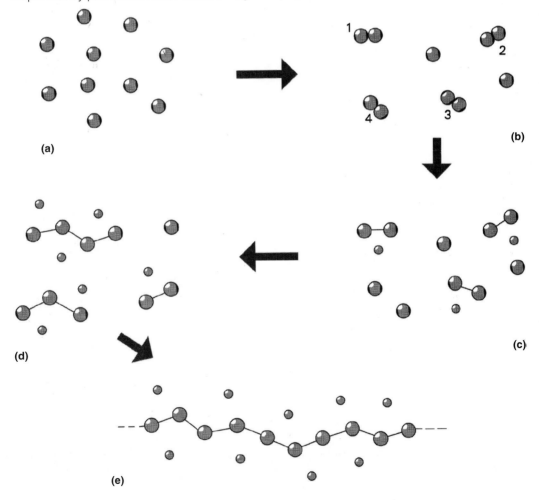

Addition polymerization differs from condensation polymerization in that no compound is split off. Monomers with the capacity to react (unsaturated monomers) can add to each other in a chemically effected chain reaction to join into a long-chain molecule. This is generally accomplished under conditions of high pressure and high temperature and in the presence of a *catalyst* (a substance that does not take part in the reaction but facilitates the reaction):

monomer		reactive monomer		reactive dimer	
+	=	+	=	+	→ *polymer*
activator		monomer		monomer	

Figure 3.3

Schematic representation of addition reaction. (a) Unreacted monomer units approached by highly reactive initiator molecule (shaded black). (b) Chemical bond formed between initiator molecule and monomer unit. The reactive site, marked by an asterisk, transfers to the opposite end of the new molecule. (c) Chain propagation, another monomer unit added. (d) Chain propagation continues with successive addition of monomer units and transfer of reactive sites. (e) End of reaction; the initiating molecule is at one end of the chain. Reprinted by permission from *Textiles Magazine,* a publication of The Textile Institute, UK.

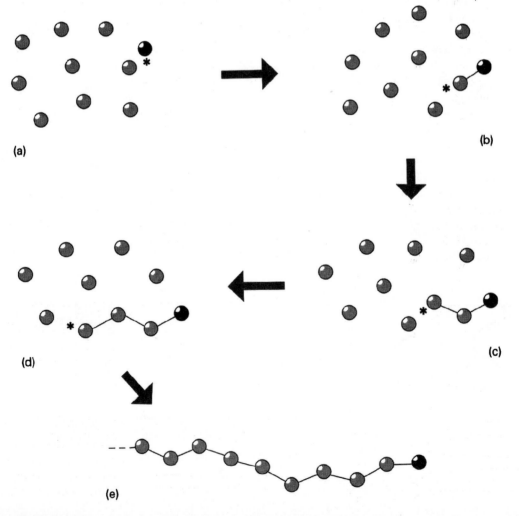

(See Figure 3.3.) An example of this process is the polymerization of acrylonitrile to create acrylic fibers. Acrylonitrile is a nitrogen-containing three-carbon molecule.

This, in highly simplified terms, is part of the chemical process that takes place in the manufacture of synthetic fibers. Most of the specific processes used by companies to make their trademarked textile fibers are carefully guarded secrets. Such confidential processes are known as *proprietary processes*. Textile chemists, however, can make reasonably accurate estimates of the processes used by each company by reading research reports and by analyzing the properties and physical structure of the fibers.

Textile Fibers

Polymers and Their Arrangement

Fibers are made up of many chemically alike polymer molecules or chains. The arrangement of the polymer chains affects many properties such as strength, elongation, absorbency, and dyeability. This arrangement can vary from random to parallel. A random, unorganized arrangement of long-chain molecules creates an *amorphous* area within the fiber (Figure 3.4). Orderly, parallel arrangement of polymer segments in a three-dimensional pattern is known as *crystallinity*, but crystalline regions may lie in a variety of positions relative to fiber length. If the crystalline structures are parallel to the length, or axis, of the fiber, they are said to be *oriented* (Figure 3.5).

Most fibers possess largely crystalline structures, but they also have some amorphous areas. The amorphous areas are weaker than the crystalline areas, and fibers with the highest levels of crystallinity are the strongest fibers. If the crystalline areas are oriented, the fiber strength is enhanced.

A good illustration of the effect of crystallinity and orientation on fiber strength is a comparison among three fibers with the same chemical structure but different polymer arrangements: cotton, flax, and rayon. They are all composed of the same polymer, cellulose. Cotton is about 70 percent crystalline and 30 percent amorphous, whereas rayon is the opposite, being only about 30 percent crystalline. The result is that cotton is stronger than rayon. Flax is slightly more crystalline than cotton, but it is considerably stronger because its polymers are oriented. In cotton, however, while some of the molecules are parallel to the fiber length, many lie at an angle. In this position they are not able to bear as much force as are more oriented molecules. It should be noted that strength is also affected by DP. Cotton and flax have higher DPs than rayon.

Figure 3.4

Amorphous arrangement of polymers within fiber.

Figure 3.5

Crystalline arrangement of molecules in fiber, with molecules oriented to fiber length.

While the crystalline areas affect fiber strength and modulus, the amorphous regions contribute other important properties. Dyes and finishes, as well as moisture, are absorbed primarily in the disordered regions. In addition, amorphous fibers are more flexible and stretchable.

The structures of some manufactured fibers have a low degree of crystallinity when they are formed. By stretching, or *drawing,* the fiber, the polymer chains become aligned and ordered, resulting in a higher degree of crystallinity. This principle can be seen by taking a strip of polyethylene plastic cut from a storage bag and slowly stretching it. As the strip narrows, the plastic becomes clearer, finer, and much stronger. (See Figure 3.6.)

Textile scientists have studied the arrangement of polymers in fibers, or *fiber morphology,* for many years. With continued research and investigation into the chemical structure of fibers, new theories and knowledge concerning the arrangement of molecules evolved. It was necessary to explain the presence of both crystalline and amorphous regions, as well as the fact that the crystalline areas, in cotton for example, were smaller than the length of the polymers. A model consistent with these observations proposed that the long polymer molecules pass in and out of crystalline regions and into amorphous regions. The *fringed fibril theory* put forth by Hearle and Peters (1963) illustrates this model (Figure 3.7). The polymers are

Figure 3.6

Effect of drawing of fibers on polymer orientation.

Figure 3.7

Fringed fibril structure.

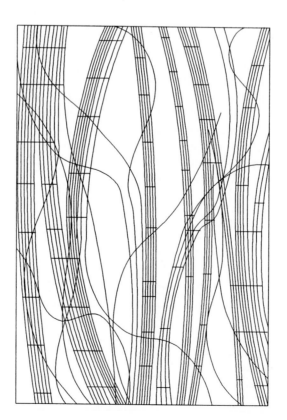

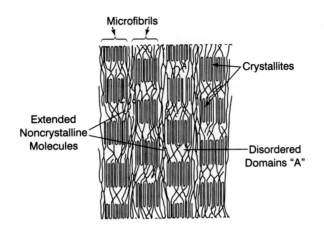

Figure 3.8

A model of the structure of polyester proposed by Prevorsek and his colleagues. Reprinted by permission from J. W. S. Hearle, "Understanding and Control of Fibre Structure," *Textile Horizons* February 1994, 11–14.

close together in the crystalline areas and then pass into more disordered regions. Morton and Hearle (1975) used the analogy of a pile of beads to describe this fiber morphology:

> If the beads have hooks on them and several people start fastening them together, each person will build up a compact region of strings of beads fastened together in regular order. But, after a time, the actions of one person will begin to interfere with those of another: it will not be possible for some chains to be fastened up any further because they are already fixed elsewhere. The hooking-together of the strings continues until finally there are several regions of beads fastened together, whereas between them the strings go off in various directions and can only be fastened together where two beads happen to pass close to one another. (p. 26)

Later work on fiber internal structure showed that crystalline areas could be formed not only from molecules close to each other but also by polymers folding back on themselves. Current theory also holds that, in many manufactured fibers, crystallites are stacked in an almost fibrillar form, tied together by polymer molecules passing through amorphous regions. (See Figure 3.8.)

Internal Bonds or Forces

Figure 3.9 shows lines representing intermolecular cross-links between the chains in the crystalline areas. In many fibers these intermolecular bonds cementing the crystalline areas are *hydrogen bonds*. Hydrogen bonds, which are about one-tenth to one-fifteenth as strong as single covalent bonds, occur in specific, highly polar compounds. The oxygen, nitrogen, or fluorine in one molecule is slightly negative and

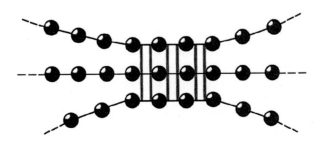

Figure 3.9

Hydrogen bonding (electrostatic attraction) between polar groups on adjacent chains. Reprinted by permission from *Textiles Magazine,* a publication of The Textile Institute, UK.

attracts the slightly positive hydrogen bonded in another molecule to an oxygen, nitrogen, or fluorine atom.

This type of bonding occurs in water (H_2O), a chemical material we experience as a gas (steam), as a liquid, and as a solid (snow and ice). The very fact that water exists as a liquid or solid means that there is something holding the individual water molecules together. That something, the polarity of the molecule, is due to the residual electrical charges found on the oxygen atom (negative) and the hydrogen atom (positive). The negative oxygen of one molecule is attracted to the positive hydrogen of another one. Hydrogen bonding also occurs in the cellulose molecule, as shown in the following illustration, where the oxygen in one molecule is attracted to the hydrogen on another molecule. This attraction holds the chains together in the crystalline areas of the fiber.

All molecules have some polarity and, thus, some tendency to stick together. When the molecules are polymers, small positive and negative electrical charges exist all along their length and provide a substantial total intermolecular bonding force. The overall effectiveness of this force depends on how strong the polarities are, how parallel the molecules are to one another, how smooth or bumpy they are, and how long the molecules are.

When long polymers are attracted to parallel long polymers by hydrogen bonds or polar forces, fibers are stronger than if short polymers are attracted to short polymers. In long molecules the area over which these forces bond is greater, increasing the cumulative effect and requiring more force to pull the chains apart. Consequently, the fiber with longer molecules bonded together is stronger. This generalization is true only up to a certain point, however. Chain length will eventually reach the point where any further increase will not result in an increase in strength. At the same time, no decrease in strength takes place either.

Although most polymers are of straight-line formation, some polymeric substances react to form side chains as well. These side chains cause the molecules to function differently than long, straight molecules. Such polymers do not crystallize as readily as do regular, unbranched polymers because the side chains prevent the polymer chains from coming in close enough contact for hydrogen bonds to operate. (See Figure 3.10.)

Another means by which molecules are held together is *cross-linking*. Cross-linking is the attachment of one polymer molecule to another by covalent chemical

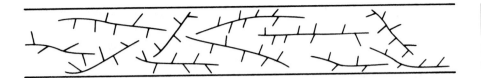

Figure 3.10

Polymers with side chains within fiber.

bonds; these bonds are equivalent in strength to those along the polymer chain. Some fibers, such as spandex, are formed with cross-links. (See chapter 12 for a discussion of spandex.) Wool and animal hair fibers have naturally cross-linked structures. It is thought that the cross-links in wool are one of the factors responsible for the excellent resiliency of this fiber. The polymers in fibers can also be cross-linked as part of an applied finish to give such properties as improved wrinkle resistance and chemical stability. The cross-links in finished cotton serve to return the molecules to their original position within the fiber after it has been bent or folded, thus providing wrinkle recovery. (See chapter 21.)

Effects of Chemical Substances on Textiles

The behavior of textile fibers depends not only on the arrangement of the polymers but also on their chemical makeup. If one were to diagram each of the smaller molecules, or monomers, from which polymers are formed, one would see precisely the elements of which they are made. When chemists see a molecular diagram or formula, they recognize that there are "functional chemical groups" within the polymer, that is, places at which chemical reactions are likely to take place. Some of these reactions take place when textiles come into contact with substances used in processing or in everyday use.

Materials with which textile fibers come into contact might be divided, roughly, into two principal groups: (1) materials used in processing fibers or fabrics, such as bleaches, dyes, or special finishes used to alter fabric characteristics such as crease resistance, soil resistance, and flame retardancy; and (2) materials used in home or professional care or cleaning of fabrics, such as soaps, detergents, cleaning solvents, and moth repellents. Some of these substances are organic and some are inorganic. Some are acid, some are alkaline, and some are neutral. Effects of some of the more important substances are discussed in the following sections.

Acids

The action of acids when they come into contact with various textile fibers varies not only with the type of textile fiber but also with the strength and type of acid. It is important for the textile manufacturer to be acquainted with the effect of acids on textile fibers to avoid damaging fibers or fabrics during finishing. Also, some specialized textile processes rely on the action of acids on various textile fibers.

Acid hydrolysis results in the breaking of long-chain molecules into shorter chains. In these cases, the bonds connecting the subunits are unstable to acid, and the result is a loss of tensile strength. If the reaction goes on for a sufficiently long time, susceptible fibers will actually be dissolved. Cellulosic fibers are damaged by strong mineral acids and are harmed even by quite diluted concentrations of these substances. Acid hydrolysis, in a highly controlled process, is used to make permanently stiffened sheer cotton fabrics. The acid is applied so that it breaks down the outermost layer of fabric. The outer layer softens, the reaction is stopped, and the fabric is given a hard press that forms the outer fabric layer into a smooth, clear, permanently stiffened finish.

Because dilute acids do not readily harm protein fibers (the bonds connecting the subunits are relatively stable to acid), especially wool, acid treatments can be used to clean vegetable matter from wool before spinning or after fabrication into cloth. The controlled acid solution destroys the sticks and burrs caught in the wool, the acid is neutralized, and the wool is left unharmed. (See the discussion of carbonization of wool in chapter 20.) Such processes are carried out under rigidly controlled conditions to avoid any harm to the fibers. Strong mineral acids will damage wool fiber.

Bases

Bases, even strong bases at high temperatures, do not appreciably harm natural cellulosic fibers. Bases do, however, cause radical physical changes that improve the strength and appearance of cellulosic fibers. For this reason, a special treatment with the alkali sodium hydroxide is sometimes given to these fibers.

Sensitivity to bases is important in the care of protein fibers (silk, wool, and animal hair fibers) in which the bonds between the subunits are broken by the alkali. Some synthetic fibers are also negatively affected by bases. Many strong soaps and detergents have alkaline material added to increase their cleaning power. These soaps and detergents should be avoided for use with fibers that are sensitive to the action of bases.

Oxidizing Agents

Many fibers are not white enough in their natural state or after manufacture to permit dyes to be fully effective. Colors and/or stains accumulated during spinning and weaving are removed by the action of bleaches that oxidize the stains or colors. The oxidation interferes with the conjugated double bonds in the colored material, converting it into a colorless substance. However, the oxidizing agent may also react with the fiber itself. If the fiber is sensitive to the action of the oxidizing agent, the fiber may be damaged.

Chlorine bleach is an oxidizing agent that may damage protein fibers and spandex. Chlorine bleach must be carefully controlled in bleaching cellulose fabric, but it does no appreciable harm to other fibers such as polyester or nylon. Other bleaching agents made from substances such as sodium perborate will oxidize stains without damage to fibers. Both the consumer and the manufacturer benefit from understanding the action of oxidizing agents on different fibers.

Solvents

Dyeing and finishing of textiles, as well as laundering and dry cleaning, involve chemical *solutions* and *solvents*. We are all familiar with water solutions of sugar or salt, in which the sugar or salt, the *solute,* is uniformly distributed in water, the solvent. Solutions where water is the solvent are *aqueous* solutions.

A substance is dissolved if it is distributed as individual atoms or molecules within the solvent. If the molecules of a substance aggregate in a solvent, they are said to be *dispersed.* Most dyes are applied to textiles from aqueous solutions. Exceptions are disperse dyes, used on polyester, nylon, and acetate, which are dispersed in water.

It is evident, therefore, that not all solvents will dissolve all solutes. An important consideration is the polarities of the solute and solvent. The rule to remember here is that "like dissolves like." As discussed earlier, water, the most common solvent, is a polar molecule. It will therefore dissolve ionic or polar molecules. Many dyes have negatively charged sulfonic acid groups ($—SO_3—$) in their structure and dissolve readily in water. Nonpolar solvents such as carbon tetrachloride or perchloroethylene are used to dissolve nonpolar substances such as oily stains on textiles.

Textiles and other materials can be classified based on their attraction for polar or nonpolar solvents. A *hydrophilic* material attracts polar water molecules, while one that is *hydrophobic* attracts and absorbs nonpolar organic solvents. Laundering, with water, removes water-based stains that are often polar in nature. Organic solvents used in dry cleaning help to dissolve oily dirt and stains. (See chapter 24.)

Some Physical Concepts

Understanding textiles requires not only some knowledge of chemistry but also an understanding of the physical world. In processing and in use, textiles are subjected to physical forces and conditions, their resistance to which determines their applicability.

Some of the physical properties of fibers that can be measured were explained in chapter 2. These measurements are expressed in units, for example inch or pound in the British system and centimeter or gram in the metric system. There are seven basic units in the SI system (described in chapter 2); these are listed, along with their symbols, in Table 3.2. These units cover the three main dimensions of the physical world: length, time, and mass. All physical quantities can be expressed in units of length, time, and mass. The speed of a car is expressed in terms of length and time, in miles per hour or in kilometers per hour. The density of fibers, explained in chapter 2, is expressed in units of length and mass: grams per cubic centimeter.

Quantity	Name	Symbol
Length	meter	m
Mass	kilogram	kg
Time	second	s
Temperature	kelvin	K
Electric current	ampere	A
Number of particles	mole	mol
Luminous intensity	candela	cd

Table 3.2

Basic Units of Measure in the SI System

Mass and Weight

Length and time are familiar concepts, but there is often confusion over the units of mass and weight. For standardization purposes mass is defined in comparison to a one kilogram standard cylinder maintained in Paris, France. Mass is really a measure of the inertia of an object, or its resistance to acceleration. This is not the same as weight, although the two are related. On earth, weight is the force with which gravity pulls on an object. Therefore, weight is mass times the acceleration due to gravity. Objects dropped from a height pick up speed, or accelerate, as they move toward the ground.

Force

When someone pulls on an object, such as a piece of fabric, he or she is exerting a *force* on the object. The resistance of a fabric to an applied force is a measure of its strength. Force is measured in terms of length, time, and mass. The standard unit of force is the *newton.* One newton is the force required to accelerate a one kilogram mass one meter per second squared. The force of gravity accelerates objects 32 feet per second squared. The strength of fiber is often measured in *grams force,* which is about one hundred times smaller than a newton.

Heat and Energy

Aside from forces, another condition to which textiles are exposed is heat. Heat is thermal energy transferred from a warm object to a cooler one. Heat, or thermal energy, may be transferred to a textile fabric from a hot iron or from an abrasive action. The molecules in fibers absorb thermal energy and may change their chemical structure or their physical arrangement. Thermoplastic polymers under high enough heat will rearrange within the fiber, often assuming a more random or amorphous form as the weakest intermolecular bonds begin to give way. The temperature at which these fibers begin to show such morphological changes, and appear to soften, is the *glass transition temperature,* abbreviated T_g. The temperature at which the fibers melt is the melting temperature, T_m.

This behavior under imposition of heat is used in heat setting fabric made from thermoplastic fibers. Not only can fibers be heat-set to make their dimensions permanent, but many fabrics can also be heat-set into pleats, creases, or other permanent shaping. For heat setting to take place, the fabric is deformed into the desired shape. When heat is then applied above the T_g but below the T_m, the molecules assume the deformed shape to accommodate the strain. Upon cooling, new intermolecular bonds form that tend to hold the molecules in their new shape. The fiber after cooling will remain in this position until the heat-setting temperature is again reached or exceeded. If the T_g of a fiber is low, the fiber cannot be successfully heat-set for ordinary uses because hot water in washing or heat from a dryer will negate the effect of heat setting.

If, in use and care, a heat-set fabric is subjected to a temperature above its respective heat-setting temperature, heat setting will be lost. Likewise, a wrinkled thermoplastic fabric lying in a very hot dryer may have wrinkles set in if the dryer temperature goes above the heat-setting temperature.

Summary

This chapter has outlined some chemical and physical concepts that are used in explaining textile properties and processes. Reference to these concepts will be made in later chapters related to particular fibers, structures, or finishes.

The importance of the chemical aspects of textile science cannot be underrated. Understanding the chemistry of fibers and finishes is important because textile products are exposed to many different chemical substances, in processing as well as in use and care. Knowing how fibers respond to acids or bases, for example, will enable wiser use of textiles and better recommendations to consumers. In addition, the chemistry involved in producing manufactured fibers, both synthetic and regenerated, affords students a better understanding of these processes.

Textiles are subjected not only to chemical effects but also to physical forces and conditions. Their responses to physical forces determine their applicability for specific end uses and thus can be used in product development and prediction of product behavior. Fabrics engineered for bullet-proof vests would be expected to have different physical properties than those designed for lingerie. Comparison of different textiles by measuring responses to different forces, to heat, or to other conditions enables appropriate selection of these products for specific applications.

References

Hearle, J. W. S., and R. H. Peters. 1963. *Fibre structure.* London: Newnes-Butterworth.

Morton, W. E., and J. W. S. Hearle. 1975. *Physical properties of textile fibres.* New York: Wiley.

Review Questions

1. What is a polymer? What is polymerization, and how is it accomplished?
2. What is the difference between addition polymerization and condensation polymerization?
3. Distinguish between homopolymers and copolymers. Name and describe three different copolymer structures.
4. Explain, in simplified terms, how seeing color is related to the chemical structure of molecules.
5. If a fiber producer wanted a strong fiber, why would the producer be likely to look for a fiber that is more crystalline and less amorphous?
6. Describe the various ways that molecules within a fiber may bond together. What advantages come from these forms of bonding?
7. Describe some of the ways in which chemical reactions between textile fibers and chemical substances such as acids, bases, and oxidizing agents can be used in textile processing.
8. What is T_g, and why is it important to textiles?

Recommended Readings

Billmeyer, F. W. Jr. 1984. *Textbook of polymer science.* New York: Wiley.

Calvert, P. 1989. Synthetic polymer self assembly. *Nature* 326 (April 9): 540.

Hearle, J. W. S. 1982. *Polymers and their properties.* Vol. 1, *Fundamentals of structure and mechanics.* Chichester, England: Ellis Horwood.

Lomax, G. R. 1987. The polymerization reaction. Part 1: Synthetic textile polymers. *Textiles* 16: 51.

————. 1987. The polymerization reaction. Part 2: Natural textile polymers. *Textiles* 16: 76.

NATURAL CELLULOSIC FIBERS

C ellulosic fibers are composed of natural cellulose, regenerated cellulose, or regenerated chemical variants of cellulose. Natural cellulosic fibers are derived from a wide variety of plant sources, which are classified as follows:

1. Seed hair fibers, or those fibers that grow in a seed pod on plants.
2. Bast fibers, or those fibers that are removed from the stems of plants.
3. Leaf fibers, or those fibers that are found on the leaves of plants.
4. Miscellaneous fibers from mosses, roots, and the like.

Manufactured cellulosic fibers include rayon, a regenerated cellulosic fiber, and acetate and triacetate, which are modified cellulosic fibers (discussed in chapter 7).

Cellulose Family

Table 4.1 lists fibers of the cellulose family. Included in this list are not only those fibers that have extensive commercial production and distribution but also fibers that have little or no importance to the consumer.

Each of these cellulosic fibers possesses distinctive qualities or properties that distinguish it from others and make it especially suitable for certain end uses. Most cellulosic fibers also share a "family resemblance" in their physical and chemical properties.

In all subsequent discussions of the properties of different fibers, statements about fiber characteristics are made in relation to the characteristics of other fibers. For example, when flax is said to be a relatively strong fiber, what is meant is that, in comparison with other fibers, flax is fairly strong. If the strength of flax were mea-

Table 4.1

Fibers of the Cellulose Family

Natural Fibers	Manufactured Fibers
A. Seed hair fibers	**A. Rayon**
1. *Major fibers*	1. Viscose rayon
Cotton	2. High-wet-modulus rayon
2. *Minor fibers*	3. Cuprammonium rayon
Kapok	4. Solvent-spun rayon
B. Bast fibers	**B. Modified cellulose fibers**
1. Flax	1. Acetate
2. Jute	Saponified rayon[a]
3. Ramie	2. Triacetate[b]
4. Hemp	
5. Kenaf	
C. Leaf fibers[a]	
1. Abaca[a]	
2. Sisal[a]	
3. Henequen[a]	
4. Piñā[a]	
D. Fruit	
Coir	
E. Miscellaneous[a]	
1. Spanish moss[a]	
2. Sacaton (root fiber)[a]	

[a]Of limited use or discontinued.

[b]No longer produced in the United States.

sured against that of a strand of steel or aluminum wire, for example, it would seem relatively weak.

General Characteristics of Cellulosic Fibers

The following discussion summarizes the general characteristics of natural cellulosic fibers and rayon as a class or group. Cellulose acetate and cellulose triacetate are chemical variants of cellulose and, as such, do not share in many of the family characteristics. Their specific fiber characteristics are discussed at length later, in chapter 7.

The density of cellulosic fibers tends to be relatively high, making fabrics woven from yarns of these fibers feel comparatively heavy. Cellulosic fibers have relatively low elasticity and resilience. As a result, they wrinkle easily and do not recover from wrinkling readily. Absorbency and moisture regain are generally high. Most cellulosic fibers are, therefore, slow to dry after wetting, comfortable to wear, and easy to dye.

Cellulosic fibers are good conductors of heat and electricity. As good conductors of heat, they carry warmth away from the body and are favored for use in hot weather and warm climates. Since they conduct electricity, cellulosic fibers do not build up static electricity, which produces shocks when garments are worn.

Cellulosic fibers tend to burn easily, with a quick, yellow flame, much as paper (which is also cellulose). Most cellulosic fibers can, however, withstand fairly high dry heat or ironing temperatures before they scorch. On an electric iron, cotton and linen settings are the highest settings on the dial.

Chemical properties of cellulosic fibers include good resistance to bases. Excessive bleaching will harm cellulosic fibers, although carefully controlled bleaching is not detrimental. Strong mineral acids are quite damaging. Most natural cellulosic fibers will withstand high water temperatures. Such properties permit laundering of cellulosic fibers with strong detergents, controlled bleaching, and hot water temperatures. Regenerated cellulosic fibers are more sensitive to chemicals and require more careful handling and gentle agitation with lower water temperatures.

Most insects do not attack cellulosic fibers. However, silverfish are likely to attack heavily starched cellulosic fabrics. Most cellulosic fabrics are susceptible to attack by fungi, especially mildew. Extended exposure to sunlight tends to damage the fibers.

Seed Hair Fibers

Seed hair fibers belong to a class in which the fibers grow from the seeds that are formed in pods on certain plants. The most widely used seed hair fiber is cotton. Other seed hair fibers include kapok, milkweed, and cattail.

Cotton

History

The cotton plant appears to have been native to the area known today as India and Pakistan, and the cultivation and use of cotton is thought to have begun there. Eventually the use of cotton spread into other areas in which the climate was compatible with its cultivation. Some archeologists and anthropologists believe that cotton was imported into South America from Asia during prehistoric times. Others, who point out that cotton plants of South America differ genetically from the Asian varieties, believe that cotton cultivation and spinning developed independently in the Western Hemisphere.

The earliest evidence of actual woven cotton fabrics was found in India during the excavation of the city called Mohenjo-Daro. The date assigned to these fabrics was the third millenium B.C., so that we know that the use of cotton for fabrics was well established by this date. Fabrics of comparable age have been unearthed in excavations of Peruvian grave sites (Barber 1991).

From India, cotton cultivation spread west to Egypt and east into China and the South Pacific. Roman writers speak of importing cotton fabrics from Egypt and the East. Since cotton cannot be cultivated in the cooler European climates, cotton fiber and fabrics used in the Middle Ages had to be imported. Because Europeans had never seen cotton plants, the belief was widespread that cotton came from the fleece of a beast that was half-plant and half-animal (Anderson 1973).

One of the purposes of Columbus's voyage was to find a shorter trade route to India to import the fine Indian cotton fabrics. When Columbus found the Indians of Santo Domingo wearing cotton garments, he was convinced that he had, indeed, discovered a new route to India.

Large-scale cotton cultivation in the American colonies is thought to have begun as early as 1556 when cotton seeds were planted in Florida. By 1616 colonists in Virginia were growing cotton along the James River.

Cotton provides an interesting illustration of the ways in which the value of a textile fiber can vary. In the eighteenth century and before the invention of the cotton gin, cotton fabric was a costly luxury used chiefly by the wealthy. After its processing became less labor intensive through mechanization, the price decreased, and for many decades cotton was a utilitarian fabric available at relatively low cost.

Since the development of manufactured fibers, cotton production and manufacture has had its ups and downs. Fluctuations in supply affect the price of cotton. But supply is not the only factor involved in establishing the price of cotton. Fashion trends toward or away from natural fibers also serve to increase or decrease demand and, thus, prices.

The Southern states of the United States proved especially hospitable to the cultivation of cotton, and the production of cotton soon became a major factor in the economy of the South. As Americans migrated westward, the cultivation of cotton also moved west in those areas where the climate was suitable. Texas is the single largest producer of cotton in the United States. During the crop years 1989–1993 (a cotton crop year runs from August to July), production in Texas averaged 4.3 million bales, or about 30 percent of total production in the United States. California was second with an average of 2.9 million bales, followed by Mississippi (1.9 million bales), Arkansas (1.3 million bales), and Louisiana (1.2 million bales). Combined, these five states accounted for 75 percent of the total U.S. cotton production for the 1989–1993 crop years.

Economic Importance of Cotton Production

Worldwide, more cotton is used than any other single fiber. From 1989–1991 cotton accounted for about 49 percent of total world fiber consumption. Outside the United States cotton made up about 52 percent of all fibers consumed. In the United States about 31 percent of the total fiber used by textile mills was cotton, while at the retail level cotton represented about 38 percent of total consumption. Among staple fibers in the United States, cotton accounted for about 48 percent of total use in 1989–1991. (Polyester staple was second with about 24 percent of the total.) Cotton consumption exceeded that for polyester staple and filament by almost 29 percent.

During the 1989–1993 crop years, total world cotton production averaged 86 million bales (18.7 million metric tons). China was the largest producer, growing 24 percent of the world total, followed by the United States (20 percent), India (12 percent), Pakistan (9 percent), and Uzbekistan (a republic of the former Soviet Union with 8 percent). On average these five countries produce almost three quarters of the world cotton crop.[1]

Botanical Information

Cotton fiber is removed from the boll, or seed pod, that grows on a plant of the botanical genus *gossypium*. (See Figure 4.1.) Cotton is a member of the mallow family, related to the common garden hollyhock, hibiscus, and okra. Each fiber is a single plant cell that develops as an elongation of a cell in the outer layer, or epidermis, of the cotton seed. (See Figure 4.2.) These seed hairs are called *lint*. A secondary

---

1. Statistics provided by the National Cotton Council of America, November 1994. (Each bale weighs 480 pounds.)

Figure 4.1

(a) Cross section of a cotton flower showing seeds in boll at the bottom of the flower; (b) closed boll; (c) mature, open boll. Micrograph (a) by J. McD. Stewart. Photographs (b) and (c) courtesy of U.S. Department of Agriculture.

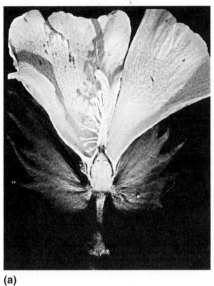

(a)   (b)   (c)

Figure 4.2

Cotton seed showing fibers growing, two days after flowering. Micrograph by J. McD. Stewart.

growth of much shorter fibers accompanies the growth of cotton lint. These fibers, which are too short to be spun into yarn, are called *linters.*

Types of Cotton

Many different species are included within the genus *gossypium,* and each species of cotton includes many varieties that will produce different results under various field and weather conditions. Robert Merkel has likened these differences to those that can be seen among wine grapes grown in different climates and soils.[2]

---

[2]Comment to author by Dr. Robert Merkel, Florida International University, in review of manuscript, spring 1985.

Cotton fibers are sometimes classified according to the length to which they grow. Longer fibers command higher prices since they are usually also finer. These are as follows:

1. *Short-staple fiber:* ⅜ to ¾ inches in length. Short fibers come from Asiatic species of cotton that are both short and coarse. (Botanically, these are either *G. arboreum* or *G. herbaceum.*)
2. *Intermediate-staple fiber:* ¹³⁄₁₆ to 1¼ inches in length. The variety known as American Upland is of intermediate length and coarseness. This variety of cotton makes up by far the largest quantity of cotton fiber grown in the United States. (Botanically, *G. hirsutum.*)
3. *Long-staple fiber:* 1½ to 2½ inches. This includes varieties known as Sea Island Egyptian and pima (or American-Egyptian), all of which are used for good-quality cotton fabric. Peruvian and Brazilian fibers also fall into this classification. However, the Peruvian variety, known as *tanguis,* has a slight crimp and rougher feel, somewhat like that of wool, with which it is sometimes blended. (Botanically, *G. barbadense.*)

Cultivation

For optimum growth the cotton plant requires a warm climate, with adequate rain or other water supply. A favorable distribution of rain is more important than is the quantity of rain because the plant needs plenty of moisture during the growing season and warm, dry weather during harvesting. For this reason, cotton is also grown successfully in warm, dry climates with adequate water for irrigation.

Blooms appear on the plant from 80 to 110 days after planting. The blooms are creamy white or yellow when they first appear. From 12 hours to 3 days after the blooms have appeared, they have changed in color to pink, lavender, or red and have fallen off the plant, leaving the developing boll on the stem. Fifty to 80 days later the pod has matured, the pod has burst open, and the cotton is ready to be picked. The mechanism that causes the opening of the cotton boll is not fully understood. It is believed to be related to hormonal changes in the maturing plant. Whatever the specific cause, the result is that the boll walls crack, the boll dries, and the cotton fiber is exposed, mature and ready for picking. (See Figure 4.1c.) Failure to pick the ripened cotton promptly detracts from the quality of the fiber.

To facilitate harvesting, plants may be treated with defoliants that cause a shedding of the leaves and prevent further development of the plant or with desiccants that kill the plant by causing a loss of water from the tissue. When desiccants are used, the leaves remain on the plant and contribute to the trash content of harvested cotton, whereas defoliants remove and thereby decrease this material.

Picking of the cotton is done either by hand or machine. In the United States a great deal of cotton production and harvesting has been mechanized (Figure 4.3), but in underdeveloped parts of the world, much of the cotton planting, cultivation, and harvesting is done by hand.

Production of the Fiber

Once the cotton fiber has been picked, it must be separated from the cottonseeds. This is accomplished by ginning. The cotton gin removes the fibers from the seeds. (See Figure 4.4.) Cotton linters, too short for spinning, are used in making rayons

Figure 4.3

Cotton harvesting machines. Photograph courtesy of Mississippi Cooperative Extension Service.

and acetates; as stuffing materials for mattresses, upholstery, and pillows; and in nontextile materials such as paper. Seeds are used in making cottonseed oil and fertilizer.

The quality of cotton fiber varies not only as to the length and variety of fiber but also as to physical condition from ginning; the amount of vegetable matter, dirt, and sand present; and color. Evaluation of cotton quality has been made easier with the introduction of high-volume instruments (HVI) for the automated measurement of length, strength, fineness, and color.

To provide an objective means of evaluating cotton quality, the U.S. Department of Agriculture established a classification system that provides information to the sellers and buyers of unprocessed cotton so that they can determine its value and the requirements for further processing. Different grades are established for different kinds of cotton, with the trash content, color, ginning preparation, and brightness being the factors taken into account. Standards for length of staple fiber have also been established.

Figure 4.4

Cotton gins in which cotton fibers are separated from cotton seeds. Photograph courtesy of Mississippi Cooperative Extension Service and Crossroads Gin, Schlater, Mississippi, owner Jack Colquett.

Measures for fineness and maturity are made by an indirect method, known as *micronaire* fineness. This is based on the air flow past a standard weight of cotton compressed to a standard volume. Under these conditions fine and immature fibers will impede the air flow more than coarser fibers because they present a more tortuous path for the air through the sample. Lower readings indicate immaturity, and higher readings may be produced by fibers that lack the fineness required for some high-quality products.

Constant inhalation of cotton fiber causes a serious lung disease called "brown lung," known medically as *byssinosis*. Toxins from bacteria or fungi associated with fibers cause the disease. In the past many individuals working in jobs where they came into contact with large quantities of "cotton dust" contracted byssinosis.

Recent developments of machinery for processing cotton have focused on closed systems that protect workers from cotton dust exposure. Air quality is monitored, and legislative requirements for safe levels of exposure have been established under the Occupational Safety and Health Act (OSHA), so that what was once seen as a pervasive problem in the cotton industry has been largely brought under control.

Molecular Structure

Cotton is composed of polymer chains of cellulose. The repeating unit of cellulose is:

The cellulosic polymers in cotton have a high degree of polymerization. The hydroxyl groups on the chains are responsible for many of the properties of cellulosic fibers. They attract water and dyes, making cotton absorptive and easy to dye. They also enable hydrogen bonding between adjacent cellulosic chains.

Cotton is about 70 percent crystalline and 30 percent amorphous (see Figures 3.4 and 3.5, page 55). Although the degree of crystallinity is high, the crystalline portions are often not oriented but are at an angle to the fiber axis.

Properties of Cotton

Physical Appearance

Color. Cotton fiber is generally white to tan in color. Recently, cottons colored brown and green have also been cultivated and marketed. Colored cottons are discussed further later in this chapter.

Shape. The length of an individual cotton fiber is usually from 1,000 to 3,000 times its diameter. The diameter may range from 16 to 20 microns. In cross section, the fiber has a U or kidney bean shape with a central canal known as the *lumen.* During growth this channel carries nutrients to the developing fiber.

After the fiber has reached its full length, layers of cellulose are deposited on the inside of the thin, waxy, exterior wall. The fiber grows much as a tree does, with concentric rings of growth (Figure 4.5). Each layer is made up of small fibrils, or minute fibrous segments. As these fibril layers are deposited, they form a complex series of spirals that reverse direction at some points. When the boll opens and the fiber is exposed to air, it dries and collapses into the flat shape seen in the microscopic view of cotton in Figure 4.6. The spiraling of the cellulose fibrils causes the characteristic twists, or *convolutions,* in the lengthwise direction of the fiber. These twists give the magnified cotton fiber the appearance of a twisted ribbon, and they make cotton easier to spin.

Figure 4.5

The structure of cotton fiber. As the cotton fiber matures, the cell formed by the primary wall (a) is filled by successive daily deposits of cellulose in layers: (d) the first layer deposited within the original cell, (b) the central layers, (c) the innermost layer, (e) and the lumen. Illustration courtesy of the National Cotton Council of America.

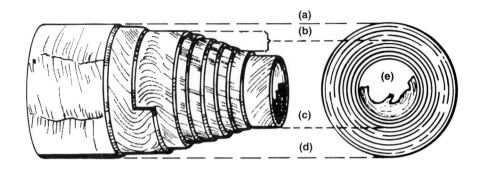

Figure 4.6

Photos of cotton fibers taken through an electron scanning microscope: (a) cross section and (b) longitudinal view. Photograph courtesy of the British Textile Technology Group (BTTG).

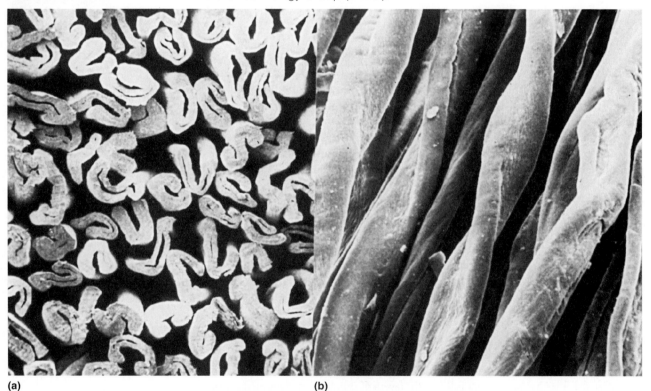

(a)   (b)

Long, staple cotton has about 300 twists per inch; short cotton has less than 200. In spite of the twisted shape of the cotton fiber, it is relatively uniform in its size.

Luster. The luster of cotton is low, unless it has been given special treatments or finishes. This is, in part, a consequence of the natural twist of cotton and its resultant uneven surface that breaks up and scatters light rays reflected from the fiber surface.

Other Physical Properties

Specific Gravity. Cotton has a specific gravity of 1.54. (Compare with that of polyester at 1.38 or nylon at 1.14.) This means that cotton fabrics will feel heavier in weight than will comparable fabrics made from polyester or nylon.

Strength. Strength of cotton on a scale of high, medium, and low would rank as medium. (Tenacity is 3.0 to 4.9 g/d.) It has a fairly high degree of crystallinity but somewhat lower orientation. The strength is increased by the length of the polymer chains. In comparison with other cellulosic fibers, cotton is weaker than flax and stronger than rayon.

Cotton is 10 to 20 percent stronger when wet than when dry. Its strength can be increased by a process called *mercerization* in which yarns or fabrics held under tension are treated with controlled solutions of sodium hydroxide. The alkali causes the fiber to swell and straighten out and to become stronger and more lustrous.

Elasticity and Resilience. Like most other cellulosic fibers, cotton has low elasticity and elastic recovery. Cotton fabrics also wrinkle easily and do not recover well from wrinkling. In stretching or wrinkling, hydrogen bonds between chains are broken and then reformed in the new position, holding in the wrinkle or other deformation. Through the application of durable press resin finishes, however, resilience can be improved. Unfinished cotton fabrics generally must be ironed after laundering.

Absorbency and Moisture Regain. Because of its many hydroxyl groups, which attract water, cotton is an absorbent fiber. Its good absorbency makes cotton comfortable in hot weather and suitable for materials where absorbency is important (such as diapers and towels). It is relatively slow to dry because the absorbed moisture must be evaporated from the fiber. For the same reason, cotton fibers take waterborne dyes readily. The percentage moisture regain of cotton is 7 to 8 percent at standard temperature and humidity.

Dimensional Stability. Cotton fibers swell considerably in the transverse direction when wet. Unfinished woven or knitted cotton fabrics will shrink in the first few launderings because the laundering releases tensions created during weaving or finishing. The relaxation of these tensions may cause changes in the fabric dimensions. Cotton fabrics can be given special finishes to prevent this *relaxation shrinkage.*

Heat and Electrical Conductivity. Cotton conducts electricity and thus does not build up static electrical charges. It has moderately high heat conductivity, which makes the fabric comfortable in hot weather.

Effect of Heat; Combustibility. Cotton is not thermoplastic and will not melt. Exposure to dry heat at temperatures about 300°F, however, does cause gradual decomposition and deterioration of the fiber. Excessively high ironing temperatures cause cotton to scorch or turn yellow.

Cotton is combustible. It burns upon exposure to a flame and will continue to burn when the flame has been removed. Burning cotton fabric smells like burning paper, and a fluffy, gray ash residue remains. It is not possible to distinguish cotton from other cellulosic fibers by burning.

Table 4.2	Reaction of Cotton to Selected Chemicals

Substance	Effect on Cotton Fiber
Acids	
Mineral acids such as sulfuric, hydrochloric, nitric, etc.	Concentrated acids destroy. Cold, diluted acids, if not
Volatile organic acids: formic, acetic	neutralized and washed out, degrade and destroy the fiber.
Nonvolatile organic acids: oxalic, citric, etc.	No harmful effect.
	Degrade fiber slightly if not removed.
Bases	
Strong bases: sodium hydroxide, etc.	No harmful effect. Causes fiber to swell and become stronger.
Weak bases: borax, soap, etc.	No harmful effect.
Oxidizing agents	
Chlorine bleaches	Destroy if uncontrolled.
Organic solvents (used in spot and stain removal)	
Perchloroethylene	No harmful effect.
Naptha	No harmful effect.

Source: Data from J. LaBarthe, *Elements of Textiles* (New York: Macmillan, 1975), pp. 22–23.

Effect of Selected Conditions on Fiber

Chemical Reactivity. Cotton that has been cleaned and bleached is about 99 percent cellulose. Its chemical reactions are typical of cellulosic materials. Table 4.2 shows the reaction of cotton to treatment with certain chemical substances in the laboratory.

Some of the chemicals listed in Table 4.2 are used in the finishing of cotton. For example, acids may be employed to stiffen permanently the cotton fabric called organdy. The reaction of cotton to strong bases, in which the fiber swells and becomes stronger with (when the process is carried out under tension) an increase in luster as well, is used for mercerization. The same process done without tension and under slightly different conditions has been used to make stretch fabrics. Dyestuffs that are too acidic in reaction cannot be applied to cotton fabrics.

Resistance to Microorganisms and Insects. Mildew grows on cotton fibers, especially if they are stored under conditions of dampness, warmth, and darkness. This fungus stains the fiber and eventually rots and degrades it. Other bacteria and fungi that grow in soiled, moist areas will also deteriorate or rot cotton fabrics.

Moths and carpet beetles do not attack cotton, but silverfish may eat the fiber. Heavily starched fabrics are liable to be damaged by silverfish.

Resistance to Environmental Conditions. Although cotton shows better resistance to sunlight than do many fibers, extended exposure to sunlight will cause weakening and deterioration of cotton fabrics. Cotton draperies will last longer if lined with another layer of fabric.

Age does not seriously affect cotton fabrics; however, it is important that the fabrics be stored in clean condition and in dry areas to prevent mildew.

Special acid-free tissue paper can be used to store antique cotton garments, cotton quilts, and spreads. Ordinary tissue paper should not be used for wrapping fabrics for long-term storage because the paper contains an acid residue that may damage the cloth.

Uses

The range of items for which cotton fabrics are used is enormous. In wearing apparel, the qualities of comfort, dyeability, and launderability have led to its wide use in articles ranging from underwear to evening gowns. In the home, bed linens, table linens, draperies, upholstery and slipcover fabrics, and towels are frequently made from cotton.

A new development in cotton production and use has been the marketing of naturally colored cotton. Available under the trademark FoxFibre®, this cotton has been developed by Sally Fox of Natural Cotton Colours, Inc., through selective breeding. Two shades of brown and two shades of green are currently available. (See Figure 4.7.) Products made from FoxFibre® include hand knitting yarns, woven and knitted apparel, upholstery fabrics, bed and bath linens, table linens, hats, and hosiery. Manufacturers and retailers have promoted these products as environmentally friendly because they do not require either dyeing or bleaching, processes that produce significant levels of pollution. Prices for products made from these fibers are higher than those of other cottons because of the more limited supply of naturally colored cottons.

Cotton has been increasingly blended with other fibers, especially with manufactured fibers. This blending may be done to create cottonlike fabrics with better wrinkle resistance and dimensional stability. Various finishes developed for cotton can also compensate for less desirable qualities. Special finishes are discussed in chapters 20 and 21.

Figure 4.7

Woven fabric with stripes created by using two different colors of FoxFibre®, a naturally colored cotton fiber.

Care Procedures

Cotton can be cleaned successfully using either synthetic-built detergents, which are generally quite alkaline, or natural soaps. The alkalinity of the detergents has no effect on the fiber. Dry-cleaning solvents do not harm cotton, so, where construction details or trim would make wet laundering undesirable, dry cleaning could be used.

Stains can be removed from white cotton by using the stronger oxidizing bleaches as long as water temperature, concentration of bleaching agent, and time of exposure are controlled. Strong chlorine bleaches should not be poured directly on cotton since pinholes can be formed in the fabric from direct contact with the bleach.

Minor Seed Hair Fibers

Kapok

Kapok, like cotton, grows in a seed pod. The kapok tree, sometimes called the silk cotton tree, is native to the tropics. Seed pods are gathered when they fall or are cut from the tree. The dried fiber is easily separated from the seeds.

The fiber has exceptional resiliency and buoyancy, but it is too brittle to be spun readily into yarns. As a result, the uses of kapok have been limited chiefly to stuffings and insulation materials. Because of its buoyancy and resistance to wetting, kapok has been used as a filling for life preservers. Having a hollow, air-filled structure, kapok can remain in the water for hours without an appreciable absorption of water, while holding up considerable weight.

Some kapok stuffings are used in household furnishings. The fibers have a tendency to deteriorate and to break down after a time. In general, kapok is little used, having been replaced by synthetic foam.

Coir

Coir is a fiber obtained from the outer hull of the coconut. Most of the coir produced is used in the geographic areas where the fiber is grown.

The production of the fiber is carried out by hand using rather primitive methods. The coconut is picked, the nut is removed, and the husks are collected. Fiber is separated from the husks by a process that includes soaking to loosen the fiber, drying, and pulling the fiber from the husks.

The brown coir fibers, which are from 5 to 10 inches long, are used for brushes, ropes, and mats. Among the useful qualities of coir are resistance to rot, lightness coupled with elasticity, and resistance to abrasion. Face yarns of coir on a polypropylene backing are being used in broadloom carpet, carpet tiles, and floor mats (Montgomery 1977). Coconut fibers are also used in geotextiles.

Bast Fibers

Bast fibers are those that grow in the stems of plants. Located in the inner bark of the stalk, these fibers are often several feet in length. The best known of the bast fibers is linen, which comes from the flax plant. Other important bast fibers include jute, ramie, kenaf, and hemp. Minor fibers of historical interest but of little or no commercial importance are urena and nettle.

Flax

History

Certain plants are native to a particular geographic area. During prehistoric times flax had the widest distribution of any of the fiber-bearing plants. The oldest archeological evidence of the use of flax shows that the flax plant stem was used in basket making long before flax fiber came into use. Techniques for removing the long fibers from flax stems were developed at a later period. At first, wild flax was gathered, but subsequent cultivation of the plant spread it rapidly throughout the Middle East, Northern Africa, and Europe.

Actual samples of woven linen fabrics have been recovered from Egyptian tombs dating from 4000 B.C. The hot, dry climate of Egypt has preserved samples of both coarse and fine linen materials. Additional samples of linen fabrics have been excavated from the dried-out lake mud of prehistoric villages in Switzerland where the mineral salts of the lakes preserved the textiles. These samples are thought to be as much as seven thousand years old (Schaefer 1945).

In Europe, before world trade routes were developed, linen fabrics were used widely for most of the items in which cotton is used today. Cooler northern climates were not suited to the cultivation of cotton, but they did permit the growth of flax. The widespread use of linen for many purposes is reflected in terminology still employed, such as *bed linens* or *table linens.* Modern bed linens and table linens are often made from fibers other than flax.

Interest in linen was stimulated in the early 1990s by ecological concerns of consumers, since flax is grown virtually free of herbicides and pesticides. The United States imports linen fibers, yarns, fabrics, and completed garments. Precise statistics on the quantity of finished fabrics and manufactured goods are hard to obtain, as economic data on all hard or leaf fibers (such as sisal) and bast fibers (such as linen and ramie) are grouped together; however, the linen share of world fiber consumption remains at about 2 percent. Countries exporting the largest quantities of linen are Poland, Ireland, Belgium, China, France, the countries of the former Soviet Union, and Egypt.[3]

Botanical Information

The botanical name of the flax plant is *linum usitatissimum. Usitatissimum* is Latin for "most useful." Before cotton was available in Western Europe, linen was used extensively in household textiles, for practical and washable garments, and for tents and sails for boats. Its many uses are clearly reflected in the Latin name given to the plant. Some varieties of the plant are grown for fiber, whereas others are grown for seeds. The plant grows to a height of 2 to 4 feet. The varieties grown for fiber have long stems, with few branches and seeds. (See Figure 4.8.)

---

3. Data provided by the International Linen Promotion Council.

Figure 4.8

Mature flax plants are harvested with machines that pull rather than cut plants. The machine forms pulled flax into bundles. Seeds, used for making linseed oil, will be removed by threshing machines. Photograph courtesy of MASTERS OF LINEN, International Linen Promotion.

Cultivation

In most countries the flax crop is sown in the early spring. The plant thrives best in temperate climates with adequate rainfall. Harvesting is done about 80 to 100 days after sowing when about one-half of the seeds are ripe and leaves have fallen from the lower two-thirds of the stem. In those countries where inexpensive labor is readily available, flax is still harvested by hand, but in developed countries, much of the labor of flax pulling is now done by machine. Whether done by hand or machine, the flax plant is pulled completely from the ground. Removing plants from the ground retains as long a stem as possible and prevents discoloration of fibers through wicking.

Stalks are dried sufficiently so that they can be threshed, combed, or beaten to remove the flax seeds, which are used for sowing future crops or for making linseed oil or livestock feed.

Preparation of the Fiber

Bast fibers require extensive processing to remove the fibers from the woody stem in which they are held. The procedure is similar for all bast fibers. The deseeded flax straw has to be partially rotted to dissolve the substances that hold the fiber in the stem. This first step in preparing the fiber is called *retting*.

Retting is accomplished through the breakdown of the materials that bind the fibers into the plant stems. Highly specific enzymes that attack only the binding materials and not the fibers are secreted by fungi and bacteria. Retting processes are of three types:

1. *Dew retting* is the process used most in Western Europe. Dew retting takes place in the field. The flax is laid out in swaths in the fields where the action of rain and dew together with soil-borne microorganisms causes the bark of

Figure 4.9

The men are loading bundles of flax into retting tanks filled with heated water. The soaking action loosens the outside flax fibers from the woody center stalk. Photograph courtesy of MASTERS OF LINEN, International Linen Promotion.

the stems to become loosened. This may take from 7 to 21 days, depending on weather conditions. After retting, the bark is removed, and retted straw bundles are set up in the fields to dry.

2. *Water retting* takes place when flax is submerged in water for from 6 to 20 days. When water temperature is cooler, the process takes the longer amount of time. Water retting may be done in ponds, in vats (Figure 4.9), or in sluggish streams. As in dew retting, the bacterial action causes the bark to be loosened.

   Water retting produces finer fiber but is more costly; therefore, the less expensive and more easily mechanized dew retting process is generally preferred except for certain qualities of fiber needed for fine, wet-spun yarns.

3. *Chemical retting* processes of several types have been developed. In one, flax is sprayed with a systemic herbicide that kills the flax as it grows. If weather conditions are right, retting takes place in the standing plant, and the dry, retted flax can be pulled. This approach, however, has been found to be too dependent on weather. Small-scale laboratory experiments have produced acceptable fiber from either simple and rapid chemical treatments or by applying enzyme mixtures to act on binding materials.

Retting only loosens the bark from the stem. (See Figure 4.10.) Following retting, *breaking* and *scutching* finish the job of separating the fiber from the stem. In breaking, the flax straw is passed over fluted rollers or crushed between slatted frames. This breaks up the brittle, woody parts of the stem but does not harm the fiber. In scutching, the broken straw is passed through beaters that knock off the broken pieces of stem (Figure 4.11). The fibers are baled and shipped to spinning mills.

At the mill the fibers go through yet another process before they are ready for spinning. The fibers are *hackled,* or combed, to separate shorter fibers (called *tow*) from longer fibers (called *line fibers*) and to align fibers parallel preparatory to spinning. Even with all this processing, individual fibers do not separate out, and bundles of fibers continue to cling together.

Linen fibers are quite long; therefore, they must be processed on specialized machinery. (See chapter 15 for discussion of spinning linen fibers.)

Figure 4.10

Diagram of a portion of a cross section of a flax stem. As a result of retting, clumps of fibers along the outer edge are starting to separate from the woody core.

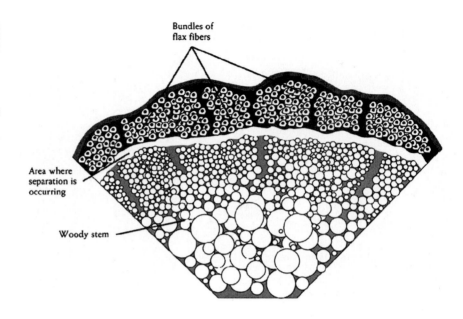

Bundles of flax fibers

Area where separation is occurring

Woody stem

Figure 4.11

Scutching separates flax fibers from the hard wooden core of the stalk by drying and grinding. Long line fibers and short tow fibers freed by scutching are then combed to cleanse and straighten them. The tow fibers are used for heavy fabrics and wall coverings, the line fibers for fine or sheer ones. Photograph courtesy of MASTERS OF LINEN, International Linen Promotion.

Figure 4.12 Photos of flax fibers taken through an electron scanning microscope: (a) cross section and (b) longitudinal view. Photograph courtesy of the British Textile Technology Group (BTTG).

(a) (b)

Properties of Linen

Physical Appearance

Color. Unbleached flax varies in color from a light cream to a dark tan. Different types of retting may produce differences in fiber color.

Shape. Fiber bundle length may be anywhere from 5 to 20 inches, but most line (longer) fiber averages from 15 to 20 inches, whereas tow (shorter fiber) is less than 15 inches. Fiber diameter averages 15 to 18 microns.

In microscopic cross section, flax has a somewhat irregular, many-sided shape. Like cotton, it has a central canal, but its lumen is smaller and less distinguishable than that of cotton. Looking at the lengthwise direction of fiber under the microscope is rather like looking at a stalk of bamboo. Flax has crosswise markings spaced along its length that are called *nodes* or *joints.* (See Figure 4.12.)

Luster. Because it is a straight, smooth fiber, flax is more lustrous than cotton. Many linen fabrics are designed to take advantage of this natural luster.

Other Physical Properties

Specific Gravity. The specific gravity of flax is the same as that of cotton (1.54). Linen fabrics are, therefore, comparable in weight to cotton fabrics but feel heavier than silk, polyester, or nylon, even in cloth of similar weave.

Strength. Flax is stronger than cotton, being one of the strongest of the natural fibers. It is more crystalline and more oriented than cotton. It is as much as 20 percent stronger wet than dry.

Elasticity and Resilience. The elongation, elasticity, and resilience of flax are lower than those of cotton because linen lacks the fibril structure that gives some resilience to cotton. Linens crease and wrinkle badly unless given special finishes.

Absorbency and Moisture Regain. Moisture regain of linens is higher than that of cotton (11 to 12 percent). Unlike cotton, linen has very good wicking ability; that is, moisture travels readily along the fiber as well as being absorbed into the fiber. The fiber gives up its moisture readily, making it quick drying. Both absorbency and good wicking ability make linen useful for towels and for warm-weather garments.

Dimensional Stability. Like cotton, linen has poor dimensional stability because the fibers swell when exposed to water. Tension from manufacturing therefore results in relaxation shrinkage of fabrics. Preshrinkage treatments can be applied to linen fabrics to prevent relaxation shrinkage.

Heat and Electrical Conductivity. Linen conducts heat more readily than does cotton and is even more comfortable for summer wear. Conductivity of electricity prevents static electricity buildup.

Effect of Heat; Combustibility. Higher temperatures are required to scorch linen than to scorch cotton. Linen is slightly more resistant to damage from heat than is cotton. The burning characteristics of linen are similar to those of cotton; it is combustible, continues to burn when the flame is removed, and burns with an odor like that of burning paper.

Effect of Selected Conditions on Fiber

Chemical Reactivity. The chemical reactions of linen closely parallel those of cotton because both are composed of cellulose. Like cotton, linen is destroyed by concentrated mineral acids, not harmed by bases or decomposed by oxidizing agents and not harmed by organic solvents used in dry cleaning. Linen could be mercerized, but because the flax is naturally strong and lustrous, mercerization offers little gain.

Resistance to Microorganisms and Insects. If linen is stored damp and in a warm place, mildew will attack and harm the fabric. Dry linen is not susceptible to attack. It generally resists rot and bacterial deterioration unless it is stored in wet, dirty areas. Moths, carpet beetles, and silverfish do not usually harm unstarched linen fabrics.

Resistance to Environmental Conditions. Linen has better resistance to sunlight than does cotton. There is a loss of strength over a period of time, but it is gradual and not severe. Linen drapery and curtain fabrics are quite serviceable.

The resistance of linen to deterioration from age is good, especially if fabrics are stored properly. Linen, however, has poor flex abrasion resistance. To avoid abrasion and cracking at folded edges, a linen fabric should not be repeatedly folded at the same place.

Table 4.3 compares characteristics of cotton and linen.

Table 4.3	Selected Properties of Cotton and Linen Fibers	
	Cotton	Linen
Specific gravity	1.54	1.54
Tenacity (g/d)		
Dry	3.0–5.0	5.5–6.5
Wet	3.3–6.4	6.0–7.2
Moisture regain	7%–11%	11%–12%
Resiliency	Poor.	Poor.
Burning	Burns, does not melt.	Burns, does not melt.
Conductivity of		
Heat	High.	High.
Electricity	High.	High.
Resistance to damage from		
Fungi	Damaged.	Damaged.
Insects	Silverfish damage.	Silverfish may eat sizing.
Prolonged exposure to sunlight	Loss of strength.	Loss of strength.
Strong acids	Poor resistance.	Poor resistance.
Strong bases	Excellent resistance.	Excellent resistance.

Source: Data on this and subsequent fiber characteristics tables (Tables 5.2, 7.3, 8.2, 9.1, 10.2, 11.1, 12.1) from *Man-made Fiber Fact Book* (Washington, D.C.: American Fiber Manufacturers Association, 1978); "Man-made Fiber Desk Book," *Modern Textiles* 62 (March 1981); "Identification of Fibers in Textile Materials," *Bulletin X-156* (Wilmington: DuPont, December 1961); *Textile Handbook* (Washington, D.C.: American Home Economics Association, 1974); R. W. Moncrieff, *Man-made Fibres* (New York: Wiley, 1975); and *Textile World Man-made Fiber Chart* 130 (August 1990).

Uses

Linen fabrics are found in wearing apparel and in household textiles. Yarns spun from flax range from very fine for weaving into sheer, soft "handkerchief" linens to coarse, large-diameter yarns for "crash," a fabric that is frequently used for making dish towels.

In wearing apparel, linen fabrics are popular for summer clothing. The major disadvantage of linen clothing, its wrinkling, may be somewhat overcome by giving the fabrics special crease-resistant finishes. Blending of fabrics with synthetics may also help to improve wrinkle recovery.

For household textiles linen fabrics are often used in table linens. The launderability of linen combined with its good luster and attractive appearance make it quite popular for use in tablecloths and place mats. Other important uses for linen fabrics in the home include tea towels; because flax fibers are longer, linen produces less lint (small bits of fiber that break off from the yarn) than does cotton and is, therefore, preferred for drying glassware. Linen is used alone or in blends for household products such as curtains and in slipcover and upholstery fabric. Linen is also used in vintage aircraft for making the wings and bodies of biplanes.

Since the fabric is in relatively short supply and the fibers require extensive processing, linen tends to be rather expensive. Both the cost factor and desirability of increasing wrinkle resistance have led to blending flax with other fibers. In those periods when a "wrinkled look" has been fashionable, garments of linen have been popular, although expensive.

Care Procedures

Linen can be dry-cleaned or laundered at home with heavy-duty detergents. Being stronger wet than dry, the fabric requires no special handling during laundering. Excessive chlorine bleaching will damage linen, but linen fabrics can be whitened by the periodic, controlled use of chlorine or other bleaches.

Even though linen can be laundered, many care labels on linen garments carry the instructions "Dry Clean Only." This is because garments are less likely to shrink and appearance is usually better. Fabrics do not wrinkle or suffer as much color loss after dry cleaning as they do after laundering.

Ironing temperatures for linen are at the highest end of the dial on electric irons. Linen fabrics can be ironed safely at a temperature of 450°F. Dryer drying at the highest setting is satisfactory.

Other Bast Fibers

Ramie

Ramie, or China grass, comes from a plant in the nettle family. The fibers are taken from the stalk. (See Figure 4.13.) A perennial shrub, the ramie plant grows in semi-

Figure 4.13

Partially retted stem of ramie plant (upper left) and fully processed strand of loosely twisted ramie fiber (lower right) are photographed against a background of fabrics made with varying proportions of ramie.

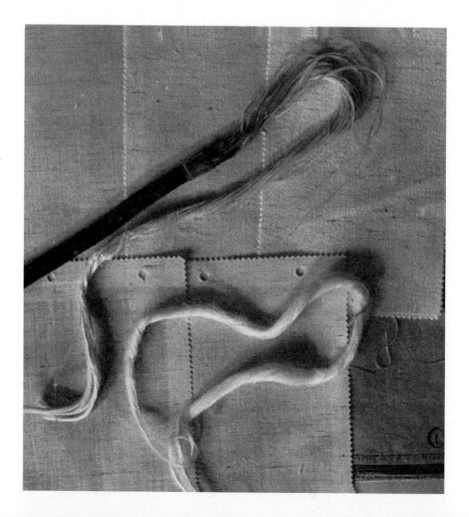

tropical regions. At the present time, ramie growth and processing are concentrated in the Philippines, Brazil, and the People's Republic of China. Hong Kong, Taiwan, Korea, and Japan process but do not grow ramie.

Ramie stalks are planted and the fiber is harvested the third year after planting. Three crops may be cut each year. After cutting the stems, the leaves of the plant are beaten off, the stems are split lengthwise, and the bark is stripped from them. This yields "ribbons" of bast that are soaked in water until the green outer layer can be scraped off. After drying, this substance, sometimes called China grass, is bundled and shipped.

Before spinning, the fiber must be retted out of the ribbons. Both dew and wet retting, similar to that used with flax, can be done. A chemical retting process that uses sodium hydroxide and an acid rinse has been patented and is used in the industrially developed countries.

Ramie has a fine diameter and high luster. It is the strongest of the natural fibers and the most crystalline. It is white in color, its absorbency is excellent, it dyes rapidly, and it has good resistance to attack by microorganisms.

The commercial use of ramie had been limited by processing difficulties that made it expensive to produce. Until the chemical retting process was developed, only hand methods could be employed to remove the fiber from the stem. Controlling fiber quality was also difficult. Researchers have developed controls for growth and processing that have made possible the production of uniform quality fibers. Advances in the processing of ramie fibers are proprietary; that is, they are not made available to the public by the manufacturers.

Ramie is used alone or in blends. Blends are most frequently made with polyester, cotton, linen, and acrylics. One hundred percent ramie fabrics do not require any special care. They are machine washable and require ironing. If blended with adequate quantities of polyester or acrylics, these fabrics will have easy-care characteristics and little shrinkage. The major use of ramie fabrics, especially ramie blends, in wearing apparel is in sweaters, suits, and pants. It is also used in table linens and fabrics for home furnishings.

The European firm Fischer Dotticon, Ltd., a major ramie producer, sees a strong future for ramie in high technology applications. Grown and processed under carefully controlled conditions, the fiber is strong and uniform. It is more rot-resistant than any natural fiber except coir. In appropriate climates it can be harvested up to six times a year and requires no pesticides. Ramie is used in geotextiles, as reinforcement fibers, and for nonwovens, where control of degumming can produce fibers that will bond with molded materials such as rubber or PVC—something synthetic fibers cannot do. Under the trademark Firon®, ramie is being used for protective gloves. It is also seen as having important environmental advantages in fishing nets where, if it becomes tangled, it will biodegrade and in the European automotive industry, where some countries are now requiring that all parts of automobiles be recyclable or reusable.

Jute

Jute fiber is taken from the stem of the jute plant. Successful cultivation of the plant requires fertile soil and a hot, moist climate. Jute is grown in India and Bangladesh and, to a lesser extent, in China, Thailand, and other southeast Asian countries.

Jute plants grow from 6 to 16 feet high. The stalks are cut just after the flowers begin to fade. Like other bast fibers, separation of the fiber requires retting. After retting, the stems are broken and the fiber is removed.

Jute is shorter than most other bast fibers. Its length is only about 150 times its breadth, which makes it difficult to spin. For this reason, it is not processed to separate out individual fibers but only to separate fiber bundles, which can be quite long.

Jute ranges in color from light to dark brown, and it is soft, fine, and lustrous, but not very pliable. On exposure to air, jute becomes somewhat brittle. It absorbs moisture readily, resists deterioration by microorganisms, and is weakened by exposure to sunlight.

Jute has long been in demand as a cheap, useful packaging material. Burlap is one of the major jute bagging fabrics. Jute has also traditionally been used for carpet backings and cordage. In recent years polypropylene, a manufactured fiber, has become a major competitor for jute in many of these uses. As a result, the jute-producing countries have been looking for additional and innovative applications. Some of these have been as geotextiles in erosion control, as a cheap replacement for cotton filling yarns in handwoven fabrics in India, and as reinforcement fiber in resin composites used to make chests and boxes for shipping tea and fruit. Some high-quality jute fabrics also have been used to make golf bags, soft luggage, and sports handbags (Atkinson 1993).

Kenaf

Kenaf is also a bast fiber, similar to jute. Botanically, it is related to both cotton and okra. Grown predominantly in Africa and India, kenaf has sparked renewed interest as an alternative crop in the south and west of the United States. When harvested, the plant stems are decorticated and then retted to obtain the fiber bundles. Fiber properties are similar to those of jute.

Traditionally, kenaf was used in making rope and twine for which its high strength was important. Recent work has focused on the use of these fibers in paper making since paper of kenaf fibers is smoother and whiter than that made from wood pulp. New methods for processing the kenaf stalks to obtain longer fibers have led to the production of nonwoven and woven textiles. For example, a nonwoven mat of kenaf fibers containing grass seeds is now marketed as a lawn starter. The woody core of the kenaf plant can be used for animal bedding and as an absorptive material for oil spill cleanup. (See Figure 4.14.)

Hemp

The hemp plant, *cannabis sativa,* is a member of the mulberry family and a type of marijuana plant. The fiber bundles come from the bast layer of the stem. Mature plants are cut off and spread on the ground where they are left to dry for 5 or 6 days. Leaves and seeds are beaten off, and bundles or sheaves of hemp are formed after additional drying. Retting, breaking, and scutching complete the fiber extraction process.

Hemp has tensile strength comparable to that of linen; it is one of the strongest of the natural fibers. It has good absorbency and poor elasticity. In its chemical properties, hemp is similar to cotton and flax.

The major uses of hemp are in the production of industrial fabrics, twine, and ropes of great tensile strength. Recently, there has been interest in processing of hemp into apparel and household textile products. (See Figure 4.15.)

Figure 4.14

Kenaf plants. Photograph courtesy of the U.S. Department of Agriculture.

Figure 4.15

(a) Hemp yarn and (b) plain-weave hemp fabric. (Products of Hemp Textiles International.)

(a)

(b)

Leaf Fibers

Leaf fibers are of limited usefulness and, for the most part, are made into cordage. They are taken from a variety of plants, most of which are perennials that produce fiber for 5 to 20 years. The leaves are harvested, and through mechanical methods, the extraneous matter is scraped and broken away from the fiber. (See Figure 4.16.)

The most widely used leaf fibers are those from cactuslike plants, such as those that have long, fleshy leaves with spiny edges (agave, henequen, sisal), yuccas, the banana family (abaca or Manila hemp), and the bromeliad family (piñā or pineapple). Piñā cloth is used in the Philippine Islands to make a sheer, lustrous fabric that is often used in Philippine national costumes.

Miscellaneous Fibers

A few fibers are obtained from roots and mosses. Sacaton, a coarse, stiff, root fiber from Mexico has been used as bristle for brushes. Spanish moss, an air plant, has been

Figure 4.16

Bales of cut henequen leaves, grown in Yucatan, Mexico, are stacked before further processing. Photograph by Robert Merkel.

used for inexpensive upholstered furniture and mattress filler. In recent years, synthetic fibers have, to a large extent, replaced these materials.

References

Anderson, F. 1973. Medieval beasties. *Natural History* 82 (January): 61.

Atkinson, R. 1993. Jute economy faces drastic industrial restructuring. *Textiles* 22 (3): 17–20.

Barber, E. 1991. *Prehistoric textiles.* Princeton: Princeton Univ. Press.

Montgomery, V. 1977. Coir yarn specialists. *Modern Textiles* 58 (February): 18.

Schaefer, G. 1945. On the history of flax cultivation. *CIBA Review* 9 (April): 1763 ff.

Review Questions

1. What are some of the physical and chemical properties common to most natural cellulosic fibers?
2. Define the following terms used in conjunction with cotton growing and processing.

   boll   byssinosis

   ginning   convolutions

   linters   naturally colored cotton

   micronaire fineness

3. What care procedures are recommended for cotton garments? How are these related to the chemical properties of cotton?
4. Compare the structural differences of cotton and flax. How do these differences affect fiber properties?
5. List the steps in processing flax. What is the purpose of each step?
6. Identify some of the uses of each of the following minor cellulosic fibers: kapok, ramie, jute, kenaf, hemp.

Recommended Readings

Buxton, A. 1988. A profile of the linen industry. *Textile Outlook International* 18 (July): 91.

Cheek, L. 1990. Dyeing and colorfastness characteristics of direct-dyed ramie in comparison to flax and cotton. *Clothing and Textiles Research Journal* 8 (Winter): 38.

Doraiswamy, I., et al. 1993. Cotton ginning. *Textile Progress* 24 (2).

Doraiswamy, I., and P. Chellamani. 1993. Pineapple leaf fibres. *Textile Progress* 24 (1).

Hickman, W. S. 1994. Linen—the way ahead. *Journal of the Society of Dyers and Colorists* 110 (5/6): 170.

Lange, M. D. 1994. U.S. cotton has challenges ahead. *America's Textiles International* 23 (March): 48.

Linen—versatility from the catwalk to the skies. 1992. *Textiles* 21 (4): 6–7.

Ramaswamy, G. N., C. G. Ruff, and C. Boyd. 1994. Effect of bacterial and chemical retting on kenaf fiber quality. *Textile Research Journal* 64: 305.

Stout, H. P. 1985. Jute and kenaf. In *Handbook of fiber science and technology.* Vol. IV, *Fiber Chemistry,* ed. M. Lewin and E. M. Pearce, 702–726. New York: Marcel Dekker.

Thompson, J. 1994. King of fibers [cotton]. *National Geographic* 185 (June): 60–87.

Wustrow, K. 1994. Quality management: Working with environmentally grown cottons. *Knitting Times* 63, (August): 14.

PROTEIN FIBERS

Protein fibers are those fibers in which the basic chemical structure is composed of amino acids joined in polypeptide chains. They may be separated into three basic groups:

1. *Animal hair fibers.* The major fiber in this group is sheep's wool. Other fibers of commercial importance come from animals such as the alpaca, camel, cashmere goat, llama, vicuña, guanaco, and the angora goat, whose fleece provides mohair. Also used are qiviut, or hair from the musk ox; angora rabbit hair; fur fiber from animals such as beaver, mink, and rabbit; and cow and horsehair.

2. *Fibers formed from extruded filaments.* Silk, produced by the silkworm caterpillars, is the only important fiber in this group. In the past such unusual materials as spider silk and byssus from mussels were said to have been made into fabrics.

3. *Fibers regenerated from vegetable or animal protein.* Corn, soybeans, and milk are some of the base materials from which regenerated protein fibers have been made.

See Table 5.1 for a list of protein fibers.

All protein fibers contain the elements carbon, hydrogen, oxygen, and nitrogen. Wool contains sulfur as well. In each protein fiber these elements are combined in different arrangements. As a result, properties of the various protein fibers may show some striking differences.

	Natural Fibers	Manufactured Fibers

Table 5.1
 	
Protein Fiber Family
	Animal hair fibers
	  Major fibers
	    Wool (from sheep)
	  Specialty hair fibers
	    Camel family
	      Alpaca
	      Huarizo
	      Guanaco
	      Misti
	      Vincuña
	      Llama
	    Goat family
	      Cashmere
	      Mohair (from the angora goat)
	      Qiviut (from the musk ox)
	      Cashgora
	    Fur fiber
	      Beaver
	      Fox
	      Mink
	      Chinchilla
	      Rabbit (especially angora rabbit)
	    Other
	      Horsehair
	      Cow hair
	Extruded fibers
	  Major fibers
	    Silk (from the silkworm)
		Regenerated protein or azlon fibers
		  Minor fibers
		    Animal protein
		      Milk protein
		      Chinon
		    Vegetable protein
		      Peanut protein[a]
		      Corn protein[a]
		      Soybean protein fiber[a]

[a]No longer in production.

Even so, these fibers share a number of common properties. Protein fibers, except silk, tend to be weaker than cellulosic fibers, and they are weaker wet than dry. Fabrics made from protein fibers must be handled with care during laundering or wet processing.

Specific gravity of protein fibers tends to be lower than that of cellulose. Fabrics made from these fibers feel lighter in weight than do comparable fabrics made from cellulosic fibers.

Protein fibers have greater resilience than cellulosic fibers. They are more resistant to wrinkling and hold their shape better. Moreover, fibers from the protein family do not burn readily. When set aflame, they may extinguish themselves. Burned fibers smell like burning hair, flesh, or feathers. Protein fibers tend to be damaged by dry heat and should be ironed with a press cloth or steam. Wool and silk require lower ironing temperatures than do cotton and linen, with recommended temperatures around 300°F.

Chemical properties common to most protein fibers include susceptibility to damage by bases and by oxidizing agents, especially chlorine bleach. Care in laundering is required to avoid damaging fibers through the use of strongly alkaline soaps and detergents and chlorine bleach. Fabrics can be bleached safely with hydrogen peroxide. Acids are much less damaging to protein fibers than to the cellulose fibers.

Sunlight discolors white fabrics made from protein fibers, turning them yellow after extended exposure. Although wool has better resistance to sunlight than does cotton, it will degrade on prolonged exposure. Silk degrades quite readily on exposure to sunlight.

Animal Hair Fibers

The hair of a number of different kinds of animals has been used for textile fibers for many centuries. It is not clear just when sheep or goats were domesticated. The ancestors of modern sheep living during prehistoric periods probably did not have the "wooly" type of fleece that modern sheep have but were covered with a straight, hair-like pelt. Straighter fibers do not spin into yarns easily, so that sheep may have originally been domesticated only for food. As woolier breeds evolved, people probably noticed these fibers could be spun into yarn and used to construct cloth. The earliest actual remains of wool fibers and fleece come from Egypt in the fourth millennium, considerably later than the first remains of flax (Barber 1991).

After people recognized that these fibers were useful in constructing cloth, sheep, goats, and other animals such as camels, llamas, alpacas, and the like were domesticated in different parts of the world, and their hair was removed for spinning and weaving. Of the many varieties of animal hair from which textile fibers are derived today, the fleece of the sheep is most widely used. In Central Asia the camel is an important source of textile fiber, and South America is the home of a number of camellike animals that produce fibers used for spinning and weaving. The alpaca and llama are native to the Andes Mountains regions and have been domesticated. Vicuña and guanaco are wild or semiwild animals from the same geographic region. Other animal hair fiber comes from domesticated goats such as the angora goat and the cashmere goat.

Hair from other wild or domesticated animals such as rabbits, musk oxen, horses, and cows have some minimal use in textile products.

Sheep's Wool

Under the Wool Products Labeling Act, wool is defined as "the fiber from the fleece of the sheep or lamb or hair of the angora or cashmere goat (and may include the so-called specialty fibers from the hair of the camel, alpaca, llama, and vicuña)" (Federal Trade Commission 1986). Fiber taken from the domesticated sheep makes up by far the largest quantity of fiber sold under the name of wool.

Approximately two hundred different breeds and crossbreeds of sheep produce wool fiber. The fiber produced by these animals varies widely in quality not only because of the conditions under which the sheep may graze and the quality of the pasture land but also because some breeds of sheep produce finer quality wool than do others.

The sheep that produces the most valuable and finest wool is the Merino variety (Figure 5.1). This type of wool accounts for about 30 percent of wool production. Merino sheep originated in Spain but are now prevalent all over the world, the largest proportion of Merino fleeces today coming from Australia. Merino wool is fine and

Figure 5.1

Merino rams with full coats of wool before shearing. Photograph courtesy of the Wool Bureau, Inc.

elastic, though relatively short—from 1 to 5 inches. French Rambouillet sheep, descendants of the Merino bloodline, were imported to the United States in 1840 and make up 27 percent of all the sheep in the United States. These, too, produce fine, high-quality wool.

A second group of sheep that originated in the British Isles produces fibers that are not quite so fine as Merino and Rambouillet but are also of quite good quality. Fibers range from 2 to 8 inches in length. Some of the breeds of sheep from this group are Devonshire, Dorset, Hampshire, Oxford, Southdown, and Wiltshire. Like Merino sheep, these breeds are raised worldwide.

Coarser, longer fiber is produced by a group of sheep known as Long British or Long Crossbreeds. The fiber length is 4 to 16 inches, and the better known breeds include Leicester, Lincoln, Cotswold, Romney Marsh, and Cheviot. Much of this fiber is made into outerwear in tweed, cheviot, homespun, and shetland fabrics.

A fourth group of sheep is made up of a variety of crossbred sheep that produce fibers, from 1 to 16 inches in length, that are coarse and have lower elasticity and strength. These wools are used largely for carpets and inexpensive, low-grade cloth.

Climatic conditions can adversely affect the quality of the wool, as can the condition of the grazing area. Australian flocks are enclosed in large fenced areas where underbrush and burrs are kept to a minimum, whereas American sheep are permitted to graze on open ranges. This free grazing results in fleece in which sticks, leaves, burrs, and other vegetable matter may be caught.

Wool Consumption

Total domestic consumer use of wool in the United States in 1993 was approximately 355 million pounds (clean wool). Of this, about 280 million pounds went into apparel and 75 million pounds into carpets. About 260 million pounds of this wool was imported; the remainder was produced domestically. About 57 percent of imported wool was used for apparel.[1]

Australia, New Zealand, and South Africa are major producers of wool. In the United States, Texas, California, and Wyoming produce the largest quantities of wool.

Fleece Removal

Sheep are sheared to remove the fleece in the spring season. (See Figure 5.2.) Expert shearers move from place to place removing fleece or clip wool. In Australia fleece is removed in sections with the underbelly section kept separate from

Worker begins to shear wool from a sheep. Photograph courtesy of the American Sheep Industry Association.

---

1. Data provided by American Wool Council.

the sides. This is done because the fleece from the undersection and legs tends to be inferior in quality to that of the sides—it contains more vegetable matter and is more tangled, matted, and torn. In the United States shearers remove the fleece in one piece.

Fleece that is sheared from sheep at 8 months of age or younger is called *lamb's wool.* Because this is the first growth of hair, it tends to be softer and finer. Products made from this soft, fine wool are generally labeled "lamb's wool."

Wool removed from animals that have been slaughtered for meat is referred to as *pulled wool.* Wool is taken from hides by one of several methods. A chemical depilatory, a substance that loosens the wool from the hides, may be used. This material does not seriously damage the hide and is the preferred method because it allows full use of both hides and fleece. Another method is to allow bacterial action to loosen the fiber so that it can be pulled from the hide.

Pulled wool is inferior in quality to fleece or clip wool because it is less lustrous and elastic. Pulled wool is generally blended with other types of wool. The chemical treatment given to the pulled wool in its removal from the skin degrades the fiber and allows the fiber to swell more readily in the dyebath. For this reason, pulled wool dyes more unevenly than does sheared wool.

Experimentation with other methods of fleece removal is ongoing. Australian researchers have been conducting field trials of a technique they call *biological wool harvesting.* A substance called Epidermal Growth Factor (EGF) is injected into sheep. Hair growth stops for one day, then resumes. The point where growth stopped creates a weak place in each hair of the fleece. In about one month when this weak point reaches the surface, the fleece can be removed by hand. This hand removal of the fleece requires less than half the time that shearing requires. However, if the fleece is removed as soon as the weak spot reaches the surface of the skin, the sheep lack adequate covering to protect them from the sun. They are provided with nets to hold the fleece in place until enough new wool is formed to protect them from sunburn! Although this method is still experimental, it may eventually have commercial application (Ryder 1993).

Grading

Grading of wool is done at the time the fleece is sheared. In grading, the fleece is judged for its overall fiber fineness and length. An alternative to grading is found in *sorting,* in which the fleece is divided into sections of differing quality. The best fiber comes from the sides and shoulders; the poorest comes from the lower legs.

Preparation for Spinning

The first step taken to prepare the fleece for use is *scouring,* which removes oil, grease, perspiration, and some of the dirt and impurities from the fleece. The fleece is washed a number of times in a warm, soapy, alkaline solution. A fleece of about 8 pounds in weight will be reduced by scouring to about 3 to 4 pounds. Much of the weight loss results from the removal of lanolin, a natural oil secreted by the sheep, which keeps the fleece soft and waterproof. This lanolin is recovered for use in cosmetics and other oil-based preparations. Even though lanolin can be recovered, the refuse produced by scouring of wool may be a cause of water pollution in areas where wool is processed.

If wool retains significant quantities of vegetable matter after scouring, it must be carbonized to remove this substance. *Carbonization* is the treatment of the fleece or fabric with sulfuric acid to destroy burrs, sticks, or other cellulosic material. Careful control is maintained to ensure that fibers are not damaged by the process. An alternative method is to lower the temperature of the fleece below freezing so that dirt, burrs, or vegetable matter become brittle and can be knocked or brushed from the fleece.

As a result of these processes, the wool may become overly dry and brittle. To avoid this, a small amount of oil is added to the fiber to keep it flexible, and the wool is kept somewhat moist during handling.

All wool fibers are *carded*. Fine wire teeth, mounted on a cylinder, separate the fibers and make them somewhat, although not completely, parallel. This procedure also helps to remove remaining vegetable matter from the fiber.

Wool Products Labeling Act of 1939

Wool fabrics can be made from new or from used wool, but one cannot tell by looking at the fabric whether the wool it contains is new or reused. To ensure that products made from used fibers are clearly labeled as such, the Wool Products Labeling Act of 1939 was enacted. This legislation regulated the labeling of sheep's wool and other animal hair fibers. The provisions of this act may be summarized as follows:

1. All wool products must be labeled.
2. The fibers contained in the product, except for ornamentation, must be identified.
3. The following terms, defined by the statute, should be used in identifying wool products (Federal Trade Commission 1986, 28).

   - The term *wool* means fiber "which has never been reclaimed from any woven or felted wool product."
   - The term *recycled wool* means (1) "the resulting fiber when wool has been woven or felted into a wool product which, without ever having been utilized in any way by the ultimate consumer, subsequently has been made into a fibrous state," or (2) "the resulting fiber when wool or reprocessed wool has been spun, woven, knitted, or felted into a wool product which, after having been used in any way by the ultimate consumer, subsequently is made into a fibrous state."
   - The terms *new wool* or *virgin wool* shall not be used when "the product or part (of a product) so described is not composed wholly of new or virgin fiber which has never been reclaimed from any spun, woven, knitted, felted, bonded or otherwise manufactured or used product."

Recycled wools are often made from the cutting scraps left from the manufacture of wool items. The fibers are pulled apart and returned to the fibrous state through a process known as *garnetting*. In the garnetting procedure, fibers may be damaged and can, therefore, be lower in quality than some new wool. Less frequently, wool is recycled from fabrics used by the ultimate consumer. These fabrics are also returned to the fibrous state by garnetting. Because these fibers have been subject to wear not only from the garnetting process but also by the normal wear and tear of a garment or product in use, these are the lowest-quality wool fibers. Recycled wools are often made into interlining materials for coats and jackets, or other inexpensive wool products. They are sometimes referred to as *shoddy*.

Although the terms *virgin wool* or *new wool* guarantee that fabrics are made from wool that has not been previously fabricated, the terms carry no guarantee of quality.

Figure 5.3

Structural formula for the wool molecule.

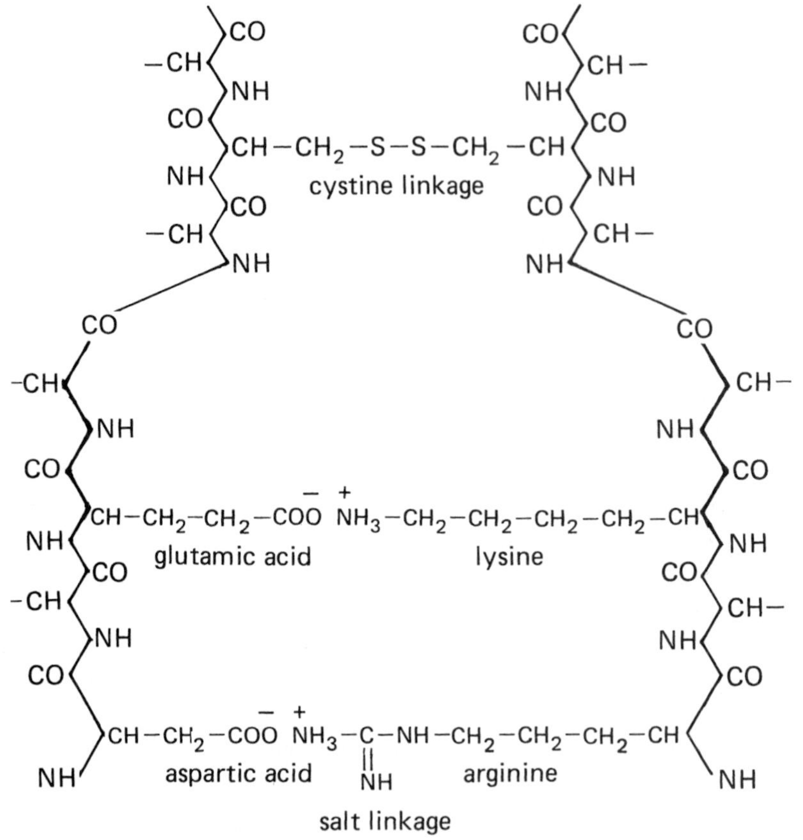

It is possible that a fabric made from poor-quality virgin wool may be inferior to one made from excellent-quality recycled wool.

In pile fabrics the face and the backing may be made of different fibers. The contents of the face and the backing may be listed separately, such as "100% wool face, 100% cotton back." If listed separately, the proportion of these fibers must also be indicated in percentage, so that in addition to the designation of "100% wool face, 100% cotton back," the label must also say "Back constitutes 60% of the fabric and pile 40%."

The contents of paddings, linings, or stuffings are designated separately from the face fabric and must be listed.

The 1984 amendments to the Wool Products Labeling Act requiring country of origin labeling are the same as those required by the TFPIA and are described in chapter 2.

Molecular Structure

Wool is made of a protein substance called *keratin,* a polymer composed of eighteen different amino acids connected by peptide bonds. Molecules composed of more than two different amino acids joined by peptide bonds are called polypeptides; therefore the wool molecule is a polypeptide. The relative amounts of amino acids vary from one type of wool to another. Within the fiber the polypeptide molecules are arranged in a helical (spiral) form, which under a tensile force can be stretched to an extended, pleated structure. The wool molecule contains three types of intermolecular and intramolecular bonds. (See Figure 5.3.) Listed in order of bond strength, these are:

- cystine or sulfur linkages where the sulfur atoms of two amino acids are covalently bonded
- ionic bonds or salt bridges between two oppositely charged amino acids
- hydrogen bonds

The sulfur bonds can be broken by chemical treatment and then reformed with the molecules in an altered position. This is the principle behind the permanent waving of hair, where hair is formed into curls, a solution is applied to break the sulfur bonds, and then a neutralizer reforms the sulfur linkages in the curled position.

The hydrogen bonds are important in shaping wool fabrics during apparel construction and also in imparting pleats and creases. The bonds can be broken by moisture and then reformed in the new position when the fabric is dried. Also, because these bonds contribute to the strength of the wool, the fiber is weaker when it is wet and the hydrogen bonds are broken. The ionic bonds are broken under either acid or basic conditions.

Because of the helical structure and bulky side chains on the polymers, wool is only about 30 percent crystalline. The high amount of amorphous material decreases the strength but increases the absorption of water and dyes.

Properties of Wool

Physical Appearance

Color. Wool fibers vary in natural color from white to creamy white to light beige, yellow, brown, and black. Wool may be dyed easily; however, it is difficult to keep white wool snow-white. The fiber tends to yellow from exposure to sunlight and with age. Bleaching is not a fully satisfactory means of keeping wool white, as chlorine bleaches are harmful to the fiber and bleaching itself tends to cause some yellowing. Among the bleaches used in textile manufacture are oxygen bleaches such as hydrogen peroxide, sodium peroxide, and sodium perborate. An alternative bleaching process is called reduction bleaching; one such process, *stoving,* uses sulfur dioxide. Peroxide is the most common treatment.

Shape. The length of the fiber depends on the breed of sheep from which it comes and on the fiber's growing time. In general, fiber length ranges from 1 to 14 or more inches, with finer fibers usually being shorter and coarser fibers usually being longer.

The diameter of the fiber ranges from 8 to 70 microns. Merino fleece fibers are usually about 15 to 17 microns in width. In cross section the fiber is oval or elliptical. The cross section may show three parts: the innermost part is called the *medulla.* Not all wool fibers possess a medulla, which is the section in which the pigment or color is carried and which provides air space. Most finer wools do not have a medulla. The next segment is the *cortex,* which makes up most of the fiber. Research has shown that the cortex is made up of microscopic cells that pack this area. The outer layer consists of a fine network of small overlapping scales. The scale structure is responsible for the behavior of wool in felting and in shrinkage. (See Figure 5.4.)

The scales on the surface of the fiber overlap "like the tiles on a roof, with the protruding end of the scales pointing toward the fiber tip" (Boston 1984, 523). Because of the way the scales are arranged, the fiber can move in only one direction. As fibers are placed close together in a mass of fiber, or in yarns, or in fabrics, they

Figure 5.4	(a) Wool fiber close-up, cross section and (b) wool fiber close-up of scale structure along the fiber length. Photographs courtesy of the U.S. Department of Agriculture.

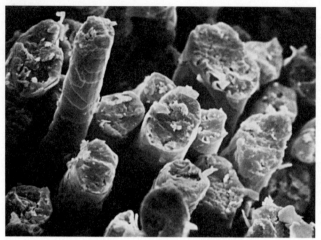

(a)

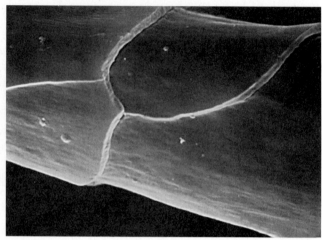

(b)

entangle with one another. During washing, the cloth is compressed and manipulated, and the individual fibers are bent. The fiber, being highly elastic, slides through the entanglement but can move only in one direction. As all the fibers exhibit this unidirectional movement, the fibers are drawn closer together, causing the whole structure to become smaller, or *shrink*.

Wool fiber possesses one further quality that is important in its physical appearance and behavior: most types have a natural crimp, or curly, wavy shape. This crimp increases the bulk and springiness of wool and makes it quite resilient. It also makes wool fiber relatively easy to spin into yarns.

Mixed into wool fleece are a number of *kemp* hairs. Kemp hairs are coarse, straight hairs that are often white and shiny and do not absorb dye easily. A large proportion of kemp hairs lowers the quality of the fleece.

Luster. The luster of wool is low because of the scaly, rough surface. Luster varies among different breeds of sheep, different sections of the fleece, and the conditions under which an animal has been raised. In general, the luster of poor-quality wool is greater than the luster of better grades of wool.

Other Physical Properties

Specific Gravity. The specific gravity of wool is 1.32. This relatively low density makes wool fabrics feel light in relation to their bulk. The ability of wool fibers to trap air also gives them an ability to provide warmth without excessive weight. This is fortunate since wool is so weak that a large amount of fiber is usually necessary to make fabrics of adequate strength.

Strength. Wool is a relatively weak fiber (tenacity is 1.0–1.7 g/d). The low strength is mainly due to the low degrees of crystallinity and orientation in the fiber. The strength decreases in wet wool because the hydrogen bonds are broken by water. Although the strength of wool is low, the fiber has high elongation owing to the helical structure.

Elasticity and Resilience. The elasticity and resilience of wool are excellent, a result of its natural crimp. Elasticity and resilience contribute to the appearance of wool products by giving them very good resistance to, and recovery from, wrinkling. Wrinkles will hang out of wool garments, especially if they are hung in a damp atmosphere, as will creases, pleats, or other shape provided by pressing.

Absorbency and Moisture Regain. Wool is a very absorbent fiber because it has a number of chemical groups that attract water and also because it has such an amorphous molecular structure. Wool also gives up its moisture slowly. Paradoxically, wool is also water-repellent. Spilled liquids run off wool because the scale structure of wool inhibits wicking of moisture along the fiber surface. Surface moisture is absorbed slowly. The behavior of wool in relation to moisture can be summarized by saying that wool is naturally water-repellent, but upon prolonged exposure to moisture, the fiber does absorb substantial quantities of water. The moisture is held inside the fiber, not on the surface. Furthermore, wool retains its resilience even when wet, so that wool can become wet yet retain the ability to insulate the wearer from cold.

Dimensional Stability. Wool has poor dimensional stability. As mentioned previously, the tendency of wool to shrink and felt can cause fabrics and garments to decrease in size. The shrinkage of wool is progressive. In the first laundering, fabrics stretched in the weaving process tend to relax. But wool will continue to shrink with subsequent launderings if it is not washed in cool water with a minimum of handling.

Consumers should preshrink wool fabrics before sewing unless the fabric is labeled as having been treated to prevent shrinkage. Purchasers of wool ready-to-wear should look for labels indicating shrinkage control. Finishes can be given to wool to render the fabric washable. Such finishes are discussed at length in chapter 21.

Heat and Electrical Conductivity. The conductivity of wool of both heat and electricity are low. Both the poor heat conductivity of wool fiber and its ability to trap air between the fibers contribute to its excellent qualities for cold-weather clothing. Even though the electrical conductivity of wool is rated as poor, wool fibers do not build up static electrical charges unless the atmosphere is very dry. The ability of the fiber to absorb moisture improves its conductivity when humidity is present in the atmosphere. For this reason, wool garments sometimes generate static electrical charges indoors in winter when central heating of homes makes them warm and dry.

Effect of Heat; Combustibility. Wool will burn if a flame is held to the fabric, but it burns slowly, and when the flame is removed, the fabric may self-extinguish. The danger of flammability exists, but this factor is not so great as with many other fabrics. Wool can be treated for fire retardancy. Dry heat damages the fiber, producing a negative effect on both appearance and strength.

Effect of Selected Conditions on Wool

Chemical Reactivity. Wool fibers are damaged quickly by strong basic solutions; even relatively weak bases have a deleterious effect on wool. Strong laundry detergents and soaps have "free" alkali added to increase their cleaning power, and extended exposure to this additional alkali may be harmful to wool. Wool fabrics should be washed with special mild detergents.

Acids do not harm wool except in very strong concentrations. This makes it possible to carbonize wool fleece to remove vegetable matter without harming the wool fiber.

Chlorine compounds used for bleaching damage wool. Hydrogen peroxide or sodium perborate bleaches can be used safely. Organic dry-cleaning solvents will not harm the fiber.

Resistance to Microorganisms and Insects. Mildew will not form on wool unless the fabric has been stored in a damp condition for an extended period of time. Fabrics should be put away only after they are completely dry.

One of the major problems in the care of wool is its susceptibility to damage from insect pests. Moths and carpet beetles are particularly destructive because the chemical structure of the cross-linkages in wool is especially attractive to these insects. Care in the storage of wool is required to minimize attack by insects. Soiled clothing is damaged more readily than are clean fabrics, as the insects may attack the spilled food as well as the wool. Wool fabrics with special finishes that prevent moth attack are referred to as being "mothproofed." Some of these finishes can be applied at the time of dry cleaning.

Consumers must exercise caution when using moth-repellents such as para-dichlorobenzene crystals or napthalene flakes. These substances are poisonous if ingested by children or animals. Because prolonged inhalation of the fumes is also dangerous, treated textiles must be placed in airtight storage containers or in areas separated from living or working space. These chemicals should be placed above the garments since their vapors are heavier than air.

Resistance to Environmental Conditions. Exposure to sunlight will cause deterioration of wool, although it is less severely affected than cotton. Sunlight also yellows white wool fabrics.

Age will not affect wool adversely. However, because of their susceptibility to attack by moths, wool fabrics require careful storage.

Uses

The excellent insulating qualities of wool lead to its use for cold-weather clothing. Winter coats, warm sweaters, and men's and women's suits are frequently made of worsted or woolen fabrics or blends of wool and other fabrics.

Wool's capacity for temporary setting makes wool ideal for tailored garments that are shaped through pressing techniques. By using different kinds of wool yarns and variations in weave, a wide variety of attractive garments and accessories are manufactured from wool.

In the home wool fabrics are made into carpets, blankets, upholstery fabrics, and sometimes draperies. Special coarse, resilient, durable wool fibers are produced for manufacture into carpets. Blankets of wool are warm without excessive weight and have the advantage of inherent flame resistance. The durability of upholstery fabrics will depend on the construction of the yarn and fabric, and those fabrics made from tightly twisted yarns with close, even weaves are most serviceable.

The disadvantages of wool used for apparel and in the home center on the tendency of fabrics to shrink and the susceptibility of wool to moth damage. Fabrics that have been finished to overcome both these problems are available, and appropriate handling during use and care will minimize these disadvantages. A disadvantage of wool for some individuals is that they may have allergic reactions from contact with the fiber. Some wool fabrics may have a rough or "scratchy" feel.

Care Procedures

Wool fabrics can be either laundered or dry-cleaned, although dry cleaning is preferable for wool fabrics that have not been specially finished to make them "washable." Dry cleaning minimizes shrinkage problems. Also, commercial dry-cleaning solvents may include mothproof finishes that will protect wool garments from moth attack during storage.

Fabrics that have been given special finishes to render them washable should be laundered according to care directions attached to the fabric. Fabrics without special finishes must be handled gently because the fabric is weaker wet than dry and also to prevent felting of fibers because of friction. Wool products should be washed in lukewarm water, and synthetic detergents without added alkali may be used. Washing can be done by hand or machine, provided that the wool fabrics are not agitated for more than 3 minutes. Agitation and friction produced in handling wool are more detrimental to the fabric than are high washing temperatures, so that care must be taken to avoid placing undue stress on wool fabrics during laundering. Knitted garments, such as sweaters, should be measured before laundering, and while the garments are drying they can be gently reshaped into their original size.

Chlorine bleach will damage wool fabrics. Hydrogen peroxide may be used for bleaching.

Solvents used for spot and stain removal do not harm wool fabrics. However, care should be taken in the application of spot remover. Excessive friction or rubbing on the fabric surface may cause matting and felting of fibers in the treated spot. Pat the fabric gently rather than rubbing hard.

Wool fabrics should not be dried in an automatic dryer. The pounding action caused by tumbling damp fabrics may cause excessive felting shrinkage of the fabrics. The dryer provides all the conditions conducive to felting: heat, moisture, and friction. Drying fabrics flat will prevent strain on any one part of the garment.

Because of the detrimental effect of heat on wool fibers, ironing temperatures should not exceed 200°F, and fabrics should always be pressed with a press cloth or steam.

Specialty Hair Fibers

Many hair fibers possess qualities similar to those of wool. These fibers are produced in comparatively small quantities, but they do have an important place in the textile industry, particularly in high-status, prestige clothing items.

Cashmere

Cashmere fiber comes from the fleece of the cashmere (or kashmir) goat, an animal that is native to the Himalaya Mountains region of India, China, and Tibet. (See Figure 5.5.) Iran and Iraq also produce cashmere fiber.

The animals are domesticated, and fiber is gathered by combing hairs from the fleece during the shedding season. Only the fine underhair is useful for cashmere fabrics, and one goat produces about 4 ounces of usable fiber each year.

The softest fibers are 1½ to 3½ inches in length. Coarser and stiffer fibers range from 2 to 5 inches. The natural color of cashmere is gray, brown, or, less often, white.

Microscopically, cashmere displays a scale structure like that of wool, but the scales are spaced more widely apart. Fibers are finer than are those in wool, about 15 microns in diameter. The cross section of cashmere fibers is round.

Figure 5.5

(a) Cashmere goat; (b) female worker in Inner Mongolia commune removes fleece from a cashmere goat, using a special handmade comb with a wood handle and an adjustable bar that allows the iron comb to open wider as the supply of fleece increases. Photographs by Boris Shlomm, President of Amicale Industries. Courtesy of Kairalla Agency.

(a)

(b)

The chemical and physical behavior of cashmere is much like that of wool, although cashmere is more quickly damaged by bases.

The softness and luster of cashmere combined with its scarcity put this fiber in the category of luxury fibers that are quite expensive. The fiber abrades easily, because of its softness, and since many of these fabrics are constructed with napped or fleecy surfaces, they require careful handling. Sweaters, coatings, and soft luxurious fabrics and yarns account for the largest proportion of the items made from cashmere.

Camel's Hair

The two-humped Bactrian camel of Central Asia is the source of the camel's hair fiber (Figure 5.6). Early accounts of the harvesting of camel's hair stated that hair was gathered during the moulting season in the spring by "trailers" who followed the camel caravans. Boris Shlomm, President of Amicale Industries, reported in an article in the *Wool Record* (1985) that on a visit to the Xinjiang Province in China he observed the processes currently used in obtaining camel's hair. Camels were shorn with hand shears similar to those used for sheep shearing before the invention of high-speed electric clippers. Shlomm speculates that the aforementioned trailers may have existed at a time when the local inhabitants were more nomadic, but that now with a more settled population the harvesting of camel's hair has become more like sheepherding. Camels are, however, also used as a means of transportation.

About 30 minutes to an hour is required for one to two people to shear one animal. Shearing takes place in May in the north and about a month earlier in the southern part of the region. Adults produce up to 10 kilograms of fiber, which is sorted by herdsmen as either coarse or fine. A re-sorting into various grades is done in a central warehouse. Within the collected hair are found both fine, soft down

Figure 5.6

Two-humped Bactrian camel being sheared by Chinese worker. Photograph by Boris Shlomm, President of Amicale Industries. Courtesy of Kairalla Agency.

called *noils,* and coarse bristly hairs. The soft noils, which make up about 30 percent of the fiber, are used for making apparel.

Under the microscope camel's hair shows a scale structure similar to that of wool, but the scales are less visible and less distinctly seen. The cortex is distinct; the medulla is discontinuous. Both the cortex and medulla are pigmented. This pigment produces the light brown or tan color associated with camel cloth, and because it is not discolored by oxidation, it cannot be removed by bleaching. Therefore, camel fabrics are usually left in their natural color or are dyed to darker shades.

Camel's hair provides excellent warmth without weight. It is said to have better insulating qualities than any of the other hair fibers. It is a relatively weak fiber and is subject to damage from abrasion because of its softness. Other physical and chemical properties of camel's hair are like those of wool.

Most fine camel's hair fiber is used for clothing, especially coating fabrics. Like other hair fibers, there is great variety in quality of camel's hair fibers, and the consumer must evaluate these products carefully. Because it is easy to dye wool camel color to blend it with camel's hair, a final product may be misrepresented as "camel's hair" when, in fact, the quantity of camel's hair is relatively low. Camel's hair fabric is expensive and should not be selected for its durability, as it tends to wear readily. Coarse camel's hair is used for industrial fiber, ropes, and paintbrushes.

Mohair

Mohair fiber is taken from the angora goat (Figure 5.7). Although South Africa produces the largest quantity of mohair (about 13.5 million pounds per year), the United States is responsible for 45 percent of world production. Of the 12 million

Figure 5.7

Angora goats, source of mohair fleece. Photograph courtesy of the Mohair Council of America.

pounds of mohair produced in the United States, 90 percent comes from animals raised in Southwest Texas. Only 2 percent of the fiber is used by the American textile industry; 98 percent is exported. Turkey, where the angora goat originates, also produces some mohair fiber.[2]

Goats are sheared in the same way as sheep. Fleece is removed twice a year. Each animal yields from 3 to 5 pounds a year of 4- to 6-inch fiber. To obtain a supply of slightly longer fiber, some goats are sheared only once a year, in which case the fibers are 9 to 12 inches in length.

The natural color of unscoured fleece is yellow to grayish white. Cleaning removes 15 to 25 percent of the weight. The clean fibers are white in color, silky, and fine in feel and appearance. Fibers are graded, with kids' or young goats' fleeces especially valued for their fineness. The cross section of the fiber is round, with the medulla being only rarely visible. Small air ducts are present between the cells of the fiber, which give it a light, fluffy feeling. The microscopic appearance of mohair is similar to that of wool.

Most of the physical and chemical properties of mohair are very similar to those of wool. The major differences between wool and mohair are the very high luster of mohair and its slippery, smooth surface. Mohair is especially resistant to abrasion. When viewed under the microscope, mohair shows fewer scales than does wool. As a result, the fiber sheds dust and soil and neither shrinks nor felts as readily as wool. Mohair is easier to launder, as well.

---

2. Data provided by the Mohair Council of America.

Figure 5.8

Fashionable sweater knitted from mohair fiber. Sweater by Kirsten Scarcelli, worn by Kim Dutton, former Miss U.S.A. and spokesperson for the Mohair Council of America.

The current uses of mohair stress products where its luster can be used to good advantage, and these include men's and women's suitings, upholstery fabrics, carpets, and draperies. Novelty yarns, such as looped or bouclé yarns, are often made of mohair, and mohair is blended with other fibers. (See Figure 5.8.)

The cost of mohair fabrics tends to be higher than that of wool. The quality of mohair can vary a good deal, so the consumer must evaluate mohair products carefully.

Qiviut

Qiviut is the underwool of the domesticated musk ox (Figure 5.9). Herds of musk oxen are cultivated in Alaska. These animals shed in the spring, at which time they are combed and the fine underwool is machine spun. Yarns are sent to Eskimo women in about 50 to 60 villages in the region, and they hand-knit a variety of products. Each village has a distinctive pattern unique to that settlement. The fiber is similar to cashmere in texture and softness. One-half pound of qiviut will make a large, warm sweater. An equivalent garment in sheep's wool would require 6 pounds of fiber.

Alpaca

Native to Peru, Bolivia, Ecuador, and Argentina, the domesticated alpaca (Figure 5.10) produces a fleece of fine, strong fibers that have a glossy luster. The alpaca is sheared once every 2 years in the spring (November and December in the Southern Hemisphere). Hairs average 8 to 12 inches in length and range in color from white to brown to black.

Figure 5.9

Domesticated musk oxen (with horns removed) being raised in Alaska.

Figure 5.10

Alpaca.

Alpaca fiber is used in suits, dresses, and upholstery fabrics. It may be made into blends with other fibers.

Llama

Another domesticated Andean animal, the llama (Figure 5.11) produces a fine, lustrous fleece, similar to alpaca. Its colors are predominantly black and brown, but some lighter colors are found. Slightly weaker than alpaca or camel's hair, llama fleece is used by many Indian artisans to produce decorative shawls, ponchos, and other products.

The fibers, which are often blended, are used for coatings, suitings, and dress fabrics.

Llamas and alpacas have been crossbred, and the resulting animals have fleece with many of the same qualities and characteristics as those of the parents. An animal with a llama sire and an alpaca dam is called an *huarizo*. One with a llama dam and an alpaca sire is a *misti*.

Figure 5.11

Llama.

Vicuña

A wild animal, the vicuña lives at very high altitudes in the Andes Mountains. (See Figure 5.12.) Although attempts are being made to domesticate this animal, most of the fiber must be obtained by hunting and killing the vicuña. One vicuña yields 4 ounces of very fine fiber and 10 to 12 ounces of less fine fiber. The Peruvian government sets a limit on the number of vicuña that can be taken in any year, so that the fiber is in very short supply.

One of the softest fibers known, vicuña is also the costliest. A vicuña coat will be comparable in cost to a good fur coat. Its use is limited to luxury items. The natural color—a light tan or chestnut brown—is usually retained, as the fiber is hard to dye.

Guanaco

Another wild animal, the guanaco, has been domesticated successfully. Although supplies of the fiber are more readily available than vicuña, it remains a relatively expensive fiber.

Guanaco is a soft, fine fleece of reddish-brown color. Often blended, guanaco is similar to alpaca in its qualities.

Cashgora

New Zealand cashgora is a relatively new specialty fiber from the cashgora goat. This animal was bred in New Zealand by crossing wild female cashmere goats and angora goats. The raw fleece consists of a small percentage of longer, stiffer hairs called guard hairs and a fine down. The guard hair is removed before spinning.

Figure 5.12   Vicuña herd. Photograph by William L. Franklin.

Cashgora fiber diameter ranges up to 22 microns. Luster is low to medium. Cashgora has a soft hand, dyes well, and is strong. Spun into either 100 percent cashgora yarn or blended, cashgora is used for knitting yarns, knitwear, blankets, and yard goods.

Fur Fiber

Fiber from the pelts of the fur-bearing animals is sometimes blended with other wool fibers. It provides interest and soft texture. Fur fibers from animals such as the beaver, fox, mink, chinchilla, rabbit, and the like are used.

Angora rabbits have long, fine, silky, white hair (Figure 5.13). These rabbits are raised in France, Italy, Japan, and the United States. The fiber is obtained by combing or clipping the rabbits. Angora rabbit fiber is exceptionally fine (13 microns) and is very slippery and hard to spin. Angora is used chiefly in novelty items and is often knitted. Sweaters are often made of angora blended with nylon and wool. The fibers tend to slip out of the yarns and increase in length on the surface of the fabrics so that some persons have the mistaken notion that angora hair "grows."

Figure 5.13

Angora rabbit. Photograph courtesy of Amicale Industries.

Fur Products Labeling Act of 1951

Relatively small quantities of fur fibers are used in the production of textiles. If fur fiber has been removed from the skin and incorporated in a textile product, it is designated as "fur fiber" and is subject to regulation under the TFPIA and the Wool Products Labeling Act. Fur that is attached to the animal skin is regulated by the Fur Products Labeling Act of 1951. This legislation requires that all fur products carry the true English name of the fur-bearing animal from which the fur comes. It also requires that furs be labeled with the country of their origin.

No fur may be given a trademark name of a fictitious or nonexistent animal. If furs have been worn or used by the ultimate consumer, they must be designated as "used fur." When fur is damaged from natural causes or from processing, it must be labeled as containing damaged fur. Any dyeing or bleaching or other treatments given to artificially color the fur must be disclosed.

Cow Hair and Horsehair

Cow hair is sometimes blended with wool in low-grade fabrics used for carpeting and blankets and in felts. Horsehair serves as a filling or stuffing material for mattresses and upholstered pieces. In the past it was woven into a stiff braid for use in millinery or dressmaking, but this use has been replaced, for the most part, by synthetic fibers. Rubberized horsehair has been used to make carpet underlays.

Silk

History of Silk Culture

Silk originated in China, the first habitat of the silkworm, which grew wild and lived on the leaves of a species of mulberry tree. Although some animal hair and flax fibers can grow to considerable length, silk is the only natural fiber that is hundreds of meters long.

Silk is made by the silkworm as it builds its cocoon. The substance is *extruded* from its body in one continuous strand from beginning to end. It is possible to unwind the cocoons and obtain long silk filaments. The Chinese discovered this process and, recognizing the potential value of the fiber it produced, guarded the method closely for hundreds of years. Silk has a natural beauty, and its history has been surrounded by legends. Chinese folklore credits the discovery of silk to Princess Si Ling Chi, who reigned about 2650 B.C. According to legend, after watching a silkworm spin its cocoon in her garden, she attempted to unwind the long filaments. After much experimentation she succeeded. She instructed her serving women in the art of weaving rich and beautiful fabrics from the long silk threads. So grateful for her discovery were the Chinese that they transformed Princess Si Ling Chi into a goddess and made her the patron deity of weaving (Lewis 1937).

History agrees with legend at least insofar as the approximate dates for the first use of silk by the Chinese. In spite of the close guarding of the secret of *sericulture,* or the controlled production of silk, other countries managed, often by somewhat devious means, to obtain silkworms. The Japanese supposedly abducted four Chinese maidens who were experts in sericulture and forced them to disclose the process. Another princess carried silkworm eggs and the seeds of the mulberry tree in her headdress when she left China to marry a prince of another kingdom. Even as late as the sixth century A.D., the secrets of silk manufacture were sought by the Byzantine emperor Justinian, who sent two monks to the East to discover how to produce and weave these handsome fabrics. The monks returned from a lengthy trip with silkworm eggs and mulberry seeds in their hollow bamboo walking sticks. From these seeds a flourishing silk industry developed in Byzantium. The cultivation of the silkworm spread to Italy and later to France (Lewis 1937).

Silk Production
Cultivation of the Silkworm

Silk is the only natural filament fiber that has significant commercial value. Produced by a caterpillar known as a "silkworm," silk can be obtained either from cultivated silkworms *(Bombyx mori)* or wild species.

Silk from wild species is limited in quantity and produces a coarser, stronger, short fiber known as *tussah silk.* Tussah silk has short fibers because the cocoons from which it is taken have been broken or pierced. When wild silk is spun by caterpillars that feed on oak leaves, the silk is light brown or tan in color and cannot be bleached.

By far the largest quantity of silk comes from sericulture, the controlled growth of domesticated silkworms to produce the silk fiber. Whether the silkworms be domesticated or wild, they go through four basic stages of development:

1. Laying of the eggs by the silk moth.
2. Hatching of the eggs into caterpillars, which feed on mulberry leaves.
3. Spinning of a cocoon by the caterpillar.
4. Emerging of the silk moth from the cocoon.

The science of sericulture has been perfected over many thousands of years. Today, all stages of development are carefully controlled, and only the healthiest eggs, worms, and moths are used for the production of silk. (See Figure 5.14.)

Selected moths of superior size lay from four hundred to six hundred eggs or seeds on prepared cards or strips of cloth. Each seed is about the size of a pinhead. These eggs can be stored in cool, dry places until the manufacturer wishes to begin their incubation.

Incubation is done in a mildly warm atmosphere and requires about 30 days. At the end of this time, the silkworms hatch. They are about ⅛ inch in length. The young silkworms require constant care and carefully controlled diets. Shredded or chopped young mulberry leaves are fed to the worms five times each day. Worms that appear to be weak or deformed are discarded. The areas in which worms are grown

Figure 5.14   (a) Silk moth laying eggs; (b) silkworms on a bed of mulberry leaves; (c) silkworm beginning to spin cocoon; and (d) completed cocoon. Photographs courtesy of the Japan Silk Association.

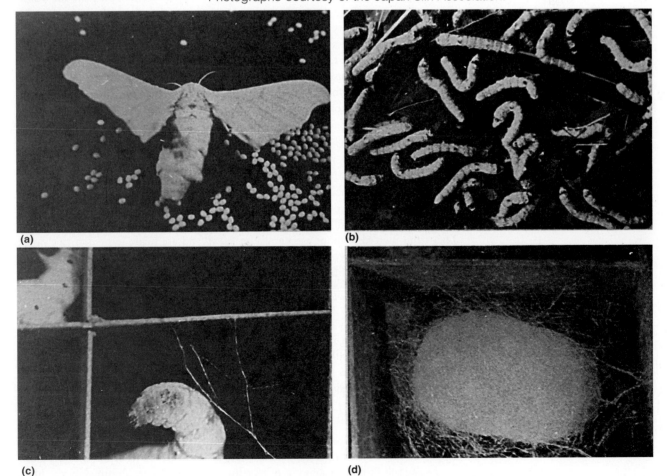

(a)

(b)

(c)

(d)

are kept scrupulously clean. For about a month the worm grows, shedding its skin four times. When fully grown, worms are about 3½ inches in length.

When its size and activity show that the worm is about ready to begin to spin a cocoon, the silkworm is transferred to a surface of twigs or straw. From two sacs located in the lower jaw, the worm extrudes a substance made up of two strands of silk (fibroin) and a gummy material (sericin) that holds them together. Moving its head in the shape of a figure eight, the worm surrounds itself with a cocoon of perhaps 1,000 meters of fiber. The completed cocoon is about the size of a peanut shell and takes 2 to 3 days to spin. If the worm is permitted to live, it will change into a pupa or chrysalis and then to a moth. After 2 weeks the moth breaks through the cocoon and emerges, mates, lays eggs, and begins the cycle again.

Only those moths selected as breeding stock are permitted to complete the cycle. These are selected from the largest and heaviest cocoons. The remainder of the cocoons are subjected to dry heat that kills the pupa.

Occasionally, two silkworms will spin a cocoon together. This produces a cocoon made of a double strand of silk and is known as *doupion* silk (*doupioni,* in Italian).

Reeling of Silk

The whole, unbroken cocoons are sorted according to color, texture, size, shape, and other factors that will affect the quality of the fiber. Reeling of silk is, to a large extent, a hand operation done in a factory called a *filature.* Several cocoons are placed in a container of water of about 140°F. This warm water serves to soften the *sericin,* the gum that holds the filaments of silk together. Very little of this gum is actually removed in reeling. The outer fibers are coarse and short and not useful in filament silk. They are separated and are used for spun silk, which is made from short fiber lengths.

The filaments from four or more cocoons are held together to form a strand of yarn. As the reeling continues, a skilled operator adds or lets off filaments as needed to make a smoother strand of uniform size. Several skeins of silk weighing 50 to 100 grams each are combined into a bundle. Each bundle is called a *book* and weighs from 5 to 10 pounds. These are packaged into bales for shipping.

Silk Yarns

The making of silk filament yarns is called *throwing.* Reeled silk filaments can be combined into yarns immediately. Short, staple-length silk fibers must be spun. Short outside fibers of the silkworm's cocoon, the inner fibers from the cocoon, and the fiber from pierced cocoons are known as *frisons* and are made into spun silk yarns. Fibers are cut into fairly uniform lengths, combed, and twisted into yarns in the same way that other staple fibers are spun.

Gum Removal

As mentioned, the sericin that holds the silk filaments in place in the cocoon is softened but not removed in reeling. This gummy material makes up about 25 percent of the weight of raw silk. It is removed before throwing, after throwing, or after the fabric has been woven. A soap solution is used to wash the gum from the silk. In some silk fabrics, called *raw silk,* the sericin has not been removed.

Regulation of Silk Weighting

During the latter part of the nineteenth century, the technique of weighting was employed extensively to add body and weight to silk fabrics after removal of the gum. In passing silk through a solution of metallic salts, the salts are absorbed by the fiber, with a corresponding increase in the weight of the fabric. Silk can absorb more than its own weight in metallic salts, so that this excess weight on the fiber will, eventually, cause the fabric to break.

This practice had become so widespread that a good deal of poor-quality fabric was being sold. Because the buyer could not tell from its appearance or hand that the silk had been weighted, the FTC, in 1938, began overseeing silk weighting by passing its pure silk regulations.

These FTC regulations are still in effect. Other than some weighting of silk for neckties and for products requiring especially heavy fabrics, few silk fabrics are now weighted. The regulations require that fabrics labeled "silk" or "pure dye silk" contain from 0 to 10 percent of weighting. All silk fabrics that have more than 10 percent weighting must be labeled as weighted silk, unless they are black in color. Black silks are able to hold a greater quantity of weighting than are other colors without degradation, and, so, black silks can be weighted up to 15 percent.

Locale of Production

Because the culture of silkworms requires so much hand labor, sericulture has been most successful in countries where labor is less expensive. No silk is produced in the United States. China is the largest silk producer in the world. India and Thailand both produce substantial quantities of silk, but most of it is consumed within those countries and is not exported. Although Japan is the world's largest consumer of silk per capita, it produces almost no silk for export. Italy is the largest exporter of finished silk goods but imports the silk fiber from which those goods are made. This is also true of England and France, which also produce finished silk fabrics.

Silk imports to the United States are in the form of raw silk in bales, spun silk and thrown silk filament yarns, woven or knitted fabrics, and completed garments or household textiles. Imports for 1993 consisted of 0.6 million pounds of silk fiber, 12.5 million pounds of spun or thrown yarns and fabrics, and 12.5 million pounds of finished goods, mainly scarves, handkerchiefs, blouses, and laces.[3] No reliable statistics were kept that record the total quantities of imported apparel and other manufactured articles made of silk.

Molecular Structure of Silk

Like wool, silk is composed of polypeptide chains, but it has fewer amino acids and no sulfur linkages. The polymer molecules are not coiled but are extended. This structure allows the chains to be more tightly packed, increasing the crystallinity of the fiber. Hydrogen bonds and salt bridges cross-link adjacent molecules, contributing to the strength.

Properties of Silk

Physical Appearance

Color. The natural color of cultivated silk is off-white to cream. Wild silk is brown.

---

3. Data from *Fiber Organon* 65 (April 1994): 75.

Figure 5.15

Photos of: (a) cross section and (b) longitudinal view of silk fibers taken through an electron scanning microscope. Photographs courtesy of the British Textile Technology Group (BTTG).

(a)   (b)

Figure 5.16

Position of silk fibers within "gum" before processing.

Silk Fibers

"Gum"

Shape. In microscopic cross section silk is triangular in shape. (See Figure 5.15.) The double silk filaments lie with the flat sides of the triangles together, surrounded by the sericin coating. (See Figure 5.16.)

The fiber has a smooth, transparent, rodlike shape with occasional swelling or irregularities along its length. It is fine, having a diameter of 9 to 11 microns, and filaments may be as short as 300 meters or as long as 1,000 meters. Individual filaments as long as 3,000 meters have been measured.

Luster. The luster of degummed silk is high but not so bright as manufactured fibers with round cross sections. Although the surface of the fiber is smooth, the roughly triangular shape changes the pattern of light reflection.

Other Physical Properties

Specific Gravity. The specific gravity of silk at 1.25 is less than that of cellulose fibers and is similar to that of wool.[4] Lightweight fabrics can be made of silk because of the fine diameter of the fiber and its high tenacity.

Strength. Silk is one of the strongest of the natural fibers. (Its tenacity is 2.8 to 5.2 g/d.) It is stronger than wool because of its higher crystallinity. Its wet strength is slightly less than its dry strength because the hydrogen bonds between protein polymers are broken by moisture.

---

4. "Identification of Fibers in Textile Materials," *Bulletin X-156.* Wilmington: DuPont, 1961. Varying sources list specific gravity of silk that ranges from 1.25 to 1.34.

Elasticity and Resilience. The elasticity of silk is good, and its resilience is medium. Creases will hang out of silk, but its wrinkle recovery is slower and not as good as that of wool.

Absorbency and Moisture Regain. The absorbency of silk is good (the moisture regain is 11 percent), making it a comfortable fiber to wear. Although silk is more difficult to dye than wool, it can be printed and dyed easily to bright, clear colors if appropriate dyes are used.

Dimensional Stability. The dimensional stability of silk is good. It does not stretch to any significant extent but may exhibit relaxation shrinkage because of its higher moisture absorbency.

Heat and Electrical Conductivity. The heat conductivity of silk is low, so densely woven fabrics can be relatively warm. However, because very sheer, lightweight fabrics also can be woven from silk, it can be used for lightweight, summer clothing.

Because the electrical conductivity of silk is not high, silk tends to build up static electricity charges, especially in dry atmospheres.

Effect of Heat; Combustibility. When placed in a direct flame, silk will burn, but when the flame is removed, the silk may self-extinguish. Therefore, silk is not considered an especially combustible fabric. Like wool, silk is damaged by dry heat and should be ironed damp, at low temperatures and using a press cloth.

Effect of Selected Conditions on Silk

Chemical Reactivity. Like other protein fibers, silk is sensitive to the action of bases. Acids will harm silk more quickly than they harm wool. Chlorine bleach deteriorates the fiber, but hydrogen peroxide or other peroxygen bleaches can be used. Organic chemical solvents used in dry cleaning will not affect silk. Perspiration will cause deterioration of the fabric. Perspiration can have a negative effect on dyestuffs, causing discoloration after repeated exposure; therefore, silk fabrics should always be cleaned before they are stored.

Resistance to Microorganisms and Insects. Mildew is not a problem with silk. Moths do not harm clean silk, but carpet beetles will attack the fabric.

Resistance to Environmental Conditions. Sunlight deteriorates silk even more rapidly than wool, causing white fabrics to yellow. Age will lead to eventual deterioration of fabric strength. Silk fabrics should be stored away from light. Antique fabrics should be sealed off from the air.

Weighting of silk causes it to crack, split, and deteriorate much more quickly than would otherwise be true. (See Figure 5.17.) Historic costumes made of silk before silk weighting was introduced are still in good condition. Weighted silk garments, made in later times, break apart into shreds.

Special Finishes Applied to Silk

Silk has long been considered a luxury fabric, delicate and requiring special care. Beginning in 1977 one company, Go Textiles, introduced popular casual garments, such as shirts and jeans, made of silk. Given a special finish called *sandwashing* (see the discussion of sueding on page 374), these garments had an attractive faded

Figure 15.7

Silk fabric from the skirt of an historic costume of the 1890s that has deteriorated as a result of silk weighting.

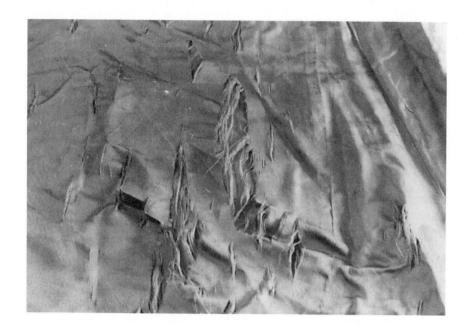

Table 5.2 Selected Properties of the Protein Fibers: Wool and Silk

	Wool	Silk
Specific gravity	1.32	1.25 (degummed)
Tenacity (g/d)		
Dry	1.0–1.7	2.4–5.1
Wet	0.8–1.6	1.8–4.2
Moisture regain[a]	About 15%	10%–11%
Resiliency[b]	Excellent.	Good.
Burning	Burns slowly, sometimes self-extinguishing when flame is removed.	Burns slowly, sometimes self-extinguishing when flame is removed.
Conductivity of		
Heat	Good insulator; low conductivity.	Moderate.
Electricity	Rather low, builds up static electricity.	Rather low, builds up static electricity.
Resistance to damage from		
Fungi	Good.	Good.
Insects	Poor; attacked by moths, carpet beetles.	Fair; not attacked by moths but attacked by carpet beetles.
Prolonged exposure to sunlight	Yellows, loses strength eventually.	Yellows and degrades.
Acids	Resists action of mild or dilute acids; damaged by strong acids.	More readily damaged by acids than wool, more resistant than cotton.
Bases	Damaged by even mildly alkaline substances.	Damaged by even mildly alkaline substances.

[a]At 70°F, 65% relative humidity.

[b]Characteristics such as resiliency, conductivity, and resistance are compared on the following scale: poor, fair, moderate, good, and excellent. Conductivity is characterized as being low or high.

appearance; they were soft, supple, and washable. Washed silks, even though expensive, became quite popular, and by the 1980s major American designers had put them into their collections.

As washable silks gained in popularity, other finishes were used to alter their hand. *Sueded silk* was finished with a slight nap. Treatment with alkali soda ash broke down the sericin coating, caused small pits in the fibers, and raised short fibers during tumble drying. To make apparel easier to care for, soil- and stain-resistant finishes were applied.

Uses

The beauty of silk fabrics is legendary. For many centuries silk was synonymous with luxury and was used for garments worn on feast days, festivals, and other occasions of great importance. Wall hangings of silk were used to decorate the homes of the wealthy, and carpets woven of silk were used in the homes of the rich in Persia and China.

In spite of the increased use of washable silk in casual clothing, the relatively smaller supplies of silk, as compared with manufactured fiber fabrics, have tended to keep silk prices relatively high. The range of apparel for which silk is used has expanded in recent years, and silk or silk blends can be found in women's dresses, blouses, slacks, and lingerie; men's trousers, shirts, and neckties; knitted cold weather underwear; and various accessories. Raw silk is popular for summer-weight suits and jackets.

Silk may also be found in some high-priced drapery and upholstery fabrics. The performance of silk fabrics in these uses is rather poor. Upholstery fabrics of silk are often made in weaves that show up the luster of the fabric but abrade rather easily. Sunlight will deteriorate drapery fabrics of silk. Draperies made of silk should be lined with some other fabric to protect the silk from constant exposure to the sun.

Table 5.2 offers a comparison of the two major protein fibers: silk and wool.

Care Procedures

Silk fabrics should be stored away from direct sunlight, both to avoid yellowing of white fabrics and to prevent loss of strength. Long-term storage of silk wedding gowns or other items is best done in containers that are sealed against air and carpet beetles.

Care labels should be followed to determine the best care procedures for individual silk garments. The following recommendations for care of silk fabrics were made by the Silk Institute.

1. Some dyestuffs used on silk are susceptible to bleeding or loss of the dyestuff. Check by wetting a small and inconspicuous spot (perhaps a seam or facing area) and blot the damp area between paper towels, pressing hard. If color appears on the paper towel, the fabric is not colorfast and should be dry-cleaned.
2. Fabrics that should generally be dry-cleaned include chiffon, georgette, taffeta, silk satin, and charmeuse; dark colors or bright patterns; those with embroidery, lace, pleats, or ruffles; items with linings, interfacings, or covered buttons.

Care of Washable Silk

Even for silk items labeled as washable, care labels should be followed closely to avoid problems. When washing items by hand, launder in a mild detergent that contains no added alkali. Use lukewarm water and handle carefully. Do not wring or scrub, especially on fabrics made from smooth, solid color filaments where wear is more likely to show. Chlorine bleach should never be used on silk. If fabrics must be bleached, use hydrogen peroxide. Rinse garments thoroughly and then roll in a clean bath towel to absorb excess moisture.

If machine washing is recommended, use a gentle, two-minute wash cycle; lukewarm water; and mild detergent. Do not tumble dry, unless care labels direct, as the surface may be abraded or the fabric may be more likely to shrink. To dry, place garment on plastic hangers (wire hangers can cause rust stains).

Iron while the garment is still damp, on the wrong side of the garment, keeping ironing temperatures low, at 300°F or lower. Test silk fabrics to be sure they will not watermark before using steam or a damp press cloth. Although badly wrinkled silk fabrics will require pressing, many creases will hang out of silk fabrics without ironing. When ironing silk, protect the fabric with a dry press cloth.

The International Fabricare Institute (IFI) has noted a number of problems with some washable silks. Dyes have actually dissolved in water, causing dye transfer to other items being washed at the same time. Pastel colors tend to be more colorfast than dark colors. Some sizings or finishes used on washable silks discolor on contact with moisture from rain, water-soluble food and beverages, or perspiration. Spilled alcohol or perfume or cosmetics that contain alcohol may remove or change colors. Dyes, especially blues and greens, may lose or change color if they come into contact with alkaline substances such as soaps, shampoos, detergents, or toothpaste. Both sunlight and artificial light will sometimes cause fading.

Washable silks should not be dry-cleaned because their dyes are often fugitive to dry-cleaning solvents. Care labels should provide thorough information about how to wash these fabrics. Products that do not perform in a satisfactory manner when directions have been followed should be returned to the retailer for a refund.

3. Among the fabrics made from silk that can often be hand-washed are China silk, India silk, crêpe de chine, pongee, shantung, tussah, doupioni, jacquard, and spun silk.
4. Raw silk garments will gradually loose the residual silk gum if laundered.

Consumer Box 5.1 discusses the care of washable silks.

Regenerated Protein or Azlon Fibers

With the commercially successful regeneration of cellulosic fibers, research was initiated to find suitable protein materials for regeneration in the hope of creating fibers with the highly desirable qualities of wool. As a base material, a protein was required that was readily available, as well as one that had a chemical structure similar to that of wool. Milk was selected, and in 1904 the first method for making filaments from the protein of milk (casein) was disclosed, but the filaments were too brittle to be used. In the 1930s a usable fiber known as Lanital® was developed in Italy, and another called Aralac® was made in the United States. Since that time other regenerated protein fibers have been made from corn, peanuts, and soybeans.

The generic name for the regenerated protein groups is *azlon*. Regenerated protein fibers had a pleasant, soft handle, but their strength was poor, and their lack of durability presented a problem. Some of the milk-based proteins also developed an unpleasant odor when wet.

Although azlon fibers have never gained a wide share of the market, information about these fibers continues to appear in the textile literature. A Polish firm is listed by the Fiber Economics Bureau (1994–95) as manufacturing a casein-based azlon fiber called *Wipolan.* The same source also lists Chinon, a graft fiber of milk protein and polyacrylonitrile manufactured and used in Japan. Chiton fibers, regenerated from the protein of beetles, have been synthesized. Chiton polymer films are being used in Japan as one of the layers in laminated fabrics for "breathable" moisture-resistant activewear.

References

Barber, E. 1991. *Prehistoric textiles.* Princeton: Princeton Univ. Press, 20–25.

Boston, W. S. 1984. Wool. In *Encyclopedia of textiles, fibers, and nonwoven fabrics,* ed. M. Grayson, 523. New York: Wiley.

Federal Trade Commission. 1986. *Rules and regulations under the Wool Products Labeling Act of 1939.* Washington, D.C. Federal Trade Commission.

Lewis, E. 1937. *The romance of textiles.* New York: Macmillan.

Ryder, M. 1993. Sheep shear thyself. *Textiles* 22 (1): 6.

Shlomm, B. 1985. Gaining an insight into camel hair production. *Wool Record,* November.

Review Questions

1. What are some of the physical and chemical properties common to most protein fibers?
2. Define the following terms that are applied to wool: lamb's wool, pulled wool, virgin wool, recycled wool, shoddy.
3. Explain how the chemical structure of wool accounts for (1) its ability to be set into pleats and creases and (2) its resiliency.
4. How does the physical structure of wool affect its properties?
5. What are the distinguishing characteristics of each of the following specialty hair fibers

cashmere	alpaca
camel's hair	vicuña
mohair	angora rabbit

6. Define the following terms that are applied to silk: degumming, raw silk, tussah silk, doupion, throwing, weighting, sandwashing, spun silk.
7. Under what conditions should silk products be dry-cleaned? Under what conditions should they be washed?
8. How are azlon fibers produced?

Recommended Readings

Burroughs, J. 1993. Making a case for mohair fashions. *America's Textiles International* 22 (November): K/A 11.

Cowan, N. 1989. The natural way into the future [cashgora]. *Textile Horizons* 9 (September): 47.

Higgs, W. 1987. The musk ox and its wool. *Journal for Weavers, Spinners, and Dyers* 142 (April): 14.

Hunter, L. 1993. *Mohair: A review of its properties, processing, and applications.* Manchester, England: Textile Institute.

Hyde, N. 1984. The queen of textiles [silk]. *National Geographic* 165 (January): 2.

McCurry, J. W. 1994. Is mohair in for more woes? *Textile World* 143 (December): 67–73.

Production of chitosan and chitin fibers. 1994. *High Performance Textiles,* July, 2.

Rasmussen, M. F., P. C. Crews, and W. H. Meredith. 1993. Chinese silk: The effects of economic reform on the silk sector of China's textile industry. *Textile Horizons,* December, 34.

Rheinberg, L. 1991. The romance of silk. *Textile Progress* 20 (4).

Rheinberg, L. 1992. *Silk the continuous filament natural fibre, Part 2. Textiles* 21(1): 6–8.

Russell, K. P. 1977. The specialty animal fibres. *Textiles* 6 (February): 8.

Sueded/sandwashed silk. 1992. *IFI bulletin: Fabrics, fashions* 2.

Wool works. 1994. *Textiles* 23(2): 14.

INTRODUCTION TO MANUFACTURED FIBERS

The chemical principles outlined in chapter 3 apply to both natural and manufactured fibers. In manufactured fibers chemists have succeeded in creating through chemical means substances that have the qualities necessary to make them useful in textiles. Manufactured fibers may be either regenerated or modified natural substances, or synthetic.

All the early procedures (in the manufactured fibers industry) started with materials similar in structure to natural fibers. These materials were dissolved chemically and were then re-formed into long, filament fibers. It was not until chemists came to understand the chemical structure of fiber molecules that they realized that it might be possible to create fibers entirely from simple chemical substances.

An analytical process called X-ray diffraction revealed that fibrous qualities depended on the presence of long-chain polymers. This understanding led to attempts to put together long-chain polymers in the laboratory from chemical materials. Chemists had synthesized a type of large molecule known as a *polypeptide*. A polypeptide is any polymer containing an abundance of amide linkages, that is, linkages made up of carbon, oxygen, nitrogen, and hydrogen (CONH). Silk and wool are, chemically speaking, polypeptides. Scientists believed that synthesis of polypeptides might lead to the invention of a totally synthetic fiber that was not derived from any natural substance.

E. I. du Pont de Nemours & Company, a chemical-manufacturing firm, had established an extensive basic research program, and those doing research in this program were given wide latitude as to the areas in which they might work. In particular, W. H. Carothers, a chemist at DuPont, chose to work in the synthesis of long-chain molecules; he was not searching for textile fibers, but the work he initiated in the formation of long-chain polymers was applied widely to the creation of a number of fibers and to their subsequent manufacture. The direction in which Carothers was working might be described as follows: "Take molecules that can react at both ends, react them, and long molecules will result. If these molecules are very long in relation to their dimensions, they will exhibit fiber-forming properties" (Moncrieff 1975, 319).

The basic research done by Carothers resulted in the invention of nylon, the first truly synthetic fiber to be marketed. Nylon is, according to chemical classification, a polyamide.

Fiber Formation

Most synthetic polymers must be converted into liquid form to be spun. This is done either by dissolving the polymer in a suitable solvent or by melting the polymer. Before actually forming the fiber, certain characteristics can be added to the polymer material. Many manufactured fibers are naturally bright, with a high luster. If dull or semidull fibers are wanted, delustering agents can be added to the molten polymer to break up light rays and decrease shine. Color can also be added.

Using one of several spinning methods, the liquid polymer is extruded through a spinneret. Each spinneret has a number of holes, and each hole produces one filament. Filament yarns are described by denier (i.e., size) and number of filaments; for example, filaments described as 70/34 represent 70 denier/34 filaments. When fibers being extruded are intended for conversion into staple lengths, spinnerets with larger numbers of holes are used to produce more filaments.

Spinneret holes are spaced to allow the filaments to be extruded without touching each other. The holes must be exactly the same size to produce uniform fibers. The metal used in the plate must be capable of withstanding high pressures.

Melt Spinning

Melt spinning takes advantage of the thermoplastic characteristics of polymers. Chips of solid polymer about the size of rice grains are dropped from a hopper into a melter where heat converts the solid polymer into a viscous liquid. The liquid forms a "melt pool" that is pumped through filters to remove any impurities that would clog the spinneret and is delivered to the spinneret at a carefully controlled rate of flow. Melt spinning is simpler and cheaper than other spinning methods; therefore, it is used except when polymers cannot be melt spun.

The spinneret holes are usually round, but noncircular holes are also used to make filaments of various cross-sectional shapes. Melt-spun fibers may be made through Y-shaped holes that yield a three-lobed fiber or C-shaped holes to produce a hollow filament, for example.

The diameter of the fiber is determined by the rate at which the polymer is supplied to the hole in the spinneret and the windup speed, not by the diameter of the hole. When the molten polymer emerges from the spinneret hole, a cool air current

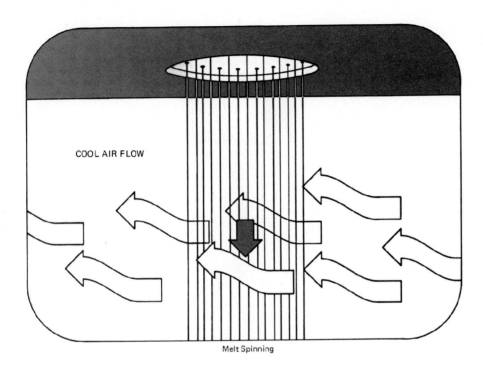

COOL AIR FLOW

Melt Spinning

Figure 6.1

Melt spinning. Illustration courtesy of the American Fiber Manufacturers Association, Inc.

is passed over the fiber, causing it to harden. (See Figure 6.1.) Failure to maintain constant feeding speed of molten polymer or changes in the temperature of cooling will cause irregularities in the diameter of the fiber. Nylon and polyester are melt-spun fibers.

One of the latest developments in melt spinning has been the significant increase in spinning speeds. Processing speed has increased from less than 1,000 meters per minute in the 1960s to over 10,000 meters/minute today. Higher speed spinning is cost-effective but does produce fibers with lower orientation and strength.

Dry Spinning

Many polymers are adversely affected by heat at or close to their melting temperatures. Polymers that cannot be melt spun undergo other methods of spinning, such as dry spinning, to produce filaments. Dry spinning requires the dissolving of the polymer in a solvent to convert it into liquid form. Substances used as solvents are chosen not only because they will dissolve the polymer but also because they are safe and can be reclaimed and reused.

The polymer and solvent are extruded through a spinneret into a circulating current of hot gas that evaporates the solvent from the polymer and causes the filament to harden. (See Figure 6.2.) The solvent is removed and recycled to be used again.

Dry-spun filaments generally have an irregular cross section. Because the solvent evaporates first from the outside of the fiber, a hard surface skin of solid polymer forms. As the solvent evaporates from the inner part of the fiber, this skin "collapses" or folds to produce an irregular shape. If the rate of evaporation is slowed, the cross section of the filament will be more nearly round. Acetate fibers and some acrylic fibers are dry spun.

Figure 6.2

Dry spinning. Illustration courtesy of the American Fiber Manufacturers Association, Inc.

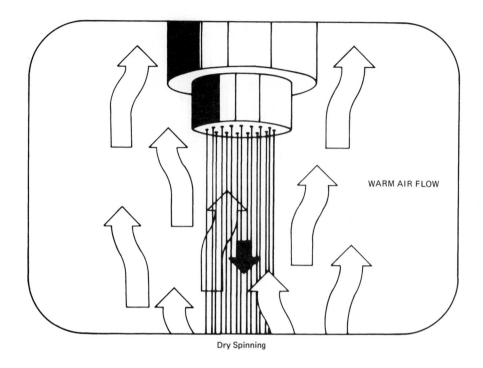

WARM AIR FLOW

Dry Spinning

Figure 6.3

Wet spinning. Illustration courtesy of the American Fiber Manufacturers Association, Inc.

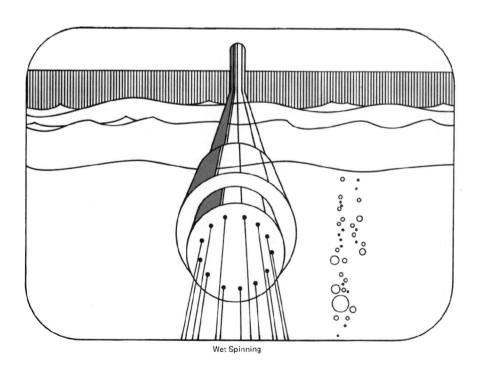

Wet Spinning

Wet Spinning

Wet-spun polymers are, like dry-spun polymers, converted into liquid form by dissolving them in a suitable solvent. The polymer solution is extruded through a jet into a liquid bath. The bath causes coagulation of the fiber. (See Figure 6.3.) Solvents are recovered from the liquid bath and are recycled. Viscose rayon and some acrylics are wet spun.

It is possible to add special chemical reagents to the liquid bath that produce selected changes in the fiber. This is done in the manufacture of some high-strength rayons, for example.

Other Spinning Methods

Although melt-, dry-, and wet-spinning techniques are used to form the vast majority of manufactured fibers, several other spinning techniques also exist and may be applied in a limited number of specialized situations. High molecular weight polymers, such as those in Spectra® polyethylene, are formed by *solution spinning* or *gel spinning*. As in wet and dry spinning, the polymer is dissolved in a solvent. The polymer and solvent together form a viscous gel that can be processed on conventional melt-spinning equipment to form a gel-like fiber strand. Later in the processing, the solvent is extracted and the fibers stretched.

Fibers made from polymers that have very high melting points and are insoluble present obvious difficulties in spinning. Such materials may be spun by a complex process called *emulsion spinning* in which small, fibrous polymers are formed into an emulsion, aligned by passing the emulsion through a capillary, then fused or sintered (combined by treating with heat without melting), passed through the spinneret into a coagulating bath, and subsequently stretched.

Hollow fibers (Figure 6.4) are made of a sheath of fiber material and one or more hollow spaces at the center. These hollows may be formed in a number of different ways. The fiber may be made with a core of one material and a sheath of another, and then the central material is dissolved out. Or an inert gas may be added to the solution from which the fiber is formed, with the gas bubbles creating a hollow area in the fiber. Other specialized techniques also appear to be used to make hollow fibers, but details of the processes are not released to the public. Hollow fibers provide greater bulk with less weight. They are, therefore, often used to make insulated cloth-

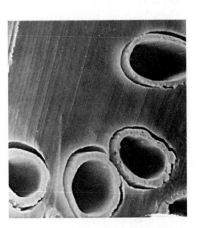

Figure 6.4

Photograph of the cross section of a hollow rayon fiber mounted in wax and photographed through a scanning electron microscope. Photograph courtesy of Courtaulds Fibers, Inc.

ing. For absorbent fibers such as rayon, hollow fibers provide increased absorbency. Some have been put to such specialized uses as filters or as carriers for carbon particles in safety clothing for persons who come into contact with toxic fumes. The carbon serves to absorb the fumes.

Microfiber Formation

Several different methods have been developed for the spinning of microfibers. Such fibers are also called *microdenier fibers* because of their small size. It is possible to produce microfibers through conventional melt spinning; however, to create such fine filaments requires very strict process controls and a uniformly high quality of polymer.

An alternative method is to use two incompatible polymers that do not adhere to each other very well. Fibers are extruded in configurations like those shown in Figure 6.5. After extrusion the individual fibers, each composed of several different polymer materials, are processed so that they split apart into individual filaments. Each filament then divides into two or more much smaller filaments.

Yet another method uses two different polymers that do not mix. One of the polymers is deposited as continuous filaments within a second or holding polymer. (See Figure 6.6.) After spinning, the holding polymer is dissolved away to leave the finer filaments. These latter two processes take advantage of technological developments in bicomponent fiber formation, discussed in chapter 14 (pages 214–217).

Figure 6.5

Method of forming microfibers by using two incompatible polymers that can be separated easily.

 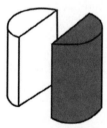

Polymer A (shaded area) is extruded from spinneret in a side-by-side configuration and separates from Polymer B (white section) to form two separate, smaller (micro) fibers.

Polymer A and Polymer B alternate segments of extruded fiber and separate to form six separate, smaller (micro) fibers.

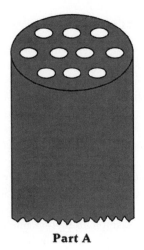

Part A

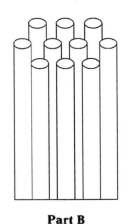

Part B

Figure 6.6

Microfibers may be formed by spinning continuous filaments imbedded in a holding polymer (shaded area in Part A). After extrusion the holding polymer is dissolved away, leaving only the microfine fibers in Part B.

Drawing or Stretching

Both crystalline and amorphous arrangements of molecules exist within newly formed filaments. It is possible to orient these molecules to make them more parallel to the walls of the filament, and therefore more crystalline and stronger, by stretching the filament before it is completely hardened. (See Figure 3.6, page 56.)

Newly formed filaments are, therefore, subjected to drawing or stretching. Depending on the fiber type, this may be done under cold or hot temperature conditions and has the additional effect of making the filament both narrower and longer. Drawing is accomplished by stretching the fibers between two rollers, called *Godet rolls,* with the first roller rotating faster. It may be done immediately after spinning of fibers or during subsequent processing as part of yarn texturing and/or spinning. Alternative treatments are discussed in chapter 15.

Not all yarns are drawn to the maximum amount possible, because when a fiber reaches its maximum length, the extensibility of the yarn and fiber are lowered. Yarns that have not been fully drawn are called *partially oriented yarns (POY).* Those that have been fully drawn are called *fully oriented yarns (FOY).* As is true of many other textile processes, precise control of the process must be maintained so that the manufacturer can achieve the qualities needed in the final product.

Other steps may be added, such as texturing (in which crimp is added to the filaments) or heat-setting treatments to ensure very low shrinkage as is required in fiber for auto tires (see next section). Sometimes two or more steps may be combined into consecutive operations to reduce manufacturing costs, so that the fibers may go from spinning directly to drawing, or from spinning to drawing to texturing.

Heat Setting

Thermoplastic manufactured fibers may shrink when exposed to heat. To prevent shrinkage, such fibers are treated with heat during manufacturing to "set" them into permanent shape. Exposure during use and care to temperatures greater than the heat-setting temperature will counteract the heat setting, resulting in fiber shrinkage or loss of heat-set pleats or creases.

High Performance Fibers

The natural fibers and fibers regenerated from natural materials are often referred to as the first generation of fibers. Second generation fibers are those manufactured fibers synthesized after Carothers's discovery of nylon. These were new generic fibers based on chemical differences. For the third generation fibers of the last two decades, technology has focused primarily on developing manufacturing processes and fiber modifications to produce *high performance fibers*. These fibers are usually developed for specific purposes or end uses. They are also called *high technology fibers* and *super fibers* (Hongu and Phillips 1990).

High technology fibers exhibit specially engineered properties such as flame resistance, chemical absorbance, or biodegradability. A polyester fiber with the cross section of silk and micro-slits to simulate silk's luster and scroop is one such high technology fiber. Microfibers are another example of high technology fibers.

Super fibers are manufactured to have exceptionally high strength (tenacities higher than 20 g/d). The gel-spinning technique described in this chapter was developed to produce very crystalline fibers with strengths in this range. Methods have also been developed to convert acrylic fibers into carbon super fibers.

Manufactured Fibers Industry Practices

Trademarks

Most companies that manufacture fibers assign trademarks to their fibers. Those trademarks are promoted to the public and within the industry. Although the TFPIA requires that both generic and trademark names be listed on labels attached to products at the point of purchase, companies are not required to list both generic and trademark names in promotional materials. As a result, companies that want to build demand for their specialized fibers often run advertisements in trade publications using only trademark names.

Frequently, fiber manufacturers will assign a trademark to a fiber that is used for particular products. For example, BASF Company manufactures nylon fibers for use in carpets and produces a series of variants of this carpet fiber, each with some properties that are unique. The company uses the name Zeftron® as a general trade-

Table 6.1			
Acronyms and Abbreviations Commonly Used in the Manufactured Fibers Industry	**Acronym or Abbreviation**	**Term**	**In-text Discussion**
	F	filament	Chapter 2, page 34
	M	monofilament	Chapter 15, page 222
	S	staple	Chapter 2, page 34
	T	tow	Chapter 15, page 235
	MD	microdenier	Chapter 2, page 35
	BF	bulked filament	Chapter 15, page 230
	FF	fibrilated film	Chapter 15, page 248
	FOY	fully oriented yarn	Chapter 6, page 131
	POY	partially oriented yarn	Chapter 6, page 131
	PT	producer textured	Chapter 15, page 230

mark for its nylon carpet fibers and then adds numbers and letters to designate the specific variants: Zeftron 200®, Zeftron 500ZX®. This makes it possible for the carpet manufacturers who are BASF's customers to more easily order the most appropriate fiber.

Terminology, Acronyms, and Abbreviations

Producers and purchasers of manufactured fibers use a number of terms and their acronyms or abbreviations to refer to fibers. These terms often are not familiar to the general public. Table 6.1 provides a brief introduction to some of the more commonly used terms and their acronyms and abbreviations. The table also provides a cross-reference to the place in the text where each concept is explored in more detail.

Summary

This chapter has provided a general introduction to the techniques used to produce manufactured fibers and to some of the specialized terminology that those working in this field use. In chapters 7 to 14, readers will be acquainted with the unique aspects of the many different types of manufactured fibers.

References

Hongu, T., and G. O. Phillips. 1990. *New Fibres*. New York: Ellis Horwood.
Moncrieff, R. W. 1975. *Man-made fibres*. New York: Wiley.

Review Questions

1. What are the differences between melt spinning, dry spinning, wet spinning, gel spinning, and emulsion spinning?
2. Describe two ways of making hollow fibers.
3. Describe two ways of forming microfibers.
4. What is the purpose of drawing or stretching manufactured fiber filaments?
5. If fibers are described as *delustered, producer textured, heat-set, microdenier* fibers, at which stage of manufacture is each of the four italicized characteristics given to the fibers?

Recommended Readings

Achwal, W. B. 1994. Microfibers—characteristics, properties, and processing. *Colourage* 41 (August): 35.
American fiber manufacturers special report [special issue]. 1994. *Southern Textile News,* December 12.
Holme, I. 1994. Microfibers: Present and future prospects. *Synthetic Fibers* 23 (April/June): 13.

Hongu, T., and G. O. Phillips. 1990. *New fibres.* New York: Ellis Horwood.

Issacs, M., and J. W. McCurry. 1994. Race is on to find new uses for microfibers. *Textile World* 144 (August): 45.

Miroslawska, M. 1990. Spinning ultrafine filaments. *America's Textiles International* 19 (January): FW–2.

Mukhopadhyay, S. K. 1993. High performance fibres. *Textile Progress* 25 (3/4).

Rudie, R. 1994. Microfibers revisited. *Bobbin* 35 (June): 12.

Talele, A. B., R. K. Datta, and R. S. Gandhi. 1994. New profiled fibers: An overview. *Textile Industry of India* 33 (March): 11.

Ultrafine microfibers. 1994. *JTN,* no. 480 (November): 49.

MANUFACTURED CELLULOSIC FIBERS

For thousands of years the only fibers used for textiles were those found in nature, even though, as early as 1664, English writer Robert Hooke suggested that people ought to be able to create fibrous materials that had the same qualities as natural fibers. However, neither Hooke nor any of his contemporaries were equal to the task. In the nineteenth century a number of scientists had begun to look seriously for techniques for creating fibers. Their search was successful. Nitrocellulose, the first rayon fiber, was obtained as early as 1832. Further experimentation and development followed, and by the end of the century, Count Hilaire de Chardonnet, a Frenchman, had set up a factory for the production of "artificial silk" (rayon), the first "man-made" fiber (Moncrieff 1975).

Rayon

The earliest processes for making rayon used natural materials that were fibrous, such as short cotton linters that could not be spun into yarns or fibrous wood pulp. Chardonnet used the pulp of mulberry trees because silkworms ate the leaves. The pulp was dissolved in chemicals that broke down the molecular structure of the fiber somewhat, while still retaining a substantial quantity of polymer molecules. The solution was forced through a metal plate that had small holes in it, exposed either to heated air or to a chemical solution, and then formed into a long, hairlike filament. This substance was called "artificial silk."

This fiber was given the name *rayon* in 1924. It is a regenerated cellulose. The specific process that was used is now obsolete in the United States and has been replaced by other methods of manufacture, but the basic principle of taking a natural material that is not usable in its original form and regenerating it into usable textile form remains the same. The manufacture of artificial silk by Chardonnet in 1891 marked the beginning of the manufactured fibers industry.

FTC definitions of generic fiber names always are written to specify the chemical makeup of the fiber. The FTC definition of rayon identifies rayon as "a manufactured fiber composed of regenerated cellulose, as well as manufactured fibers composed of regenerated cellulose in which substituents have replaced not more than 15 percent of the hydrogen of the hydroxyl groups." The major fiber groups that fall within this definition are viscose rayon, cuprammonium rayon, high-tenacity rayon, lyocell, and high-wet-modulus rayon. Viscose rayon accounts for by far the largest amount of rayon manufactured.

Viscose Rayon

Raw Materials

Wood pulp is the major source of cellulose used to produce viscose rayon. Cotton fibers, especially the short cotton linters, can also be used. Most of the timber used comes from eight- to twelve-year-old eucalyptus, spruce, or southern pine trees that are raised in nurseries. Harvested trees are stripped of their bark, sun-dried, then cut into strips, and finally reduced to chips. Chips are treated to remove lignin (binding agents) and to remove as much of the resin as possible.

The resulting pulp consists of about 94 percent cellulose. It is pressed and cut into blotterlike sheets for further processing.

Manufacture

The following steps are employed in the process for manufacturing viscose rayon from these sheets of cellulose. The purpose is to produce a soluble form of cellulose so that it can be spun into fibers.

Slurrying. The quantity of cellulose is measured carefully by weight and then placed in a soaking press, or slurry press, where it remains immersed in a solution of caustic soda (sodium hydroxide) for about an hour. The excess solution is pressed out of the pulp material, leaving a slurry consisting of a substance called alkali cellulose.

Pre-ageing. Alkali cellulose is shredded into small fluffy particles called *white crumbs.* These are aged under carefully controlled conditions for several days. During this time the cellulose chains are broken into shorter polymers that can be dissolved more easily.

Xanthation. Carbon disulfide is then added to the white crumbs, which produces sodium cellulose xanthate and changes the color to bright orange-yellow. Cellulose xanthate is soluble in sodium hydroxide.

Dissolving and Ripening. The orange-yellow crumbs are placed in dissolving tanks of dilute sodium hydroxide. The resulting solution is thick and viscous and is known as viscose. In color, it is gold with a consistency similar to that of honey.

Deaeration and Filtration. The viscose is filtered to remove any insoluble particles. This is important because the particles would clog the spinneret holes and interfere with the spinning process. It is at this point that delustering agents (such as titanium dioxide) or pigment dyes for coloring the fiber may be added.

Extrusion. The final step in the formation of the fiber is the forcing of the viscous liquid through the spinneret. The solution is wet spun into a dilute sulfuric acid bath. The acid hydrolyzes the xanthate, thereby reversing the xanthate formation and regenerating the cellulose in the form of long, continuous filaments that are then washed to remove chemicals or other impurities. Figure 7.1 shows the process in a flowchart.

Molecular Structure

Rayon is composed of cellulose, like cotton. In viscose rayon, however, the cellulosic chains are much shorter. The degree of polymerization is only about 400–700, compared to 6,000–10,000 for cotton. The molecules are also less ordered, and the fiber has a higher amount of amorphous material.

Properties of Viscose Rayon

In the production of manufactured fibers, many qualities can be built into the fiber. For this reason, it is difficult to generalize about all rayon fibers, since each manufac-

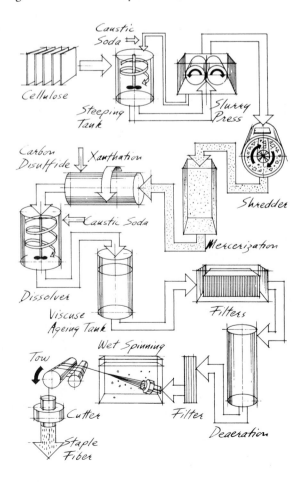

Figure 7.1

Flowchart showing the manufacture of viscose rayon fiber. Following wet spinning, fibers can be cut into tow (as shown on this chart) or wound onto packages as uncut filaments. Illustration courtesy of the American Fiber Manufacturers Association, Inc.

turer may produce viscose rayons that differ somewhat. The following discussion refers to the properties of viscose rayon that has not had any special modifications.

Rayons have generally been used in many of the same kind of products for which cotton is used. When compared with cotton, rayons have displayed certain disadvantages. They are not equal in firmness and crispness; they have poorer dimensional stability, stretching and shrinking more than cotton; and they lose strength when wet so that rayons must be handled carefully both in industrial processing and in home laundering.

Physical Appearance

Color and Luster. Rayon fibers are normally white in color. The luster of rayon can be modified by adding titanium dioxide, a delustering agent, to the solution before the fibers are extruded.

Shape. Manufactured fibers can be manufactured in any length and diameter. In cross section the viscose rayon fibers appear as irregular circles with serrated edges. When lengthwise fibers are examined microscopically, longitudinal lines called *striations* are seen. (See Figure 7.2.) The striations on the surface of viscose rayon are a visual effect caused by the appearance of the serrations created when the skin of the fiber formed at a faster rate than the core. When the core is formed, the skin, which is larger, collapses slightly to form an irregular "wrinkled" surface.

Variations of cross-sectional shapes can be created by modifying the extrusion process. Changing the conditions in the coagulating bath can affect the rate of formation of the fiber so that fiber surface would be more serrated than usual. Use of spinnerets with slits, E-, H-, X-, or Y-shaped holes can produce fibers with noncircular shapes.

If carbon dioxide or some other gas-generating material such as sodium carbonate is injected into the viscose solution, that gas will be trapped inside the fiber when it is extruded. Depending on how this process is controlled, the resulting fibers may be hollow or may have hollow spaces (cells) within the fibers. (See Figure 6.4, page 129.)

Other Physical Properties

Specific Gravity. The specific gravity of rayon is 1.51. Rayon fibers are comparable in specific gravity with cotton and linen (1.54). Viscose, cotton, and linen fabrics of similar weave and construction will be of comparable weight.

Figure 7.2

Photomicrographs of regular viscose rayon in: (a) a cross section and (b) a longitudinal view. Photomicrographs courtesy of the DuPont Company.

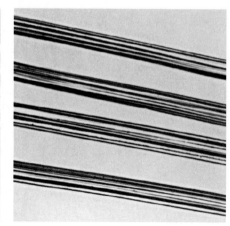

(a)   (b)

Strength. The strength of viscose rayon is low due to its lower polymer chain length (when compared with cotton and flax). Furthermore, rayon is weaker than cotton because its physical structure is different. During the growing process, cotton develops a fibril structure, the layers or rings of which protect the fiber and provide greater strength. Ordinary rayon has no fibril layers in which the crystallinity of the physical structure is increased. Instead, rayon has a more amorphous inner structure. There is a considerable decrease in strength when the fiber is wet. Rayon fabrics must be handled carefully during laundering. Figures cited by manufacturers of regular-tenacity rayons available in the United States range from 1.0 to 2.5 g/d for dry fibers, and for wet tenacity, .5 to 1.5 g/d.[1]

Exceptionally high-tenacity rayons are also manufactured. These are generally used in specialized and industrial applications. Tenacities for such viscose fibers range from 3.0 to 5.7 g/d, dry, and 1.9 to 4.3 g/d, wet.

Elasticity and Resilience. The elastic recovery of rayon is low, as is its resiliency. Untreated rayons tend to stretch and wrinkle badly. Durable press finishes are generally not applied to viscose rayon because they weaken the fiber.

Absorbency and Moisture Regain. The molecular structure of viscose is more amorphous than is that of cotton or linen, making the viscose fibers more absorbent than the natural cellulosic fibers. Moisture regain is 11 percent. Viscose accepts dyes readily, because of its increased accessibility. Also, fibers with larger surface areas dye more readily, and the serrated edge of the rayon fiber provides greater surface area. The absorbency of the fiber makes clothing of viscose comfortable to wear.

Dimensional Stability. Viscose rayons stretch and, having low elastic recovery, tend to remain stretched. For some time after stretching, the distorted fabric tends to "creep" toward, but not completely to, its original length.

Fabrics may be stretched during processing and exhibit relaxation shrinkage upon a first laundering. Fibers may continue to shrink in subsequent launderings, as the creep effect continues. Special finishes can be given to viscose to overcome some of the problems of shrinkage. Treating fabrics with resin finishes has been the most commonly used means of stabilizing viscose rayon fabrics.

Heat and Electrical Conductivity. The conductivity of both heat and electricity of viscose rayon is satisfactory, so that the fiber is reasonably comfortable in hot weather and does not build up static electricity.

Effect of Heat; Combustibility. Viscose fabrics must be ironed at lower temperatures than cotton. Too-high ironing temperatures will produce scorching. The recommended ironing temperature of viscose rayon is 250°F. Long exposure to high temperatures deteriorates the fiber.

The fibers burn with characteristics similar to those of cotton. Viscose rayon fabrics continue to burn after the source of the flame has been removed, and burning fabrics have the odor of burning paper. A soft, gray ash remains after burning.

Effect of Selected Conditions on Fiber

Chemical Reactivity. The amorphous molecular structure of viscose makes it more susceptible to the action of acids and bases. Acids attack viscose more readily than cotton or other cellulosic fibers. Viscose is more susceptible to damage from bases as well.

---

1. Data from *Textile World Man-made Fiber Chart* 130 (August 1990).

Resistance to Microorganisms and Insects. Viscose is subject to damage from mildew and rot-producing bacteria. Silverfish will attack the fiber. Care in storage is necessary to prevent exposure of the fabric to conditions that encourage mildew and silverfish.

Resistance to Environmental Conditions. Exposure to sunlight will deteriorate viscose rayons more rapidly than cotton. Although it is often used in curtains and draperies, viscose rayon is not especially satisfactory for these products unless they are lined to protect against sunlight. Age has no deleterious effect on viscose rayons if care is taken to be sure fabrics are stored in a clean, dry condition.

Uses

Viscose rayon is used in fashionable wearing apparel, ranging from millinery to lingerie, suits, dresses, and sportswear. Viscose rayon is often blended with other fibers. In the home rayon fabrics or blends of rayon and other fibers can be found in tablecloths, slipcovers, upholstery, bedspreads, blankets, curtains, and draperies.

Rayon fibers have also been used in the manufacture of a wide variety of nonwoven fabrics, both disposable and durable. Rayon has also been used as a starting material for carbon fibers (see page 206), and for the "cotton balls" sold for cosmetic uses.

Care Procedures

Fabrics made from rayon have had a broad range of quality and price. For optimum serviceability rayon fabrics should have special finishes to control shrinkage and wrinkling. Consumers should be sure to follow care-labeling instructions closely. Some rayon requires dry cleaning for best results, whereas others can be laundered quite successfully.

Laundering requires care because the fiber is weaker when wet and can be damaged more easily by rough handling. Drying in an automatic dryer may accentuate rayon's tendency to shrink. When pressing rayon fabrics, use lower ironing temperatures. Chlorine bleaches must be controlled carefully to avoid fabric deterioration. Oxygen (or perborate) bleaches are safer for rayon fabrics, if bleaching must be done.

The Future of Viscose Rayon

Although viscose rayon declined in popularity for apparel after the introduction of synthetic manufactured fibers in the 1940s, it made a strong return for fashionable clothing in the 1980s. One of the largest American manufacturers of viscose rayon, Avtex, decided to cease manufacture of viscose rayon for apparel in July 1989. The company had, for some time, been having difficulties in meeting local environmental standards for air and water pollution.

When Avtex ceased rayon production, there were concerns that rayon would become scarce. To date, rayon has remained both popular and available. Economists have noted, however, that shipments of rayon for the first four months of 1994 decreased 20 percent when compared with the same period in 1993 (Maycumber 1994).

High-Wet-Modulus Rayon

Attempts have been made to produce rayon fibers that possess some of the advantages of cotton. These experiments have centered on the development of rayon fibers with fibril structures similar to that of the natural cellulose fibers.

A Japanese researcher, S. Tachikawa, discovered a process for manufacturing rayon that develops a physical structure more like that of cotton. In this process the severity of the chemical processing was decreased, the manufacturing time was decreased, and careful control was maintained over the chemical materials used. More specifically, Tachikawa's process eliminated the aging of alkali cellulose, dissolved the cellulose xanthate in water rather than in caustic soda, and eliminated the ripening of cellulose xanthate. A lower concentration of acid was used in the spinning bath with little or no salts.

These rayons are known as *high-wet-modulus rayons,* which means rayons that have greater resistance to deformation when wet. They are also called *polynosic rayon.* Although high-wet-modulus rayons are no longer manufactured in the United States, they are manufactured abroad. The Lenzing Fibers Corporation of Austria manufactures *modal* fibers, a European generic name for high-wet-modulus fibers, and distributes these fibers in the United States.

Properties of High-Wet-Modulus Rayon

The strength of high-wet-modulus fibers is higher than that of viscose rayon and somewhat lower than the manufactured fiber lyocell (discussed later). Its resilience and elastic recovery are better than viscose rayon. These fibers do not stretch or shrink excessively, can tolerate ironing temperatures slightly higher than those suitable for cotton, and can be mercerized. Although deteriorated by sunlight, they resist sun better than viscose rayon.

Absorbency is similar to that of viscose rayon. Lenzing recommends them for blending with cotton, as they have similar dyeing characteristics.

Uses

In the United States modal fibers are currently being used almost exclusively for apparel. According to Lenzing, they are quite successful in Europe in lingerie and knit tops, and the company anticipates that such products made from modal will also be available soon in the United States. The price of these fibers is midway between the lower price of viscose rayon and the higher cost of lyocell.

Lyocell

Courtaulds, a fiber manufacturer, developed and introduced the trademarked fiber Tencel®, which is produced by a process known as solvent spinning. This fiber has been given the generic fiber designation *lyocell* in Europe. Application by Courtaulds for this generic fiber designation is now pending before the FTC in the United States.

The Lenzing Company expects to be selling a lyocell fiber in the U.S. market by 1996. The company calls its product "Lyocell by Lenzing."

Manufacture

The raw material for lyocell, like that for viscose rayon, is wood pulp. Amine oxide, a solvent, dissolves cellulose chains directly, omitting the more degradative steps required in the viscose process. The resulting clear, viscous solution is filtered, then extruded into a bath of dilute amine oxide in which the cellulose is precipitated as a fiber. (See Figure 7.3.)

Figure 7.3

Flowchart showing the spinning process for Tencel® lyocell fibers. Illustration courtesy of Courtaulds Fibers, Inc., Mobile, Ala.

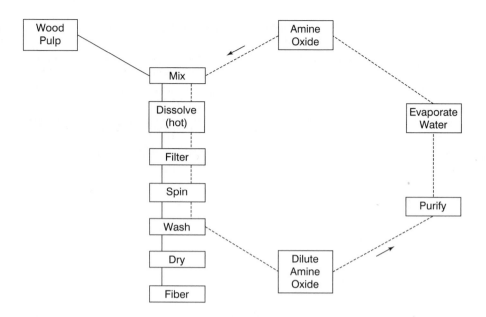

A major advantage of this process is that it is self-contained. The amine oxide in the fiber-forming bath is reclaimed and recycled. Solvent-spinning technology can more readily meet the even stricter environmental regulations likely to be enacted in the future.

Properties of Lyocell

Tencel® has a smooth cross section, without the serrations characteristic of viscose rayon. It is a high-strength, high-modulus fiber with a high degree of crystallinity. Dry strength is 5.9 g/d, and wet strength can be up to 4.3 g/d. Courtaulds describes Tencel® as closer to cotton than to rayon in its characteristics.

Uses

Tencel® is used in men's and women's apparel such as shirts, blouses, pants, dresses. (See Figure 7.4.) It also is used in some household textiles. The producer sees its major uses in high-end, microfiber products. Lyocell by Lenzing is expected to have somewhat different aesthetics than Tencel®, and the manufacturer says it will be used in products for a broad market.

Care Procedures

Lyocell fabrics may be given finishes that make them either washable or dry-cleanable, so consumers should follow care labels. IFI notes that garments should not be washed commercially but only under normal home washing conditions. If fabrics that require dry cleaning are washed, they may shrink and become quite wrinkled.

Figure 7.4

Apparel made from Tencel®
fibers. Photograph courtesy of
Courtaulds Fibers, Inc.,
Mobile, Ala.

Cuprammonium Rayon

The manufacture of cuprammonium rayon was discontinued in the United States
in 1975. It is still being manufactured in Italy, Japan, and eastern Germany. Water
waste from the cuprammonium process is contaminated with chemicals, mainly
copper, that must be removed to meet clean-water standards in the United States.
The cost of removing chemical pollutants from the water is significant, and it is
this factor that has resulted in discontinuance of its manufacture in the United
States.

Properties of Cuprammonium Rayon

Properties of this type of rayon are quite similar to those of viscose rayon. The fiber
has a somewhat more silklike appearance and feel and is often manufactured in finer
diameters. It is also stronger.

Under the microscope cuprammonium rayon appears to have a round cross section and a smooth, longitudinal appearance. No striations, or very fine striations, appear on the surface.

The fiber can be made into very lightweight fabrics. A good conductor of heat and fairly absorbent, it is especially suitable for use in warm-weather clothing. Consumers may find cuprammonium rayon fibers labeled as *cupro*. Films and hollow fibers of cuprammonium rayon are used in making artificial kidneys as they exhibit superior performance in removing impurities and cause less blood clotting than do other manufactured fibers.

Fibers Derived from Cellulose: Cellulose Acetate and Cellulose Triacetate

In the 1920s experimentation with regeneration of cellulosic materials led to the discovery of a by-product called cellulose acetate. This substance, a chemical derivative of cellulose, was used as a coating for the fabric wings of World War I airplanes. It caused the fabric to tighten up and become impervious to air. After the war the demand for this material decreased, and the manufacturers of cellulose acetate sought another market for their product. Intensive research yielded a process for converting cellulose acetate into a fiber with high luster and excellent draping qualities. Like rayon, acetate was known as "artificial silk."

The resulting confusion between real silk and artificial silk led the FTC to establish a separate name for the manufactured fibers. In 1924 the term *rayon* was established to include both regenerated cellulose and cellulose acetate. In 1953 an FTC ruling established separate categories for rayon and acetate and for triacetate, another derivative cellulose fiber.

Cellulose acetate and cellulose triacetate are classified as *derivative cellulose fibers*. These fibers should be distinguished from the rayons, which are *regenerated cellulose fibers*. The production of both fibers begins with cellulose but, unlike rayon, the chemical composition of acetate and triacetate fibers is not cellulose but a chemical variation of cellulose known as an ester. For this reason, the behavior of cellulose acetate and cellulose triacetate differs somewhat from the other cellulosic fibers.

Manufacture

In the chemical reactions that take place during the manufacture of cellulose acetate (and cellulose triacetate), acetyl groups

$$(CH_3-\overset{\overset{\textstyle O}{\|}}{C}-O-)$$

are substituted for —OH groups on the cellulose molecule. This process is known as *acetylation*.

All three hydroxyl groups in the cellulose molecule are acetylated. When a substance is formed from cellulose in which all three hydroxyl groups have been acetylated, the material is called cellulose triacetate. If one-third of the acetyls are removed by hydrolysis, the substance is called cellulose acetate or cellulose diacetate. Both are used in forming textile fibers, but triacetate is no longer produced in the United States.

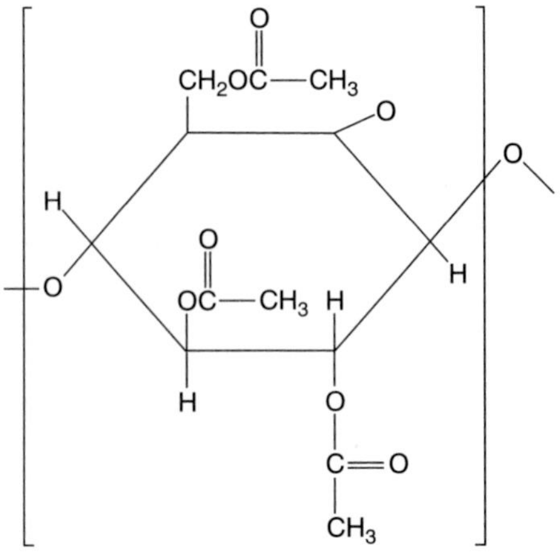

cellulose triacetate

The initial stages of formation of both cellulose acetate and cellulose triacetate are the same. Cotton linters or wood pulp are treated to remove any impurities. In making acetate, the purified cellulose is steeped in acetic acid for a time to make the material more reactive. After further treatment with still more acetic acid, acetic anhydride is added. This mixture is stirred until it is thoroughly blended, but no reaction takes place until sulfuric acid is added to the mixture. The sulfuric acid begins the acetylation reaction. The temperature is kept low, and the mixture stands for 7 or 8 hours until it takes on a thick, gelatinlike consistency. The material formed is triacetate, also known as the primary acetate. From this point, the procedure differs, depending on whether cellulose acetate or triacetate is being made.

Cellulose triacetate having been formed, water is added to the viscous solution. The triacetate can no longer be held in this weak solution and precipitates out in the form of small, white flakes. These flakes are collected, dried, and then dissolved in a solution of methylene chloride and a small quantity of alcohol. The fibers are dry spun through a spinneret into warm air, solidified, and are formed into yarns.

To follow the steps in the spinning of regular acetate, we must return to the formation of triacetate, or the primary acetate. The next step is the conversion of the base acetate into a diacetate. The primary acetate (triacetate), excess acetic acid, and acetic anhydride from the first reaction are combined with sufficient water to produce a 95 percent solution of acetic acid. This mixture stands for 20 hours, during which time acid hydrolysis takes place and some of the acetylated hydroxyl groups are reconverted to their original form. This mixture is tested constantly so that the reaction is stopped at the appropriate joint. The mixture is poured into water, and the cellulose acetate precipitates into chalky white flakes that are collected, washed, and dried. This is the secondary acetate, or cellulose acetate.

Flakes from different batches of cellulose acetate are mixed together to maintain a uniform quality of acetate. The flakes are soluble in acetone. Before spinning, the flakes are dissolved in acetone to form the solution, or dope. This takes about 24 hours. The dope is filtered and then extruded through spinnerets into warm air that evaporates the acetone. In winding the fiber into yarns, fibers are given a slight stretch that orients or parallels the molecules, making the fiber somewhat stronger. (See Figure 7.5.)

Flowchart showing the manufacture of cellulose acetate. Illustration courtesy of Eastman Chemical Company.

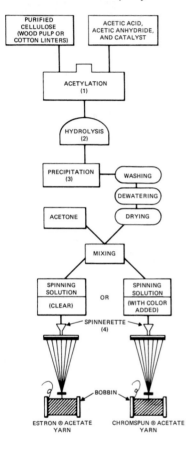

Properties of Acetate and Triacetate

Physical Appearance

Shape. In microscopic appearance cellulose acetate and cellulose triacetate are very similar. Normally, both fibers are clear and have an irregular, multilobed shape in cross section rather like popcorn. Acetate may be manufactured in other cross sections as well; however, most commercially available acetate fibers with unusual cross-sectional shapes have been withdrawn from manufacture.

The longitudinal appearance of regular acetate and triacetate fibers shows broad striations. It is not possible to distinguish regular acetate fibers from triacetate fibers by microscopic examination. (See Figures 7.6 and 7.7.)

Luster and Color. If acetate and triacetate have not been treated to decrease luster, both fibers will have a bright appearance and good luster. Fibers that have been delustered show small, black spots of pigment in the microscopic longitudinal view and cross section. Fibers are white unless they have been solution dyed.

Other Physical Properties

Specific Gravity. Acetate and triacetate are both lower in specific gravity, at 1.32 and 1.3, respectively, than is rayon or cotton. Comparable fabrics, therefore, feel lighter when made of acetates or triacetates than if they are woven of cotton, linen, or rayon.

Strength. Both acetate and triacetate have very low strength. Both are weaker wet than dry. The abrasion resistance is poor. Nylon hosiery wearing against acetate satin linings in coats provides sufficient abrasion to cut these fibers.

Elasticity and Resilience. Acetate and triacetate differ markedly in their elastic recovery and resilience. Acetate has poor elastic recovery and poor wrinkle recovery. By contrast, triacetate has increased elastic recovery, is resilient, and has good wrinkle recovery.

Absorbency and Moisture Regain. Acetate is more absorbent than is triacetate. (Acetate has a moisture regain of 6.3 to 6.5 percent, whereas triacetate regains only

Photomicrographs of cellulose acetate fiber in: (a) a cross section and (b) a longitudinal view. Photomicrographs courtesy of the DuPont Company.

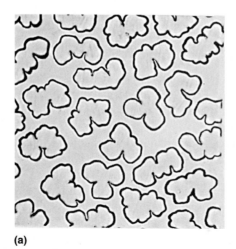

(a)

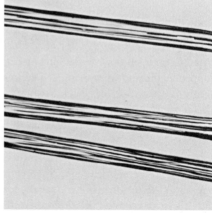

(b)

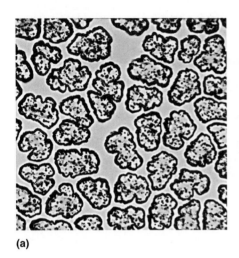

(a)

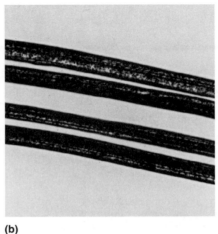

(b)

Figure 7.7

Photomicrographs of delustered cellulose triacetate fiber in: (a) a cross section and (b) a longitudinal view. Photomicrographs courtesy of the DuPont Company.

3.5 percent of moisture.) Acetate has more of the cellulose hydroxyl groups remaining for attracting water.

Dimensional Stability. Triacetate fibers have good resistance to stretch or shrinkage. Acetate fabrics may exhibit relaxation shrinkage on laundering unless they are pretreated. Knit fabrics are especially prone to relaxation shrinkage, showing as much as 10 percent shrinkage during laundering. Exposure to high temperatures may also cause acetates to shrink.

Heat and Electrical Conductivity. Neither heat nor electrical conductivity of acetate and triacetate is as good as the conductivity of other cellulosic fibers. Both fibers tend to build up static electricity charges, and neither acetate nor triacetate is as cool to wear as cotton, linen, or rayon.

Effect of Heat; Combustibility. Both acetate and triacetate are thermoplastic fibers; they will soften and melt with the application of heat. Triacetate is normally given a special heat-setting treatment that makes it much less sensitive to heat than acetate. Surface designs such as moiré can be heat-set in acetate. If triacetate is stretched during heat treatment, the crystallinity of the molecule can be increased. Along with the increase in crystaline structure, the moisture regain decreases. Heat-treated triacetate can be permanently set into pleats or other shapes. Table 7.1 contrasts the effect of heat on each fiber.

If ignited, acetate and triacetate burn with melting. When the flame has been put out, a small, hard, beadlike residue remains at the edge of the burned area.

Effect of Selected Conditions on Fiber

Chemical Reactivity. Table 7.2 compares the chemical reactivity of acetate and triacetate.

Acetate	Triacetate
Sticks at 350°F to 375°F	464°F (after heat treatment)
Melts at 500°F	575°F

Table 7.1

Effect of Heat on Acetate and Triacetate

Table 7.2	Chemical Reactivity of Acetate and Triacetate	
	Acetate	**Triacetate**
Effect of acids	Resistant to cold, dilute acids. Decomposed by strong acids; dissolves in acetic acid.	Resistant to cold, dilute acids. Damaged by strong acids; slightly better acid resistance than acetate.
Effect of bases	Good resistance to weak bases. Saponified (acetate groups removed) by strong bases.	Like acetate.
Effect of bleach	Hydrogen peroxide or sodium perborate bleach recommended at temperatures below 90°F.	Like acetate.
Effect of organic solvents	Petroleum products safe for use; dissolved by acetone, an ingredient in some fingernail polish remover, and in cresol, phenol, and some lacquer solvents.	Like acetate—partially dissolved by acetone with heat.

Resistance to Microorganisms and Insects. Mildew will grow on acetate or triacetate if the fabrics are incorrectly stored. The growth causes discoloration of the fabric but no serious loss of strength. Triacetate is more resistant to mildew than is acetate.

Moths or carpet beetles do not attack either fiber. However, heavily starched or sized acetates are prone to attack from silverfish.

Resistance to Environmental Conditions. Extended exposure to sunlight will cause a loss of strength and deterioration of acetate fabrics. Draperies should be lined to protect them from the sun. Triacetate has moderate resistance to sunlight. The resistance of acetate to ultraviolet light is decreased if the fiber has been delustered.

Acid fumes in the atmosphere may adversely affect some dyes used for acetates. The chemical nature of acetates requires that they be dyed with a type of dye known as *disperse dye.* Certain of these dyes are subject to atmospheric fading, or *fume fading.* Blue and gray shades, after exposure to atmospheric gases produced by heating homes with gas, turn pink or reddish. Greens may turn brown.

To overcome this problem, acetate fibers may be colored in the solution before the fiber is extruded from the spinneret. Pigment that is added to the acetate solution is locked into the fiber permanently and cannot change in color.

In addition to solution dyeing, special finishing agents called diethanolamine or melamine can be applied to acetate and triacetate fabrics to stabilize colors and prevent fume fading. Also some blue dyes that are not reddened by gas fumes have been developed.

Acetate does lose some strength through aging. Triacetates resist deterioration with age.

Uses

Acetate is used for many household and apparel textiles because it has an attractive appearance and pleasant hand. Decorative fabrics are woven to take advantage of the high luster and wide color range available in acetate fabrics. Poor abrasion resistance limits their use in products where abrasion resistance is important, such as upholstery.

Acetates are used for items of clothing such as blouses, dresses, and lingerie (Figure 7.8). Handsome drapery and upholstery fabrics are often made of acetate brocade, taffeta, or satin. Acetate yarns are used in some fabrics together with yarns of other fibers to provide a contrast between the luster of acetate and dull appearance of, for example, cotton or rayon. Cigarette filters are a major and growing use of acetate tow. Filament acetate is produced by Eastman Chemical Company under the trademarks of Chromspun®, a producer-colored fiber, and Estron®. Hoechst Celanese makes these acetate fibers: Celebrate!®, which is produced as filament, staple, and tow and Microsafe AM®, an antimicrobial fiber produced in filament or staple.

Triacetate fabrics have the advantage of being able to be heat-set. Apparel in which pleat or shape retention is important is often made from triacetate. The major use of this fabric is in wearing apparel; however, the manufacturer recommends its use for comforters, bedspreads, draperies, and throw pillows, as well. Triacetate is manufactured in Belgium, Japan, and the United Kingdom.

Table 7.3 gives a comparison of the properties of the major manufactured cellulosic fibers.

Figure 7.8

Fashionable blouse, vest, and wide-legged pants made from Celebrate!® acetate fiber. Photograph courtesy of Hoechst Celanese Fibers Group. Outfit by G.S.L. of California.

Table 7.3   Comparison of Characteristics of Regenerated Cellulosic Fibers and Cellulose Derivative Fibers

	Regular-Tenacity Viscose Rayon	High-Wet-Modulus Rayon	Lyocell[a]	Acetate	Triacetate
Specific gravity	1.51	1.51	1.56	1.32	1.3
Tenacity (g/d)					
Dry	1.0–2.5	2.5–5.5	5.9	1.2–1.4	1.1–1.3
Wet	0.5–1.5	1.8–4.0	Up to 4.3	0.8–1.0	0.8–1.0
Moisture regain	11%–14%	11%–14%	11%	6%	4%
Resiliency	Poor.	Fair.	Good.	Poor.	Fair.
Burning	Burns, does not melt.	Burns, does not melt.	Burns, does not melt.	Burns, melts at 500°F.	Burns, melts at 575°F.
Conductivity of					
Heat	High.	High.	High.	Moderate.	Moderate.
Electricity	High.	High.	High.	Moderate.	Moderate to high.
Resistance to damage from					
Fungi	Damaged.	Damaged.	Damaged.	Fair resistance.	Resistant.
Insects	Attacked by silverfish.	Attacked by silverfish.	Attacked by silverfish.	Silverfish may eat sizing.	Silverfish may eat sizing.
Prolonged exposure to sunlight	Loss of strength.	Some loss of strength.	Some loss of strength.	Some loss of strength over time.[b]	Moderate resistance.
Strong acids	Poor resistance.	Poor resistance.	Poor resistance.	Poor resistance.	Poor resistance.
Strong bases	Poor resistance.	Excellent resistance.	Excellent resistance.	Causes saponification and eventual loss of strength.	Causes saponification and eventual loss of strength.

[a]Data provided are for Tencel® fiber produced by Courtaulds.

[b]Sunlight-resistant acetate is available for draperies.

Care Procedures

Acetate

If handled with care, acetates can be laundered successfully. However, acetates that have not had special shrink-resistant finishes should be dry-cleaned. Woven acetate goods may shrink as much as 5 percent and knits as much as 10 percent in laundering.

During laundering, acetate fabrics should not be subjected to undue stress through wringing or twisting. Fibers are weaker wet than dry, and acetates will wrinkle badly if creased or folded when wet.

Hydrogen peroxide or sodium perborate bleaches can be used if necessary for whitening of fabrics. Bleaching should be carefully controlled. Ironing temperatures for acetates must be kept low. The fabric will stick if ironed at temperatures about 350°–375°F and will melt at 500°F.

Acetone, a component of some fingernail polishes and polish removers, will dissolve acetate. Care should be taken to avoid spilling acetone-containing substances on the fabric.

Triacetate

Triacetate fabrics can be hand or machine washed. Hydrogen peroxide and sodium perborate bleaches can be used. Triacetates have better wrinkle recovery and crease resistance than acetates. If the fabrics require touch-up ironing after laundering, triacetates can be ironed at the rayon setting on the iron dial.

Dry-cleaning solvents will not harm triacetates. These fabrics can be successfully dry-cleaned.

Acetone will also damage triacetate fabrics. Spills from nail polish or remover that contains acetone will dissolve the fabric.

References

Maycumber. 1994. 1994 turning into a banner year for fibers. *Daily News Record*, 24 June, 8.

Moncrieff, R. W. 1975. *Man-made fibers.* New York: Wiley: 147.

Review Questions

1. In what ways are cotton and viscose rayon different? How does the molecular structure of these fibers account for these differences?
2. What was the reason for the development of high-wet-modulus rayon? What advantages does it offer?
3. Why is solvent-spun regenerated cellulosic fiber considered to be an environmentally friendly fiber?
4. Why is cuprammonium rayon no longer manufactured in the United States?
5. What is the difference in chemical composition of regenerated cellulosic fibers and cellulose derivative fibers? What generalizations can you make about the differences in properties of those fibers that are regenerated and those that are derivative?
6. What differences in fiber properties of acetate and triacetate can be explained by differences in chemical structure?

Recommended Readings

Artificial silk. 1967. *CIBA Review* 2.

Cumberbirch, R. J. E. 1984. High absorbency viscose fibers. *Textiles* 11 (Autumn): 58.

Japanese cellulosic fibers. 1994. *JTN,* no. 474 (May): 31.

Kumar, A., and C. Purtell. 1994. Enzymatic treatment of man-made cellulosic fabrics. *Textile Chemist and Colorist* 26 (October): 25.

Lenzing developing new lyocell. *Daily News Record* 196 (14 October): 8.

Richmond, M. L. 1987. Diverse rayon comes of age. *California Apparel News* (16–22 January): 6.

Rudie, R. 1993. Tencel—debut of a fiber. *Bobbin* 34 (February): 10.

Summers, T. A., B. J. Collier, J. R. Collier, and J. L. Haynes. 1993. History of viscose rayon. In *Manmade fibers: Their origin and development,* ed. R. B. Seymour and R. S. Porter, 72. London: Elsevier.

Thornton, A. 1993. A cellulosic fibre for the 21st century. *Textile Month,* February, 42.

NYLON AND ARAMID FIBERS

Nylon

Under the most recent FTC definition, nylon is "a manufactured fiber in which the fiber-forming substance is a long-chain synthetic polyamide in which less than 85 percent of the amide (—C—NH—) linkages are attached directly to two

$$O$$

aromatic rings." This definition covers a variety of structures, two main classifications of which are used in the United States: nylon 6 and nylon 66. Figure 8.1 shows the overall steps in producing nylon.

Nylon 66 and nylon 6 are isomers; that is, each polymer contains the same elements by weight, but the polymers' molecules are arranged differently. Such differences in structural arrangements cause some differences in fiber properties. However, in an article comparing the two types of nylon, R. A. F. Moore (1989) concluded that "the properties of these two types of nylon are more similar than dissimilar" (p. 22).

Although the processes for making both nylon 66 and nylon 6 have been known since the earliest experimentation on nylon, DuPont, which pioneered the development of nylon in the United States, chose to utilize the nylon 66 process. Nylon 66 predominates in the United States, whereas nylon 6 predominates in Europe, although a number of U.S. textile companies produce nylon 6.

The generic name *nylon* was proposed by DuPont in 1938 for the first commercially produced fibers. The company had considered such names as *Delawear* (for the tate in which the DuPont laboratories were located) and *Duparooh* (for "*Du*Pont *pulls a r*abbit *out of h*at") before settling on *nylon*.

Flowchart showing the manufacture of nylon 66. Illustration courtesy of the DuPont Company.

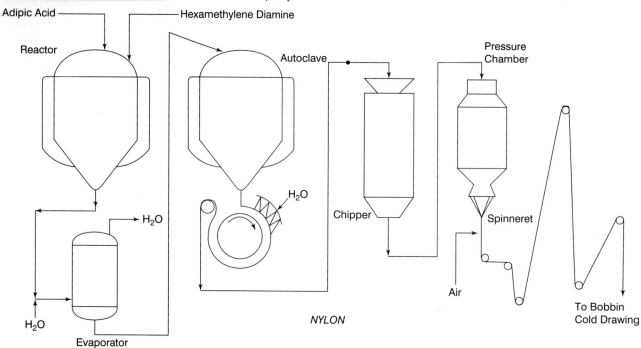

Manufacture

The chemicals from which nylon 66 is synthesized are adipic acid and hexamethylene diamine:

Adipic acid	Hexamethylene diamine
$COOH(CH_2)_4COOH$	$NH_2(CH_2)_6NH_2$
$1 + 4 + 1 = 6$	(6)

Note that there are six carbon atoms in each molecule of adipic acid and six carbon atoms in each molecule of hexamethylene diamine. For this reason, this nylon was designated as nylon 6.6 (six carbons in each molecule of reacting chemical). In time it came to be known as nylon 66. These materials are synthesized from benzene.

Nylon 6 is made from *caprolactam,* which has the following chemical structure:

$$
\begin{array}{c}
CH_2 \\
CH_2 \quad\quad C{=}O \\
\quad\quad\quad NH \\
CH_2 \quad CH_2 \\
CH_2
\end{array}
$$

Since there are six carbons in caprolactam, the fiber is known as nylon 6.

Because DuPont pursued development of nylon 66, the development of nylon 6 was left to researchers in Europe, where it became the most common type of nylon manufactured. In recent years the high costs associated with the disposal of a large amount of ammonium sulfate (a by-product of the manufacture of caprolactam) have made nylon 6 somewhat more costly to produce than nylon 66.

Polymerization of Nylon 66

The first step in the manufacturing process is to cause the reacting materials to form polymers. Nylon is formed by condensation polymerization. The reaction of adipic acid and hexamethylene diamine takes place in an air-free atmosphere. Water, which is split off during polymerization, is allowed to escape from the reacting tank. If the manufacturer wishes to produce a delustered nylon, titanium dioxide can be added to the material during this step.

The molten polymer that forms is extruded from the tank as a ribbon, several inches in width. The material is quenched in cold water, which reduces the size of the crystals formed. The ribbon is broken into smaller nylon "chips."

Polymerization of Nylon 6

Caprolactam is polymerized by one of two methods. In one, caprolactam is melted, heated, and filtered under high pressure, during which process condensation polymerization takes place. In the second method, water in the amount of 10 percent of the weight of the caprolactam is added, after which the water and caprolactam are heated to a high temperature, steam escapes, and polymerization takes place.

In both of these methods, a certain amount of monomer material remains. The polymerized material is given a water bath in an extractor to remove the monomer, which, if it remained, would weaken the final fiber. The polymer is dried and made into nylon chips.

Spinning

Both nylon 66 and nylon 6 are melt spun, although nylon 66 has a higher melting point (482°F) than nylon 6 (415°F). The chips fall onto an electrically heated grid that is too small to allow the chips to pass through until they have been melted. The melted polymer is delivered from an extruder, from a metal grid melter, or directly from a polymerizer and then passes through a filter that removes any impurities on to a metering pump. The pump delivers measured polymer to the *pack,* which consists of a small filter and spinneret.

As they exit from the spinneret, the molten filaments enter a chimney where they are air cooled and simultaneously stretched. Spin finish (a complex mixture of oil lubricants emulsified in water together with additional materials such as wetting agents, antistatic agents, and adhesives) is coated onto the fiber. The finish lubricates fibers for subsequent processing and disperses static electrical charges that would interfere with yarn formation. The finish is eventually washed from the fabric.

Drawing

After addition of the finish, the fiber is wound onto a bobbin. In this state, nylon is not especially strong or lustrous, so fibers are heated and stretched to 400 to 600 percent of their original length. The stretching orients the molecules, making the fiber more crystalline, increasing luster, and improving tensile strength. (See Figure 8.1.)

Molecular Structure

The polyamide chains in nylon are fairly highly oriented in a crystalline structure. When the molecules are straightened during the drawing process, they have no bulky side groups to prevent them from packing closely together. So, the crystalline areas form easily, and hydrogen bonds form between the amide links of adjacent polymers. The fibers are 50 to 80 percent crystalline, depending on the amount of drawing. In the amorphous areas the polymers are coiled, allowing for fiber stretch and recovery. Nylon 66 and 6 differ in the chain packing because of differences in the order of groups in the amide linkages.

Properties of Nylon

Physical Appearance

Normal nylon in microscopic appearance looks like a long, smooth cylinder. Its cross section is circular, and it is naturally lustrous, unless it is delustered. (See Figure 8.2.)

Other Physical Properties

Specific Gravity. A relatively low-density fiber, nylon has a specific gravity of 1.14, which is lower than most other fibers. (Rayon, for example, has a specific gravity of about 1.5, polyester 1.22 or 1.38.) Nylon can be made into very light, sheer fabrics, of good strength.

Strength. The strength of nylon is excellent. It is produced in a variety of tenacities. Regular tenacity of nylon 66 is 3–6 g/d; of regular nylon 6, 4–7 g/d. High-tenacity nylon 66 that has been drawn more during spinning is rated 6.0–9.5 g/d. The exceptional strength of nylon has led to its use not only for tire cords but also for a variety of industrial items. Its abrasion resistance is superior, being four to five times that of wool. The strength and abrasion resistance plus the elasticity of nylon have led to its predominance in the field of women's hosiery. Since the fibers are so strong, they can be made in very fine deniers required for sheer hosiery and lingerie. A low modulus makes nylon easy to stretch with little force.

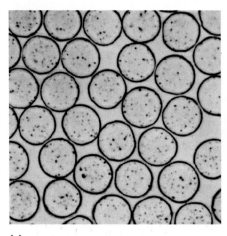
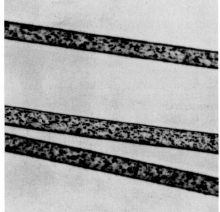

Figure 8.2

Photomicrographs of delustered, regular nylon 66 in: (a) a cross section and (b) a longitudinal view. Photomicrographs courtesy of the DuPont Company.

(a)

(b)

Elasticity and Resilience. The elasticity of nylon is very high. Its resilience and wrinkle resistance are good. Its exceptional compressional resilience has led to its prominence in carpets and rugs. Elastic recovery of nylon 6 is claimed to be slightly better than in nylon 66.

Absorbency and Moisture Regain. Nylon is moderately hydrophilic, having better moisture regain than many manufactured fibers. Nylon fabrics dry quickly after laundering.

Dimensional Stability. Nylon has good dimensional stability at low to moderate temperatures, neither shrinking nor stretching out of shape. At high temperatures nylon fabrics may shrink. Washing and drying temperatures should be kept low. The moderate regain prevents a high degree of relaxation shrinkage when fabrics are wet.

Heat and Electrical Conductivity. Nylon is a poor conductor of electricity, and it builds up static electricity, especially when humidity is low. Nylon serves as a good insulator in electrical materials because of its nonconducting qualities. Some special nylons have been manufactured to improve conductivity and decrease static electricity. Heat conductivity is also low.

Effect of Heat; Combustibility. The melting point of nylon 66 is about 500°F. It will soften and may start to stick at 445°F. Nylon 6 is even more heat sensitive. If a hot iron is used on nylons, the fibers may glaze, soften, or stick. The fiber burns in a flame but usually self-extinguishes when the flame is removed. However, nylon fibers do melt, and as with any fiber that melts, if the molten fiber drips onto the skin, it may cause serious burns. The thermoplasticity of nylon allows it to be heat-set.

The decreased thermal stability of nylon 6 places some limitations on its uses. It is not used in industrial applications in which thermal resistance is essential, and it is more difficult to process into textured yarns for hosiery and to finish in yarns blended with other fibers, such as spandex.

Effect of Selected Conditions on Fiber

Chemical Reactivity. Like most synthetics, nylon is chemically stable. Dry-cleaning solvents will not harm the fiber. It is not seriously affected by dilute acids but is soluble in strong acids. Treatment with concentrated hydrochloric acid at high temperatures will break nylon 66 down into adipic acid and hexamethylene diamine, the substances from which it is made. This reaction could be used to reclaim these basic materials and permit this fiber to be recycled after use. Prolonged exposure to acidic fumes from pollution will decrease the dyeability of nylon.

Resistance to Microorganisms, Insects, Sunlight, and Aging. Moths, mildew, and bacteria will not attack nylon. The fiber is degraded by long exposure to sunlight, but age has no appreciable effect if fabrics are stored away from sunlight. Sheer nylon fabrics are unsuitable for use in curtains.

Variations of Nylon 66 and Nylon 6

Varying the cross-sectional shape of a manufactured fiber is one means of producing fibers that may have some particularly desirable appearance or performance quality.

Both nylon 66 and nylon 6 are made in varieties that are designed for some special purpose. For example, nylon 66 is sometimes made in tribal or multilobal forms. The trilobal shape, similar to that of silk, reflects more light, thereby increasing luster. Table 8.1 lists some of the trademark names of nylon fiber variants.

Uses

The availability of a wide variety of types of nylon (from fine to coarse, from soft to crisp, from sheer to opaque) has resulted in the use of nylon in an enormous range of products for apparel, the home, and industry. (See Figure 8.3.)

Nylon has long been of major importance in the manufacture of women's hosiery because it can be heat-set and is strong and elastic. Sheer fabrics of nylon have been popular because of their inherent strength and abrasion resistance. Special-pur-

Table 8.1	Nylon Trademarks of U.S. Manufacturers	
Manufacturers and Trademarks	**Type of Fiber or Yarn**	**Special Features and Specialized Uses**
Allied Signal Fibers		
A.C.E.®	Nylon 66: filament.	—
Anso®	Nylon 66: bulked filament, staple.	—
Capima®	Nylon 66: producer textured.	—
Caplana®	Nylon 66: filament.	—
Caprolan®	Nylon 66: filament, monofilament.	—
Caprolan Sea Gard®	Nylon 66: partially oriented yarn, filament.	—
Captiva®	Nylon 66: filament.	—
Creme de Captiva®	Nylon 66: filament.	—
Hydrofil®	Nylon 66: filament.	—
Patina®	Nylon 66: filament.	—
Stay Gard®	Nylon 66: filament.	—
Tru-Ballistic®	Nylon 66: filament.	—
BASF Corporation Fiber		
Products Division		
Crepeset®	Nylon 6: filament.	Permanently creped, semi-dull nylon yarn. Uses: primarily in intimate apparel.
Matinesse®	Nylon 6: filament.	Matte luster, fine denier nylon yarn, compatible with spandex. Uses: primarily in intimate apparel.
Shimmereen®	Nylon 6: filament.	Bright luster, fine denier nylon yarn, compatible with spandex. Uses: primarily in intimate apparel.
Silky touch®	Nylon 6: filament.	0.8 dpf microdenier, compatible with spandex. Uses: primarily in intimate apparel.
Zefsport®	Nylon 6: filament.	Bright or matte luster, compatible with spandex. Uses: primarily swimwear and activewear.
Resistat®	Nylon 6: filament and staple.	Conductive nylon.
BASF Carpet Products		
Group		
Zeftron® fiber series	Nylon 6: bulked filament, staple (depending on variant).	Carpets.
Zeftron® 200	Nylon 6.	Solution dyed.

pose nylons have been manufactured for upholstery and carpets. Nylon is often used in blends for abrasion resistance.

Nylon is one of several fibers being made in microfiber sizes. To date, nylon microfibers are mostly being used in active sports apparel, ski wear, camping apparel, and sleeping bags. These applications take advantage of the high strength of nylon.

Care Procedures

Nylon is considered to be an easy-care fiber. Most nylon items are machine washable and can be tumble dried at normal drying temperatures.

However, some aspects of the care of nylon require special attention. Like many synthetics, nylon has an affinity for oil-borne stains. These should be removed with a grease solvent before laundering.

Table 8.1	Nylon Trademarks of U.S. Manufacturers *(continued)*	
Manufacturers and Trademarks	**Type of Fiber or Yarn**	**Special Features and Specialized Uses**
Berkley Inc.		
Trilene®	Monofilament.	—
Trimax®	Monofilament	—
Camac Corporation		
Lexes®	Nylon 66: producer textured	—
DuPont		
Antron® series	Nylon 66: bulked filament, filament, and Staple (depending on variant.)	— —
Cordura®	Nylon 66: bulked filament	—
DriSilque	Nylon 66: Certification mark, filament	—
Jentell	Nylon 66: Certification mark, filament	—
Microsupplex®	Nylon 66: filament	Microdenier
Supplex®	Nylon 66: filament	—
Tactel®	Nylon 66: filament	—
Tactel® Microfiber	Nylon 66: filament	Microdenier
Monsanto Fibers Division		
No-Shock®	Filament	—
Ultron®	Staple, filament	—
Ultron 3 D®	Staple, filament	—
Wear Dated® Carpet	Staple, filament	Carpet
Wear-Dated Π™	Staple, filament	Carpet
Wear-Dated FREEDOM™ carpet	Staple, filament	Carpet
Traffic Control Fiber System™	Staple, filament	Carpet
Wellman Inc		
Wellon®	Staple	—
Wellstrand®	Staple, tow	—

Source: Data provided by fiber manufacturers.

Figure 8.3

A few of the very diverse uses of nylon fibers: (a) tires made with tire cord of A.C.E.® nylon, AlliedSignal; (b) tent, a geotextile made of A.C.E.® nylon, AlliedSignal; (c) residential carpet made with the Anso® brand nylon family of fibers, tough and fashionable carpet fibers from AlliedSignal Fibers; and (d) nightgown made of Patina® nylon, AlliedSignal. Photographs courtesy of AlliedSignal Fibers.

(a)

(b)

(c)

(d)

Nylon has a tendency to "scavenge" colors, picking up surface color easily from other fabrics. This is why many white nylons gradually become gray or yellowed; therefore, it is advisable to wash white nylons alone, never with other items of color.

Nylon's resilience usually precludes its ironing, but if pressing seems necessary, the heat sensitivity of nylon requires that it be pressed with a warm, not hot, iron. Also, nylon items should be removed from the dryer as soon as the cycle is ended. Nylons that remain in a hot dryer in a wrinkled condition may retain these wrinkles until the item is pressed.

Spun yarns may tend to pill, as the fabric wears. Pilling on synthetics including nylon is a particular problem because the strength of the fibers causes tangled fiber ends to cling tightly. These fiber ends do not fall off, which makes wearing apparel unsightly.

Other Types of Nylon

Nylon 612, a low-moisture variant, and nylon 11 or Rilsan®, a French product made from castor oil and having a relatively low melting point, are commercially available in the United States but are not used in apparel or household textiles. Other nylon variations cited in the literature but not available to the public at this time include nylon 7, which is being developed in Russia. It is claimed to be more stable to heat and light than is nylon 6.

Nylon 4 was developed by the General Aniline and Film Corporation. The advantage of nylon 4 is said to be an increased moisture regain, which decreases static buildup. Nylon 4 is supposedly closer to cotton in its physical characteristics than are other nylons.

Aramid

In a 1974 revision of generic fiber categories, the FTC established a separate category of fibers that is designated *aramids*. Like nylon, aramid fibers are polyamides. However, in its redefinition, the FTC separated polyamides into those in which *less* than 85 percent of the amide linkages are attached directly to the aromatic rings (nylon) and those in which 85 percent or *more* of the amide linkages are attached to two aromatic rings (aramid). Nomex® and Kevlar® are DuPont trademarks of fibers that belong to the aramid classification.

Characteristics of aramids include high strength and good dimensional stability. The higher strength and thermal stability are due to the aromatic rings that make the polymer chains stiffer. Standard moisture regain is 5 percent; absorbency is moderate. Figure 8.4 shows a cross-sectional view of Nomex® aramid fiber.

The outstanding properties of aramid fibers are their heat and flame resistance, and toughness. Aramid fibers have no melting point (they do not melt), and they have extremely low combustibility. The fiber decomposes at a temperature above 700°F. Selected aramid and nylon characteristics are compared in Table 8.2.

Aramids degrade and lose strength on exposure to ultraviolet rays. Their resistance to radiation from gamma, beta, and X rays is, however, excellent, and this resistance is utilized for some industrial applications. Their resistance to most chemicals and organic solvents is generally good, but like nylons, they are degraded by strong acids.

Aramid fibers are used in industrial and military protective clothing. Nomex® has very good thermal stability and so is used by firefighters, race car drivers, petro-

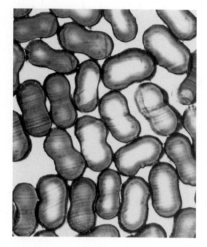

Figure 8.4

Photomicrograph of a cross section of Nomex® aramid fiber. Photomicrograph courtesy of the DuPont Company.

chemical and refinery workers, utility workers, U.S. Forest Service personnel, military flight personnel, and NASA astronauts. It is made into a wide variety of garments, including hoods, shirts, lab coats, jackets, parkas, aprons, gloves, pants, coveralls, jumpsuits, and socks. Kevlar®, with high strength and modulus, is used in safety gloves, boots, clothing, chain saw chaps, firefighter clothing, military helmets, and bullet-resistant vests (IFI 1991).

Other uses of aramid fibers include industrial hot-air filtration fabrics, ropes, cables, sailcloth, and marine and sporting goods. Nomex® aramid is used in applications that take advantage of its flame resistance. For example, highly temperature-resistant papers are made from Nomex®.

Kevlar® aramid is being used in products that take advantage of its strength and toughness. In industry it may reinforce plastics with strong but lightweight fiber material. It is substituted for glass fiber in the aircraft industry because it is lighter in weight than glass. Sports equipment, such as sailboats, hockey sticks, tennis racquets, fishing rods, and golf clubs, also make use of Kevlar® fibers. Kevlar® is used for canoes because it is both light and strong. Whereas aluminum canoes weigh 70 to 80 pounds and fiberglass 50 to 70 pounds, a Kevlar® canoe of the same size will weigh only 40 to 50 pounds. It will, however, cost almost twice as much as the heavier canoes (Figure 8.5). It is also used in automobile tires.

The color range of aramid fibers is limited. Nomex® garments are now available in a number of colors. Kevlar® color range is more limited, generally limited to gold, sage green, royal blue, or black. Some dyes increase aramid flammability.

With increased usage of aramid fibers in protective clothing, consumers and professional launderers and dry cleaners are encountering garments made from these fibers. The International Fabricare Institute makes the following recommendations about caring for garments made from aramid fibers (IFI 1991). Nomex® and Kevlar®

Table 8.2   Selected Properties of Nylon and Aramid Fibers

	Nylon 66 (regular tenacity)	Aramid (Nomex® filament)
Specific gravity	1.14	1.38
Tenacity (g/d)		
Dry	3.0–6.0	4.8–5.8
Wet	2.6–5.4	3.8–4.8
Moisture regain	4.0%–4.5%	5%
Resiliency	Excellent.	Excellent
Burning characteristics	Burns slowly with melting in flame, usually self-extinguishing after flame is removed.	Low flammability.
Melting point	482°F (nylon 66)[a]	Decomposes above 700°F; does not melt.
Conductivity of		
Heat	Low.	Low.
Electricity	Low.	Low.
Resistance to damage from		
Fungi	Excellent.	Excellent.
Insects	Excellent.	Excellent.
Prolonged exposure to sunlight	Degrades.	Degrades.
Acids	Degraded by concentrated acids.	Degraded by hot, concentrated acids.
Bases	Degraded by hot, concentrated bases.	Degraded by hot, concentrated bases.

[a]The melting point of nylon 6 is 415°F.

Figure 8.5

Canoeist easily portages lightweight Kevlar® aramid canoe between lakes or around impassible stretches of water. Photograph courtesy of We-No-Nah Canoe, Inc.

garments can be machine washed and dried in home laundering, but they must be washed separately so that they do not pick up lint from other garments. The lint will impair their flame resistance. Garments soiled with grease or oil can be dry-cleaned. Chlorine bleach should not be used, but oxygen bleaches are safe.

References

IFI. 1991. Nomex® and Kevlar®. *International Fabricare Institute Bulletin,* September.
Moore, R. A. F. 1989. Nylon 6 and nylon 66: How different are they? *Textile Chemist and Colorist* 21 (February): 19.

Review Questions

1. Compare the characteristics of nylon 6 and nylon 66. In what ways are they different? In what ways similar?
2. What properties of nylon make it especially useful in (a) women's hosiery and (b) carpets.
3. Identify some of the products in which Nomex® aramid fibers are used and some in which Kevlar® aramid fibers are used. What differences in the properties of these two fibers account for the different kinds of products in which they are used?

Recommended Readings

Bardsley, T. 1994. Nylon: The name. *Textile Horizons,* December, 34.

Hillermeier, K. 1984. Prospects of aramid as a substitute for asbestos. *Textile Research Journal* 54 (September): 575.

Meikle, J. L., and S. M. Spivak. 1988. Nylon: What's in a name? *Textile Chemist and Colorist* 20 (June): 13.

Morris, W. J. 1988. Nylon at 50: An industrial success and a personal tragedy. *Chemtech* 18 (December): 725.

Nylon-11: An agro-based polymer. 1994. *Manmade Textiles in India* 37 (May): 207.

The Nylon Revolution. 1988. *America's Textiles International* 17 (April): 28.

Yang, H. H. 1989. *Aromatic high strength fibers.* New York: Wiley Interscience.

———. 1995. *Kevlar aramid fiber.* New York: Marcel Dekker.

POLYESTER FIBERS

Polyester

In his first experiments with the synthesis of polymers, W. H. Carothers concentrated his attention on compounds called polyesters. Encountering some difficulties in this research, he turned his attention to polyamides, from which he synthesized nylon.

After the discovery of nylon, a group of English researchers at Imperial Chemical Industries (ICI) concentrated on the polyester group. Their experimentation led to the development and subsequent manufacture of polyester fibers. DuPont bought the English patent, and the first DuPont plant for the production of Dacron® polyester in the United States opened in March 1953.

The FTC defines polyester fibers as "a manufactured fiber in which the fiber-forming substance is any long-chain synthetic polymer composed of at least 85 percent by weight of an ester of a substituted aromatic carboxylic acid, including but not restricted to substituted terephthalate units p($-$R$-$O$-$C$-$C$_6$H$_4$$-C-O-$) and

$$p(-R-O-\underset{\displaystyle \overset{\|}{O}}{C}-C_6H_4-\underset{\displaystyle \overset{\|}{O}}{C}-O-)$$

parasubstituted hydroxybenzoate units p($-$R$-$O$-$C$_6$H$_4$$-C-O-$)" (as amended

$$p(-R-O-C_6H_4-\underset{\displaystyle \overset{\|}{O}}{C}-O-)$$

September 12, 1973). British publications may refer to polyester as Terylene, an ICI trademark.

Manufacture

The raw material from which most polyesters are made is petroleum, from which the constituent acids and alcohols are derived. The most commonly used acid is terephthalic acid or its dimethyl ester. The processes that are used for manufacturing different types of polyesters vary. Many of the details of these processes are not known because the companies that hold the patents on the manufacturing processes have not released full information on precisely how these processes are carried out. A generalized description of the process for synthesizing polyesters follows.

Polymerization

The major polyester in manufacture and use is polyethylene terephthalate, abbreviated PET. It is formed by the reaction of terephthalic acid and ethylene glycol. Condensation polymerization takes place during the reaction of terephthalic acid and alcohol, in a vacuum, at high temperatures. Polymerized material is extruded in the form of a ribbon onto a casting wheel or cooling trough. The ribbon hardens, and small polyester chips are cut from the ribbon.

Spinning and Drawing

The chips are dried to remove any residual moisture and are then put into hopper reservoirs ready for melting. The melted polymer (polyester is melt spun, like nylon) is extruded through the spinnerets, solidifies on hitting the air, and is wound loosely onto cylinders. How the solidified filaments are processed next depends on the projected end use of the fiber.

If filaments are to be made into staple fiber, several sets of filaments, each containing 250 to 3,000 filaments, are brought together and coiled in a large can in preparation for drawing. The yarns are heated, drawn to several times their original length to orient the molecular structure, and then allowed to relax to release stresses and strains and reduce shrinkage of drawn fibers. Drawn tow is crimped, dried, and heat-set for stability. At this point, tow may be cut into required staple lengths, usually 38 to 152 millimeters (1.5 to 6 inches) in length, and baled, ready for sale.

Fiber intended for continuous filament yarn is either drawn directly and packaged for sale or wound on bobbins preparatory for draw twisting or draw texturing. Yarn for weaving or knitting or yarn intended for texturing is often processed on a draw twister that heats, draws the fibers, and imparts a small amount of base twist. Additional heating and drawing is given to high-strength industrial yarns in a second stage of processing.

Although draw-twisted yarns can also be textured, recent developments in spinning polyester have led to the use of an alternative process. High-speed spinning processes yield partially oriented yarn (POY), which is preferred for draw texturing because it eliminates the expensive draw-twisting operation and allows the POY to be both drawn and textured in the same operation, one in which the drawing, texturing, and heat-setting operations are carried out in an integrated manner. Chapter 15 gives a fuller discussion of texturing. The diagram in Figure 9.1 summarizes the manufacture of polyester.

Molecular Structure

In polyester fibers the long polymers of PET are arranged in amorphous and crystalline regions, the extent of which is dependent on the amount of drawing during manufacture. Polyester does not crystallize as easily as nylon because of its aromatic

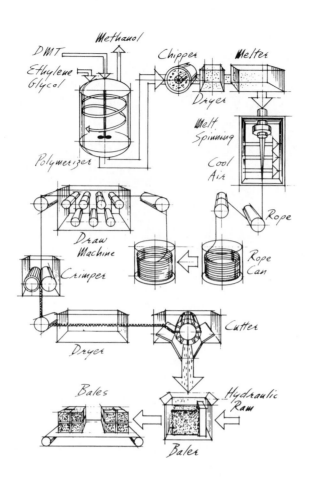

Figure 9.1

Steps in the production of polyester staple fiber. Polyester also can be produced in filament form. Illustration courtesy of the American Fiber Manufacturers Association, Inc.

rings, which are bulky and inhibit alignment of the molecules. In addition, there are no polar groups in the polyester polymers to form hydrogen bonds between the polymers. The aromatic rings do, however, provide stiffness to the polymer chains, which contributes to modulus, strength, and thermal stability.

Properties of Polyesters

Physical Appearance

Polyester fibers are manufactured in a variety of cross sections, including round, trilobal, pentalobal, and hollow shapes. Under the microscope round fibers appear as long, smooth rods, with spots of pigment if the fiber has been delustered. This pigmented appearance decreases the luster or brightness of polyesters. Longitudinally, multilobal fibers appear striated. (See Figure 9.2).

Other Physical Properties

Specific Gravity. Specific gravity (1.38 or 1.22, depending on type) is moderate. Polyesters have a specific gravity greater than nylon (1.14) and lower than rayon (1.50). Fabrics made from polyesters are medium in weight.

Strength. The strength, or tenacity, of polyester varies with the type of fiber; however, as a general category, polyester would be considered a relatively strong fiber. Its

Figure 9.2

Photomicrographs of regular Dacron® polyester in: (a) a cross section and (b) a longitudinal view. Photomicrographs courtesy of the DuPont Company.

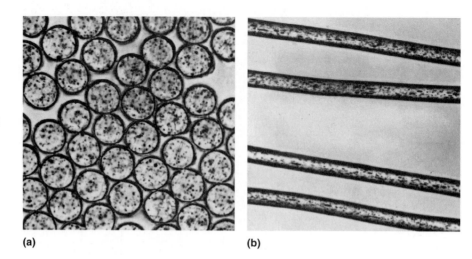

(a)   (b)

strength is not affected by moisture. Regular filaments have a breaking tenacity of 4–7 g/d; high-tenacity filaments are rated at 6.3–9.5 g/d.

Elasticity and Resilience. The elasticity of polyester is generally good. Polyester recovers well from stretching but is inferior to nylon in its elasticity. Resilience is excellent. For this reason, polyesters are often blended with less wrinkle-resistant fibers to make easy-care fabrics.

Absorbency and Moisture Regain. The moisture regain of polyester is low, only 0.2 to 0.8 percent. Although polyesters are nonabsorbent, they do have wicking ability. This quality makes polyester relatively comfortable to wear in warm weather, as perspiration is carried to the surface of the fiber and evaporated. Multilobal fiber cross sections improve the wicking qualities of polyesters. Special finishes can be applied to polyester to make it more hydrophilic.

Dimensional Stability. Polyesters that have been given heat-setting treatments have excellent dimensional stability, so long as the heat-setting temperature is not exceeded. If polyester fabrics have not been heat-set, they may shrink at high temperatures. Because of its low moisture regain, polyester does not shrink when wet and can stabilize fabrics when it is blended with other fibers.

Effect of Heat; Combustibility. The melting point of polyester is close to that of nylon, ranging from 480° to 550°F. Polyesters usually need no pressing because of their excellent wrinkle recovery. If they must be pressed, it should be with a warm, not hot, iron. Polyesters can be heat-set into pleats with especially good results. Not only will heat setting stabilize size and shape, but wrinkle resistance of polyesters is enhanced by heat setting.

Polyester shrinks from flame and will melt, leaving a hard black residue. The fabric will burn with a strong, pungent odor. Some polyesters are self-extinguishing. Melted polyester fiber can produce severe burns.

Effect of Selected Conditions on Fiber

Chemical Reactivity. Polyesters are not harmed by solvents used in professional dry cleaning nor are they susceptible to damage from bleaching. Although polyesters are not harmed by acids, they may be adversely affected by strong bases. Alkalinity encountered in detergents is not harmful.

Table 9.1	Selected Properties of Polyester Fiber

	Polyester
Specific gravity	1.22 or 1.38[a]
Tenacity (g/d), filament	
Dry	4.0–7.0 (regular tenacity); 6.3–9.5 (high tenacity)
Wet	4.0–7.0 (regular tenacity); 6.3–9.5 (high tenacity)
Moisture regain	0.4–0.8[a]
Resiliency	Excellent.
Burning and melting point	In flame, burns slowly with melting; melts at 482°–550°F[a]
Conductivity of	
Heat	Low.
Electricity	Low.
Resistance to damage from	
Fungi	Excellent.
Insects	Excellent.
Prolonged exposure to sunlight	Good if behind glass.
Acids	Good.
Bases	Good to weak alkali.
	Poor to strong alkali.

[a]Depending on type.

Resistance to Microorganisms, Insects, Sunlight, and Aging. Bacteria, mildew, and moth larvae will not attack polyesters. Although the fibers will degrade after long exposure to sunlight, they have better sun resistance than do most fibers. This resistance is enhanced when the fibers are placed behind glass that screens out some of the harmful ultraviolet rays. Polyesters are, therefore, quite suitable for use in curtains and draperies.

Age has no appreciable effect on polyesters.

Table 9.1 summarizes selected characteristics of polyester.

Varieties and Modifications of Polyesters

Among manufactured fibers polyester dominates the market. In 1993 polyester claimed 42 percent of the domestic apparel market. United States polyester capacity as of November 1994 was 4,469 million pounds. U.S. polyester production in the first quarter of 1994 represented 15 percent of the global total.[1]

The quantity of polyester in use is a reflection of its versatility. It is produced as staple, filament, tow, and fiberfill, which may be made in either filament or crimped staple form. Filament yarns are textured to create stretch yarns or filament yarns with the aesthetic qualities of yarn spun from staple fibers. Such yarns decrease pilling, which can be a problem in staple polyester yarns.

Cross-sectional shape can be modified to create fabrics for special purposes. Japanese manufacturers have varied cross-sectional shape to produce fabrics with especially attractive hand and drape. These fabrics, called *Shingosen fabrics,* are sold in Japan and abroad. Teijin, a Japanese company, manufactures and sells Wellkey®, a

---

1. Data provided by Fiber Economics Bureau, December 1994.

Figure 9.3

Polyester fibers with unique cross sections intended for special purposes. (a) Wellkey® fiber, which has a hollow center and modified surface designed to absorb perspiration. (Illustration courtesy of Teijin American Inc. (b) Cross section of polyester Type 4DG®, a deep-groved fiber. Photograph courtesy of Eastman Chemical Company.

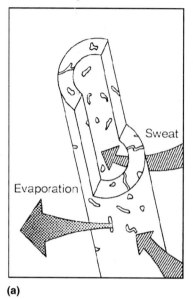

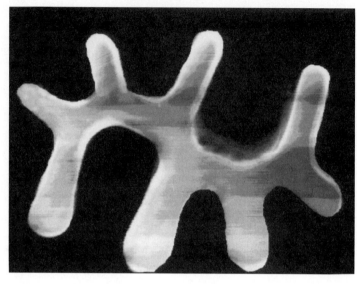

(a)   (b)

hollow polyester with minute holes in the cross section that are intended to absorb perspiration (Figure 9.3a). Hollow polyester fibers are made into fiberfill with good insulating qualities. Eastman Chemical Company recently introduced a deep-grooved polyester with a novel cross section that, according to Eastman, has these characteristics: moves fluids, stores and traps substances, provides large surface area, and provides more bulk and cover than round fiber (Figure 9.3b).

Polyester's surface can be modified with alkaline treatments with the objective of creating silk, wool, or linenlike qualities. Other treatments improve affinity for moisture or weaken fibers to decrease pilling. Polyester microfibers are produced by a number of manufacturers and used in high-density fabrics for sportswear and rainwear and other apparel such as blouses, shirts, and dresses.

Several polyester manufacturers have introduced polyester fibers made from recycled plastic soda bottles (see page 476). These fibers are frequently used in outdoor clothing and are advertised as environmentally friendly. Table 9.2 lists trademark names for polyester fibers produced in the United States.

Uses

Polyester is used in a wide range of wearing apparel, home furnishings, and industrial products, either alone or in blends. The exceptional resilience of polyester makes it especially suitable for use in easy-care fabrics. (See Figure 9.4.)

Blends of polyester with other fibers are made to take advantage of durability and easy maintenance. Durable press fabrics are frequently made from blends of cotton and polyester. Wool and polyester blends have a wool-like feel and appearance and some of the easy-care aspects of polyester. Furthermore, creases and pleats can be

Table 9.2   Polyester Trademarks of U.S. Manufacturers

Manufacturers and Trademarks	Type of Fiber or Yarn	Special Features and Specialized Uses
AlliedSignal Fibers		
A.C.E.® series	Filament.	—
Compet®	Filament.	—
DSP®	Filament.	—
Stay Gard®	Filament.	—
American Micrell		
Micrell®	Partially oriented yarn, producer textured.	Microdenier.
DuPont		
Dacron®	Partially oriented yarn, filament, staple, tow.	—
Coolmax	Certification mark: filament, staple.	—
Hollofil®	Staple.	—
Micromatique®	Filament, staple.	Microdenier.
Softec Dacron	Certification mark: filament.	—
Thermostat	Certification mark: filament, staple.	—
Thermax	Certification mark: staple.	—
Eastman Chemical Company		
4DG®	Staple.	Moves fluids spontaneously; grooved; high surface area, high bulk. Uses: insulation in footwear and apparel; filtration, medical, industrial and personal care products.
Firestone Fibers and Textiles Co.		
FiberBrite 2000®	Filament.	Solution dyed. Uses: webbing, cordage, wire and cable, fabrics.
Hoechst Celanese		
ESP®	Partially oriented yarn, staple, monofilament.	—
Pentron®	Staple.	—
Polarguard® series	Staple.	—
Pro Earth®	Recycled staple blend.	Made with recycled fibers.
Trevira® series	Depending on variant: partially oriented yarn, filament, staple, monofilament.	Available in microdenier.
Trevira II®	Recycled staple blend.	Made with recycled fibers.
Universe®	Staple.	—
Nan Ya Plastics Corp., America		
Tairilin®	Partially oriented yarn, staple.	Microdenier; used in textile fabrics.
Wellman Inc.		
Comfortrel®	Staple.	—
Fitwell®	Staple.	—
Fortrel® series	Depending on variant: partially oriented yarn, staple.	Available in microdenier.
Fortrel EcoSpun®	Staple.	Made from recycled plastic bottles.
Polystrand®	Staple.	—
Wellene®	Staple, tow.	—
Martin Color-Fi Inc.		
NatureTex®	Staple (solution dyed or natural). or spun yarn	Made of 100% recycled fibers with a minimum of 50% post-consumer content.

Source: Data provided by fiber manufacturers.

Figure 9.4

Raincoat made of Trevira Micronesse® 0.7 denier polyester microfiber. Designed by Donna Karan. Photograph courtesy of Hoechst Celanese.

heat-set through the thermoplastic properties of polyester. Other blends with rayon and with acetate as well as blends with other synthetics such as acrylics and with natural fibers such as silk, flax, and ramie are produced.

Polyesters and their blends are used for carpets, curtains, draperies, sheets, and pillowcases for the home furnishings market. Sleeping bags, insulated outdoor clothing, and pillow and comforter fillings of polyester are being promoted by manufacturers as easy-care, nonallergenic substitutes for goose down. Hollow polyester fibers are said to offer advantages in this use over traditional polyester fiber forms.

Industrial uses of polyesters include fire hoses, power belting, ropes, base fabrics for coating, and nets. Tire cord for automotive uses and sails for sports are also made from polyester fibers. Nonwoven polyester fiber webs may be used in construction projects for reinforcement.

The relatively low cost of polyester fiber makes it the fiber of choice for many of the foregoing applications.

Care Procedures

Polyester is blended with so many other fibers that consumers should consult labels for specific instructions on care. Those procedures that are appropriate for 100 percent polyester fabrics may not be suitable for the fibers with which polyester is blended.

Polyester fabrics are generally machine washable. Water temperatures should be warm, not excessively hot. Ordinary laundry detergents can be used. Household bleaches will not harm white fabrics. Oily stains should be removed before laundering by treatment with a grease solvent.

Polyesters should be dried at moderate temperatures, and items should be removed from the dryer as soon as the cycle is complete to avoid creases that must be removed by ironing. As a general rule, polyesters should not require pressing after drying, although polyester fabrics may be ironed on the wrong side with a moderately warm iron. Some blends of polyesters and cottons can be difficult to iron because the suitable ironing temperature for polyester fibers may not be high enough to press wrinkles from cotton, whereas the cotton temperature is too high for the polyester.

Most fabrics made from polyesters can be dry-cleaned safely. Some polyester double knits printed with pigment colors cannot be dry-cleaned. Care labels should be checked to determine whether dry cleaning should be avoided.

Polyester Marketing Problems

"Polyester gets no respect!" This was the lead sentence in an article discussing manufacturers' efforts to enhance the image of polyester. After more than two decades of constant growth in demand for and use of polyester by consumers, apparel manufacturers in the 1970s flooded the market with polyester double knits. The public came to associate polyester with these garments, many of which had questionable design quality, aesthetics, and comfort. With the advent of microfibers and special finishes to improve the aesthetics of polyester, attitudes toward polyester have been changing, and in certain markets, such as high tech clothing for outdoor activities, it is often the fabric of choice. Nevertheless, industry executives feel that polyester's marketing problem has not been entirely overcome, and organizations such as the Polyester Council continue to carry out public relations campaigns designed to enhance the image of this fiber.

Review Questions

1. What is POY, and why is it preferred over other forms of the fiber for draw texturing?
2. If you had three fabrics that were the same in all other respects but one was made of polyester, one of nylon, and one of rayon, which would feel heaviest? Why?
3. Describe step-by-step care procedures that could be used for a 100 percent polyester garment that can be laundered at home. For each step that you describe, identify one or more properties of polyester that make this type of care appropriate.
4. What are some of the modifications of polyester fibers that can be made to produce fabrics with specific characteristics? To what uses are these modified fibers put?
5. How are the properties of polyester related to its chemical structure?

Recommended Readings

Brunnschweiler, D., and J. W. S. Hearle. 1993. *Polyester: 50 years of achievement.* Manchester, England: Textile Institute.

Callahan, P. 1994. The fabric of our lives? Polyester makes a comeback. *Forbes* 153 (9 May): 64.

Janeck, C., and H. Lunde. 1983–84. Hydrophilic finishes: Effect on selected properties of polyester fabric. *Clothing and Textiles Research Journal* 2 (Fall/Winter): 31.

Matsudaira, M., et al. 1993. The effect of fibre cross-sectional shape on fabric mechanical properties and handle. *Journal of the Textile Institute* 84 (3). 376.

Meyer, D. G., and H. Koopman. 1993. Marketing polyester in the 1990's. Part 7: Business and economics. In *Polyester: 50 years of achievement,* ed. D. Brunnschweiler and J. W. S. Hearle, 323. Manchester, England: Textile Institute.

Miyoshi, T. 1993. Functional polyester developments. *Textile Asia* 24 (July): 71.

Nishimura, M. 1993. Wedge-shaped polyester microfilaments of 0.1 Dtex. *Textile Technology International* 53.

Thomas, M. 1993. At 50 years polyester gains new fashion vitality. *Textile World* 143 (December): 62, 65.

Zeronian, S. H., and M. J. Collins. 1989. Surface modification of polyester by alkaline treatments. *Textile Progress* 20 (2).

ACRYLIC AND MODACRYLIC FIBERS

CHAPTER

10

A crylic fibers are defined by the FTC as "manufactured fibers in which the fiber-forming substance is any long-chain synthetic polymer composed of at least 85 percent by weight of acrylonitrile units (—CH$_2$—CH—).

$$|$$
$$CN$$

Acrylics

Although acrylonitrile, the polymer of which acrylic fibers are composed, had been synthesized earlier, it could not be melt spun because it tends to decompose if melted. Suitable solvents for the polymer were not found until the 1940s. A number of different fiber producers had been working independently to develop and patent processes for spinning fibers from the acrylonitrile polymer, each proceeding along somewhat different lines. As a result, seven separate production processes were patented: six using wet spinning and one using dry spinning.

The second synthetic fiber to be produced commercially by DuPont, Orlon® acrylic fiber entered production in 1950. DuPont announced in 1990 that it would phase out its acrylic business by the end of that year. Monsanto entered the acrylic field in 1952 with Acrilan® acrylic, and American Cyanamid introduced Creslan® acrylic in 1958. Both Monsanto and American Cyanamid are currently producing acrylic fibers. First targeted for outdoor uses, acrylic fiber ultimately found its major applications in apparel and carpets.

Manufacture

Acrylic fibers are produced from acrylonitrile usually in combination with one or more comonomers. The reaction that takes place during polymerization is an addition reaction. After the acrylic polymer is made, it is dissolved in dimethyl formamide (DMF). Some acrylics are dry spun into heated air (Figure 10.1); others are wet spun into baths of lower DMF concentration. Most acrylics are used in staple form, and the fiber is crimped before cutting.

A number of variations in the processes used to manufacture acrylic fibers are possible. Many of these processes are proprietary, and their details are not available. The general characteristics common to most acrylic fibers are as follows.

Molecular Structure

Acrylonitrile polymers in acrylic fibers are highly crystalline because the chains pack together tightly. Most fibers contain up to 15 percent of another monomer to interrupt the regular packing of the polymers and reduce the brittleness of the fiber. Different producers use different comononers, resulting in some variation of fiber properties and processing. Fibers that are 100 percent acrylonitrile are stronger and more thermally stable than copolymer acrylic fibers, but they are also more brittle.

Figure 10.1

Flowchart depicting manufacture of acrylic fiber by the dry-spinning process. Illustration courtesy of American Fiber Manufacturers Association, Inc.

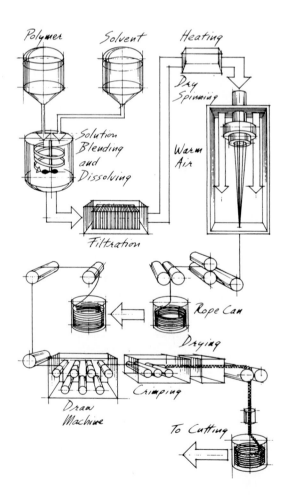

Properties of Acrylics

Physical Appearance

The microscopic cross section of acrylic fibers may be round, bean shaped, dog-bone shaped, or multilobal, depending on the manufacturing process. Likewise, the longitudinal appearance of acrylics is either smooth or twisted and may have wide striations (lengthwise markings). (See Figure 10.2.)

Other Physical Properties

Strength. Standard breaking tenacities of acrylic fibers are reported as ranging from 2.0–3.6 g/d. The fibers are weak and are therefore not appropriate for end uses requiring high strength.

Specific Gravity. Specific gravity ranges from 1.14 to 1.19, making acrylics lightweight.

Elasticity and Resilience. The elasticity of acrylic fibers varies from one trademarked fiber to another. In general, however, elastic recovery is lower than that for most other synthetic fibers. Resilience ranges from good to excellent.

Absorbency and Moisture Regain. The moisture absorption of acrylics is low, with a moisture regain of 1.0 to 2.5 percent.

Dimensional Stability. Heat setting will produce good dimensional stability in fabrics made of acrylics. Because of the fiber's low moisture absorbency, acrylic fabrics do not shrink when wet. However, there are many varieties of acrylics with somewhat different performance in regard to their dimensional stability. For this reason, instructions on care labels should be followed carefully in laundering acrylics. For example, some fabrics are manufactured from specially crimped fibers that require machine drying after laundering to restore the crimp. If hung wet on a line, some of these fabrics may stretch out of shape.

Electrical Conductivity. The low electrical conductivity of acrylics is related to their low moisture absorption. Antistatic finishes may be added to fibers to eliminate static electricity buildup.

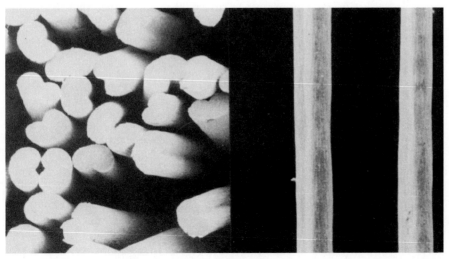

(a)   (b)

Figure 10.2

Photographs of acrylic fibers taken through an electron scanning microscope: (a) cross section and (b) longitudinal view. Photographs courtesy of the British Textile Technology Group (BTTG).

Effect of Heat; Combustibility. Although the literature reports melting points ranging from 450° to 497°F, depending on the specific type of fiber, manufacturers report that acrylics do not exhibit typical melting points but rather tend to decompose over a wide temperature range and eventually char to a brittle residue. Untreated acrylic fibers ignite and burn, leaving a hard, black bead residue at the edge of the fabric. Flame-retardant finishes can be given to acrylics. Fibers shrink in steam but can be safely ironed at 300°F. Exposure to high, dry heat may cause yellowing. Acrylic fibers and fabrics can be heat-set.

Effect of Selected Conditions on Fiber

Chemical Reactivity. Acrylics are very resistant to acids, except to nitric acid in which they dissolve. Resistance to bases is moderate, and degradation by sodium hydroxide at high concentrations and/or temperatures is cited by Moncrieff (1975) for Acrilan® and Creslan®. Solvents used in commercial dry cleaning do not affect the fiber adversely. Most acrylics are not harmed by household bleaches.

Resistance to Microorganisms, Mildew, Sunlight, and Aging. Mildew, microorganisms, and moths will not harm acrylic fibers. Resistance to sunlight ranges from very good to excellent. Age has no detrimental effect on fabric strength.

Bicomponent Acrylics

Acrylic fibers may be made in bicomponent varieties. (See chapter 14 for full discussion of bicomponent fibers.) Bicomponent acrylic fibers are created by extruding two different types of acrylic material together as one fiber from the spinneret. Each has somewhat different shrinkage properties, and when the fiber is subjected to heat and moisture during processing, one polymer shrinks more than the other and produces a permanent spiral crimp. The crimp provides increased bulk and resilience. Bicomponent acrylics are most often used in knitted goods such as sweaters and socks. Care instructions provided with bicomponent acrylic fibers often indicate that they must be laundered and tumble dried. During laundering the fibers swell, relieving tensions placed on the fibers during use, and the tumble drying is necessary to return fibers to their crimped and bulked shapes. Because line drying will not produce the same results, consumers should be sure to follow care instructions.

Uses

Acrylic fibers as a class are used in a wide variety of different apparel and home furnishings products. Their wool-like handle and bulk combined with easy-care characteristics make them popular for use in sweaters, fleece fabrics, hand-knitting yarns, blankets, and carpets. Resistance to degradation by sunlight leads to use of acrylics in drapery and upholstery fabrics. Acrylic fibers are fabricated into woven and knitted cloth constructions in a variety of textures and weights that are used for apparel, home furnishings, and industrial end uses. Acrylic fibers can be used alone or in blends. (See Figure 10.3.) Table 10.1 lists trade-marked acrylic fibers.

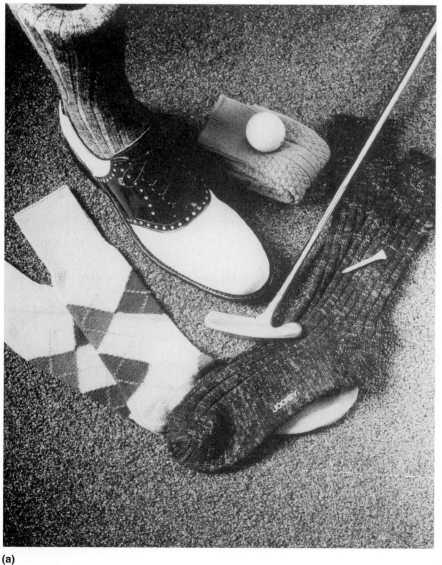

(a)

(b)

(c)

Figure 10.3 Three of the common types of apparel in which acrylic fibers are used: (a) hosiery, (b) knitted sportswear, and (c) high-pile fabrics for warmth. Photographs courtesy of the Acrylic Council.

Care Procedures

Different acrylic fibers may vary in their care requirements. For this reason, it is especially important to follow care labels of these fabrics. In general, acrylic fabrics can be laundered and dry-cleaned. They do not shrink in laundering but may be sensitive to heat, so that when machine drying is recommended for acrylic products, low heat settings should be used, and fabrics should be removed from the dryer immediately after tumbling. Pressing temperatures should not exceed 250° to 300°F.

Table 10.1	Acrylic Trademarks of U.S. Manufacturers	
Manufacturers and Trademarks	**Type of Yarn or Fiber**	**Special Features and Specialized Uses**
Cytec Industries		
Bulkaire®	Staple.	Medium bulk that makes it especially suitable for athletic socks.
Creslan®	Staple, tow.	Available in both natural and producer-colored fibers.
MicroSupreme®	Staple.	Microdenier; available in both natural and producer-colored fibers; high transport properties.
CFFR®	Fibrillated fiber.	High tech fiber for applications requiring good heat stabilization.
CTF®	High tech fiber engineered to meet defined requirements.	Especially used in filter bags, paper processing.
CPF®	High tech fiber engineered to meet defined requirements.	Especially used in processing products.
CYLIGHT®	Staple.	Light stabilized fiber for outdoor furniture market.
Monsanto, The Chemical Group, Fibers Division		
Acrilan®	Staple, tow.	—
Bi-loft®	Staple, tow.	—
Duraspun®	Tow.	Highly durable yarn used in socks.
Fi-Lana II®	Staple, tow.	—
Pil-Trol®	Staple, tow.	Resists pilling.
Sayelle®	Yarn.	Bicomponent yarn used in craft yarns.
Sno-Brite®	Staple.	Optic white.
So-Lara®	Staple, tow.	Producer dyed.
Wintuk®	Yarn.	Bicomponent blend used in craft yarns, sweaters.

Source: Data provided by fiber manufacturers.

Modacrylics

Modacrylic fibers were first manufactured commercially by Union Carbide Company in 1949 before the production of acrylics. Because the composition of modacrylics is very similar to the acrylics, both fibers were at first included in the acrylic classification, but in 1960 the FTC ruled that a separate category should be established for them.

Modacrylics are defined by the FTC as "a manufactured fiber in which the fiber-forming substance is any synthetic polymer composed of less than 85 percent but at least 35 percent by weight of acrylonitrile units (—CH—CH$_2$—) except

$$\underset{\text{CN}}{|}$$

fibers under category (2) of paragraph (j) of Rule 7 of the Textile Fiber Products Identification Act."[1]

---

1. This exception refers to certain synthetic rubber products that have a substantial quantity of acrylonitrile in their composition.

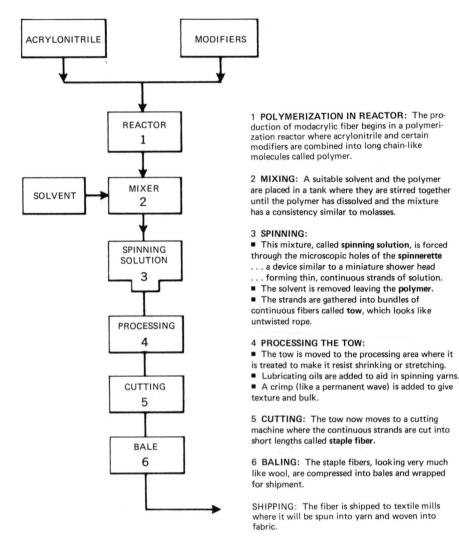

Figure 10.4

Flowchart for the manufacture of modacrylic fiber. Illustration courtesy of the Technical Committee of the American Fiber Manufacturers Association, Inc.

1 **POLYMERIZATION IN REACTOR:** The production of modacrylic fiber begins in a polymerization reactor where acrylonitrile and certain modifiers are combined into long chain-like molecules called polymer.

2 **MIXING:** A suitable solvent and the polymer are placed in a tank where they are stirred together until the polymer has dissolved and the mixture has a consistency similar to molasses.

3 **SPINNING:**
- This mixture, called **spinning solution**, is forced through the microscopic holes of the **spinnerette** . . . a device similar to a miniature shower head . . . forming thin, continuous strands of solution.
- The solvent is removed leaving the **polymer**.
- The strands are gathered into bundles of continuous fibers called **tow**, which looks like untwisted rope.

4 **PROCESSING THE TOW:**
- The tow is moved to the processing area where it is treated to make it resist shrinking or stretching.
- Lubricating oils are added to aid in spinning yarns.
- A crimp (like a permanent wave) is added to give texture and bulk.

5 **CUTTING:** The tow now moves to a cutting machine where the continuous strands are cut into short lengths called **staple fiber**.

6 **BALING:** The staple fibers, looking very much like wool, are compressed into bales and wrapped for shipment.

SHIPPING: The fiber is shipped to textile mills where it will be spun into yarn and woven into fabric.

Manufacture

Modacrylic fibers are made from chemicals derived from natural gas, coal, air, salt, and water. Combinations of acrylonitrile and other materials, such as vinyl chloride, vinylidene chloride, or vinyl bromide, are made in a polymerization reactor. The polymer formed in the reaction is dissolved in an appropriate solvent, and the fiber is spun, drawn, and cut into staple lengths. Varying degrees of crimp may be added to the fiber depending on its projected end uses. Modacrylics can be produced by dry- or wet-spun processes but are sold only as staple products.

Modacrylics were produced in the United States by Union Carbide (Dynel®), Eastman Kodak (Verel®), and Monsanto (SEF®). Union Carbide and Eastman have terminated production, leaving Monsanto as the only domestic producer. Figure 10.4 diagrams the modacrylic manufacturing process.

Properties of Modacrylics

Physical Appearance

The microscopic appearance of various types of modacrylics differs. Cross sections range from an irregular flat shape, through a U shape, to a peanut shape. The longi-

Figure 10.5

Photomicrographs of modacrylic fiber in: (a) a cross section and (b) a longitudinal view. Photomicrographs courtesy of Monsanto, The Chemical Group, Fibers Division.

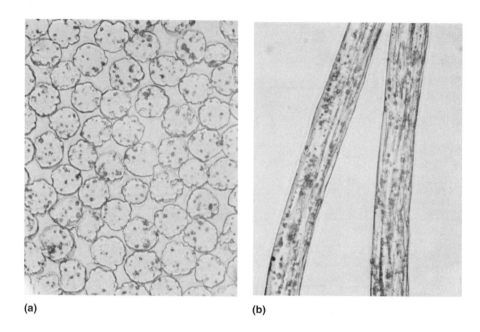

(a)

(b)

tudinal appearance usually shows some striations, or it may have a grainy effect. (See Figure 10.5.)

Other Physical Properties

Specific Gravity. The specific gravity of modacrylics is 1.3, which is comparable to wool, so that the fibers feel light but also have good insulating qualities.

Strength. The strength of SEF® modacrylic is 2.3 g/d, similar to acrylics. Abrasion resistance is moderate.

Elasticity and Resilience. The resilience is high, and the combination of high resilience with abrasion resistance makes modacrylic fibers especially suitable for use in high-pile fabrics. Elastic recovery is good.

Absorbency and Moisture Regain. The absorbency of the fibers is low, and the moisture regain is 2.5 percent. As a result, the stain resistance to water-borne soil is good.

Dimensional Stability. Modacrylics have good dimensional stability. However, their sensitivity to heat may result in some shrinkage if they are dried in a dryer at high temperatures.

Effect of Heat; Combustibility. While SEF® and most other common commercial modacrylic fibers are copolymerized with halogenated monomers to impart flame retardance, not all modacrylics are inherently flame retardant. Most modacrylics currently available will burn when placed in a direct flame but will self-extinguish as soon as the flame is removed.

The melting point of modacrylics is low (about 370° to 410°F). Only the olefins and saran are more sensitive to heat. If modacrylic fabrics are ironed, very low temperature settings must be used. If a dryer is used, temperatures should be set for low or no heat.

Effect of Selected Conditions on Fiber

Chemical Reactivity. Dry-cleaning solvents will not affect modacrylics adversely. Some modacrylics may be discolored by strong bases. Their resistance to acids is good to excellent. At some times and in some processes, acetone has been the solvent used in spinning acrylic fibers. While this is not the case for SEF® modacrylic, some modacrylic fibers processed using acetone may be soluble in acetone.

Resistance to Environmental Conditions. The resistance to deterioration from light is fairly good. Neither moths nor mildew attack modacrylics. Age has no apparent effect.

Uses

The major areas of use for modacrylic fibers include wall coverings, pile and fleece fabrics for apparel, blankets, flame-resistant draperies and curtains, paint roller covers, filters, wigs, and hairpieces. Because modacrylics have a low softening temperature and a high thermal shrinkage potential, a variety of texturizing treatments can be given to the fibers that allow them to simulate the textures and characteristics of fur fibers. Most simulated fur fabrics are made from modacrylic or acrylic fibers. The same characteristic of modacrylics makes it possible to create hairlike fibers, which leads to their use in wigs and hairpieces. They are also used in some industrial fabrics that take advantage of their flame resistance and good chemical resistance. Monsanto also produces a pigmented modacrylic under the trademark SEF Plus® that is suitable for outdoor applications, such as awnings and boat covers.

Care Procedures

Deep-pile garments must be cleaned professionally to avoid crushing or altering the appearance of the pile. Other modacrylic fabrics are machine washable, but special care should be taken to avoid exposing them to very high temperatures because of their heat sensitivity. Low dryer temperatures must be used, and ironing should be done only with a warm, not hot, iron. Some modacrylic fibers are discolored by the use of chlorine bleaches. Table 10.2 compares selected properties of acrylic and modacrylic fibers.

Table 10.2	Selected Properties of Acrylic and Modacrylic Fibers	
	Acrylic	Modacrylic
Specific gravity	1.14–1.19	1.30–1.37
Tenacity (g/d)		
Dry	2.0–3.5	1.7–3.5
Wet	1.6–2.9	1.5–3.5
Moisture regain	1.0–2.5	0.4–4.0
Resilience	Good.	Good.
Burning and melting point	In flame, burns with melting, continues after flame removed; softens at 450° to 497°F; indeterminate melting point.	In flame, burns very slowly with melting; self-extinguishing after flame removed; melting point 371° (approximate) to 410°F.
Conductivity of		
Heat	Low.	Low.
Electricity	Low.	Low.
Resistance to damage from		
Fungi	Excellent.	Excellent.
Insects	Excellent.	Excellent.
Prolonged exposure to sunlight	Excellent.	Excellent.
Acids	Good, except nitric.	Good.
Bases	Good to weak bases.	Moderate.

Reference

Moncrieff, R. W. 1975. *Man-made fibres.* New York: Wiley.

Review Questions

1. What are some of the outstanding properties of acrylic fibers? What are some of the end uses for acrylic fibers, and how do the outstanding properties you have identified contribute to these uses?
2. What cautions must be exercised in caring for acrylics?
3. What are some of the outstanding properties of modacrylic fibers? What are some of the end uses for modacrylic fibers, and how do the outstanding properties you have identified contribute to these uses?
4. What cautions must be exercised in caring for modacrylics?
5. How are bicomponent acrylics different from regular acrylic fibers?

Recommended Readings

Acrylic Council sponsors blind sock test, survey with young football players. 1994. *Southern Textile News,* 10 October, 5.

Bajaj, P. 1994. Absorbent acrylic fiber launched. *Textile Month,* August, 38.

Ford, J. E. 1992. Acrylic fibres. *Textiles* 21(2):12.

Hobson, P. H., and A. L. McPeters. 1994. Acrylic and modacrylic fibers. In *Encylopedia of textiles, fibers, and non-woven fabrics,* ed. M. Grayson, 1. New York: Wiley Interscience.

Improved heat resistance and luster for acrylic. 1990. *High Performance Textiles* 3 (March): 8.

Masson, J. C. 1995. *Acrylic fiber technology and applications.* New York: Marcel Dekker.

Scalco, M. 1991. Pil-Trol®. *International Fabricare Institute Bulletin,* September.

Tsai, J.-S. 1994. Influence of spinneret dimensions on modacrylic fiber. *Textile Research Journal* 64 (October): 611.

OLEFIN FIBERS

Although olefin monofilaments have been manufactured for specialized applications since 1949, the widespread use of olefin fibers for a variety of textile products has been a relatively recent development. (British publications may refer to these fibers as *polyalkenes*.)

The FTC definition of olefin fiber is "a manufactured fiber in which the fiber-forming substance is any long-chain synthetic polymer composed of at least 85 percent weight of ethylene, propylene, or other olefin units, except amorphous polyolefins qualifying under category (1) of paragraph (j) of rule 7."[1]

Two major categories of olefin fibers exist. One is polypropylene; the other is polyethylene. Of the two, polypropylene is used far more extensively for textiles and constitutes the larger quantity of olefin fibers in use today.

Polypropylene Fibers

Manufacture

Polypropylene flakes and chips are manufactured from polypropylene gas, a component of natural gas, or from the cracking of naptha, a product of crude oil refining. After polymerization the fiber is formed by one of two means: polypropylene may be

---

[1]This exception refers to a type of synthetic rubber with a substantial proportion of polyolefin material.

melt spun as filaments, or it may be mechanically fibrillated. Fibrillated fibers are created by first extruding a film of polypropylene. This film is either stretched and split or slit and drawn into a network of fibers. (See chapter 15 for a discussion of film fibrillation.)

The properties of the melt-spun fibers and fibrillated fibers differ somewhat. The denier (size) range of melt-spun fibers is greater than is that of fibrillated fibers. Fibrillated fibers have a branchlike structure that may eliminate the need to add texture to the fiber. Also, fiber-to-fiber interlocking is better in fibrillated films, but fiber length is not so uniform, and fibrillated fibers are less regular in shape than are those from melt-spun fibers. Spun fibrillated yarns are smoother and softer.

Properties of Polypropylene Fibers

Physical Appearance

In microscopic appearance (Figure 11.1) the polypropylene fiber may have any of several cross-sectional configurations, depending on the shape of the holes of the spinneret used in extruding the fibers. Under the microscope the surfaces of polypropylene fibers appear to be smooth; however, under the greater magnification of electronmicroscopy, pigmented fibers may have protuberances along the fiber surface that are thought to be either clumps of pigment particles or part of the fiber structure.

Other Physical Properties

Specific Gravity. The density of polypropylene is especially low. Its specific gravity is 0.92, or less than that of water. As a result, olefin fabrics float on water when they are washed. The low density of polypropylene also is related to the relatively low cost of olefin fiber, as a small weight of raw materials can be used to produce a large volume of fiber.

Figure 11.1

Photomicrographs of Marvess® olefin fiber in: (a) a cross section and (b) a longitudinal view. Photomicrographs courtesy of Amoco Fabrics and Fibers Company.

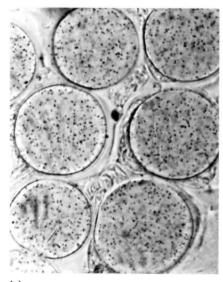

(a)

(b)

Strength. Polypropylene olefins are strong. The breaking strength of polypropylene filaments is from 2.5–5.5 g/d (regular-tenacity nylon 66 is 3.0–3.6 g/d), and the abrasion resistance is good.

Elasticity and Resilience. The elastic recovery of polypropylene olefin fibers is excellent. The resilience of the fiber is good.

Absorbency. Almost completely nonabsorbent, polypropylene is difficult to dye. Best results in coloring fibers are attained when pigment is combined with the polymer before the fibers are formed. Low absorbency also makes the fiber exceptionally resistant to water-borne soil and stains. Grease and oil do stain polypropylene fabrics, and since they are oleophilic (or oil attracting), stains may be difficult to remove. Olefin fabrics have good wickability.

Dimensional Stability. The dimensional stability of heat-set polypropylene is good, as long as it is not subjected to temperatures above 250°F. Elevated temperatures will result in fabric shrinkage. Wet stability is good.

Electrical Conductivity. The electrical conductivity of polypropylene is poor. Its low absorbency contributes to problems of static electricity buildup, although finishes used in the spinning and processing of the fiber can overcome this problem in the finished product.

Effect of Heat; Combustibility. The melting point of polypropylene is quite low: 338°F. Hot bacon fat dropped on olefin carpets will melt fibers. Olefins are combustible and melt as they burn. They produce a sooty smoke.

Effect of Selected Conditions on Fiber

Chemical Reactivity. In general, polypropylene's resistance to bases and to acids is good. Some organic solvents used in dry cleaning may affect the fabrics adversely. Perchloroethylene should not be used. However, Stoddard solvent will not deteriorate the fibers. Home laundering is preferable to dry cleaning in the care of polypropylene fabrics.

Resistance to Environmental Conditions. Mold, mildew, and insects do not attack olefins. Sunlight does gradually deteriorate the fabric, and age has no appreciable effect. Hindered amine light stabilizers, a newly introduced product, can be added to the fiber to control light degradation.

The characteristics of polypropylene fibers are summarized in Table 11.1.

Uses

Propropylene fibers are used in the manufacture of carpets, especially indoor/outdoor carpeting. Being nonabsorbent and having good weather resistance, polypropylene can be made into carpets that will withstand exposure to outdoor conditions in areas where sunlight is not intense or prolonged. However, without ultraviolet light stabilizers such carpets will deteriorate in climates like those of the American Southwest.

Table 11.1		
Selected Properties of Regular Polypropylene Fibers		
Specific gravity	0.92	
Tenacity (g/d)[a]		
Dry	2.5–5.5	
Wet	2.5–5.5	
Moisture regain	None.	
Resiliency	Good.	
Burning and melting point	In flame, burns with melting; continues to burn after flame is removed; melts at 325° to 335°F.	
Conductivity of		
Heat	Low.	
Electricity	Low.	
Resistance to damage from		
Fungi	Excellent.	
Insects	Excellent.	
Prolonged exposure to sunlight	Slowly loses strength but can be ultraviolet stabilized effectively.	
Acids	Excellent.	
Bases	Excellent.	

[a]Filaments.

Figure 11.2	Carpet and upholstery fabrics made from polyolefin fiber. Photograph courtesy of the American Polyolefin Association.

When polypropylene is used for traditional indoor carpets, soil- and water-borne stain resistance are exceptional. Other characteristics such as good abrasion resistance, good lightfastness if solution dyed, and resistance to moths have contributed to the successful use of polypropylene for carpetings (Figure 11.2).

Upholstery fabric manufacturers have made extensive use of polypropylene in a variety of fabrics including velvets. Again, stain resistance and resistance to abrasion are important in this application. Automotive interior fabrics represent a major market for olefin fabrics.

Other products made from polypropylene include blankets and wall coverings, and polypropylene serves as replacement for jute and other bast fibers in twine, rope, carpet backings, and the like. It is also used in a variety of nonwovens, including industrial filters and diaper stock, where thermobondability is an essential property. Good wicking qualities also contribute to its use in diaper liners (Figure 11.3).

Industrial applications of olefins are numerous and include ropes, cordage, filter paper, netting, and bagging. Nonwoven olefin geotextile materials are used in road construction and in other engineering projects. For example, the geotextiles can prevent erosion by stabilizing soil in road beds, embankments, and other building sites.

Although industrial and home furnishings areas are the major outlets for polypropylene fiber, it is also an apparel fiber. Well established for activewear products (Figure 11.4) such as underwear that are the first layer against the skin, thermal garments, hosiery, and wet suit liners, polypropylene is also beginning to penetrate other markets such as lingerie, bathing suits, and children's clothing. It is also being used as effect and design yarns.

Figure 11.3

Polyolefins are widely used in diaper stock and diaper liners. Photograph courtesy of the American Polyolefin Association.

Activewear and sportswear use polyolefin fibers because of their excellent moisture transport qualities. Photograph courtesy of the American Polyolefin Association.

Characteristics that encourage activewear applications are excellent wicking qualities (by which moisture is transmitted to the outer surface, thereby reducing the cold, clammy feeling next to the skin), good thermal insulating qualities, and excellent abrasion resistance.

Fine denier filament polyolefin is difficult to produce as high-quality filament yarn, although research in this area continues. Staple fiber yarns are more easily produced, and most apparel is made from staple yarns. Because the polymer must be colored before it is extruded, polypropylene has the advantage of absolute colorfastness but the disadvantage that decisions about color must be made long before the fabrication of final products. Given the impact of fashion on apparel, this may be a limiting factor in use in highly fashion-oriented garments.

Polypropylene may be blended with wool, particularly for men's hosiery. Wool and polypropylene blends are being evaluated for possible use in blankets. The low specific gravity of polypropylene together with its low thermal conductivity would offer the advantage of a lighter blanket that retains the desirable properties of a heavier all-wool blanket.

Table 11.2   Polypropylene Olefin Trademarks of U.S. Manufacturers

Manufacturers and Trademarks	Type of Yarn or Fiber	Special Features	End Uses
Amoco Fabrics and Fibers Co.			
Alpha®	Bulked filament.	—	—
Essera®	Producer textured.	—	—
Marquesa Lana®	Bulked filament.	—	—
Marvess®	Bulked filament, filament, staple.	—	—
Patlon III®	Bulked filament.	—	—
Trace®	Bulked filament, producer textured.	—	—
Fibres South Inc.			
Crown Fiber®	Monofilament, fibrillated film, staple.	—	—
Filament Fiber Technology			
Salus®	Filament.	High vapor transport, low thermal conductivity, low specific gravity, solution dyed, stain and odor resistant.	Hosiery, socks, thermal underwear, apparel, automotive upholstery, wall coverings, medical and industrial applications.
Telar™	Filament.	Same as above.	Same as above.
Hercules Incorporated			
Herculon®:			
Types T-136, T-162	Staple.	Solution dyed, abrasion and chemical resistance, color matched to customer specifications.	Home furnishings and contract carpet.
Type T-116	Staple.	Low moisture absorption, fade resistant.	Apparel.
Types T-144, T-145, T-150	Staple.	Moldable, stain resistant, solution dyed, low shrinkage.	Automotive.
Type T-734	Bulked filament.	Colorfast, stain resistant, mildew and insect resistant.	Home furnishings and automotive.
Types T-101, T-158	Staple.	Chemically inert, moisture resistant.	Industrial fabrics (general purpose, wet lay nonwovens, asphalt and concrete additive.)
Type 104	Staple.	High stretch, hydrophobic, thermally bondable.	Hygenic fabrics.
Type 186	Staple.	Hydrophilic, thermally bondable.	Hygenic fabrics, wet lay nonwovens, industrial fabrics.
T-190™	Staple.	High strength, hydrophobic, thermally bondable.	Hygenic fabrics.
T-196™	Staple.	High strength, hydrophilic, thermally bondable.	Hygenic fabrics.
Polyloom Corporation of America			
Polyloom®	Fibrillated film.	—	—
Synthetic Industries			
Fibrilon®	Filament, staple, monofilament, fibrillated film.	—	—

Source: Data provided by fiber manufacturers.

Olefin fibers are also being used for insulation materials for gloves, footwear, and apparel. Very fine olefin and polyester fibers are made into a nonwoven batting that the manufacturer, 3M, calls Thinsulate®. The batting provides, according to the manufacturer, approximately two times the thermal insulation of competitive materials, including 100 percent polyester fiberfill, down, and wool. One advantage, therefore, is that warmth without excessive bulk is possible.

DuPont manufactures Tyvek®, a spunbonded polyolefin (see chapter 18 for discussion of spunbonding) for use in barrier garments such as clean suits, protective garments for toxic waste cleanup, and the like. One of the major advantages of the fiber is the low cost of production.

Table 11.2 lists trademarked polypropylene fibers.

Care Procedures

Polypropylene carpet and upholstery fabrics are relatively care free. Stains can be wiped off with a damp cloth. Routine vacuuming and periodic shampooing will help to maintain and preserve both appearance and durability.

Garments and other items such as blankets can usually be laundered. Polypropylene is injured by some dry-cleaning fluids. Care labels should be checked carefully, as blends of polypropylene with other fibers may require special care.

All polypropylene fabrics can be laundered at moderate temperatures. This fiber is heat sensitive at about 250°F. Most dryers do not exceed temperatures of 180° to 190°F so that drying at low temperatures is permissible; however, line drying may be preferable as it generally eliminates any need for pressing. Hot irons will damage these fabrics, so only cool iron temperatures should be used for pressing.

Polyethylene Fibers

Polyethylene shares many qualities in common with polypropylene and exhibits some differences, including a lower melting point and some tendency to be deformed if stretched more than 10 percent. Melt-spun polyethylene has not been a textile fiber of major importance, being used mostly for plastic films and packing materials. Recently, however, several companies have developed high-strength polyethylene fibers. AlliedSignal Fibers produces Spectra®, a gel-spun polyethylene fiber with an exceptionally high degree of polymer chain orientation.

Spectra® and other high-strength polyethylene super fibers manufactured abroad are characterized not only by high strength and modulus but are also less brittle than many competing high technology fibers. They resist moisture, chemicals, and ultraviolet light and are lightweight. Disadvantages are a low melting point (300°F or 147°C) and, for some varieties of the fiber, a tendency to "creep," or elongate, under load over a long period of time.

Products for which these fibers are being used include ropes, cables, sailcloth, cut-resistant clothing, gloves, backpacks, body shields, and a wide range of fiber composite materials for industry (Figure 11.5).

Figure 11.5 High-strength products made from Spectra® polyethylene fiber range from (a) protective gloves and sleeves to (b) backpacks considered to be the toughest, lightest internal frame packs ever produced. Photograph (a) courtesy of Golden Needles Knitting & Glove Company. Photograph (b) courtesy of AlliedSignal, Inc.

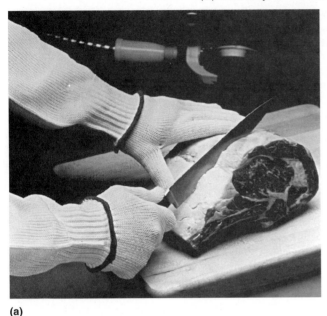

(a)

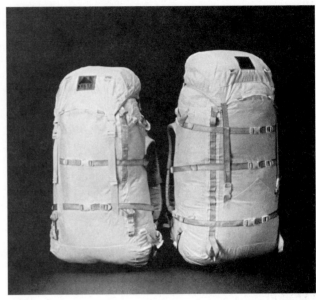

(b)

Review Questions

1. Which properties of polypropylene fibers contribute to their use in the following products?

   carpets

   upholstery

   thermal underwear

2. What care procedures are recommended for polypropylene garments?

3. What properties of high-strength polyethylene fibers contribute to their use in the following products?

   cut-resistant clothing

   composite materials for industry

Recommended Readings

Barish, L. 1989. Sunlight degradation of polypropylene textile fibers: A microscopial study. *Journal of the Textile Institute* 80 (1): 107.

Cheng, C. Y., and C. R. Davey. 1994. Effects of recycling on polypropylene properties. *International Nonwovens Journal* 6 (Summer): 38.

Dobson, S. 1994. Polypropylene fibers for technical textiles. *Technical Textile Markets* 19 (October): 48.

Douglas, B. A. 1989. Polypropylene: The new wonder fiber. *Southern Textile News* 45 (2 October): 8.

———. 1992. Telar: The newest olefin textile fiber. *Southern Textile News* 48 (9 March): 8.

Ford, J. E. 1988. Polyethylene textiles. *Textiles* 17 (2): 31.

———. 1988. Polypropylene fibres. *Textiles* 17 (1): 2.

Mansfield, R. G. 1994. Polypropylene use in apparel grows. *America's Textiles International* 23 (January): K/A 8.

Elastomeric Fibers

Elastomeric fiber is defined as fiber made of "a natural or synthetic polymer which at room temperature can be stretched repeatedly to at least twice its original length and which after removal of the tensile load will immediately and forcibly return to approximately its original length" (American Society for Testing and Materials 1986, 262).

Natural rubber has been made into fiber for many years. Natural rubber has certain disadvantages in fiber use, however. It is difficult to dye, has poor abrasion resistance, is deteriorated by sunlight, and has relatively poor chemical resistance. Textile chemists have synthesized several new fibers that compare favorably in elasticity with rubber without some of its disadvantages.

Three generic fiber classifications have been established for elastomeric fibers: spandex, rubber, and anidex. Other elastomeric fibers have been made by modifying cellulose fibers, and still other elastomers are in experimental stages of development. Of these generic fiber groups, only rubber and spandex are currently being manufactured.

Rubber Fibers

The FTC category of *rubber fibers* divides the fibers into three subcategories: natural rubber and two kinds of synthetic rubber.

Natural rubber comes from rubber plants. From a liquid form, the rubber can be extruded into fibrous form. For many years natural rubber was used as the core for fiber-covered elastic materials. Its advantages include elasticity, flexibility, good strength, and nonabsorbency. Its disadvantages include deterioration by temperatures above 200°F and by sunlight, oils, petroleum, and aging.

Globe Manufacturing Company, the largest domestic producer of natural latex rubber-based thread, indicates that these products are used in such areas as hosiery, elastic waistbands for underwear, foundation garments, surgical support stockings, stretch bandages, and industrial stretch items.

A variety of synthetic rubber products was marketed after World War II. These products are made from hydrocarbons such as polyisoprene, polybutadiene, and noncrystalline polyolefins. Copolymers of dienes and hydrocarbons are also used in the manufacture of some synthetic rubber.

The FTC also identifies synthetic rubber made from "polychloroprene or a copolymer of chloroprene in which at least 35 percent by weight of the fiber-forming substance is composed of chloroprene units." Synthetic rubbers exhibit similar characteristics to natural rubber in their behavior but in general show better resistance to deterioration than does rubber.

Spandex

Manufactured in the United States since 1959, spandex fibers have attained extensive use in stretch fabrics for foundation garments, sports apparel, fashionable clothing, and other products where elasticity is important.

The FTC defines spandex fiber as "a manufactured fiber in which the fiber-forming substance is a long-chain synthetic polymer comprised of at least 85 percent of a segmented polyurethane." Spandex is a block copolymer with rigid aromatic segments connected by urethane linkages to aliphatic polyester or polyether segments. The rigid segments act as cross-links providing strength. The amorphous segments assume a coiled position when fibers are relaxed, but when fibers are stretched the coils straighten, thereby providing the elongation characteristic of spandex. Upon the release of tension, the amorphous, or "soft," segments coil up again, returning the fibers to their prestretched position.

Properties of Spandex

Physical Appearance

The microscopic appearance of spandex fibers differs from one trademarked fiber to another. In cross section some are round, some are shaped like peanut shells, and others are shaped like dog bones. Longitudinal views display even, smooth, or striated surfaces. (See Figure 12.1.)

Other Physical Properties

Because spandex is selected for use in many products in which rubber might be used, it is helpful to compare the properties of spandex to rubber as well as to other fibers. It should be noted, for example, that spandex can be made in much finer deniers than rubber.

Specific Gravity. Spandex has a moderate density. Specific gravity is 1.0–1.2, depending on pigmentation.

<table>
<tr><td>

Figure 12.1

</td><td>

Two cross-sectional views of Lycra® spandex fibers: (a) fibers magnified 500 times and (b) fibers magnified 150 times. Photomicrographs courtesy of the DuPont Company.

</td></tr>
</table>

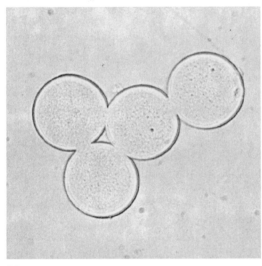

(a)

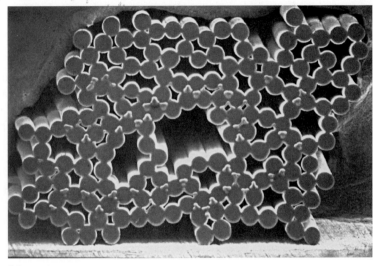

(b)

Strength. Spandex is relatively weak when compared with nonelastomeric fibers. It is about twice as strong as rubber. Breaking strength ranges from 0.7 to 1.0 g/d, depending on type.

Elasticity and Resilience. The most important property of spandex is its ability to stretch and recover. It will stretch 500 to 600 percent without breaking. This amount of stretching is comparable to that of rubber. Recovery from stretching is slightly better for rubber than for spandex. The improved strength of spandex combined with its excellent elongation gives it an advantage over rubber. Other properties of spandex described in the following paragraphs also make spandex more practical to use than rubber.

Absorbency and Moisture Regain. Although the moisture regain of spandex fibers is low (<1.0%), water will penetrate the fiber.

Effect of Heat; Combustibility. Spandex fibers will burn. The melting point varies from trademarked fiber to trademarked fiber, and the specific melting point is difficult to ascertain. Most spandex fibers melt at temperatures of about 450° to 520°F. These fibers stick at temperatures around 340°F.

Spandex can be heat-set. Spandex fibers can be dried safely in an automatic dryer.

Effect of Selected Conditions on Fiber

Chemical Reactivity. The resistance to chemicals is generally good. Chlorine compounds in strong concentrations will cause the fiber to be degraded and yellowed, but spandex will withstand chlorine concentrations such as those used in swimming pools. Chlorine bleaches should be avoided.

Seawater has no deleterious effect on spandex fibers. Perspiration and suntan oils do not seriously affect spandex, although some suntan oils may cause yellowing of white fibers. (Suntan oils *do* deteriorate rubber.)

Resistance to Microorganisms and Light. Spandex has satisfactory resistance to microorganisms. Extended exposure to light may cause discoloration of some types of white spandex but does not deteriorate the fiber seriously. The characteristics of spandex are summarized in Table 12.1.

Uses

Spandex fibers are always used in conjunction with other fibers. This combination may be made in one of several ways. The spandex fiber may be used as bare yarn, single-covered yarn, double-covered yarn, or core-spun yarn. Fine denier spandex is used to give stretch with sheerness in products such as ladies' hosiery.

Bare core spandex yarns are uncovered filaments. They may be woven or knitted into fabrics in combination with other yarns. This provides additional strength to the spandex and stretch to the fabric. Often, the spandex filament is covered with another fiber, and the spandex serves as the core. Single-covered yarns have one layer of another filament fiber wrapped around the spandex core. In double-covered yarns one layer is twisted around the core in one direction, and the second layer is twisted around the core in the opposite direction. These can be made into very sheer yarns and are often used for support hose. Where it is desirable, two different types of fibers can be used, one in each layer. Core-spun yarns are made by holding spandex filaments at tension while a staple fiber is spun around the core. (See Figure 12.2.)

Spandex yarns are woven or knitted into a variety of garments in which stretch is desirable. These may include power nets for foundation garments, woven or crocheted fabrics for underwear waistbands, tricot or circular knits for lingerie, and activewear used in sports such as swimming, skiing, golf, and tennis. (See Figure 12.3.) Attractive stretch laces and other decorative fabrics may be made with spandex.

Table 12.1		
Selected Properties of Spandex Fibers	Specific gravity	1.21 (for dull)
	Tenacity (g/d)	
	Dry	0.7–1.0
	Wet	0.7–1.0
	Moisture regain	1.3%
	Breaking extension	500%–600%
	Elasticity and resilience	Excellent.
	Burning and melting point	In flame, burns with melting; continues to burn flame is removed; melts at 450° to 520°F. after
	Conductivity of	
	Heat	Difficult to assess because fiber is used in combination with other fibers.
	Electricity	Difficult to assess because fiber is used in combination with other fibers.
	Resistance to damage from	
	Fungi	Excellent.
	Insects	Excellent.
	Prolonged exposure to sunlight	Resists degradation but some varieties may discolor.
	Acids	Good—acid fumes may cause yellowing.
	Bases	Fair.

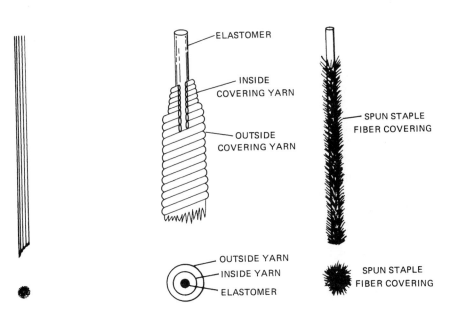

ELASTOMER
INSIDE COVERING YARN
OUTSIDE COVERING YARN
SPUN STAPLE FIBER COVERING

OUTSIDE YARN
INSIDE YARN
ELASTOMER

SPUN STAPLE FIBER COVERING

Bare Filament   Covered Yarn   Core-spun Yarn

Figure 12.2

Types of elastomeric yarns (length and cross section).

Figure 12.3

Bathing suit that achieves a close fit and also permits freedom of movement by using Lycra® spandex fiber. Photograph courtesy of the DuPont Company.

The cost of spandex fibers is relatively high. As a result, spandex is used chiefly in those applications where alternative forms of providing stretch, such as stretch-texturing nylon or polyester, are inadequate.

Care Procedures

Because spandex fibers are used in combination with other fibers, care must take into account not only the characteristics of spandex but also those of the other fibers. Spandex should not be subject to excessive heat in ironing. It is recommended that ironing temperatures not exceed 300°F or the "synthetic" setting on a hand iron. Dryer temperatures should be moderate. Chlorine bleaches should not be used in laundering spandex.

Trademarks of Spandex

Commercial trade names for spandex fiber include Lycra®, a DuPont trademark, and Glospan® and Cleerspan® by Globe Manufacturing Company.

Reference

American Society for Testing and Materials. 1986. *Compilation of ASTM standard definitions.* 6th ed. Philadelphia: ASTM.

Review Questions

1. What is the definition of an elastomeric fiber?
2. What are the advantages of using spandex fibers instead of rubber fibers in bathing suits?
3. Describe the various ways in which spandex is used in combination with other fibers.
4. How are care procedures for fabrics that include spandex determined?

Recommended Readings

Barnes, P. 1994. Sensational Lycra. *Textiles* 23 (Spring): 9–10.

Davidson, W. A. B. 1994. Spandex markets are heating up. *America's Textiles International* 23 (September): 49.

Rudie, R. 1992. Love affair with Lycra® spandex far from over. *Bobbin* 33 (May): 19.

Ultee, A. J. 1986. Fibers, elastomeric. In *Encyclopedia of polymer science and engineering,* 2d ed., Vol. 6. New York: Wiley.

Inorganic, Metallic, and Carbon Fibers

The small number of natural fibers that can be classified as mineral fibers might also be called inorganic fibers, because these fibers lack carbon, the essential element in the chemical composition of organic fibers. Of these, only asbestos is found in the fibrous state. Glass and metal fibers are considered to be manufactured fibers because they are subjected to processing to make them into fibrous form.

Most of the applications of the fibers discussed in this chapter are to be found in products used in industry, in building and construction materials, by the law enforcement community and the military, in recreational equipment, or in geotextiles. These and some fibers with similar end uses are the high performance fibers introduced in chapter 6. While few consumers will select or purchase many of the products made from these fibers, we increasingly depend on the machines, equipment, tools, and structures that incorporate these fibers in our homes, our work environments, and our leisure time pursuits. As these segments of the textile industry grow, larger numbers of graduates of textile technology programs are likely to find employment in the management, manufacture, and distribution of geotextiles and high performance textiles.

Asbestos

Asbestos fiber comes from mineral deposits. As it is naturally fireproof, it had been used alone or in blends to make textile products in which fire resistance was important, for example, in fire curtains for theaters, insulating materials, and household products such as ironing board covers or pot holders.

Continued inhalation of asbestos fiber can cause serious lung disease, and asbestos fiber is considered to be carcinogenic. For this reason, the use of asbestos fiber is being limited to products in which persons are not exposed to the fiber. The consumer, therefore, is unlikely to encounter new products made from asbestos, although it continues to have some industrial applications.

Glass Fiber

During World War I, the Germans found that they were running short of asbestos fiber. In an effort to find a substitute fiber that was noncombustible, they attempted to make fibers from glass, with only a limited success.

Following World War I, researchers continued to look into ways of using glass to produce fibers. This technology had been sufficiently advanced by the late 1930s, when the Owens-Corning Glass Company initiated the mass production of glass fiber.

Glass fiber is made from glass that has been melted and extruded into long, fine filaments. Glass is made from silica sand and limestone, plus small amounts of other constituents such as soda ash, borax, and aluminum hydroxide. The quantities of these ingredients are varied depending on the qualities desired in the glass fiber.

Production

Glass fiber can be produced in both continuous filament form and in staple lengths. Selected ingredients are mixed together, and that mixture is melted in a high-temperature furnace. Molten glass is then drawn from the furnace in the form of filaments, the diameter of which is controlled by the viscosity of the glass melt, the rate of extrusion, and the size of the spinneret hole.

If staple fiber lengths are required, an air jet "cuts" the filaments and pulls the fibers onto a revolving drum from which they are gathered into a strand. Filament fibers are wound onto a spool by high-speed winders. Bare glass fibers have poor abrasion resistance, so a sizing or lubricating material is applied to fibers to provide some degree of protection. Fibers made of glass are subject to the usual textile processes for making yarns and for weaving.

Properties of Glass Fiber

Physical Appearance

Under the microscope glass fibers look like small glass rods (which is just what glass fibers are). The fiber diameter is determined by the size of the orifice through which it is extruded. Size is selected according to the end use of the fiber.

The longitudinal view of the fiber shows a very smooth, round surface that produces a high luster. The fiber is colorless, unless a ceramic pigment has been added to the glass melt before it is formed into fibers.

Other Physical Properties

Specific Gravity. Glass fibers have a specific gravity of from 2.5 to 2.7, making them very heavy.

Strength. Glass fiber has exceptionally high breaking strength and has been called the strongest fiber. Nevertheless, one of the major problems encountered in glass fabrics is their lack of flex abrasion resistance. They tend to break where creased and to wear at points where the fabric rubs against other objects.

Dimensional Stability and Resiliency. Glass has excellent dimensional stability but lacks resilience and stretch.

Absorbency. Glass fiber is completely nonabsorbent and, therefore, has no affinity for dyes. For best colorfastness color can be added to the molten glass before it is spun by incorporating ceramic pigment into the glass melt.

Heat and Electrical Conductivity. Glass fiber conducts neither heat nor electricity. For this reason, it is used in staple form in a variety of insulation materials.

Effect of Heat; Combustibility. The fiber is completely noncombustible. When held in a flame, the finish of the fabric will darken as the pigments and resins used in finishing are destroyed, but the fibers, yarns, and woven structure of the fabric will remain intact. Glass fiber softens at 700°C or 1,350°F or above.

Effect of Selected Conditions on Fiber

Chemical Reactivity. Acids do not generally affect glass fiber; however, bases can have a deleterious effect. Organic solvents do not affect the fiber.

Resistance to Insects, Microorganisms, Sunlight, and Aging. Glass fiber is attacked by neither mildew nor insect pests. Sunlight does not damage the fabric nor is it harmed by aging.

Uses

Except for special items of protective clothing in which glass fiber is one component, glass fiber has never been used for wearing apparel. If the ends of the fibers are broken, they scratch or irritate the skin. Also, glass fiber has poor resistance to abrasion, is not absorbent, and lacks stretch. At one time glass fiber was used fairly extensively in draperies, curtains, lampshades, and window shades; however, at the present time, except for some institutional curtain and drapery products, the only significant applications of glass fibers for home use are in vertical blinds. The glass fiber batting material used for insulation in buildings is not classified by the glass fiber industry as a textile fiber.

Today, glass fiber is most widely used for products in aerospace, construction, the electrical industries, transportation, recreation, packaging, and filtration for insulation purposes. Yarns made from glass fiber are used for reinforcement and in the growing field of composites (Figure 13.1). (Chapter 19 gives a detailed discussion of such fiber-reinforced composites.)

Glass fibers also find applications in the field of fiber optics. Scientists learned that light could be transmitted over long distances through fine strands of transparent materials. These beams of light can be used to carry messages. Glass fiber has proved to be a particularly effective carrier. The strands of glass fiber that form the light-transmitting core of fiber optic cable are surrounded by a sheath that keeps the light from dispersing or straying (Figure 13.2).

Figure 13.1

Strands of glass fiber roving are woven into fabric that is used in reinforced plastic boats, containers, parts for trucks and recreational vehicles, home furnishings equipment, sporting goods, and corrosion-resistant products such as storage tanks. Photograph courtesy of PPG Industries, Glass Group.

Figure 13.2

In an optical fiber electrical signals are converted into light that can be transmitted by the optical fiber; the light can then be converted back into an electrical signal. Cladding helps keep most of the light inside of the fiber by reflecting light waves toward its center as they pass through it. Reprinted courtesy of The National Science Foundation.

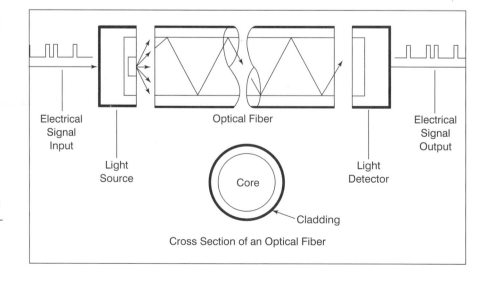

Electrical Signal Input

Light Source

Optical Fiber

Light Detector

Electrical Signal Output

Core

Cladding

Cross Section of an Optical Fiber

Other Inorganic Fibers

Several other types of fibers have been developed for use in the aerospace and aircraft industries. These fibers are not used for commercial textile products for the home or in garments. They include the following:

1. *Aluminum silicate fibers.* Used in high-temperature insulation, filters. Spinning is similar to that of glass fiber.
2. *Ceramic fibers.* Used in the aerospace program or in aircraft. A modification of the viscose process is used to spin a fiber with a proportion of cellulose and of metal oxides. The cellulose is burned off to yield ceramic fiber.
3. *High-purity silica fibers.* Produced by purifying glass of specified composition through an acid leaching treatment, the resulting fibers are composed of 99 percent silica. These fibers will withstand very high temperatures.
4. *Silicon carbide fibers.* These fibers serve as reinforcement materials in resins, some ceramics, and metals.
5. *Boron fibers.* Made by depositing boron vapor onto fine tungsten wire, these fibers have uses in reinforcement, especially of aluminum. Cloth made in part from boron fibers was used in the drill stems for collecting lunar rock samples during NASA's moon mission.

Metallic Fibers

Metallic fibers were the first manufactured fibers. Gold and silver "threads" have long been used to decorate costly garments, tapestries, carpets, and the like. These threads were made either by cutting thin sheets of metal into narrow strips and weaving these strips into decorative patterns or by winding a thin filament of metal around a central core of another material.

Examination of historic costumes and fabrics reveals the disadvantage of using metals in this way. Except for gold, the metals tended to tarnish and become discolored. Yarns were relatively weak and broke readily. Durability was limited, and, of course, the cost of precious metals was very high.

Fashion fabrics today make use of a wide variety of metallic fibers that are both inexpensive and decorative. Other metallic fibers are used for purely practical purposes. Many decorative metallic fibers are made in the form of large monofilaments. These are discussed later under the heading of "Monofilament Yarns" in chapter 15.

Forming fibers from metal is difficult; therefore, metal fibers are largely limited to those made from steel (carbon, stainless, and low-alloy types), aluminum, iron, nickel, and cobalt-based superalloys. These particular metals lend themselves most readily to fiber formation. The manufacture of fibers from metal is usually done by one of three methods. A rod of metal may be used as the starting material, and from this rod fine-dimension metal wire is drawn to form fibers. Another method begins with the formation of metal foil that is sheared or slit into fibers. Metal as a substance does not lend itself well to the traditional method of forming manufactured fibers from a liquid melt; however, research has resulted in the development of some specialized techniques by which this can be done.

Most applications of metal fibers are for aerospace and other industrial applications where such products as filters, seals, abrasives, and insulation are used. The automotive industry uses metal fibers in products such as tires and brake linings. Some limited applications of metal fibers are made in consumer products, particularly in certain household textile products. Superfine filaments of stainless steel and aluminum are made and are added to fabrics in any one of a number of ways. Sometimes metal fibers are used as the core of yarns, sometimes they are wrapped around other core yarns, and sometimes they are used alone. Steel and copper and aluminum fibers are being blended into some industrial carpets where they cut down on static electricity buildup and have the side effect of decreasing flammability. As the heat of a fire increases, the metallic fibers conduct some of the heat away from the fire, thereby decreasing the heat of the flame. This tends to slow the rate of burning or to lower temperatures below the kindling point. Other projected end uses for metal fibers include upholstery, blankets, and work clothing and in blends with polyester for hospital gowns.

Carbon Fibers

Carbon fibers, like other fibers discussed in this chapter, find their major applications in industrial uses. Within the industry the terms *carbon fibers* and *graphite fibers* are sometimes used interchangeably, but graphite fibers are actually a special type of carbon fiber that has a crystal or *graphitic* structure unique to true graphite fibers (Figure 13.3).

Manufacture

Carbon fibers are made either from rayon or polyacryonitrile (PAN) fibers or from pitch, coal tar, or petroleum-tar base material. Rayon or PAN fibers are carbonized at temperatures over 1,000°C, leaving only carbon atoms. On further heating to 2,500°C, a crystalline graphite structure develops. Similar processing is given to pitch, which can be formed into fibrous materials. Because the raw material is less expensive, substantial quantities of industrial and general grade materials are manufactured from pitch.

Properties of Carbon Fibers

Carbon fibers are black in color, with a silky appearance. They have a stiff hand, possess high strength, and are light in weight. The high tenacity (>10 g/d) and modulus are due to the crystalline structure of the fiber.

Figure 13.3

Photos of carbon fibers in a composite structure taken through an electron scanning microscope: (a) cross section and (b) longitudinal view. Photographs courtesy of the British Textile Technology Group (BTTG).

(a)   (b)

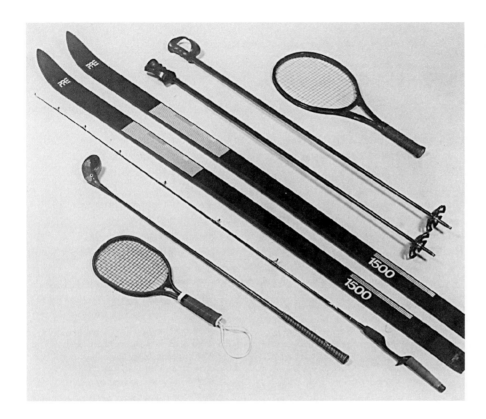

A variety of sports equipment that is made using graphite fibers. Photograph courtesy of Hercules Aerospace Products Group.

Uses

Carbon fibers are most often used as a reinforcing material in plastic composites. The high strength of the fiber increases the toughness of the composite material, and the black color is not a detriment because the fibers are embedded in the matrix. Carbon fiber reinforced composites are used in lightweight structures for aircraft and space-craft and as brake discs for jet airplanes. Carbon fibers see use in such diverse areas as sporting goods (Figure 13.4), the construction industry, the automotive industry, and medicine. For example, the spinnaker pole of the yacht *Intrepid* contained 23 miles of graphite yarn. Golf club handles have been made with carbon fibers, and tennis racquets and fishing poles are made of carbon. Carbon fibers are used for the reinforcement of bridges and buildings, and graphite materials have been used for implantation to replace bone. Many industrial composites use carbon fibers in their structure.

Summary

Inorganic and carbon fibers have little use in ready-to-wear and household textiles. Even though they are used in sporting goods and a wide array of industrial textiles, consumers are generally not aware of them. These fibers, however, do demonstrate clearly the enormous range of textile fiber uses in a technological society.

Review Questions

1. What properties of glass fiber prevent it from being used in wearing apparel?
2. Describe the ways in which fibers can be formed from metal.

3. Identify at least three uses of carbon fibers and explain which properties make carbon fibers a good choice for these uses.

Recommended Readings

Budnelskii, G. A., V. S. Matveev, and M. E. Kozamakov. 1994. Carbon fibers and materials based on viscose fibers. *Fibre Chemistry* (May): 360.

Demodaran, S. et al. 1990. Chemical and physical aspects of the formation of carbon fibers from PAN-based precursors. *Journal of the Textile Institute* 81 (4): 384.

Fiber glass: a different breed of fiber. 1990. *Textile World* 140 (February): 70.

Ford, J. E. 1988. Metalized textiles. *Textiles* 17 (3): 58.

Glass fibers and materials based on them. 1994. *Fibre Chemistry,* September, 48.

High-performance carbon fibres. 1975. *Textiles* 4 (January): 2.

How fiber optics works. 1988. *High Technology Business* 8 (February): 38.

Huang, Y., and R. J. Young. 1994. Microstructure and mechanical properties of pitch-based carbon fibers. *Journal of Materials Science* 29: 4027.

Prescott, R. 1989. Carbon fibers. *Modern plastics encyclopedia* 66 (October): 198.

Weddell, J. K. 1990. Continuous ceramic fibers. *Journal of the Textile Institute* 84 (4): 333.

Wirtner, M. 1989. Ceramic fibers. *Modern plastics encyclopedia* 66 (October): 199.

OTHER MANUFACTURED AND BICOMPONENT FIBERS

I n addition to the manufactured fibers discussed in earlier chapters, there are other generic types of fibers that have somewhat limited use or represent relatively recent developments in the technology of manufactured fiber production. These include a number of synthetic fiber types that are manufactured either in the United States or abroad.

Saran

Saran is a textile fiber of limited use. It is defined by the FTC as "a manufactured fiber in which the fiber-forming substance is any long-chain synthetic polymer composed of at least 80 percent by weight of vinylidene chloride units ($-CH_2-CCl_2-$)." Introduced by Dow Chemical Company in 1941, saran is now made in the United States by Pittsfield Weaving Company. It is a stiff, nondrapable fiber with specialized uses in agricultural and industrial fabrics. Upholstery fabrics for deck chairs and garden furniture have been made from saran.

Production and Processing

The molten vinylidene chloride/vinyl chloride copolymer is forced through the spinneret, air spun into cold air, quenched in water, and stretched. Saran fibers can be delustered and/or spun dyed. This polymer, extruded as a thin film, forms the plastic wrap used for the storage of food.

Properties of Saran

Physical Appearance

In microscopic view, filaments of saran have a round cross section. The longitudinal view shows a smooth surface. Saran can also be produced in flat and oval shapes.

Other Physical Properties

Specific Gravity. A high-density fiber (specific gravity is higher than most other synthetics at 1.70), the weight and inflexibility of saran eliminate it from use in apparel fabrics.

Strength. Saran is generally made as a large diameter monofilament, so that its strength is very good. It also has excellent tear and abrasion resistance.

Elasticity and Resilience. Fibers made of saran have excellent elastic recovery and are quite resilient.

Absorbency and Moisture Regain. Saran is nonabsorbent. The moisture regain is less than 0.1 percent.

Dimensional Stability. If saran is not exposed to excessive temperatures, its dimensional stability is good.

Heat and Electrical Conductivity. Because of the low heat and electrical conductivity of saran, it may be used for insulation purposes.

Effect of Heat; Combustibility. Saran burns very slowly if placed in a direct flame. The fiber is self-extinguishing after removal of the flame. The melting point of the fiber is relatively low: 335°F.

Effect of Selected Conditions on Fiber

Chemical Reactivity. Neither acids nor bases affect the fiber adversely to any extent.

Resistance to Insects, Microorganisms, and Sunlight. Saran is not attacked by moths, mildew, or bacteria. Sunlight resistance is very good, although some discoloration may take place after long exposure to the sun.

Uses

Upholstery fabrics made from saran have been used for public conveyances, deck chairs, garden furniture, and the like. Its low absorbency, good sunlight and weather resistance, and strength and abrasion resistance make saran appropriate for this use.

Agricultural fabrics take advantage of the weather and flame-resistant characteristics of saran. Such fabrics are used to provide shade for growing plants. The chemical resistance of the fiber results in a variety of industrial uses. Saran grille fabrics are used in sound systems because they distort sound less than other materials do. Saran in combination with other fibers, such as modacrylics, is used for making drapery fabrics that are flame resistant.

Furniture with saran webbing can be cleaned easily with soap and water. Because the fiber is nonabsorbent, these items will dry quickly. They do not stain readily.

Generic Fiber Names Added In 1986

Sulfar

Sulfar is defined by the FTC as "a manufactured fiber in which the fiber-forming substance is a long synthetic polysulfide in which at least 85% of the sulfide (—S—) linkages are attached directly to two (2) aromatic rings." This fiber is described as having tenacity, elongation, modulus, elastic recovery, boiling water shrinkage, and moisture regain that are satisfactory for textile applications. Its melting point is very high (545°F, 285°C); chemical resistance is described as excellent.

Suitable applications for the fiber include filter bags for filtration of high-temperature materials, woven and nonwoven filter fabrics for gas and liquids, paper-maker felts, and protective clothing.

Manufacturers suggest that sulfar has advantages over competing high-temperature–resisting, chemically resistant fibers in that it is less expensive and easy to process.

Sulfar fibers are manufactured under the trademark name of Ryton® by Amoco Fabrics and Fibers Company and under the trademark PPS® by Shakespeare Monofilaments. Albany International Monofilaments and Johnson Filaments also manufacture sulfar fibers.

PBI

PBI is defined by the FTC as "a manufactured fiber in which the fiber-forming substance is a long-chain aromatic polymer having reoccurring imidazole groups as an integral part of the polymer chain." The letters PBI are an abbreviation of polybenzimidazole.

PBI entered commercial production in May 1983. The largest present end use of PBI is in civilian and military protective apparel. It is being used as a successful alternative to asbestos in protective gloves, gaskets, and packing materials in industrial applications and to construct fire-blocking material in places such as aircraft (Figure 14.1).

The fiber is nonflammable in air, emits little or no toxic gases or smoke up to temperatures of 1,040°F, and has excellent resistance to acids, organic solvents, and fuels. The fiber is currently produced by Hoechst Celanese in staple form.

Generic Fibers Not Currently in U.S. Production

The production of novoloid, vinal, vinyon, and nytril fibers has been discontinued in the United States. Imported items made from vinal and vinyon can sometimes be purchased, but novoloid, a noncombustible high technology fiber, and nytril, a soft apparel fiber with a very low melting point, are no longer being manufactured.

Figure 14.1

PBI blends are used extensively in applications such as firefighters' turnout gear (shown here) and industrial protective clothing. Photograph courtesy of Hoechst Celanese Corporation.

Vinal

The FTC calls vinal "a manufactured fiber in which the fiber-forming substance is any long-chain synthetic polymer composed of at least 50 percent by weight of vinyl alcohol units (—CH_2—CHOH—) and in which the total of the vinyl alcohol units and any one or more of the various acetal units is at least 85 percent by weight of the fiber."

Most of the development of vinal has taken place in Japan. The fiber has a melting point close to that of nylon 6 (around 425°F) and very good chemical resistance and is especially resistant to rot-producing microorganisms.

The use of vinal fibers is largely in industrial applications, although some blends of vinal fiber with cotton, rayon, or silk have been used abroad. Vinal fibers are manufactured in China, Germany, and Japan. Imported apparel, especially scarves, made from 100 percent vinal or vinal blends can sometimes be purchased in the United States. In some countries vinal fibers are called polyvinyl alcohol fibers. A water-soluble form of vinal fibers has found specialty end uses discussed later in this chapter under "Soluble Fibers".

Vinyon

Vinyon fibers are used most frequently in industrial applications where their high resistance to chemicals is useful. Vinyon has a low melting point and is, therefore, useful as a bonding agent in nonwoven fabric construction.

The FTC defines vinyon as "a manufactured fiber in which the fiber-forming substance is any long-chain synthetic polymer composed of at least 85 percent by weight of vinyl chloride units (—CH$_2$—CHCl—)."

The low melting point of vinyon has prevented its use to any extent in apparel in the United States. (The fiber is combined with vinal, however, in making the biconstituent fiber Cordelan®, discussed later in this chapter.) Vinyon has high resistance to chemicals. Major uses are as a bonding agent in industrial nonwoven applications and for tea bags and other specialty uses. Vinyon is manufactured in Japan.

Fibers for Industrial or Specialty Uses

The FTC has discouraged the proliferation of generic fiber categories. For this reason, fibers may not have been given generic designation if it has been deemed that "disclosure of the fiber content is not necessary for the protection of the ultimate consumer."[1] Some such fibers, use of which is limited to industrial and/or specialized uses and those which have not been extensively commercialized, are discussed in the following section.

Soluble Fibers

Fibers that will dissolve are useful for rather specialized applications in the textile industry. Alginates, regenerated fibers made from seaweed, are soluble. In a preliminary step during manufacture, a soluble form of vinal fiber is created. Nonsoluble vinals or polyvinyl alcohol (PVA) fibers are formed after additional treatments.

Production of alginates reportedly has stopped in the United Kingdom, where their manufacture had been concentrated. PVA fibers, manufactured in Japan, seem to have superseded the alginates in most uses.

Soluble yarns of PVA may be used as "support" yarns in fabric constructions where open, sheer, or lacelike effects are desired but are not attainable through normal weaving processes. The fabric is woven and then laundered, causing the soluble yarns to dissolve, leaving only the insoluble yarns in a lacy, open pattern.

Soluble yarns may also be used when wool socks are manufactured in a continuous "string" with a few rows of stitches between the toe of one sock and the top of the next. The socks are cut apart, and when subjected to finishing processes, the remaining soluble threads dissolve out, leaving a smoothly finished edge. Only hot water is required to dissolve polyvinyl alcohol fibers, whereas alginates must be laundered in water with dilute sodium carbonate or sodium phosphate added.

---

1. Section 12, Part II (b) of the Textile Fiber Products Identification Act.

Fluorocarbon Fibers

Polymers containing fluorine, based on the substance called polytetrafluoroethylene (PTFE), have been used in some textile applications. The polymeric material may be formed into fibers by the emulsion spinning process (see page 129) or may be formed into sheets, extruded in molded form, or applied as a coating to other substances.

Consumers may know Teflon®, a fluorocarbon manufactured by DuPont as a coating for cooking utensils. Teflon® fluorocarbon polymer is also made into a thin microporous membrane. This membrane with very tiny openings or pores is used in making Gore-Tex® fabrics, which have wide use in outdoor apparel. (See page 393 for a discussion of Gore-Tex® fabrics.)

Fluoropolymers other than Teflon® may differ somewhat in chemical composition but have generally similar properties and can be used in comparable applications. All have excellent chemical resistance, are usable over a wide temperature range, resist abrasion, and are nonabsorbent. Industrial uses include pump and valve packing, gaskets, filtration materials, bearings, and office copy equipment.

Other Fibers

A number of other fibers should be mentioned briefly. These fibers either have quite specialized uses or are available in the United States on a rather limited basis. They include:

Polyetheretherketone (PEEK) fiber is a heat-resistant fiber that is generally used for engineering applications. It is manufactured usually either as monofilaments or tow in the United States by Albany International Monofilaments, Ketema Inc., and Shakespeare Monofilaments.

Polyimide fibers, manufactured by the Austrian firm Lenzing A. G., are used for flame-retardant, high-temperature applications.

Chlorofibre, a synthetic fiber made up of at least 50 percent or more of polyvinyl chloride (PVC), is manufactured in France and used for apparel and household textiles, some of which may be imported into the United States. Dry cleaners have reported problems with shrinkage from the heat of steam finishing during dry cleaning of these fabrics. They wash well but cannot be dry-cleaned with chlorinated solvents. Although they resist burning, they soften and melt at relatively low temperatures. Tenacity is medium; elongation is high.

Inidex, a fiber developed by Courtaulds, is described as a cross-linked polyacrylate fiber that does not burn, melt, or give an afterglow. It is suggested for uses in nonwoven fabrics in areas where poisoning by smoke and toxic fumes might be a hazard.

Bicomponent Fibers

As the technology for producing manufactured fibers has become more highly developed, manufacturers have turned to increasingly sophisticated techniques for creating new fibers. Not only are new generic fibers being created but also different polymers or variants of the same polymer can be combined into a single fiber to take advantage of the special characteristics of each polymer. Such fibers are known as bicomponent fibers. ASTM defines a bicomponent fiber as "a fiber consisting of two polymers which are chemically different, physically different, or both."[2]

Bicomponent fibers can be made from two variants of the same generic fiber (for example, two types of nylon, two types of acrylic) or from two generically different fibers (for example, nylon and polyester or nylon and spandex). The latter are called *bicomponent bigeneric fibers.*

Components in bicomponent fibers may be arranged either side by side or as a sheath core. In making a *side-by-side bicomponent fiber,* the process requires that the different polymers be fed to the spinneret orifice together so that they exit from the spinneret opening, side by side. (See Figures 14.2 and 14.3.)

Sheath-core bicomponent fibers require that one component be completely surrounded by the other, so that the polymer is generally fed into the spinneret, as shown in Figure 14.2. Variation in the shape of the orifice that contains the inner core can produce fibers with different behavioral characteristics.

Most bicomponent fibers are made to provide stretch or crimp to the fiber. Each of the polymers used in the bicomponent fiber has slightly different characteristics. Often one polymer is made to shrink in heat or chemical treatment more than the other, which pulls the fiber into a permanent crimp. If sufficient crimp is provided or

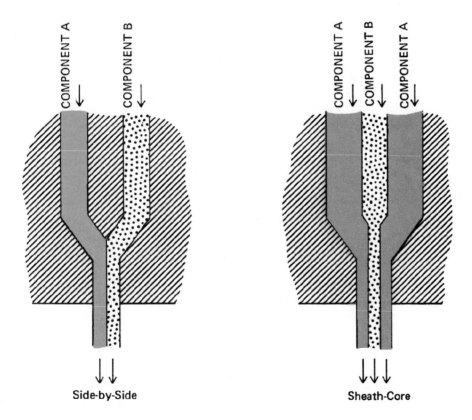

Figure 14.2

Formation of bicomponent fibers.

Side-by-Side   Sheath-Core

---

2. Reprinted, with permission, from the Annual Book of ASTM Standards (1994), copyright 1994 American Society for Testing and Materials, 1916 Race Street, Philadelphia, PA 19103.

Figure 14.3

Photomicrograph of cross section of Monvelle® biconstituent fiber. The spandex portion of the fiber shows as black; the nylon is transparent. This fiber is no longer manufactured. The photograph shows clearly how different constituents can be combined. Photomicrograph courtesy of Monsanto, The Chemical Group, Fibers Division.

if the fiber is elastic, the bicomponent fiber may also have increased stretchability. Other uses for bicomponent fibers have been suggested. For example, components with different melting points could be used to bond fibers together in the construction of nonwoven fabrics. When heat is applied, one fiber softens, serving as a glue to hold the other fiber in place. A less absorbent core fiber could be sheathed in a more absorbent fiber to increase comfort or increase dyeability.

Another type of bicomponent fiber is the *matrix fiber* in which one polymer is dispersed within the other before they are extruded. Figure 14.4 illustrates the structure of a matrix fiber. Few commercial matrix fibers have been manufactured. One, Cordelan®, a Japanese fire-retardant fiber recommended for children's sleepwear, was distributed in the United States for a time but is no longer available.

Under the TFPIA those products made from bicomponent bigeneric fibers must have listed on their labels the generic fibers present. Constituents are to be listed in the order of "predominance by weight" and must state the "respective percentages of such components by weight." The ruling goes on to state, "If the components of such fibers are of a matrix-fibril configuration, the term 'matrix-fibril' or 'matrix fiber' may be used."

Figure 14.4

Longitude and cross section of matrix fiber structure. The black areas represent fibrils of one generic fiber; the second fiber is represented by the white.

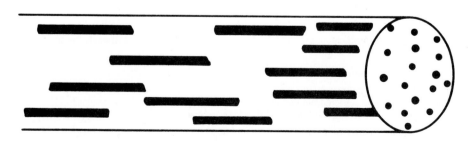

The label of a Cordelan® fiber product might, therefore, read as follows:

100% matrix fiber
(50% vinal, 50% vinyon)

Bicomponent fibers made from the same generic fiber are not covered by this regulation. They are composed of the same generic fiber type throughout, even though the different types of the same polymer may each exhibit somewhat different characteristics.

The Future of Manufactured Fiber Technology

Using the concept of fiber generations introduced in chapter 6 as a platform from which to look into the future, one can see that "synthetic fibers of the third generation are not simply alternatives to natural fibers as were synthetic fibers of the second generation" (Hongu and Phillips 1990, 3). The future is likely to bring not only modifications of existing generic fibers that will enhance fiber aesthetics and performance for the general consumer but also a wide array of high technology and super fibers with ever expanding applications in fields ranging from biotechnology to space exploration. As protecting the environment becomes increasingly important, fibers made from recycled materials and environmentally friendly processes are likely to thrive. Products that now seem exotic, such as fibers that protect the wearer from the damaging ultraviolet rays of the sun, absorb perspiration during exercise, or release perfumed oils, will become commonplace. As the technology for producing manufactured fibers continues to be refined, consumers will find that both visible and invisible textile fibers are a part of every aspect of their lives, often in places that they least suspect!

Reference

Hongu, T., and G. O. Phillips. 1990. *New fibers.* New York: Ellis Horwood.

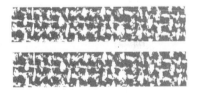

Review Questions

1. Which of the following fibers are consumers likely to find in apparel? Which in household products? Which ones are consumers unlikely to encounter in products they purchase and why?

saran	fluorocarbon fibers
sulfar	PEEK
PBI	polyimide
vinal	chlorofibre
vinyon	inidex

2. Define the following terms, and explain how and why these fibers might be used.

bicomponent fibers	side-by-side bicomponent fibers
bicomponent bigeneric fibers	matrix fibers
sheath-core bicomponent fibers	

3. What are some uses for soluble fibers?

Recommended Readings

Collier, B. J., et al. 1993. Adhesion promotion in rayon/nylon skin/core bigeneric fibers. *Clothing and Textiles Research Journal* 11 (Summer): 18.

Ford, J. E. 1989. Chlorofibre. *Textiles* 18 (2): 30.

Mukhopadhyay, S. K. 1993. High performance fibers. *Textile Progress* 25 (3/4): 1.

Smith, C. 1988. High performance polymers. *Chemtech* 18 (May): 290.

MAKING FIBERS INTO YARNS

I f fibers are to be woven or knitted into cloth, they must be formed into long continuous strands called *yarns.* Fiber for yarns is supplied either in long filaments or short staple lengths. The type of yarn chosen for a fabric affects its appearance, durability, and hand and draping characteristics. Yarn construction can serve either to enhance or detract from the inherent qualities of the fiber from which the yarn is made. The term *spinning* is generally used to describe the conversion of fibers into yarn.

Steps in the Historical Development of Spinning

Hand Spinning

Before the invention of manufactured fibers, all yarns except those made from silk had to be spun from short, staple fibers. At first these staple fibers were twisted together by hand. A simple experiment will easily demonstrate how this can be done. Take a small bunch of cotton from a roll of absorbent cotton. Pull off a long strand and begin to twist the fibers in one direction. You will soon find that you have a rather short, coarse, but recognizable, cotton yarn. Rolling the fiber between the hand and the leg is another primitive method of spinning. Hand twisting by an experienced spinner can produce an acceptable yarn. Ancient textiles have been found in Peruvian graves that were woven from hand-twisted cotton yarns of excellent quality.

Before fibers could be twisted into yarns, some attempt had to be made to bring them into a more parallel alignment. This could be done by hand by running fingers through a bundle of fibers in order to straighten the fibers somewhat. Tools were designed to do the job more efficiently, and hand spinners still use an ancient device called a *carder,* a pair of wooden paddles on which is mounted a leather piece set with bent wire hooks. The process of straightening fibers before spinning, done by hand or machine, is called *carding* (Figure 15.1).

A small quantity of fiber was placed on one carder. The second carder was laid against the first, and each was pulled in the opposite direction. This process was repeated several times until the fibers were roughly parallel and any extraneous material had fallen out. The carded fibers were put aside for spinning.

Fibers could be made more completely parallel by a further step called *combing.* Combing was generally reserved for fibers of longer lengths, and the process, using a device shaped like a comb, pulled the fibers into alignment.

After the fiber had been carded or carded and combed, the actual twisting together of the fibers was begun. The spinner who twisted fibers together by hand needed a place to put the completed yarns. The solution was to wind them onto a stick. In time, the stick itself became a tool for spinning. By notching the stick to hold the thread and by adding a weight (called the *whorl*) to the end of the stick, a spindle was made. With the whorl to provide momentum, the spinner could use the stick to help in twisting the yarn. The spinner stood erect and held the mass of fiber under the left arm, leaving both hands free to work. A long, untwisted strand of fiber was fed to the spindle by the left hand. With the right hand, the spinner gave the stick a twist and let it fall, whirling, toward the ground. The momentum and weight of the falling spindle twisted the fibers into a continuous yarn. The right hand was used to control the quantity of fiber feeding onto the spindle. When the spindle reached the ground, the spinner bent over, picked up the spindle, and wrapped the newly made yarn around the stick. Pulling out a new bunch of fiber, the spinner twisted the end of the unspun fiber to the end of the completed yarn and began the process again.

For better control of spinning, bundles of fiber were mounted on a long staff. The staff also prevented the fibers from becoming entangled. The Old English word for a bundle of flax was *dis,* and so the staff on which the fiber was placed came to be known as the *distaff* (Figure 15.2).

So closely were women associated with the tasks of spinning that many of these terms have taken on interesting connotations in modern language usage. The spinning was often done by the unmarried girls and adult women, and so the term *spinster* has become a synonym for an unmarried woman. The distaff was used almost exclusively by women, and in time the term has come to connote women's activities or interests.

For many thousands of years, this hand method of spinning was the only way in which yarn could be made. A major improvement in this technique originated in India when the action of a wheel was added to the spinning of the yarn. The Indian *charka,* or spinning wheel, seems to have been invented sometime between A.D. 500 and A.D. 1000 (Born 1939). Since the production of cotton was paramount in India, this wheel was devised to spin cotton. The spinning wheel did not come into wide use in Europe until the fourteenth century, and it is thought to have been carried to Spain by way of the Arab countries that occupied Spain until the late 1400s. The original Indian wheel that had been used for cotton was small and close to the ground. A modification of this wheel that allowed the spin-

Figure 15.1

Woman uses hand carders to card wool before spinning. The uncarded fiber is placed in a basket to the right of the picture, and rolls of carded fiber are seen on top of a basket to the left.

ner to stand was made in Europe, but the same basic wheel, with minor modifications, was used for spinning flax, cotton, or silk. Wool, however, required a bigger wheel, and the wool spinning wheel was always made with a much enlarged wheel. (See Figure 15.3.)

With the earliest European wheels, the spinner had to move back and forth in front of the wheel, turning it first in one direction to spin, then in the opposite direction to wind the yarn. Modifications of design produced a treadle mechanism for turning the wheel, and this made it possible for the spinner to sit at the wheel to spin. Another advance came in the sixteenth century with the invention of a "flyer and detachable bobbin" mechanism. This device allowed the simultaneous spinning and winding of yarn onto the bobbin, thus eliminating the interruptions occasioned by the older operation in which (1) the yarn was spun, (2) the spinning was interrupted to wind the thread, and then (3) the spinning was begun anew.

Throughout the development of all these processes, power was always supplied by the spinner, either through hand or foot and hand motions.

Mechanized Spinning

The invention of the spinning wheel may be thought of as the first mechanization of spinning. In 1741 John Wyatt and Lewis Paul built the first of a series of machines for spinning cotton yarn. Wyatt and Paul used a roller-drafting principle; that is, they fed a long strand of carded or combed fibers through a series of rollers. Each set of rollers moved at a different speed, thereby drawing out or elongating the strand of fibers. This strand of fibers was called the *roving*. From the roller the strand of fibers was stretched to a bobbin-and-flyer twisting mechanism, like that of a spinning wheel. Arkwright used this same principle in 1769 when he constructed a spinning machine called the "water frame," which was given this name because it was operated by water power.

Figure 15.2

Hand spinning with spindle and distaff. The woman holds the distaff under her left arm, draws fibers from the bundle tied to the distaff, and spins fibers into a yarn by lowering the spindle with a spinning motion. Spun yarn is wrapped around the spindle as it is formed.

Figure 15.3

Spinning wheels. The wheel on the left is a flax wheel. On the ground under the wheel stands a device for winding skeins of yarn and one for hackling (carding) flax fibers. The wheel on the right is a wool wheel.

WHEEL, CARD, AND REEL.   WOOL WHEEL.

A second spinning machine was invented by James Hargreaves sometime in the 1760s. Utilizing the basic principles of the spinning wheel, Hargreaves's "spinning jenny" made eight yarns at the same time. A later patent shows that the number of yarns that could be made was increased to sixteen, and eventually the jenny was modified to make as many as one hundred yarns.

Both the spinning jenny and the Arkwright machine had certain limitations. Yarns made on these machines were not as strong as hand-spun yarns and were, therefore, not as suitable for use in the warp where greater tension was placed on each one.

Samuel Crompton combined the Arkwright machine and the spinning jenny into one basic machine that used both rotating rollers in drawing out the yarn and a moving carriage that provided the twist needed to make strong, fine yarns. This machine, known as the spinning mule, was the basic machine for producing cotton yarn in England until well into the twentieth century.

Although each of these methods made it possible for the quantity of yarn produced by one spinner to be enormously increased, they still required supervisory personnel to keep the machines operating. In about 1830 a device was developed that could be added to the spinning mule to make its operation completely automatic. These first machines were made for spinning cotton yarns, but the spinning jenny and subsequent modifications of this machine allowed the mechanization of wool spinning as well.

At about the same time that the automatic spinning mule was developed, an American inventor named John Thorpe devised a ring spinning machine. This machine has been used in the United States since about 1830 and is a basic machine used for spinning cotton and other staple fibers today.

The most recent development in the spinning of yarns from staple fibers is a process known as *open-end spinning*. In this method of spinning, air suction takes the fibers through a spinning tube in which twist is imparted to the fiber.

Types of Yarn

Filament Yarns

Filament yarns are made from long, continuous strands of fiber. *Monofilament yarns,* those made from a single filament, find limited use in nylon hosiery (where an exceptionally sheer fabric is wanted), in some open-work decorative fabrics, and in saran fabric webbing (used in some lightweight beach or casual furniture) as well as in a variety of industrial uses. Monofilament yarns can be made by the extrusion of large single filaments from spinnerets. The slit film technique in which a film of synthetic polymer is cut into strips will also make single filaments, each of which can be used as a monofilament yarn.

More commonly, many filaments are joined to form *multifilament yarns.* Multifilament yarns can be made more cohesive by twisting them together loosely or more tightly. The amount of twist together with the characteristics of the fibers (luster, handle, cross-sectional shape, etc.) will determine the appearance and feel of the yarn. For example, a loosely twisted smooth filament yarn made from a bright fiber would be characterized by marked luster, resistance to pilling, and a smooth surface.

Sometimes filament yarns are put through an additional process called *texturing.* Texturing modifies the feel and bulk of filament yarns.

Staple Yarns

Being short, staple fibers must be held together by some means in order to be formed into a long, continuous yarn. Although the multiple processes required to make staple yarn add significantly to the cost of the yarn, the aesthetic qualities such as comfort, warmth, softness, and appearance make these yarns highly desirable in many products. Natural fibers, except for silk, are all staple fibers. Silk and manufactured fibers can be cut or broken into staple fibers, so that it is possible to spin any natural or manufactured fiber into a staple yarn.

In addition to identifying yarns as being made from either filament or staple fibers, yarns are also classified based on a number of other characteristics. Authorities often differ when they define yarn types. The following are the most common classifications.

Yarns Classified by Number of Parts

Yarns that have been classified by the number of parts they possess are divided into *single, ply,* and *cord yarns.* A single yarn is made from a group of filament or staple fibers twisted together. If a single yarn is untwisted, it will separate into fibers. A single yarn might be identified as either a single yarn of staple fibers or a single yarn of filament fibers.

Ply yarns are made by twisting together two or more single yarns. If ply yarns are untwisted, they will divide into two or more single yarns, which, in turn, can be untwisted into fibers. Each single yarn twisted into a ply yarn is called a *ply.*

Cord yarns are made by twisting together two or more ply yarns. Cord yarns can be identified by untwisting the yarn to form two or more ply yarns. Cord yarns are used in making ropes, sewing thread, and cordage and are woven as decorative yarns into some heavyweight novelty fabrics. (See Figure 15.4.)

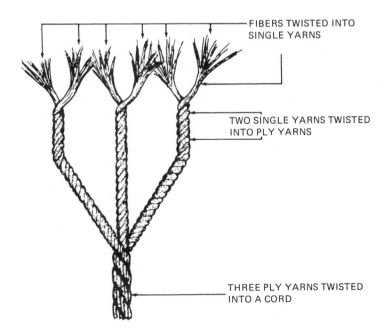

FIBERS TWISTED INTO SINGLE YARNS

TWO SINGLE YARNS TWISTED INTO PLY YARNS

THREE PLY YARNS TWISTED INTO A CORD

Figure 15.4

Single, ply, and cord yarns.

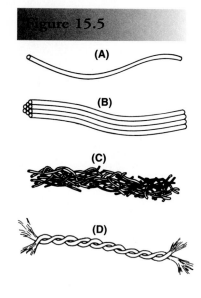

Yarns depicted are: (a) monofilament—solid single strand of unlimited length, (b) multifilament—many continuous filaments, (c) staple—many short fibers twisted together, (d) two-ply—two single yarns twisted together. Reprinted by permission from B. C. Goswami, J. G. Martindale, and F. L. Scardino, *Textile Yarns: Technology, Structure, and Applications* (New York: Wiley, 1977), 2. Copyright 1977 by John Wiley & Sons, Inc.

Yarns Classified by Similarity of Parts

Simple yarns are those yarns with uniform size and regular surface. They have varying degrees of twist, ranging from loose to moderate, tight or hard twist. Single, ply, and cord yarns can all be simple yarns if their components are uniform in size and have a regular surface. When one strand of fibers is twisted together evenly, it is classified as a simple single yarn. Two simple, single yarns twisted together create a simple ply yarn. (See Figure 15.5.)

Yarns made to create interesting decorative effects in the fabrics into which they are woven are known as *novelty yarns*. Some authors also call these yarns *complex yarns*. Novelty yarns can be single, ply, or cord, staple or filament.

In the industry novelty yarns tend to be referred to as *fancy yarns*. Terminology identifying these yarns is confusing. A Saurer Corporation (manufacturers of spinning equipment) spokesperson commented on the difficulties in a 1982 presentation, saying "it is most difficult to find the correct terminology, due to the fact that, say, five twisting specialists may have about seven terms for the same yarn alone." The following list of terms and their definitions represent an attempt to define these terms as they appear to be accepted by most authorities.

1. BOUCLÉ YARN[1]

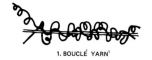

2. FLAKE, FLOCK, OR SEED YARN[1]

3. NUB, SPOT, OR KNOP YARN[1]

4. SLUB YARN[1]

1. *Bouclé yarns* are ply yarns. An effect yarn (so-called because it is used to create decorative effects) forms irregular loops around a base yarn or yarns. Another yarn binds or ties the effect yarn to the base. Some sources use the terms *loop* or *curl yarns* interchangeably with bouclé (Potter and Corbman 1967). *Ratiné yarns* are similar to bouclé in construction. The loops in ratiné yarns are spaced evenly along the base yarn.

2. *Flake, flock,* or *seed yarns* are made of loosely twisted yarns that are held in place either by a base yarn as it twists or by a third or binder yarn. These yarns are relatively weak and are used in the filling to achieve decorative surface effects.

3. *Nub yarns* are ply yarns in which an effect yarn is twisted around a base yarn a number of times in a small area to cause an enlarged bump or "nub." Sometimes a binder yarn is used to hold the nubs in place. The spacing of the nubs may be at regular or irregular intervals. Nubs are often different colors than the base yarn. The terms *knot, spot,* or *knop* are also applied to this type of yarn.

4. *Slub yarns* may be either ply or single yarns of staple fibers. The slub effect is created by varying the twist in the yarn, allowing areas of looser twist to be created. This produces a long, thick, soft area in the fabric called a slub. Slub yarns are irregular in diameter. The surface of fabrics woven with slub yarns shows these irregularities. Yarns made in this way have areas of varying twist, causing weaker areas in the yarn. In many fabrics slub yarns are placed in the filling direction where fabrics receive less strain. Slubs are the same color as

[1]Reprinted by permission from B. C. Goswami, J. G. Martindale, and F. L. Scardino, *Textile Yarns: Technology, Structure, and Applications* (New York: Wiley, 1977), 6. Copyright 1977 by John Wiley & Sons, Inc.

the rest of the yarn and cannot be pulled out of the fabric without damaging the structure of the fabric. Filament yarns can be spun with varying degrees of twist. These yarns also create a slubbed appearance in fabrics. Such filament yarns are known as *thick-and-thin yarns.*

5. *Snarl yarns* are ply yarns in which two or more yarns held at different tension are twisted together. The varying tension allows the effect yarn to form alternating unclosed loops on either side of the base yarn.

6. *Spiral,* or *corkscrew, yarns* are made of two plys, one soft and heavy, the other fine. The heavy yarn winds around the fine yarn.

7. *Chenille yarns* are made by a totally different process and require several steps in their preparation. First, leno-weave fabric is woven (see page 290). This fabric is cut into strips, and these strips, which have a soft pile on all sides, are used as yarns. These are not yarns in the traditional sense of twisted fiber but have been taken through a series of preliminary stages before being readied for use.

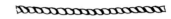

6. SPIRAL OR CORKSCREW YARN[1]

7. CHENILLE YARNS[1]

Core-Spun Yarns

Core-spun yarns do not fall into the category of novelty yarns, but are yarns made with a central core of one fiber around which is wrapped or twisted an exterior layer of another fiber. Core-spun yarns may be made with an elastomer core, such as spandex, covered by another fiber to produce a stretch yarn. Other core-spun yarns include sewing thread made with polyester cores and cotton cover. (See Figure 12.2, page 199.)

Thread

The terms *yarn* and *thread* are sometimes used interchangeably. However, a distinction should be made between yarns, which are fiber assemblies intended for weaving, knitting, or otherwise combining into a textile fabric, and sewing threads, which are used for sewing together sections of garments or other products.

Sewing threads may be made from one or more kinds of fiber. The most important threads have been those made from cotton or from a multifilament core of polyester covered with a cotton, rayon, or spun polyester. Except for yarns made from nylon or polyester, single yarns are not suitable for sewing threads; therefore, two or more plys are used.

To perform well, sewing threads must have high stability to bending, good strength, limited elongation, minimal shrinkage, and good abrasion resistance. Consider the stresses to which sewing thread is exposed. On the sewing machine, it must slide through various thread guides, it is hit back and forth under tension by the sewing machine needle, and it is permanently held in a bent position as it interlocks with the thread from the bobbin. Seams in tarpaulins, shoes, pants, and safety belts are subject to considerable tension and abrasion. If threads used shrink more or less than the fabrics in garments, puckering and wrinkling will appear at seam lines.

Home sewers purchase thread for their personal use, but 95 percent of the sewing thread produced goes to industry. The development of high-speed industrial sewing machines requires manufacturers of sewing thread to improve constantly the quality and performance of these products. A surface lubricating finish must be applied to industrial thread to minimize frictional heating of the sewing needle that could fuse or damage thermoplastic materials.

---

[1]Reprinted by permission from B. C. Goswami, J. G. Martindale, and F. L. Scardino, *Textile Yarns: Technology, Structure, and Applications* (New York: Wiley, 1977), 6. Copyright 1977 by John Wiley & Sons, Inc.

Effects of Twist

The degree of twist given to a yarn affects a number of aspects of its appearance, behavior, and durability. The bulkiness of yarns is related to twist. As a general rule, increasing twist decreases apparent yarn size. This can be demonstrated easily by taking a strand of loose fiber, such as absorbent cotton, and twisting it. The more one twists, the smaller in diameter the "yarn" will become.

Strength increases in staple yarns as twist increases up to a certain point. Beyond this point, the strength of the yarn begins to decrease, and yarns with exceptionally high, tight twist may become brittle and weak. Filament yarns are stronger untwisted.

Elasticity is increased if yarns are twisted very tightly. Very tightly twisted yarns are known as *crepe yarns,* which are generally very fine. The twist of crepe yarns is so high that they curl up unless they are held under tension, as they would be on a loom during weaving. A simple and easy test to identify crepe yarns is to unravel a yarn from the fabric and run it between the fingernails, thus removing the tension produced by sizing material. If the yarn curls up into corkscrewlike curls, it has been creped. This tendency of crepe yarn to twist makes fabrics constructed from these yarns less dimensionally stable than other fabrics, as they are more elastic, and they have an uneven fabric surface.

More tightly twisted yarns shed soil more easily. Because their surface is smoother, there are fewer loose fiber ends to attract and hold soil. In yarns made from absorbent fibers, absorbency is lower in more tightly twisted yarns.

Abrasion resistance is increased by tighter twist. This is a logical result because in a more tightly twisted yarn many fibers are held in such a way that they appear on the surface, then into the center of the yarn, and then back to the surface again. As a result, more fibers are subject to a relatively even distribution of abrasion. Loose surface fibers in low-twist yarns also snag and pull up, creating points of wear.

Keeping these points in mind is helpful when evaluating products in relation to performance. For example, abrasion resistance is important to consider when selecting an upholstery fabric, as abrasion is related to the durability of a product on which people will sit. Not only can the consumer look for a fiber that has reasonably good abrasion resistance but also for a yarn that has reasonably high twist. Low-twist yarns abrade and snag more easily than do those with higher twist. Also, tighter-twist yarns shed soil more readily.

The appearance of a fabric is determined to a large extent by the twist of the yarn. For example, if filament yarns of higher luster are only given very low twist, they will reflect greater quantities of light in mirrorlike fashion and, therefore, appear brighter than the same yarns when they are more tightly twisted. Crepe fabrics achieve a nubby, somewhat crinkled, effect by using creped yarns that have a less even surface texture. Loosely twisted worsted yarns produce a smooth, more even surface. The fabric designer takes advantage of these effects to create a wide variety of surface textures and designs. (See Figure 15.6.)

Direction of Twist

In twisting fibers together to form yarns, the fibers can be twisted either to the right or to the left. In textile industry terminology this twist is called *S* or *Z twist* (Figure 15.7). Z twisted yarns are twisted so that the direction of the twist follows the center bar of the letter Z. Z twist is also known as *right twist.* In S twist yarn, the twist direction follows the center bar of the letter S. S twist is also known as *left twist.* This concept will be more easily understood if the reader takes a small bunch

(a) Tightly twisted crepe yarns are used to create a pebbly surface texture; (b) loosely twisted silk slub yarns are used to produce a fabric of the shantung type.

Figure 15.6

(a)

(b)

Figure 15.7

S and Z twist.

of absorbent cotton and makes a vertical line on the fibers with a pen. Then, suspending the fibers from the thumb and forefinger of the left hand to that of the right, rotate the fibers to the right with the upper left-hand fingers. The line you have made will take a diagonal direction similar to that of the bar in a Z. If the upper fingers are twisted to the left, the line will follow the bar of the S.

Most yarns are made with a Z twist. However, in certain fabric constructions special effects can be achieved by combining yarns in which the fibers have been twisted in either the same or opposite directions.

The amount of twist in a given yarn can also be measured. The ASTM standard definition of twist is "the number of turns about its axis per unit length observed in a yarn or other textile strand" (ASTM 1986, 839). Twist may be expressed as turns per meter (tpm), turns per centimeter (tpcm), or turns per inch (tpi).

Size of Yarns

Because the textile industry requires some means for distinguishing between yarns of different sizes, standards of measurement have been established. There are different systems of measurement for cotton-type yarn and wool-type yarn, and still other systems for filament yarns.

This variety of measurement systems may seem unnecessarily complicated. The systems had their origins in measurements that were appropriate for particular uses in isolated textile manufacturing localities and may go back for hundreds of years. The present trend is toward use of metric measurements, but one will still encounter the use of traditional terminology.

The basic principles underlying these systems that should be borne in mind are these: the system is different for each type of fiber, is different for staple and filament yarns, and may be either a direct measure of size or an indirect measure.

Direct methods of measurement rely on the measurement of fixed lengths of yarn. A specified length of yarn is measured, and this length is weighed. The measures used are tex or denier. As explained earlier, tex is the weight in grams of a 1-kilometer (1,000-meter) length of yarn, and denier is the weight in grams of 9,000 meters of yarn. Yarns may also be specified in *decitex*, which is the weight of 10,000 meters. In all these measures, the higher the number, the coarser the yarn.

Indirect methods of measurement rely on the measurement of fixed weights of yarn. The numbering system establishes a number of hanks (skeins) of yarn that make up either a pound or a kilogram of yarn weight. Pounds are used for measurements in the English system and kilograms for measurements in the metric system. The size of the hanks used is different for each kind of fiber, with the measures being as follows: cotton count equals the number of hanks of 840 yards in 1 pound; linen count (also called *linen lea*) equals the number of hanks of 300 yards in 1 pound; woolen count equals the number of hanks of 1,600 yards per pound; worsted count equals the number of hanks of 560 yards per pound. All these yarn numbers are reported in technical or research literature followed by the abbreviation *Ne,* which stands for "number in the English system." Metric yarn numbers in the indirect measurement system equal the number of 1,000-meter hanks in each kilogram, and this measurement is followed by the abbreviation *Nm,* which stands for "number in the metric system."

Because different lengths of yarns are used to establish yarn numbers in the varying systems, yarn numbers are not directly comparable unless one uses a table such as Table 15.1. Looking at that table, one can see, reading across the table, that depending on the system being used, comparably sized yarns can have widely divergent numbers assigned. Nevertheless, regardless of the specific yarn numbers, certain basic principles apply. In the direct system the lower numbers indicate fine yarns; higher numbers indicate coarser yarns. Just the opposite is true in the indirect system, where higher numbers indicate finer yarns and lower numbers coarser yarns. For example, if 7 hanks of one linen yarn weigh 1 pound, and 50 hanks of another linen yarn weight 1 pound, obviously the yarn with the higher number (50) would be finer than the yarn with the lower number (7).

| Table 15.1 | | Comparable Yarn Numbers in Major Direct and Indirect Systems of Yarn Numbering | | | | |

Direct Methods		Indirect Methods			
Tex (weight in grams of 1,000 m of yarn)	Denier (weight in grams of 9,000 m of yarn)	Worsted (no. of 560-yd hanks per lb)	Woolen (no. of 1,600-yd hanks per lb)	Cotton (no. of 840-yd hanks per lb)	Linen (no. of 300-yd hanks per lb)
thinnest					**thinnest**
5.6	50	160	56	106	298
8.3	75	106	37	71	198
11.1	100	80	28	53	149
16.6	150	53	19	35	99
22.2	200	40	14	27	74
33.4	300	27	9.3	18	50
44.4	400	20	7	13	37
55.5	500	16	5.6	11	30
77.7	700	11.4	4	7.6	21
111	1000	8.0	2.8	5.3	15
166	1500	5.3	1.9	3.5	10
222	2000	4	1.4	2.7	7
coarsest					**coarsest**

Source: Adapted from J. Pizzuto, *Fabric Science* (New York: Fairchild, 1974), 88.

Yarn Production Methods: An Overview

The pages that follow provide an overview of the techniques used to transform fibers into yarns. The following outline may help the reader to understand the sequence of that discussion.

Making filament fibers into yarns.

Making bulk filament yarns.

Transforming filaments into tow.

Making staple fibers into yarns.
    Preparation of staple fibers for spinning.
        Blending staple fibers.
        Breaking and opening bundles.
        Cleaning fibers.
    Systems for processing different types of staple fibers.
        Fiber preparation by the cotton system.
        Fiber preparation by the woolen system.
        Fiber preparation by the worsted system.
        Processing of linen fibers.
    Insertion of twist into yarns.
        Ring spinning.
        Open-end spinning.
    Ply yarns.
    Other methods of manufacturing yarns.

In the chapters devoted to various types of fibers, the term *spinning* was used to describe the formation of manufactured fibers by extruding them through a spinneret. This usage of the word should not be confused with the term *spinning* as it is used to describe the formation of a yarn from fibers. Newly formed manufactured fibers were also described as being *drawn*. This term also has two meanings: (1) the drawing of manufactured fibers to orient the molecules within the fiber and (2) a step in certain of the processes for creating yarns from staple fibers.

Making Filament Fibers into Yarns

In creating manufactured fibers for use in filament yarns, spinnerets are used that have the exact number of holes (usually from 20 to 120) needed for a particular type of yarn. Following extrusion, the fibers may be drawn or, alternatively, the drawing may take place during a subsequent step. This is true, for example, of partially oriented yarns (POY) of polyester. The drawn filaments may be twisted together either tightly or loosely, depending on the characteristics desired in the resulting yarn.

Much of the silk fiber produced is processed into filament yarns, although short silk fibers can also be made into staple yarns. Creation of filament yarns of silk can be done immediately after reeling fibers from cocoons or later, after the gum has been removed.

Making Bulk Filament Yarns

Yarns made from straight filament fibers are smooth and slippery to the touch. They lack the warmth, bulk, and comfort of yarns spun from staple fibers. Manufactured yarns can be treated with processes that use heat setting or mechanical entangling of fibers to alter their texture.

Texturing of manufactured filament yarns can produce softer, bulkier yarns, with increased warmth, comfort, and absorbency; can decrease pilling of the fibers; or can impart stretch. Texturing may be done by the fiber manufacturer (*producer textured* yarn) or at some later step in the manufacture of the yarn.

The ASTM assigns textured yarns to the general category of bulk yarns. In the ASTM compilation of standard definitions, *bulk yarns* are described as yarns prepared to have greater covering power or apparent volume than similar conventional yarns with normal twist. The category of bulk yarns is further subdivided into *bulky yarns, textured yarns,* and *stretch yarns* (ASTM 1986).

Bulky Yarns

Bulky yarns are formed from fibers that are inherently bulky and cannot be closely packed because of such characteristics as cross-sectional shape, fiber resilience, natural crimp, or some other quality. No special treatments are needed for bulky yarns to make them bulky, although the fibers may have been engineered to obtain some of the aforementioned qualities. Bulky yarns are used in those applications in which bulk is more important than stretch, although many bulky yarns do have moderate stretch. Products in which bulky yarns are most often found are sweaters, warm hosiery, carpets, wool-like knits, and upholstery.

Textured Yarns

Textured yarns may be filament or spun yarns that have been given "noticeably greater volume" through physical, chemical, or heat treatments or a combination of these. In the ASTM standard definitions compilation, textured yarns are separated into the categories of *loopy yarn, high-bulk yarn,* and *crimped yarn.*

Loopy yarns have a relatively large number of randomly spaced and sized loops along the filaments or fibers and very little stretch. Loopy yarns may be produced through air-jet texturing in which texture is produced not by heat but by feeding yarns into a system in which slack filaments are formed into loops by jets of air (Figure 15.8). Loopy yarns can also be made by core-spun processes.

High-bulk yarns have a random crimp produced by the combination of fibers that shrink markedly with those that do not tend to shrink. The fibers or parts of fibers that shrink pull the other fibers or fiber sections into a permanently crimped position. High-bulk yarns do not usually exhibit a great deal of stretch.

Crimped Yarns

Crimped yarns are often made from thermoplastic fibers. These yarns are deformed from a straight configuration to a saw-toothed or curled shape. Heat setting of the fibers in the deformed position makes these shapes permanent.

At the present time the dominant process used for texturing crimped yarns is the *false-twist* process. The means of inserting twist vary depending on the process. Some machines use a series of disks over which the yarn passes, others use a friction belt device, and others a spindle. No matter how the twist is developed, the yarn is heat-set in the twisted position and then untwisted, whereupon it kinks. Unless a yarn with stretch is required, this textured shape is treated to stabilize it. (See Figures 15.9, 15.10, 15.11.)

Other processes that introduce crimp include the *stuffer box* process, in which fibers are fed into a small chamber in which the crimped shape is heat-set. The *gear crimp* process imparts crimp by passing filaments between the teeth of two heated gears. In *knit-deknit,* yarns are knitted into a fabric, the fabric is heat-set, then yarns are unraveled and retain crimp formed in the knitted configuration (Figure 15.12). These last-mentioned processes account for only about 5 percent of textured yarns (Wilson and Kollu 1987, 1).

In an earlier process, the edge-crimp process, heated thermoplastic yarns were drawn over a sharp knife edge, causing some areas of the fiber to fuse slightly and imparting a spiral-like curl to the yarn. This process is now considered to be obsolete. Likewise, the separation of texturing into a three-stage process has been superceded by continuous processes.

It should be noted that texturing filament yarn is much less expensive than spinning staple yarns. Customers seem to show a preference for spun yarns in many applications; thus, texturing filament yarns, especially those of polyester, has become an important manufacturing step. With the widespread use of POY (see chapter 9 for fuller discussion), the texturer, who may also be the fiber producer, simultaneously draws and textures the yarn.

Stretch Yarns

ASTM defines stretch yarns as yarns with a high degree of potential elastic stretch and rapid recovery. They are said to have a high degree of yarn curl achieved by deforming the yarn and heat-setting the yarn in this position. When the yarn is placed under stress, it will stretch, flattening the curls; but when stress is removed, the yarn returns to the permanent heat-set shape. False-twist processes can produce stretch yarns.

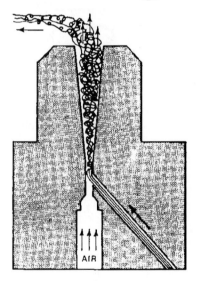

Figure 15.9

Friction false twisting. Illustration courtesy of Hoechst Celanese Corporation.

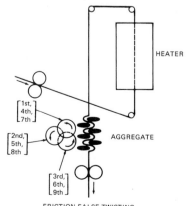

Figure 15.10

Disk system for insertion of false twist.

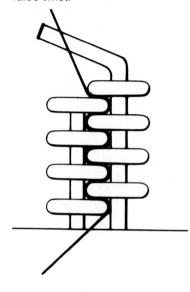

Figure 15.11

Yarn is twisted by "twister belts" as it passes between them. Illustration courtesy of Murata of America, Inc.

Figure 15.12

Texturing of yarns through the knit-deknit process. From "Yarn" by Stanley Backer. Copyright © 1972 by Scientific American, Inc. All rights reserved.

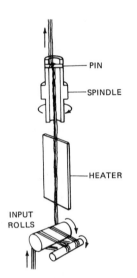

PIN

SPINDLE

HEATER

INPUT ROLLS

Consumers as well as those in the textile industry use the term *stretch* more broadly, applying it to any yarn or fabric that exhibits stretch and recovery. Most of these alternative routes to provision of stretch are discussed elsewhere, and they include the use of elastomeric fibers (chapter 12), bicomponent fibers with differential shrinkage (chapter 14), and treatment of fabrics to provide moderate amounts of stretch (chapter 20).

Transforming Filaments into Tow

Tow is filaments that have been broken or cut into staple lengths. One of the advantages of starting with tow for spinning a staple yarn is that, unlike cotton, wool, and other natural fibers, the tow fibers are aligned and parallel and need not be combed or carded to make them ready for spinning. The fibers can be said to go from tow to *sliver,* a continuous rope of staple fibers, in one operation. The industry terms the process "tow-to-top." Specialized machines make this conversion. For example, the Pacific converter cuts a flat web of tow into the desired staple length. Fibers may be cut into uniform or variable lengths. The web of cut fibers is then rolled into a *sliver* of staple fibers (Figure 15.13).

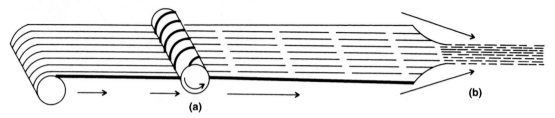

Figure 15.13 Filaments are converted to tow. Continuous filaments are fed under a roller (a) with sharp blades that cut the filaments into short lengths. Cut fiber is rolled into a sliver (b).

A second method of converting tow-to-top is to break the fibers into staple lengths. The Perlock system applies tension to the tow and pulls the stretched tow across a tow breaker wheel, a cog wheel with sharp, protruding edges. The filaments then break on the sharp edges of the tow breaker wheel. Stretch breaking is most effective with synthetic fibers, less useful in cutting regenerated cellulose. A variation of this process, the Turbo-stapler process, is used for producing high-bulk yarns, especially from acrylics.

During stretch breaking, the fibers are extended and must be treated to relax the fiber or yarns will show a good deal of relaxation shrinkage. In the Perlock process, breaking is followed by adding crimp to the fiber, heat-setting the crimp, and relaxing the fiber by a steam heat treatment. If a sliver of stretch-broken, crimped, relaxed staple is blended with a sliver of stretch-broken, crimped, but not relaxed staple, the bulking properties of the resulting yarns are much improved.

The yarns made in this way are woven or knitted into a garment, the garment is treated with hot water, and the unset fibers shrink, causing the preshrunk fibers to stand up in bulky, fuzzy surface texture.

Making Staple Fibers into Yarns

Preparation of Staple Fibers for Spinning

From the time staple fibers are supplied to the manufacturer until they have been made into yarns, they go through a series of steps. Some steps are required for all yarns and fibers, and some are optional.

Blending Staple Fibers

It is sometimes desirable to blend two or more different fibers into one yarn. Frequently, manufactured fibers are blended with natural fibers to take advantage of the best qualities of each fiber. In other blends the combination may be made to reduce the cost of the fabric by blending a less expensive fiber with a more expensive one, or blending may be done to achieve decorative effects.

Blending may be done at one of several steps in the preparation of yarns from staple fibers: during opening, during carding, or during drawing out. No matter when blending is done, quantities of each fiber to be used are measured carefully, and the proportions of one fiber to another are consistently maintained.

Figure 15.14

Bales of fiber are opened. Much of this operation is done automatically to avoid exposing workers to cotton dust. Photograph courtesy of American Textile Manufacturers Institute, Inc.

Breaking and Opening Bundles

Bales of fiber may be opened either by hand or by machine (Figure 15.14). Many modern textile mills have completely mechanized this process. The trend toward mechanization of opening cotton bales has been accelerated by the requirements of the Occupational Safety and Health Act that workers' exposure to cotton dust be limited. As noted earlier, high levels of cotton dust appear to be associated with a lung disease called byssinosis.

Cleaning Fibers

Cotton contains impurities such as sand or grit and particles of leaf, stalk, and seeds. New wool that has not previously been cleaned contains vegetable matter, sand, dirt, and grease. Both may require special cleaning after the bales have been opened.

Manufactured fibers do not require cleaning, but if they have been compressed for packing and shipping, they need to be opened and the fibers separated so that bunches of fibers do not cling together and form thick areas, or *slubs,* in the yarn.

Systems for Processing Different Types of Staple Fibers

Processing of fibers in preparation for spinning may be done on one of three major spinning systems: the cotton, the woolen, or the worsted (also called long-staple) system. These systems were developed at the time when only natural fibers were in use; therefore, the different characteristics of the fibers, including their length, helped to shape the processes used. Manufactured staple fibers can be handled on any of these systems. More yarn is produced on the cotton system than on the worsted or woolen systems.

Fiber Preparation by the Cotton System

Increased automation in yarn production has largely eliminated initial steps of loosening and separating lumps of fiber and the subsequent formation of a *lap,* a flattened fairly uniform layer of fibers. Instead, the opening and transport of fiber to the carding machine are done in a more or less closed system.

Carding. The carding machine consists of an inner cylinder and an outer belt, both set with hundreds of fine wires. The intermeshing wires separate the fibers and pull them into somewhat parallel form. The wire teeth also remove trash and entangled lumps of fibers called *neps.* A thin web of fiber is formed in this machine, and as the web is moved along, it passes through a funnel-shaped device that forms it into a ropelike strand of roughly parallel fibers. (See Figure 15.15.)

Blending can take place at the point of carding by joining quantities of different fibers. Carding mixes the blend fibers together, distributing them evenly throughout the mass of fiber.

Combing. Whereas carding is a step in the production of all fibers, combing is an optional step in the preparation of some yarns. When a smoother, finer yarn is wanted, fibers are subjected to a further paralleling called *combing.* A comblike device arranges fibers into parallel form. At the same time it removes the short fibers as well as most remaining neps or impurities. (See Figure 15.16.)

Combed yarns have smooth surfaces and finer diameters than do carded yarns. Since the shorter fibers have been removed, fewer short ends show on the surface of the fabric, and the luster is increased. Combed yarns are more expensive to produce, and fabrics made from combed yarns are, therefore, higher in price. Far more of the yarn produced on the cotton system is carded than that which is both carded and combed.

Drawing Out. Carding or combing transforms a fiber mass into a sliver. Several slivers are combined in the drawing-out process. Blending of fibers can be done by combining slivers of different fibers. During the drawing out, a series of rollers rotating at different rates of speed elongates or draws out and attenuates the sliver into a single more uniform strand that is fed into large cans.

Within the card sliver is a substantial proportion of fibers with hooked ends. These hooks are formed as the fibers are moved along by the carding machinery.

Figure 15.15

Cleaning and separation of individual fibers takes place in the carding machine. A web of fibers is formed into a thin, ropelike strand called a sliver. Photograph courtesy of the National Cotton Council.

Their presence reduces the effective length of the fiber, and if these hooks are not removed, the yarns produced will be weaker. Subsequent drawing steps help to eliminate some hooks.

Carded slivers are drawn twice following carding. Combed slivers are drawn once before combing and twice more after combing.

Roving. The sliver is fed to a machine called the *roving frame*. Here, the strands of fiber are elongated still more by a series of rollers. As they are wound on the bobbins, they are given a slight twist. The product of the roving frame, an elongated, slightly twisted strand of fibers, is called the *roving*. (See Figures 15.17, 15.18, 15.19, and 15.20.)

Fiber Preparation by the Woolen System

A wide range of wool types, but generally the shorter fiber varieties, can be spun on the woolen system. Manufactured staple fibers can be blended with the wool fibers and spun on the woolen system as well.

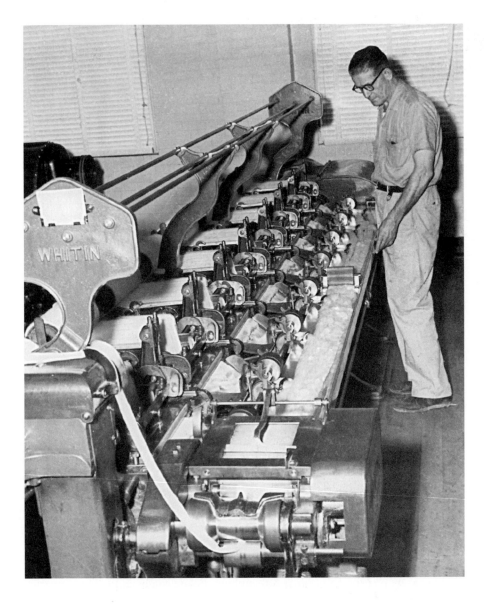

Figure 15.16

If combed yarns are being made, a lap composed of slivers is passed through a comb that combs out short fibers. The output of the comb is formed again into a sliver. Photograph courtesy of the National Cotton Council.

After cleaning, the fibers are blended, a small amount of oil is added to the fiber to facilitate processing, and the fibers are carded. The carded web is divided into strips by a *condenser,* following which a very slight amount of twist is introduced by subjecting the strips to a rubbing motion to form rovings. Final twist and yarn formation are subsequently imparted, usually on a ring spinner. Some authors prefer to call the woolen system the "condenser system" because fibers other than wool are often prepared by this system.

Woolen yarns are soft and bulky. They have many fiber ends on the surface of the yarn, giving them a fuzzy appearance and handle. This results from omission of the drawing-out processes that would have straightened the fibers. Woolen yarns are weak and have poor abrasion resistance.

Fiber Preparation by the Worsted System

The worsted system is used for longer varieties of wool and can also be used for manufactured staple fibers in appropriate lengths. If wool fiber is being processed, it is

Figure 15.17

Sliver, pulled from large cans, is fed into the roving frame. Photograph courtesy of the National Cotton Council.

cleaned and then processed either dry or with oil added to lubricate the fibers. Carding is followed by preparation of fibers for combing. Before combing, the fibers are subjected to *gilling* (comparable to drawing out). The fibers pass through gill boxes in which pins control the movement of short fibers and minimize the development of unevenness in slivers while also assisting in straightening of fibers. Slivers are subjected to three gillings, after which they are combed, gilled again, drawn, and, finally, spun.

Worsted yarns are smooth, sleek, and compact in appearance, with few fiber ends on the surface of the yarn. Their strength is better than that of woolen yarns and their hand is crisper. Figure 15.21 provides a comparison of woolen and worsted yarns.

The *semiworsted system* is a variation of worsted spinning that omits combing. Yarns produced are not as smooth, lean, or lustrous as worsted yarns, but processing is cheaper.

Processing of Linen Fibers

The length of linen fibers requires that they be processed somewhat differently from either wool or cotton. The final cleaning of flax is accomplished by a hackling machine, a device that has a revolving belt set with pins that remove short fibers, entangled fibers, and vegetable matter. The pins bring the linen fibers into alignment.

Figure 15.18

On the roving frame, fibers are twisted slightly and drawn into a smaller strand. Photograph courtesy of the National Cotton Council.

Linen fibers that are comparable to carded fiber after hackling are referred to as tow or hackled fibers; those comparable to combed fibers are referred to as line or well-hackled fibers. The same terms are applied to the yarns made from these fibers. Table 15.2 summarizes the terms used in referring to combed and carded yarns from different fibers.

The processes used in preparing linen fiber for spinning are intended to take advantage of the strength and luster of these long fibers. Precise steps vary, depending on whether tow or linen fibers are being handled. Also, either a wet or dry processing can be utilized. Wet processing produces the finest, strongest, and smoothest yarns.

Figure 15.22 compares steps in the major yarn preparation processes.

Insertion of Twist into Yarn

The aforementioned systems for preparation of fibers for spinning are preliminary to the final yarn formation. A variety of different means can be used to join fibers

Figure 15.19

Sliver that has been given some twist is wound onto bobbins. Textile plants that use open-end or air-jet spinning do not need the roving process. Open-end and air-jet machines spin yarn directly from the card sliver. Photograph courtesy of the American Textile Manufacturers Institute, Inc.

together to form a yarn. Some of these yarn-forming methods are well established, others are beginning to be used commercially, while still others are in various stages of noncommercial research and development.

The predominant commercial systems of yarn formation are ring spinning and open-end spinning. The following text summarizes the methods of spinning that are now used or that are likely to be commercialized in the near future. The major focus of discussion is ring and open-end spinning because of their dominant position in the industry.

Ring Spinning

The ring spinner is made up of the following parts:

1. Spools on which the roving is wound.
2. A series of drafting rollers through which the roving passes.
3. A guiding ring or eyelet.

Roving is fed to ring spinning frame where it is drawn out to final size, twisted into yarn, and wound on bobbins. Photograph courtesy of the National Cotton Council.

Figure 15.21

Diagrams of: (a) yarn spun on the woolen system and (b) yarn spun on the worsted system. Illustration courtesy of the American Wool Council.

A

B

4. A stationary ring around the spindle.
5. A traveler, a small, U-shaped clip on the ring.
6. A spindle.
7. A bobbin.

The roving is fed from the spool through the drafting rollers. The rollers elongate the roving, which passes through the eyelet, moving down and through the traveler. The traveler moves freely around the stationary ring. The spindle turns the bobbin at a constant speed. This turning of the bobbin and the movement of the traveler impart the twist to the yarn. The yarn is twisted and wound onto a bobbin in one operation. (See Figures 15.23 and 15.24.)

Table 15.2

Terms for Combed and Carded Yarns from Different Fibers

Fiber	Term for Carded Yarn	Term for Combed Yarn
Linen	Tow or hackled yarn	Line or well-hackled yarn
Wool	Woolen yarn	Worsted yarn
Cotton and other staple fibers	Carded yarn	Combed yarn

Figure 15.22   Comparison of the steps in the major yarn preparation systems.

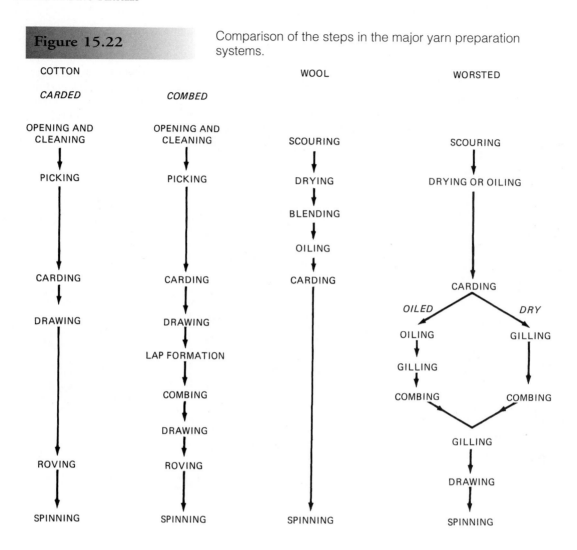

Bobbins must be removed from the machine when full, a process called *doffing*. From here, bobbins are transported to a *winding* machine where yarn is wound onto packages. Automated systems for doffing and winding have been developed and are widely used. Winding is considered an important step. It provides an opportunity to *condition* yarn, that is, to bring the yarn into equilibrium with the moisture in the atmosphere, and to add wax or other coatings that will facilitate weaving. Winding also allows the identification of flaws in the yarn.

The ring spinning technique produces finer and stronger yarns than can be made on other competing processes. However, by the 1960s the rotation speed of the spindle (which began at 4,000 revolutions per minute) seemed to have reached an upper limit at about 12,000 rpm. At higher speeds the traveler burns and must be replaced frequently. These maximum speed limitations gave impetus to the development of alternate twisting systems that operated at higher speeds. Although ring spinning continued to hold an important place in the production of yarns, other systems, most notably the open-end spinning systems, seemed likely to replace ring spinning for certain sizes and types of yarns. Recently, ring spinning has made a comeback, however, for the following reasons. Japanese manufacturers of spinning machinery were able to improve ring spinning technology so that maximum speeds have increased to 21,000 rpm. Demand for finer count yarns has increased in the last several years. Increased automation and improved quality control have helped to lower costs of manufacturing.

In 1993 a German firm, Fehrer A. G., together with the Reiter Company, announced its intention to begin extensive practical trials and to subsequently bring to market a machine that eliminates steps in the transport of sliver to the ring spinning machine. The companies call this the *DREF compact spinning process.* The same system also automates transport of bobbins from the spinning machine to the winding machine.

The consensus in the textile industry seems to be that ring spinning will continue to have an important place in the production of yarns and will continue to dominate the fine count area. As Dr. Ernst Fehrer stated, "Even today and in spite of its 'old age' of more than 100 years, ring spinning remains the model for all new spinning systems invented in the past decades. . . . Thus, the textile properties of yarns produced by rotor, air jet, or friction spinning machines are mostly compared with ring-spun yarns" (Fehrer 1989).

Open-End Spinning

Because of the speed limitations in ring spinning, researchers concentrated on developing techniques for inserting twist into yarns that would permit more rapid production. A result of this search was the introduction, in the 1960s, of the *open-end spinning machine,* which operated at higher speeds but that produced a yarn with slightly different characteristics than conventional ring-spun yarns.

Open-end spinning omits the step of forming the roving. Instead, a sliver of fibers is fed into the spinner by a stream of air. Figure 15.25 shows an open-end spinner of the rotor type and describes its operation. The sliver is delivered to a rotary beater that separates the fibers into a thin stream. It is carried into the rotor by a current of air through a duct and is deposited in a V-shaped groove along the outer edge of the rotor. Twist is provided by the turning of the rotor.

Fibers fed to the rotor are incorporated into the rapidly rotating "open end" of a previously formed yarn that extends out of the delivery tube; hence, the name open-end spinning. As the fibers join the yarn, which is constantly being pulled out of the delivery tube, twist from the movement of the rotor is conveyed to the fibers. A constant stream of new fibers enters the rotor, is distributed in the groove, and is removed at the end of the formed yarn, becoming part of the yarn itself.

The fineness of the yarn is determined by the rate at which it is drawn out of the rotor relative to the rate at which fibers are being fed into the rotor. In other words, if fewer fibers are being fed in while fibers are being withdrawn rapidly, a thinner yarn will result, and vice versa. The twist is determined by the ratio of the rotor turning speed to the linear or withdrawal speed of the yarn (i.e., the higher the speed of the rotor, the greater the twist).

Theoretically, a variety of different means may be used to form the yarn and insert twist. These have been divided into the following categories: mechanical spinning (of which rotor spinning is an example), electrostatic spinning, fluid spinning, air spinning, and friction spinning. Of these, only rotor and friction open-end spinning machines have been commercialized, and most of the open-end spinning machines now in use are of the mechanical rotor spinning type. Friction open-end spinning machines are also available.

Friction spinning systems use friction to insert twist. A mixture of air and fibers is fed to the surface of a moving, perforated drum. Suction holds the fibers against the surface while a second drum rotates in the opposite direction. Twist is inserted and the yarn begins forming as the fibers pass between the two drums. The newly

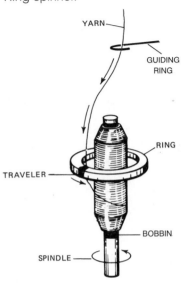

Figure 15.23

Ring spinner.

Figure 15.24

Ring spinning machine in operation. Note the cones of roving at the top of the machine. The filled bobbins of spun yarn are being removed automatically at the center of the picture, with new bobbins at the bottom ready to be moved into position for spinning. Photograph courtesy of Zinser Textilmaschinen GmbH.

forming yarn is added to the open end of an already-formed yarn, and the completed yarn is continuously drawn away. (See Figure 15.26.)

The advantages of open-end spinning are that it increases the speed of production, eliminates the step of drawing out the roving before spinning, and permits finished yarns to be wound on any sized bobbin or spool (Figure 15.27). As a result, it is less expensive. It produces yarns of more even diameter than does ring spinning. Yarns are more uniform in diameter, bulkier, rougher, more absorbent, and less variable in strength than are ring-spun yarns.

Fabrics made from open-end spun yarns compared with ring-spun yarns are more uniform and more opaque in appearance, lower in strength, less likely to pill, and inferior in crease recovery. A number of sources indicated that they are more subject to abrasion.

Neither friction nor rotor spinning will produce yarns as fine and strong as ring-spun yarns. Open-end spun yarns have a handle that has been characterized

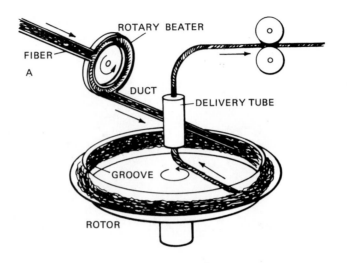

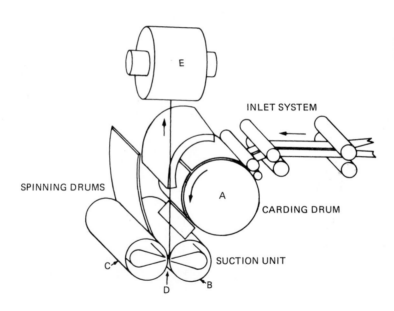

Figure 15.26

DREF-2 spinning system, which uses friction as the means of inserting twist. A mixture of air and fibers is fed to a moving, perforated surface (A). Suction holds the fibers against the drum (B). A second perforated drum rotates in the opposite direction (C). Twist is inserted as the fibers pass between the two drums (D). The newly forming yarn is added to the open end of an already-formed yarn, and the yarn is continuously drawn away and wound (E). Illustration courtesy of Fehrer A. G.

as "harsh." Some of the kinds of products that seem to be especially well suited to the use of open-end spun yarns are in filling yarns for fabrics where yarn strength is not a factor, toweling pile yarns, denim, and heavier weights of bed sheeting. The yarns' even surface makes them desirable as base fabrics for plastic-coated materials. On the other hand, the more acceptable feel of ring-spun yarns has led knitwear manufacturers to prefer them, and they are better for fine blends of polyester and cotton.

Ply Yarns

Ply yarns are made from two or more single yarns that are twisted together. Ply yarns are much more expensive than single yarns but are nevertheless often produced to achieve certain benefits. Ply yarns made from identical single yarns are more regular in diameter and are stronger. Ply yarns are often made to achieve particular decorative effects.

| Figure 15.27 | Room equipped with open-end spinning machines. Compare this photo to Figure 15.24, and note that fibers are fed directly from the cans to the machine and that it is not necessary to mount spools of roving on the machine. Photograph courtesy of the American Textile Manufacturers Institute, Inc. |

In general, the steps involved in creating ply yarns include:

1. winding single yarns and clearing any flaws.
2. placing the required number of component yarns alongside each other, in place, ready for supplying to the machine.
3. insertion of twist to form the ply yarn by any of a number of different machines.
4. winding the finished yarn on a cone or package for delivery to the customer.

A number of different machines are used in making ply yarns, which may also be referred to as *folded yarns*. Ring-folding machines, for example, operate on the same principle as ring-spinning machines except that instead of a roving being fed to the traveler, the single yarns to be combined are both fed together for twisting.

A variant on this process is *Sirospun yarn*. To strengthen worsted warp yarns sufficiently to withstand the stresses of weaving, the yarns generally must be *two-folded* or double ply. Instead of feeding two single yarns into the spinning system, two rovings are fed into the ring-spinning machine. Naturally occurring variations in the density of fiber strands and in tension cause randomly inserted levels of twist to be incorporated. The end result, Sirospun yarn, is very similar to a single yarn yet has enough of the characteristics of a ply yarn to be satisfactory for weaving.

Other Methods of Manufacturing Yarns

In addition to ring and open-end spinning, techniques that insert true twist into yarn, there are other types of yarn construction. Three of those that have some current commercial application are described in the following sections: false-twist, or self-twist, spinning; yarn wrapping; and splitting or slitting films made from synthetic polymers. Assessment of the viability of these processes for commercial purposes varies.

False-Twist, or Self-Twist, Spinning

Self-twist spinning, also called false-twist spinning, is used to make ply yarns. The process follows these steps:

Two rovings are used. Each one is passed through a pair of rollers that are both rotating and oscillating. Each set of rollers twists its roving in a direction opposite to the other. The uneven motion of the rollers forms a yarn that has both twisted and untwisted areas. Adjacent ends of the two yarns are allowed to untwist around each other. Care must be taken to space the untwisted areas of each yarn in such a way that a loosely twisted section of one yarn never coincides with a loosely twisted section of the other yarn, or a weak spot would result. (See Figure 15.28.)

Repco® is the trademark of one commercially available self-twist spinner. Officials of the manufacturer cite the following benefits from the use of self-twist yarns: less space required for producing the same weight of yarn, reductions in annual maintenance costs and time, less waste in spinning, lower power utilization, and lower labor costs. This system is currently being used in Europe for worsted and acrylic manufacture (Tewksbury 1981).

Self-twist yarns can, of course, be used only in those fabrics that require two-ply yarns. The process also requires that fiber lengths not be too short. Wool and long manufactured staple fibers are especially suitable.

Yarn Wrapping

Yarns can be made from a bundle of parallel fibers held in place by surface wrapping of other staple or filament fibers. The first of these wrapped yarns were made by

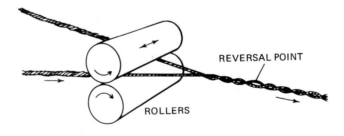

Figure 15.28

Self-twist spinning. Two separate rovings are fed between a pair of rollers that move both forward and side to side. The twisted rovings, each with opposite directional twist, when placed side by side, twist around each other to form a ply yarn. From "Yarn" by Stanley Backer. Copyright © 1972 by Scientific American, Inc. All rights reserved.

Figure 15.29

Diagram of the structure of a fasciated yarn.

DuPont and were called *fasciated yarns.* (See Figure 15.29.) The term derives from the Latin word *fasces,* meaning "a bundle of rods wrapped with ribbons." Such yarns are no longer made by DuPont; however, wrapped or covered yarns, similar in concept, are being produced.

Air-Jet Spinning. The Murata Company, a Japanese firm, has commercialized an air-jet spinning machine that functions as follows. A largely untwisted sliver is fed into the machine. Two nozzles, each forcing an air jet against the sliver from opposite directions, cause fibers from the outer layer of the sliver to wrap around the interior fibers, thereby forming the yarn (Figure 15.30).

Hollow Spindle Spinning. In hollow spindle spinning, a sliver of core fibers is fed through a hollow spindle where it is wrapped by a filament yarn unwinding from the spindle.

An interesting application of the technique has been in the manufacture of towels and other fabrics, in which the wrapped yarns are used in the pile. In this instance, the wrapping yarn is made from polyvinyl alcohol fibers, which are soluble. After the fabric has been put through the finishing processes, these yarns dissolve, leaving a soft, all-cotton twistless and absorbent yarn in the pile.

Figure 15.31 illustrates the differences in appearance of ring-spun and wrap-spun yarns.

Core Spinning. Core-spun yarns are usually made with a continuous filament core surrounded by twisted fibers or other yarns. (See Figure 12.2, page 199.) Recently, core-spun yarns with a staple core of one fiber and an outer sheath of another fiber have been produced by an adaptation of ring spinning. Two rovings, one of polyester and one of cotton, are fed through drafting rollers and then pass through separate channels before being wound on the spindle. The channel for the cotton sheath is longer, assuring that it will wrap around the polyester core as the twist is inserted. Fabrics from staple core yarns are more durable and more easy-care features than those of 100 percent cotton yarns.

Making Yarns from Films

Recently, various new techniques have emerged that allow yarns to be formed directly from synthetic polymers without the formation of fibers or the twisting of fibers into yarns. These processes include the formation of yarns by the split film and slit film processes. Slit film yarns could be classified as monofilaments. Yarns made by the split film process do not fit neatly into the categories of staple or filament yarns.

Split Films. In the creation of yarns by the split film technique, a sheet of polymer is formed. The formed sheet is drawn in the lengthwise direction. Through drawing, the molecules in the polymer are oriented in the direction of the draw, causing the film to be strengthened in the lengthwise direction and weakened in the crosswise direction. This causes a breakdown of the film into a mass of interconnected fibers, most of which are aligned in the direction of the drawing, but some of which also connect in the crosswise direction. The process is known as fibrillation (Figure 15.32).

Figure 15.30

Diagram of Murata jet spinner for wrap spinning.

Sliver Delivery

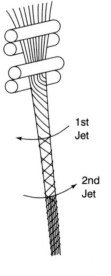

1st
Jet

2nd
Jet

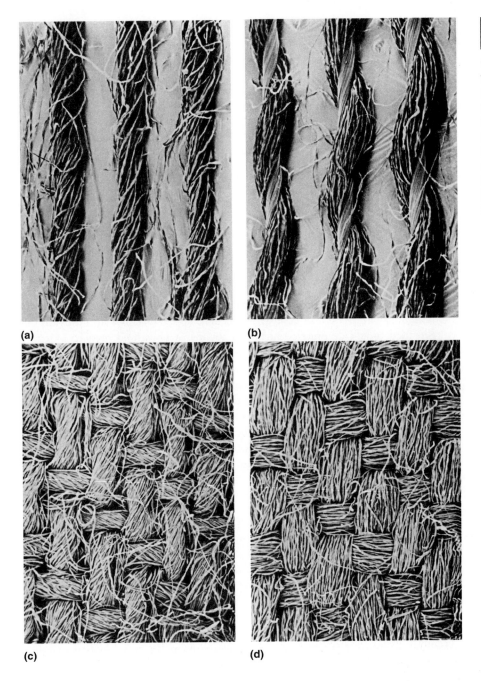

(a)

(b)

(c)

(d)

Figure 15.31

Comparison of ring-spun and wrap-spun yarns. (a) Ring-spun yarns. (b) Wrap-spun yarns with soluble filament wrapping. (c) Ring-spun yarns made into plain-weave fabric. (d) Plain-weave fabric of wrap-spun yarns with filament wrapping dissolved. Micrographs courtesy of George F. Ruppenicker.

The fibrillated materials can be twisted into strings or twines or other coarse, yarnlike materials. The usefulness of split film yarns is limited because the yarns created are coarse. Olefins are made into split film yarns for use in making bags, sacks, ropes, and other industrial products.

Slit Films. Slit films are made by cutting film into narrow, ribbonlike sections. Depending upon the process used for cutting and drawing the film, the tapes may display some degree of fibrillation, like that described for split films. When tapes are made that do not fibrillate, they are flatter and are more suitable for certain uses. Flat tapes are used as warp yarns in weaving and can be made into carpet backings that will be very stable, remain-

Figure 15.32   Film fibrillation.

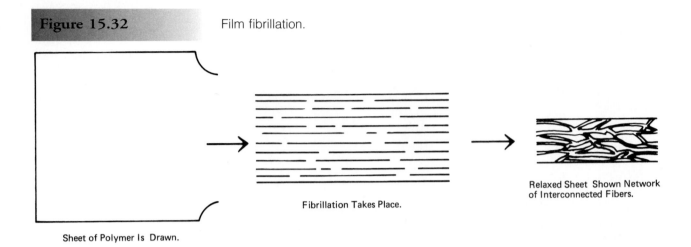

Sheet of Polymer Is Drawn.

Fibrillation Takes Place.

Relaxed Sheet Shown Network
of Interconnected Fibers.

ing flat and even. All types of tape yarns are used in making wall coverings, packaging materials, carpet backing, and as a replacement for jute in bags and sacks.

Lurex®, a flat, ribbonlike yarn with a metallic appearance, is a slit film yarn that is often used to add decorative touches to apparel or household textiles. Lurex® is made from single or multiple layers of polyester film. Multilayered types are made by placing a layer of aluminum foil between two layers of polyester film. Mono-ply types are cut from metallized polyester film, protected by a clear or colored resin coating. The natural color of Lurex® is silver. Other colors are produced by adding pigments to the lacquer coating or to the bonding adhesive. The width of these yarns ranges from 0.069 to 0.010 inches. The manufacturer claims that the use of polyester film yields a strong, flexible yarn that can be woven or knitted without support, but notes that these yarns are decorative rather than functional.

Blends

Blending is the process of mixing fibers together. As noted earlier, it can take place at any of several points during the preparation of a yarn. The ASTM differentiates between *blended yarn,* which it defines as "a single yarn spun from a blend or mixture of different fiber species," and *self-blended yarn,* which is defined as "a single yarn spun from a blend or mixture of the same fiber species" (ASTM 1986, 898).

The purposes of blending are (1) the thorough intermixing of fibers and/or (2) combining fibers with different properties to produce yarns with characteristics that cannot be obtained by using one type of fiber alone. Self-blending of bales of the same fiber is done routinely in processing natural fibers because the fibers may vary from bale to bale. In this type of blending, the mixing of as many bales as possible is done early in the processes preparatory to spinning so that the subsequent steps can help to mix the fiber still more completely.

For the same reasons, even when two or more different fiber types are combined, blending is done as early as possible. Carding helps to break up fiber clusters and intermix fibers more thoroughly. However, if the fibers being blended require different techniques for opening, cleaning, and carding, as with polyester and cotton, then slivers can be blended. For blended yarns of different fibers, the *blend level* is the percentage by weight of each fiber.

Blending is not limited to staple-length fibers. Filament fibers of different generic types can be combined into a single yarn. This can be done either by extruding these fibers side by side during drawing or during texturing.

Sometimes a blended yarn is core spun with one fiber at the center and a different fiber as the covering or is wrapped with one fiber making up the central section and another the wrapping yarn. As yarn spinning and texturing technologies grow more sophisticated, we expand the possibilities of combining several different fibers into one yarn. For example, using air to entangle two different generic fibers is another technique that has had some commercial applications.

It should be noted that fabrics woven from two or more yarns each made of different fibers are not considered blends. These fabrics are, instead, called *combination fabrics*. They do not behave in the same way as those fabrics in which the fibers are more intimately blended and may require special care procedures. Regrettably, the TFPIA labeling requirements do not distinguish between blended fabrics and combination fabrics when fiber percentage contents of fabrics are given.

The properties affected by blending may be aesthetic or functional or both. Among the aesthetic qualities that may be affected by blending are luster, texture, hand or draping qualities, and color. Blending for color may be done to combine already-colored fibers or those that will show different affinities for dyestuffs when they are dyed subsequently.

Functional qualities that may be affected by blending include strength, resilience, abrasion resistance, absorbency, or any desirable quality that any fiber used in the blend will confer. Blending less expensive fibers with more costly fibers may be done to lower the cost of fabrics.

Properties of Blended Fibers

Fibers with different characteristics, blended into a yarn, can each contribute desirable properties to the final textile material. The ultimate performance is an average of the properties of the component fibers. For example, a fabric of 50 percent cotton and 50 percent polyester would have an absorbency intermediate between that of cotton or polyester. In some cases, however, the observed fabric property is not determined simply by the relative amounts of each fiber in the blend. In blends of nylon with cotton, the tenacity of the blended yarn initially decreases with increasing amounts of nylon because of differences in the breaking elongation of the two fibers. At the breaking strain of the cotton fibers, the nylon fibers are not assuming their share of the stress, leaving the cotton to bear the load.

The stage at which blending occurs also affects the properties of the fabrics. In general, the more intimate the mixing of fibers in the blends, the better the resulting properties. Yarns blended at the fiber stage exhibit a more effective averaging of properties than ply-blended yarns.

Even though considerable study and evaluation have been made of optimum fiber proportions required to achieve desired results in blends, no certain conclusions have been reached. It is clear that very small proportions of fibers have no appreciable influence on performance, although they may have some effect on appearance.

References

ASTM. 1986. *Compilation of ASTM standard definitions.* Philadelphia: American Society for Testing and Materials.

Born, W. 1939. The Indian hand-spinning wheel. *CIBA Review* 28 (December): 988 ff.

Fehrer, E. 1989. The DREF Ring Spinning Machine. *Textile Month,* January.

Potter, M. D., and P. B. Corbman. 1967. *Textiles, fiber to fabric.* New York: McGraw-Hill.

Tewksbury, C. G. 1981. New spinning systems. *American Fashions and Fabrics,* no. 123, p. 17.

Wilson, D. K., and T. Kollu. 1987. The production of textured yarns by methods other than the false-twist technique. *Textile Progress* 16 (3).

Review Questions

1. Describe the steps in hand spinning that are required to form a yarn. What is the purpose of each step? Which of these steps are also used in mechanized spinning?
2. What are the differences between filament and staple yarns? single, ply, and cord yarns? simple and fancy or novelty yarns? thread and yarn? S and Z twist yarns?
3. What differences would you expect to find between low-twist and high-twist yarns?
4. How do direct and indirect yarn numbering systems differ?
5. What are the differences between bulky yarns, textured yarns, and stretch yarns? What properties of manufactured fibers are used in texturing yarn?
6. Compare the steps in the cotton spinning system, the woolen spinning system, and the worsted spinning system.
7. For what types of end uses are open-end spun yarns best suited. Why?
8. What is the purpose of blending fibers? What is the difference between a blended yarn and a self-blended yarn? What are some of the factors that affect the properties of blended yarns?

Recommended Readings

Abend, J. 1994. Towing the line. *Bobbin* 35 (April): 56.

Backer, S. 1993. Staple fibers—the story of blends. Part 2: Development and the future. In *Polyester—50 years of achievement,* ed. D. Brunnschweiler and J. W. S. Hearle, 94. Manchester, England: Textile Institute.

Barella, A. 1993. The hairiness of yarn. *Textile Progress* 24 (3).

Catling, H. 1983. A history of spinning and weaving. *Textiles* 12 (Spring): 20.

Dupeuble, J. C. 1994. HT heaters boost draw texturing operating parameters. *Textile World* 144 (February): 82–85.

Floyd, K. L. 1988. Carding. *Textiles* 17 (2): 34.

Horridge, P., and S. Khan. 1994. Physical properties of cotton-wool blend fabrics. *American Dyestuff Reporter* 83 (July): 38.

Ishida, T. 1990. An introduction to textile technology: Yarn manufacturing—filament yarns. *JTN,* no. 424 (March): 98.

———. 1990. An introduction to textile technology: Yarn manufacturing—spun yarns. *JTN,* no. 423 (February): 98.

Krause, H. W. 1985. Staple fiber spinning systems. *Journal of the Textile Institute* 76 (2): 185–195.

Meier, K. 1994. Methods of producing filament yarns from thermoplastic polymers. *International Textile Bulletin (Yarn and Fabric Form)* 40 (2d Quarter): 8.

Nikolic, M., J. Cerkvenic, and Z. Stejepanovic. 1993. Formation models: Comparing yarn qualities and properties. *Textile Horizons,* December, 47.

Sawhney, A. P. S., K. Q. Robert, and G. F. Ruppenicker. 1989. Device for producing staple-core/cotton wrap ring spun yarns. *Textile Research Journal* 59 (9): 519.

Sawhney, A. P. S., et al. 1991. Comparison of fabrics made with cotton covered polyester staple core yarn and 100% cotton yarn. *Textile Research Journal* 61 (2): 71.

Wilson, D. K., and T. Kollu. 1991. The production of textured yarns by the false-twist technique. *Textile Progress* 21 (3).

CHAPTER 16

WOVEN FABRICS

Fabrics can be constructed in a variety of ways, ranging from the matting together of fibrous materials to the intricate interlacing of complex yarn systems. The following discussion outlines and defines the major classifications of fabric constructions. The specific techniques and processes by which these different fabrics are made are discussed in the chapters that follow.

Woven Fabrics. Weaving of fabrics consists of interlacing systems of yarn. By varying the interlacings, a wide variety of different fabric constructions can be made.

Looped Fabrics. Fabrics can be constructed from one or more continuous yarns by the formation of a series of interconnected loops. Knitting, though a complex form, is one type of looping construction. Crochet is another.

Knotted Fabrics. Some fabrics are created by knotting yarns together. Lace, nets, macramé, and tatting are created by knotting.

Braided Fabrics. Fabrics may be created by plaiting together yarns or strips of fabrics. The components are interlaced in a diagonal pattern over and under one another to form a flat or tubular fabric of relatively narrow width.

Films. Since films are not made from fibers, they are not considered to be true textiles. They are sometimes laminated to textiles and therefore may be part of the structure of some textile products. They are synthetic polymers extruded in the form of

sheets rather than as fibers. In some cases, these films are eventually made into fibrous form by a process called fibrillation or by cutting the sheet into fibers.

Fiber Webs. Masses of fibers can be held together into a fabric by interlocking of fibers by mechanical action or by fusing fibers together with heat, adhesives, or chemicals. Examples of a few fabrics constructed by these means include felt, bark cloth, spun lace, spunbonded and needle-punched fabrics, and bonded webs. In the textile literature these structures are most commonly referred to as *nonwovens.*

Stitch-Through Fabrics. Stitch through or stitch bonding is a relatively new technique for constructing fabrics in which two sets of yarns or masses of fibers are stitched together into a fabric structure by another set of yarns.

Textile Composites. These materials generally consist of one or more textile components impregnated with or embedded in a resin matrix. Textile composites are generally used for high technology products for industry, the military, and aerospace.

The Creation of Woven Fabrics

Fabrics can be woven from yarns on a simple hand loom or on a highly complex, totally automated power loom. In either case, the fabric that is produced will be made by interlacing one yarn with another. The lengthwise-direction yarns in a woven fabric are called the *warp yarns* or *ends*. Crosswise yarns are called *filling yarns, weft yarns,* or *picks.* Warp and filling yarns normally interlace with each other at right angles.

The Hand Loom

Weaving requires that the warp yarns be held under tension. Having stretched out one set of yarns, the weaver then takes a second yarn and interlaces it with the warps. The simplest interlacing is made by moving the filling over the first warp, under the second, over the third, and under the fourth, and so on. In the second row, the filling moves under the first warp, over the second, under the third, and so on. The third row repeats the pattern of the first, and the fourth row repeats the pattern of the second row. Known as a *plain weave* or *tabby,* this is the simplest form of weaving.

An ancient craft, hand weaving was well known in North America, South America, and the Middle East at least eight thousand years ago. Two separate types of looms developed in different geographic areas. These looms differ in their means of providing tension to the warps. Northern Europeans used warp-weight looms, a vertical type of loom on which the warps were suspended from an upper bar and weighted at the bottom by small stone or clay loom weights. The force that gravity exerted on the weights provided the tension. (See Figure 16.1a.)

The second type of loom was the *two-bar loom* in which the warps stretched from one bar to another. This loom could be made either vertically or horizontally, as a frame of stakes in the ground held the two bars taut. Looms from Asia, the southern shores of the Mediterranean, and South America were of this type. South American looms often added a waist strap to the lower bars. The weaver suspended one bar from a tree or wall, and by placing the strap around the waist, the weaver could increase or decrease tension on the yarns by moving backward or forward. (See Figure 16.1b.)

The filling yarns, those running at right angles to the warps, could have been introduced by hand, but it was easier to use a needle or to wrap the yarns around a stick. This latter method had the advantage of allowing the yarn to be unwound as the stick was moved through the warps. Ultimately, yarn was wound onto a bobbin, and the bobbin was placed into a boatlike *shuttle.* The pointed end of the shuttle

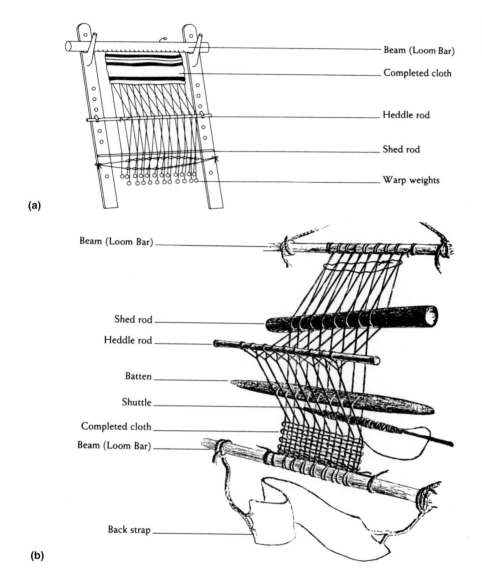

(a)

(b)

Figure 16.1

Two varieties of the hand loom:
(a) warp-weight loom and
(b) back strap loom.

Labels in figure (a): Beam (Loom Bar), Completed cloth, Heddle rod, Shed rod, Warp weights

Labels in figure (b): Beam (Loom Bar), Shed rod, Heddle rod, Batten, Shuttle, Completed cloth, Beam (Loom Bar), Back strap

allowed the carrier to move smoothly, while the bobbin allowed the yarn to unwind as it was needed.

Filling yarns tended to be somewhat loose in placement and had to be pushed into place more firmly. The earliest weavers painstakingly pushed each yarn into place with a small stick. A later, more efficient method used a wooden stick, shaped like a sword, that was slipped behind the filling yarns and pushed them tightly against the fabric that had already been woven. This weaver's sword, or *batten,* became a permanent part of the loom, although its shape was transformed gradually into a comblike device called a *reed* that was mounted on a frame. The frame retained the name *batten,* and a pull of the hand on the batten frame moved the reed forward, swinging the reed against the filling yarn and pushing it ("beating up") firmly into place.

The finished cloth on both horizontal and vertical looms was at first most probably the same dimensions as the loom. At some point, this changed and horizontal looms were adapted to making lengths of fabric longer than the loom. Egyptian fabrics of quite long dimensions have been found, and it is possible that they may have used a roller beam system. A beam with warp yarns wrapped around it allowed yarns to be fed continuously to the weaver, and as the fabric was woven, it was wrapped around a roller at the other end of the loom. In this way continuous lengths of fabric, longer than the loom, could be constructed.

As long as each warp yarn had to be raised by hand before the filling was interlaced with it, the process of weaving remained slow and tedious. Inventive weavers improvised a means of speeding up the procedure of raising and lowering warp yarns. Alternate rows of warps were placed over a *shed rod,* a stick that lifted them above the level of their neighboring yarns. This formation of raised and lowered warp yarns is called the *shed.* The bobbin could be thrust across the entire width of the cloth through the shed without stopping to raise each individual warp yarn. The alternate set of warp yarns was threaded through a series of string loops that were tied to another rod. This rod could raise the second set of yarns past those on the shed rod, and now by thrusting the bobbin under this second set of yarns that had been raised by an upward pull on the rod, the filling interlaced with an alternate set of yarns. Alternate raising and lowering of the rod made it possible to interlace warp and filling yarns quickly and efficiently. The rod that held the second set of warps was called a *harness;* the loops were called *heddles.* Heddles were used in Egypt before 2000 B.C. and in Peru at a comparable period (Albers 1957, 20). Variety in weave could be achieved through the use of multiple harnesses, each raising a different set of warps.

The widespread use of silk probably brought about certain improvements in loom structure. Since silk filament yarns were fine and slippery, use of the shed rods made weaving more difficult. In silk weaving, the shed rod was replaced by a second harness, as the smooth, fine yarns tended to slide against the shed rod, while the heddles held them securely.

The change from hand manipulation of harnesses to operation by foot treadle was another improvement. The loom was constructed so that pressure on a foot treadle raised and lowered the harness frame. This released the hand to operate the shuttle and the batten and increased the speed with which the weaver could work.

Probably the single most important invention that preceded automation of the loom was the flying shuttle. The *flying shuttle,* designed by John Kay and patented in 1733, was a device with a spring mechanism that threw the shuttle across the loom from one side to the other. In hand weaving, Kay's device was activated by a cord on either side of the loom that was pulled by the weaver. When the machine was mechanized, the flying shuttle was incorporated into the loom and operated mechanically.

Figure 16.2 depicts the basic hand loom that had developed by the time of the Industrial Revolution. Hand looms used by weavers today have the same type of structure.

Automation of Weaving

To transform weaving from a hand to a mechanical operation, several conditions had to be satisfied. The various motions made in hand weaving had to be automated. The *Encyclopedia of Textiles* (1980) notes that "the power loom of today is essentially the hand loom adapted to rotary driving" (p. 30).

A further requirement of power looms was that a power-operated loom had to stop automatically when a warp or filling yarn had broken. If the loom continued to function, the cloth would be flawed.

The first automatic loom was devised by Edmund Cartwright in 1784. Although it had a number of defects, this loom did work well enough to demonstrate that automatic loom weaving was feasible. Gradually, inventions by different individuals each contributed to the development of an economically viable automatic loom.

| Figure 16.2 | Eighteenth-century loom. Illustration courtesy of Museum of American Textile History. |

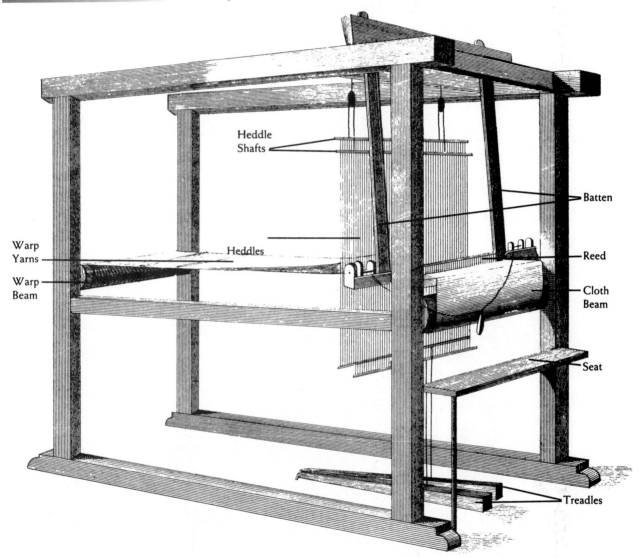

Eventually, upper limits on production speed of shuttle looms were reached. Also, shuttle looms are extremely noisy. To overcome these deficiencies, looms were invented that transported filling yarns without a shuttle. These shuttleless weaving machines are faster and less noisy than are shuttle looms. Currently, their operations are monitored by computers.

Modern Weaving Processes

Present-day looms can be divided between two major classifications: those that produce cloth in flat form and those that produce cloth in tubular form. Looms that produce flat woven cloth predominate. Flat looms can be further subdivided into two categories: (1) those that use a shuttle to transport filling yarns and (2) shuttleless looms, those that use some other means for carrying the filling from side to side.

Preliminary Steps

Preparing the Warp Yarns for Weaving

Before their use on the loom, warp and filling yarns must be prepared for weaving (Figure 16.3). The essential characteristics of suitable warp and filling yarns differ. Warp yarns undergo greater stress and abrasion during weaving than do filling yarns; therefore, warp yarns must be strong enough to withstand these pressures. Warp yarns must be clean, free from knots, and uniform in size. A single warp yarn is called an end.

To strengthen and lubricate warp yarns, *sizing* or *slashing* is added. Size is made up of starches, resins, or gums that act as lubricants. The yarns are passed from one warp beam through a solution of sizing material. The sized yarns are dried immediately after treatment and are wound onto another warp beam. Sizing is not always required on filament yarn warps.

The warp beam containing the sized yarns is placed on the loom. In preparation for weaving, each warp end (yarn) must be threaded through its own drop wire, heddle eye, and reed dent. The *drop wire* is a device that will stop the loom if an end

| Figure 16.3 | Warp beam being prepared from several hundred "cheeses" of yarn. Photograph courtesy of the National Cotton Council of America. |

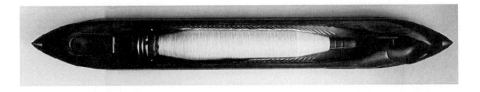

Figure 16.4

The wooden shuttle (into which is fitted a quill, or pirn, on which yarns are wound) carries yarn across the loom. Photograph courtesy of Steel Heddle.

should break, the *heddle eye* is the opening in a heddle that carries the yarn, and the *reed dent* is an opening in the reed, the comblike device that will push each filling yarn close against the completed fabric.

Placing the warp yarns on the loom is done either by *drawing-in* or by *tying-in*. If warp yarns from a previously woven fabric are in place and if that fabric had the same number of warps, the new warps are tied into place by attaching them to the warps already on the loom.

If the new warp is different from that previously woven or if there is no warp on the loom, then the warps must be drawn-in. To draw-in or tie-in each end by hand would be enormously time consuming; therefore, a variety of machines has been developed for drawing-in. A separate machine can be used for each step (i.e., drawing through the drop wire, the heddle eye, and the reed dent), or one machine can perform all three steps. When a loom makes the same fabric, warp after warp, the new warp can be tied-in to the old.

Heddle wires are held in frames called *harnesses*. The number of harnesses required for the loom is determined by the weave.

Preparing the Filling Yarns for Weaving

Yarn that is to be used for the filling must be packaged in some form that allows it to be unwound easily for transport through the shed. In shuttle looms the device that carries the yarn across the shed is called a shuttle and is made up of a wooden carrier into which a *quill*, or *pirn*, is placed (Figure 16.4). The filling yarn is wound onto the quills from larger packages of yarn. For shuttleless looms this step of winding quills is unnecessary because filling yarn is drawn directly from large packages carrying two to three pounds of yarn that are mounted on the sides of the loom. If yarn that has been prepared for use in the filling is not to be used immediately, it is usually conditioned, kept in a room with hot, humid air. Conditioning allows yarn to relax and helps to prevent the formation of kinks.

Basic Motions of Weaving

Loom Operations

Once the filling yarns have been prepared and the warp yarns have been set into place, the loom goes through a series of motions: shedding, picking, beating up, and letting off (Figure 16.5).

Shedding

The shed is formed by raising the harnesses to form an open area between the sets of warps. The formation of the shed is known as *shedding*.

Figure 16.5

Steps in the action of a loom when a filling yarn is inserted in a plain-weave fabric: (a) shed is formed by separating warp yarns to create space through which the shuttle can travel; (b) shuttle is projected through the shed; (c) beating up of yarn takes place to push new filling firmly against the others already in place; (d) positions of warp yarns are reversed to reform shed, and the process is repeated with the shuttle traveling in the opposite direction.

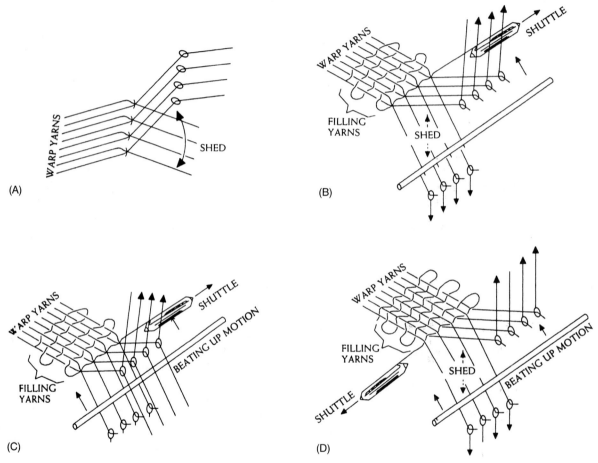

Picking

While the shed is open, the yarn is transported across the opening, laying a filling yarn across the width of the loom. The insertion of the filling is known as *picking*. A single filling yarn is known as a pick. Speed of weaving machines is generally expressed as the number of picks per minute or yards or meters of filling inserted per minute. Speed obviously is related to the width of the loom. Wider looms, weaving wider fabrics, would require more time for one filling insertion.

Beating Up

Beating up is done by the reed, the comblike device that pushes the filling yarn close against the woven fabric.

Letting Off

As the woven fabric is formed, it must be moved or *let off* the loom and *taken up* on the cloth beam to make room for the formation of more fabric. All these functions are synchronized so that they occur in the appropriate sequence and do not interfere with one another.

Monitoring Yarn Breakage

There is always the danger that a warp or filling yarn may break during weaving, causing a flaw in the cloth. To monitor this, warp yarns are threaded through drop wires, small metal plates with holes, which are drawn down when a yarn breaks. Modern looms use electronic scanners that indicate when a yarn is broken. Through signals resulting from either the drop wires or a break in the electronic contact, the loom is shut off, allowing the broken yarn to be repaired.

Yarn Transport Methods

The carrier used for transporting the filling yarn may differ from one kind of loom to another. The different devices used form the basis for classifying different types of looms. Within the industry many people refer to newer equipment as *weaving machines* rather than looms. Weaving machines vary from older, shuttle looms to modern shuttleless machines with sophisticated electronic controls. This newer equipment now predominates in the U.S. textile industry.

Shuttle Looms

In shuttle looms the shuttle traverses the cloth, and the filling yarn unwinds from the quill. Quills in the shuttle must be replaced when the yarn supply is exhausted. The frequency with which a quill has to be replaced depends on the fineness of the filling yarn. Coarse yarns require more frequent replacement; finer yarns need to be replaced less often.

In the mechanical changer, full quills are kept ready in a revolving case. The machine rams them into the shuttle when the shuttle comes to rest briefly after crossing the yarn. The pressure of the full quill crowds the empty quill out of the shuttle. It falls through a slot into a container under the loom. The new quill is pushed mechanically into place in the shuttle, which has a self-threading device that automatically picks up the yarn when the new quill is inserted. This allows the weaving to continue without a stop.

A specialized process has been developed that allows winding of quills to take place at the loom. In the *Unifil system,* empty quills are carried on a conveyer belt to a point where yarn from a large package is wound onto an empty quill that is then returned to a position where it can be placed in the shuttle. This system requires that fewer wound quills be supplied, but it has several limitations. It is useful only for single color picks, and because the cost of the system is high, it is most economical for coarse yarns that would require especially frequent quill replacement. (See Figure 16.6a.)

Picking when two or more different colors or types of filling yarn are used requires two or more shuttles and a more complex and costly type of loom arrangement. A conventional shuttle loom has one shuttle box on each side of the machine. (See Figure 16.6b.)

| Figure 16.6 | (a) Modern box loom. Quills being filled on the Unifil system are visible at the point indicated by the arrow. Photograph courtesy of Picanol Corporation. (b) Filled quills are mounted, ready for insertion into the shuttle, which is not visible. Photograph courtesy of MASTERS OF LINEN, International Linen Promotion. |

(a)   (b)

To insert yarns of different colors or types, a number of shuttle boxes must be moved up and down to bring shuttles into position to create the pattern. Such looms are often called *pick and pick looms*. Among the advantages of most shuttleless looms is that they draw yarn for each pick directly from yarn packages, making it easier and less costly to insert a number of different types of yarn.

The rapid crossing of the shed by the shuttle leaves a layer of filling yarn. When the shed is changed, the yarn is locked into place by the change in warp positioning. However, to make the yarn lie flat and in its proper position, it must be beaten into place.

Shuttleless Weaving Machines

Shuttleless weaving machines were invented to increase the speed of weaving and reduce the literally deafening noise. The modern loom with a shuttle, although much faster in operation than the earliest automatic looms, is not susceptible to further increases in speed because of the variety of operations that the machine must perform. Time is required for stopping the shuttle and accelerating it in the other direction. For this reason, future loom developments are likely to be in the area of shuttleless weaving.

Shuttleless machines may be classified as to the method used in inserting the filling yarns. Four basic types have been developed:

1. Machines with grippers or projectiles (throw across) (Figure 16.7a).
2. Machines with mechanically operated gripper arms or rapiers (reach across) (Figure 16.7b).
3. Machines employing water or air jets to carry the filling (spit or blow across) (Figure 16.7c).
4. Machines that form multiple sheds (multiphase) (Figure 16.8).

In hand weaving and automatic shuttle weaving, the filling yarn is continuous and runs back and forth across the fabric, but in most shuttleless weaving, the filling

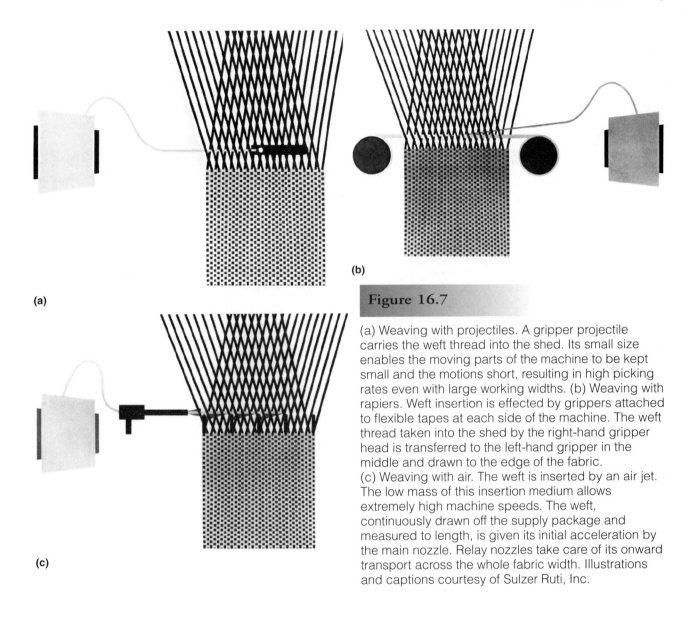

(a)

(b)

(c)

Figure 16.7

(a) Weaving with projectiles. A gripper projectile carries the weft thread into the shed. Its small size enables the moving parts of the machine to be kept small and the motions short, resulting in high picking rates even with large working widths. (b) Weaving with rapiers. Weft insertion is effected by grippers attached to flexible tapes at each side of the machine. The weft thread taken into the shed by the right-hand gripper head is transferred to the left-hand gripper in the middle and drawn to the edge of the fabric.
(c) Weaving with air. The weft is inserted by an air jet. The low mass of this insertion medium allows extremely high machine speeds. The weft, continuously drawn off the supply package and measured to length, is given its initial acceleration by the main nozzle. Relay nozzles take care of its onward transport across the whole fabric width. Illustrations and captions courtesy of Sulzer Ruti, Inc.

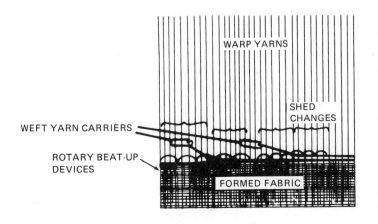

WARP YARNS

SHED
CHANGES

WEFT YARN CARRIERS

ROTARY BEAT-UP
DEVICES

FORMED FABRIC

Figure 16.8

Multiphase loom continually inserts weft yarns from yarn carriers. Rotary beat-up devices press inserted yarn firmly against previously formed cloth. If the pattern requires frequent shed position changes, small groups of yarns are changed into a new shedding position after each new yarn carrier has passed.

yarn extends only from selvage to selvage, as it is cut off before it passes across the shed. In all shuttleless weaving, the yarn for the filling is unwound from large, stationary packages of yarn that are sometimes set on one side and at other times set on both sides of the loom. Since loom speed depends on fabric width, there is every incentive to build wider looms for more efficient filling insertion.

Gripper Loom

In the gripper or projectile type of loom, a small hooklike device grips the end of the filling yarn. As the gripper is projected across the warp shed, it tows the filling behind it. The gripper can move more quickly than a conventional shuttle because of its decreased size; it can travel farther more easily, thereby making possible the weaving of wider fabrics, and it does not require the step of filling the shuttle; it pulls the yarn directly from a prepared yarn package.

Two types of gripper looms are used. In one, the gripper travels only in one direction. It is returned to the starting point by a conveyor belt. To maintain the speed of weaving, each loom must have several grippers, although only one is in use at any one time.

In the other, a single gripper inserts one filling yarn alternately from the right- and left-hand side of the loom. The gripper serves the same function as a conventional shuttle, but instead of holding a quill, it carries the yarn behind it. Packages of yarn must, therefore, be placed on both sides of the loom.

The gripper loom not only weaves fabric more quickly than does the shuttle loom, but it runs with less noise, making it possible for manufacturers to comply more easily with government regulations that restrict noise levels.

There is also a saving in power costs for wide-width fabrics. Narrow fabrics are not economically woven on this loom since too much time is spent in periods of acceleration of the gripper. Wide fabric widths are quite productive, as the power consumed is less than that for a conventional shuttle loom of the same size. Sheets are woven side by side on some of these looms to take advantage of these savings. According to data from producers of these machines, operation is at speeds of up to 1,400 meters of yarn per minute.

Rapier Loom

As in the gripper loom, a stationary package of yarn is used to supply the filling yarns to the rapier loom. One end of a *rapier,* a rod or steel tape, carries the filling. The other end of the rapier is connected to the control system. The rapier moves across the width of the fabric, carrying the filling across through the shed to the opposite side. The rapier is then retracted, leaving the new filling in place.

In some versions of the loom, two rapiers are used, each half the width of the fabric in size. One rapier carries the yarn to the center of the shed, where the opposing rapier picks up the yarn and carries it the remainder of the way across the shed. A disadvantage of both these techniques is the space required for the machine if a rigid rapier is used. The housing for the rapiers must take up as much space as the width of the machine. To overcome this problem, machines with flexible rapiers have been devised. The flexible rapier can be coiled as it is withdrawn and will therefore require less space. However, if the rapier is too stiff, it will not coil; if it is too flexible, it will buckle. The double rapier is used more frequently than the single rapier. (See Figure 16.9.)

Rapier looms operate at speeds of up to 1,260 meters of filling per minute.

Figure 16.9

In the two-rapier type of shuttleless machine, one rapier (a) carries the yarn to the center of the shed where a second rapier (b) grasps the yarn and carries it across the rest of the width of the fabric. Photographs reproduced by permission of American Dornier Machinery Corp.

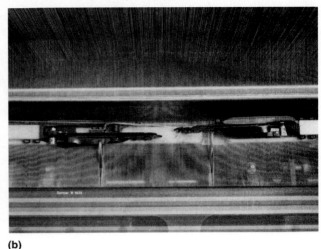

(a)   (b)

Water-Jet Loom

Water-soluble warp sizings are used on most staple warp yarns. Therefore, the use of water-jet looms is restricted to filament yarns, yarns that are nonabsorbent, and those that do not lose strength when wet. Furthermore, these fabrics come off the loom wet and must be dried. In this technique a water jet is shot under force and, with it, a filling yarn. The force of the water as it is propelled across the shed carries the yarn to the opposite side. This loom is quite economical in its operation. A water jet of only 0.1 centimeter is sufficient to carry a yarn across a 48-inch shed. The amount of water required for each filling yarn is less than 2.0 cubic centimeters. Water-jet looms are exceptionally fast: 2,160 meters of filling per minute.

Air-Jet Loom

Air-jet looms operate in a manner similar to water-jet looms. Instead of projecting a stream of water across the shed, a jet of air is projected. The initial propulsive force is provided by a main nozzle (Figure 16.10). Electronically controlled relay nozzles provide additional booster jets to carry the yarn across the shed. Data from manufacturers indicate that air-jet looms operate at speeds of up to 630 picks per minute, or a production rate of up to 1,960 meters of filling inserted per minute. They can weave multicolored yarns to make plaids and are available with both dobby and jacquard patterning mechanisms.

Multiphase Loom

All the weaving techniques discussed thus far require that the shed be open all the way across the loom for the device carrying the filling yarns to pass through the shed. This imposes a limit on loom speed.

The multiphase loom overcomes this limitation by forming many different sheds at different places across the loom and forming these only as the filling yarn is inserted. In this way, a number of filling yarns can be inserted, one behind the other.

Figure 16.10

Air-jet nozzles spaced across the weaving machine transport filling yarns. Photograph courtesy of Sulzer Ruti, Inc.

As a section of the shed opens, the filling passes, and the shed closes, opening again in the new pattern as the next filling yarn arrives. (See Figure 16.8.) Speed is increased because of the number of yarns that can be inserted almost simultaneously one right after the other, but the actual speed of movement of the filling yarns is lower than in other types of looms. For this reason, filling yarns that are weaker can be used. Nuovo Pignone, the manufacturer of a multiphase loom, states that its loom will insert up to 2,000 meters of filling per minute.

Selvages

Many shuttleless weaving machines insert filling yarns from one side. In the shuttle type of loom, the carrying of the continuous filling back and forth across the fabric creates a closed selvage edge, with no loose yarn ends to fray or ravel. In shuttleless looms, however, one or both of the selvages is fringed. It is necessary to reinforce this edge if the fabric is not to fray at the edges. Methods of reinforcement include providing for tucking the yarns at the open edge or use of a *leno selvage,* a self-selvage in which two warp yarns at the edges of the fabric twist around each filling. The tucked-in finish is the more durable. For heavy industrial fabrics made from heat-sensitive or thermoplastic fibers, hot melting devices cause the yarns to fuse together to form a tight selvage. (See Figure 16.11.)

Figure 16.11

Alternative selvage finishes.

NORMAL SELVAGE FRINGED SELVAGE TUCKED SELVAGE LENO SELVAGE

Advantages of Shuttleless Weaving Machines

When patterned fabrics are woven on shuttleless weaving machines, colors can be changed more easily. Unlike shuttle looms in which a different shuttle must be provided for each different color, the shuttleless machines can be provided with a variety of colors directly from yarn packages. Other advantages include lower power requirements, lower sound levels, smaller space requirements, and higher speeds of fabric production. On the other hand, the higher production rates of shuttleless machines require that yarn quality be high to assure trouble-free operation. Over the coming years most shuttle looms will be replaced by one or another shuttleless type.

Control of Loom Motions

The essential motions in loom operation are the motion of the harnesses to form the shed and the activation of devices for carrying the filling through the shed.

Cam Loom

In the past the motions in most simple weaves were controlled by mechanical devices called *cams*. Such looms are rapidly being replaced by more modern machines with electronic control of motions. The shape or profile of the cam is followed by a device called the cam follower, and the irregularities in the cam shape are translated by the cam follower into the motions of the loom (Figure 16.12). In this way simple repeat patterns can be created. Repeats are limited to six or fewer picks, but this includes a substantial majority of the most commonly used fabrics. More complex designs require dobby or jacquard looms.

Dobby Loom

The *dobby loom* is a conventional loom with a somewhat enlarged dobby "head" (Figure 16.13). The dobby mechanism uses a pattern chain on which there are pegs. Nee-

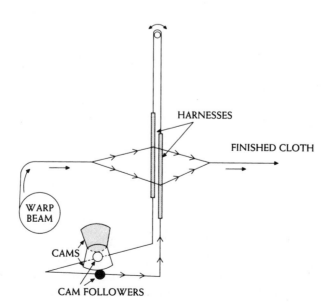

Figure 16.12

Cam follower translates the motion of the cams to the harnesses, which are raised and lowered according to the "instructions" transmitted by the shape of the cam. In this way variations in the weave can be achieved.

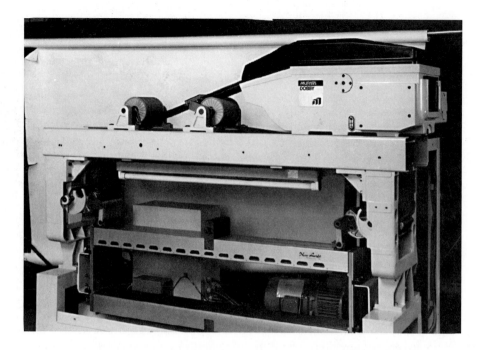

dles or feelers contact the pegs in the pattern chain and are positioned by the pegs. The feelers cause hooks within the dobby head to be connected or disconnected, and the motion of the hooks is translated to the harnesses that move from up to down or to in-between positions as dictated by the pattern.

From twenty-four to thirty shedding combinations are controlled in this way, so that the repeats are limited to about thirty rows in size. A machine called the double-cylinder dobby loom has been developed that approximately doubles the size of the repeat that can be made. The fabrics woven on this loom are less complex than are jacquard patterns and usually consist of small fancy or geometrical figures or designs. Plain terry towels are also woven on dobby looms. With the development of electronic jacquard looms that can make both jacquard and dobby fabrics, dobby looms are becoming less important.

Jacquard Loom

The *jacquard loom* (Figure 16.14) is the descendant of an oriental loom, the draw loom, which was used to weave complex patterned fabrics. Operation of the draw loom required two workers: the weaver who threw the shuttle and operated the batten and a *drawboy* who raised and lowered a series of cords that controlled the pattern. The drawboy had to work from a platform above the loom while the weaver sat below.

Since the drawboy could make mistakes in the selection of cords, later modifications of the loom structure introduced a mechanical device for raising and lowering the cords. In 1805 Joseph Jacquard, a Frenchman, perfected the principle of the mechanical draw loom. To this day, this same type of loom used in weaving complex patterns is known as the jacquard loom and the weave is known as the *jacquard weave*.

The ability of the jacquard loom to weave a variety of complex fabrics is a result of the ability of this machine to control each warp yarn separately. Each warp yarn is threaded through a loop in the end of a leash or cord.

Figure 16.14

Jacquard weaving machines with two different configurations. (a) Dornier rapier jacquard weaving machine, Type HTV8J with a Stäubli electronic head. Photograph courtesy of American Dornier Machinery Corporation. (b) Bonas U.S.A. electronically operated jacquard loom. Photograph courtesy of Bonas U.S.A., Inc.

(a)

(b)

Before the loom is set up, a design is worked out on graph paper, and the position of each of the yarns in the design is analyzed. A punched card is prepared that corresponds to each of the filling yarns. The card contains a "code," a set of punched holes that will determine which warp yarns must be lifted for each passage of the filling. The punched cards are laced together in the correct order for the design. As each card advances to the operating position, needles rest against the card. The needles are held under the pressure of a spring. When a needle position coincides with a hole in the card, the needle moves through the hole. The movement of the needle engages a hook, which in turn lifts the cords attached to the hook. The cords raise the yarns they hold to form the shed. When the filling has been inserted, the needles retract, the cards move to the next position, and different sets of needles engage holes in the next card. This, in turn, causes other warp yarns to be lifted to form a different shed.

Some electronically operated jacquard machines require far less space than mechanically operated jacquards (Figure 16.14). Other advantages of electronic machines are increased speed of operation and the ability to change patterns with greater ease, which makes possible the production of short runs of fabric.

The Weaves

Basic Concepts and Terminology

Woven fabrics, with a few exceptions (such as triaxial fabrics, discussed later in this chapter) are constructed by interlacing warp (lengthwise) yarns and filling (crosswise) yarns at right angles. In theory, warp and filling yarns should intersect at right angles. When this relationship is perfect, the fabric is said to be on *true grain* or *grain perfect*. As a result of the stresses and strains imposed during weaving or finishing, these yarns may not lie in the proper position, and when this occurs, the fabric is said to be *off grain*.

The off-grain relationship of warp and filling yarns is described by different terms, depending on how the distortion lies. Warp yarns are usually straight, as they are subject to lengthwise tension throughout the processing of fabrics. Filling yarns are usually responsible for the distortion, but they may be distorted in a straight line *(skewed)* or in a curved line *(bowed)*. (See Figure 16.15.)

Within the textile and apparel industries, comparative measurement systems are necessary. The concept of yarn size expressed as yarn number has been discussed in chapter 15. When dealing with fabrics, comparisons of size are made in terms of the number of yarns per inch or fabric count, the width of the fabric and the weight of the cloth.

The closeness of the weave is expressed as the *fabric count*. With a small magnifying glass calibrated in inches or centimeters, it is possible to count the number of yarns in 1 inch or centimeter of warp and in 1 inch or centimeter of the filling. When the number of yarns in the warp is similar to the number of yarns in the filling, the weave is said to be a balanced weave. The fabric count is often expressed in numeri-

Figure 16.15

Grain positions. (a) Warp and filling interlace at 90° angle. Fabric is on true grain.
(b) Filling is off the square, skewed. Though straight, the filling is not at 90° to the warp.
(c) Filling is bowed, i.e., straight for part of the way, then curved toward one selvage. (d) Filling is bowed, curved from selvage to selvage.

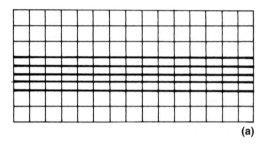

(a)

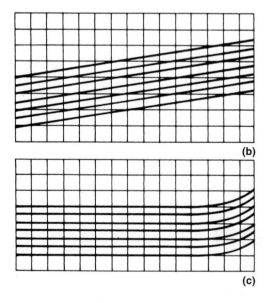

(b)

(c)

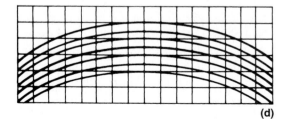

(d)

cal form as 80 × 64, indicating that there are 80 warp yarns per inch by 64 fillings. When warp and filling are perfectly balanced, or equal, the count may be stated as 80 square, meaning there are 80 yarns per inch in the warp and 80 yarns per inch in the filling. Alternatively, the number may be doubled, in which case a count of 180 would indicate a count of 90 yarns per inch in each direction. Balanced-weave fabrics with the same type of yarns in warp and filling are more durable because the fabric wears evenly in both warp and filling directions.

Fabric count is usually measured with a calibrated, square magnifying glass called either a *linen tester* or *pick glass* (Figure 16.16). The glass is marked off in fractions of an inch or in centimeters, and the number of warp and filling yarns beside these calibrations can be viewed in magnified form with the glass and counted.

In those fabrics where fabric counts are not balanced, the larger number of yarns will usually be found in the warp direction. Unbalanced fabrics usually exhibit so-called rib effects created when numerous finer warp yarns cross over coarser filling yarns. Costs increase more rapidly as the number of picks (filling yarns) per inch increases; therefore, fabrics with balanced weaves or those with more yarns in the filling than in the warp are more costly to manufacture.

Counts are taken in the greige (i.e., unfinished) goods, and since fabrics may shrink during finishing, the count provided may not be exactly accurate. If only one number appears, it can generally be assumed that the fabric has a balanced weave.

Fabric widths will vary with the size of the loom on which they were woven. Since the introduction of automated looms and with improvements in the technology for transporting the filling yarns, fabric widths have increased dramatically. A survey of the specifications of air-jet shuttleless looms, for example, notes width possibilities of as much as 157 inches, while narrow looms are available for weaving specialty items such as tapes.

Fabric weight is expressed as ounces per linear (running) yard, yards per pound, or ounces per square yard. Woolens, worsteds, and fabrics of similar weight made from blends or manufactured fibers are often measured in ounces per yard. For example, one may see designations such as a 14-ounce tweed or an 8-ounce tropical worsted. In this system of measurement, the higher the number, the heavier the fabric. As measurements tend to move to the metric system, these weights may be expressed in grams per square meter rather than in ounces.

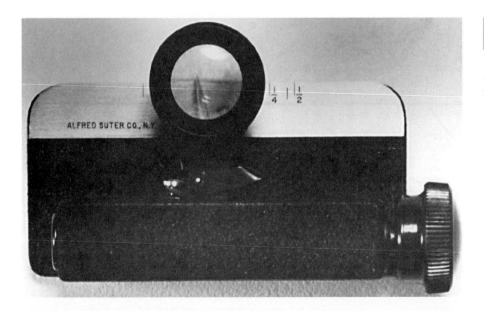

Figure 16.16

Pick glass used to facilitate counting yarns per inch or wales and courses (lengthwise and crosswise stitches) of knitted goods. Photograph courtesy of Alfred Suter Co., Inc.

Yards per pound is a measure of the number of yards of cloth in 1 pound. In this measure, higher numbers indicate lighter weight fabrics. This system of measurement is used mostly for cottons, cotton blends, or lightweight manufactured fabrics.

When measuring ounces per yard or yards per pound, the width of the fabric is not taken into account. These measures are, therefore, less precise than is the measure of ounces per square yard, which is the weight of a piece of fabric measuring 36 inches by 36 inches.

Fabric weights may range widely. Fabrics weighing less than 1 ounce per square yard would be very lightweight, as for example in some sheer curtain fabrics, gauzes, or even mosquito netting. Fabrics weighing from 2 to 4 ounces per square yard are also relatively lightweight. These are often referred to in the industry as *top-weight* fabrics and are typically used for shirts or blouses. Medium-weight fabrics, 5 to 7 ounces per square yard, are referred to as *bottom-weight* fabrics and are used for items such as skirts or slacks. Heavyweight fabrics range from 9 to 11 ounces (e.g., some jeans), and weights over 14 ounces are classified as *very heavyweight* (perhaps for upholstery).

The number and placement of yarns will affect the handle, the draping qualities, and the appearance of fabrics. As warp yarns are placed on the warp beam, they must be spaced so as to allow room for the filling yarns to interlace. In a *jammed* weave with minimum possible space for interlacing, a stiff, less flexible structure will be created. In general, it is true that those fabrics with fewer interlacings and more space between the yarns will be softer and more supple and will drape better. Fabrics with closer, denser weaves are likely to be more durable than those with loosely woven, open weaves. Higher count fabrics have higher strength.

Three types of weave structure form the basis of even the most complex weaves. Known as basic weaves, these are the *plain weave,* the *twill weave,* and the *satin weave.*

Visual representation of weaves is often made on graph paper. Each square of the paper represents the yarn that appears on the upper side or surface of the fabric. Darkened squares represent the warp yarns crossing over filling yarns.

Diagramming of weaves on graph paper is a useful exercise, but students will probably find that the concepts relating to weaves are made clearer if they use colored yarns or strips of colored paper to create small samples of each of the basic weaves. A small hand loom, or a child's loom, can be used for this purpose.

Basic Weaves

The Plain Weave

The plain weave is the simplest of the weaves and the most common. It consists of interlacing warp and filling yarns in a pattern of over one and under one. Imagine a small hand loom with the warp yarns held firmly in place. The filling yarn moves over the first warp yarn, under the second, over the third, under the fourth, and so on. In the next row, the filling yarn goes under the first warp yarn, over the second, under the third, and so on. In the third row, the filling moves over the first warp, under the second, and so on, just as it did in the first row. (See Figure 16.17.)

The weave can be made in any type of yarn. Made with tightly twisted, single yarns that are placed close together both in the warp and filling, and with the same number of yarns in both directions, the resulting fabric will be a very durable, simple, serviceable fabric. If, however, the warp were to be made from a single yarn and the filling from a colorful bouclé yarn, a quite different, much more decorative fabric would result. Both are the product of the same, basic, plain weave.

Plain-weave fabrics are constructed from many fibers and in weights ranging from light to heavy. Weaves may be balanced or unbalanced. Decorative effects can be achieved by using novelty yarns or yarns of different colors. Together with many

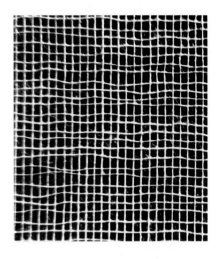

(a)   (b)

Figure 16.17

(a) Diagram of the plain weave and (b) close-up photo of plain weave.

of these novelty fabrics, a number of standard fabric types are made in the plain weave. In the past these standard fabrics were always constructed from specific fibers. At present suitable manufactured fibers are also woven into many of the standard fabric constructions.

Plain-Weave Fabrics

The balanced weaves are the most common. Unbalanced weaves, or *rib weaves,* and another variation, *basket weaves,* will be discussed later. It is helpful to classify balanced plain weaves by weight as light, medium, or heavy.

Lightweight Plain-Weave Fabrics. Lightweight plain-weave fabrics may be light in weight because they have either a low fabric count or are constructed of fine yarns. The following low-fabric-count balanced plain weaves have somewhat specialized uses.

- *Cheesecloth* is very open weave soft fabric originally used in producing cheese, serving as a wrapper or strainer for curds (Figure 16.17b).
- *Crinoline* and *buckram* are heavily sized to serve as stiffening fabrics.
- *Gauze,* with a higher count than cheesecloth, is used in theatrical costumes and medical dressings, as well as for blouses and dresses.

The following are high-count balanced plain weaves with fine yarns.

- *Chiffon* is made from fine, highly twisted filament yarns. Because of the tightly twisted crepe yarns, chiffon has excellent drape, and although it is delicate in appearance, it is relatively durable. Sheer evening dresses, blouses, lingerie, and other dressy apparel are constructed from the fabric.
- *Ninon,* a sheer plain weave of filament yarns, is often used in sheer curtains and draperies.
- *Organdy* is a sheer cotton fabric that is given a temporarily or permanently stiffened finish.
- *Organza* is a stiff sheer fabric made of filament yarns.
- *Voile,* a soft fabric with somewhat lower fabric count and higher twist yarns, has a distinctive two-ply warp and good drapability.

Medium-Weight Plain-Weave Fabrics. Medium-weight balanced plain weaves usually have fairly high fabric counts, contain medium-weight yarns (12–29 tex), and are opaque. Distinguishing characteristics may be design, color, finish, or fabric count.

- *Calico* is a closely woven fabric with a small printed design.
- *Chambray* fabrics have colored warp yarns and white filling yarns that produce a heather appearance.
- *Chintz* is a fabric printed with large designs that is often given a polished or glazed finish. Solid color glazed fabrics are called *polished cotton.*
- *Gingham* is a woven check or plaid design made with yarns of different colors.
- *Muslin,* generally woven from cotton or cotton blends, is made in both heavily sized, bleached qualities and in better grades for sheets and pillow cases. Muslin sheets are not combed and have a lower count (128 to 140 total yarns per inch) than do percale sheets.
- *Percale,* a closely woven, plain weave of cotton or blended fibers, is made from yarns of moderate twist. Percale yard goods are generally carded, but percale sheets are finer and more luxurious in feel and are made of combed yarns. Percale sheets have a count of 180 to 200 yarns (warp plus filling) per inch.

Heavyweight Plain-Weave Fabrics. The following are common heavyweight plain-weave fabrics.

- *Butcher linen* is a plain, stiff, white fabric made from heavy yarn.
- *Crash* is made from thick and thin yarns, giving the fabric a nubby look.
- *Homespun* is a furnishing fabric made with irregular yarns to resemble hand-spun and hand-woven fabrics.
- *Osnaburg* is made of low-quality cotton for industrial use and in interior fabrics for upholstered furniture.

Plain-Weave Variations

Rib Variations. Ribbed fabrics have an unbalanced weave with many small yarns crossing over a fewer number of large yarns. Most unbalanced weaves have a larger number of warp yarns than filling, forming a crosswise rib. Ribs can be relatively small or quite pronounced (Figure 16.18). *Corded fabrics* can be created by grouping yarns together in one direction before they are crossed by yarns in the other direction or by using large yarns at intervals (Figure 16.19). Following are some standard rib-weave fabrics.

- *Bengaline* and *ottoman* heavyweight fabrics with large ribs, are used mostly in upholstery and furnishings.
- *Broadcloth* is a medium-weight unbalanced plain weave with fine ribs. The rib weave makes it crisper than medium-weight balanced weaves. It is often made from cotton or cotton blends.
- *Faille* has a prominent rib and is made with fine filament yarns in the warp and heavy spun yarns in the filling. It is usually heavyweight, although lighter weight *tissue failles* are also produced.
- *Grosgrain* has very prominent ribs and is usually woven in narrow ribbon widths.
- *Poplin,* a bottom-weight rib weave, is usually made from cotton or cotton blends.
- *Shantung* has a nubby, irregular rib in the filling. Formerly made almost exclusively of silk, shantung is now made from a variety of manufactured fibers as well.
- *Taffeta* is a medium-weight weave made from filament yarns that is often used for evening wear.
- *Bedford cord* is a sturdy fabric constructed with a pronounced lengthwise cord.

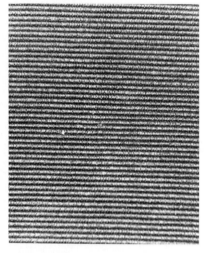

Figure 16.18

Faille fabric with pronounced crosswise rib.

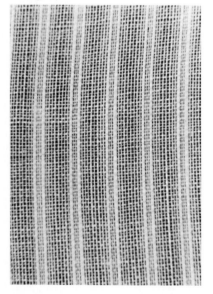

Figure 16.19

Dimity fabric with pronounced lengthwise cord.

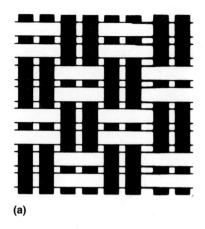

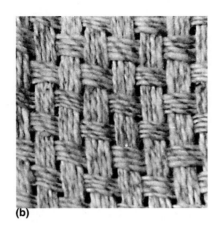

(a)   **(b)**

Figure 16.20

(a) The basket-weave variation of the plain weave and (b) monk's cloth, a basket-weave fabric with four warp and four filling yarns.

- *Dimity,* a sheer cotton fabric, is often made with a lengthwise cord effect. Some dimity fabrics use larger yarns in both the warp and filling direction to achieve a checked, or *barred,* effect.

Basket Weave. Using the principle of the plain weave, variations are made. The basket weave uses two or more warp and/or two or more filling yarns side by side as one yarn (Figure 16.20a). The resultant cloth is fairly loose in weave.

The following are among the more common basket-weave fabrics.

- *Monk's cloth* is a coarse cloth of large yarns (Figure 16.20b). Monk's cloth uses four or more yarns as one in the weave. Its major uses are in household textiles such as curtains, spreads, and the like.
- *Hopsacking* is made of many different fibers. This fabric simulates the fabrics used in bags for gathering hops. It has a 2-2 or 3-3 basket weave and is commonly used in upholstery.
- *Modified basket weaves* may use double yarns in one direction but not in the other. *Oxford cloth,* which is made in this way, is a soft fabric, often made of cotton or cotton blends, that is used for shirts. Frequently, it is made with narrow colored stripes in the warp, or a colored warp.
- *Duck* and *canvas* are heavy, tightly woven, and very stiff plain-weave fabrics made of even yarn for industrial use. Because of the tight weave, these fabrics are often used for outdoor purposes.

Twill Weave

Twill fabrics are readily identified by the diagonal lines that the weave creates on the surface of the fabric. Because there are fewer interlacings, the yarns in twill fabrics can be spaced closely together, packed tightly, and held firmly in place. Therefore, twill fabrics are usually quite strong and durable, while at the same time they are supple and drape well. Most twill-weave fabrics are made in bottom weight. The compact structure of twill fabrics enables them to shed soil readily, although when soiled they may be difficult to get clean. Depending on their construction, twill fabrics generally show good resistance to abrasion. Twill fabrics are often used for tailored garments, particularly when made of worsted wool yarns.

The simplest twill weave is created by the warp yarn crossing over two filling yarns, then under one, over two, under one, and so on. In the next row, the sequence begins one yarn down. (See Figure 16.21.) The area in which one yarn crosses over several yarns in the opposite direction is called a *float.*

Figure 16.21

Right-handed, warp-faced twill weave.

Figure 16.22

Left-handed twill weave.

The lines created by this pattern are called *wales.* When the cloth is held in the position in which it was woven, the wales (diagonal lines) will be seen to run either from the lower left corner to the upper right corner or from the lower right to the upper left. If the diagonal runs from the lower left to the upper right, the twill is known as a right-hand twill. About 85 percent of all twill-woven fabrics are right-hand twills (American Fabrics 1980, 325). When the twill runs from the lower right to the upper left, the twill is known as a left-hand twill (Figure 16.22).

There are a number of types of twill weaves. All use the same principle of crossing more than one yarn at a regular, even progression. Descriptions of twills may be made in terms of the pattern of warp yarns crossing filling yarns. The description of twill weaves is notated as 2/1, 2/2, 3/2, and so on. The first digit refers to the number of filling yarns crossed over by the warp and the second digit to the number of filling yarns the warp passes under before returning to cross the filling again. When the crossing is over and under the same number of yarns, the fabric is called an even or even-sided twill. When warps pass over a larger or smaller number of filling yarns than they pass under, the fabric is called an uneven twill.

Even-sided Twill. The even-sided twill has the same number of warp and filling yarns showing on the face of the fabric. Figure 16.23 shows how such a weave is achieved in a 2/2 twill. Even-sided twills are reversible unless printed or finished or one side.

- *Serge* is a popular basic twill fabric made from any number of different fibers. When serge is made from wool, it is often woven from worsted yarns. Serge will take a crease well, but wool serge tends to become shiny with wear. It tailors well.
- *Flannel,* if made of wool, is usually a twill weave with a napped finish.
- *Plaids* or tartan patterns are yarn-dyed even-sided twills.

Warp-faced Twill. Warp-faced twills have a predominance of warp yarns on the surface of the fabric, with patterns of 2/1, 3/1, 3/2, and so on. (See Figure 16.24.)

- *Denim* is a durable heavyweight twill with colored warp yarns and white filling yarns. Since it is a warp-faced twill, the colored warp yarns predominate on the face and the white filling yarns on the back.
- *Drill* is another heavyweight fabric, usually of a solid color.
- *Jean* is a lighter weight twill.
- *Gabardine* is durable and closely woven. It is made into a variety of weights from many different fibers such as wool, rayon, cotton, and manufactured fibers.

Filling-faced Twill. Filling-faced twills have a predominance of filling yarns on the surface of the fabric. Filling yarns are generally weaker than are warp yarns, so that relatively few filling-faced twills are made.

Herringbone Twill. In a herringbone twill the direction of the twill reverses itself to form a broken diagonal that appears like a series of V's: herringbone patterns create a decorative effect (Figure 16.25). Herringbone twills are very common in suiting fabrics.

Twill Angles. When the face of a twill fabric is examined, the diagonal of the wales will be seen to move at a more or less steep angle. The steepness of the angle is dependent on two factors in the construction of the fabric: the number of warp yarns per inch of fabric and the number of steps between movement of yarns when they interlace.

The more warp yarns in the construction, the steeper the angle of the wales, provided that the number of filling yarns per inch remains the same. This is because the

Figure 16.23

Right-handed, even-sided twill (2/2).

points of interlacing of the yarns will be closer together, thereby making a steep climb upward. When the steepness of the angle is the result of close spacing of warp yarns, these steeper angles are an indication of good strength. If the angle the wale makes with the filling yarn is about 45°, the fabric is a *regular twill.* Fabrics with higher angles are *steep twills,* and those with smaller angles are *reclining twills.*

Generally, the interlacing of yarns in a twill changes with each filling yarn. There are, however, fabrics in which the interlacing of yarns changes only every two filling yarns or every three filling yarns. The less often the interlacing changes, the steeper the angle of the twill will be.

Satin Weave

Satin-weave fabrics are made by allowing yarns to float over a number of yarns from the opposite direction. Interlacings are made at intervals such as over four, under one (using five harnesses); over seven, under one (eight harnesses); or over eleven, under one (twelve harnesses). Floats in satin fabrics may cross from four to twelve yarns before interlacing with another yarn. No pronounced diagonal line is formed on the surface of the fabric because the points of intersection are spaced in such a way that no regular progression is formed from one yarn to that lying next to it.

When warp yarns form the floats on the face of the fabric, the fabric is a *warp-faced satin* (Figure 16.26). When filling yarns float on the face, the fabric is a *filling-faced satin* (Figure 16.27). Satin-weave fabrics made from filament yarns are called *satins;* those from spun yarns are *sateen.* Most warp-faced weaves have filament yarns because filament yarns do not require a tight twist to serve as warp yarns, whereas cotton, being a staple fiber, must be given a fairly high degree of twist if it is to serve as a strong warp yarn. Therefore, sateen fabrics are usually filling faced, although some warp sateens are made.

Satin-weave fabrics are quite decorative. They are usually made from filament yarns with high luster to produce a shiny, lustrous surface and tend to have high fabric counts. They are smooth and slippery in texture and tend to shed dirt easily. The

Figure 16.24

Right-handed, warp-faced twill weave (2/1).

Figure 16.25

Herringbone twill fabric.

Warp-faced satin weave. Warp yarns form floats, crossing over seven filling yarns between every interlacing.

Filling-faced weave. Filling yarns form floats, crossing over four warp yarns between every interlacing.

long floats on the surface are, of course, subject to abrasion and to snagging. The longer the float, the greater the likelihood of snags and pulls. Satins are often used as lining fabrics for coats and suits because they slide easily over other fabrics. The durability of satin-weave fabrics is related to the density of the weave, with closely woven, high-count fabrics having good durability. Satins made from stronger fibers will, of course, be more durable than those made from weaker fibers.

Following are some names given to satin fabrics.

- *Antique satin,* a satin made to imitate silk satin of an earlier period, often uses slubbed filling yarns for decorative effect.
- *Peau de soie* is soft, closely woven satin with a flat, mellow luster.
- *Slipper satin* is strong, compact satin, heavy in weight. It is often used for evening shoes.

In *crepe-backed satin,* loosely twisted, lustrous warp yarns are combined with tightly twisted, creped filling yarns. The floats on the surface are created by the warp, so that the face of the fabric is chiefly made up of warp yarns with a satin appearance, whereas the back of the fabric is made up largely of tightly twisted filling yarns that produce a crepe or rougher surface texture with a flat, less shiny appearance.

Novelty Fabrics from Basic Weaves

Novelty effects in fabrics are in large part a result of selection of novelty yarns for incorporation into fabrics made in one of the basic weaves.

Crepe Fabrics. *Crepe fabrics* may be defined as fabrics characterized by a crinkled, pebbly surface (Figure 16.28). Originally, crepe fabrics were made from crepe yarns, that is, yarns with an exceptionally high degree of twist, up to 65 turns per inch. Most standard crepe fabrics were made in the plain weave, some with rib effects, and some in satin weave, as in crepe-backed satin. With the advent of synthetic fibers, however, many *crepe effects* are achieved through the use of textured yarns, bicomponent yarns in which uneven shrinkage creates a crepelike surface, or embossing or stamping a crepelike texture on the surface of the fabric. Most fabrics made from these more recent processes will be durable only if they are made from heat-treated thermoplastic fibers. Another method is to use a special crepe weave that breaks up the surface of the cloth into a random sequence of interlacings. Careful examination of fabrics having a crepelike appearance will reveal that relatively few of them are actually woven with crepe yarns.

Seersucker. Another plain-weave fabric, seersucker is created by holding some warp yarns at tight tension, some at slack tension. Those at slack tension puff up to form a sort of "blister effect." Seersucker surface effects are permanent. Often the slack and tight yarns are each made from a different colored yarn, to provide a decorative striped effect. Seersucker should not be confused with fabrics having puffed effects created by chemical finishes, such as *plissé* or *embossing,* which are much less durable.

Variations of the Basic Weaves

Dobby Fabrics

The dobby weave is rather like a jacquard weave in miniature. The patterns created by the dobby weave are small, repeated patterns, usually geometric in form (Figure 16.29).

The following are some of the fabrics made on the dobby loom.

Crepe fabric with a pebbly surface created by using tightly twisted crepe yarns.

- *Bird's eye,* a cloth made with small diamond-shaped figures, has a weave that is said to resemble the eye of a bird. Bird's eye is also called *diaper cloth.*
- *Piqué* is a medium- to heavyweight fabric, often of cotton, with a pronounced lengthwise cord, often combined with other small figures or patterns such as honeycomb or waffle effects.
- *White-on-white* has a white dobby figure woven on a white background and is often used for men's shirting.

Figure 16.29   Close-up photographs of two different fabrics woven on the dobby loom.

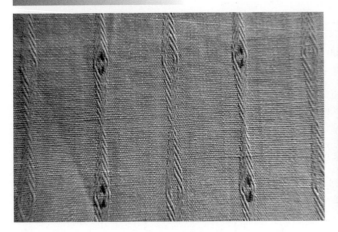

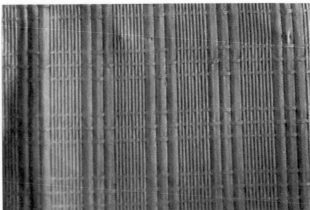

Jacquard Fabrics

The operation of the jacquard loom has been described earlier in this chapter. Jacquard patterns, when carefully analyzed, may be seen to contain combinations of plain, twill, and satin weaves, even in the same crosswise yarn. Many decorative fabrics are made by the jacquard technique (Figure 16.30). Jacquard woven fabrics should not be confused with true tapestries even though some fashion promotions may refer to jacquard fabrics as being "tapestry fabrics."

The following are some of the best-known jacquard patterns.

- *Brocade* features an embossed appearance. Elaborate patterns, often of flowers and figures, stand out from the background. Pattern and ground are usually different weaves. Brocades are made from a wide range of fibers and with a wide range of price and quality. Fabrics are used for upholstery, draperies, and evening and formal clothing.
- *Brocatelle* is similar to brocade, but with figures or patterns standing in high relief. Brocatelle is used mostly for upholstery fabrics and draperies.
- *Damask* is a flatter fabric than brocade and often has a fine weave. Damask figures often use a satin weave to reflect light from the pattern, whereas the background is made in a plain or twill construction. Linen damasks have long been used for luxurious tablecloths. Damasks are reversible. Cotton and linen damasks are made either with four-yarn float or a seven-yarn float in the satin weave. The longer floats are more lustrous, but the shorter floats are more durable, as they are less likely to snag or be subject to abrasion. (See Figure 16.31.)

Tapestries

Tapestry weaving differs from jacquard weaving in that the former is essentially a hand technique. Whereas jacquard weaving uses repeated patterns of finite size, tapes-

Figure 16.30

Photograph of fabric "picture" woven on a jacquard loom that illustrates the complexity of designs that can be woven on the jacquard loom.

Figure 16.31

Damask fabric woven on a jacquard loom.

try weaving is used to produce enormous fabrics that can be one, large picture. Tapestry weaving may be compared to painting with yarn. (See Figure 16.32.) Since it is basically a hand technique, tapestry is made on a very elementary loom.

In the weaving of European tapestries, the loom followed the basic form of the two-bar loom. The loom was set up either vertically or horizontally, and warp yarns were measured and affixed to the loom. Filling yarns were prepared in the appropriate colors. The design of the tapestry was first worked out in a drawing, or *cartoon,* as it was called. The artist who created the drawing may have been one of great stature, and painters such as Raphael and Rubens served as designers of sixteenth- and seventeenth-century tapestries. The cartoon was sometimes traced onto the warp yarns. In other instances it was mounted behind the loom, and the tapestry weaver looked through the warp yarns to the design, following the plan of the drawing. The tapestry was woven with the wrong side facing the weaver. Sometimes a mirror was set up beneath the tapestry so that the weaver could check the progress on the right side.

The various colors of yarns were wound onto sharp, pointed bobbins that were introduced into the warp, and the weaver proceeded to fill in the area of that particular color. When the weaver reached the end of one color, a new bobbin was used for the next section. This created a problem, because as the weaver worked back and forth in a particular segment of the design, the yarns of one color did not join with the yarns of the adjacent color. This produced slits in the fabric at the place where each new color began. Sections of the tapestry could be sewn shut, but this caused the fabric to be weaker at the spots where the fabric was seamed together. Two other methods were also used to prevent the formation of slits. Where the color of one section ended and another began, both the old and the new color could be twisted around the same warp yarns. This system worked well except that it created a slightly indistinct or shadowy line. Where clear, well-defined lines were required, the yarns of adjacent colors were fastened together by looping one yarn around the other.

In tapestry weaving, all the warp yarns are completely covered by filling yarns, so it is the filling yarns that carry the design. The warp yarns serve only as the base.

Figure 16.32

French or Flemish tapestry of the late fifteenth century woven from wool and silk with metal threads. Photograph courtesy of the Metropolitan Museum of Art, the Cloisters Collection. Gift of John D. Rockefeller, Jr., 1937.

Leno-Weave Fabrics

The leno weave is the modern descendant of a technique called *twining* that was used thousands of years ago for making fabrics. In leno-weave fabrics, the warp yarns are paired. A special attachment, the *doup* or *leno* attachment, crosses or laps the paired warp yarns over each other, while the filling passes through the opening between the two warp yarns. (See Figure 16.33.)

Leno-weave fabrics are made in open, gauzelike constructions. The twined (not twisted) warp yarns prevent the filling yarns of these open fabrics from slipping. Curtain fabrics are often made with leno weave. Two of the more popular leno-weave fabrics are *marquisette* and *grenadine*. Many fruit sacks are leno-woven of slit films.

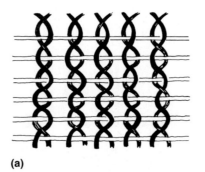

(a)

Figure 16.33

(a) Structure of a leno-weave fabric and (b) close-up of a leno-weave fabric with bouclé yarns in the crosswise direction.

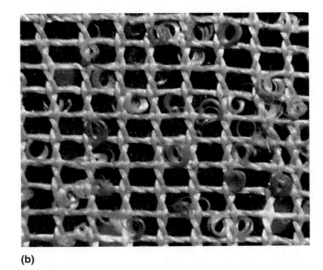

(b)

Woven Pile Fabrics

Pile fabrics have been defined as "fabrics(s) with cut or uncut loops which stand up densely on the surface" (Klapper 1967, 64). Pile fabrics may be created by weaving or through other construction techniques, such as tufting, knitting, or stitch through. To create the loops that appear on the surface of woven pile fabrics, the weaving process incorporates an extra set of yarns that form the pile. Construction of woven pile fabrics, therefore, represents a complex form of weaving in which there are at least three sets of yarns.

Woven pile fabrics are divided into two categories depending on whether the extra set of yarns is in the warp direction or the filling direction. *Warp pile fabrics* have two sets of warp yarns and one set of filling yarns. *Filling pile fabrics* have two sets of filling yarns.

Pile fabrics are woven by one of several methods, depending on whether they are warp pile or filling pile fabrics.

Warp Pile Fabrics. Warp pile can be made by the wire method, the double-cloth method, or by slack tension weaving.

In the wire method one set of warp yarns and the filling yarn interlace in the usual manner and form the "ground" fabric in either a plain or twill weave. The extra set of warp yarns forms the pile. When the pile yarns are raised by the heddles, the machine inserts a wire across the loom in the filling direction. When the

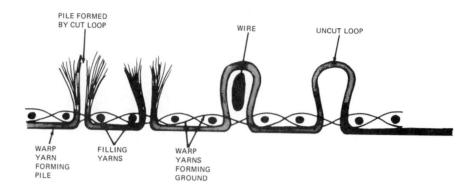

warps are lowered, they loop over the wire to make a raised area. The next several filling yarns are inserted in the usual manner. The wire is then withdrawn, leaving the loop, which is held firmly in place by the other yarns. Frisé, a fabric often used for upholstery, is an example of an uncut, looped pile fabric that can be made by the wire method. If the fabric is to have a cut pile, the wire has a knife blade at the end that cuts the yarns as the wire is withdrawn. *Velvets* may be made in this way. (See Figures 16.34 and 16.35.) If the fabric is to have an uncut pile, the wire has no cutting edge.

The double-cloth method is used for cut pile fabrics. Here, two sets of warps and two sets of fillings are woven simultaneously into a layer of fabric. A third set of warp yarns moves back and forth between the two layers of fabric, holding them together and being held by each fabric. The resultant fabric is cut apart by a sharp knife, thereby creating two lengths of fabric, each with a cut pile. (See Figure 16.36.)

Figure 16.36

Construction of pile fabric by the double-cloth method. Illustration courtesy of Crompton Company, Inc.

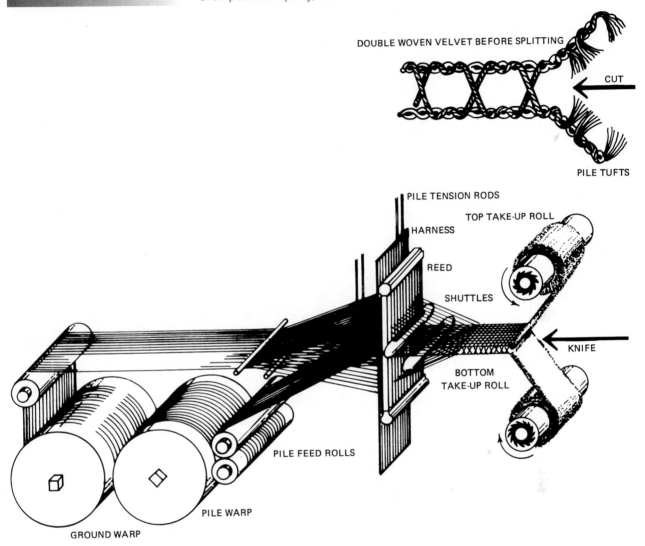

DOUBLE WOVEN VELVET BEFORE SPLITTING

CUT

PILE TUFTS

PILE TENSION RODS

TOP TAKE-UP ROLL

HARNESS

REED

SHUTTLES

KNIFE

BOTTOM TAKE-UP ROLL

PILE FEED ROLLS

PILE WARP

GROUND WARP

Velvets and *plushes* can be made with the double-cloth method. Velvets are usually made of filament yarns. Other nonpile fabrics can be made by the double-cloth method. These are discussed later in this chapter.

Terry cloth is made by the slack tension method. Terry cloth is made with uncut loops. Usually, two sets of warps and one set of filling yarns are used; however, more expensive fabrics may use two sets of yarns in each direction. The ground of the fabric is of warp yarns held under tension, the pile of warp yarns that are allowed to relax. Periodically (usually after every three picks), tension is released on the warp pile yarns at the same time as the next three filling yarns are pushed firmly into place. The first two of each three picks are only beaten up part way. The loose warp yarns loop up on the surface to form the terry pile.

Loops may remain uncut to form the traditional terry cloth with loops on both sides (Figure 16.37). Sometimes one side is sheared to make an attractive *velour* face. Such fabrics do not wear as well as uncut loop fabrics. Pile yarns in velour toweling

Figure 16.37

Terry cloth fabric. Ground is visible in the spaces between the uncut loops of the pile.

tend to become dislodged more easily, thereby shortening the wear life of the material. Terry pile may appear on one or both sides of the fabric.

Filling Pile Fabrics. Filling pile fabrics are woven by the filling pile method. In this method there are two sets of filling yarns and one set of warp yarns. The extra set of filling yarns forms floats that are from four to six yarns in length. The floating yarns are cut at the center of the float, and these ends are brushed up the surface of the fabric (See Figure 16.38.)

In some filling pile constructions, the filling yarn that makes the pile is interlaced with the ground one time before it is cut; in others, the filling pile interlaces twice. Those fabrics in which there are two interlacings are more durable than when only one interlacing has taken place.

Floats for *corduroy* are placed in lengthwise rows, and floats for *velveteen* are spaced to produce an overall pile effect. Velveteens are characterized by a uniform, overall pile. The even spacing of corduroy floats produces a strip or wale characteristic of this fabric. Corduroys are given names according to the numbers of wales. *Feathercord* corduroy has about 20 to 25 lengthwise wales per inch; *fine wale* or *pinwale* corduroy, about 16 to 23 wales; *mid, medium,* or *regular wale* corduroy, about 14 wales; *wide wale* corduroy, about 6 to 10 wales; and *broad wale* corduroy, about 3 to 5 ribs per inch. Novelty wale corduroys are also produced in which thick and thin wales are arranged in varying patterns (Figure 16.39). Some corduroy fabrics are now made with 100 percent cotton yarns in the pile filling and polyester and cotton blends in the ground yarns. Other decorative effects can be achieved by cutting floats selectively to vary pattern and texture. Most filling pile fabrics are made from spun yarns.

Figure 16.38

Construction of corduroy by the filling pile method.

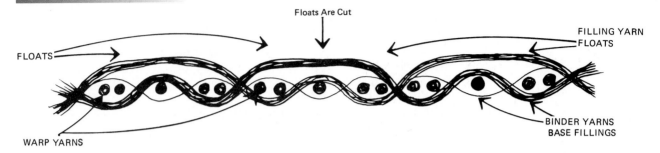

Floats Are Cut

FLOATS

FILLING YARN FLOATS

WARP YARNS

BINDER YARNS
BASE FILLINGS

Cut Floats Form Pile

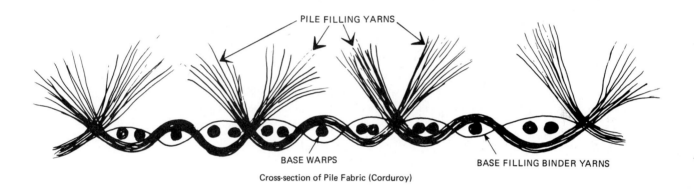

PILE FILLING YARNS

BASE WARPS

BASE FILLING BINDER YARNS

Cross-section of Pile Fabric (Corduroy)

Chenille

Chenille fabrics have a pile that is created by the use of chenille yarns. (See chapter 15.) The loose yarn ends that fluff up on the surface of the chenille yarn to form "caterpillars" create a soft, cut pile when woven into fabrics. The pile in this case is created not by the fabric structure but by the characteristics of the yarn which is itself a narrow strip of leno-woven fabric. Chenille fabrics may be woven or knitted.

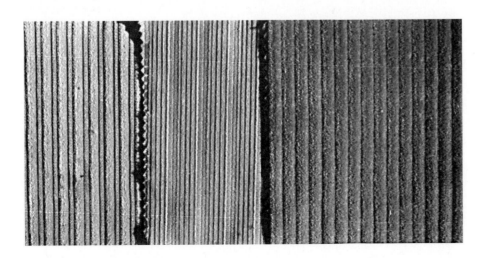

Figure 16.39

Corduroy fabric made with wales of three different widths and types.

Decorative Surface Effects

Woven Effects

Hand embroidery has been used for many centuries to add decoration to fabrics. With the invention of the automatic loom came the invention of looms that would create ornamental effects similar to that of embroidery.

Clipped or Unclipped Spot Weave

Embroiderylike designs may be achieved through the use of extra warp and extra filling yarns. In the clipped spot weave, either an extra shuttle or an extra set of warp yarns interlace to create a simple woven design. The extra yarns are carried along as a float on the wrong side of the fabric when they do not appear in the design. After the cloth is completed, the long floats may be cut away (clipped) or left uncut (unclipped). If clipped, which is the most common practice, the yarns form a characteristic "eyelash" effect. Sometimes these fabrics are used inside out for design interest. (See Figure 16.40.)

The durability of the design depends on the closeness of the weave of the fabric into which it is woven. Some domestic dotted swiss fabric is constructed by the clipped spot weave. This sheer cotton fabric uses small clipped spot yarns in contrasting color to create a dotted surface design (Figure 16.41). Dotted swiss may also be made with flocking or with plastic dots, much cheaper options.

Figure 16.40

Clipped spot design.

Figure 16.41

Close-up of dotted swiss made by the clipped spot method.

Swivel Weave

Similar fabrics can be made in the swivel weave, which is now relatively rare. The design is made by supplying an extra filling yarn on a small shuttle or swivel. The filling design yarns are carried several times around a group of warps by the motion of the swivel to prevent the yarn from pulling out of the background fabric. The long floats between designs are knotted and clipped off. Occasionally, some imported dotted swiss fabrics are found that use a swivel weave rather than a clipped spot weave. The swivel weave is more durable than is the clipped spot weave because the design yarns are woven in and cannot pull out of the fabric as easily as in the latter method. (See Figure 16.42.)

Lappet Weave

Lappet weave uses an extra warp yarn that may interlace in both the warp and filling direction with the ground fabric. The extra set of warps is threaded through needles set in front of the reed. The yarns are carried in a zigzag direction, back and forth to form an embroiderylike design. The design is created on the right side of the fabric, the excess yarn being carried along on the wrong side. Extra yarn is not clipped away from the back of the fabric but can be seen as it is carried from one design area to another. Imported Swiss braids often use the lappet weave, but it is seldom found on merchandise sold in the United States.

Interwoven, or Double-Cloth, Fabrics

Interwoven fabrics are also called double-cloth fabrics. They are made with three, four, or five sets of yarns.

Double-faced fabrics are made with three sets of yarns. Woven either from two sets of warp yarns and one filling yarn or from two sets of filling yarns and one warp yarn, the effect of the weave is to produce the same appearance on both sides of the fabric. Some blankets and double-faced satins are examples of fabrics that are woven in this way.

Fabrics made with four sets of yarns use two sets of warp yarns and two sets of filling yarns. Yarns from both layers move back and forth from one layer to another, as required by the design. In some areas the two fabrics are totally separated; in others, all four sets of yarns are interwoven. *Matelassé* is one fabric made by this process (Figure 16.43a). The two layers of these fabrics cannot be separated without destroy-

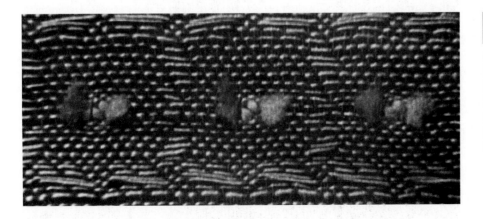

Figure 16.42

Close-up of dotted swiss made by the swivel weave. Note that in Figure 16.41 the fibers only interlace under one warp yarn, whereas in this figure the yarns appear to wrap around the warp yarns.

Figure 16.43

(a) Matelassé fabric produced with four sets of yarns. In flat areas all four yarns interlace to form a single layer; in raised areas two separate fabrics are formed. (b) Double-woven fabric made with five sets of yarns. Each side of the fabric is a different color, and at the lower right corner the two fabric layers have been pulled apart and the yarns that hold them together can be seen.

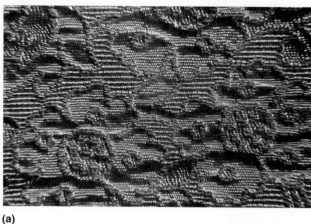

(a)

(b)

ing the fabric. The cut edge of the fabric will show small "pockets" where fabric layers are separate. The pocket boundaries are the point at which yarn sets interchange from one side of the fabric to the other.

Fabrics with five sets of yarns are produced in the same way as double-woven pile fabrics. Two separate fabric layers are constructed. Extra yarns travel back and forth between the two layers to hold them together. These fabrics are often reversible, with one side being of one color and one side of another color. If the connecting yarn is cut, the two segments of the fabric can be separated into two individual pieces of cloth. (See Figure 16.43b.)

Triaxally Woven Fabrics

Research and development of new fabric construction is constantly in progress. Several recent methods of fabric construction that are related to knitting are discussed in chapter 17. There is, however, another method of constructing fabrics that is closely related to traditional weaving, and it is known as *triaxial weaving*. The term is derived from *tri-* meaning "three" and *axial*, meaning "of or pertaining to the axis or center line." In other words, triaxial fabrics have three axes or center lines (Figure 16.44). Traditionally, woven fabrics have a biaxial form or two axes, the lengthwise and crosswise axes.

Triaxial fabrics are usually woven by interlacing two sets of lengthwise yarns with one set of crosswise yarns. Special cams in the loom manipulate the yarns so that the double set of yarns is carried in a diagonal direction. All three sets of yarns interlace.

Triaxial weaves are not entirely new. Snowshoes and some forms of basket work sometimes have been made using a triaxial construction. The major advantage of triaxial weaving is in its stability against stretching not only in the length and crosswise directions but also in the bias. Even those biaxial fabrics with good stability in the warp and filling will stretch in the bias direction. Triaxially woven fabrics have high burst resistance and strong resistance to tearing and raveling. Strength is uniform in all directions.

Figure 16.44

Triaxial fabric structure.

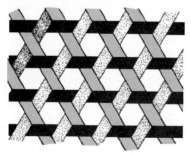

Evaluation of Woven Fabrics

Textile fabrics may be evaluated by a variety of textile tests. The results of these tests may be used by product manufacturers in determining whether textiles meet the standards they have specified for use in their products and by scientists conducting research.

Strength

Fabric strength evaluations are made in terms of breaking strength, tearing strength, or bursting strength. A variety of machines is used to measure strength, and fabric samples are prepared for testing according to ASTM test method procedures.

Breaking strength, the force required to break a woven fabric when it is pulled under tension, is measured on a tensile testing machine (Figure 16.45). The strength is reported in pounds or newtons of force required to break the fabric. Half the specimens are prepared with warp yarns running in the direction of stress, and the other half have the stress in the filling direction.

Figure 16.45

Instron Tensile Tester with fabric specimen mounted in clamps. Photograph by Prather Warren, LSU Public Relations.

The tearing strength of a fabric, expressed in pounds or grams, is the pressure required to continue a tear or rip already begun in a woven fabric.

If yarns in one direction have low tearing or breaking strength, performance will be affected. High levels of strength in one direction do not counterbalance low strength in the other.

Bursting strength is the pounds or grams of pressure required to rupture a woven fabric. Force is applied to the fabric from below or above the fabric as it is held flat.

Elongation and Recovery from Stretching

At the same time that breaking strength is being tested on a tensile testing machine, the degree of elongation that the fabric undergoes before breaking may be determined. Force required to break the sample and the inches of elongation before the sample broke are recorded. The percentage of stretch the sample underwent is calculated.

Fabrics may also be tested for recovery from elongation. Samples are stretched to a certain percentage of their original length (often 2 percent) and then permitted to recover for a specific length of time. A remeasurement is made, and the percentage of recovery is calculated by determining the length before stretching, length after stretching, and length after recovery. Since some fabrics recover gradually from stretching, measurements of recovery may be made after varying periods of time.

Figure 16.46

CSI Surface Abrader for testing surface abrasion. Other instruments will test for flex abrasion and edge abrasion. Photograph courtesy of Custom Scientific Instruments, Inc.

Abrasion Resistance and Pilling

Abrasion resistance is tested on different types of abrasion-testing machines (Figure 16.46). The results of tests run on different machines cannot be compared, as each machine tests with a different motion and each holds the fabrics in different positions. (See discussion of abrasion in chapter 2.) Machines such as the Brush Pilling Tester or Random Tumble Pilling Tester are used to evaluate the tendency of fabrics to pill (Figure 16.47).

Abrasion is one of those factors most likely to be affected by each individual's unique use of textiles. For example, the linings of overcoats are subject to abrasion from garments worn beneath them. A person who favors soft, smooth-textured clothing would subject the lining of a coat to considerably less abrasion than one would who prefers coarse-textured, rough-surfaced textiles.

Figure 16.47

Random Tumble Pilling Tester for determining the pilling and fuzzing characteristics of all types of fabrics. Photograph courtesy of Atlas Electric Devices Co.

References

Albers, A. 1957. *On weaving.* Middletown, Conn.: Wesleyan University Press.

American Fabrics and Fashions Magazine, ed. 1980. *Encyclopedia of textiles.* 3d ed. Englewood Cliffs, N.J.: Prentice Hall.

Klapper, M. 1967. *Fabric almanac.* New York: Fairchild.

Review Questions

1. Explain the basic principle of operation of a hand loom weaving a plain-weave fabric. In what ways does the operation of a modern shuttleless machine differ from the hand loom?

2. When would it be necessary to use a jacquard loom? A dobby loom? What are the names of some kinds of fabrics that are made on each of these looms?

3. Identify the various methods of transporting the filling yarns through the shed in automated weaving.

4. What is the difference between a fabric that is on *true grain* and one that is *bowed* or one that is *skewed?*

5. Define *fabric count.* How is fabric count measured? What is meant by a *balanced* fabric count?

6. Explain the differences between a plain weave, basket weave, twill weave, satin weave, jacquard weave, and leno weave. Give the names of at least two standard fabrics made with each of these weaves.

7. Describe the different methods by which pile fabrics can be made.

8. Explain what is meant by each of the following: clipped spot weave, swivel weave, lappet weave, double-cloth fabric, triaxial weave.

9. How can fabric strength, elongation and recovery from stretch, and abrasion resistance be measured?

Recommended Readings

Broudy, E. 1979. *The book of looms.* New York: Van Nostrand Reinhold.

Catling, H. 1984. The development of modern weaving machines. *Textiles* 13 (Spring): 5.

Chadwick, A. 1987. Weaving. *Textiles* 16 (3): 63.

D'Harcourt, R. 1962. *Textiles of ancient Peru and their techniques.* Seattle: Univ. of Washington Press.

Emery, I. 1966. *The primary structure of fabrics.* Washington, D.C.: The Textile Museum.

Ishida, T. 1993. Historical developments in weaving machinery: Part 3. Modern weaving machinery, today and tomorrow. *JTN The International Textile Magazine,* no. 458 (January): 108.

Marks, R., and A.T.C. Robinson. 1986. *Principles of weaving.* Manchester, England: Textile Institute.

Men's dress shirts. 1993. *Consumer Reports,* August, 504.

Mueller, C., and O. Bissmann. 1993. Letters, figures, interweaving: An easy task. *Textile World* 143 (November): 61.

Schwartz, P., T. Rhodes, and M. Mohamed. 1982. *Fabric forming systems.* Park Ridge, N.J.: Noyes.

KNITTED FABRICS

Few segments of the textile industry have grown so rapidly in recent years as has the knitting industry. Advances in knitting production techniques along with the use of synthetic fabrics, such as acrylics and polyesters, for knit goods have led to the manufacture of knitted items, including such diverse products as men's tailored suits, table linens, blankets, bedspreads, carpeting, wall coverings, upholstery, shipping sacks, paint rollers, and vacuum cleaner bags.

The apparel knitting industry may be divided into four branches: knitted outerwear, knitted yard goods, knitted hosiery, and knitted underwear. Knitted yard goods mills produce a wide variety of fabrics in either flat or circular form that can be cut and sewn into apparel and other items. Those mills that produce outerwear, hosiery, or underwear may knit the item directly or may knit sections of a garment (such as sleeves, body sections, and the like) that are sewn, or cut and sewn, together. These mills complete the garment from knitting right through to assembly in the same mill.

Historical Development of Knits

Although fragments of knitted cloth have been found at the site of Dura Europos, an ancient Syrian city founded in 280 B.C., and other examples from the Middle East date from the middle of the third century A.D., hand knitting seems to have come to Europe only during the Middle Ages. Apparently, the Arab conquerors of Spain imported the technique of knitting from their homeland sometime after A.D. 1000.

Knitting spread gradually to the rest of Europe. Because knits were more elastic than woven goods, they gained popularity, especially for making stockings and gloves.

Today one thinks of hand knitting as a process that uses two or more knitting needles, but the earliest hand knitting was done not on needles but on a frame into which a series of pegs had been set. Yarn was looped around each peg. To make the stitches, the knitter pulled a new loop of yarn through the old loop encircling the peg and placed the new loop around the peg while slipping the old loop off the peg with a hooked needle. The gradually increasing rows of loops formed the fabric. Eventually, a long, pointed knitting needle, such as those used today, replaced the pegs for holding the loops, and a second needle replaced the hook for adding and subtracting loops.

The use of two needles or the knitting frame made a flat fabric. A round tube of fabric could be made by using a circular needle, a round frame, or a set of four needles.

Since the knitting process was relatively simple, it lent itself to mechanization somewhat more easily than did weaving. By the late 1500s a knitting frame machine had been invented by William Lee. This machine made mechanically all of the kinds of knits that had previously been made by hand. Lee's machine continued in use until further refinements of machine knitting were made during the Industrial Revolution. (See Figure 17.1.)

Knitting: Some Basic Concepts

"Knitting is the process of making cloth with a single yarn or set of yarns moving in only one direction. Instead of two sets of yarns crossing each other as in weaving, the

Figure 17.1

Knitted cap made in Italy in the seventeenth century.
Photograph courtesy of the Metropolitan Museum of Art, Rogers Fund, 1927.

single knitting yarn is looped through itself to make a chain of stitches. These chains or rows are connected side by side to produce the knit cloth" (American Fabrics 1980, 370). The interlocking of these loops in knitting can be done by either vertical or horizontal movement. When the yarns are introduced in a crosswise direction, at right angles to the direction of growth of the fabric, and run or interlock across the fabric, the knit is known as a *weft knit.* (Some sources may refer to these knits as *filling knits,* but the term *weft knit* is used in the knitting industry.) When the yarns run lengthwise or up and down, the knit is known as a *warp knit.*

In knitting terminology, the rows of stitches that run in columns along the lengthwise direction of the fabric are known as *wales.* This corresponds to the warp direction of woven fabrics. Crosswise rows of stitches or loops are called *courses.* The direction of the courses corresponds to the filling of woven goods. (See Figure 17.2.)

Both warp and weft knits are made by machine. Knitting machines may be either flat or circular. The flat-type knitting machine has needles arranged in one or two straight lines and held on a flat needlebed. The cloth is made by forming stitches on these needles. The resulting fabric is flat. Machines with flatbeds are used to make both warp and weft knits.

The circular knitting machine has needles arranged in a circle on a rotating cylinder. The resulting fabric is formed into a tube. Circular knitting machines produce weft knits almost exclusively. (See Figure 17.3.)

For nearly two hundred years after its invention in 1589, Lee's machine was used without further improvement. Using a *spring beard needle,* Lee's machine produced flat knitted fabrics by mechanically passing one loop of yarn through another.

Figure 17.2

Rows of stitches that run in a vertical column along the lengthwise direction of the fabric are called wales; crosswise rows of stitches or loops are called courses.

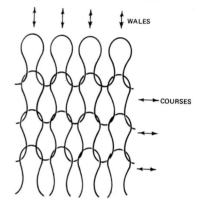

Figure 17.3

(a) Electronically controlled circular weft knitting machine. This model, Monarch F–LPJ/3A, is a 72-feed 37-step double knit machine. The yarn is held on the spools on a frame at the left of the machine. The completed fabric emerges in tubular form at the bottom of the machine. Photograph courtesy of Monarch Knitting Machinery Company; photographed at Alandale Knitting Co., Inc., Troy, N.C.

(a)

Figure 17.3 *(continued)*

(b) Electronically controlled flat-weft knitting machine. Photograph courtesy of H. Stoll GmbH & Co.

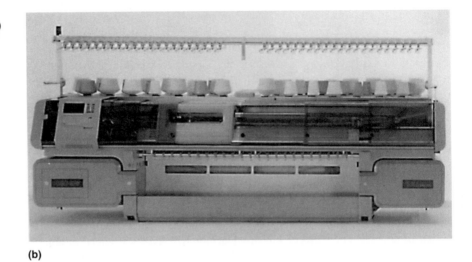

(b)

Figure 17.4

Formation of a loop by a spring beard needle.

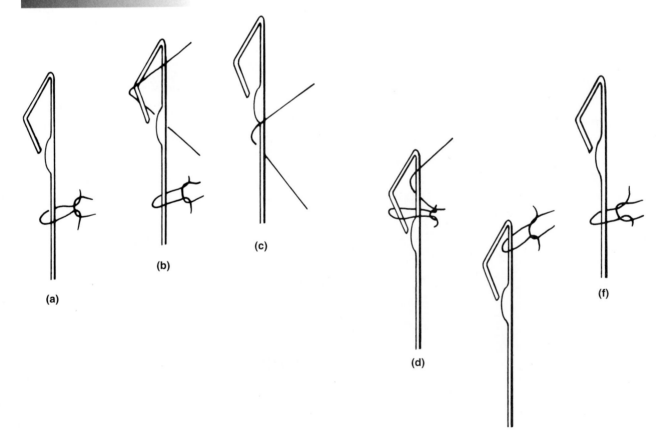

(a)

(b)

(c)

(d)

(e)

(f)

Loop Formation

The spring beard needle is formed from one piece of thin wire. One end of the needle is drawn into thinner dimensions and is curved to form a hook. The flexible outer side of the hook can be pressed against the stem of the needle to close the hook. Figure 17.4 illustrates the steps in loop formation:

1. The old loop is held on the stem of the needle below the hook. (a)
2. A new loop is formed around the outside of the hooked section of the needle. (b)
3. The needle rises, dropping the new loop to the stem. (c)
4. The needle falls again to bring the new loop into the hook. (d)
5. At the same time a presser comes in, closing the hook so that the old loop is held outside the hook. (d)
6. The needle falls further, sliding the old loop off the needle. The new loop is now held inside the hook. (e)
7. The needle is now ready to repeat the cycle. (f)

In 1847 Matthew Townshend invented a different type of hook known as the *latch needle,* which has come to be the most widely used type of needle. Its operation is similar to that of the spring beard needle, except that instead of having to mechanically press the flexible wire of the needle closed so that the new yarn loop will not slide off, a latch closes to hold the yarn in place. Figure 17.5 illustrates the steps in the cycle of the latch needle:

Figure 17.5 Formation of a loop by a latch needle.

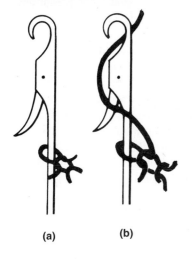

(a)

(b)

(c)

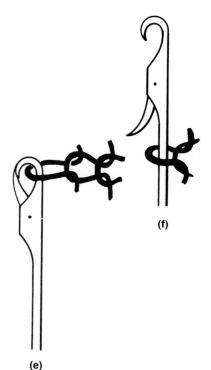

(d)

(e)

(f)

Figure 17.6

Tongue (a) of compound needle moves into position against the hook (b) to close the needle.

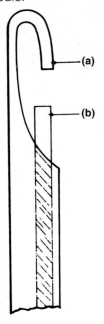

1. The old loop is held on the stem of the needle. The latch is open. (a)
2. A new loop is formed around the hook of the needle. (b)
3. The needle falls, the old loop rises, closing the latch of the needle. (c)
4. The old loop is cast off (d and e), the new loop pushes the latch open, the needle rises, and the new loop slides down to the stem of the needle. (f)
5. The needle is now ready to repeat the cycle. (f)

Yet a third type of needle, the compound needle, is used almost exclusively for warp knitting. The compound needle has two components, a tongue and a hook (Figure 17.6). Its motion is as follows:

1. The old loop encircles the hook; the tongue is in such a position as to leave the hook open.
2. Both tongue and hook rise; a new yarn is fed to the hook.
3. Both tongue and hook descend, but the tongue descends more slowly, thereby closing the hook.
4. As the needle descends, the held loop slides off, forming a new loop.
5. The needle returns to its initial position, the hook ascending more rapidly, thereby opening the hook again.

For weft knitting with either needle type, a cam system provides the action for lifting the needles as the yarn is fed in. A small projection called a butt is located at the bottom of the needle. The butt is held in a groove formed by a system of cams or shaped pieces. The movement of the butt in the grooves between the cams causes the needle to rise and fall. (See Figure 17.7.)

The engaging by the needle of a new piece of yarn is called *feeding*. Devices called feeders are located to introduce the yarn to the needles. The number of feeders can vary, but obviously the more feeders a machine has, the higher will be the speed of fabric forming on the machine, since each needle produces a loop each time it is activated and if many needles are activated more frequently, many courses can be formed at the same time.

Another important element of some knitting machines is the sinker. The already-formed fabric may need to be controlled as the subsequent knitting action takes place. A thin steel device, the sinker may be used to hold the fabric as the needle rises, support the fabric as the needle descends, and push the fabric away from the needle after the new loop has been formed. Sinkers are generally mounted between the needles. (See Figure 17.8.) Some machines, however, do not use sinkers but instead use the tensions placed on the completed fabrics for control.

The size of the needle and the spacing of the needles on knitting machines determine the number and size of the knit stitches and their closeness. Each wale is formed on one needle. The number of needles is equal to the number of wales. The closeness of the stitches determines whether a knit fabric will be lightweight and open or heavier and more dense. The term *gauge* is used to describe the closeness of knit stitches. Gauge is the number of needles in a measured space on the knitting machine. Higher gauge fabrics (those with more stitches) are made with finer needles; lower gauge fabrics are made with coarser or larger needles.

The term *cut* is also used to designate the number of needles per inch in the needlebed of a circular weft knitting machine. To describe the stitch density of a single or double knit fabric, the fabric may be designated as an 18-, 20-, 22-, or 24-cut fabric. The higher the cut, the closer the stitches; the lower the cut, the coarser the fabric.

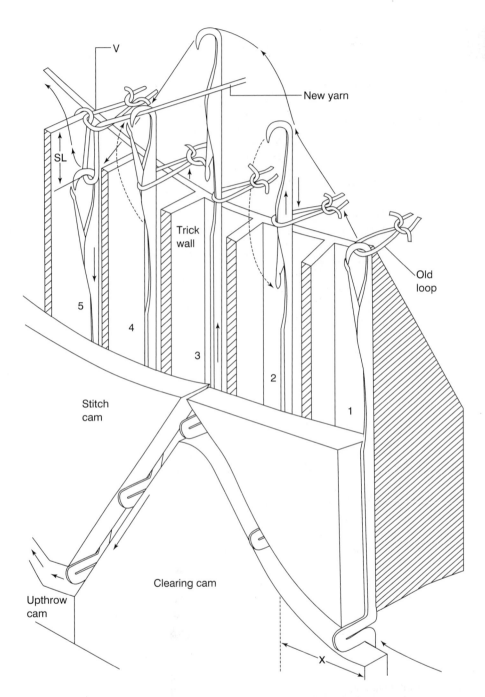

V

New yarn

SL

Trick
wall

5

4

3

2

1

Stitch
cam

Old
loop

Upthrow
cam

Clearing cam

X

Figure 17.7

Cam system for control of
needle action in weft knits.
Reprinted by permission from
D. J. Spencer, *Knitting
Technology,* 2d ed. (Oxford:
Pergamon, 1989), 20.
Copyright © 1989 by
Butterworth-Heinemann Ltd.

Varying types of knitting machines measure gauge over different distances on the machine. For example, circular knit hosiery measures the number of needles in 1.0 inch, full-fashioned knitting in 1.5 inches, and Raschel knits in 2.0 inches. Because of these differences, it is best to keep in mind the generalized principle that the higher the gauge, the closer the stitches.

The quality of needles used in manufacturing knit goods is related directly to the quality of the fabric produced. Needles of uneven size and quality will produce knit fabrics with uneven-sized stitches and imperfect surface appearance.

Figure 17.8

Sinkers used for weft knits, with latch needles in position ready for formation of new loop.

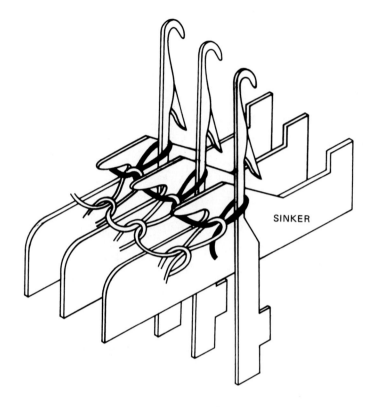

SINKER

In warp knits, those knits in which the yarns interlace in the long direction, one or more yarns are allotted to each needle on the machine, and those yarns follow the long direction of the fabric. For weft knits, those in which the yarns interlace crosswise or horizontally, one or more yarns are used for each course, and these yarns move across the fabric. In weft knits, one yarn may have from twenty to several hundred needles associated with it. To summarize, weft knits can be made with one yarn, but warp knits must have a whole set of warp yarns, that is, one or more for each needle.

Once the basic distinction between warp and weft knits has been made, further subdivisions of knit classifications are usually based on the types of machines used in their production. The majority of knit fabrics are named after the machines on which they are constructed. For this reason, the discussion of knitted fabrics that follows is organized around the types of machines used in manufacturing knit fabrics and the types of knit fabrics made on these machines.

Weft Knits

The most important difference among weft knitting machines is in the number of needlebeds and the number of sets of needles used. On these bases, weft knits are divided among those made on each of these machines:

1. Flat or circular jersey, or single knit, machine: one needlebed and one set of needles.
2. Flat or circular rib machine: two needlebeds and two sets of needles.
3. Flat or circular purl, or links-links, machine: two needlebeds and one set of needles.

Jersey, or Single, Knits

Machines with one needlebed and one set of needles are called jersey machines or single knit machines. With one set of needles and one needlebed, all needles face the same direction; all stitches are pulled to the same side of the fabric. As a result, jersey fabrics have a smooth face with a vertical grain on the right side of the fabric and a widthwise grain on the back side. The loops formed by the jersey machine are formed in one direction only (See Figure 17.9), which gives a different appearance to each

| **Figure 17.9** | Plain, or jersey, knit stitch. Illustrations courtesy of the National Knitwear Manufacturers Association. |

(a)

TECHNICAL FACE

(b)

(c)

TECHNICAL BACK

(d)

side of the fabric. The basic fabric produced by this machine is known alternately as a *plain, single knit,* or *jersey:* the terms are interchangeable.

Jersey stretches slightly more in the crosswise than the lengthwise direction. If one stitch breaks, the fabric may ladder, or *run.* A great many items of hosiery, sweaters, and other wearing apparel are made in the plain knit. Jersey fabrics, also tend to curl at the edges and are less stable than are some other types of knits. This is the result of the pressures exerted during knitting. Special finishing techniques are used to overcome these tendencies and maintain fabric stability; the principal ones use starches, gum mixtures, polyvinyl acetate emulsions, and resins.

Plain knit fabrics can be made into designs of two or more colors by use of a patterning mechanism that controls the selection and feeding of yarns and types of stitches to create jacquard knits. (See Figure 17.10) Jersey machines can also produce terry, velour, fleece, and sliver knit fabrics.

High-Pile Fabrics

High-pile fabrics, such as imitation furs and plushes, are usually knitted by a jersey machine. While the knitting is taking place, a sliver of staple fiber is fed into the

Figure 17.10 Sides of a jacquard-patterned plain knit fabric: (a) face and (b) reverse.

(a) (b)

Figure 17.11   A jersey knit, high-pile fabric: (a) back and (b) face.

(a)

(b)

machine. These fibers are caught in the tight knit and are held firmly in place. Although any staple fiber can be used for the pile, the greatest quantity of these fabrics are made with acrylic and modacrylic fibers in the pile. (See Figure 17.11.)

By using staple fibers of varying lengths, adding color through fiber dyeing or printing on the surface of the pile, and by shearing or brushing the pile, an enormous variety of effects can be achieved. The use of knitted pile fabric ranges from excellent imitations of furs, such as leopard, tiger, mink, or mouton, to colorful pile outerwear, coat linings, or pile carpet fabrics.

Knitted Terry, Velour, and Fleece

Jersey knits can also be made in the form of knitted terry fabrics and knitted velours. Two yarns are fed into the machine simultaneously, picked up by the same needle, and knitted in such a way that one of the yarns appears on the face of the fabric, the other on the back. The yarn that forms the pile is pulled up to the surface of the fabric. If the pile remains uncut, the resulting cloth is like a one-sided terry cloth. If the pile is cut, the fabric is called *velour*. (See Figure 17.12.)

Terry fabrics made by this process are not as durable as are woven terry cloth, nor do they hold their shape as well. On the other hand, they have softer draping qualities. The knitted velours are softer and more flexible than are woven pile fabrics, such as velveteen. Major uses for both fabrics are for sports and loungewear, for infants' and children's clothing, and for household items such as towels and slipcovers.

The soft, fleecy effect produced on the inside of sweatshirts is achieved by much the same techniques as in making velours. The fleece is created by cutting and brushing the loops that are formed on the underside of the fabric.

Figure 17.12

A jersey knit, velour fabric:
(a) back and (b) face.

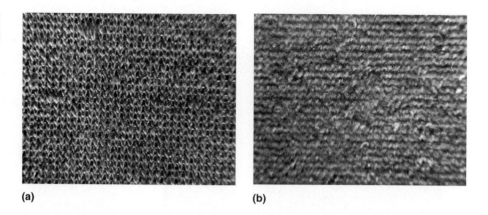

(a)　　　　　　　　　(b)

Plated Fabrics

In creating plated fabrics, the knitting machine feeds two separate yarns at the same time. The two yarns are in the same loop, one behind the other. By varying the color, texture, or type of yarn, interesting decorative effects can be achieved. It is also possible to use one yarn as the face yarn and another as a backing yarn. Using an expensive face yarn with an inexpensive backing yarn can help to keep the cost of the fabric lower. Plating varies from relatively simple construction to very intricate pattern designs.

Two-Bed Knits

The *Knitting Encyclopedia,* (Reichman 1972) states, "From a purely technical point of view, a double knit fabric is any knitted cloth or garment section that has been produced on any type of opposed bed knitting machine with two sets of needles of any range of fineness or coarseness" (p. 96). Those which have the greatest commercial interest can be classified as:

1. narrow and broad rib knits
2. nonjacquard and jacquard double jersey (commonly called double knits)
3. interlock knits

The machines used to produce rib knits, double jerseys, and interlock knits differ from the machines used for plain knits in that they have two needle-holding beds and two sets of needles. For circular machines one set of needles is located on the needle cylinder in the same way as in plain knit machines, and the second set is placed in a dial positioned over the cylinder much as a lid would be placed over a cylindrical jar. The dial is grooved, as is the cylinder, and needles lie within the grooves, called *tricks,* in such a way that the hooks of the horizontal dial needles and those of the vertical cylinder needles are perpendicular to each other. (See Figure 17.13.) The fabric created between the two sets of needles will have the appearance of the technical face on both sides.

In flat-bed machines the needlebeds are placed so the two rows of needles form an inverted V. These machines are known as *vee bed machines* (Figure 17.14).

Rib Knits

"A rib knit fabric is characterized by lengthwise ribs formed by wales alternating on the face and back of the cloth. If every other stitch alternates from front to back, it is

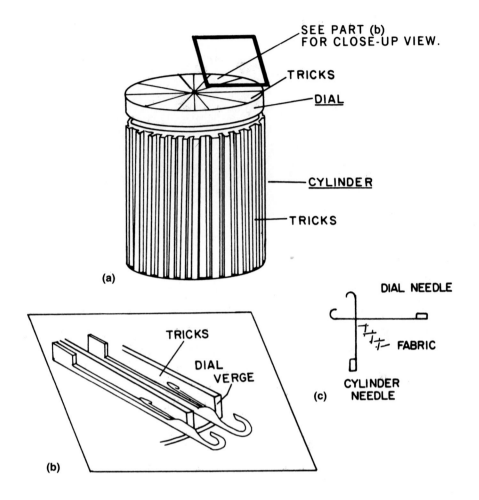

SEE PART (b)
FOR CLOSE-UP VIEW.

TRICKS

DIAL

CYLINDER

TRICKS

(a)

TRICKS

DIAL
VERGE

(b)

DIAL NEEDLE

FABRIC

CYLINDER
NEEDLE

(c)

Figure 17.13

Diagrams of (a) a cylinder and dial arrangement for a circular knitting machine, (b) close-up view of needles placed inside the tricks, and (c) the relative positions of dial and cylinder needles. Diagrams from *Fabric Forming Systems* by Peter Schwartz, Trevor Rhodes, and Mansour Mohamed. Reproduced by permission of Noyes Publications.

called a 1 × 1 rib. If every two stitches alternate, it is called a 2 × 2 rib." (Reichman 1972, 354) The larger the number of stitches that alternate, the more pronounced the rib. A 1 × 1 rib made in a fine gauge may hardly be visible to the eye. Fabrics may appear to be a jersey on both sides. Rib knits are made on a two-bed machine with one set of needles forming the loops for one wale and the other set of needles forming the alternating wale.

Rib knits have greater elasticity in the width than in the length. They are stable and do not curl or stretch out of shape as do the jersey knits. For this reason, they are often used to make cuffs and necklines on weft knitted garments. (See Figures 17.15 and 17.16.) Rib knits are reversible unless the number of stitches in the alternating wales is uneven, as in a 2 × 3 rib.

Double Jersey Fabrics

The term *double knit* is generally applied by consumers to fabrics that are, technically, double jersey fabrics. Double jersey fabrics are also made on two-bed knitting machines, but the arrangement of the needles is different from that for knitting rib fabrics. The layers of loops alternate from one side to the other, locking the two layers together. Double knit fabrics have the same appearance on both sides of the fabric, that is, exhibiting the appearance of the face or outer side of a single knit on both sides. Twice as much yarn is incorporated into double knit fabrics as into comparable

Figure 17.14

Diagrams of (a) a vee bed and (b) relative positions of needles from front and back beds. Diagrams from *Fabric Forming Systems* by Peter Schwartz, Trevor Rhodes, and Mansour Mohamed. Reproduced by permission of Noyes Publications.

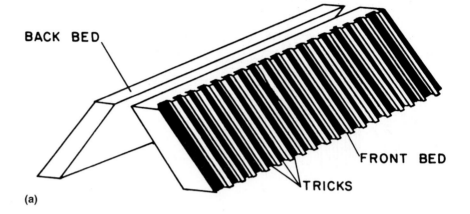

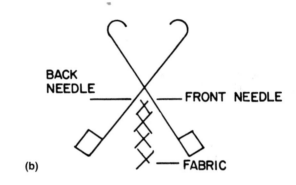

Figure 17.15

1 × 1 rib fabric structure. Illustration courtesy of National Knitwear Manufacturers Association.

1 X 1 RIB FABRIC

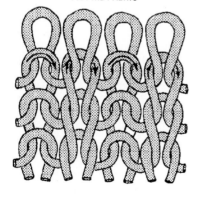

single knits. (See Figure 17.17.) Double knit fabrics are more stable than plain knits. When made from synthetic yarns, double knits should be heat-set for better dimensional stability. They do not run and are easier for the home sewer to handle. During periods when double knits have been fashionable, textured synthetic yarns and wool have been favored for double knit apparel. The home furnishings industry also has utilized double knit fabrics for upholstery.

A wide variety of decorative effects are possible in double jersey fabrics. These include "blister" fabrics with sculptured or raised surface effects and elaborate patterns called "jacquard" patterns because of their similarity to jacquard-woven patterns.

Interlock Knits

Interlock knits are produced on a special machine that has alternating long and short needles on both beds. Long and short needles are placed opposite each other. Long needles knit the first feeder yarn; short needles knit the second feeder yarn. (See Figure 17.18.) The fabric created is an interlocking of two 1 × 1 rib structures.

The resulting fabric, like double knit fabrics, is thicker than single knit fabric, and more stable in the widthwise direction. Interlock fabrics have been traditionally used for underwear. They are produced more slowly than are other rib knits and are generally made in plain colors or very simple patterns because the addition of pattern slows down the manufacture even further. (See Figure 17.19.)

Purl Knits

Purl machines have two needlebeds and one set of needles. Because the machine moves only to the left, it is also called a *links-links machine. Links* is the German word for "left."

Figure 17.16

2 × 2 rib fabric.

Figure 17.17

(a) Diagrammatic representation of a double knit and (b) close-up photograph of a double knit showing face (left) and back (right).

(a)

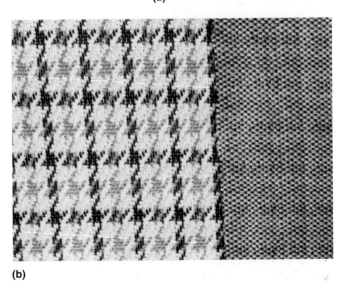

(b)

Figure 17.18

Diagram of interlock knitting. Short needles are labeled S and long needles, L. The first feeder yarn is white, the second dark. Reprinted by permission from D. J. Spencer, *Knitting Technology,* 2d ed. (Oxford: Pergamon, 1989), 63. Copyright © 1989 by Butterworth-Heinemann Ltd.

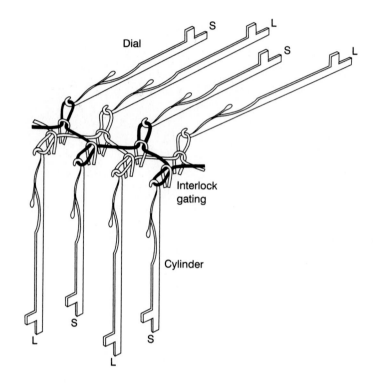

Figure 17.19

(a) Diagrammatic representation of an interlock knit. Reprinted by permission from D. J. Spencer, *Knitting Technology,* 2d ed. (Oxford: Pergamon, 1989), 61. Copyright © 1989 by Butterworth-Heinemann Ltd. (b) Photograph showing both sides of an interlock knit fabric. Left is underside of fabric; right is top side.

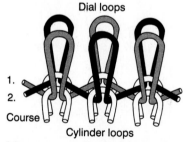

(a)

(b)

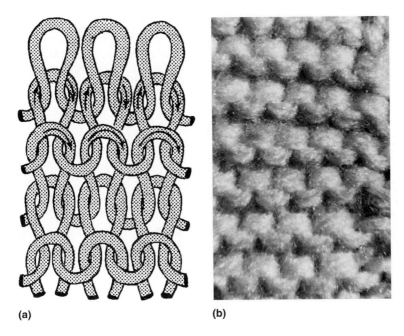

(a)   **(b)**

Figure 17.20

(a) Purl knit structure.
Illustration courtesy of the
National Knitwear
Manufacturers Association.
(b) Close-up view of stitches in
a purl knit fabric.

The links-links machine operates somewhat more slowly than do other knitting machines, causing the price of purl fabrics to be higher than those of other knits. The machine has a latch-type knitting needle with a hook on either end that allows the needle to pull stitches to either the back or the face of the fabric. This makes possible the construction of stitches on alternate sides of the fabric. The double needle arrangement makes this the most versatile of the weft knitting machines, as it can make plain, purl, or rib knits.

The simplest purl fabric is made by alternating courses so that every other course is drawn to the opposite side of the fabric, thereby producing a fabric with the same appearance on both sides. The raised courses produce a somewhat uneven texture. (See Figure 17.20.)

Purl knit fabrics have high crosswise and lengthwise stretch. They are often made into a variety of decorative sweaters. Interesting textures can be achieved by the use of fluffy, soft yarns. The versatility of the machine makes possible the creation of a variety of patterns in these knits; however, relatively small quantities of fabrics are made in the purl stitch.

Weft Knit Stitch Variation

The basic loop formed in the plain knit serves as the starting point for a wide range of weft knit stitches that can be used to vary the surface texture of weft knits. These include miss or float stitches, tuck stitches, and open stitches variously known as transfer or spread stitches. (See Figure 17.21.)

In miss or float stitches, some needles are immobilized, and instead of catching the stitch, they allow the yarn to be carried across the back of the fabric. The float stitch can be used to hide colored yarns at the back of the fabric when they do not appear in the design on the face. When long, straight floats are used, the elasticity of the fabric is reduced, and long floats are likely to be caught or snagged in use.

The tuck stitch is made by programming certain needles to hold both an old loop and a new yarn without casting off the old stitch. This creates an elongated stitch that appears in the fabric as an opening or variation in the surface pattern.

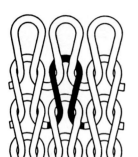

Figure 17.21 Basic weft-knitted stitches viewed from the front of the fabric. (Note that only a single purl stitch is shown here. This should not be confused with a purl fabric, shown in Figure 17.20, which is made from many purl stitches.) From J. A. Smirfitt, *An Introduction to Weft Knitting*. Copyright © Merrow Publishing Co., Ltd. Reproduced by permission.

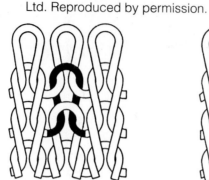
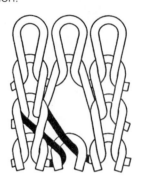
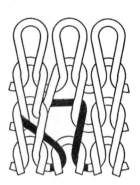

PLAIN   PURL   TRANSFER   SPREAD

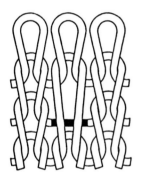
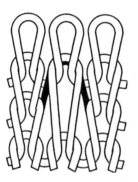
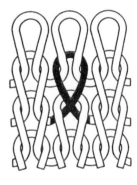

MISS OR FLOAT   TUCK   CROSS

Loops can be transferred sideways to create decorative effects or open spaces. Transfer of loops can also be used in shaping of knits, as in *full-fashioning*, which is accomplished on specialized machines. Combinations of the tuck, miss, and other stitches with basic rib, plain, or purl knit stitches can create such varied effects as raised cables, open work alternating with plain knit, and a wide range of other decorative fabrics. An almost infinite variety of patterns can be created by combining different colored or textured yarns and various stitches.

Weft knits are usually circular unless they are made on full-fashioning machines. In hosiery and sweaters the item itself or sections of the item are made on the specialized knitting machines. When sweaters or stockings are knitted, the desired shape of the fabric piece may be created by increasing or decreasing the number of stitches.

Where stitches have been dropped or added, *fashion marks* appear. Fashion marks—small alterations in the surface caused by the shifting of the needles and the change in position of the yarns—are an indication of better quality in that the consumer can be sure that the shaping of the garment is permanent. Items made in this way are referred to as *full-fashioned*. Some manufacturers will create mock fashion marks at seamed areas to give the appearance of better quality. A careful examination of the area will show that in a true full-fashioned item, the number and direction of

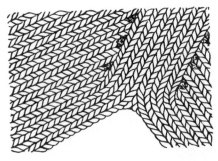

Figure 17.22

Fashion marks contrasted with mock fashion marks. Illustrations courtesy of the DuPont Company.

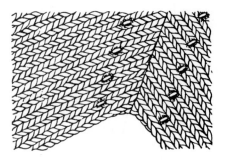

FASHION MARKS

MOCK FASHION MARKS

stitches change. In mock fashion marks, this does not occur. Mock fashion marks are usually produced by embroidery and have a long yarn float on the wrong side between marks. (See Figure 17.22.)

Three-Dimensional Knitting

The techniques employed for full-fashioned garments are also being used to produce three-dimensional knitted structures. Complex shapes can be knitted that serve as reinforcement in molded parts for industrial applications. Covers for chairs and seats can be knitted as one piece, eliminating the cutting and sewing of fabric pieces to fit the forms. (See Figure 17.23.)

Consumer Box 17.1 discusses one of the common products made from weft knits.

Warp Knits

In warp knitting, each yarn is looped around one needle at a time. The guide bar that carries the yarns moves sideways as well as forward and back so that the yarns are carried both lengthwise and, to a limited extent, diagonally. This diagonal motion is needed to assure that the yarns interlace not only with the loop directly below in the same wale but also with loops to the side in adjacent wales. If the yarn interlaced only vertically, there would be no point at which each individual chain of stitches was attached to its neighboring chain.

This construction provides resistance to laddering (running), since each stitch is most directly connected not only with the stitch beneath but also with a stitch placed diagonally and lower. In forming the stitch, diagonal underlay moves the yarn from loop to loop.

Several types of warp knits are made on a number of different warp knitting machines.

Tricot

Tricot machines account for the largest quantity of warp knits. Tricot fabric is knit flat. On the face side the wales create the appearance of a fine, lengthwise line. On the back side crosswise ribs appear in a horizontal position.

In the manufacture of tricot, guide bars move the yarns from side to side. The tricot machines may have from one to four guide bars. The greater the number of bars, the greater the distance the yarn moves between stitches. In moving from one placement to the next, underlay yarns are carried across the back of the fabric. This extra yarn creates heavier weight fabrics. (See Figure 17.24.)

Figure 17.23

Computer-aided three-dimensionally knitted upholstery fabric in which a two-tone effect is achieved by using both lower luster and bright yarn of the same color and different stitch structures. Photograph courtesy of Teknit, suppliers of 3-D knitted covers for the office furnishing industry in Europe and America.

Tricot fabrics are identified as one-bar, two-bar, three-bar, or four-bar, depending on the number of guide bars used in their manufacture. One-bar, or single-bar, tricot is relatively unstable and is seldom used for garments. It is, however, used as backing for some bonded fabrics. It will run, because the loops interlace close together. Two-bar tricot is stable and fairly light in weight and is used extensively in lingerie, blouses, and the like. Three- and four-bar tricots are used for dresses and men's wear and are heavier than two-bar tricot. (See Figures 17.25 and 17.26.)

In addition to the basic tricot fabric, a number of variations can be made. A tricot satin is produced by allowing yarns to float further across the back surface of the fabric before they interlace. Other textured tricots known as *brushed tricots* are made with raised, napped surfaces or with small loops. The fabric as knitted is smooth on both sides. The surface effects are achieved during finishing when the fabric is passed through a special machine equipped with wire rollers that either pull loops to the surface of the fabric or break some of the filaments to give a "brushed," soft, napped surface. Brushed and looped tricot fabrics are made with long underlaps that form the pile or loops.

17.1   T-shirts

T-shirts began life as white knitted cotton undergarments for men during World War II. By the 1990s they were being worn as undergarments and outergarments by men, women, and children; printed with logos and messages; dyed to a wide range of colors; decorated with embroidery, sequins, and beading; and cut to fit loosely or tightly. Between April 1990 and April 1991, more than one billion T-shirts were sold in the United States (Lonsinger 1993.)

The classic T-shirt is constructed of tubular jersey fabric. It has short sleeves set into the body of the garment. Sleeve and bottom hems are usually sewn flat. The neckline consists of a 1 × 1 rib knit strip sewn onto the body of the shirt. Some shirts have pockets sewn onto one or both sides of the front. T-shirts are sometimes made of fine rib knits that, even on close examination, are hard to distinguish from jersey knits. Long-sleeved T-shirts are also made, and these usually have an attached 1 × 1 rib knit cuff.

The characteristics of jersey and rib knits make them the fabric of choice for T-shirts. Jersey knits stretch, moving comfortably with the body. They are resilient, returning to their original shape after stretching. If laundered and tumble dried, they generally require no ironing. The widthwise elasticity of rib knits allows the T-shirt to stretch as it is pulled over the head or wrists but then return to a close fit.

Although many fibers can and have been used to make T-shirt–like garments, the classic T-shirt is usually made from 100 percent cotton or from blends of cotton and polyester. The most common blend is 50/50. Some manufacturers are also making T-shirts of 90 percent cotton and 10 percent spandex for increased stretch and recovery.

The quality of T-shirts depends on the quality of the fibers, yarns, fabric, and construction. Long-staple pima or sea island cottons may be used for high-quality products. Cotton yarns may be mercerized for increased strength, luster, and durability. Yarns may be carded, which will leave more fuzzy fiber ends on the surface of the fabric, or combed for a smoother surface.

Jersey knits can be made in various weights. Those with more stitches per inch and heavier yarns will feel heavier and will be more durable, although in hot weather they will also feel warmer because they allow less air penetration. Less densely constructed knits are likely to snag and pull more readily. If a knit stitch breaks, a run can form, but unlike sheer nylon stockings where the slippery nature of the fiber allows runs to form quickly, the friction of cotton yarns makes runs travel less readily and for less distance.

The major performance problem consumers experience with T-shirts is shrinkage, which occurs during the first several launderings. Jersey knits undergo relaxation shrinkage as a result of the relaxation of tensions placed on fabrics during processing. Shrinkage is usually more pronounced in the lengthwise direction and is often accompanied by growth in the crosswise direction as the knitted loops broaden. Retailers generally anticipate shrinkage of 8–10 percent in both width and length, although high-quality knit goods manufacturers try to limit product shrinkage to 5 percent. To ensure satisfactory performance, consumers should look for labels that indicate fabrics have been treated to prevent shrinkage.

In satisfactory construction seams are sewn flat and not puckered, and stitches are close and even. Seams at the back of the neck and also at the shoulder may be covered with a strip of knitted tape, which is more comfortable against the skin than a seam. The tape also prevents the shoulder seam from stretching excessively.

T-shirts can generally be machine washed and tumble dried; however, printing of logos and slogans, and novelty trimmings such as sequins, beads, or embroidery, may require special handling. Consult care labels for recommended procedures.

Three- and four-bar tricot constructions permit the carrying of hidden yarns through the fabric. Monofilaments that stabilize the fabric or spandex filaments for stretch may be concealed in the complex structure of the tricot fabric.

Tricot fabrics can be made with a variety of open effects to create interesting lacelike patterns, as well. Figure 17.27 depicts a tricot knitting machine.

Figure 17.24

Guide bars on warp knitting machine move from side to side while needles move up and down. Follow the path of each yarn as it changes its position in the fabric structure.

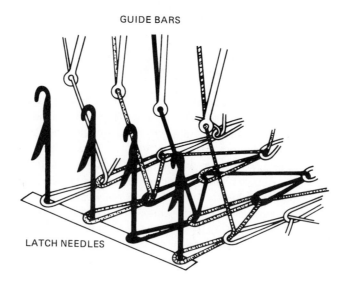

LATCH NEEDLES

Simplex Knits

Simplex knitting machines create warp knits similar to tricot but with a more dense, thicker texture—a sort of double knit tricot. Simplex knits are used in products requiring heavier fabrics, such as women's gloves, handbags, and simulated suede-textured apparel fabrics.

Raschel Knits

Raschel knits can range from finely knitted laces to heavy-duty fabrics. Elaborately patterned surface effects can also be achieved with the Raschel machine. The fabrics have lengthwise rows of loops held together by laid-in yarns and may, to the eye, have the appearance of woven goods or lace.

Raschel knitting machines are flat beds with two to forty-eight guide bars. A mechanism called a *fall plate* controls the placement of the laid-in yarns. In the normal knit stitch formation, the needle moves up and down, looping yarns on and off the needle to form a continuous chain. In Raschel machines the fall plate is lowered to prevent the laid-in yarn behind it from forming a normal loop. Instead, the yarn

Figure 17.25

(a) The simplest single-bar tricot construction and (b) diagram of three-bar tricot. Darker areas show how one yarn is carried throughout the fabric. Illustration (b) courtesy of National Knitwear Sportswear Association.

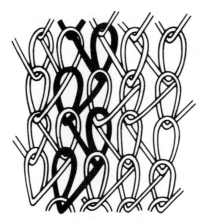

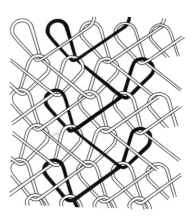

(a)   (b)

Figure 17.26

Tricot knitting cycle: (a) the needle is in the up position, old loops are on the needle stems, and guides (bars) are ready to swing through the needles to the back; (b) the guides are at the back and sideways one space; (c) the yarns are laid across the needles; (d) the needle has risen to get the yarns around the stem; (e) the needle falls, moving the yarn into the hook of the needle while the presser bar presses the needle closed so that the new loops are held inside the hook; (f) a backward motion of the sinker moves the old loops over the closed needle; and (g) the old loops have been cast off, and the needle is ready to rise into position as in (a). From D. G. B. Thomas, *An Introduction to Warp Knitting.* Copyright © Merrow Publishing Co., Ltd. Reproduced by permission.

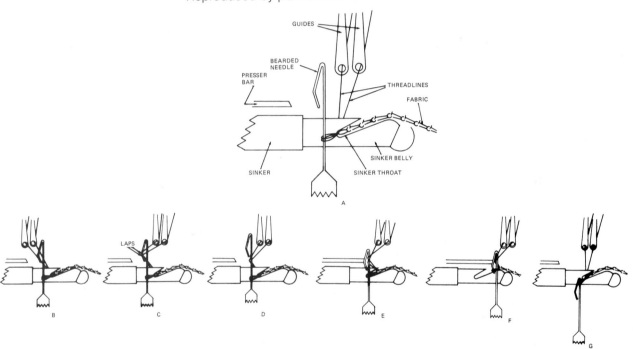

Figure 17.27

Tricot warp knitting machine. Example shown is Type HKS-2/3. Photograph courtesy of Karl Mayer Textilmaschinenfabrik GmbH.

Figure 17.28

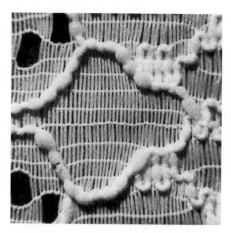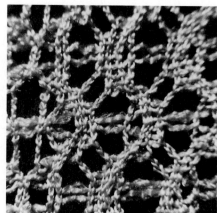

Figure 17.28

Close-up views of two open-structured Raschel knit fabrics.

is carried along in the fabric in a horizontal or diagonal direction, according to the pattern desired. In some fabrics this technique is used to simulate the effect of embroidery; in others, it gives a woven appearance (Figure 17.28).

Among the most popular types of Raschel fabrics are power net of elastomeric yarns for foundation garments and swimsuits, thermal cloth for cold-weather underwear, lace, and tailored menswear fabrics. Pile warp knits for fake fur fabrics are made by incorporating an extra yarn in the structure that is then brushed. In power nets for foundation garments, the laid-in yarns are spandex core yarns.

Crochet Knits

An especially versatile variation of the Raschel knitting machine is used to make fabrics that simulate hand-crocheted fabrics. Although the mechanism of the machine varies slightly from that of an ordinary Raschel knitting machine, the principle of forming lengthwise loops held together by laid-in yarns is the same in both machines. The resulting textiles range from narrow trimmings, including those with fancy fringes, to wider fabrics (25 to 75 inches) used for apparel or household textiles.

Creating Pattern and Design in Knitted Goods

Finished knit goods can be dyed. Patterns can be created by printing on the fabric or through the manipulation of differently colored yarns.

Weft knits are easily knitted into stripes. These stripes always run across the fabric, since the pattern is achieved through varying the colors of the yarns in the different courses. Since the yarns interlace horizontally, it is not possible to knit a vertical stripe in weft single knits.

A jacquard attachment for weft knit machines makes possible the knitting of a wide variety of patterned fabrics. Like woven jacquard patterns, jacquard knit designs are plotted on paper and then are transferred to the jacquard mechanisms where the machine automatically activates the appropriate needles and colored yarns. Electronically controlled machines are widely used in the knitting industry (See Figure 17.10).

The structure of patterns in warp knitting is determined by a system known as the *link-chain system*. Chains with links of variable heights control the movement of the guide bars. The height of the link transfers a motion to the guide bars. The guide

bars set the yarn in position over a group of needles to form the pattern, but pattern variations are limited.

Performance and Care of Knitted Fabrics

Although there is a great variety in the quality of knitted goods sold, and the performance of any individual knit may differ markedly from that of other knits, some general guidelines for the care of knitted goods can be observed. The problems that consumers seem to encounter most often in the performance of knitted fabrics are in the areas of dimensional stability, snagging, and pilling.

Dimensional Stability

One reason for the popularity of knits for wearing apparel is their comfort. The looped construction of knit fabrics permits the fabric to give with the body as it moves. But the stretchiness of knits also results in lessened dimensional stability. Consumers have complained about shrinkage, stretching, and distortion of knits, although some interlock and double knit fabrics display little or no shrinkage.

Shrinkage control treatments, heat setting of synthetics, and special resin finishes can provide good dimensional stability for knits. Unfortunately, not all manufacturers provide such treatment for their products. Consumers should check labels for percentage of shrinkage or for other special treatments to judge potential dimensional stability. (About 3 percent shrinkage is one garment size.) If products fail to live up to specified performance standards, items should be returned to the retailer or the manufacturer.

Knits are considered to be easy-care fabrics, and many care labels recommend machine washing. Some labels will also specify that the fabric can be dried in an automatic dryer. In general, however, knits will shrink more in the dryer than if air dried. Knits maintain their shape best if they are dried flat. The weight of a wet knit, hung on a line, may cause the fabric to stretch out of shape. The dimensions of knits usually will be retained best by professional dry cleaning.

Hand knits, sweaters of wool or animal hair fiber, and other knits with a very open construction may require special hand laundering and blocking (stretching back into shape). Such items should be laid on a sheet of wrapping paper before washing, and the outlines traced. After washing, the garment should be stretched out on the paper to dry. While still damp, the garment should be gently stretched to fit the outline of the original dimensions.

In general, knits made of synthetics will have better resistance to stretching out of shape than will cotton, acetates, and rayons. Blending of synthetics with cottons, acetates, and rayons will improve the resiliency and dimensional stability of knitted fabrics made from these fibers. Price is a good guide—especially for children's knits.

Knit fabrics have better wrinkle recovery than woven fabrics because the yarns can move more freely.

Mechanical Damage

The loop structure of knitted fabrics makes them especially susceptible to snagging. If a loop catches on another object, it may be pulled up from the fabric surface and a long snag, or pull, of yarn may be formed. If the yarn that has been snagged is not broken, it can be pulled to the back of the fabric. It may be possible to gently stretch the fabric and work the pulled yarn back into place. This is difficult to do with very tightly knitted fabric structures. Spun yarns are weaker and are more easily broken than filament yarns.

Figure 17.29

Diagram shows how markings are made on fabrics being tested for skewness, or twisting. Skewness is calculated by subtracting the length of BD from the length of AC and dividing by the sum of the two lengths. It can be seen that if there is no skewness after laundering, BD will equal AC, and the skewness change will be zero. AATCC Test Method 179–1994; illustration reproduced courtesy of the American Association of Textile Chemists and Colorists.

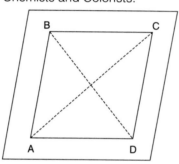

Figure 17.30

Structure of weft insertion warp knit fabric. Illustration courtesy of National Knitwear Manufacturers Association.

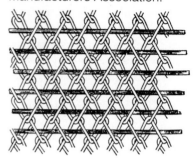

If the yarn has been broken, the snag may produce a hole in the fabric. A few hand stitches with needle and matching thread should be made to secure the yarns so that the hole does not become enlarged during wearing or laundering.

Synthetic double knits or knits made from loosely twisted yarns may be subject to pilling. As the fabric is subjected to abrasion during wear, the short fiber ends that work their way to the fabric surface are rubbed into a small ball that hangs onto the fabric surface. Weaker fibers, such as cotton, rayon, acetate, and wool, generally break off the fabric. But the stronger synthetic fibers cling to the fabric, making an unsightly area on the fabric surface. The use of textured yarns for knitting synthetics decreases the likelihood of pilling.

Knits may be damaged by sharp objects puncturing the fabric. If yarns are cut, a hole will result, and further pressure and strain on the fabric may enlarge the open area, as loops are dropped in the interlocking structure.

Evaluation of Knitted Fabrics

Knitted fabrics, like woven fabrics, may be evaluated through established testing procedures (see chapter 16). Bursting strength is one of the tests frequently used to evaluate the strength of knitted fabrics.

Dimensional stability and skewness resulting from laundering are also tests that relate to end-use performance of knits. In calculating dimensional stability, shrinkage is determined by measuring a marked square on the fabric before and after laundering and reported as percent shrinkage or growth.

A newly developed AATCC test method determines the skewness change in fabric—the twist that develops in garments after laundering. The diagonal lines of a marked square are measured, and the percent change in their length calculated (Figure 17.29).

Warp and Weft Insertion

Processes have been developed that allow the insertion of warp or weft yarns into knitted structures. Some of these variations of knitting have been purely experimental; others have been commercialized for a time. Their purpose is to provide increased stability to knitted structures. This is accomplished by integrating warp or filling yarns part or all of the way into the lengthwise or crosswise direction of a knitted structure, which holds them in place.

Presently, only weft insertion systems have any substantial commercial distribution. A separate magazine feeds weft yarns to a tricot or Raschel warp knitting machine. The weft yarn crosses the entire width of the fabric. When the fabric is viewed from the back side, it can be seen that the weft always passes under the underlap of the knit stitch and over the loops, as shown in Figure 17.30.

Manufacturers of magazine weft insertion machines recommend the fabrics for a wide variety of apparel, household textile, and industrial applications. The textile literature describes their potential for use in processing high-tenacity yarns that are difficult to handle in ordinary weaving. High-tenacity yarns will lose some strength as a result of stresses imposed by the interlacing of yarns required in weaving. In weft insertion, the knitting yarns serve to hold the weft yarn in place, and full advantage can be taken of the strength of the inserted yarn.

References

American Fabrics and Fashions Magazine, ed. 1980. *Encyclopedia of textiles.* 3rd ed. Englewood Cliffs, N.J.: Prentice Hall.

Lonsinger, K. 1993. T-shirts and underwear: The building blocks of fashion. *Knitting Times* 62 (August): 21.

Reichman, C., ed. 1972. *Knitting encyclopedia.* New York: National Knitted Outerwear Association.

Review Questions

1. What is the difference between a weft knit and a warp knit?
2. What determines the number, size, and closeness of knitting stitches? What terms are used to describe the closeness of knit stitches?
3. Describe the various ways that differences in pattern and surface texture can be achieved in weft knits.
4. Which of the following weft knits are made with one needlebed and one set of needles, which are made with two needlebeds and two sets of needles, and which are made with two needlebeds and one set of needles?

jersey knits	velour knits
purl knits	high-pile knits
interlock knits	double knits
rib knits	

5. Explain the differences in weft knit and warp knit structures that make warp knits less subject to developing runs.
6. Identify some of the common end uses of Raschel knit fabrics, and explain why Raschel knits are often used for these products.
7. Assuming comparable quality and fiber content, compare knitted and woven fabrics in terms of their performance in regard to comfort during physical activity, dimensional stability, snagging, wrinkle recovery, and pilling. Explain what accounts for these differences.

Recommended Readings

Cegielka, L., ed. 1988. The knitting industry: Present needs and future requirements. *Textile Progress* 19 (1).

Ghosh, S., and P. K. Banerjee. 1990. Mechanics of single jersey weft knitting process. *Textile Research Journal* 60 (April): 203.

How to buy a sweater. 1994. *Consumer Reports,* December, 791.

King, M. W., R. Guidoin, and B. Soares. 1993. Designing fabrics for hernia repair. *Canadian Textile Journal* 110 (October): 18.

Knitting in the third dimension. 1994. *Textile Horizons* (December): 22.

Schwartz, P., T. Rhodes, and M. Mohamed. 1982. Knitting and knit fabrics. In *Fabric forming systems,* 76–151. Park Ridge, N.J.: Noyes.

Smith, S. 1994. The history of hosiery in America. *Southern Textile News,* 8 August, 2.

Spencer, D. J. 1989. *Knitting technology,* 2d ed. Oxford: Pergamon.

———1989. The basic principles of knitting. *Textiles* 18 (1): 15.

Weft-insertion warp-knits for industrial fabrics. 1983. *Textile Industries,* March, 56.

Willis, D. 1993. More than just T-shirts. *Canadian Textile Journal* 110 (October): 15.

CHAPTER 18

NONWOVEN FABRICS

Although woven and knitted goods make up the largest quantity of fabrics produced, various other construction methods are also used for the fabrication of textiles. Many of these techniques derive from processes used since prehistoric times, others have been developed more recently, and some are the result of new technology within the textile industry. It has become customary within the industry to refer to most of these fabrics as *nonwovens* even though, strictly speaking, knitted fabric is also a "nonwoven" textile.

The fabrication methods discussed in this chapter may be divided into several broad classifications: fabrics made by knotting, by looping, by stitching yarns or fibers together, and by bonding together a web of fibers. Netting, macramé, and lace are created by knotting, either by hand or by machine. Crochet, essentially a hand technique, is made from a series of loops in a process that is similar to knitting. A new fabric construction technique, known either as stitch bonding or stitch knitting, combines yarns and/or fibers by sewing them together. Ancient techniques such as felt making or bark cloth construction are similar in principle to the manufacture of modern nonwovens, fibers held together in a flexible web.

Fabric Webs

Felt

Although the evidence is scanty, it is believed that the first means of making fibers into cloth was through felting. Prehistoric remains of felt materials have been found in such diverse parts of the world as Anatolia, Siberia, Europe, Southeast Asia, and South America. To understand the process by which felt is formed, it is necessary to review the structure of the wool fiber from which it is made.

The surface of the wool fiber is covered with a fine network of small scales. This scaly structure causes wool fibers to cling closely together, as the scales from one fiber interlock with the scales of another. Furthermore, the natural crimp of wool assists in felting. When masses of wool fiber are placed together, the crimped fibers become entangled. Friction increases this tangling. If the wool is subjected to conditions of heat and moisture, the scales open wider, interlocking with still more scales from neighboring fibers. Wool scales are so oriented that each fiber moves in its root direction, causing the mass to hold together more tightly. When pressure is added, the mass is flattened, producing a web of tightly joined fibers, or felt. The factors essential for producing natural felt from wool are pressure, which increases the tangling, heat, and moisture.

It is not too difficult to imagine a situation in which felt might have been produced accidentally. Suppose a horse rider placed a sheep fleece on the back of a horse as cushioning material. The body of the horse is both warm and moist; the rider provides the pressure and the friction. Over time, the fleece becomes matted, producing a primitive form of felt. Frequent repetition of the procedure could lead to the recognition that this material had potential for some of the same uses as the fleece from which it was made.

Eventually, the natural process was reduced to a series of steps that included applying heat and moisture to a mass of wool fiber, placing the batt (or mass) of fibers on flat stones, and pounding the fibers with hammers or beaters. To vary the texture and quality of the material, fur fibers might have been added, but it was the wool that served to hold the substance together.

In the commercial production of felt, a batt of cleaned wool fiber is fed into a carding machine that lays down a web of fairly even thickness. To improve strength and dimensional stability, two webs of carded fiber are laid across each other with the fibers of one web at right angles to the fibers of the other web.

Steam is forced through the mass of fiber, after which a heavy, heated plate or rollers are lowered onto the fibers. The plate or rollers are moved about to produce mechanical motion. The moisture, heat, and friction effectively interlock the fibers.

Following this operation, the fabric is passed through a solution of soap or acid that causes the fabric to compact further. From this stage the fabric goes to a "fulling mill" in which the fabric is subjected to further agitation, pounding, and shrinkage. After felting is complete, the fabric can be dyed or given any of the traditional finishes used on wool.

To decrease costs, manufacturers may blend other fibers with wool. A woven scrim (a plain, open, woven fabric) may sometimes be added as a framework to support felt to increase its strength.

Felt has the advantage of being easily cut, and because it has no yarns, it will not fray at the edges. Felt can be molded into shape and, so, has wide use in making hats. Because of its densely packed fibers, felt provides a good deal of warmth, and it is not easily penetrated by water. On the other hand, felt is a relatively weak fabric, may tear under pressure, and is subject to pilling. Being rather stiff, felt does not fall into graceful folds. Its use, therefore, is somewhat limited. Modern manufacturers of wool felt supply material not only for hats and fashion accessories but also for a wide range of industrial uses.

Bark Cloth

A process similar to that used for felt produces bark cloth or, as it is called in the Polynesian Islands, *tapa*. This nonwoven fabric was also known during prehistoric times in areas as widespread as Asia, Africa, Europe, South and Central America, and the South Pacific.

Made from certain trees, among them the paper mulberry, breadfruit, fig, or related species, bark cloth is produced by first removing strips of the inner layer of bark from the tree. This substance is softened by soaking it in water. The softened bark is placed on an anvil or other flat surface, and special beaters are then used to pound the bark strips to interlace the fibers. When the mass is sufficiently integrated, the material is dried, producing a sheet of fabric. Special texture or surface markings are achieved by pounding the material with incised hammers or embossing the flat surface on which the fibrous materials are spread to be beaten and to dry.

The process is similar to that used in making paper, and the resulting fabric is somewhat like a soft, supple paper. Printed designs are added to the surface. Although woven cotton goods replaced native bark cloth in the South Pacific in the nineteenth century, small quantities are still made for native religious garb and as an example of native handicrafts.

Like felt, tapa has limited usefulness. In medium to heavy weights, it does not drape or sew particularly well and so is used chiefly for simple unsewn garments such as ponchos, sarongs, loincloths, or turbans. On the other hand, because pieces of tapa can be joined without sewing, simply by wetting the edge of two pieces and pounding them together, large pieces of fabric can be made without seams.

Other Fiber Webs

Techniques by which fabrics are made directly from fibers, bypassing both spinning and weaving, have been used for centuries in the production of felt and bark cloth. With the development of manufactured fibers, and, in particular, the synthesis of thermoplastic fibers, technologies have evolved that have made possible the large-scale production of nonwoven fabrics. Marketed extensively for both durable and disposable items, nonwoven fiber webs range from disposable diapers to blankets, from industrial filters to tea-bag covers.

The ASTM defines nonwoven textile fabrics as textile structures "produced by bonding or interlocking of fiber, or both, accomplished by mechanical, chemical or solvent means and combinations thereof" (ASTM 1986). Excluded from this class are paper; fabrics that have been woven, knitted, or tufted; or those made by wool or other felting processes.

Paper is formed by a process very much like that described in Figure 18.1(c), and it is difficult to make a clear division between some paper and some nonwoven textile products.

American Fabrics (1974) magazine had recommended that nonwoven fabrics be classified as durable products or disposable products. They defined a durable product as "one which is multi-use. It is not manufactured to be thrown away after a single application" (p. 40). Examples of this type of product are blankets, carpet backings, and furniture padding.

Disposable products were defined as "made to be disposed of after a single or limited number of uses" (p. 40). These are exemplified in disposable diapers, towels, or tea-bag covers. Some items, *American Fabrics* pointed out, are disposable not because of their durability but because of their purpose. Medical gowns, for example, or airplane and train headrests, might withstand multiple use, but for sanitary reasons they have limited use periods.

Nonwoven fabrics are made from both staple fibers and filaments. Filament fibers are made into fabrics by spunbonding, which is discussed later in this chapter. Staple fibers may be made into fabrics by several different processes.

Staple Fiber Web Formation

Both durable and disposable staple fiber nonwovens are manufactured in several stages. The first step, the forming of the web of fibers, is done by either *dry forming* or *wet forming*. Either of two different dry-forming processes, carding or air laying, may be used. Fiber-forming processes are explained in the following pages through the use of diagrams and captions reproduced courtesy of INDA (Association of the Nonwovens Fabrics Industry). This material appeared originally in INDA's publication *The Nonwovens Handbook,* 1988. (See Figure 18.1.)

Binding the Fibers Together

Once a web has been formed, some treatment must be given to bind the fibers together. This can be done by using a bonding, or adhesive, material or by entangling fibers.

Bonding. Bonding may be achieved by applying an adhesive material to the web and then setting the adhesive. This, in essence, "glues" the fibers together. (See Figure 18.2.) When adhesive is applied to the surface of the fiber web, it tends to make the

Figure 18.1

Schematic representation of different methods of web forming. Following web formation, the web must be treated to bond fibers together.

(a) Web forming by the dry laying, carding (or garnetting) method. Fine wires and teeth comb fibers from the bale into parallel arrays.

(b) Web forming by air laying method. Fibers from opened bales are suspended in air and then collected on a screen.

(c) Web forming by wet laying method. Fibers are suspended uniformly in water and collected to form a sheet by filtering onto a screen. Figure reproduced courtesy of INDA, Association of the Nonwovens Fabrics Industry.

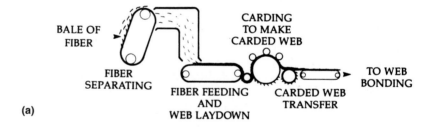

(a)

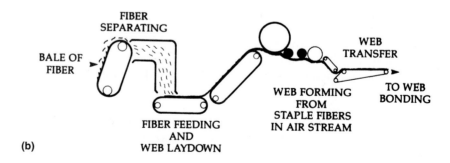

(b)

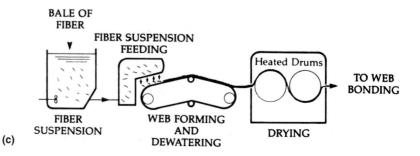

(c)

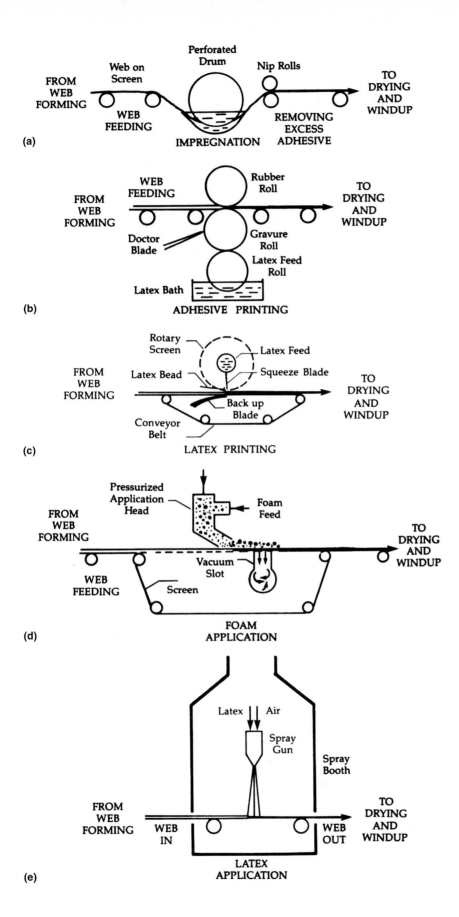

(a)

Web on Screen

Perforated Drum

Nip Rolls

FROM WEB FORMING

TO DRYING AND WINDUP

WEB FEEDING

IMPREGNATION

REMOVING EXCESS ADHESIVE

(b)

WEB FEEDING

Rubber Roll

FROM WEB FORMING

TO DRYING AND WINDUP

Doctor Blade

Gravure Roll

Latex Feed Roll

Latex Bath

ADHESIVE PRINTING

(c)

Rotary Screen

Latex Feed

FROM WEB FORMING

Latex Bead

Squeeze Blade

TO DRYING AND WINDUP

Back up Blade

Conveyor Belt

LATEX PRINTING

(d)

Pressurized Application Head

Foam Feed

FROM WEB FORMING

TO DRYING AND WINDUP

WEB FEEDING

Vacuum Slot

Screen

FOAM APPLICATION

(e)

Latex Air

Spray Gun

Spray Booth

FROM WEB FORMING

TO DRYING AND WINDUP

WEB IN

WEB OUT

LATEX APPLICATION

Figure 18.2

Fiber webs are most frequently bonded by applying an adhesive binder called latex. Methods of applying the latex include: (a) saturation bonding, (b) gravure printing, (c) screen printing, (d) foam bonding, and (e) spray bonding. Figure reproduced courtesy of INDA, Association of the Nonwovens Fabrics Industry.

327

fabric stiff and more rigid. Also, fabrics exhibit the characteristics of the adhesive material on the surface rather than those of the original fiber. To overcome this disadvantage, adhesives may be imprinted onto the surface in selected areas. The printing patterns are developed carefully to assure that adequate bonding takes place among fibers to maintain fabric strength. Such fabrics are less rigid and have better drapability and a more pleasant surface texture than do those that have been completely coated by an adhesive.

Instead of adhesive bonding, fibers may be bonded by spraying a mixture of chemicals and water onto the surface of the fibers. When subjected to heat, the water evaporates and the chemical vaporizes, dissolving a small amount of fiber, usually where one fiber crosses another. When the dissolved fibers resolidify, bonds are formed that hold the fibers together.

Thermoplastic fibers may be bonded by heat. The application of heat causes the fusing together of heat-sensitive fibers, which effectively fastens them together. As in bonding with adhesives, heat may be applied in a pattern to provide sufficient bonding for durability and to allow greater flexibility and softness in the end product. Nonwovens can also be formed with a small percentage of binder fiber of lower melting point than the predominant fibers. When the web is heated, the binder fibers melt, providing the necessary adhesion. (See Figure 18.3.)

Entangling Fibers. Fiber webs produced by the dry-web methods may be joined by entangling the fibers in some way. One of these methods is discussed later in the section on stitch bonding. It is the process (with the Maliwatt and the Arachne machines) of *chain stitching,* or knitting through a batt of fibers.

Another method, known as *needle punching,* has wide use in the home furnishings industry. (See Figure 18.4.)

Figure 18.3

Two methods of thermal bonding of fiber webs: (a) through-air bonding and (b) calender bonding. Figure reproduced courtesy of INDA, Association of the Nonwovens Fabrics Industry.

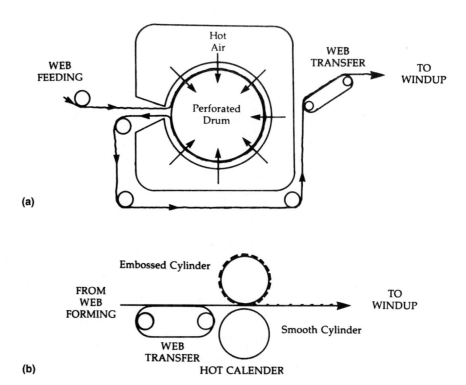

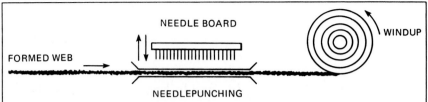

Process: A needle punched fabric is produced by introducing a fibrous web—already formed by cards, garnetts, or air laying—into a machine equipped with groups of specially designed needles. While the web is trapped between a bed plate and a stripper plate, the needles punch through it and reorient the fibers so that mechanical bonding is achieved among the individual fibers. Often, the batt of fibers is carried into the needle punching section of the machine on a light-weight support material or substrate. This is done to improve finished fabric strength and integrity.

Fabric characteristics: The needle punching process is generally used to produce fabrics that have high density yet retain some bulk. Fabric weights usually range from 1.7 to 10 ounces per square yard. Thicknesses generally range from 15 to 160 mils.

Typical end uses: Blankets, filter media, coated fabric backings, carpeting and carpet backings, automobile landau top substrates, apparel interlinings, road underlay, auto trunk liners.

Figure 18.4

Needle-punched process. Figure reproduced courtesy of INDA, Association of the Nonwovens Fabrics Industry.

Spunlaced, or *hydroentangled,* goods are made by fluid entanglement. High-speed jets of water hitting a fibrous web bind fibers together by causing them to knot or curl around each other. No binder is required. Patterns can be created by the use of perforated, patterned screens that support the fiber web. As the fibers become entangled, they assume the pattern of the supports. Depending on the patterns used, spunlaced fabrics may have an appearance similar to fabrics woven from yarns. (See Figure 18.5.)

Direct Laid Processes

Direct laid processes have the economic advantage of taking the fiber directly from the spinning stage to the fabric-forming stage without costly intermediate processing. Direct laid processes currently in use are spunbonding, melt blowing, and film fibrillation.

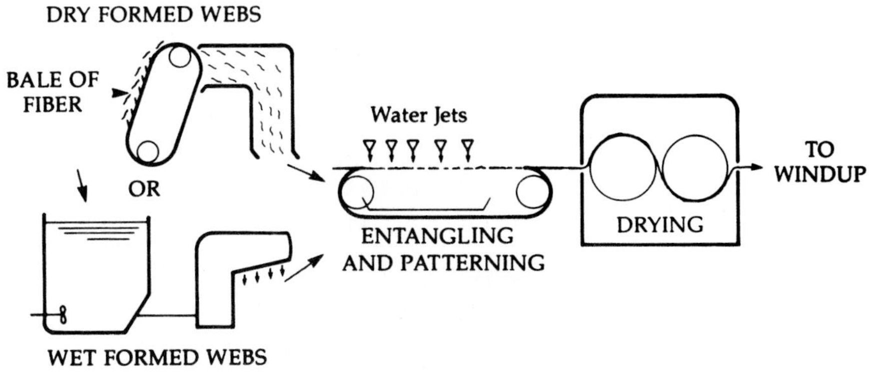

Figure 18.5

Web forming and bonding by the spunlacing, or hydroentangling, process. Figure reproduced courtesy of INDA, Association of the Nonwovens Fabrics Industry.

Spunbonding. Spunbonded fabrics are manufactured from synthetic filament fibers. Continuous filaments are formed by extrusion through spinnerets, and the filaments are blown onto a moving belt where they form a web. As the still hot and partially molten filaments touch, they bond. Polymers most often used are polypropylene and polyester. (See Figure 18.6.) Spunbonded fabrics are used for a wide variety of products ranging from apparel interlinings, carpet backing, furniture and bedding, bagging material, and packing material. Spunbonded fabrics may be used in geotextiles to control erosion or in constructing roads. Some spunbondeds made from olefins are used as a tough, especially durable substitute for paper in wall coverings, charts, maps, tags, and the like.

Melt Blowing. Melt blowing also forms fabrics directly from fibers, but it differs from spunbonding in that molten fiber filaments are broken into short lengths as they exit from the spinnerets. Cool air distributes the fibers onto a moving screen. As the fibers cool they bond, forming a white, opaque web of fine fibers. (See Figure 18.7.)

Passing the spunbonded or meltblown fiber webs between heated cylinders bonds fabrics more completely. Design effects can be produced if these cylinders have patterns embossed on their surfaces.

Specialty products can also be made by layering spunbonded and meltblown fabrics or by entrapping absorbent fibers or other materials within the meltblown structure.

Film Fibrillation. Film fibrillation as a means of forming yarns is discussed in chapter 15. Film fibrillation can also be used to create fabrics directly from polymer films.

Figure 18.6

Web forming and bonding by the spunbonding process. Figure reproduced courtesy of INDA, Association of the Nonwovens Fabrics Industry.

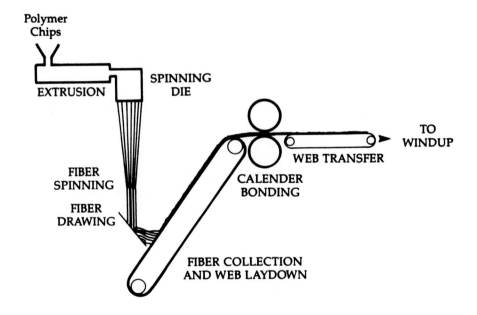

Figure 18.7

Web forming and bonding by the melt blowing process. Figure reproduced courtesy of INDA, Association of the Nonwovens Fabrics Industry.

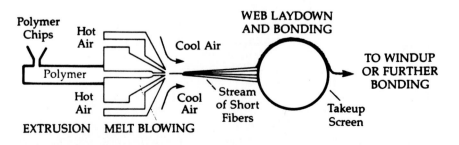

After extrusion the films are embossed, thereby thinning them in selected areas. The embossed film is then stretched in the lengthwise and crosswise directions, and the film breaks apart in the weak areas to form a netting. The fabrics produced by this means may be used alone, as facings for other fabrics, or as supporting scrims between layers of fabric.

Stitch Bonding

A process known variously as *stitch bonding, stitch through, stitch knitting,* or *mali* (from one machine used in its manufacture) produces fabrics for industrial, household, and, to a lesser extent, apparel uses. Heinrich Mauersberger, an East German inventor, developed the stitch-bonding concept after observing his wife mending a fabric in which the filling yarns had been worn away. Mauersberger assigned the trademark Malimo to his process and the fabric it produced.

Stitch bonding offers manufacturers the advantages of faster speeds than knitting or weaving and can be produced at lower costs, not only because of increased volume of production but also because less fiber or yarn is required. Some stitch-bonded fabrics have greater bursting strength and tear strength than comparable woven fabrics.

One group of stitch-bonding machines constructs fabrics from yarn. Warp and filling yarns are laid loosely, one over the other. A third set of yarns stitches the warp and weft yarns together. (See Figure 18.8.) It is also possible to use filling yarns alone,

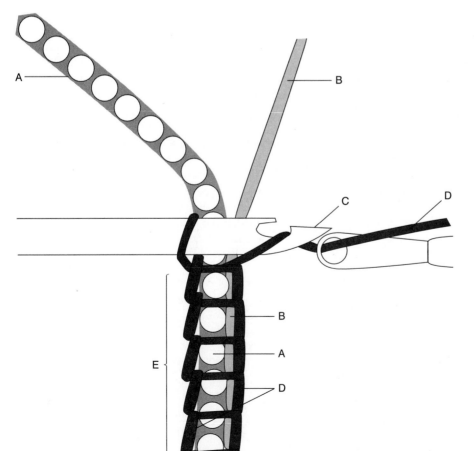

Figure 18.8

Schematic showing how stitch-bonded fabrics are made from warp and filling yarns: (a) filling yarns, shown in cross section, being fed into the mechanism; (b) warp yarn; (c) compound loop-forming hook; (d) stitch-bonding yarn; and (e) completed fabric with warp and filling yarns held together by stitch-bonding yarn.

Figure 18.9

Fabrics constructed by the stitch-through technique.

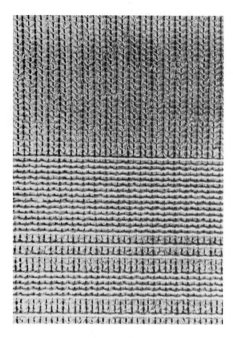

holding them in place with overstitching. These fabrics are called Malimo fabrics by the Mayer Textile Machine Corporation, which has acquired what was the Malimo Company. The fabrics find use in such applications as industrial textiles, furnishing fabrics, and household textiles. (See Figure 18.9.)

Another yarn-based stitch-bonding technique, Malipol, creates single-sided pile fabrics by stitching pile yarns onto a woven, knitted, nonwoven, or stitch-bonded fabric base. The resulting fabrics have the appearance of plush, terry cloth, or velour and are used in apparel and as lining fabrics, upholstery fabrics, and imitation fur fabrics. The Schusspol stitch-bonding machine also produces pile fabrics by stitching warp, filling, and pile yarns together at the same time, and it does not require a pre-formed base fabric. Applications include carpets and other floor coverings, upholstery, and terry fabrics.

Another group of stitch-bonding techniques works with fiber webs. In Maliwatt fabrics fiber webs are stitched together. (See Figure 18.10.) The resulting fabrics are used as lining fabrics, furnishing fabrics, insulating materials, base fabrics for tufted goods, and in industrial and geotextiles. Malivlies fabrics, used in felts, packing materials, insulation materials, and utility textiles, are created by forming stitches from the

Figure 18.10

Schematic showing how fiber webs may be held together by stitch bonding. Figure reproduced courtesy of INDA, Association of the Nonwovens Fabrics Industry.

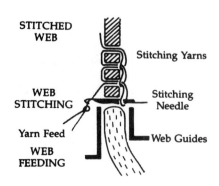

fibers of the web itself. No additional yarns are required. In the Voltex process, fibers are intermeshed with a backing fabric to form a voluminous pile fabric. Applications include imitation furs, lining fabrics, plushes, and blankets.

The newest developments in stitch bonding are the Kunit and Multiknit processes. (See Figure 18.11.) Kunit fabrics are formed by feeding a web of fibers into

(a) Maliwatt

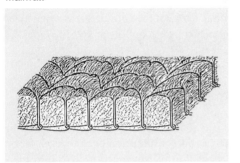

Cross-lapped carded fleece with mechanical compacting be additional stitchbonding.

(b) Malivlies

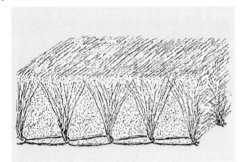

Cross-lapped carded fleece. The mechanical compacting is effected by partial stitching of the fiber structure.

(c) Kunit

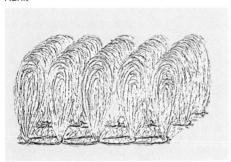

Length-oriented carded fleece. The mechanical compacting is effected by stitching of the fiber structure to pile loops of pre-determined height.

(d) Multiknit

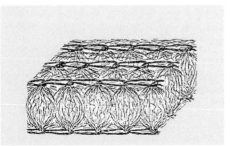

The ground fabric is Kunit and in a connected process it is subsequently stitched on top of the loops, resulting in two identical plain fabric surfaces.

Figure 18.11

Cross-sectional diagrams of pile fabrics made by the stitch-bonding process. Illustrations courtesy of Karl Mayer Techmaschinenfabrik GmbH.

a machine where a type of compound knitting needle (see chapter 17, page 307) forms knitting stitches from the fiber web. These stitches hold the web together and form a fabric that may have either a plushlike, furlike, or flat appearance. Uses include linings for clothing and shoes, plush for toys, automotive interior fabrics, acoustical and thermal insulation, packaging material, and base fabrics to which coatings may be applied. In the Multiknit process, two fabrics formed by the Kunit process are united into a double-sided, multilayered fabric with knitting stitches made by a compound needle with a sharp point that can penetrate both fabrics. Applications include insulation materials, garment interlinings, base materials for molded textile composites, and as a replacement for foam in car and furniture upholstery.

The Place of Nonwoven Fabrics in the Textile Industry

Figure 18.12 shows clearly the rapid increase in consumption of nonwoven fabrics in the United States since 1970 and the prediction of continued growth into the next century. INDA reports that the first nonwoven consumer product, an interlining fabric for the apparel industry, was introduced in 1952. By 1960 nearly 50,000 tons of nonwoven products were being produced. It is estimated that the volume will reach 1,125 thousand metric tonnes by 2000 (INDA 1992).

Table 18.1 provides a summary of the pervasive nature of nonwovens in the United States at the present time. Many of the applications would be considered industrial fabrics, as they are not used for clothing or home furnishings. An area of strong growth in industrial textiles has been the products known as geotextiles.

Figure 18.12

U.S. nonwoven volume output. Figure reproduced courtesy of INDA, Association of the Nonwovens Fabrics Industry.

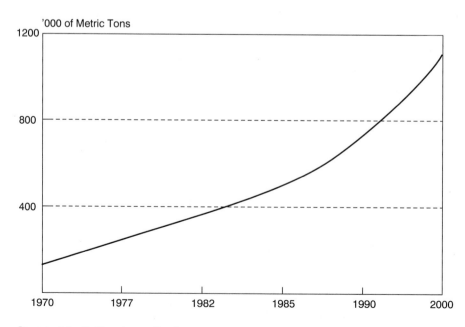

Source: John R. Starr, Inc. estimates

Table 18.1	Products That Use Nonwovens

Agriculture
- Seed strips
- Greenhouse covers

Automotive
- Sound and heat insulation
- Interior trim
- Battery separators
- Vinyl roofs
- Upholstery
- Carpet backing

Civil Engineering
- Road and railroad beds
- Soil stabilization
- Drainage
- Dam and stream embankments
- Golf and tennis courts
- Artificial turf
- Sedimentation and erosion control

Clothing
- Interfacings
- Skiwear
- Insulated clothing, gloves
- Swimwear
- Imitation fur
- Underwear
- Bra and shoulder padding
- Robes
- Handbags
- Tailors' patterns
- Shrouds, casket liners
- Shoe liners, insoles
- Rainwear

Construction
- Roofing and tile underlayment
- Acoustical ceilings
- Insulation

Home Furnishings
- Upholstery backings and webs
- Slipcovers
- Wallcovering backings
- Quilts, blankets, bedspreads
- Mattresses, mattress covers, tickings
- Pillows, pillowcases
- Lampshades
- Window shades
- Draperies
- Carpet backings

Household
- Wipes: wet, dry, polishing
- Aprons
- Scouring pads
- Glove liners
- Laundry softeners and antistatics
- Dust cloths, mops
- Tea and coffee bags
- Doormats, bathmats
- Garment bags
- Placemats, napkins
- Ironing board pads
- Laundry bags
- Washcloths
- Tablecloths
- Cheese wrap

Industrial, Military
- Coated fabrics
- Filters
- Clean room apparel
- Air conditioning
- Military clothing
- Abrasives
- Parachutes
- Cable insulation
- Reinforced plastics
- Tapes
- Protective clothing, labcoats

Leisure, Travel
- Sails, kites
- Sleeping bags
- Tarpaulins, tents
- Artificial leather, luggage
- Art canvases
- Airline headrests
- Fiberglass boats

Health Care
- Surgical: caps, gowns, masks, shoe covers
- Sponges, dressings, wipes
- Orthopedic padding
- Bandages, tapes
- Dental bibs
- Drapes, wraps, packs
- Sterile packaging
- Bedpan covers
- Instrument pads
- Privacy curtains
- Bed linen, underpads

- Examination gowns, slippers
- Filters for IV solutions, blood oxygenators and kidney dialyzers
- Transdermal drug delivery

Personal Care and Hygiene
- Buff pads
- Diapers
- Sanitary napkins, tampons
- Incontinence products
- Dry and wet wipes
- Cosmetics applicators, removers
- Bibs
- Vacuum cleaner bags
- Tea, coffee bags

School, Office
- Bookcovers
- Mailing envelopes, labels
- Maps, signs, pennants
- Floppy disk liners
- Towels
- Promotional items

Note: Reproduced courtesy of INDA, Association of the Nonwovens Fabrics Industry.

Geotextiles

Geotextiles perform functions such as filtration, separation, or reinforcement in ground and soil applications. Although the development of geotextiles is recent, there are historic examples of such textile applications. Hannibal's army in the third century B.C. spread blankets and coats over a marshy battleground before fighting.

Geotextiles can be woven or nonwoven fabrics of polyester, nylon, or polyolefin. The cheaper processing and the wide variety of possible products of nonwovens make them ideal for the large-volume applications in geotextiles. Rugged nonwoven fabrics can be used to stabilize roads by providing a separation layer between the asphalt and

Figure 18.13

Typar® nonwoven geotextile provides a tough, durable permeable separation layer, used here in road construction. (a) Road surface without Typar® layer. Soil contaminates and weakens aggregate base placed beneath pavement. (b) Road surface with Typar®. Aggregate will not sink into and intermix with subsoil. Illustrations courtesy of LINQ Industrial Fabrics, Inc.

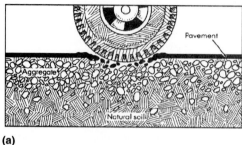
(a)

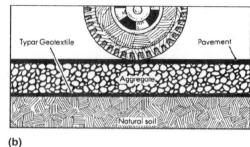
(b)

Figure 18.14

Geotextile earth embankment application. (1) gravel sand, (2) geotextile fabric, (3) embankment, and (4) subsoil. Reprinted by permission from Jarmila Svedova, ed., *Industrial Textiles,* vol. 9 of *Textile Science and Technology,* 285 (Amsterdam: Elsevier, 1990). Copyright 1990 by Elsevier Science.

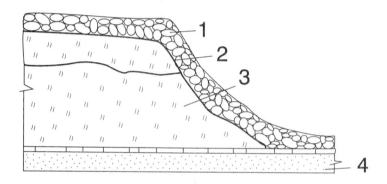

the soil road bed. The geotextile prevents the asphalt aggregate from mixing into the soil and weakening the road surface. (See Figure 18.13.)

Another growing application for nonwoven geotextiles is in soil erosion control. The geotextile fabric, when placed under the sand or gravel cover on an embankment, can prevent soil erosion by holding the soil underneath. (See Figure 18.14.) Nonwoven geotextile mats of biodegradable natural fibers can also be placed on top of newly seeded construction sites to hold the soil until vegetation can grow.

Nets, Macramé, Lace, and Crochet

Nets

Nets are created by looping and knotting a continuous strand of yarn into an open mesh. In use since prehistoric times for trapping fish, birds, and other small animals, nets also have a long history as decorative fabrics. Egyptian burial chambers, for example, contained fabric made from open-work net with embroideries of pearls and precious stones.

Most netted fabrics are made with either a square or diamond-shaped mesh. The hand process is a fairly simple one of looping and knotting to form an open-work fabric. The decorativeness of the net can be increased by embroidering designs on the open mesh. The terms *filet* work or *lacis* are applied to decorated nets, and they are often classified as a type of lace. (See Figure 18.15.)

Machine-made nets are manufactured on a bobbinet lace machine. Raschel or compound needle tricot knitting machines also produce fabrics similar in appearance

Figure 18.15

Examples of lacis, or embroidered net fabric, from the sixteenth century. Photograph reprinted by permission of the Metropolitan Museum of Art. Gift of Mrs. Magdalena Nuttall.

but with different structures. Net fabrics range from lightweight tulles to heavy fishing nets.

Macramé

Macramé might be considered as a variation of the principle used in making nets. Like netting, macramé uses the techniques of looping and knotting yarns. Unlike netting, however the decorative qualities of macramé are determined by the selection and use of a variety of ornamental knots. In netting, it is the open area that is important. In macramé the closed or knotted areas are emphasized.

The word *macramé* seems to be Arabic in origin, and the process itself probably was brought to Europe from the Arab world. Like filet or lacis, macramé may be classified as a lace. Its first use was in finishing off the unwoven yarns at the end of a fabric. In time, macramé was constructed separately and attached to linens or garments in the same way that other trimmings were sewn into place.

The first major surge of interest in macramé came during the seventeenth century during a period of emphasis on lace making in general. Since that time macramé has experienced periods of great favor and periods of relative obscurity. During the nineteenth century it was an important decoration for clothes and household items. Fashion magazines of the 1800s were filled with instructions for macramé work. Macramé was not used widely during the early 1900s, but since the late 1960s there has been a resurgence of interest in the technique.

Since macramé does not require specialized tools, it can be made with a minimum of equipment. During the eighteenth and nineteenth centuries sailors on whaling ships often occupied their spare time by making macramé items that they bartered when they reached port.

The yarns or cords that are used in macramé are fastened to a holding cord, which in turn is clamped or pinned securely so that the cords will not slip. For complex work, the yarns are wound onto bobbins so that they do not become entangled. The work is done by creating a variety of knots that join the cords at different intervals. Placement of the knots and judicious selection of the type of knots make possible the creation of a variety of textures and decorative effects. Macramé is essentially a handcraft technique. (See Figure 18.16.)

Lace

Because of its delicate beauty, lace has been one of the most sought-after fabrics. The precise origins of lace making are unknown, but its development was related not only to knotting and netting but also to embroidery. Among the earliest lacelike fabrics were those that were called *drawn work*. In drawn work, individual yarns were unraveled from a woven fabric, and embroidery stitches were used to fasten groups of these yarns together into a decorative pattern. *Cut work* was also a forerunner of lace. In cut work, areas of fabric are cut out to form a pattern, and the raw edges around the open areas are embroidered both to prevent them from fraying and to add decoration. Ornamentation can be increased by throwing threads across the open area to form geometric patterns, by weaving in and out, or by embroidering over the threads that bridged the gap.

Although fabrics decorated by each of these techniques bear certain similarities to lace, true lace making dispensed with the base fabric and created the design from

| Figure 18.16 | Macramé fabric, knotted from ivory cotton by an American artist in the late nineteenth century. Photograph reprinted by permission of the Philadelphia Museum of Art. Given by Mrs. Edward F. Bailey, 1955. Copyright © 1955 by the Philadelphia Museum of Art. |

the threads alone. Laces are generally divided into two categories, according to their construction. One is called *needlepoint lace,* the other *bobbin lace.*

Needlepoint lace, which is slightly older than bobbin lace, probably originated in Venice sometime before the sixteenth century (Goldenberg 1904). In making needlepoint laces, the design for the lace was first drawn on parchment or heavy paper. A piece of heavy linen was sewn to the back of the parchment to hold it straight. Threads were then laid along the lines of the pattern and basted lightly onto the parchment and linen. None of these threads was attached to any other. The lace was created by embroidering over the base threads with decorative stitches. These embroideries connected the base threads. The areas between the threads could also be filled in with fancy needlework, according to the requirements of the pattern. When the embroidery was complete, the basting threads that held the lace to the paper were clipped, and the finished lace was released.

Bobbin lace or, as it is also termed, *pillow lace* uses twisted and plaited threads. It is more closely related to netting and knotting, whereas needlepoint lace stems more from embroidery. Again the design is drawn on stiff paper. Holes are pricked into the paper in the area of the pattern. This pattern is then stretched over a pillow, and small pins are placed at close intervals through the holes in the paper. The pins go through the paper and into the pillow. The thread is wound onto bobbins, and the threads are worked around the pins to form meshes, openings, and closed areas. Bobbin lace seems to have originated in Flanders or Belgium. (See Figure 18.17.)

The techniques for making both bobbin lace and needlepoint lace quickly spread throughout Europe. Each town developed its own style of lace, which had its traditional patterns and construction features. It is this localization of design that has given us the names for most laces. Chantilly lace, for example, was first made in the French city of Chantilly, Venice point lace originated in Venice, and Val lace was first made in Valenciennes, France.

The production of lace by machine began soon after 1800. Although an earlier machine had had good success in producing manufactured nets, machine-made laces

Figure 18.17   Lace making using a lace pillow and bobbins. Yarns from the various bobbins are knotted together following the pattern drawn on a sheet of parchment paper placed over the pillow. The pins hold the knotted yarns in place.

were not perfected until John Leavers invented a machine that could make as much lace in one day as a skilled handworker would produce in six months (Schwab 1951). Only an expert can tell the difference between machine- and handmade lace. Most modern laces are produced by machine on the Leavers machine. Knitted laces may be made on the Raschel machine, and some lacelike embroidered fabrics are produced by the Schiffli machine. Schiffli fabrics, however, are not true laces; rather, they are embroidered, woven fabrics.

Crochet

The origins of crochet are obscure. The technique of creating fabric by pulling one loop of yarn through another with a hook was brought to the United States by Irish immigrants of the nineteenth century. The craft was evidently practiced in Irish convents as an efficient means of copying lace fabrics. During the potato famine of the 1840s, the nuns taught many poor Irish women to crochet so that they could supplement the family income. When these families came to America, they brought Irish crochet with them, and soon women throughout the United States had learned to crochet.

Crocheting is closely related to knitting. Both join together a series of interlocked yarn loops into a variety of open and/or closed patterns. Crochet is made with a single needle or hook, whereas knitting uses several needles.

References

American Fabrics, ed. 1974. AAF appraises the non-wovens. *American Fabrics,* no. 101 (Summer): 40.

ASTM. 1986. *Compilation of ASTM standard definitions.* Philadelphia: American Society for Testing and Materials.

Goldenberg, S. L. 1904. *Lace: Its origin and history.* New York: Brentanos.

INDA. 1992. *The nonwoven fabrics handbook.* Cary, N.C.: Association of the Nonwovens Fabric Industry.

Schwab, F. R. 1951. *The story of lace and embroidery.* New York: Fairchild.

Review Questions

1. Explain how the physical properties of wool fibers make the production of felt possible.
2. How can fibers be held together in the manufacture of fiber webs made from manufactured fibers?
3. What are the economic advantages of processes such as spunbonding, melt blowing, and film fibrillation?
4. Explain the basic principles of forming fabrics by stitch bonding.
5. What are the differences in the techniques for making pillow lace and needlepoint lace by hand?
6. What is the difference between the techniques for making macramé and crochet?
7. How are nonwovens used in geotextile applications?

Recommended Readings

Bark fabrics. 1940. *CIBA Review,* May.

Conley, J. T. 1984. Modern air forming. *Nonwovens Industry* 15 (March): 68.

DiStefano, F. V. 1985. Chemical bonding of air laid webs. *Nonwovens Industry* 16 (June): 16.

Felt. 1958. *CIBA Review,* no. 129 (November).

Griggs, D. 1989. Machine lace manufacture. *Textiles* 18 (2): 32.

Levey, S. M. 1983. *Lace: A history.* London: Victoria and Albert Museum.

Mansfield, R. G. 1993. Spunlaced fabric production rising. *America's Textiles International* 22 (November): FW 2.

———. Nonwovens industry continues market focus. *America's Textiles International* 23 (October): 59.

Nonwovens, a growth market. 1992. *Textile Horizons,* December, 83.

MULTICOMPONENT FABRICS

When readers reach this point in the text, they will have learned how fibers are produced, how yarns are made from those fibers, and how fabrics can be made from yarns or fibers by weaving, knitting, or other processes. It is also possible to create products by combining two or more of these textile materials (fibers, yarns, and fabrics) into a single material. Materials created by combining several different textile products can be called *multicomponent fabrics*. Some multicomponent materials have been used for centuries. For example, quilts have long been made by placing a batt, a sheet of matted fibers, between two layers of (ordinarily) woven fabric. Other multicomponent fabrics may rely on high technology to create composite structures of fibers held within a polymer matrix and shaped within a mold.

Embroidery

The technique of embroidery, which is not a method of constructing fabrics but a method of decorating them, uses two components: a fabric base and a yarn that decorates it. The effects it produces are similar to those achieved by the surface weaves discussed in chapter 16. Embroidery is often used in conjunction with appliqué.

Appliqué also uses two components: a fabric base and small decorative pieces of cloth. The cloth is cut and attached to the surface of the larger textile to create a design. The decoration of fabrics by appliqué is an old technique. Archeologists have identified appliqués from as early as the fifth century B.C. These very early forms were wall hangings or carpets in which the base material was felt and the designs were formed with other, smaller pieces of multicolored felt.

Since appliqués are most often attached to the base fabric by hand stitches, they are often combined with embroidery. Embroidery is the use of yarns applied with a needle in a variety of stitches to form a decorative pattern. Embroidery is a skill that has been practiced for many centuries. The translation of writings from classical Greece includes many references to fine embroideries. The ancient Greeks considered weaving and embroidery to be fitting occupations for goddesses and noblewomen. One interesting Greek textile showing evidence of embroidery has been dated at 500 B.C. and provides some of the earliest evidence of the embroidery skills. It is believed, however, that embroidery was practiced long before this date (Wace 1948).

A wide variety of different types of embroidery and embroidery stitches has been developed in all parts of the world. Each area originated a style with a distinctive repertory of stitches and decorative motifs.

One of the most famous decorated textiles ever made was created by embroidery. Called the Bayeux tapestry, this representation of the conquest of Britain by the Normans is actually a large embroidery, not a tapestry. On its 231-foot length and 20-inch width, seventy-two embroidered pictures show the sequence of events that led to the Battle of Hastings and the conquest of England by William the Conqueror in 1066. The embroidery, made almost nine hundred years ago and now discolored with age, is still displayed in the Cathedral at Bayeux, France.

American embroidery forms originated in Europe, especially in England. From the general category of embroidery, a number of specialized forms have broken off to become separate art crafts. These include crewel embroidery, cross-stitch embroidery, and needlepoint.

In embroidery a wide variety of stitches is used to outline and fill in the design. The choice of stitch is usually related to the effect the sewer wants to achieve. The yarns may be made of any fiber.

Crewel embroidery is done with crewel wool, a loosely twisted fine yarn that probably was named after the English town of Crewel. Traditional crewel embroidery uses stylized forms and a repertory of specific basic stitches.

Made of two stitches that cross in the center to form an X, the cross-stitch is one of the simplest of the embroidery forms. In Colonial American times it was the first embroidery technique taught to young girls. Combinations of the X-shaped stitches were used to make samplers or to decorate all kinds of household articles.

Needlepoint embroidery covers a canvas base with thousands of tiny stitches. Queen Elizabeth I of England was said to have preferred it to all other embroideries, and in the 1920s, Alice B. Toklas, companion to the writer Gertrude Stein, made a number of needlepoint chair covers after designs created for her by Picasso. Needlepoint has its own repertory of specialized stitches that are selected according to the pattern they will make in the often-complex needlepoint design.

Machine-Made Embroidery

When machines create embroidery, the embroidery is not accomplished as an integral part of the weaving process but is applied to the cloth after it is completed. (See Figure 19.1.) The Schiffli embroidery process, developed in Switzerland, requires as many as a thousand needles. Designs can be applied to all weights and types of fabrics. When

Figure 19.1

Machine-made Schiffli embroidery.

used on sheer fabrics, these embroideries can have the appearance of lace. Schiffli is the predominant method used for applying embroidered designs to fabric yardage.

Other machines are used to embroider individual apparel items or decorative textiles. A recently developed embroidery process can create designs from a number of colored threads with only a single needle, as it automatically changes colors and splices yarns together. (See Figure 19.2.) Not all hand embroidery stitches can be created by machines, but through computer technology design changes and stitch variations can be accomplished quickly and easily.

Tufted Fabrics

Tufting is the process of punching a first component, loops of yarn, through a second component, a woven or nonwoven backing material. Hand-tufting is often used in "hooking" or tufting rugs. A hook is passed through the backing material, a loop is formed on the outside of the backing, and the needle is pulled back to the wrong side, leaving the loop to form the pile on the surface of the fabric. Loops can be left uncut or be cut to create a fluffy surface.

Machine-made tufted fabrics are created in much the same way as hand-tufted fabrics except that many needles punch through the fabric at the same time. A hook holds the loop in place when the needle is withdrawn. If a cut pile is being made, this hook has a small blade that cuts the loop. Tufted fabrics are identified easily by the parallel rows of stitches on the wrong side of the fabric. (See Figure 19.3 on page 347.)

Carpet Manufacture

More than 90 percent of the carpet produced in the United States is constructed by tufting. Tufts of pile yarn are punched through a woven primary backing of jute, heavy cotton, polypropylene, or other synthetic. The back of the carpet is given a

Figure 19.2

Embroidery machine that can embroider up to 18 colors with one needle by automatically re-threading the needle with each color change. Photograph courtesy of Melco Embroidery Systems.

coating of latex for greater stability and strength and to hold in the tufts. A secondary backing fabric may also be applied and bonded by the latex.

Compared to more traditional methods of pile carpet construction, tufting is faster, does not require such highly skilled craftspersons, and requires less-expensive equipment to manufacture. Although lower in cost than most other constructions, tufted carpet is not necessarily inferior in quality. The quality of carpets is more dependent on the fibers, yarns, and backing materials and the closeness of the pile than on the construction.

The major limitations in tufting are in the area of design. Jacquard-type designs cannot be made, although design variations can incorporate cut and uncut pile or higher and lower levels of loops or cut pile. Designs can also be printed on the surface of the carpet.

Most tufted carpet manufacturing in the United States takes place in or near the town of Dalton in northeast Georgia. Tufting of bedspreads and other items began as a handcraft in that area in the early twentieth century. The process was mechanized and adapted for carpets in the 1950s.

Carpets are often made in *pile constructions*. In addition to tufting, several other major types of pile carpet construction are available to consumers. The names of the processes used for weaving carpets have become standard terminology in the carpet industry.

Figure 19.3

(a) In tufting process, looper below primary backing holds loop of yarn as needle withdraws. (b) For cut pile carpet, a knife cuts the loop as the needle withdraws. Illustrations reprinted by permission of the Monsanto Company.

(a) Uncut pile

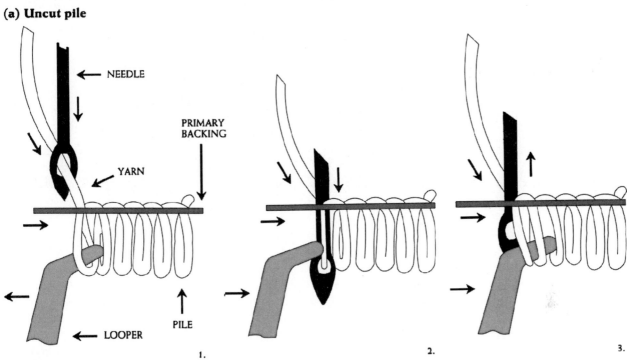

NEEDLE

PRIMARY BACKING

YARN

PILE

LOOPER

1.

2.

3.

(b) Cut pile

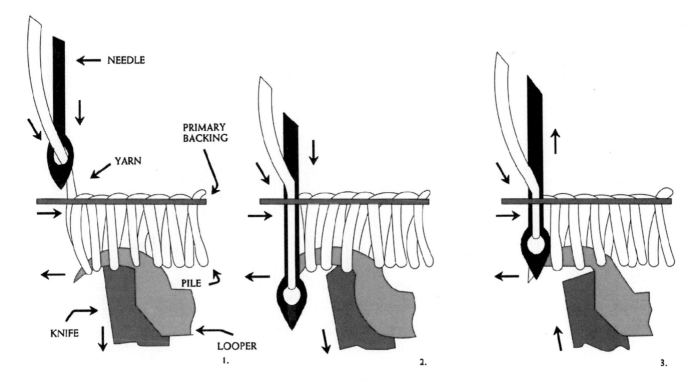

NEEDLE

PRIMARY BACKING

YARN

PILE

KNIFE

LOOPER

1.

2.

3.

Figure 19.4

Velvet carpet construction.
Illustration courtesy of
Bigelow-Sanford, Inc.

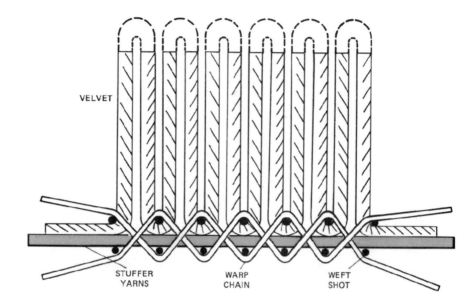

Velvet-weave carpets should not be confused with velvet-surface carpets. The term *velvet weave* refers to the construction of the carpet, the pile of which may be either cut or uncut. Simple in construction, the weave is similar to the construction of lighter weight pile fabrics made by the wire method. (See Figure 19.4.) The pile is formed by wires inserted between the pile warp and ground yarns. The loops that are formed are held in place by the interlocking of filling yarns with the pile. The ground warps are also interlocked with the filling. Velvet-weave carpets are usually made in solid colors, but tweed effects can be created with multicolored tweed yarns. The cost of these carpets is moderate to low.

Wilton carpets are made on a special Wilton loom. This loom is essentially a velvet loom with a jacquard attachment that can work with up to six different colors. Patterns in Wilton carpets are woven, not printed. When yarns are not utilized in the surface design, they are carried along in the back of the carpet. This makes for a dense, strong construction. Wilton carpets of good quality are among the longest-

Figure 19.5

Wilton carpet construction.
Illustration courtesy of
Bigelow-Sanford, Inc.

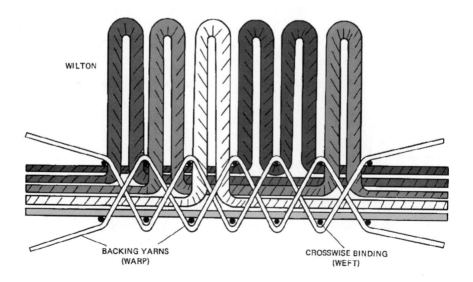

wearing machine-made domestic rugs. Piles may be cut or uncut; loops may be high or low. (See Figure 19.5.)

Both velvet-weave and Wilton carpets are very durable and are often found in offices and public buildings ("contract installations" as opposed to home, or "domestic," use).

Axminster carpets have the greatest versatility in machine-produced carpets in utilizing color. The loom draws pile yarns from small spools wound with yarns of various colors as they are needed for the design. The pile is a one-level, cut pile, although textured effects may be attained by varying the twist or type of yarn used. Carpets made on an Axminster loom are readily identifiable because the construction produces a heavy ridge across the back of the carpet, and the carpet can be rolled only in the lengthwise direction. The quality of carpets made on the Axminster loom is medium, but they are the only machine-made carpets that can have woven-in designs similar to those in oriental carpets. (See Figure 19.6.)

Chenille carpets are the most expensive and the most luxurious of all machine-made carpets and are rarely found. They are constructed on two looms. On one loom a fabric called a chenille blanket is woven. This blanket is cut into long strips called *caterpillars,* which have a fuzzy surface. A second loom weaves the strips into the carpet. These strips are used in the filling direction, and are actually sewn into place. Chenille carpet pile is cut, carpets are made in solid colors, and the pile is dense, close, and velvety in texture.

Consumer Box 19.1 discusses the construction and use of residential wall-to-wall carpet.

Carpets can also be made by knitting, needle punching, and flocking, as discussed earlier in this and previous chapters. Designs can be added to carpets by printing as well as by weaving.

In addition to mass-produced, machine-made carpets, there are a number of one-of-a-kind, hand-woven carpets. The bibliography for this chapter includes some references for further reading about hand-woven and specialty carpets.

Many hand-woven carpets are made in the Near or Far East, using traditional designs, and are known as *oriental carpets.* Both antique and contemporary versions of these traditional design carpets can be purchased. Oriental designs can be printed

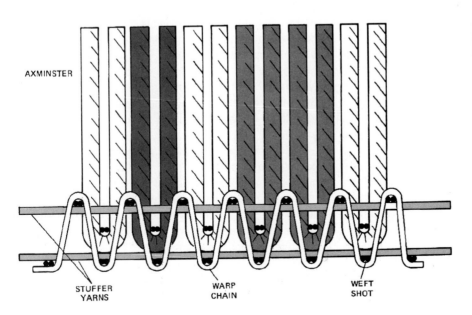

AXMINSTER

STUFFER YARNS   WARP CHAIN   WEFT SHOT

Figure 19.6

Axminster carpet construction. Illustration courtesy of Bigelow-Sanford, Inc.

Residential Wall-to-Wall Carpet

Textile floor coverings are generally referred to as carpets or rugs, terms that are often used interchangeably. The term *wall-to-wall carpet* is used to distinguish carpeting that covers the entire floor of a room from an *area carpet,* a rug that covers only part of the floor. Although the following discussion focuses on wall-to-wall carpet, the principles would apply to area rugs of the same construction as well. Wall-to-wall carpet is one of the most costly textile products purchased by consumers. For such a major investment, informed purchase is essential.

The first step in making an informed choice is to analyze the area to be carpeted. What kinds of activities will take place in the area? What will the traffic patterns be? Who will use the area—adults? children? pets? Armed with a thorough understanding of the demands that will be made on the carpet, the consumer can move on to examine available alternatives.

Carpet is usually made from nylon, olefin, polyester, acrylic, or wool fibers. (Individual chapters on fibers give detailed description of their properties.) The qualities of these fibers contribute to their use in carpets.

Nylon accounts for about 80 percent of carpet pile fibers. It resists abrasion, wear, and staining; dyes to a wide variety of colors; and is easy to clean. Olefin (polypropylene) resists abrasion and is readily cleaned. Generally, the color is added before the fiber is formed, making it quite colorfast. Quite resistant to stains, moisture, and mildew, olefin carpeting is often used outdoors as well as indoors, especially in areas such as playrooms and kitchens. Polyester can have an attractive texture, clear colors, and high luster. It is resilient, resists water-soluble stains, and is easily cleaned. Acrylic fibers resist moisture, mildew, and water-soluble stains. They can look and feel much like wool. The vast majority of carpets are made from manufactured fibers such as these; only about 3 percent are wool, which is generally more expensive. Wool is resilient and durable, can be dyed a wide range of colors, and has a luxurious appearance.

Many fiber manufacturers produce trademarked fibers specially for carpet use. Retailers can readily supply information about whether fibers have been engineered or carpets finished to incorporate antistatic or anti-soiling qualities.

This chapter describes in detail the manufacture and construction of the various types of carpet. The type of pile will affect the appearance and performance of the carpet. Pile can be cut or uncut (also called *loop pile*) or a combination of *cut and loop pile,* which produces a sculptured surface effect. *Single level loop pile* has a smooth surface with all loops the same size. In *multilevel loop pile,* the loops are two or three different heights, often producing an interesting patterned effect on the surface. Cut pile carpets include *velvet* (not to be confused with velvet construction), or *plush,* surfaces. Their yarns have little twist and a level surface. *Saxony pile* carpets, made with yarns of two or more plys heat-set to lock in twist, produce a texture in which individual yarns are more distinct than velvet pile. *Frieze pile* yarns are tightly twisted to produce a nubby effect. Figure 19.7 illustrates some common varieties of carpet pile.

The most important factor in durability is pile density: the closer and more dense the pile yarns, the better a carpet will wear. To evaluate pile density, fold the carpet back upon itself and look through the pile at the backing. The more visible the carpet backing, the lower the density of the pile. Pile with yarns of the same length distributes wear evenly across the surface of the pile. Footprints do not cause flattening or shading of pile made with tightly twisted yarns, like those in frieze and some uncut pile carpet, which tend to be more durable and suitable for high-traffic areas.

Generally, wall-to-wall carpet is installed over a carpet pad or cushion. The carpet manufacturer will have informed the retailer of the type of padding appropriate for a particular carpet. Incorrect installation or use of improper padding may void carpet warranties; therefore, purchase from and installation by a reputable dealer is essential.

Although construction, fiber content, and installation determine the wear life of a carpet, its selection is based to a very significant extent on the consumer's preferences for certain colors, textures, or printed or woven designs. A natural characteristic of cut pile fabrics is the "shaded" effect that results from light reflecting off different areas of pile, which do not all fall in the same direction. Footprints are more apparent in cut pile carpets.

Color and design are related not only to appearance but also to performance. Soil is generally tracked onto carpets from uncarpeted areas or from the out-of-doors. Consumers living in geographic locations where the soil is dark will find darker colored carpets more practical, but those with light-colored soil will notice that dark carpets will show soil, dust, and lint. For these consumers lighter colors may be more practical. Tweeds, multicolored patterns, and nubby textures tend to hide soil. Many carpets sold today have been treated with a stain-blocking finish.

Other than soiling, the most serious consumer concern with cut pile carpeting is wear. In heavy traffic areas carpet will begin, after some time, to look worn down and matted. This is because the tips of the pile yarns untwist and flatten, becoming entangled with their neighbors. When this happens, the yarns have lost their tuft definition, and the carpet has lost its new appearance. Carpets with higher twist pile yarns, and higher pile densities, will retain a better appearance longer because the yarns will not untwist as easily.

Proper care can extend the wear life of carpeting. Soil accumulating at the base of carpet pile abrades and cuts the fibers, so frequent vacuuming to remove soil particles is important. Stains should be removed immediately. Carpets also require periodic cleaning that goes beyond vacuuming. The Carpet and Rug Institute recommends that deep cleaning be done once every 12 to 18 months. If you do it yourself, check with your retailer about procedures. Do not rub carpeting vigorously, either to remove stains or for general cleaning, as this will accelerate the loss of tuft definition. Most communities have reputable professional carpet cleaning services.

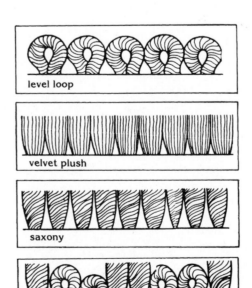

Figure 19.7

Various types of carpet pile. Reprinted by permission from the Carpet and Rug Institute, *How to Choose Carpets and Rugs* [brochure].

or woven into machine-made carpets, but true orientals are made by hand-knotting a pile of wool or silk to a woven base of cotton or wool. The quality of these carpets depends on the density rather than the length of the pile. There is a lively trade in new and antique oriental carpets, and prices are high. Purchasers should deal only with reputable merchants who can be depended on not to sell counterfeit merchandise.

Rya rugs, another hand-made area rug type, are imported from the Scandinavian countries. These rugs have a long "shag" pile and are generally woven in contemporary designs.

Some traditional early-American–style rugs are made not by weaving but from strips of cloth braided or sewn together. Still others are made by hooking, a hand process similar to tufting in which yarn or fabric strips are punched or pulled through a woven backing with a special hook.

Quilted Fabrics

Quilted fabrics have been made for centuries. Quilted fabrics use at least three components, as a general rule. A filling material (usually cotton batting, wool, or down) is sandwiched between two layers of decorative outer fabric. These layers are sewn

Figure 19.8   Nineteenth century appliquéd and pieced quilt. From the collection of the Huntington Historical Society, Huntington, N.Y.

together with strong thread in selected areas to keep the filling material from shifting about. The location of the stitches forms a padded design that might take geometric, floral, or other shapes. (See Figure 19.8.)

Many quilted fabrics are produced commercially for apparel or household use. Synthetic fiberfill has, to a large extent, replaced the natural fillers because of its easy-care aspects.

The performance of quilted fabrics is related to the closeness of the quilting stitches, the size of the stitches, the type of thread used for stitching, and the durability of the outer fabric. If stitches are spaced too far apart, the filling will shift about and become uneven. If quilting stitches are too large, stretching of the cloth will tend to break the thread. The outer fabric layer should have high fabric count and a balanced weave. Well-balanced fabrics will have better abrasion resistance and durability. A close weave is also important if the filling is not to work its way out through the covering fabric. Down-filled comforters or quilts require the use of an inner layer of downproof ticking, a dense, closely woven fabric that prevents the escape of small bits of down.

New Techniques of Quilting

Changes have taken place in the methods by which some quilted fabrics are produced. Instead of sewing quilted fabrics with thread, bonding may be done with heat or adhesives. Thermal bonding requires that all components be thermoplastic. The heat application causes the components to fuse together in the heat-stitched areas. One of these techniques uses high-frequency, ultrasonic vibrations to generate the heat in the stitching device. This *sonic sewing* can be used to construct apparel and household textiles made from synthetic fibers. (See Figure 19.9.)

Another technique used to produce raised surface patterns with layered fabrics places a layer of fabric that is not thermoplastic over fabric, foam, or fiberfill that is thermoplastic. A design is printed on the fabric with a special chemical, which

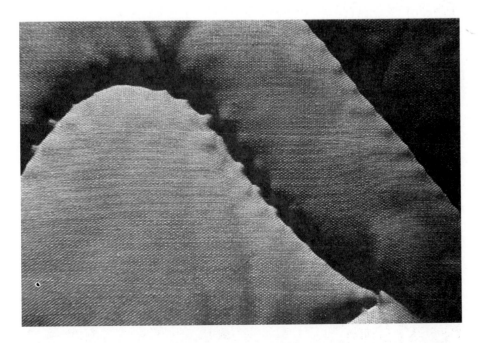

Figure 19.9

Close-up photograph of a sonically quilted fabric in which heat has been used to fuse thermoplastic elements of the quilt.

holds the layers together in the printed area. The fabric is subjected to heat, which causes the backing fabric to shrink, thereby producing a raised pattern on the face fabric.

Laminated or Bonded Fabrics

The terms *laminated* and *bonded* have been defined by the ASTM (1986, 290) as follows:

> *bonded fabric*—a layered fabric structure wherein a face or shell fabric is joined to a backing fabric, such as tricot (a knit fabric), with an adhesive that does not significantly add to the thickness of the combined fabrics.
>
> *laminated fabric*—a layered fabric structure wherein a face or outer fabric is joined to a continuous sheet material, such as polyurethane foam, in such a way that the identity of the continuous sheet material is retained, either by the flame method or by an adhesive, and this in turn normally, but not always, is joined on the back with a backing fabric such as tricot.

Several different methods can be used to join fabric to fabric, fabric to foam, or fabric to foam to fabric.

Fabric-to-Fabric Bonding

When two layers of fabric are joined, the purpose is to provide greater stability and body to the face fabric or to create a self-lined fabric. The underlayer in bonded fabrics is often knitted tricot or jersey, used because they have good flexibility, are relatively inexpensive, and slide readily, making them easy to don over other garments. For the most part, fabrics used in bonding are less expensive and lower quality fabrics that can be upgraded by this process.

Two methods can be used for attaching fabric to fabric. The *wet-adhesive method* places an adhesive material on the back of the face fabric, and together the fabrics are passed between heated rollers that activate and set the adhesive.

The second method is known as the *flame-foam method*. A thin layer of polyurethane foam is melted slightly by passing it over a flame. The two layers of fabric are sandwiched around the foam, which then dries, forming the bond between the two layers of fabric. Ideally, the layer of foam should be so thin that it virtually disappears. (The foam in the finished fabric is about 0.010 inches thick.) The foam does, however, add body to the fabric and produces a somewhat stiffer fabric than does the wet-adhesive method. It is preferable that the flame-foam method not be used with open-weave fabrics because of the possibility that some of the foam may appear on the surface of the fabric. (See Figure 19.10.)

Fabric-to-Foam Lamination

Fabrics are laminated to polyurethane foam when it is desirable to provide some degree of insulation. Winter coats and sportswear, for example, are made from these fabrics. The flame-foam process can be used to manufacture such fabrics. A thick layer of foam is utilized. Only one side of the foam, that to which the fabric attaches, must be heated. Still another foam process flows the sticky foam onto the fabric, cures the fabric, and causes the foam to solidify and adhere to the fabric at the same time.

Figure 19.10

Flame-foam and wet-adhesive bonding. Illustration courtesy of Hoechst Celanese Corporation.

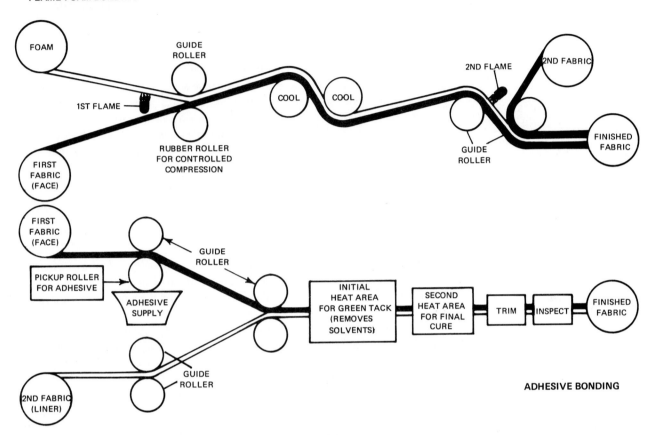

When laminates first entered the retail market, customers found wide variation in the permanence of the bonding. Some fabrics separated during laundering, others separated during dry cleaning, and still others separated during use. Often the backing and face fabrics shrunk unevenly, causing wrinkling and puckering. Today, many of these problems have been overcome. Although laminated fabrics of varying quality are still sold, many of these fabrics are labeled with guarantees of serviceability. The label term *Certifab* guarantees bonding and dimensional stability in dry cleaning or laundering for one year. *Celabond* offers the same guarantee but is applied to fabrics laminated with certain acetates.

Recent Developments in Lamination

The older technique of lamination has been applied to some newer materials. With the success of Gore-Tex®, special attention has been given to the creation of fabrics made by layering conventional fabrics with very thin, microporous films that transmit moisture. (See discussion of water repellency in chapter 21.) Such fabrics require extreme precision in application of adhesive materials if the finished product is to transmit vapor and also drape well. In addition to its use in rainwear, vapor-transmitting film laminates are used in clean room clothing, medical barrier products, and molded automotive parts.

Lamination of extremely thin films to fabrics of Lycra® spandex/nylon has been used in the manufacture of lightweight, stretchable fabrics. The Lycra®/nylon layer is laminated to urethane film with a special urethane adhesive system. Marketed under the trademark of Darlexx®, these fabrics are capable of passing moisture vapor for comfort. Darlexx® fabrics are said to be particularly suitable for active sportswear, in particular for racing swimwear and wind surfing suits.

Yet another area for which laminates are currently being made is molded automobile seats, which traditionally required a labor-intensive sewn upholstery process. Molded seats are covered with a film component to which a urethane foam is attached, and then the upholstery fabric is laminated to the urethane foam.

Fiber and Textile Wall Coverings

Textile products used in interior design include laminated materials that are affixed to walls. They are generally made by attaching fibers or fabrics to cloth, foam, or paper backings. The backing is attached to the wall with adhesives. Often-used fibers include linen, silk, cotton, wool, jute, manufactured fibers, or blends. Other popular materials include simulated suede produced by flocking and flocked printed designs.

When selecting textile wall coverings, consumers should avoid those made in very wide sections, as the fabrics may sag. Fibers or fabrics that do not shrink are important if climates are humid and because moisture from the water-based adhesives can pass through to the surface. Woven fabrics should have a close weave and be of at least medium weight so that stains from the adhesive will not pass through the fabric.

Many of these wall coverings are treated so that they are washable. Selection of fiber or fabric wall coverings should take into account the properties and characteristics of fibers, yarns, and fabric structure as it relates to the anticipated use of the areas where they are placed. For example, if fabrics, especially simulated suede or flocked materials, are located in high-traffic areas where they are subject to abrasion, the surface fibers may wear off. Wall coverings made from fibers that are damaged by sunlight or fabrics colored with dyes that are not colorfast to sunlight should not be used in areas that have extended exposure to direct sunlight.

Hybrid Fabrics Using Polymer Films

Fabrics coated with polymer films are used for a variety of products ranging from apparel to tablecloths. (See chapter 21 for a fuller discussion of coated fabrics.)

Coated fabrics and *poromerics,* products with microscopic, open-celled structures, are used to produce leatherlike materials. Vinyl-coated fabrics may have an imitation leatherlike grain embossed on the surface. These are the least satisfactory leather imitations both in terms of aesthetics and performance. Fabrics are cold and hard to the touch and do not allow the transmission of moisture vapor.

Expanded vinyl is manufactured so as to have internal air bubbles that improve flexibility and cause the material to feel warmer and softer. Urethane-coated fabrics are even more leatherlike in their qualities.

Apparel items made from film-coated fabrics vary in their care requirements. Consumers should follow care label instructions carefully as some products must be laundered; others can withstand dry cleaning.

Poromeric structures more closely match the moisture vapor permeability and other qualities of real leather. Many of their applications fall outside of areas that would be considered as textile products. In simplified terms, the process of producing poromerics consists of forming a microporous web of urethane which is extruded onto a suitable support, usually a woven, knitted, or nonwoven fabric structure. A suedelike finish may be achieved by brushing and napping the polyurethane surface.

Certain of the techniques for creating suedelike fabrics, however, rely on recently developed, highly sophisticated fiber-forming technologies. Ultrasuede®, the trademark name of a suede-type fabric, is manufactured in Japan and distributed in the United States by the Skinner Division of Springs Mills. While the specifics of the manufacturing process are not released by the manufacturer, the general approach could be described as follows.

Matrix fibers are formed from two polymers, with one polymer distributed within the other in the "islands in the sea" form. (See Figure 14.4, page 216.) The "sea" phase is dissolved, leaving only the "islands" phase, a network of very fine fibers. A nonwoven fabric is formed by needle-punching or hydroentangling a crosslapped or a randomly laid web. The fabric is then impregnated with polyurethane and the surface brushed to create the suedelike texture.

Promotional materials from Skinner indicate that Ultrasuede® will not stretch out of shape, pill, fray, crock (lose color through rubbing of the surface), or wrinkle. It is hand or machine washable, dry-cleanable, colorfast, and will not water spot or stiffen.

Ultrasuede® is used for apparel of all kinds, for furniture, wall coverings, and for luggage. Special care must be used by home sewers using this fabric. In the fabric all face fibers run in the same direction, so all garment pieces must be cut in the same direction. Needle and pin holes will remain, so care must be taken to avoid ripping and pinning in areas where holes would be evident.

Fiber-reinforced Composites

Fiber-reinforced composites (FRC) are among the newest technological developments in the textile field. Except for potential applications in automobile parts and bodies and in sporting goods, applications for these products may be unknown to the average consumer. Those persons entering careers in the textile field, however, are likely to see significant growth in this sector of the textile industry. Many graduate programs in textile science are currently involved in research and development of composite materials using textile fibers. For example, the College of Textiles at North Carolina State University is engaged in research aimed at developing the technology to create composite materials for a NASA manned flight to Mars, possibly as early as 2010 (Dockery 1988).

The following is intended to provide a brief introduction to the complex area of FRCs. FRCs generally consist of one or more textile components impregnated

Figure 19.11

Structure of a fiber-reinforced composite in which fibers are imbedded in a matrix. Reprinted by permission from *Textiles Magazine,* a publication of the Textile Institute, UK.

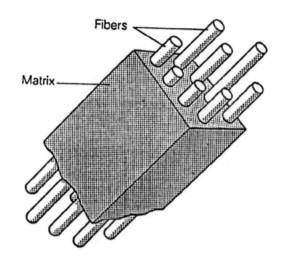

with or imbedded in a resin matrix. (See Figure 19.11.) The textile components may be fibers, yarns, nonwoven mats, or woven fabric structures. The resulting products have high strength and light weights and can be molded into a variety of shapes. In most FRCs the fibrous materials make up 65 percent or less of the total volume.

Briefly summarized, the process for forming FRCs includes these steps. Fibers, yarns, or fabrics are impregnated with resin. Any of a number of high technology fibers can be used, but at present these are most likely to be glass, carbon, or aramid fibers. Cellulosic fibers are also being used in composites. The most commonly used resins are polyester resins, epoxy, or phenolic resins. Resin application may be done by a wet lay-up system, or materials may be delivered as already resin-impregnated sheets called *pre-pregs.*

The fiber resin layer is placed on a mold of the selected shape. Layers can be arranged as required for purposes of the final product. For example, reinforcing fibers may be laid one over the other with fibers running in the same or different directions to provide strength in a particular area. The layer or layers are pressed into the mold. After or during this shaping, heat is applied which cures the resin and sets the shape. Additional curing processes may be needed, depending on the resin that was used.

If hollow or spherical components are required, an alternate construction method called *filament winding* may be used. In this process a continuous yarn or roving is fed through a resin bath, then wound on a form of the correct shape. When the desired thickness is reached, the FRC is cured.

One of the most important factors in FRC production is the adhesion between the reinforcing material and the matrix. The reinforcing fibers are required to increase the tensile, compressional, or impact strength of the matrix material. To do this, the load must be transmitted from one phase to the other. If the fiber and resin phases separate, the load sharing is not maximized. Glass fibers, for example, are treated with coupling agents to increase their adhesion to polyethylene and polyester resins.

Readings included in the bibliography at the end of the chapter provide a more detailed discussion of FRCs.

References

ASTM. 1986. Compilation of ASTM standard definitions. Philadelphia: American Society of Testing and Materials.

Dockery, A. 1988. N.C. State works on composites for NASA spacecraft. *America's Textiles International* 17 (November): FW 2.

Wace, A. T. B. 1948. Weaving or embroidery? Homeric references to textiles. *American Journal of Archeology* 52 (1): 51.

Review Questions

1. What are the limitations of machine embroidery as compared with embroidery done by hand?
2. What types of designs are possible on carpets that are made by tufting?
3. What should a consumer look for when examining a carpet sample to determine its probable quality and durability?
4. What should a consumer look for when examining a quilt to determine its probable quality and durability?
5. What is the difference between a laminated and a bonded fabric? Give an example of one kind of product in which each process would be used.
6. How have new fiber-forming technologies been used to create suedelike fabrics?
7. Describe the general process used to create fiber-reinforced composites.

Recommended Readings

Computers weave materials for the space age. 1989. *New Scientist,* no. 1660 (April 15): 16.

Devine, J. 1994. Understanding ultrasonics. *Bobbin* 35 (March): 74.

Easton, P. M. 1986. Fibre-reinforced composites. *Textiles* 15 (2): 35.

Fulmer, T. D. 1994. Coated fabric use increasing. *America's Textiles International* 23 (June): 86.

Hahn, H. T., et al., eds. 1989. *Mechanical Behavior and Properties of Composite Materials.* Vol. 1 of *Delaware Composites Design Encyclopedia.* Basel, Switzerland: Technomic Publishing.

Kirby, J. 1993. Fibre and textile wallcoverings. *Textiles* 22 (1): 22.

Lomax, G. R. 1992. Coating of fabrics. *Textiles* 21 (2): 18–23.

Mansfield, R. 1990. Specialty composites. *America's Textiles International* 19 (June): 88.

Mohamed, M. 1990. Weaving of fabrics for composite applications. *America's Textiles International* 19 (February): 55.

Novina, T. 1993. Quilting market a rising star. *America's Textiles International* 22 (December): 82.

Sabo, L. R. 1994. Decorative stitching gains ground. *Bobbin* 35 (June): 86.

Southern, J., et al. 1991. Fundamental physics of carpet performance. *Journal of Applied Polymer Science* 47 (1991): 355.

Toon, J. 1993. A boost for composites. *Canadian Textile Journal* 110 (June): 36.

Von de Wiele, M. 1994. Carpet weaving technology expands. *America's Textiles International* 23 (August): 36.

Walter, B. J., and J. O. Wheeler. 1984. Localization economics in the American carpet industry. *Geographical Review* 74 (2): 183.

Wyner, D. 1990. Succeeding with sensitive laminates. *America's Textiles International* 19 (May): 74.

ROUTINE FINISHES AND THOSE AFFECTING HAND AND APPEARANCE

T he finishing of woven, knitted, and nonwoven textiles consists of the application of a wide variety of treatments and special processes that give to the fabric some quality that is needed to enhance its aesthetic or performance properties. Some finishes modify appearance, some modify behavior, and some modify both appearance and behavior.

Classification of Finishes

Finishes may be classified on several bases. Certain finishes are routinely given to fabrics before dyeing or final processing. These are sometimes referred to as steps in fabric preparation rather than finishes. Other finishes involve the mechanical manipulation of the fabric. Still others are chemical treatments that produce some change in fabric properties. Chemical treatments may be topical and applied to the surface of the fabric, or they may form chemical bonds with the fabric. In some instances, a finishing process may be both mechanical and chemical.

Finishes are also separated into those that are permanent, those that are durable, and those that are temporary. Permanent finishes will last for the lifetime of the product, durable finishes can be expected to function reasonably well for most of the lifetime of the fabric, and temporary finishes are removed after one or more launderings or dry cleanings. Renewable finishes can be added to fabrics when through use or care processes the original finish has been diminished or destroyed.

Some finishes are made permanent by utilizing the thermoplastic characteristics of synthetic fabrics. When heat-sensitive fibers are subjected to finishes involving heat treatment, the fabric may be permanently "set" in such a way that new characteristics are established. For example, in many finishes patterns are heat-set into thermoplastic fabrics by the use of heated, patterned rollers.

A single fabric can be given several finishes that are each intended to accomplish different purposes. For example, a fabric may be bleached to enhance whiteness and then given a durable press finish to make it resist wrinkling. Few fabrics are manufactured that do not undergo some type of finishing. The discussion in this chapter concentrates on routine finishes and those that affect fabric hand and appearance. Chapter 21 covers finishes that improve or alter performance or function, usually as a result of chemical treatment.

Application of Finishes

The application of finishes from a solution is generally accomplished through the steps of padding, drying, and curing. Figure 20.1 depicts the traditional process. In the padding stage, the fabric is wet by the finishing solution. Then, as the fabric passes between two rolls, the excess liquid from the padding solution is squeezed out. The fabric is dried in an oven. Fabrics treated with finishes that react chemically with the fibers undergo curing at a higher temperature as a final step.

Considerable amounts of energy are required to dry the fabric after padding. Because energy use contributes significantly to the cost of making textiles, manufacturers have devoted a good deal of effort to the development of processes that are less energy intensive. A basic goal in developing these finishes is to decrease drying time. This is done by removing substantial quantities of liquid from the fabric before drying, wetting the fabric less during finishing, or combining several finishes into one so that instead of drying fabrics several times, they need be dried only once. Figure 20.2 shows a number of variations of the low-wet-pickup processes. Similar principles and techniques are used in some types of dyeing to save energy.

Figure 20.1

Pad-dry-cure textile finishing. Reprinted by permission from M. Grayson, *Encyclopedia of Textiles, Fibers, and Nonwoven Fabrics* (New York: Wiley, 1984), 468. Copyright © 1984 by John Wiley & Sons, Inc.

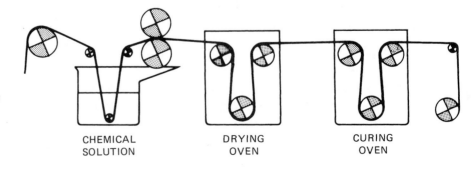

CHEMICAL SOLUTION   DRYING OVEN   CURING OVEN

Figure 20.2

Low-wet-pickup techniques in finishing. (a) Fiber-coated, high extraction roll. Highly porous, rubber-coated fiber rolls produce a suction effect that helps to remove more water. (b) Pad/vacuum extraction. After padding, fabric is carried over a vacuum slot where a portion of the pad liquor is removed, filtered, and recirculated for reuse. (c) Transfer padding. A continuous loop belt of material revolves through the finishing liquor, picks up the liquor, and then is brought into contact with the fabric that is to be finished. The dry fabric picks up the finishing liquor from the wet belt. (d) Kiss roll. Partially submerged roll picks up finishing solution as a film and carries it to the fabric. (e) Spray. Finishing solution is sprayed onto the surface of the fabric. (f) Engraved roll. An engraved metal roll passes through the pad mix, picking up finishing material in the engraved areas. A doctor blade removes excess finishing material before the fabric passes between the engraved roller and a rubber roller that facilitates transfer of the liquor evenly. *(figure continues)*

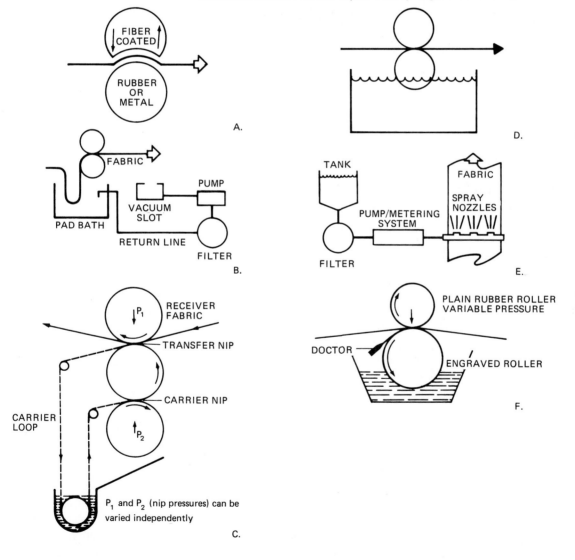

Figure 20.2

(continued) Foam finishing techniques. Finishing material is formed into foam by incorporation of air. Application of the foam can be made by any of the following techniques: (g) knife over a roll, (h) horizontal pad, (i) transfer from a roll, (j) through a screen using a squeegee to force foam onto the fabric, (k) printed onto the fabric surface, or (l) using foam applicators that coat first one side, then the other. (In the diagrams, shaded areas represent the foam finishing material.) Reprinted by permission from T. D. Fulmer, "Low-Wet-Pickup Techniques in Finishing," *America's Textiles* (May 1984): 62, 64.

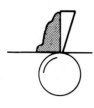

G. KNIFE OVER ROLL

H. HORIZONTAL PAD

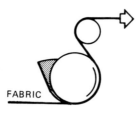

I. TRANSFER FROM ROLL

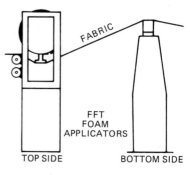

FFT FOAM APPLICATORS

L. FFT 2-SIDED APPLICATION

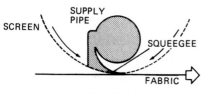

J. ROTARY SCREEN

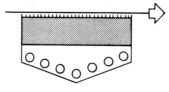

K. PRINTAIRE

Drying

Every type of fabric is dried at least once and often more times during processing. Drying is costly both in terms of time and energy. As the application of heat to dry the cloth is the most costly part of this operation, mechanical devices such as mangles, which squeeze off water; suction dryers, which pull off water by vacuum extraction; or centrifuges, which spin off water, may be used to remove as much water as possible before thermal drying.

Thermal drying requires the application of heat. Passing the cloth over heated cylinders is one such drying technique. This would be comparable, in principle, to ironing a wet garment to dry it. This drying technique is not suitable for pile fabrics, as it would crush the pile.

Among the recent technological advances in drying of textile products has been the use of radio frequencies to dry fabrics. Described as being similar to microwave ovens in that only the material being processed and not the equipment itself is heated, radio frequency drying is said to have a number of advantages over conventional drying systems. These include faster drying, greater economy of energy consumption, flexibility of design, and selective drying of damp areas.

Another method uses hot air in a tentering machine (Figure 20.3). Tentering both dries and stretches the fabric smooth and free from wrinkles. Fabrics are stretched between two parallel chains of correct width. The fabric is held in place on the tenter frame by pins and clips. Examination of the selvage of fabrics dried in tentering frames will usually reveal either small pinholes or marks from the clips.

Figure 20.3   Fabric entering tenter frame. Photograph courtesy of West Point–Pepperell, Inc.

The tenter frame carries the fabric into a drying apparatus, where the fabric is dried under tension and made wrinkle free. Fabrics that have not been set on the tenter frame straight will be off-grain. That is, the warp and filling yarns will not cross at right angles. Some fabrics that are off-grain can be straightened by pulling the yarns into the correct or straight position. However, fabrics that have had heat-setting or resin treatments cannot be straightened and will always be off-grain. The serviceability and aesthetic qualities of fabrics are, therefore, adversely affected by poor tentering.

Drying fabrics with hot air is more expensive than drying with heated rollers. For this reason, some fabrics may be tentered after being passed over heated rollers for preliminary partial drying. In any case, after the last drying, the fabric should have a controlled width and length.

Preparation of Fabrics

The processing of natural fibers removes impurities such as grease and vegetable matter in wool, gum in silk, or vegetable matter in cotton. Optimum conditions for spinning fibers into yarns, however, require some lubrication of fibers. Also, in synthetic fibers some means must be found to decrease the static electricity that builds up during spinning. For these reasons, natural lubricating substances in cotton are not removed before spinning, and other fibers generally have had substances added that aid in spinning. During weaving, temporary starches (called sizings) or other special additives such as identifying dyes may have been used. If fabrics become soiled dur-

Figure 20.4 Fabric passes over gas flame that singes or burns off excess surface fiber. Photograph courtesy of West Point–Pepperell, Inc.

ing weaving, these substances and soils must be removed before further treatment is given to the fabrics. The specific fabric preparation steps will vary, depending on the fibers from which the cloth is made.

Cotton and Cotton Blends

Singeing

To produce a smooth surface finish on fabrics made from staple fibers, fabrics are passed over a heated copper plate or above a gas flame. The fiber ends burn off. The fabric is moved very rapidly, and only the fiber ends are destroyed. Immediately after passing the flame, the fabric is passed through a water bath to put out any sparks that might remain. (See Figure 20.4.)

The burning characteristics of fibers must be taken into account when this process is applied, as heat-sensitive fibers melt, forming tiny balls on the surface of the fabric. These balls interfere with dye absorption, so that, as a general rule, heat-sensitive fibers would be singed after dyeing or printing. The tendency of some manufactured fibers to pill may be decreased by singeing.

Filament yarns do not require singeing, as there are no short fiber ends to project onto the surface of the fabric. Fabrics that are to be napped are not singed.

Desizing

In order that subsequent dyeing and finishing materials can be absorbed as evenly as possible, all sizing material must be removed from fabric completely and uniformly. These materials are removed either by a hot water wash or by enzymes, depending on the sizing materials that were used. The most commonly used sizing materials are starches or polyvinyl alcohol.

Scouring

Scouring removes waxes and destroys vegetable matter residues in cotton and cotton blend fabrics. Sodium hydroxide is used to saponify the fats on the fibers. The soap that is formed then serves to emulsify the remaining waxes and wash away any dirt or other impurities. Scouring may be done in a *kier vat,* a large iron vessel in which the fabric is boiled in the alkaline solution, or in a *J Box* for continuous scouring and bleaching of full-width fabrics (Figure 20.5). Knitted goods are

Figure 20.5 Fabric is scoured on a continuous basis as it passes through cleansing solution. Photograph courtesy of West Point–Pepperell, Inc.

processed in a beck/jet machine in which the process is integrated with dyeing of the fabric.

Bleaching

Cotton fabrics are naturally off-white to tan in color, depending on the amount of pigmentation in the fiber. Problems can arise in dyeing if any small amount of impurity that is highly colored remains. Even manufactured fiber fabrics, especially those that have been heat-set, may become yellowed as a result of processing. Therefore, fabrics may require bleaching or whitening to prepare them for dyeing or printing or to produce a clear white fabric. Bleaches are chemical substances that oxidize colored compounds, removing the color. Most bleaches used by industry are either chlorine bleaches or peroxygen bleaches. The peroxygen bleaches, and particularly hydrogen peroxide bleaches, are used most frequently in commercial bleaching of greige (untreated) goods, although for some fabrics other types of bleaches must be used.

Mill processes include saturating the fabric with the bleaching agent, steaming it to effect the bleaching reaction, and washing the fabric thoroughly, usually with a dilute mineral acid to neutralize any residual alkali. This last step is called *souring* and in earlier times was done with buttermilk. (Home bleaching is discussed in chapter 24.)

Mercerization

Singeing, desizing, scouring, and bleaching are routine finishing processes, whereas *mercerization* is an optional step in the finishing of cotton and cotton-blend fabrics. In 1851 John Mercer discovered that the treatment of cotton with a strong solution of sodium hydroxide altered the strength, absorbency, and appearance of the fabric. Because fabric treated in this way shrunk as much as 25 percent of its length, the finish was not applied commercially until an English chemist, H. A. Lowe, discovered that applying the finish under tension not only minimized shrinkage but also increased luster.

In mercerization, as this finish is called, the cotton fabric is immersed under tension in a strong solution of sodium hydroxide for a short, controlled period of time (usually 4 minutes or less), the alkali is washed off, and any excess alkali is neutralized. The sodium ions in the solution displace the hydrogens on the cellulose—OH groups, pushing the polymeric chains farther apart and swelling the fiber.

Mercerized cotton fabrics have greatly increased luster. During mercerization the fiber swells, the natural convolutions of cotton are largely lost, and the fiber retains a fuller, rounded diameter. This smooth surface reflects more light than does the untreated, flatter fiber.

The strength of the fiber is increased as much as 20 percent. The cotton becomes more absorbent and has a greater affinity for moisture and for dyestuffs. Vat-dyed cotton fabrics that have been mercerized have excellent colorfastness, and less dye is required to produce colors. Some decorative effects can be achieved by combining mercerized yarns and unmercerized yarns in one fabric because mercerized yarns dye to darker shades than untreated yarns.

Mercerized fabrics are also more reactive. As a result, they are more easily damaged by acids and oxidizing agents, but mercerized fabrics are more receptive to resin finishes.

Mercerization can be applied to either yarns or fabrics. Most good-quality cotton sewing threads are mercerized to improve their strength. *Slack mercerization,* or mercerization of fabrics that are not held under tension, can be used to produce stretch fabrics. During slack mercerization yarns shrink and develop a good degree of elasticity. The finished fabric can be stretched, and when the tension is removed, the goods will return to their original length. Yarns that have been slack mercerized do not have the high luster of yarns mercerized under tension. This process is not widely used.

Mercerization is both inexpensive and permanent, and for these reasons it is widely used on cotton goods. Linen can also be mercerized, and since it has a natural luster and good strength, the major advantage of mercerizing linen is to improve the dyeability and receptivity of linen to other finishes.

Silk

In addition to removing the soil or additives used while weaving silk, scouring removes any sericin (gum) that remains on the silk. Often a quantity of the natural gum has been allowed to remain on the silk fiber to give it additional body and to make it easier to handle in spinning and weaving. Although for raw silk fabrics the gum is retained purposely to provide body or produce a different texture, most silk fabrics are degummed as a part of the finishing process. The resultant fabric has a much softer hand and a whiter appearance. Silk is usually bleached with dilute solutions of hydrogen peroxide.

Wool

Carbonizing

Wool fabrics that have some vegetable matter clinging to the woven or knitted yarns must be *carbonized*. Carbonizing is accomplished by the immersion of wool in sulfuric acid or hydrochloric acid. Because strong acids readily attack the cellulose of the vegetable matter and do not immediately harm protein fibers like wool, the burrs, sticks, leaves, and the like that remain in the wool are destroyed. The treatment is carried out under carefully controlled conditions so that the wool is not damaged, and the fabric is given a careful scouring afterward to remove or neutralize all the acid that remains.

Scouring

The scouring of wool is done in solutions of less concentration and at lower temperatures than the scouring of other fibers because the alkalinity of most scouring solutions damages wool. Mild detergents and sodium carbonate are frequently used.

Fulling

Wool fabrics are *fulled,* or *milled,* to give the fabric a more compact structure. In a type of preshrinking, fabrics are subjected to moisture, heat, soap, and pressure. In the milling machine, the wet fabric is pounded with hammers or is alternately stretched and compressed for mechanical action.

Fulling causes the yarns to shrink and to lie closer together and gives the fabric a denser structure. Wool cloth may be given more or less fulling, depending on the desired characteristics of the resultant fabrics. Melton cloth, for example, is one of the most heavily fulled wool fabrics and has a dense, feltlike texture.

Bleaching

Although wool fabrics often are finished in the natural color or dyed without bleaching, sometimes bleaching may be necessary. Traditionally, wools were bleached by a process called stoving, which exposed the fabric to sulfur dioxide. Current processes use hydrogen peroxide and mild temperatures.

Basic Finishes That Affect Appearance

Optical Brighteners

In addition to being bleached, many white fabrics are treated with fluorescent whiteners known as optical brighteners to enhance their whiteness. Optical brighteners are not bleaches but are dyelike compounds that emit a strong bluish fluorescence. This causes the white to appear whiter (a "bluish-white" instead of a "yellow-white") and brighter. Optical brighteners are most effective in daylight; they are not effective in artificial light, which does not contain ultraviolet light.

Optical brighteners are only moderately fast to laundering and are not fast to chlorine bleaching. Since most detergents contain optical brighteners for cellulose in their formulation, any loss of the original brightener is usually replaced in laundering. Wool fabrics treated with optical brighteners may develop a brown discoloration when the brighteners fade as a result of exposure to sunlight.

Delustering

Many of the manufactured fibers have a high natural luster or brightness. Some manufactured fibers are treated to reduce this luster before the fiber is formed by adding titanium dioxide pigment, which causes the fiber to reflect less light and thereby decreases the brightness. Other methods of delustering fibers include etching or roughening of the fiber surface by chemical treatment to produce a more irregular surface that does not reflect but scatters light.

Fabrics may be delustered by applying a delustrant to the surface of the fabric and fixing it in place with a resin binder. Any process that roughens or brushes fibers onto the fabric surface will also reduce luster. (Brushing, napping, and other surface modification processes are discussed later in this chapter.)

Basic Finishes That Affect Hand or Texture

Stiffening

Sizing

To add body to fabrics, some type of sizing is often applied. This may be in the form of starch, gelatin, or resin or a combination of these with softening substances such as oils or waxes.

Starches and gelatins are temporary sizings and are removed during laundering or dry cleaning. Inexpensive cotton or rayon fabrics are often heavily starched and after laundering may become quite limp. For fabrics sized with starch or gelatin, it is possible to determine how heavily sized a fabric is by rubbing hard at a section of the fabric. If small flakes of starch can be removed, the fabric has obviously been sized. If the same fabric is held up to the light, one can often see more light through the area in the section from which the sizing has been removed than in other areas.

Gelatins are used as sizing on rayons because they are clear in color and do not dim the luster of the fabric. The application of the sizing, plus a hard press, may create a deceptively full hand and surface luster that is lost after laundering.

Various resins can also be used to add body to fabrics. These resins produce a durable finish. The resin attaches to the surface of the fiber or actually impregnates the fiber. Sometimes resins are used in combination with starches to produce a reasonably durable finish in which the resin serves to "bind" the starch to the fiber.

Permanent Stiffening of Cottons

By a special acid treatment known as *parchmentizing,* some cottons are given a permanently stiff character. The application of a carefully controlled acid solution causes the surface of the yarn to become softened and gelatinlike. An afterwash in cold water causes the gelatinous outer surface to harden, forming a permanently stiffened exterior. Permanently finished organdy, for example, is made by this process. Acid finishes are also used to create certain decorative effects, which are discussed later in this chapter.

Weighting of Silk

The sericin in raw silk comprises from 25 to 30 percent of its weight. When the fiber is cleaned, this gum is removed. Silks may be weighted both to enable the producer to regain some of the loss in fiber weight and to add greater body to fabrics. Silk weighting is discussed at length in chapter 5.

Softening

Heat setting of manufactured fabrics, durable press finishes, and some treatments given to acrylic fabrics may produce a harsh and unpleasant hand. Application of fabric softeners during finishing can overcome these negative qualities. The chemical compounds used penetrate intersections between yarns to allow a certain amount of yarn slippage, thereby creating a more supple, smoother, and more pleasant-feeling fabric.

Some of these products are available for use in home laundering. These are discussed in chapter 24, "The Care of Textile Products."

Surface Finishes

Many finishes are used because of the effect they have on the appearance of the fabric. Sometimes these finishes produce a related change in texture or hand, as well.

Calendering

Calendering is a broad, general term that refers to a mechanically produced finish achieved by passing fabrics between a series of two or more rollers. The object of calendering is to smooth the fabric and/or create interesting surface effects.

Simple Calendering. The simplest form of calendering is comparable to ironing a fabric. The calender rolls are heated, and the dampened cloth is passed between the cylinders to smooth and flatten the fabric, producing a wrinkle-free, slightly glossy surface.

Glazing. A special calender called a *friction calender* produces fabrics that have a highly glazed or polished surface, such as chintz or polished cotton. Before passing the fabric through the calender, the cloth is saturated with either starch or resin. The fabric is dried slightly and then fed into the machine in which a rapidly moving, heated roller polishes the surface of the more slowly moving fabric. If starch is used to produce the glaze, the finish is temporary. If resins are used, the glaze is durable.

Ciréing. Ciré fabrics are characterized by a high surface polish. A fashion term, "the wet look," has sometimes been used to describe ciré fabrics. Made by much the same process as friction calendering, ciré effects on natural fibers or rayon are produced with waxes and thermoplastic resins. Heat-sensitive synthetics are given a permanent wet look when the thermoplastic fibers fuse slightly under the heat of the rollers.

When hydrophobic fibers are given a ciré finish, some degree of water repellency is provided. This occurs as a result of the slight glazing or fusing that the fabrics undergo.

Embossing. Embossed designs are produced by pressing a pattern onto fabrics. Like other calendered finishes, the designs may be permanent when applied to thermoplastic fibers, durable when applied to fabrics that have been resin treated, and temporary on other fabrics.

Some embossed designs are relatively flat, as in a velvet with flattened embossed areas. The pattern is created by running an embossed roller with a raised pattern across the fabric. The opposite roller is made of paper and has a smooth surface. Because the paper roll can "give" with the pressure, the embossed roller "prints" the colorless design by flattening some sections of the cloth.

Three-dimensional embossed designs are made with embossed rollers also. In this method the embossed roller first presses the design onto the surface of the paper roller; then, when the fabric is passed between the rollers, both the engraved roller and the shaped paper roll work together to mold the shape of the pattern into the cloth.

Embossed designs provide surface texture at a lower cost than do woven designs. If applied to nonthermoplastic fibers without special resin finishes, the embossing will be lost sooner or later. Embossed fabrics should not be ironed or pressed, as the design may be diminished by the pressure. (See Figure 20.6.)

Schreinering. The Schreiner calender produces fabrics with a soft luster and a soft hand. One of the calender rolls is embossed with about 250 fine diagonal lines per inch. This roller passes over the fabric, flattening the yarns and producing a more opaque fabric with soft luster and hand. Unless the fabric is thermoplastic, the finish is a temporary one. Thermoplastic fibers are set permanently into position by the Schreiner calender's heat. If fabrics are given a resin treatment before Schreinering, the finish will be fairly durable.

Figure 20.6

Embossed cotton fabric.

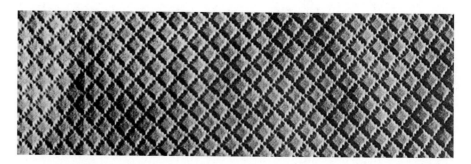

Figure 20.7

Faille fabric with a moiré finish.

The Schreiner finish is designed to give fabrics a soft luster. Damask table linens and cotton sateens are among the fabrics given this finish routinely. Thermoplastic tricots are treated with the finish to enhance surface luster.

Moiré. The fashion side of moiré fabrics has a watered or clouded surface appearance that is sometimes called a "wood grain" pattern (Figure 20.7). The original technique for producing moiré fabrics is an old one and was used in many luxurious silks of the eighteenth and nineteenth centuries.

The moiré pattern is temporary, durable, or permanent depending on the fiber and/or chemicals used. In watermarked moiré, such as those used a hundred years ago, the pattern would be destroyed by laundering. Resin treatment makes the pattern reasonably durable to cleaning and laundering, and the use of heat setting of thermoplastic fibers creates a permanent finish.

To achieve an effective moiré pattern, ribbed fabrics such as taffeta, faille, or bengaline are usually selected. One of two methods is employed. The first, and more traditional method, places two lengths of a fabric from the same bolt face to face, with one layer slightly off-grain in relation to the other. Enormous pressure is put on the fabrics by the smooth moiré rollers, and the ribs of one fabric press down on those of the other, flattening each other in some areas and causing the fabrics to reflect light differently across the surface of the fabric. The moiré produced in this manner has a random pattern with no discernible repeats.

The second method uses a roller with a moiré pattern etched into its surface. In this procedure the roller flattens or distorts one area more than another, creating the same effect as in the first method. Here, however, the patterns are repeated at regular intervals.

Beetling

Linens and cottons that are intended to look like linens are beetled, a process in which the fabric is pounded (in a machine equipped with hammers that strike over the surface of the fabric) to flatten the yarns and make them smoother and more lustrous. Unless a resin treatment has been given to the fabric before beetling, the finish is temporary. (See Figure 20.8.)

Figure 20.8

Lustrous linen damask fabric reflects light as a result of beetling.

Napping and Sueding

Napped and sueded fabrics are fabrics in which fiber ends are brushed up onto the surface of the fabric. Napping and sueding are applied to woven or knitted goods, and although the term *pile* is often used to refer to the fiber ends that appear on the surface of the cloth, these fabrics should not be confused with pile fabrics in which a separate set of yarns is used to create the pile through weaving.

Sueding develops a very low pile on the surface of the fabric, and the surface of the fabric can be finished to look and feel like suede leather. An abrasive material, a type of sandpaper, is used to achieve the finish. The fabric is rotated against the abrasive material, and the hand and appearance of the fabric are determined by the type of fiber used, the size of the yarn, and the intensity of the contact between the fabric and the abrasive material. This process is sometimes referred to as *sanding,* and it is one of the ways that so-called sandwashed silk is produced.

In periods when suedelike fabrics have been fashionable, woven and knitted fabrics finished on sueders have been widely available. Attempts to simulate suede leather have ranged from the development of nonwoven fabrics such as Ultrasuede®, which approximates the hand and appearance of suede leather closely, to those in which finishing with a sueder provides the appearance of suede surface while maintaining the hand and drapability of woven or knitted cloth.

Napped fabrics, like suede fabrics, have a pile or nap on the surface of the fabric. Napping generally develops a deeper nap and is produced by machinery different from sueding.

Napped fabrics are used for clothing and household textiles in which warmth is desired. The loose fiber ends trap air that serves as insulation. Blankets, sleepwear, coating fabrics, sweaters, warm activewear, and the like are often made from napped fabrics.

The nap is created by rubbing the surface of the fabric with a rough device. Napped fabrics are generally made from yarns with a fairly loose twist, so that the surface fibers will brush up easily. Long ago this was done with teasels (plant heads with many fine, hooklike, sharp projections). Today, napping is more likely to be done with machines set with small, fine wires that approximate the teasel spine. These small, hooklike projections catch fibers and pull them up to the surface of the fabric, creating a fuzzy, soft layer of fibers on the surface that are also caught into the yarn. Some very fine napped wools are still made by using natural teasels. The terms *gigging* and *raising* may also be used to describe the napping process. Excessive napping may tend to weaken fabrics by pulling up too many fibers, thereby weakening the

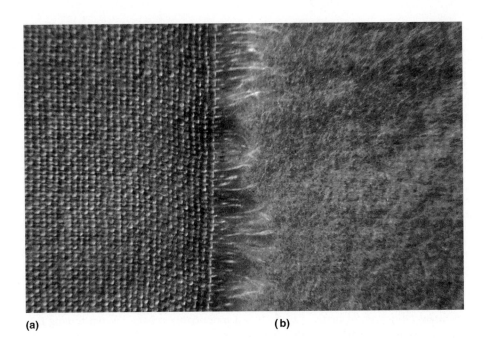

(a)   **(b)**

Figure 20.9

Cotton fabric (a) before napping and (b) after it has been napped on one side.

basic structure of the fabric. Fabrics intended for apparel are generally napped on one side, whereas those for blankets are napped on both sides. (See Figure 20.9.)

Brushing

Fabrics made from staple fibers may be brushed to remove loose fiber from the surface of the fabric. This is done to improve the appearance of the fabric.

Some fabrics with names such as *brushed denim* or *brushed tricot* are created by napping or sueding or brushing fibers up onto the surface of the fabric to create a soft surface texture. The surface fibers are less dense than in napped or sueded fabrics.

Many napped and pile fabrics are brushed in such a way that the nap or pile runs in one direction. When this has been done, the fingers can be run across the surface of the fabric to feel that the fabric is smooth in one direction and rougher in the other direction. Items cut from such fabrics must be handled so that the direction of all pieces is the same. If this is not done, a fabric in which the grain runs down may reflect light differently from one in which the grain runs up. This difference in light reflection may cause pieces placed side by side to appear to be different in color.

Shearing

Shearing removes unwanted fibers projecting onto the surface of fabrics.

Napped or pile fabrics may be sheared to make the nap or the pile the same thickness in all parts of the fabric. The shearing is done in a machine in which sharp, rotating blades cut off fibers or cut the pile or nap to the desired length. The machine has been compared by Potter and Corbman (1967) to a lawn mower. If some sections of the pile or nap are flattened, and other areas sheared, brushing up the uncut sections can achieve a sculpted effect.

Flocking

A surface effect that is similar to a nap or a pile may be created by flocking, a process in which short fibers are "glued" onto the surface of fabrics by an adhesive material. If the adhesive coats the entire surface of the fabric, the flocking will cover the entire surface of the fabric, but if the adhesive is printed onto the fabric in a pattern of some sort, the flock will adhere only in the printed areas (see Figure 23.10, p. 436). All-over flocked fabrics may have a suedelike appearance.

Short lengths of fiber flocking can be made from any generic fiber type. Rayon is often used for flocking. Nylon may be selected for situations that require good abrasion resistance.

Fibers for flocking are made from bundles of tow fiber (continuous filament fibers without twist). The tow is fed through a finish removal bath and then into a bank of cutters that cut flock of the desired length. The fibers may be dyed before they are attached to the fabric, or the completed fabric may be dyed.

The application of the flock to the fabric is done by either of two methods (Figure 20.10). The mechanical flocking process sifts loose flock onto the surface of the fabric to be coated. A series of beaters agitate the fabric, causing most of the fibers to be set in an upright position, with one end of each fiber "locked" into the adhesive.

The second method causes the fibers to be attached in an upright position by passing them through an electrostatic field. The fibers pick up the electric charge and align themselves vertically. One end penetrates into the adhesive, and the flock is formed. Electrostatic flocking ensures more complete vertical positioning, and the resultant fabrics are of better quality. It is a more costly process. When buying fabrics, a consumer cannot tell which process was used.

The durability of flocked fabrics depends largely on the adhesives that hold the flock firmly during either laundering or dry cleaning. In some cases, flock may be removed by dry-cleaning solvents. Permanent care labels should tell the consumer how flocked fabrics ought to be handled. A second factor in the durability of flocked fabrics has to do with the fiber from which the flock has been made.

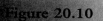

Figure 20.10   Application of flock to fabrics.

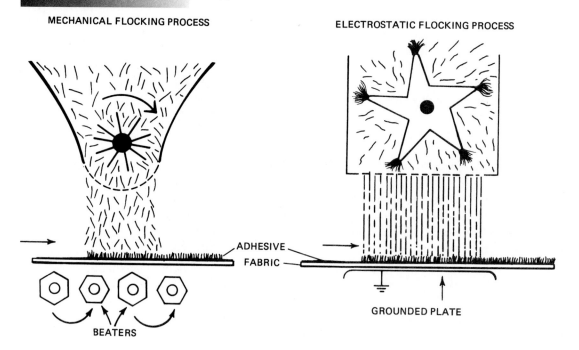

Burn-out Designs

Chemicals that will dissolve some fibers can be used to produce alterations in fabric appearance. It is possible, for example, to create open areas in fabrics by imprinting a cellulosic fabric with a sulfuric acid paste that dissolves the printed area. Such fabrics are likely to fray around the edges of the dissolved area and are not especially durable.

In blended fabrics, this technique can be used to create a number of interesting effects. Two different fibers are used. When the dissolving material is imprinted on the fabric, one of the fibers is dissolved while the other is unharmed. Those areas that have not had chemical imprinted on them remain intact and create the design. By contrasting texture, luster, or color of the fiber to be "burned out" with that of the second fiber, a number of attractive decorative effects can be achieved (Figure 20.11).

Plissé Designs

A puckered effect called plissé is achieved in some fabrics by imprinting them with chemicals that cause the fabric to shrink. When these chemicals are printed in a design, some areas of the fabric shrink while others do not. This causes untreated areas to pucker or puff up between the treated areas (Figure 20.12). Cottons and rayons react in this way when treated with sodium hydroxide, an alkali, as do nylons that have been printed with phenol, an acid substance. Although this is a fairly durable finish, plissé fabrics should not be ironed because the pressing of the plissé flattens the surface. Thermoplastic fibers can also be embossed to simulate plissé.

Acid Designs

In addition to stiffening the fabric, the acid treatment of cotton fabric causes it to become more transparent. The action can be utilized to create fabrics with a "frosted" design. Areas of the fabric are coated with acid-resistant materials. When the finish is applied, these areas remain opaque, while the acid-treated areas become quite transparent.

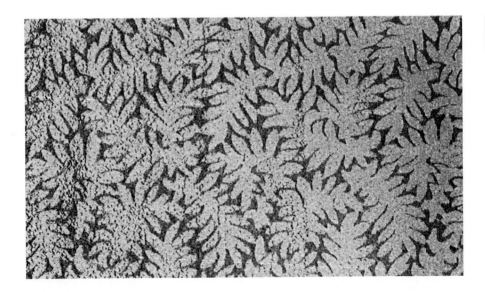

Figure 20.11

Burn-out design. Chemicals printed onto this fabric have dissolved away the dark-appearing sections. For photographic purposes the fabric has been placed against a dark background, but when the fabric is in use those areas would be more sheer and translucent than the leaf-shaped design.

Figure 20.12

Cotton plissé puckered design created by printing with sodium hydroxide on the background to shrink the fabric, leaving puffed, untreated areas between.

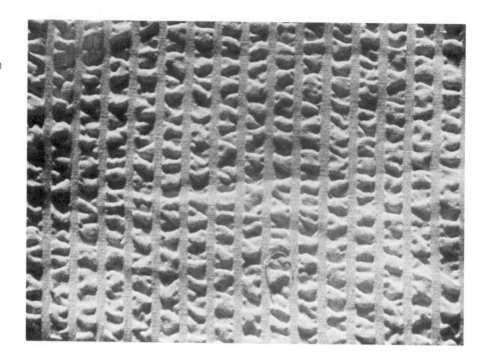

Enzyme Treatment

Cellulase enzymes are used in finishing cotton, rayon, and lyocell to produce smoother surfaces, softer hand, and a decrease in pilling. The cellulase enzymes hydrolize cellulosic fibers on the surface of the fabric, and mechanical action removes the weakened fibers from the surface. As a result, the fabric becomes softer and smoother. The Danish firm Novo Nordisk calls its enzyme finishing process *BioPolishing*.

If enzyme finishing is applied after fabrics or garments have been dyed with vat, sulfur, or pigment dyes, the effect is similar to that of stone washing (see page 422). The treatment does result in some loss of strength and reduction in weight. It is most frequently applied to denim.

A Few Other Finishing Steps

Before a fabric is ready to leave the factory, a visual or electronic inspection of the goods is made (Figure 20.13). If done by a worker, the fabric is run over a roller. The process is called *perching*, and the machine used is known as a perch. The perch resembles the uprights on a football goal.

Electronic scanning is done by laser that generates selvage markings of defective areas and a computer map showing where all the defects in a roll are located. This map can be used by apparel manufacturers using computer-controlled cutting systems that will cut automatically around defects in the cloth. The data generated by electronic inspection can help to pinpoint sources of defects so that these can be corrected.

For woolens and worsteds, both *specking* and *burling* may have to be done. Specking is the removal from woolens and worsteds of burrs, specks, or other small objects that might detract from the final appearance of the fabric. It is usually done with a tweezers or a burling iron.

| Figure 20.13 | Photograph of inspection of fabrics. Photograph courtesy of West Point–Pepperell, Inc. |

Burling is the removal of loose threads and knots from woolens and worsteds by means of a burling iron, a type of tweezer. Many knots must be pulled or worked to the back of the fabric because pulling them out might leave a small hole in the fabric.

The finishes described in this chapter are well described by *A Dictionary of Textile Terms* (1967): "the application of a pleasing or appealing effect to the fabric, comparable with the application of cosmetics to improve the facial effects of those who use them" (p. 41).

References

A dictionary of textile terms. 1967. Danville, Va.: Dan River Mills.
Potter, M. D., and B. P. Corbman. 1967. *Textile, fiber to fabric.* New York: McGraw-Hill.

Review Questions

1. Describe the ways that finishes can be classified. Identify the classifications into which the following finishes would fall, and explain why you have placed them into those classifications:
   - singeing
   - embossing of cotton fabric that has been given no special finishes
   - moiré finish on acetate
   - napping a wool flannel

2.   What is meant by low-wet-pickup finishes? Why is the textile finishing indus-
     try placing emphasis on these finishes?

3.   Identify those finishes that are routinely applied to textile fabrics. Give the pur-
     poses of each of these finishes and the types of fabric to which they are applied.

Recommended Readings

Abrahams, D. H. 1994. Improving on mercerizing processing. *American Dyestuff
    Reporter* 83 (September): 78.

Bio-polishing. 1994. *Textile Horizons,* April, 42.

Cook, F. L. 1994. Less is more in applying chemicals to textiles. *Textile World* 144
    (January): 59–65.

Computer-aided fabric inspection developed through AMTEX project CAFE puts
    U.S. textiles on quality's top shelf. 1994. *Southern Textile News* 50 (13 June): 2.

Cowhig, W. T. 1974. What is moiré? *Textiles* 4 (June): 46.

Finishing fabrics in the nineties. 1994. *Canadian Textile Journal* 111 (November): 28.

Goldstein, H. E. 1993. Mechanical and chemical finishing of microfabrics. *Textile
    Chemist and Colorist* 25, (February): 16–21.

Hodgson, A. 1982. Desizing and bleaching. *Textiles* 11 (Spring): 10.

Kumar, A., et al. 1994. Enzymatic treatment of man-made cellulosic fabrics. *Textile
    Chemist and Colorist* 26 (October): 25.

Peters, R. H. 1967. *Textile chemistry. Vol. II: Impurities in fibres, purification of fibres.*
    Amsterdam: Elsevier.

Tyndall, R. M. 1992. Improving the softness and surface appearance of cotton fab-
    rics and garments by treatment with cellulase enzymes. *Textile Chemist and Col-
    orist* 24 (June): 23.

FINISHES THAT AFFECT PERFORMANCE

A lthough chapter 20 describes preparatory treatments and mechanical finishes and this chapter concentrates on finishes that are more functional than aesthetic and that are achieved chiefly through the use of chemical applications, there are some finishes that defy strict classification. Mercerization, for example, uses chemical treatment as part of a preparatory process and could be classified as a chemical finish. Likewise, finishes for shrinkage control include both mechanical techniques or chemical finishes or a combination of both.

Shrinkage Control

A reduction in the length or width of a fiber, yarn, or fabric is known as shrinkage. If fabrics shrink after they have been made into garments or household items, they may decrease in size to such an extent that the item is no longer serviceable. For example, a garment with a 25-inch waist size will decrease by 1¼ inches if it shrinks 5 percent. *Growth* occurs when a fabric increases in dimensions.

Some fibers such as wool, cotton, and rayon swell more in water than do others. Fabrics made from these fibers will shrink more than fabrics made from fibers with lower moisture absorbance.

Wetting a fabric causes the tension that has been applied during its manufacture to be relaxed, so that fabrics generally shrink after the first and up to the fifth laundering. As discussed in chapter 2, this type of shrinkage is known as relaxation shrinkage. It occurs because the moisture within the fibers allows them to return to the dimensions they occupied before they were stretched during processing. The amount of relaxation shrinkage depends on the amount of stretching the fibers underwent during manufacturing. Wool and rayon, which are more extensible, will stretch more and therefore have greater potential for relaxation. Successive heating and drying cycles may produce progressive shrinkage, where the fabric continues to shrink.

The warp yarns of woven fabrics are subject to greater tension than are filling yarns because they are pulled through the machines; consequently, the fabrics generally shrink more in the warp than in the filling direction. Knit goods tend to stretch more during manufacture than do woven goods, and therefore knit goods are likely to shrink and change shape even more than woven goods.

Procedures and solvents used in commercial dry cleaning, as a rule, do not permit fabrics to relax, as washing does, so that items that are dry-cleaned may not shrink as readily. Shrinkage in dry cleaning generally results from the high moisture content in the solvent or from steaming during pressing.

Compressive Shrinkage Control

For fabrics subject to relaxation shrinkage, such as cotton, linen, and rayons, it would seem logical to "wash" or wet the fabrics to allow them to return to their true dimensions. This is not, however, practical for the manufacturer, not only because the process would be time and energy consuming but also because the required equipment would take up a great deal of space. Instead, a method has been devised in which the fabric is mechanically reduced to its correct dimensions.

A sample of fabric is measured, the measurements are recorded, and the fabric is laundered in such a way as to produce maximum shrinkage. The shrunken fabric is measured, and the percentages of warp and filling shrinkage are calculated. This tells the processor how much to compress the fabric.

In compressive shrinkage control processes, the fabric is dampened and is placed on a machine equipped either with a continuous woolen or felt blanket or with a rubber pad. These pads are constructed so that they can be both stretched and compressed. The fabric is carried on top of the blanket or pad, meeting the pad or carrier at a point where it is stretched around a curve. As the carrier moves from the curve to a straight area, it squeezes or compresses into a smaller, flat area. When the carrier compresses, the fabric it carries is also compressed. The fabric is then set into this compressed position. The machines used are engineered to provide the degree of compression needed for each type of fabric. The various patented processes of the compressive shrinkage type guarantee residual (or remaining) shrinkage of less than 1 percent unless the fabric is tumble dried.

The Sanforized Company has developed a number of different compressive shrinkage control processes for different types of fabrics. All provide for shrinkage of less than 1 percent. The trademark Sanforized® is used on woven cotton and cotton blends. Sanfor-set® is used on easy-care 100 percent cotton and cotton blends. In this latter process, cotton fabric is treated with liquid ammonia, which causes the fiber to swell and relax. Then, the fabric is subjected to mechanical, compressive shrinkage control treatment. When the treatment is complete, the ammonia is removed from the cotton and recycled. The resulting fabric is both shrinkage and wrinkle resistant. It can be laundered in the same way as any cotton fabric: washed and tumble dried, although prompt removal from the dryer is recommended.

Shrinkage Control for Knits

During knitting and finishing, knit fabrics are subject to tension and stretching, especially in the lengthwise direction. The construction of most knits allows for greater stretch. They often shrink far more than comparable woven goods. Shrinkage may be particularly pronounced in the lengthwise direction, often accompanied by growth in the crosswise direction.

Techniques used to control shrinkage in knitted fabrics include subjecting fabrics to treatment with resin-containing solutions, wetting then drying fabrics to relax tensions applied during processing, and compressive shrinkage processes similar to those described for woven fabrics.

Excellent results can be obtained by wetting fabrics to at least 40 percent humidity and then drying them in a rotary tumbler, but while dimensional stability of fabrics is excellent, the process is costly because lots must be small and fabrics tend to become knotted or tangled during tumbling. Knots must then be untangled manually. A variation of this process called the VH-Tric-O-Dry system utilizes the same principle. Fabrics are wet to at least 40 percent humidity then passed through a closed channel system in which fabrics bump against the walls of the channel, rather than tumbling; and are relaxed and dried in a larger chamber so that knots do not form. The manufacturer of the equipment indicates that larger lots can be processed, also (Skieller 1989).

Compressive shrinkage processes for knits use different methods to return fabrics to their relaxed position. Among these is a process that feeds fabric through a machine in which a series of rollers operating at different speeds causes the fabric to become compressed. In another, knitted fabrics are stretched in the crosswise direction.

Sanfor-Knit®, another shrinkage control process of the Sanforized Company, addresses the problem of knit shrinkage in both length and width. In this process, test garments that have had compressive shrinkage control treatment are made up in the desired size, washed, tumble dried, and checked by a testing instrument called the Knitpicker. The test instrument determines whether the garments have held both the length dimension and the elasticity in girth that will provide comfortable wear. If the garment does not meet the established standard, the knitter is advised as to changes that should be made in construction, yarn characteristics, or production techniques. Sanfor-Knit® garments are available in men's T-shirts, athletic shirts, polo shirts, briefs, and sports knits.

Still another technique for controlling shrinkage in knits is known as Micrex® shrinkage control. Fabrics are moved between two conveyors, each 6 inches apart. The cloth is kept in constant motion, both vertically and horizontally, by hot air from a high-energy nozzle system. This action allows the relaxation of the tensions that were imposed in previous operations, thereby allowing the fabric to relax to its original dimensions.

Synthetic knits are stabilized by heat setting. If heat setting has not been done, the fabrics will shrink. Low-priced double knits, for example, may display shrinkage as a result of inadequate heat setting.

Shrinkage Control for Rayon Fabrics

Viscose rayon fabrics may shrink progressively, although high-wet-modulus rayon fabrics exhibit less shrinkage. Shrinkage control for rayons is most effective when compressive shrinkage control treatments are followed by a resin finish to stabilize the fabric.

Careful control is needed in the application of chemical resins, as excessive concentrations can lower the quality and durability of the fabric. However, if applied correctly, chemical resins penetrate the fibers to prevent further shrinkage.

Shrinkage Control for Wool

Wool and animal hair fibers are among those few fibers that show progressive shrinkage. This continuous shrinkage is due to the scale structure of the wool fiber, which also causes felting.

In addition to felting shrinkage, wool fabrics display the same type of residual shrinkage from relaxation that other fibers show. Unlike cotton fabrics, however, wool may continue to shrink if the relaxation of the fibers is not complete after one or two washings. Shrinkage treatments for wool are of two types: those that alleviate the problems of relaxation shrinkage and those that eliminate or ameliorate felting shrinkage.

Relaxation Shrinkage

The following methods can be used to eliminate relaxation shrinkage in wool. Because these processes do not protect against felting shrinkage, fabrics that have these finishes should be dry-cleaned or handled carefully during laundering.

1. *Damp relaxing or steam relaxing.* High-quality worsted fabrics are subjected to a step that permits them to relax before they are cut into garments. The fabric is dampened or steamed and then permitted to dry in a relaxed state. The tensions applied to the fabric during processing are thereby removed. The process is sometimes called *London shrinking,* although this British term is not often used by American textile manufacturers.
2. *Cylinder method.* In this method wool fabric is passed across perforated cylinders. Jets of steam are released through the holes in the cylinders, causing the fabric to be dampened. The damp fabric, which relaxes in size, is dried without tension.

Washable Wools

Attempts to produce washable wool fabrics that will not show felting shrinkage have led to the development of processes that alter the scale structure of the fiber.

Degradative Processes. Because the wool scale structure is thought to cause shrinkage, a number of techniques have been developed to alter the scale structure in some way. Used alone, these processes may not meet "machine washable" standards, but they are adequate for products designated as "hand washable."

The most popular degradative processes use chlorine gas or liquid chlorine compounds to apparently partially dissolve the edges of the wool fiber scales, thereby decreasing their tendency to catch on each other. This chemical is, however, destructive, and unless the process is carefully controlled, it can weaken or seriously damage the cortex of the fiber. The texture of the fabric tends to become rough and harsh.

Fibers that have been subjected to chlorination are often blended with other wool or manufactured fibers. When blended with other wool fibers, chlorinated fibers may lead to problems in dyeing. Chlorinated fibers tend to accept dyes more readily than do untreated fibers, thereby causing an unevenness in color.

Alternative processes utilize other oxidative or reductive agents.

Polymer-based Processes. A second method for the creation of washable wools is the application of a thin polymeric layer to the surface of the fabric. The polymer coats the scales, inhibiting the interlocking action. Fibers can also be "spot welded" with synthetic resins to prevent their migration within the fabric structure.

Different processes utilize varying resins. Problems encountered in the use of resins or polymers include a tendency for the fabrics to become stiff or harsh to the touch when enough resin or polymer is used to make the fabrics completely shrinkproof. Also, some resin or polymer is lost after a number of launderings.

Combination Processes. Still other techniques consist of a degradative treatment followed by a polymer finish. Superwash® is a finish that uses chlorination followed by a resin finish. It is used especially for sweaters and knitwear.

Shrinkage Control through Heat Setting

Synthetic fabrics may be stabilized through heat setting. Synthetics can be permanently set into shape by subjecting them to heat near their glass transition temperature. The heat allows the molecules to relax so the fiber will not exhibit further shrinkage. This process is used to establish permanent dimensions for these fabrics. Synthetic knits, for example, are relatively free from shrinkage problems during laundering if they are properly heat-set. They may, however, undergo thermal shrinkage when subjected to high heat.

Finishes That Minimize Fabric Care

Wrinkle Recovery

Resistance to the formation of persistent wrinkles can be imparted to fabrics by different means. First, the fiber itself may recover naturally from wrinkling because of its resiliency. This is true of many synthetics and of wool. Second, because of their construction, certain fabric types recover from or disguise wrinkling. Terry cloth, knits, seersucker, plissé, and some "busy" prints are such fabrics. Or special finishes may be applied to fabrics to improve their wrinkle resistance.

Since cellulosic fibers are most prone to wrinkling, most wrinkle-resistant finishes were applied to fabrics made from these fibers or their blends. Wrinkle-resistant finishes date back to 1929 when Tootal Broadhurst Lee Ltd. patented a finish that could be used on cottons and rayons. The Tootal process utilized urea-formaldehyde resin. According to the theory behind this process—accepted at the time the process was developed—the resin penetrated into the fiber and formed a polymeric resin inside the fiber. Once inside, the resin was thought to "stuff" the fiber so that it was less flexible and therefore resisted wrinkling.

Recent textile finishing processes designed to secure wrinkle resistance in cellulosic fibers also utilize similar compounds. However, researchers today believe that wrinkle resistance and recovery are achieved by chemical reactions between the resins and the molecular structure of the fiber.

Moreover, although resin finishes improve wrinkle resistance, finishing reduces the absorbency, abrasion resistance, and strength of treated fibers. The blending of cellulose with resilient synthetic fibers may have the effect of improving wrinkle resistance. Blended fabrics abrade less readily, but the use of synthetics does nothing to improve absorbency. Even though most of the resin finishes are classed as durable, some loss in effectiveness is generally observable over the lifetime of the item.

Wash and Wear

Wash-and-wear finishes were an outgrowth of wrinkle-resistant finishes, and, historically, this name was given to the next group of easy-care finishes to be developed. In the 1950s much effort was put into developing finishes that would eliminate the need for ironing after items were laundered. Many of these wash-and-wear finishes (as they were called) did require some touch-up pressing before use.

Permanent Press or Durable Press

In spite of problems of adequate performance, of yellowing and degradation of fabrics that were bleached with chlorine bleach, and of a harsher hand, consumer acceptance of wash-and-wear fabrics was enthusiastic. Continued research to improve these resin finishes led eventually to the development of finishes that came to be known as permanent or durable press. Unlike the wash-and-wear and easy-care processes that were applied to flat goods, durable press finishes can be applied to constructed garments and products. This provides durably set shaping and creases. When laundered correctly, durable press garments require no ironing.

The terms *permanent press* and *durable press* are often used interchangeably by consumers, advertisers, and the textile industry. Durable press is a more accurate term, as some of these finishes are diminished over the lifetime of the garment. It is important to remember that, although synthetic fibers may be blended with cellulosics for durable press fabrics, the finishes themselves react only with the cellulose component. Like the crease-resistant and wash-and-wear finishes, durable press finishes rely on the properties of fibers, fabric construction, and/or treatment with synthetic resins or other chemicals.

Utilizing Fiber Properties

Heat setting of synthetic fibers can provide durability for creases and pleats. Furthermore, synthetic fibers that are quite resilient may not require ironing after laundering. These fabrics are not given chemical finishes.

Resin Treatments

By far the largest quantity of durable press is achieved through resin treatment of cellulosic and cellulosic-blend fabrics. The resin compounds used have at least two functional groups that react with adjacent cellulose molecules. Strong covalent bonds replace the weaker hydrogen bonds, cross-linking the cellulose chains and providing greater stability in the position of the molecules. Upon deformation, the molecules are pulled back into alignment, preventing the formation of wrinkles.

The most commonly used resin treatment is dimethyloldihydroxyethyleneurea (DMDHEU). It has two—OH (hydroxyl) groups and two—NH_2OH (methylol) groups that can react with cellulose. When blends consisting of cellulose fibers and synthetic fibers are treated, the resin reacts only with the cellulosic fibers in the blend.

The manufacturer applies the resin treatment, dries the fabric, and then follows with a "cure" period at higher temperature. It is during the curing step that the chemical reaction takes place. The cure may be applied either before the goods are constructed into garments or other items or after construction. (See Figure 21.1.)

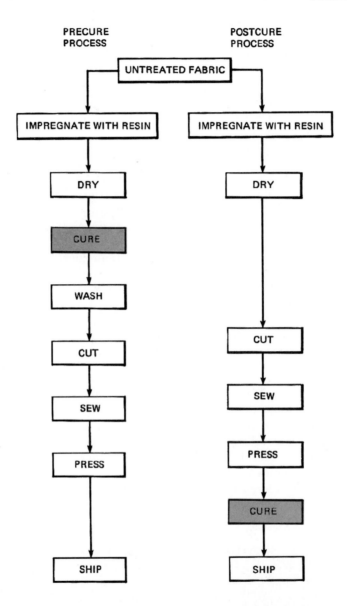

Figure 21.1

Comparison of the processing sequences of precure and postcure durable press treatments.

Precure, or Flat-Cure, Durable Press. Fabrics given a *precure* (also called *flat-cure*) treatment are finished before delivery to the manufacturer. The resin is impregnated into the fabric and cured, setting the fabric in a flat position. "Durable press" yard goods used by home sewers are made by the precure process.

When precured goods of blended fibers are used in manufactured items, the items are pressed with a hot-head press. The heat and pressure of the press shape the item, chiefly by heat-setting the thermoplastic fibers in the blend. Precured fabrics have been made into plain dresses or blouses, curtains, table and bed linens, and draperies, all of which require relatively little shaping.

Postcure Process. Manufacturers found that precured fabrics were difficult to handle in manufacture. Furthermore, these fabrics were difficult to press into permanent shape because they had been set as "flat." An alternative method of producing durable press items was, therefore, required.

In this new method, known as the *postcure* process, the fabric is impregnated with resin and dried. In this state, treated but not cured, the fabric is shipped to the manufacturer. Garments or other items are manufactured from the cloth, and then the finished items are cured in a special curing oven. Creases, pleats, hems, and the like are "permanently" set in this way. Care must be taken to be sure that the fabrics are free from wrinkles or puckers, or these, too, will be permanently set.

Problems of Durable Press

Manufacturing. The production of durable press items raises the cost of manufacture. The additional steps required and the cost of special equipment for finishing both contribute to this increase in price that is passed along to the consumer. Most consumers, however, appear to be willing to pay more for a product that requires less care.

In constructing items, the garment manufacturer must make changes in sewing techniques. Stitching of long seams may cause puckering unless special thread is used and unless changes in sewing machine tension, type of needle, and length of stitching are made.

It is also important for the garment manufacturer to select findings such as interfacings, linings, hem tape, and the like that will be compatible with durable press. They must not wrinkle or shrink differently from the fashion fabric.

Use and Care. Durable press fabrics, like their forerunners the crease-resistant and wash-and-wear fabrics, exhibit some loss in strength and particularly a decrease in abrasion resistance. One hundred percent cotton fabrics have been known to undergo loss in strength as high as 50 percent when given durable press finishes. In blends, areas such as collars and cuffs of men's shirts or the knees of children's pants often show the results of abrasion by fraying or frosting. Frosting is a change in color that results from the breakage and loss of fibers because of abrasion. The soft, fuzzy ends of the fibers give abraded areas a lighter or darker shade of color, depending on the color of the synthetic fibers that have not been worn away (Figure 21.2).

Figure 21.2

Close-up view of durable press fabric in which frosting has taken place. Darker cotton fibers have worn away, leaving a line of lighter polyester fiber.

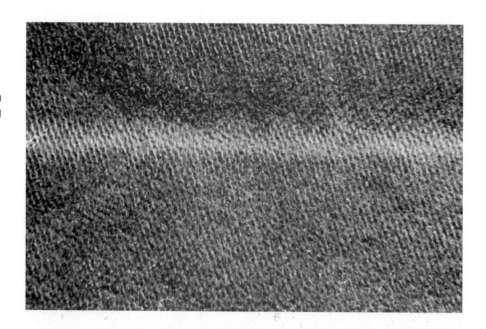

Blending of cellulosic fibers with synthetics, especially with polyesters that have increased abrasion resistance, can overcome the abrasion problem to a great extent. Even with blends, however, the problem of different rates of abrasion for each fiber remains.

A variety of different blends of thermoplastic and cellulosic fibers are used for durable press. The most common of these are polyester (from 40 to 75 percent) and cotton (from 25 to 60 percent), polyester (from 50 to 65 percent) and high-wet-modulus rayon (from 35 to 50 percent), and varying other combinations such as rayon or cotton with nylon. Spandex is sometimes incorporated for its stretch properties.

A number of problems with durable press finishes were noted in the 1970s. One was increased attraction of oils and reduced water penetration. As a result, oil-borne soils were absorbed by durable press fabrics, and since the fabrics resisted wetting, laundering (even with detergents that would normally remove oil-based soils) did not clean them effectively. Special soil-releasing finishes (discussed later in this chapter) were developed to overcome these difficulties.

Another problem was that the quantities of resin needed to produce satisfactory durable press made some of these fabrics rather stiff. They did not drape as well and were less comfortable to wear in warm weather than untreated fabrics. Also, if fabrics were not given an adequate after rinse, they had a "fishy" odor. This odor was generally lost after one or more launderings. Many of these problems have been overcome with the development of better finishes, such as DMDHEU, and by using lower levels of finish.

Safety. Formaldehyde is an important component of easy-care and durable press finishes. Under hot, humid conditions, the reaction forming the finish can reverse, releasing formaldehyde. Debate has focused on what constitutes a safe level of formaldehyde in the environment, and revised OSHA standards may mandate still lower levels in the workplace. Manufacturers have thus decreased the amount of formaldehyde-containing finishes being applied to fabrics and are developing newer finishes without formaldehyde.

One approach has been to alter the methylol groups in DMDHEU that are the source of formaldehyde. Finishes based on this approach show minimal formaldehyde release but are not as cheap or effective as the traditional commercial finish. Current research is focused on polycarboxylic acids, compounds with multiple acid groups that can react with cellulose molecules forming ester bonds. Fabrics finished with polycarboxylic acids have good durable press features with better strength retention and abrasion resistance but are either expensive or cause yellowing of the fabric.

Consumer Box 21.1 summarizes performance and care aspects that consumers should be aware of when selecting products made from 100 percent cotton durable press fabrics.

Testing of Wrinkle-Resistant Finishes

Garments treated with wash-and-wear or durable press finishes are expected to look reasonably free of wrinkles after laundering. AATCC test methods have been developed to evaluate garments and other textiles treated with these finishes. The tests include a test for the appearance of durable press fabrics after repeated home laundering, a test evaluating the appearance of seams in wash-and-wear items after home laundering, a test for the appearance of creases in wash-and-wear items after home laundering, and a test evaluating the appearance of apparel and other textile products after repeated home launderings. The specifics of these test methods can be found in the AATCC *Technical Manual,* published annually.

CONSUMER BOX 21.1   Durable Press Fabrics of 100 Percent Cotton

Cotton fabrics, as we all know, become wrinkled during use and after laundering. The cause of this wrinkling is described in chapter 4. Durable press finishes were developed to provide cotton fabrics that did not require ironing after washing. These finishes react chemically with the cellulose chains in cotton fibers to prevent deformation of the fibers, which results in wrinkling of the fabric.

Consumers like the comfort of all-cotton fabrics for apparel as well as for home furnishings items such as sheets. Application of durable press finishes to cotton fabrics increases their consumer acceptance in many end uses. Products made from the finished fabric may be designated as *wrinkle resistant, wrinkle-free,* or *easy-care.*

Current commercial finishes can be applied to both cotton and cotton blend fabrics. Blending synthetic fibers, such as polyester, with cotton enhances the fabric's smooth-drying properties, and such blends require less of the durable press finishing material. All-cotton fabrics finished with durable press resins exhibit significantly higher wrinkle resistance after washing and drying than unfinished fabrics. These wrinkle-resistant cotton garments are enjoying a market surge, especially in men's casual clothing. The cost is slightly higher for durable press products, but consumers seem willing to pay for the convenience of easy care. Labels on such products should tell consumers that the products are wrinkle resistant or wrinkle-free.

Both precure and postcure processes are used for durable press cotton products. The precure process is best for fabric that will be made into items without creases or pleats. These include sheets, shirts, and knits. Postcuring is used for products that have permanent creases or pleats, such as men's pants. For both processes accurate control of the curing step is the key to ensuring high-quality manufactured products.

Even though the wrinkle-resistant properties of cotton are enhanced by durable press finishes, the fabrics may still need touch-up ironing, especially at seams and other stitched areas, to achieve the appearance desired by some consumers. The finishes will therefore be more effective on cotton garments or other home furnishings with less stitching and fewer details.

Durable press finishes also allow the setting of durable creases and pleats in garments of 100 percent cotton. The postcuring process, for example, can set creases in pantlegs of men's trousers. However, once creases and pleats are permanently set, making alterations to garments is difficult. It is easier to shorten skirts or trousers than it is to lengthen them, even though it may be difficult to get as crisp a press as the fabric had when it came from the manufacturer. The crease mark of the original hem will always show in a lengthened garment. For these reasons, durable press garments should be bought to fit and should not be given extensive alterations.

In addition to testing that evaluates the appearance of garments, devices have been developed that will evaluate recovery of fabrics from wrinkling. The AATCC Wrinkle Tester allows an evaluation of wrinkle recovery by first subjecting a sample of fabric to wrinkling and then allowing a period of recovery. Finally, samples are evaluated by comparing them to specified visual standards (replicas of fabrics with varying degrees of wrinkling) and rating the samples.

Soil and Water Repellency

Soiling results when a textile comes into contact with soiled surfaces or with air- or water-borne soils. Soil is retained either by mechanical entrapment of soil within the yarn or fabric structure or by electrostatic forces that bond the soil to the fabric.

Durable press finishes not only produce wrinkle resistance, they also inhibit shrinkage, a property which has led to increased use of these finishes in knit goods. Cotton knits do not wrinkle as much as woven cotton fabrics, but they usually shrink more, and the durable press finishes stabilize the fabric dimensions. Several companies are beginning to market 100 percent cotton knit shirts with shrinkage control.

Special care in home laundering is required to produce optimum durable press performance. Washing should be done at warm rather than hot temperatures. Best results are seen when a warm wash cycle is followed by a cool rinse. Durable press finishes are designed for use in automatic laundering equipment, especially tumble dryers. If items must be line dried, they should be washed in a durable press cycle or removed from the washer before the spin cycle, in which fabrics may become creased.

Dry fabrics should be removed from the dryer immediately after the cycle ends to keep creases from forming while the item lies wrinkled at the bottom of the dryer. Durable press cycles, a feature of most modern dryers, have an initial warm-drying phase, followed by a cool-air phase that prevents this problem. If items do become wrinkled, they can be placed in a warm dryer for a few minutes with a damp item and then immediately removed.

Although durable press resins increase the smooth-drying property of cotton fabrics, they also decrease their strength and abrasion resistance. Some of the earlier wash-and-wear finishes caused losses in fiber strength and toughness. Consumers should recognize that although this problem is no longer so severe, the wear life of cotton durable press fabrics is shorter than that of unfinished fabrics. The problem is greater with shirt-weight fabrics because they are weaker to begin with than the heavier weight fabrics used for pants and trousers.

Cotton fabrics with a durable press finish may have decreased absorbency. The decrease, however, is not large and should not noticeably affect the comfort of the fabrics. Finished cotton fabrics also have an increased attraction for grease and oil. To improve performance in this area, most manufacturers couple the wrinkle-resistant finish with a soil-release finish.

Another problem with durable press cotton fabrics has been the release of formaldehyde from the finish under hot, humid conditions. Garments, curtains, or sheets that have been stored in plastic wrappers for some time may release detectable formaldehyde when the plastic is opened. The improved finishing methods that are currently used have significantly decreased the formaldehyde release, but to minimize exposure consumers should prewash any durable press items before use. Research has shown that laundering easily removes released formaldehyde. Researchers are experimenting with finishes without formaldehyde, but such finishes are not yet commercially available.

One way to approach the problem of soiling is to prevent its deposition on the fabric. Another is to seek ways to facilitate its removal. Special finishes have been developed that have taken both of these approaches (Figure 21.3).

Stain Repellency

Scotchgard® and other finishes that repel water and oil may be classified as stain-resistant finishes. These finishes decrease the surface energy of the fabric so that water or oil beads up rather than penetrating the fiber. They are applied to fabrics used in products such as upholstery and tablecloths to prevent soiling by staining. They may be applied to an upholstery fabric at the time of manufacture in a liquid form or sprayed onto the fabric after the fabric has been applied to a piece of furniture. Aerosol spray containers of some of these finishes can be purchased for home

Figure 21.3

(a) The drop of liquid on the left is oil; the right, water. Note how the fluorochemical stain-resistant finish enables this nylon upholstery fabric to resist both oil- and water-based stains and soil. (b) The silicone finish applied to this nylon upholstery fabric enables it to resist only water-based stains. Oil-based stains are absorbed by the silicone-treated fabric. (Note, however, that application of silicone finishes over fluorochemical finishes will cancel out oil repellency.) Photographs courtesy of 3M Company.

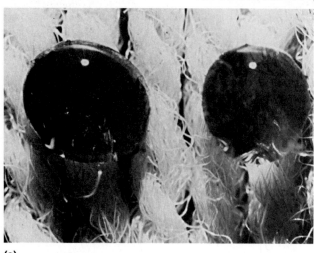

(a)

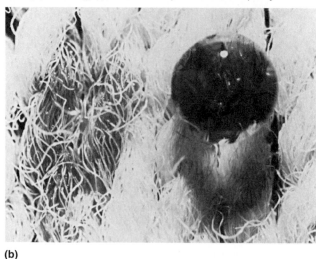

(b)

application. The finish tends to diminish with laundering, but it can be renewed by using the sprays.

Soil-Releasing Finishes

Soil-releasing finishes were developed largely as a result of the tendency of durable press and polyester fabrics to absorb and hold oil-borne stains. The soil-releasing finish should not be confused with stain-repellent finishes, although Scotchgard® is both stain resistant and soil releasing.

Soil-releasing finishes may be of two types. The first type prevents soil from entering the fabric by coating the surface of the fibers and yarns. Soil and stains are held on the surface of the fabric. When the fabric is laundered, the soil and stains are readily lifted away by the washing action.

Alternatively, soil-release finishes alter the characteristics that cause soil to bond to the fibers. Polyester presents particular soiling problems because oily soil has an affinity for the fiber surface. Agents such as nonionic polyethylene glycol derivatives may be added to the polymer solution before extrusion to make the fiber more hydrophilic.

One type of finish that forms hydrophilic grafts on the fiber results in improvements in soil release and soil redeposition. Most soil-releasing finishes for polyester are applied during the finishing of the fabric and are compatible with durable press finishes.

At the same time that soil-releasing finishes increase the receptivity of fibers to water, a second benefit is gained. Static electricity buildup is decreased as absorbency is increased. Increased absorbency also increases the comfort of the garment in warm weather. Fuzzing and pilling seem to be decreased by soil-releasing finishes as well, as the finish almost lubricates the fabric.

Effective soil-releasing finishes should result in fabrics from which common soil is removed during home laundering with normal detergents. Oily stains, often hard to remove from durable press fabrics, should be removable in home laundering. The disadvantage of most of these finishes is that they are gradually diminished through laundering.

Stain-Resist Finishes

Stain-resist finishes for nylon carpets were developed to increase the resistance of these carpets to food and other common stains. The finishes are generally sulfonated aromatic condensation (SAC) compounds that function essentially as colorless dyes. The stain blockers, which have negative charges, are attracted to the positive sites in the nylon fibers, tie up the dye sites, and set up a barrier layer to staining materials. Food stains, for example, which are anionic like the stain-resistance molecules, are not absorbed as easily.

Today, stain-resist finishes are used on most nylon carpets for residential use. Trademarks are DuPont's Stainmaster® and Monsanto's StainBlocker®.

Water Repellency

Waterproof Fabrics

A fabric that is waterproof allows no water to penetrate from the surface to the underside. Coated fabrics can be waterproof. Coatings made from rubber or synthetic plastic materials can create fabrics that are completely waterproof; however, these fabrics tend to be warm and uncomfortable because they create a barrier that traps air and perspiration close to the body.

Recent advances in fabric coating and laminating have led to the development of fabrics that are described as *waterproof and breathable (WP/B)*. The general principle behind these fabrics is that they keep out water from rain and snow but allow the passage of moisture vapor from perspiration. They are promoted for use in outdoor clothing and for active sports. One of the first of these products was Gore-Tex®, made by placing a membrane of PTFE fluorocarbon underneath a layer of outer fabric. The membrane is porous. The pores are smaller than a drop of water that contains many water molecules, but they are larger than a molecule of water vapor. This structure keeps out rain but allows moisture from perspiration to escape (Figure 21.4).

The success of Gore-Tex® has led to the production of a number of products using similar principles. Many of these use polyurethane coatings with microscopic pores. Sympatex®, a polyester membrane for lamination, has a "no pores" structure, but uses a "combination of chemistry and physics" described as follows. The membrane has a positive charge on the outside. Water molecules, with a negative charge, are attracted to and drawn through the membrane. Also helping to "push" moisture vapor through is the high vapor pressure on the body side (Sympatex 1988).

Performance of waterproof garments is closely related to their construction. Seamlines must be sealed, so that water does not pass through the fabric by way of the holes left by the sewing needle. Tears, rips, or worn spots are also areas in which leaks can occur. The manufacturer recommends that Gore-Tex® garments not be laundered in liquid detergents, as these tend to leave surfactants on the surface that may allow the wetting of the fabric. Instead, use cold-water temperatures and powdered detergent.

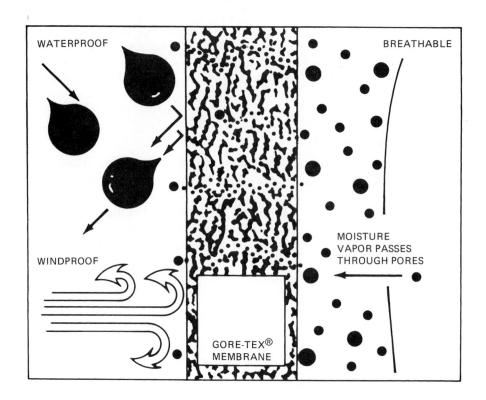

Figure 21.4

Manufacturer's diagram shows how Gore-Tex® membrane repels water but allows moisture vapor to pass through pores that are too small to permit passage of water. Illustration courtesy of W. L. Gore and Associates.

Water-Repellent Fabrics

The term *water repellent* should not be confused with the term *waterproof.* Water-repellent fabrics resist penetration by water but are not completely waterproof. Such fabrics represent a practical alternative to fabrics that keep out water and air, since they resist wetting and also allow the passage of air. The passage of air is imperative if one is to have a garment that is comfortable to wear.

Water repellency is conferred through a combination of the principles of fabric construction, the application of one of the finishes that are classified as either renewable finishes or durable finishes, and appropriate selection of fiber content.

Renewable Finishes. Renewable water-repellent finishes are removed during laundering and dry cleaning. These are relatively inexpensive and easily applied, so that they can be renewed after each laundering or dry cleaning.

Either wax emulsions or metallic soaps are used to secure renewable water repellency. Both these materials are naturally water repellent, and when they are applied in such a way that they coat the yarns of the fabric, they permit the passage of air between the yarns but prevent the passage of water. If the fabric on which they are coated has a close, compact weave, water repellency is improved. Of course, in conditions in which the fabric is subjected to long periods of exposure and sufficient force, water will eventually penetrate any water-repellent fabric.

Durable Finishes. As in renewable finishes, the effectiveness of durable water-repellent finishes is maximized if fabrics with high yarn counts and close weaves are selected. Although the first water-repellent finishes were of the renewable type, subsequent research has concentrated on effective durable finishes. A number of different materials have been developed that confer a more permanent finish.

1. *Finishes That Provide Water Repellency.* Many of these finishes begin with fatty or oily substances that possess natural water repellency; these substances are then treated with other chemicals to form compounds that can be absorbed by the fiber and are also insoluble in dry cleaning or soap solutions. Pyridinium compounds, methylol stearamides, and ammonium compounds are used. Silicone compounds are also effective in producing durable water-repellent fabrics. Trade names for silicone finishes include Cravanette®, Hydro-Pruf®, and Syl-mer®.

2. *Finishes That Provide Water and Oil Repellency.* Most of the finishes under discussion thus far repel water, but they do not repel oil. They are quite serviceable for products in which only water repellency is required. However, by using fluorochemical compounds, it is possible to produce finishes that repel both water and oil. Scotchgard® is one trade name of such finishes. (See Figure 21.3.)

Some of the durable finishes are durable only to laundering or only to dry cleaning. It is especially important, therefore, for the consumer to follow care instructions attached to these products.

Flame Retardance

Flame-Retardant Finishes

Finishes that make fabrics flame retardant have gained in importance since the passage of a series of laws known as the Flammable Fabrics Act. The act provided for the setting of certain standards in regard to flammability that must be achieved in wearing apparel, carpets, mattresses, and children's sleepwear.

The terminology employed in a discussion of flame retardancy can be confusing. To clarify the following discussion, a series of definitions is provided.

1. *Flame resistance* is defined by ASTM (1994) as "the property of a material whereby flaming combustion is prevented, terminated, or inhibited following application of a flaming or non-flaming source of ignition, with or without the subsequent removal of the ignition source." The material that is flame resistant may be a polymer, fiber, or fabric.

2. A *flame retardant* is "a chemical used to impart flame resistance" (ASTM 1994).

3. *Self-extinguishing* material (fabric or garment) is one that, when ignited at the bottom edge in a vertical position, does not continue to burn after the source of ignition is removed (Clark and Tesoro 1974).

4. *Thermally stable* material (fiber or polymer) is one that has a high decomposition temperature and is thus inherently flame resistant because of chemical structure (rather than through the presence of added flame retardants) (Clark and Tesoro 1974).

Thermally stable materials include fibers such as asbestos and glass fiber and certain synthetic fibers that have been developed for the aerospace industry, such as Kevlar® and Nomex® aramid. These could be called fireproof substances that will not burn. Glass fiber has many industrial uses and may be used to a limited extent in household textile products such as window shades or lamp shades. Thermally stable synthetic fibers have not been developed for general use but for specialized protective clothing for industrial and military uses. Not only are they expensive, but they lack the aesthetics that would make them useful in consumer products.

Some synthetic fibers are flame resistant. Many modacrylics offer adequate flame resistance at a moderate cost and have some use in carpets, curtains, and children's sleepwear. Vinyon fibers and Cordelan®, a biconstituent matrix fiber, also exhibit flame-resistant qualities. These last two fibers are not especially useful in carpets, as their resilience is not adequate, but they can be made into children's sleepwear.

If inherently flame-resistant or -retardant fibers are not used, flame-retardant textiles can be produced by either (1) incorporating a flame-retardant additive during or immediately after polymerization to produce modified manufactured fibers or (2) applying flame-retardant finishes to fiber, yarn, or fabric.

Polyester, acrylic, rayon, cellulose acetate, and triacetate are produced in flame-retardant fiber varieties. Polyester, polyester and cotton blends, cellulosics, and nylon are treated with finishes applied to fiber, yarn, or fabric. Wool is inherently moderately resistant to burning.

In addition to these so-called durable fire-retardant finishes, a solution of 30 percent boric acid and 70 percent borax can be used as a rinse for products. This rinse will provide temporary flame retardancy, but it produces a decrease in the softness and drapability of the fabric to which it is applied.

Factors Affecting Flame Retardance

Flame retardancy conferred through finishing, as opposed to that achieved by use of thermally stable and inherently flame-resistant materials, may be lost or diminished through normal use and care of products. Use of chlorine bleach, soaps, low-phosphate detergents, and some fabric softeners may result in loss of flame-retardant finish. Laundering in hard water will also diminish the effectiveness of the finish.

Blends of synthetic and natural fibers also create problems in relation to flame retardancy. The finishes that are effective on cellulose fibers, for example, may not be effective when those fibers are blended with polyesters. Polyester retardants may also be rendered ineffective when the polyester is combined with cotton.

Yet other hazards result when layers of different fibers are combined. A cotton dress worn over a nylon slip will burn very differently from a cotton dress worn over a rayon slip. Often the effect of these combinations is not fully understood. These problems and others regarding flammability have yet to be overcome.

Flammable Fabrics Act

Flammability of textiles is an important contributor to serious injuries and loss of life and property in fires. After a number of injuries and deaths due to highly flammable garments, the Flammable Fabrics Act of 1953 was passed. In this legislation the use and sale of *highly* flammable materials for clothing were banned. This law was amended in 1967 to extend coverage to (excluding some types of accessories) carpets, draperies, bedding, and upholstery.

The Flammable Fabrics Act is a federal law. Local and state laws and other regulations may impose restrictions on the use of flammable textile materials in public buildings, but there is no *national* regulation of such items as draperies or curtains for home or public places, other than that they may not be "highly flammable."

Since 1967 the regulations have been modified yet further. Originally only those materials that are *highly* flammable were prohibited, but now the manufacture of *all* flammable carpets, mattresses, and children's sleepwear (sizes 0 to 14) is banned.

In 1972 responsibility for administering and enforcing the law was given to the federal Consumer Product Safety Commission (CPSC). Products found to be in violation of the law may be confiscated and destroyed. Persons found guilty of "manufacturing for sale, offering for sale, or selling items that do not comply with the law" are subject to fines and/or imprisonment. The secretaries of the Commerce and Health and Human Services departments are required to sponsor research concerning fire-related hazards. When, on the basis of these investigations, the Secretary of Commerce determines that a new standard is needed, the National Institute of Standards and Technology (NIST) is given the responsibility of conducting research analyses and developing test methods.

Standards that products must meet are established in a two-step procedure. Notice is given by the commission that there may be a need for a new standard, and a proposed standard is set forth. Individuals are invited to offer their opinions about the proposals. Finally, the standard and test method(s) are announced together with effective dates.

Standards of Flammability

A publication setting forth the text of the law, rules and regulations, and detailed description of the standards that must be met is available from the CPSC. Specific test methods and apparatus to be used are described at length. Amendments to the Flammable Fabrics Act have expanded and refined the standards and testing procedures. At the present time there are standards for clothing textiles (Part 1610 of the Act), vinyl plastic film (Part 1611), children's sleepwear, sizes 0 to 6X (Part 1615) and sizes 7 to 14 (Part 1616), carpets and rugs (Parts 1630 and 1631), and mattresses and mattress pads (Part 1632.)

Clothing Textiles

The standard for this part of the law conforms to the standard set forth when the law was first enacted. It requires that "a piece of fabric placed in holder at a 45 degree angle and exposed to a flame for 1.0 second must not spread flame up the length of the sample in less than 3.5 seconds for smooth fabrics or 4.0 seconds for napped fabrics." (CPSC 1974, 1). Five specimens measuring 2 inches by 6 inches are required for each test. The time of flame spread is taken as an average of five specimens.

In 1983 the CPSC issued a rule that allows persons and firms performing testing of fabrics to use apparatus and procedures other than the ones specified in the standard, "provided that the apparatus or procedure is as stringent or more stringent than the apparatus and procedure prescribed by the Standard."

Carpets

Carpet standards (16 CFR Parts 1630 and 1631) require that manufacturers test samples of carpet before marketing. Eight samples are tested by the "methenamine pill" test. This pill, which simulates a source of flame such as a match, is placed in the center of a bone-dry sample of carpet and ignited. If the resulting flame does not extinguish itself before it spreads 3 inches in more than one of the samples, the carpet will not pass the test and must not be sold in the United States.

The pill test determines only surface ignition. It does not assess the contribution of carpets to the spreading of fires, the behavior of carpets in an environment created by a general fire, or the toxicity of the fumes produced.

Other test methods are used to assess the performance of carpets during fires. These test methods are controversial and are not accepted by all authorities as valid. They are not required by the Flammable Fabrics Act. The most widely used test of this type is called the Flooring Radiant Panel Test, which is said to simulate conditions of interior fires more effectively than other carpet tests. As a result, it is likely to be used by governmental and other regulatory agencies that require the more extensive product evaluation that carpeting installed in hospitals and facilities participating in Medicare and Medicaid programs must meet.

There are several exceptions to carpets covered under flammable fabrics legislation. One-of-a-kind carpets need not meet the standards. Handcraft items, oriental carpets, and the like are not covered by this law. Carpets that are 6 feet by 6 feet or smaller than 24 square feet that do not pass the pill test may be sold, provided that they are clearly labeled as being flammable.

Children's Sleepwear

Since 1972 children's sleepwear in sizes 0 to 6X (16 CFR Part 1615) has been regulated under the Flammable Fabrics Act. For the first year that the law was in effect, sleepwear that did not meet the standards established had to be labeled as flammable. After July 1973 flammable children's sleepwear was banned. Coverage under the law was extended in May 1975 to sleepwear sizes 7 to 14 (16 CFR Part 1616).

Standards for children's sleepwear sizes 0 to 6X and for sizes 7 to 14 are virtually the same.

The general requirements of the standard are described as follows: "Five conditioned specimens, 8.9 × 25.4 cm. (3.5 × 10 in.) are suspended one at a time vertically in holders in a prescribed cabinet and subjected to a standard flame along their bottom edge for a specified time under controlled conditions. The char length is measured." Test criteria that must be met are:

1. Average char length of five specimens shall not exceed 17.8 cm (7 in.).
2. No individual specimen shall have a char length of 25.4 cm (10 in.). (Code 1989, 517)

These standards must be met not only by new fabrics but also by those that have been laundered fifty times. All sleepwear must be labeled permanently with instructions as to the care required to maintain the flame-retardant finish. Both manufactured sleepwear items and fabrics intended for use in sleepwear must meet the standard. This includes fabrics and wearing apparel such as pajamas, nightgowns, robes, sleepers, and underwear that is sold in children's sleepwear departments. The CPSC is seeking to define "sleepwear" and "playwear" to eliminate confusion in the marketplace.

In August 1994 the CPSC voted to extend a stay of enforcement and continue a rule-making process that will most likely result in excluding sleepwear for children under six months of age from the standard. The rationale for this change is that infants six months or younger do not have sufficient mobility to come close to sources of ignition. The Commission took the same action on exempting tight-fitting children's sleepwear because "tight-fitting garments can reduce the amount of trapped air needed for combustion, reduce the possibility of contact with a flame, and shorten the reaction time of the wearer" (CPSC 1994).

Mattresses and Pads

After December 1973 it became illegal for manufacturers to make mattresses and mattress pads that are combustible. The flammability of mattresses is tested using lighted cigarettes, which were selected as a source of ignition because statistics showed that the greatest number of mattress fires were caused by smoking in bed.

This testing procedure requires that nine cigarettes be placed at various points on the mattress and another nine cigarettes between two sheets on the mattress. To pass the standard (16 CFR Part 1632), the char length on the mattress surface may not be more than 2 inches in any direction from any cigarette. The legislation applies to mattress ticking filled with "any resilient material intended or promoted for sleeping upon" and includes mattress pads. Pillows, box springs, and upholstered furniture are excluded.

Other Standards

Consideration has been given to extending regulations to include other products.

Upholstered Furniture

In November 1978 the CPSC considered a draft of a mandatory standard for flammability of upholstered furniture. In response to this move by the CPSC, the Upholstered Furniture Action Council (UFAC), a trade organization for the furniture industry, proposed that a voluntary plan devised by the industry be utilized. The industry plan, as it evolved, included a fabric rating system, criteria for construction of furnishings, a labeling plan, and compliance procedures.

The CPSC gave the industry an opportunity to try the voluntary plan. The rating system grouped all upholstery fabrics into one of two classes, based on fiber content. Fabrics containing at least 50 percent of thermoplastic fibers, which are less likely to ignite, are placed in Class I; all other fabrics are placed in Class II. Class II fabrics can be upgraded to Class I if they can pass a cigarette ignition test. Cigarettes are responsible for many of the fires that start in upholstered furniture.

Furthermore, various components of furniture such as welting, filling and padding, decking materials, and substances placed as a barrier between Class II fabrics and the cushion filling must be able to withstand cigarette ignition tests. Only furniture meeting the Class I standards could carry the UFAC approval label.

Compliance was monitored through the UFAC by periodic inspections. The Commission considered that the voluntary standard provided adequate protection and did not impose a mandatory standard for furniture.

On May 12, 1994, following a petition by the National Association of State Fire Marshals requesting mandatory standards to reduce the risk of upholstered furniture fires caused by cigarettes and small open flames, the CPSC voted to take the first steps required in the procedures that could lead to making a ruling. At the present time the Commission is collecting information on the effectiveness of and industry compliance with the existing voluntary standard. Whether the CPSC will eventually enact mandatory standards will depend on their findings in this and subsequent steps in the regulatory process.

Nightwear for the Elderly

As a group the elderly, like children, are considered to be at greater risk of injury from flammable nightwear than other age groups. Voluntary standards, similar to those used for upholstery, had been proposed. The Intimate Apparel Council (IAC) of the

American Apparel Manufacturers Association submitted a counterproposal that the CPSC mandate that all adult sleepwear carry a label warning consumers to keep garments away from open flame or other ignition sources (CPSC 1989). It was the IAC's position that such labeling would be a less onerous burden on the industry than classification of adult nightwear in terms of their flammability hazard. Such classifications would require extensive testing of products. Furthermore, they felt, it would be easier to understand than a label conveying test results. Industry representatives also recommended a program of education of consumers about flammability hazards associated with sleepwear.

After consideration of various alternative proposals, the Commission rejected both voluntary standards proposed by Commission staff and the mandatory labeling proposal of the IAC. Instead, the Commission recommended that the voluntary education proposals made by the industry be pursued (ATMI 1990, 1).

Flammability Testing

Testing for flammability is required under the Flammable Fabrics Act. The requirements of that legislation and the performance standards that materials are required to meet are set forth by the CPSC in its publications. In addition to the tests required by law, a wide variety of additional tests for flammability can be conducted. (See Figure 21.5.)

Researchers have devised a number of techniques to study flammability. Most of these devices require test samples of considerable size or even whole garments. They are intended to provide more extensive information about the effects of burning fabrics.

DuPont, Eastman Kodak, and the University of Minnesota have developed "thermal" manikins with heat sensors located in various parts of the figure. Tests performed using these figures can determine not only the combustibility of the fabric being tested but also the location of hot spots and data about the transfer of heat.

Another device is called the *mushroom tester*, or the MAFT. The device consists of a hollow cylindrical tube. A circular platform is mounted at the top of the tube. The sample to be tested is wrapped around the platform and hangs down (much as a skirt would hang from a person's waist). An air space is formed between the sample and the vertical tube. Temperature sensors are located in the tube and in the platform, and the device measures time of ignition and transfer of heat from the burning fabric.

Consumer Reaction

Consumer and research interest in fabric flammability reached its peak in the ten-year period beginning in the late 1960s. In 1977, however, TRIS, one of the chemicals used in some finishes given to polyester, acetate, and triacetate fabrics, was banned after it was shown to have possibly mutagenic effects. TRIS-treated fabrics and garments were withdrawn from the market. Much of the public quickly became suspicious of fire-retardant treatments in general. As a result, interest in fire retardancy has waned. In spite of the obvious hazards from textile combustibility to persons in certain high-risk groups such as the elderly, the disabled, and cigarette smokers, there is little likelihood of increased regulation of textiles in regard to flammability at the present time.

Figure 21.5

Flammability tester used to test vertically oriented textile products, in this case a plush child's toy. The specimen is mounted on the rectangular frame at the center of the upright section of the tester. Ignition is from the small nozzle just below the foot of the toy. Photograph courtesy of James H. Heal & Company, Ltd.

Antistatic Finishes

Synthetic fibers, being poor conductors of electricity, tend to build up static electric charges. Electricity causes garments to cling or to build up charges that are dissipated through unpleasant, though mild, electric shocks when the wearer touches a conductor such as a metal doorknob or another person's hand.

Some finishes have been developed that attempt to decrease static buildup. However, these finishes tend to have limited effectiveness, largely because they are gradually lost during laundering. The antistatic finishes work on either of two principles: either they coat the surface of the fiber with a more conductive substance, or they attract to the fiber small amounts of moisture that increase its conductivity.

More successful cutdown in static buildup of synthetics is achieved through the modification of the polymer before extrusion. These finishes, which are permanent, incorporate compounds in the fiber structure that increase the moisture absorbency, which, in turn, increases conductivity.

Another approach is to use special, high performance antistatic fibers. Metal, metallized, and bicomponent fibers containing metal or carbon are among those used. A small proportion of these fibers is blended with conventional synthetic fibers. Being more conductive, they serve to dissipate the static charges.

Antistatic sprays can be purchased for home use. Fabric softeners applied in the final rinse during laundering will also provide some reduction in static buildup.

Special-Purpose Finishes

A number of finishes have been developed to overcome problems of individual fibers or to meet a particular need. Such finishes are applied on a fairly limited basis to particular fibers, yarns, or fabrics, many of which are intended for rather specialized uses.

Finishes That Increase Absorbency

Cellulosic fibers that are being used for diapers, towels, or other items in which absorbency is important may have ammonium compounds applied to them. These compounds increase the absorbency of the fabrics somewhat.

Increasing the absorbency of synthetic fibers has had some success. Antistatic finishes and soil-releasing finishes do make them more hydrophilic. Surface hydrolysis of polyester using sodium hydroxide can also increase absorbency, although this process is not used on a large scale.

Antislip Finishes

Smooth, filament yarns may have a tendency to slide against one another, creating flawed areas in a fabric or problems of seam slippage. This is known as yarn *slippage*. Resins coated on the surface of these fabrics will keep the yarns in place, as the resin holds yarns together at the points where the yarns interlace. Resin antislip finishes are durable.

Other antislip finishes can be created by coating silica compounds on fabrics. However, these are only temporary finishes.

Antimicrobial Finishes

Antimildew and Antirot Finishes

Mildew, a fungus or mold, is a whitish growth that affects certain textile fibers when they are stored in a damp condition in a warm place. This growth damages the fiber and causes serious staining. Cellulosic fibers are most susceptible to mildew. Protein fibers are less likely to be attacked.

The best protection against mildew is to make certain that the fabrics are dry and clean when stored and that they do not become damp during storage. Mildew is an especially serious problem in warm, humid climates. Mildew weakens fabrics, and home treatments to remove mildew stains may be degrading to them as well.

Rotting is an acute problem with bast fibers, such as jute and hemp, when they are used for bags, ropes, and other materials that are exposed for long periods to water, damp soil, or wet floors. Rot- and mildew-resistant fabrics can be made by treating the fabrics with antiseptic substances. Since copper has bactericidal power, copper solutions may be used to confer rot resistance to fabrics. A variety of other chemical substances (among them phenol, formaldehyde, and pentachlorophenol) that are not harmful to the fabric and inhibit the growth of microorganisms are also used.

Experimentation with melamine resin finishes for crease resistance revealed that these finishes retarded mildew and rotting. Home processes can be used to guard against mildew. An after-rinse with boric acid will retard the formation of mildew.

Antibacterial Finishes

Chemical substances that inhibit the growth of bacteria are also used to finish goods that will be used in health care products, apparel, home furnishings, or fabrics used in the hotel/restaurant industry. These can be metal compounds that are toxic to bacteria or organic substances such as phenols and anilides.

Although these finishes are classified as either renewable or durable, even so-called durable finishes are removed gradually during laundering. Renewable finishes can be replaced during laundering.

Certain specific organic ammonium compounds are known to combat diaper rash. Many diaper services routinely apply this finish to the diapers that they launder. Antimicrobial finishes are being applied to nonwoven fabrics used in surgical and medical products such as instrument packs, surgical packs, and surgical draping fabrics.

Mothproofing Finishes

Wool and other animal hair fibers are attacked by the larvae of the clothes moth. Silk is not attacked by moths as it lacks cystine, a sulfur-containing amino acid moths seem to require.

Finishes to prevent moth damage operate according to one of two basic principles. Either the finish is a substance (an insecticide) that is poisonous to the moth larvae, or the finish alters the fiber in some way that makes the wool unpalatable to moth larvae, thereby starving the grubs.

The insecticide finishes may be applied during manufacture or during dry cleaning. Some of these finishes are durable, whereas others must be renewed with each cleaning.

The second type of finish effects a change in the chemical structure of the fiber. Through chemical treatment, the disulfide cross-linkages, which are attacked by the moth larvae, are changed and are replaced by longer linkages that the moths cannot digest. These finishes are permanent.

Temperature-Adaptable Finishes

Temperature-adaptable fabrics are finished with polyethylene glycol (PEG) polymers that are cross-linked on the fabric. The polymer is applied along with a methylol agent such as DMDHEU to cross-link the PEG. The result is a network polymer that is insolubilized on the surface of the fibers. The cross-linked polymer absorbs and holds heat energy at high temperature and then releases the stored energy under cool conditions. The finish, marketed under the name Polytherm® is durable to wear and laundering.

Not only do these finishes help to warm or cool the body, they also increase the moisture absorbency of fabrics, thereby further enhancing comfort. Other improved properties are resistance to static, wrinkling, abrasion, pilling, and soil. Temperature-adaptable finishes have been used on T-shirts, underwear, socks, activewear, and biomedical products.

Heat-Reflectant Finishes

An increased level of insulation can be provided in garments and draperies by the addition of heat-reflectant finishes. Most of these products are treated with a spray coating of metal and resinous substances. The heat-reflectant material is sprayed onto the surface of a closely woven fabric. The finish is designed to keep heat either on one side or the other of the fabric. The finish is effective only with radiated heat.

Lining fabrics are usually constructed so that the finish is applied to the inside of the fabric. The finish reflects the body heat back toward the wearer, thus providing added warmth. In protective clothing to be worn under hot conditions, the finish is worn to the outside to deflect heat away from the body. Draperies may also be treated to provide greater insulation for homes. Treated draperies placed inside windows may serve to keep heat inside the home or to reflect heat outward, preventing it from warming the house.

Some of the processes designed to produce heat reflectance use aluminum in the finish, as it provides excellent reflectancy. The trade name for this process is Milium®.

A variant of this principle is utilized in fabrics coated or laminated with a thin layer of aluminum, foams, resins, or synthetic rubber.

Light-Reflectant Finishes

Light-reflectant finishes are created by the application of microscopic reflective beads to the surface of a fabric. The increased number of persons who jog or ride bicycles after dark is probably responsible for the application of this finish to a variety of garments for sports and to other items such as backpacks. A reflective finish called Scotchlite® is produced by the 3M Company. The manufacturer notes that the finish does not alter the color or appearance of the garment by day, but after dark the fabric "lights up" when directly in the path of the lights of an oncoming vehicle (Figure 21.6).

Light-Resistant Finishes

Many textile fabrics are deteriorated by exposure to sunlight, so attempts have been made to protect fabrics from light damage. Of the rays in the spectrum of the sun, the ultraviolet are the most destructive of fibers. Although antilight finishes have yet to be perfected, those that are being tried either coat the fabric or impregnate the fibers with materials that absorb ultraviolet rays but are not themselves damaged by or removed by exposure to these rays. Such finishes are particularly important in olefin fabrics, which are degraded by sunlight unless ultraviolet stabilizers are added. Such additives to olefin fibers are permanent and are not lost during usage.

Synthetics that have been delustered with titanium dioxide are especially subject to damage from sunlight. This chemical apparently accelerates damage to the fiber and fading of dyes. The addition of certain chemical salts to the melt solution before spinning can ameliorate this problem.

The relationship between exposure to the ultraviolet light of the sun and skin cancer is well known. Many people assume that fabrics prevent exposure to any part of the body that is covered; however, research shows that fabrics do allow passage of ultraviolet light. Knitted fabrics, which usually have a more open structure, generally allow more ultraviolet light through than woven fabrics; lightweight summer fabrics allow more than heavier fabrics with more opaque yarns.

Figure 21.6

Runner wears garments with Scotchlite® light reflective finish. At night, light is reflected from headlight beams to alert motorists to the presence of the wearer. Photographs courtesy of 3M Company.

Ultraviolet protection is now being built into fibers and fabrics. Most of the techniques are proprietary processes, so details of how the protection is provided are limited. Kuraray, a Japanese firm, produces Esmo®, a polyester staple fiber to which powered ceramics have been added to absorb and reflect ultraviolet rays. A similar fiber called Aloft® is produced by Toray, and other Japanese firms produce fabrics that are given special protective finishes (Development 1992).

Australian researchers have developed a chemical finish called Rayosun® that is said to be washfast, colorfast, and lightfast. The finishing material contains a "two-part molecule," one part of which absorbs ultraviolet rays while the other reacts with the fabric, thereby making this a finish that "will bond with the fibre for the life of the garment" (Sun-proof clothing 1993, 72).

Other Specialty Finishes

Several additional finishes produce special effects. In one, a powdered material is applied to fabrics to decrease the loss of body heat. In another, the finishing material contains microencapsulated fragrances that gradually release perfumed oils as the fabric is abraded during wear.

Textile Tests Evaluating Finishes

It is sometimes desirable to determine whether special finishes have been applied to textiles. The presence of some finishes, for example, would interfere with textile recycling. The identification of such finishes is difficult. Except for mechanical finishes that can easily be identified by eye (such as embossing and napping), the determination of chemical finishes may require extensive laboratory procedures. AATCC Test Method 94-1987 outlines a variety of tests for the identification of textile finishes.

Researchers may use testing methods to make comparisons between control samples of unfinished fabrics and fabrics with finishes. Tear and breaking strength tests and abrasion tests, for example, may be used to ascertain whether finishes used to improve wrinkle recovery will affect the durability of fabrics.

A number of tests have been devised to determine the effectiveness of finishes. These tests cover such areas as durability of applied designs and finishes to dry cleaning, oil repellency, soil release, water resistance and repellency, and weather resistance. Specific instructions for testing in these and other areas are included in the AATCC's *Technical Manual* and in the *Book of ASTM Standards.*

Summary

Whereas the finishes discussed in chapter 20 were compared with "cosmetics," used to enhance the physical properties of fabrics, the finishes discussed in this chapter are designed to modify the actual behavioral properties of textiles. Although finishes may change the appearance, texture, and hand of a fabric, they do so for more than cosmetic reasons. Finishes that modify, or in some way improve, inherent fiber properties may result in an increase in price and/or a change in care requirements, but consumers have generally been receptive to the improvements and are willing to pay for them. But the costs of some finishes cannot be measured only by a price increase on the product. Durable press finishes do result in shorter wear life and may result in more frequent replacement of garments, and there are other kinds of trade-offs involved. For example, proper laundering of some fire-retardant products requires the use of phosphate-containing detergents. Phosphates have been cited as a cause of water pollution. The choice is between one kind of hazard and another. There are no easy answers and no simple solutions.

References

ASTM. 1994. *Compilation of ASTM standard definitions.* Philadelphia: American Society for Testing and Materials.

ATMI. 1990. *Textile Trends* [newsletter of American Textile Manufacturers Institute] 38 (5).

Clark, J. E., and G. Tesoro. 1974. Textile flammability. Paper presented to the American Chemical Society's State of the Art Symposium on Man-made Fibers, held in Washington, D.C., June.

Code of Federal Regulations. 1989. 16 CFR, Chapter 11, January 1.

CPSC. 1974. *Fact sheet.* Washington, D.C.: Consumer Product Safety Commission, June.

CPSC. 1989. U.S. Consumer Product Safety Commission memorandum, 13 July.

CPSC. 1994. CPSC votes to continue rulemaking on children's sleepwear. *News from CPSC*, 3 August.

Development of new fibers with sophisticated functions as high added-value products. 1992. *Knitting International* 99 (June): 42.

Skieller, E. 1989. Eliminating shrinkage problems in knitted cotton fabrics. *American Dyestuff Reporter* 90 (September): 30.

Sun-proof clothing. 1993. *Textiles* 22 (3): 6.

Sympatex: Breathable fabrics without pores. 1988. *America's Textiles International* 17 (November): 72.

Review Questions

1. Explain the difference between relaxation shrinkage, progressive shrinkage, and consolidation shrinkage.
2. Identify and describe the ways that fabrics can be preshrunk without being made wet. Why is it not desirable to wet or launder fabrics to prevent shrinkage?
3. How is the largest quantity of fabric given durable press finishes? Explain the chemical changes that take place within the fibers, and identify other properties that may be affected.
4. What is the difference between stain-repellent and soil-releasing finishes? Explain how each is achieved.
5. What is the difference between a fabric that is waterproof and one that is water repellent? What is the difference between a fabric that is waterproof and one that is waterproof and breathable? How is breathability achieved?
6. Which generic fibers are flame resistant? How can other fibers or fabrics that are not flame resistant be made safer?
7. What kinds of products are subject to strict regulation under the Flammable Fabrics Act and must meet specified standards? What kinds of products are encouraged to meet voluntary standards?
8. Identify five or more finishes that have been developed to improve specific properties of fibers that consumers find troublesome. Explain which properties the finish changes and how.
9. Identify two finishes that might be described as providing additional safety or protection to consumers who wear apparel made from these products. How do these finishes function?

Recommended Readings

Abend, J. 1994. Wrinkle resistant, ironing out the process. *Bobbin* 35 (July): 30.

Andrews, B. A. K. 1992. Safe, comfortable, durable press cottons: A natural progression for a natural fiber. *Textile Chemist and Colorist* 24 (November): 17.

Brown, R. O. 1994. Enhancing the performance of wrinkle resistant cotton garments. *American Dyestuff Reporter* 83 (September): 106.

Cook, F. L. 1994. Less is more in applying chemicals to textiles. *Textile World* 144 (January): 59–65.

De Boos, A. G. 1989. Finishing wool fabrics to improve their end-use performance. *Textile Progress* 20 (2).

Dockery, A. 1993. New process lets polyester breathe. *America's Textiles International* 22 (October): K/A 12.

Ferguson, C. 1982. Hydrophilic finishes for polyester: Durability and processing advantages. *American Dyestuff Reporter* 71 (June): 43.

Flame retardant fibers for interior use. 1990. *JTN,* no. 426 (May): 43.

Hamlyn, P. F. 1990. Talking rot . . . and mildew. *Textiles* 19 (2): 46.

Holme, I. 1993. New developments in the chemical finishing of textiles. *Journal of the Textile Institute* 84 (4): 520.

Huang, X. X., Y. K. Kamath, and H.-D. Weigmann. 1993. Photodegradation and the loss of stain resistance of stain blocker treated nylon. *Textile Chemist and Colorist* 25 (November): 293.

Mansfield, R. G. 1994. Fighting wrinkles is big business. *America's Textiles International* 23 (May): K/A 12.

McNamara, M. 1994. Makers say U.S. made rayon quite safe. *Women's Wear Daily* 168 (23 August): 13.

North, B. F. 1991. Reactants for durable press textiles: The formaldehyde dilemma. *Textile Chemist and Colorist* 23 (October): 21–22.

Pollack, A. 1993. A dream unfolds for cotton shirts. *New York Times,* 29 December, D1.

Pratt, H. T. 1994. Some milestones in the history of bleaching. *Textile Chemist and Colorist* 26 (11): 21–27.

Rudie, R. 1993. Permanent press makes a smooth comeback. *Bobbin* 34 (May): 66.

Sabia, A. J. 1994. Use of silicones to enhance the aesthetic and functional properties of microfibers. *Textile Chemist and Colorist* 144 (August): 13–16.

Sun-protective children's wear? 1994. *Canadian Apparel Manufacturer* 18 (March/April): 18.

Townsend, M. W. 1983. Moths and wool. *Textiles* 12 (Spring): 9.

CHAPTER 22

ADDING COLOR TO TEXTILES

Most objects made by human beings are decorated in some way. Textiles are no exception. The decoration of textiles may be achieved through varying the construction of the fabric, by adding color through dyeing, or by applying color in patterns by printing.

Even the earliest fabrics excavated by archeologists show evidence of ornamentation, through the use of natural fibers of contrasting colors or by embroidery or dyes. Cave paintings made by prehistoric peoples of at least twenty-five thousand years ago clearly demonstrate that these people knew how to make pigment colors from natural materials. Pottery from many cultures was painted with designs. Probably the first addition of color to fabrics was made by painting designs on the cloth.

Dyeing

Natural Dyestuffs

The paints used on pottery or stone were not always serviceable on fabrics, but certain substances did have a particular affinity for cloth. These dyestuffs came from a wide variety of animal, vegetable, and mineral matter. The difficulty with most of the natural dyestuffs was that they lacked colorfastness. As a result, those dyes that proved to have excellent colorfastness became important items of international trade.

Few of these early dyes could be relied on to produce strong colors on all fibers. The coloring of fibers results from the chemical or other reaction of the functional groups within the fibers and those within the dyestuff. The varying chemical composition or structure of the natural fibers caused each to react differently with the chemicals in each of the dyestuffs then available. The treatment of the fabrics with certain natural acids or oxides did, however, improve their colorfastness. These substances, called *mordants,* react both with the dyestuff and the fiber to form a *colored lake,* an insoluble compound, thereby "fixing" the color within and on the fiber. The effect of mordants probably was discovered accidentally when it was realized that washing undyed fabrics in the water of some streams (those high in certain metallic compounds) resulted in their taking and holding colors better.

Some mordants were more effective on animal fibers such as silk and wool; others were preferable for cotton and linen. Those who worked in the dyer's trades developed skill in using mordants to make fabrics of fairly good colorfastness, although it was not possible to obtain consistently excellent colorfastness until after the invention of synthetic dyes in the nineteenth century.

There were many sources of natural dyes. Vegetable dyes could be made from flowers, leaves, berries, barks, roots, grasses, weeds, vines, and lichens. The most famous of the traditional dyes made from plants included woad, indigo, madder, fustic, logwood, cutch, and safflower. The woad plant was cultivated in European villages for its blue color made from the bark of the plant. Its production continued from Roman times until the end of the Middle Ages, when woad was supplanted by indigo, a blue dye imported from India. The compound in the woad plant that creates the blue color is present in much greater concentrations in indigo. Madder was a source of reds, but it also had the peculiar quality of producing several different colors or color intensities when it was employed in combination with different mordants. The chemical reaction of the metallic salts in the various mordants with the chemical compound in madder resulted in colors that ranged from yellow to rose to red. Fustic for yellow, logwood and cutch for browns, and safflower for red were other widely known dyes. By combining the primary colors of red, blue, and yellow, it was possible to create additional colors in the green, purple, and orange ranges. A good, fast, dark black was exceedingly difficult to achieve.

Some iron oxides were employed, but in general mineral colors were less often used than were plant or animal substances. Animal sources provided some of the most effective dyestuffs. Kermes, a brilliant scarlet dyestuff, was obtained in ancient times from the bodies of small insects that lived in oak trees. This dye was replaced by cochineal from small insects that are native to South America and that had been used by the Indians as a dyestuff for many centuries. This cochineal bug, which became a major item of trade between the New and Old Worlds, produced a vivid red of excellent fastness.

The color purple has been associated with royalty for centuries. The origins of this association are based on the production of Tyrian purple, a color made from the juice secreted by a small shellfish. The technique for making the dye was known as early as 1000 B.C. and required a lengthy and complex series of steps. First, the dye was "milked" from the shellfish. This white liquid, as it oxidized, turned from milky white to green, to red, to deep purple. Careful control of the color range could be used to produce a wide range of red-purple colors, the most desirable being a deep, rich red-purple. The process was time consuming, difficult, and the supply of the dye limited. Fabrics dyed with Tyrian purple were very costly and therefore available only to the rich and, in particular, to the nobility. Royalty eventually gained a monopoly on the color, and so it has come to be known as "royal purple" (Gerhard 1964).

Synthetic Dyes

William Perkin, an English chemist, discovered that a coal tar derivative, *aniline,* colored white silk. After further experimentation, Perkin was able to make a dyestuff that had potential commercial application. It was a reddish-purple in color, called mauve.

Perkin's discovery in 1856 stimulated additional research with other coal tar derivatives and related compounds, and the synthesis of a wide range of manufactured dyestuffs resulted. Gradually, an enormous range of synthetic dyes made from many chemical substances was developed. These have almost completely replaced natural dyes for commercial production.

The selection of dyestuffs for coloring fabrics is a decision requiring the attention not only of the highly trained dye technician but also of designers, stylists, and business managers who are knowledgeable about current fashion trends. Although some types of dyed fabrics can be bleached and redyed another color, or designs printed over plain-colored fabrics, dyeing a fabric to an unpopular color may spell financial disaster for a manufacturer of piece goods.

In addition, the choice of hue is only the first of many decisions about adding color to fabrics. It must be decided at what point the color will be added and the type of dyestuff that will be used.

Each fiber reacts differently to dyestuffs; therefore, the use of an appropriate dye is crucial to colorfastness. Since loss of color in use is a major source of consumer dissatisfaction, reputable manufacturers must choose dyes carefully.

Color is one of these areas in which the chemistry of textiles is particularly important. The combination of fibers with dyestuffs may involve not only physical but also chemical reactions.

Dyestuffs and Colorfastness

The science of dyeing is highly complex, and the mechanisms of dyeing are not completely understood. This discussion is necessarily superficial and does not provide an in-depth exploration of the subject. For additional background, readers may consult the sources listed at the end of the chapter.

To be usable in coloring fabrics, dyes and pigments must have these properties: they must be highly colored, and they must yield goods with resistance to color change or loss in use and care. This latter quality is known as *colorfastness.* Furthermore, dyes must be soluble or capable of being made soluble in the medium in which they are applied, or they must themselves be molecularly dispersible into the fibers. The medium most often used for dyes that require a solvent is water. Dyes derive their color from the conjugated double bonds in their molecular structure.

The rate of dyeing depends on three factors. The first, the rate of migration of dye onto the fiber surface, is assisted by the agitation of the dyebath. The second, the rate of dye penetration into the fiber, is fairly rapid in most cases; and the third, the rate of diffusion within the fiber itself, varies greatly from one type of fiber to another but increases with the temperature of dyeing.

Exhaustion is the amount of transfer of dye from the bath into the fiber. It is possible for all the dye to be removed from the bath and for the dyebath to be clear at the end of the process. Some dye classes exhaust better than others. *Leveling* is the uniformity of shade throughout the textile. Uneven leveling will result in a streaked appearance of the cloth. Dyes that have been absorbed by fibers may migrate back to the surface when the textile is dried, resulting in uneven dyeing.

A number of chemical reagents or auxiliaries are used in the dyeing process. These chemical auxiliaries act in a variety of ways, ranging from softening water or assisting with dye leveling to increasing dye solubility or the rate of penetration into the fiber. Substances that increase the acceptance of the dyestuff are called mordants. The temperature of the dyebath may also have an effect on the receptivity of the fiber to the dyestuff, although the optimum temperature will differ not only with the type of dye but also with the kind of fiber being dyed.

Once the dye has entered the amorphous regions of fiber, it must be retained within the fiber not only during the dyeing but also when fabrics are laundered or dry-cleaned during use. Several factors make for dye retention. In general, the number of chemically reactive sites in the fiber is the most crucial element in dyeability. Dyes may be physically bound to fibers by forces such as hydrogen bonding or ionic forces. Ionic forces are the attraction between positively and negatively charged ions, one on the dye, the other on the fiber. The chemical structure of dyestuff and fiber may allow the formation of covalent chemical bonds between fiber and dye. Dyes may be carried in a temporary solvent that, when removed, leaves the dye stranded within the fiber. Individual dye molecules may aggregate.

Colorfastness

A fabric that retains its color during care and use is said to be *colorfast*. Fastness of dyestuffs is related to the chemical and physical forces holding the dye within the fiber, the stability of the combination of dye and fiber to environmental factors, and the location of the dye within the fiber. Small aggregates of dyestuff molecules distributed evenly throughout the fiber make for a more satisfactory result than do surface applications of color.

Fabrics may be more or less colorfast to a variety of different substances or conditions. The importance of colorfastness depends on the use of the fabric. Colorfastness to laundering is, of course, important in those garments and household textiles that must undergo frequent laundering. Some colors are not fast to laundering but are fast to dry cleaning, or vice versa.

Perspiration may cause some color change and/or color transfer, and many colors are not fast to light. Ascertaining the colorfastness to sunlight of curtains, draperies, carpets, or other items that have prolonged exposure to sunlight may be important in evaluating the usefulness of fabrics for these items. Some colors may be lost or diminished by heat.

Some dyes tend to *crock,* or rub off on fabrics or other materials with which they come in contact. Others will *bleed* into water during laundering and may be picked up by lighter-colored fabrics. Chlorine bleaches will remove color from most dyed fabrics, but some types of dyestuff are more sensitive than others to the action of chlorine bleaches.

Even dyes that belong to the same class of dyestuffs can have differing degrees of colorfastness to the same condition, so that the consumer has no real guarantee of color permanence unless a label specifies that a particular fabric is colorfast. Dye performance labeling is not required by any form of legislation or regulation. Some manufacturers do, however, include colorfastness information on labels. Such labels will generally describe the conditions under which the fabric is colorfast, such as "colorfast to laundering, but not to chlorine bleaching" or "colorfast to sunlight." A few terms may be found on labels that carry an assurance of colorfastness, such as trademarks that have been applied to spun-dyed synthetic fibers. The colorfastness of one class of dyes, the vat dyes, is so consistently good for laundering that the term "vat dyed" on labels has come to be accepted as an assurance of good color-fastness.

Testing for Colorfastness

The colorfastness of fabrics to a variety of substances and conditions can be measured by the use of specific testing methods and machinery. The details of these test methods are described in the *Technical Manual* published by AATCC.

Color change is ascertained by keeping a *control,* an untreated sample of the fabric being tested. Tested samples are then checked against the original. A scale called the *Gray Scale,* established by AATCC, makes it possible to determine more precisely the degree of color change that has taken place. Samples of both treated and control samples are compared under standard lighting conditions, and the standard scales and numerical ratings are applied. (See Figure 22.1.) Although visual evaluation can yield reasonably consistent results, computerized color evaluation instruments are more accurate, and visual evaluations are being superseded by electronic measurement.

Atmospheric conditions may result in color loss in some fabrics. Fume fading, or gas fading—loss of color caused by exposure to acidic atmospheric gases (specifically oxides of nitrogen) and to ozone—can be measured in a device called a *gas fading chamber.* Fabrics in this enclosed chamber are exposed to these gases, and their color loss is determined.

Fading from exposure to sunlight is measured in a machine that simulates, at an accelerated rate, the fading action of the sun. Samples can be exposed for varying periods of time and tested samples compared to control samples. Among the machines most often used for such tests are the Fade-Ometer and the Weather-Ometer.

Both wet and dry crocking can be tested on a device called a Crockmeter that rubs the test sample across a white fabric sample. Color transfer from the test sample to the white sample indicates that the test sample is subject to crocking. (See Figure 22.2.)

Colorfastness to laundering and dry cleaning are done in machines such as the Launder-Ometer. Similar procedures are used to ascertain fastness to dry cleaning. Instead of water and detergent, dry-cleaning solvents are used. Test specimens are

Figure 22.1

MacBeth Color Matching Booth for evaluation of color change. Photograph by Prather Warren, LSU Public Relations.

examined for color loss. If samples of a special cloth containing yarns made of a number of different fibers are included along with test specimens, it is possible to determine whether other fabrics are likely to pick up color from the tested fabric during laundering or dry cleaning.

A device called the AATCC Perspiration Tester evaluates not only colorfastness to perspiration but also to chlorinated water (as in swimming pools), seawater, water spotting, and the like. The fabric sample is soaked in one of these liquids and then subjected to heat and pressure. Up to twenty specimens can be tested simultaneously. (See Figure 22.3.)

Types of Dyeing

Color may be added to fabric at any one of four steps in its processing. Color can be added to manufactured fibers before the fiber is extruded, or dyes can be applied to fibers, to yarns, or to constructed fabrics or finished products.

Addition of Color Before Extrusion

When color is added to manufactured fibers before they are extruded, the fibers are known as *spun-dyed, solution-dyed* or *dope-dyed* fibers. Pigment is dispersed throughout the liquid fiber solution. When the fiber is extruded, it carries the coloring material as an integral part of the fiber.

This "locked-in" color is extremely fast to laundering (i.e., it will not diminish); however, such colors can be sensitive to light and bleaching or may fade. The range of colors in which solution dyeing is done is rather limited for economic reasons. The fiber manufacturer must produce substantial quantities of fiber to justify the expense of adding an extra step during the manufacturing process. Furthermore, fiber production takes place well in advance of the time when fabrics reach the market. Fash-

Figure 22.3

AATCC Perspiration Tester
for testing colorfastness to
perspiration and to chlorinated
pool, sea, and distilled water.
Up to twenty specimens can
be tested simultaneously.
Photograph courtesy of Atlas
Electric Devices Co.

ion color trends may change fairly rapidly, so that, by the time a spun-dyed fabric
reaches the market, the color may be out of fashion and not salable. For this reason,
spun-dyed fabrics are generally produced in basic colors.

Spun dyeing is used on acetate to prevent gas fading. Gas fumes in the air may
turn some blue or green dyes used for acetate to pink or brown.

Addition of Color to Fibers

When color is added at the fiber state, this process is known as *fiber dyeing* or *stock
dyeing.*

Loose (usually staple) fibers are immersed in a dyebath, dyeing takes place, and
the fibers are dried. This is a relatively expensive type of dyeing because it takes longer
to dye the fibers than it would to dye a comparable quantity of yarn or fabric and
because it costs more to reopen the containers that hold the fibers when dyeing is
complete. Dye penetration into the fiber is high, however, and fibers tend to take up
the dye evenly.

Stock-dyed fibers are most often used in tweed or heather effect materials in
which delicate shadings of color are produced by combining fibers of varying colors
(Figure 22.4). The yarns in Harris Tweed fabrics are a distinctive example of fiber

22.4

Tweed effect created by using filling yarns made from stock-dyed fibers.

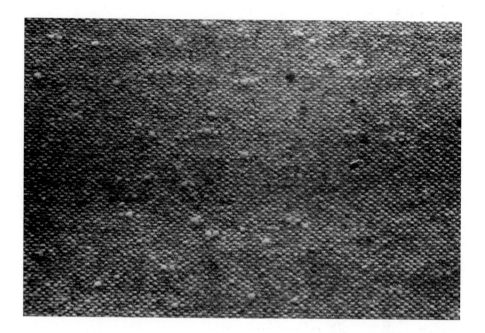

dyeing. Fiber-dyed fabrics can be identified by untwisting the yarns to see whether the yarn is made up of a variety of different colored fibers. In solid-colored yarns untwisted stock-dyed fibers will be uniform in color, with no darker or lighter areas.

Fibers for worsted fabrics are sometimes made into a sliver before they are dyed. This variation of fiber dyeing is known as *top dyeing*. By dyeing the fibers after they have been combed, the manufacturer avoids the wasteful step of coloring the short fibers that would be removed in the combing process.

Yarn Dyeing

If color has not been added either to the polymer or the fiber, it can be applied to the yarns before they are made into fabrics. Usually yarns are dyed to one solid color, but in a variant of the technique called *space dyeing,* yarns may be dyed in such a way that color-and-white or multicolored effects are formed along the length of the yarn.

Many types of fabrics utilize yarn of differing colors to achieve a particular design. Stripes in which contrasting sections of color alternate in the length or crosswise direction, chambrays in which one color is used in one direction and another color is used in the other direction, complex dobby or jacquard weaves, and plaids may all require yarns to which color has already been added.

Yarns may be dyed in skeins, in packages, or on beams. (See Figure 22.5.) Special dyeing equipment is required for each of these processes. In skein dyeing, large, loosely wound skeins of yarn are placed in a vat for dyeing. In package dyeing, the yarn is wound onto a number of perforated tubes or springs. The dye is circulated around and through the tubes to assure that the yarns have maximum contact with the dyestuff. Beam dyeing is a variation of package dyeing, which uses a larger cylinder onto which a set of warp yarns is wound.

Yarn-dyed fabrics may be identified by unraveling several warp and several filling yarns from the pattern area to see whether they differ in color. Not only will each yarn be a different color, but the yarns will have no darker or lighter areas where they have crossed other yarns. (See Figure 22.6.)

Figure 22.5 Package dyeing of yarns.

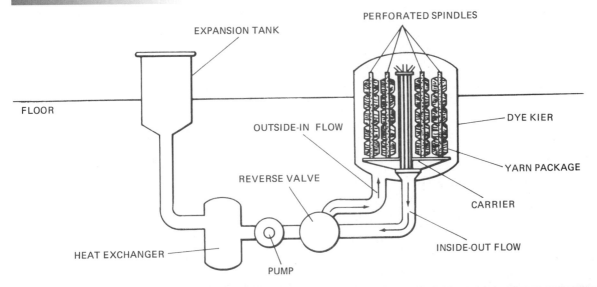

PERFORATED SPINDLES

EXPANSION TANK

FLOOR

OUTSIDE-IN FLOW

DYE KIER

YARN PACKAGE

REVERSE VALVE

CARRIER

HEAT EXCHANGER

INSIDE-OUT FLOW

PUMP

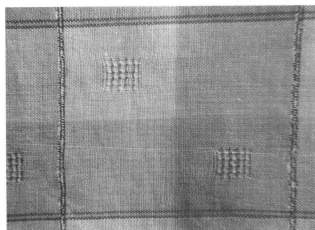

Figure 22.6

Examples of fabrics in which designs were created by using yarns dyed to different colors.

Piece Dyeing

Fabrics that are to be a solid color are usually piece dyed. In piece dyeing, the finished fabric is passed through a dyebath in which the fabric absorbs the dyestuff. A number of different methods are used for piece dyeing, each of which differs slightly in the way in which the fabric is handled. This is the cheapest dyeing method.

Fabrics may be dyed either continuously or in batches. In continuous dyeing, the cloth continually passes through the dyestuff. Where possible, this method is used for dyeing large yardages. Batch dyeing is used for shorter fabric lengths, for yarn dyeing, and for dyeing individual items such as hosiery. Some fabrics are dyed in open, flat widths. Knitted fabrics and those woven materials that are not subject to creasing are handled in "rope" form, that is, bunched together and handled as a narrower strand. Some of these methods are especially suitable to certain types of fabrics and unsuitable for others. Many different kinds of machines can be used for piece dyeing.

A process known alternately as *beck, box,* or *winch dyeing* is frequently used in batch dyeing wool fabrics and knits, as it places relatively little tension on the fabric during dyeing (Figure 22.7). Fabric is formed into an endless, circular chain and is rotated through the dye. Up to twelve ropes of fabric can be dyed side by side at the same time. Devices in the machine keep the ropes separate.

Jet dyeing is a relatively new method that uses jet propulsion to improve dye penetration. Dyeing takes place in a closed system that carries a fast-moving stream of pressurized dye liquor.

A fluid jet of dye penetrates and dyes the fabric. After it passes through this jet, the fabric is floated through an enclosed tube in which the fluid moves faster than the fabric. This prevents the fabric from touching the walls, keeping it constantly immersed in the dyebath. Turbulence is created by locating elbows in the tube. The turbulence aids in diffusing dyes and other chemicals. Since no pressure is put on the fabric, even very delicate fabrics can be dyed by this process. Jet dyeing has the advantage of being economical in operation and at the same time allowing a high degree of quality control. (See Figure 22.8.)

Jig dyeing is a process that places greater tension on the fabric than either of the aforementioned processes. Fabrics are stretched across two rollers that are placed above a stationary dyebath. At regular intervals the fabric is passed through the dyebath. The tension created by placing the fabric on the rollers means that this process must be reserved for fabrics with a fairly close weave that will not lose their shape under tension.

Beam dyeing, which is used for lightweight, fairly open-weave fabrics, utilizes the same principle as beam dyeing of yarns. The fabric is wrapped around a perforated

Figure 22.7

Sideview diagram of a typical dye beck showing movement of fabric through the dyebath.

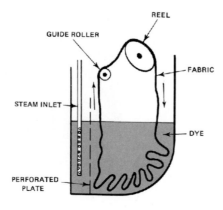

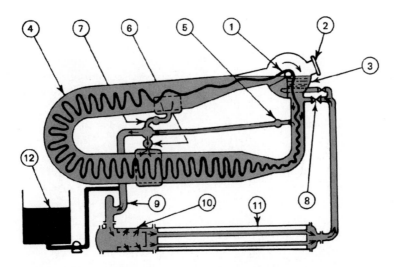

Figure 22.8

Hiska jet-dyeing machine. Illustration reprinted by permission of the National Knitwear and Sportswear Association.

1. Fabric guide roll
2. Loading and unloading port
3. Header tank
4. "U" tube
5. Suction control
6. Suction control
7. Suction control
8. Delivery control
9. Main Pump
10. Filter
11. Heat exchanger
12. Service tank

beam and immersed in the dyebath. Tightly woven fabrics would not allow sufficient dye penetration; hence, this method must be applied to loosely woven cloth. It has the added advantage of not putting tension or pressure on the goods as they are processed. (See Figure 22.9.)

Pad dyeing is a continuous process used in producing large quantities of piece-dyed goods that can withstand tension and pressure. Fabrics pass through a dyebath, then through pads or rollers that squeeze out the excess dye, and finally into a steam or heated chamber in which the dye is set.

Vacuum impregnation is a dye system introduced to improve the dyeing of heavy-weight fabrics. Because of their thickness, fabrics such as corduroy, sateens, and heavyweight ducks have been resistant to good dye penetration. Trapped air, caught in these denser fabrics, makes dyeing them difficult. In this vacuum system, the fabric comes in contact with a perforated stainless steel cylinder into which a vacuum pump draws air. At the same time, the dye liquor is applied to the other side of the fabric, resulting in more thorough dye penetration. The vacuum system has been particularly useful in dyeing corduroy fabrics and other pile fabrics as it allows equal dye penetration of both the pile and the ground fabric.

Foam dyeing is a continuous process for applying color to the surface of fabrics. Currently used on a limited basis in the carpet industry, foam dyeing has been compared to spreading colored shaving cream over the face of the carpet. The foam bubbles break down and deposit dye liquor over the surface of the fabric. The advantage of foam dyeing is that even though the material being dyed must be wet before foam application, the wet pickup is much reduced, and less time and energy are required to dry the dyed carpet. Foam can be applied in different colors and in selected areas to create designs. Only those dyestuffs that use a wet fixation technique can be applied through the foam process; therefore, neither vat nor sulfur dyes can be applied. One

Figure 22.9   Beam dyeing of fabric. Photograph courtesy of Allied Corporation and Steinfeld Mills, Oxford, N.C.

problem with foam dyeing has been the difficulty in achieving even color distribution.

Cross-dyeing

The increased use of blended fabrics, that is, fabrics composed of two or more different fibers, has created problems for the dyer and yet has led to new techniques. Dyeing of piece goods is less expensive than fiber or yarn dyeing. Cross-dyeing uses piece-dyeing techniques to produce a multicolored fabric, thereby decreasing the higher costs of production in yarn or fiber dyeing.

Cross-dyeing is done by mixing several dyes, each of which is specific to one fiber, in one dyebath. A blended fabric is passed through a single dyebath, and each fiber picks up only its specific dye. For example, if a black/red/gray tweed effect using a blend of rayon, acrylic, and nylon fibers is desired, the fabric could be passed through a dyebath in which there was a black dye specific to rayon, a red specific to acrylics, and a gray specific to nylon. The resulting fabric would be made up of black rayon, red acrylic, and gray nylon fibers. Plaids or stripes can be created by alternating yarns of different fibers, so that, for instance, nylon yarns are dyed red and polyester yarns are dyed blue to make a blue and red stripe.

Union Dyeing

Conversely, the dyer has difficulty in piece dyeing solid-colored, blended fabrics because each fiber takes up the dye differently. It is sometimes necessary for the dyer to select several different types of dyes of the same color, mixing them together in the same dyebath, to achieve a uniform color in a fabric that is made of several different fibers. This type of piece dyeing, called *union dyeing,* requires careful selection of dyes to match colors. Another way to achieve solid colors on blends is with resin-bonded pigments (discussed later in this chapter).

Tone-on-Tone Dyeing

A more subtle method of creating pattern with color is seen in *tone-on-tone fabrics.* Here, two different types of the same generic fiber might be used. Both types respond to the same type of dye, but one may be less reactive so that, for example, a lighter and darker shade of the same color results.

Garment Dyeing

Except for dyeing socks and narrow fabrics, *garment dyeing,* or the process of dyeing completed garments, remained a rather unimportant novelty until the second half of the 1980s. Industry sources credit two factors with a sharp increase in the amount of garment-dyed apparel. First, fashion demanded small lots of garments from fabrics with stonewashed, ice-washed, tie-dyed, overdyed, and distressed effects. These effects were more readily achieved through garment dyeing than traditional dyeing methods. The second factor was the ability of manufacturers to achieve Quick Response or Just-In-Time production (discussed in chapter 1) through garment dyeing.

The lead time required for delivery of orders in the traditional dyeing system is about eight weeks. For garment-dyed products lead time is about two weeks. Although the process of garment dyeing is more costly than traditional piece dyeing (estimated at $1 to $3 per item), savings are achieved in the long run because manufacturers and retailers need not maintain large inventories. If undyed merchandise is left from one season, it can be dyed for sale the following season. However, if it has already been dyed and a different color is wanted, it must be overdyed, given a second dyeing to a different color. Manufacturers can be more responsive to fashion trends by producing small dye lots.

Garment dyeing is primarily applied to cotton fabrics; however, high-pressure equipment can be used to process polyester and cotton blends. To achieve consistently good results with garment dyeing, manufacturers must exercise care in a number of areas.

- *Fabric.* All fabric used in one garment must come from the same bolt of fabric. If, for example, one trouser leg of a pair of jeans is cut from one bolt of fabric, and the other from another bolt, each leg may dye to a different shade. The result would be jeans in which the legs do not match.
- *Shrinkage.* Fabric must also be tested for shrinkage before cutting of garments, and garments must be cut large enough to allow for shrinkage so that sizes will be accurate.
- *Thread.* Thread must be chosen carefully and tested to be sure it will accept the dye in the same way as the fabric. One hundred percent cotton thread is preferred, but even with all-cotton thread there may be problems. For example, mercerized thread will dye to a darker shade

than unmercerized garment fabric. This will make the stitching stand out from the background fabric.
- *Labels, buttons, zippers.* All of these supplies must be compatible with the garment fabric in terms of reaction to the dye and shrinkage.

The machines used for garment dyeing are called *paddle machines.* To avoid entanglement during dyeing, garments are generally placed inside of bags. Paddle devices in the machine rotate, changing directions periodically, to make sure that all pieces being dyed are equally exposed to the dye liquor. Garments are generally washed before dyeing to remove any finishing materials that would interfere with dyeing and after dyeing to remove excess dye.

Special Washing Techniques

The fashions that provided the impetus for the growth in garment dyeing often had a distressed look in which garments had uneven colors. To achieve this effect, denim or other fabric was treated to destroy color randomly on the garment. Although the most widely used term for this process was *stone washing,* other names to describe the random removal of color included ice washing, white washing, acid washing, frosting, super washing, and snow washing.

Both indigo and sulfur-dyed denims lose color when exposed to oxidative bleaches. Stone washing is most commonly done by soaking a rather porous pumice stone in sodium hypochlorite or potassium permanganate, adding these stones to a load of garments in a type of washing machine without any water, and running the machine for a specified time. The contact of the cloth with the bleach removes color at random on the garment. This treatment is followed by another wash (in a different machine, as a rule) to remove any excess bleach.

Cellulase enzymes (see chapter 20, page 378) are also used to produce a stone-washed appearance on vat-dyed, sulfur-dyed, or pigment-dyed fabrics. If cellulase enzymes are used in combination with stone washing, the capacity of processing machines can be increased, thereby speeding up production.

Dye Classes

Dyestuffs are divided into a number of classifications. Within each of these classifications there exists a range of colors, and each of these colors may vary somewhat in its fastness to different conditions. The names given to the dye classes generally relate to the method of application and, to a lesser extent, the chemical composition of the dye class. All currently used dyes are listed by class in the *Colour Index,* a set of volumes published by the Society of Dyers and Colourists in the United Kingdom.

The ability of the fibers to accept each of these dye classes, called *substantivity* or *affinity,* depends on several factors. One is the availability of appropriate chemically reactive groups in both the fiber and the dyestuff, and another is the chemical composition of the dye liquor. Dyes that must be applied in an alkaline medium, for example, are difficult to use on protein fibers because the alkalinity of the dyebath may harm the fiber. Likewise, dyebaths that are strongly acidic may be harmful to cellulose fibers.

In the following discussion of specific dye classes, these classes are grouped according to the fiber types for which they are most widely (though not exclusively) used.

Dyes Most Often Used on Cellulosic Fibers

Azoic Dyes. Azoic dyes (also called naphthol dyes) are used primarily on cotton fibers, but they can also be applied to acetates, olefins, polyesters, and nylons. The reaction that produces dyeing takes place when two components, a diazonium salt and a naphthol compound, join together to form a highly colored, insoluble compound on the fabric.

These dyes are also known as *ice dyes* because the reaction takes place at lowered temperatures. Their colorfastness is good to laundering, bleaching, alkalis, and light. They do tend to crock somewhat, however. The color range is broad, although somewhat deficient in blues and greens.

Direct, or Substantive, Dyes. Direct dyes, also called substantive dyes, are water-soluble dyes used primarily for cotton and rayon, although some polyamide and protein fibers are also dyed with these compounds. These dyes have the advantage of being applied directly in a hot aqueous dye solution in the presence of common salts required to stabilize the rate of dyeing, making the process relatively inexpensive. They also possess the disadvantage of poor fastness to laundering because they are primarily physically bound to the fibers. An aftertreatment with copper salts is sometimes used to form a more stable dye compound. This improves colorfastness by forming a chemical compound of the dye molecule, the cellulose, and the copper salts. Other special finishes have also been developed to make the dye color more stable.

Vat Dyes. Vat dyes are insoluble in water. By chemical reduction they are converted to a soluble form. The dye is applied to the fibers, and then the dye, now within the fiber, is reoxidized to the insoluble form. This creates a color that is fast to both light and washing.

Because vat dyes must be applied in an alkaline solution, they are not suitable for use with protein fibers. Primarily used with cottons and rayons, vat dyes are also used on acrylics, modacrylics, and nylon. These dyes provide a wide range of colors except for reds and oranges. Indigo, used on denim, is a vat dye.

Sulfur Dyes. Sulfur dyes produce mostly inexpensive dark colors, such as black, brown, or navy and are applied in an alkaline solution to cottons and rayons. Fabrics dyed with sulfur dyes must be carefully processed or a buildup of excess chemicals on the fibers will eventually weaken the fibers. Like vat dyes, sulfur dyes are applied to textile materials in a soluble form and then oxidized to an insoluble form within the fiber. Colorfastness of sulfur dyes is good to washing and fair to light. Black and yellow sulfur dyes may accelerate light degradation of cellulosic fibers.

Reactive Dyes. In this class of dyes, the dyestuff reacts chemically with the fiber to form covalent bonds. Reactive dyes are applied most commonly to the cellulosic fibers, cotton, rayon, and linen. Some colors are appropriate for use on wool. Wools that have been chlorinated, bleached, or shrink-proofed may present difficulties in colorfastness as they tend to have poor wetfastness. Reactive dyes can produce good wetfast colors on wool and silk. Nylons and acrylics can be dyed to some shades with reactive dyes, although the dyes are difficult to apply evenly on synthetics. Because of the strong covalent bonds, colorfastness of these dyes is generally good to all types of use.

Dyes Used Primarily for Protein Fibers

Acid Dyes. Acid dyes have one to four negatively charged functional groups. Applied in acid solution, they react chemically with the basic groups in the fiber structure to form ionic bonds. Because wool has both acid and basic groups in its structure, acid dyes can be used quite successfully on wools. These dyes are also utilized for dyeing nylon and, to a lesser extent, for acrylics, some modified polyesters, polypropylene, and spandex. Acid dyes cannot be used on cellulosic fibers because these fibers are susceptible to damage from acids. Colorfastness of acid dyes varies a good deal, depending on the color and the fiber to which the dye has been applied.

Metal complex dyes, or *premetallized dyes,* are usually classified with acid dyes. These are dyes that have been reacted with a metal mordant, such as chromium or cobalt, before application to the fiber. Resulting dyes are very stable, with excellent light and wash fastness, but the resulting colors are not as bright as those of true acid dyes. Major applications are to protein fibers and nylons.

Chrome, or Mordant, Dyes. Used on the same general group of fibers as acid dyes, chrome dyes (also called mordant dyes) use a metallic salt that, when applied with the dye molecule, reacts to form a relatively insoluble dyestuff with improved wet- and lightfastness. As the name of the dye indicates, chrome salts are most often used for the process, but salts of cobalt, aluminum, nickel, and copper can also be utilized. Especially effective for dyeing wool and silk, these dyes have excellent colorfastness to dry cleaning, but residual metals may be harmful, especially to silk fabrics.

Dyes Used Primarily for Manufactured Fibers

Basic Dyes. Basic dyes contain positively charged amino groups that are attracted to negative groups in fibers; for this reason, they are also known as cationic dyes. Wool and silk have negative acid groups and acrylic fibers usually have sulfonic acid groups added to the polymer for dyeing with basic dyes. Modified nylon and polyester fibers can also be dyed with basic dyes.

The colors that these dyes produce are exceptionally bright. Unfortunately, in natural fibers basic dyes have rather poor colorfastness to light, laundering, or perspiration. As a result, they are rarely used for silk and wool any more. Recent developments of basic dyes for synthetics produce excellent colorfastness.

Disperse Dyes. Developed for coloring acetates, disperse dyes are now used to color many other manufactured fibers. The dye is almost insoluble in water. Particles of dye disperse in the water without dissolving but, rather, dissolve in the fibers.

Disperse dyes can be applied to a wide variety of fibers, including acetate, acrylic, aramid, modacrylic, nylon, olefin, polyester, saran, and triacetate, and are really the only practical means of coloring acetate and polyester fibers.

Disperse dyes can be applied in an aqueous dispersion, through a special process developed by DuPont called the Thermosol® process, and by heat transfer. (See chapter 23 for discussion of heat transfer printing.) In the Thermosol® process no dyebath is used. Instead, the fabrics are padded with dye and then passed through an oven in which temperatures of 390° to 420°F cause fixation of color to fabric. Dye *carriers* are solvents that may be used to swell the fibers before penetration by the dye.

Colors produced with disperse dyes cover a wide range and generally have good fastness. Blues, however, tend to be discolored by nitrous oxide gases in the atmosphere and may gradually fade to a pinkish color. Greens may fade to brown. This is known as fume fading. The main source of fumes in homes is gas-fired stoves and heaters (see chapter 7).

Pigment Colors. Pigment colors are not soluble, cannot penetrate fiber surfaces, and therefore must be attached to the surface of the fabric by a binder. A polymeric resin serves as the binder. When the resin is cured, or permanently fixed to the fabric, the dye is also fixed on the fabric surface. The colorfastness of pigment colors is dependent on the durability of the binder, not the pigment. Pigment colors provide an easy way to get uniform solid colors on fabrics made from blends.

Fugitive Tints

Colors that are not permanent are sometimes called *fugitive tints*. In most dyeing processes, the manufacturer wishes to produce a color that is permanent and one that will not disappear in use or in processing. An exception is found in the use of fugitive tints such as Versatint®, a range of colors produced by Milliken Chemical Company.

These dyes are used to identify fibers or yarns during the manufacture of fabrics. By coloring fibers or yarns of a particular generic type to a specific tint, the manufacturer has a readily identifiable color code. When the processing of the materials is complete, the manufacturer can remove the color by a simple wash, often in cold water.

Reference

Gerhard, P. 1964. Emperor's dyes of the Mixtecs. *Natural History* 73 (January): 26.

Review Questions

1. Before the discovery of synthetic dyes, what kinds of substances were used to dye fabrics? When were the first synthetic dyes made, and what were they made of?
2. Define the term *colorfastness*. What are some of the conditions that may affect the colorfastness of dyed textiles?
3. What are some of the factors that make for good dye retention in a textile fabric?
4. Identify the stages of fiber and fabric manufacture at which color can be added to a textile.
5. Explain the difference between cross-dyeing and union dyeing.
6. What is the basis of the names given to the various dye classes? Explain why all dye classes are not equally useful for fabrics made from all textile fibers.
7. What are the advantages and disadvantages of garment dyeing?

Recommended Readings

Aspland, J. R. 1991–1993. Series of articles on dyeing. *Textile Chemist and Colorist.* Appearing monthly from October 1991 (vol. 23) to November 1993 (vol. 25). See individual issues for a wide range of specific topics.

Bide, M. 1992. Wool dyeing: What's new? *Textile Chemist and Colorist* 24 (April): 17–22.

Broadbent, A. D. 1994. Colorimetry. Part 1: Factors involved in the perception and measurement of color. *Canadian Textile Journal* 111 (March): 15.

Fox, M., and J. Pierce. 1990. Indigo: Past and present. *Textile Chemist and Colorist* 22 (April): 13.

Fulmer, T. D. 1993. Dyeing textiles for automotive interiors. *America's Textiles International* 22 (December): 88.

Garment dyeing. *Textile Progress* 19 (2).

Hori, T., and H. Zollinger. 1986. The role of water in the dyeing process. *Textile Chemist and Colorist* 18 (October): 19.

Hunt, P. K., and J. N. Etters. 1994. The dyeing process in wearable art. *American Dyestuff Reporter* 83 (September): 112.

Lopez, J., and J. Farrell-Beck. 1992. What colored the transition from madder to alizarine? *Clothing and Textiles Research Journal* 10 (Spring): 36–43.

Perenich, T. A., et al. 1991. The effects of chlorinated pool water on the lightfastness properties of fiber reactive dyed cotton knit fabrics. *Textile Chemist and Colorist* 23 (August): 14.

Perkins, W. S. 1991. A review of textile dyeing processes. *Textile Chemist and Colorist* 23 (August): 23.

Rivlin, J. 1992. *The dyeing of textile fibers: Theory and practice.* Philadelphia: Philadelphia College of Textiles and Science.

Taylor, G. 1988. Dyeing in Britain from Roman times to the advent of synthetic dyes. *Textiles* 17 (2): 51.

Water-soluble dyes. 1992. *Clothes Care Gazette,* no. 65 (December).

Zimmerman, K. 1993. Cellulase enzymes won't leave your laundry washed up. *Bobbin* 35 (December): 62.

CHAPTER 23

TEXTILE PRINTING AND DESIGN

Important decisions in the creation of a textile product must be made when its design and/or its color are chosen. Although many thousands of yards of fabrics are processed in solid colors, thousands more yards of fabric have designs applied through printing.

The application of a pattern to fabric by the use of dyes, pigments, or other colored substances may be effected by a variety of hand or machine processes. Freehand painting of designs on fabrics is probably the oldest technique for applying ornament, but hand painting is a time-consuming procedure. Furthermore, it does not always result in a uniform repeat of a motif that is to be used more than once. If a design is transferred to a flat surface that can be coated with a dye and then stamped onto the fabric, the same design can be repeated many times over simply by pressing the decorated surface against the fabric. This process is known as *printing*. Over many centuries a variety of techniques for printing designs have evolved. Printing can be applied to warp yarns, to fabrics, or to apparel pieces—for example, slogans or pictures on T-shirts.

In general, printing is a cheaper way of creating designs on fabric than weaving or knitting with different colored yarns.

Early Forms of Printing

Block Printing

Block printing appears to be the most ancient of these techniques. Some experts assign a date of 2000 B.C. to printed fabrics from the Caucasus in Russia. Blocks that were used in printing textiles have been recovered from Egyptian graves of the fourth century A.D. (Haller 1939). This is the simplest of the printing techniques and requires only a limited technology. A block of material (usually wood) has a design drawn on one flat side. The design is carved by cutting away the spaces between the areas that form the pattern, thus placing the design in a raised position. Color is applied to the surface of the block, and the block is pressed onto the cloth. Anyone who has ever made a potato or linoleum print should recognize the technique. Sometimes during printing, the block was tapped with a mallet to assure complete contact of the block with the fabric.

To make the best possible print, the dye had to be in a viscous or pastelike form; otherwise, the incised areas would have been filled in by the dye mixture, and the block would not have carried sufficient dye to make a clear image.

Mordant Printing

Inventive printers found another means of combining printing and dyeing to add color patterns to fabrics. Colorfastness without mordanting was very poor. The printer learned to print the mordant onto the surface of the fabric and then to pass the entire cloth into the dyebath. The mordanted areas absorbed the dye permanently; the rest of the cloth picked up dye only on the surface. When the fabric was rinsed after the dyebath, the dye washed out of the unprinted areas and left a colorful design on the section that had been impregnated with the mordant.

By using different mordant materials, different colors could be produced from the same dyestuff. Madder was especially useful in this respect. When the dyer printed the surface with several different mordants, immersed the fabric in the dyebath, and rinsed away the excess dye, a fabric printed with two or three different colors resulted. This process was evidently used in Egypt during Roman times. The Roman writer Pliny describes a mysterious process in which an "invisible ink" (the mordant) was painted onto fabric and the fabric passed through another solution (the dye). After rinsing, a multicolored fabric "magically" appeared (Lewis 1937).

Resist Printing

In resist printing, a substance coats the fabric in preselected areas, thus preventing the fabric from absorbing dye in the areas. Resist materials have included starch, clay, and wax. The technique has been used to produce designs in textiles in many different cultures, including those of Persia, India, South America, Egypt, and the Far East. Although the pattern of the resist material can be said to be "printed" onto the fabric, the application of color takes place by dyeing, just as in mordant printing.

Batik

Today, the best known wax-resist process is that used for the making of *batik*. The name *batik* originates in the Indonesian Archipelago, where resist printing has become an important art form. An analysis of the batik method shows clearly how resist printing is done. Wax is applied to the areas that the printer does not want to dye. In Indonesia a small, spouted cup with a handle is used to apply the wax. As the wax is heated, it melts, and the liquid wax is poured from the cup, or *tjanting*, onto the cloth (Figure 23.1). When it hardens, the wax coats the fabric so that the dye cannot reach the fibers.

If several colors are to be used, the process becomes somewhat more complex. For example, if a fabric is to be colored white, red, and blue, the artisan begins with a creamy-white cotton cloth. Those areas that are to remain white are coated with wax, and the areas to be red are also covered. Only the area to be colored blue remains exposed. The fabric is now subjected to a blue dyebath, and the exposed areas take on the blue tint.

Next, the wax is boiled off and reapplied to the blue and white areas. The fabric is placed in the red dyebath. Since both the blue and white areas are covered with wax, the red color penetrates only the uncovered areas of the design. After dyeing is complete, the fabric is treated with a fixative (a mordant) to make the colors fast, and a final rinse in hot water removes all traces of wax.

For faster production a technique was devised whereby the wax could be printed onto the surface of the fabric with a device called a *tjap*. As in block printing, the design is carved on a tjap block. The block is dipped in wax, the block is pressed onto the fabric, and the molten wax is thus imprinted on the cloth. Well-to-do Indonesians look upon the tjap-printed fabrics as inferior in quality, although to the untrained eye they look much the same as those made with the *tjanting*.

Figure 23.1

Indonesian woman uses tjanting for applying wax to a batik fabric. Photograph courtesy of Exxon Corporation.

Figure 23.2   A tie-dyed fabric. Reprinted by permission from the Metropolitan Museum of Art. Gift of Fay Halpern, 1972.

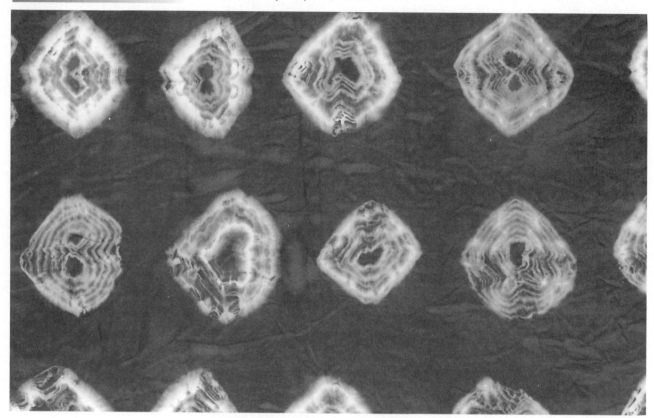

Tie and Dye

Resist designs can be produced by the tie-and-dye method in which parts of the fabric are tightly wound with yarns, or the fabric may be tied into knots in selected areas. When the fabric is placed in a dyebath, the covered or knotted areas are protected from the dye. Careful attention to the shape of the wrapping and the placement of the tied areas can produce intricate and attractive patterns. In Indian textiles the tie-and-dye method is known as *bandanna.* (See Figure 23.2.)

Ikat

A complex and unusual variation of resist printing has been practiced in many places. The process, called *ikat,* required the weaver to prepare the warp yarns on the loom. Selected sections of the yarns were then covered with a resist material—wax, clay, or other yarns as in tie and dye. The warps were dyed, and the covered area did not absorb the dye. If a more complicated pattern were required, the warp yarns might be treated several times, as in the batik procedure. When dyeing was completed, the resist material was removed, and the filling was woven into place. This produced a fabric design of blurred, indistinct patterns. Ikat fabrics often have a shimmering, soft quality that is very beautiful (Figure 23.3a). The technique called *warp printing* grows out of the ancient ikat process (discussed later in this chapter).

Block printing, batik, and tie-dyeing are methods of color application used largely by either natives from Africa, South America, and the Orient or by persons

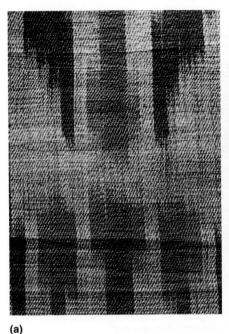
(a)

(b)

Figure 23.3

(a) Ikat fabric and (b) printed fabric made to imitate a woven ikat fabric.

using these techniques as hobbies or art forms. Such fabrics are sometimes produced commercially in small quantities, usually at very high prices.

Industrial Printing Processes

Screen Printing

Silkscreen, or screen, printing is a method of applying a colored design created either by hand or by an automated process. In hand screen printing, the fabric to be printed is spread out on a long table. A screen is prepared for each color of the design. At the time this procedure was developed, fine screens of silk were used—hence the name silkscreen printing. Today, screens of synthetic fibers or metal mesh are more likely to be used.

A lacquer coating closes off all areas of the screen except the area through which one of the colors of the design is to be printed. For example, if a red rose with green leaves is to be printed, one screen is made that closes off all but the red rose area, and another is made that closes off all but the green leaves.

A screen is prepared for each color of a design by coating it with a photosensitive material, covering it with a negative, and exposing it to light. The light degrades the coating in the exposed area, afterwards the coating can be washed out.

The printer takes the screen for one color, which is mounted on a frame, and places it in the correct position above and against the fabric. A viscous dye paste, rather than an aqueous dye solution, is used to prevent running of the applied design. The dye paste is coated on the top of the screen; the fabric is underneath. A squeegee is run across the screen and presses the dye through the open area of the screen, onto the fabric. To color the next section of the fabric, the screen is moved farther along the fabric. After one color has been applied, a second color is added as are additional colors if they are required.

Figure 23.4

Silkscreen printing of carpets. Courtesy of *Modern Textiles* magazine.

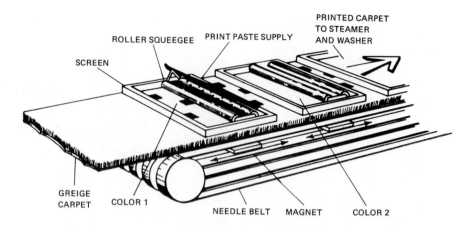

Flat-bed Zimmer carpet printing machine lays down each color separately form printing paste applied by means of two magnetic roller squeegees. Pressure is controlled by the selection of heavy or light squeegees and by varying the current going to the electromagnet. Endless belts fitted with needles assure a positive drive for good register.

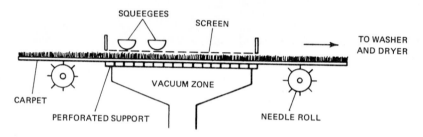

The BDA Screen printer uses a series of screens, one for each color; the basic unit is sketched above.

Hand screen printing is a slow process. Automation has been achieved in the manufacture of flatbed screen prints by making the frames stationary and moving the fabric along on a belt from screen to screen. The squeegee action, too, is done automatically. Flatbed screen printing machines can print from 10 to 15 meters per minute (Datye and Vaida 1984, 353). This is a limited production when compared with rotary screen printing and roller printing, but flat screens allow very large design repeats. (See Figure 23.4.)

Rotary Screen Printing

In addition to flatbed screen printing, a rotary screen printing technique has been developed that makes possible an output of quantities of 25 to 100 meters per minute. Instead of using a flat screen, screens are shaped into cylinders or rollers (Figure 23.5). As in the hand process, a screen is prepared for each color. The dye feeds through the unscreened area, pushed out from inside the roller by a squeegee. Fabrics move continuously under the rollers, and up to twelve colors may be printed on one fabric. The maximum length of the design repeat is limited to the circumference of the roller. The production of screens for rotary screen printing is less costly than the engraving of the heavy copper rollers used for roller printing, and the use of rotary screen printing techniques is increasing.

Roller Printing

Like rotary screen printing, roller printing uses a series of rollers, each imprinting a different color on the fabric (see Figure 23.6 on p. 434). Up to sixteen different col-

Figure 23.5

Rotary screen printing machine. Each cylinder on the machine adds a different color and a different part of the total pattern. Photograph courtesy of the American Textile Manufacturers Institute.

ors can be used on one fabric. As with rotary screen printing, the length of the repeat is determined by the circumference of the roller. Printing speeds of 100 to 150 meters per minute are possible (Datye and Vaida 1984, 353).

The rollers are made of copper, plated with chromium for durability. The design of each color is transferred accurately to the roller by one of several processes. In photoengraving, a photographic image of the design is etched onto the roller, or a pantograph may be used to transfer the design from a flat surface to the roller. This device allows markings to be made on the roller simultaneously with the tracing of the design from a master design.

Once the rollers have been prepared, they are installed in exact position on the printing machine. The fabric to be printed moves over a rotating drum. Behind it is placed a layer of fabric that will absorb excess dye and keep it from being deposited on the drum. The design roller also rotates, moving against a rotary brush that rotates in a tray of print paste. This brush furnishes color to the roller. A *doctor blade* scrapes off excess dye from the roller, and the roller then rotates against the cloth and the

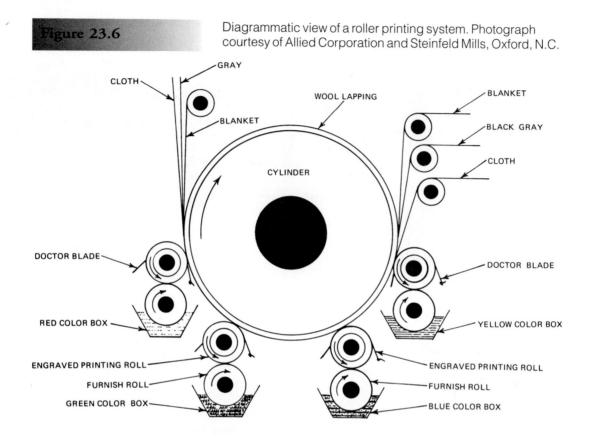

Diagrammatic view of a roller printing system. Photograph courtesy of Allied Corporation and Steinfeld Mills, Oxford, N.C.

design is imprinted. The fabric moves on to the second roller where a second color is imprinted, and so on, in a continuous printing operation.

Rollers must be aligned perfectly to keep the print in registration. If rollers are not positioned correctly, the resulting print will have one or more colors that do not fall in quite the correct position, causing the print to be distorted. The printed cloth is dried immediately and then passes to a chamber in which steam or heat sets the dye.

Roller printing is superior to other types of printing for fine or precise designs. However, roller printing requires skilled labor and much heavy manual work in the changing of the color troughs and rollers. The initial investment of time and money in the preparation of rollers for roller printing and in setting up the machine is such that production of small quantities of printed cloth is not economical. Roller printing is used more advantageously for lengthy runs of the same pattern.

Use of roller printing is declining in the United States. Rotary screen printing, by contrast, has overtaken roller printing and is continuing to increase.

Variations of Printing

Duplex Printing. Duplex printing is done on a special machine that imprints designs on both sides of the fabric at the same time. Most often, the same design is printed on opposite sides, although different designs can be printed on each side. The resulting fabric looks like fabric with a woven design (Figure 23.7). This process is seldom used now, as it is almost as expensive to create duplex prints as it is to weave designs.

Figure 23.7

Duplex print. Note that the same design has been printed on both sides of the fabric, thereby giving the appearance of a woven design.

Blotch Prints. In blotch prints, both a colored background and design motifs are printed onto the fabric. These prints should be differentiated from *overprinting,* or printing of a design on a fabric that has already been piece dyed. Blotch prints can generally be distinguished from overprinting by a close examination of the fabric (Figure 23.8). Background colors of blotch-printed fabrics usually have a lighter color on the wrong side than on the right side of the fabric. Sometimes, too, minute, uncolored areas appear between the sections of background color and the design. Blotch prints can be made on either a rotary screen printing machine or on a roller printing machine. Blotch-printed fabrics made by screen printing may have better color penetration in background color areas than those made by roller printing.

Discharge Printing. Piece-dyed fabrics may be printed with a substance known as a *discharge paste* that removes color from specific areas of the fabric. Discharge printing

(a)   (b)

Figure 23.8

Blotch print. In blotch prints, background color is lighter on the underside of the fabric, whereas in an overprinted fabric the background has the same depth of color on both face (a) and back (b) sides.

Discharge print. This fabric has been dyed, and then the light area has had the color removed to create the design. (a) Face and (b) back.

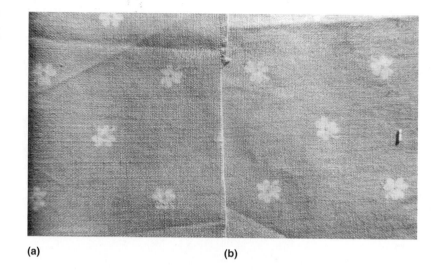

(a)   **(b)**

is used only for small, light-colored or white designs on dark background. If fabrics are not processed carefully to remove all the discharge paste, these chemicals may eventually weaken the fabric in the areas from which color has been discharged. Discharge prints are recognizable because the color of the background design of the fabric is the same on both the front and back sides (Figure 23.9).

Flock Printing. By imprinting an adhesive material on the surface of a fabric in the desired pattern, and then sprinkling short fibers over the adhesive, a flocked print may be created (Figure 23.10). Flocking as a type of finish is discussed at length in chapter 20.

Resist Printing. Resist printing is a combination printing and dyeing method. A substance that resists dyes is printed onto the fabric in selected areas. Later, when the fabric is passed through the dyebath, the resist material prevents the fabric from absorbing the dye, thereby creating a design. This machine process follows the principle used in handmade batik fabrics.

Flocked design printed on a sheer nylon fabric.

| **Figure 23.11** | (a) Warp-printed silk fabric and (b) roller-printed cotton fabric made to simulate indistinct pattern of a warp-printed fabric. |

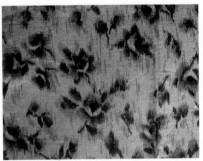

(b)

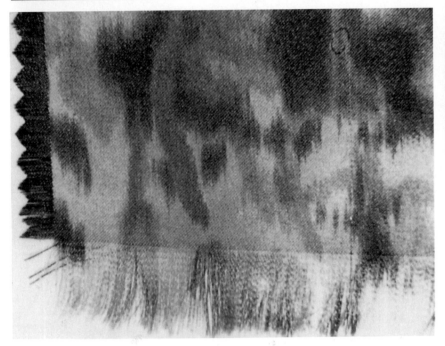

(a)

Warp Printing. Warp yarns can be printed before they are woven into the fabric. The resulting fabrics have a delicate, shimmery quality that is achieved by the indistinct patterns created in warp printing (Figure 23.11). Warp printing is applied to higher-priced fabrics.

Heat Transfer

Heat transfer printing, or sublimation printing,[1] is a system in which dyes are printed onto a paper base and then transferred from the paper to a fabric. The transfer of colors takes place as the color sublimes through vaporization. This is achieved by rolling the paper and the fabric together under pressure and at high temperatures (424°F or 200°C). (See Figure 23.12.)

Initially, heat transfer dyes were disperse dyes mostly effective on nylons and polyesters. Disperse dyes can also be used on acrylics, triacetates, and polyester and cotton blends where the proportion of polyester is relatively high. In the early 1990s development of several alternative processes have extended heat transfer printing to silk, cotton and other cellulosic fabrics, and wool.

Sublimation printing achieves a sharpness and clarity that other types of printing cannot match. All colors are applied to the fabric at the same time, thereby simplifying the operation and requiring lower processing costs, with fewer personnel required. Production can change rapidly from one design to another simply by

---

1. Sublistatic printing, a term often used in conjunction with heat transfer printing, is the trademark of the Sublistatic Corporation, a major producer of heat transfer printing paper.

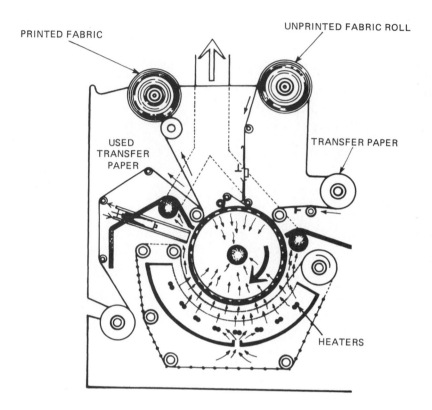

Figure 23.12

Heat transfer printing. This schematic diagram shows transfer printing process. Unprinted fabric roll is at top to the right of the heat outlet. Gray fabric moves down to the drum where it is almost immediately joined by transfer paper from the right. The two pass through a bank of infrared heaters. Used transfer paper exits left and to the bottom, while printed fabric goes to roll at top left of the heat outlet. Reprinted by permission from *Textile World* magazine. Copyright © 1972 by McGraw-Hill, Inc.

changing the design paper, whereas in roller or screen printing, each separate roller or screen must be removed from the machine and the machine set up for a new design with different rollers or screens. Short runs are feasible, fast deliveries are possible, given shorter time for processing, and companies need not keep costly inventories of fabric in stock.

Heat transfer printing has proved especially successful in printing knitted fabrics. Knitted goods are less dimensionally stable than are woven fabrics. Manufacturers using conventional screen and roller printing techniques on knit fabrics experienced difficulties in making multicolor prints in which the segments of the print must fit together accurately. In sublimation printing, all parts of the design are applied at once, eliminating the problem of fabrics stretching as they move from one roller to another.

On the other hand, heat transfer printing is slower than is either roller or screen printing. Ten to 15 meters of printed fabric are produced per minute in transfer printing operations, whereas roller printing can produce 100 to 150 meters of fabric per minute and rotary screen printing can produce up to 100 meters of fabric per minute.

Losses of fabric through faulty printing are substantially lower during heat transfer printing than are losses in conventional roller printing. Energy requirements are also lower. Garments and garment pieces can be printed, and precise placement of decorative motifs on a completed garment is possible.

One disadvantage of heat transfer printing is off-grain printing. Some dyes used on nylons and acrylics have displayed variations in shade depth and, in some cases, problems with fastness to laundering. A yard of paper is required for each yard of fabric to be printed, so the disposal of paper also can become a problem. On the other hand, conventional dyeing and printing systems produce problems of water pollution, whereas paper can be recycled.

Growth of heat transfer printing has not been as dramatic in recent years as it was when the technique was first introduced. This is probably due to the limited types of fabrics that can be produced.

Other Special Printing Techniques

Photographic printing is done in a manner similar to the photochemical preparation of screens for screen printing. A photosensitive dye is coated on the fabric, a negative is placed over the fabric, light is applied, and a photographic type of printing takes place. (See Figure 23.13.)

Electrostatic printing is an experimental process in which a plate with an electrostatic charge is placed behind the fabric. A stencil in the form of the pattern is placed over the fabric. Special powdered inks that can be attracted by the electrostatic charge are passed over the surface fabric, and the inks are attracted into and color the fabric in the open areas of the stencil.

Ombre printing is the printing of a rainbow or varying tone effects. The tone may change from light to dark shades of one color, or vice versa, or the effect may be shading from one color into another. Ombre effects can also be obtained by weaving fabrics from yarns that have been yarn dyed into shaded colors.

Polychromatic printing, or *polychromatic dyeing,* is actually a dyeing method that achieves a printed effect. Several different streams of different colored dye liquors are utilized. The dye liquor is run over the surface of the fabric. By controlling the direction and flow of the dye, a variety of different effects can be achieved. Polychromatic® is a trademark of the ICI Company.

Figure 23.13

Cotton fabric with a photographic print of citrus fruits.

Foam printing, a variant of the foam dyeing process (see chapter 20), can be used to apply dye to selected areas of fabric to create a multicolored effect. Foam printing offers the same energy-saving advantages as foam dyeing.

Another technique uses *heat-sensitive inks* that contain thermochromic liquid crystals to print colors and designs that reflect different wavelengths of light at different temperatures. The inks are sensitive to either body or atmospheric heat. They can be applied either by screen printing or heat transfer printing. Care labels generally recommend that garments colored with these inks should be washed in cold water without bleach, and that the fabrics not be ironed. Some trademarks and trade terms applied to these products include Hypercolor® and chameleon colors.

Printing Techniques for Carpets

Recent style trends have led to the production of substantial quantities of patterned carpet. Rotary screen and flatbed screen techniques can be used for printing carpets, though they require some special adaptations. Heat transfer printing is also applied to small area rugs and to floor carpet tiles. Foam and polychromatic coloring techniques can be used on carpeting, also.

A number of specialized processes used chiefly for carpets have gained acceptance over the last several years. One such process, the Kustur TAK® process, is based on the use of a device that sprinkles droplets of dye solution onto a predyed or prepadded carpet. The simplest of these machines can produce two colors, plus the base shade. The Multi-TAK® machine allows the application of dye liquor to specific areas of the carpet to produce a random pattern. Other variants of the process can create a multilayered color effect by applying a gum that resists the dye to the surface of the carpet, while allowing the TAK® droplets to penetrate below the surface.

Traditional roller printing on pile carpets would flatten or crush the pile; therefore, raised pattern areas are now being produced by mounting hard and soft rubber

Figure 23.14

Carpet printed by the Millitron® printing machine is inspected. Photograph courtesy of Milliken and Company.

materials on a wood roller. These materials take up the dye from a dye trough and apply them to the carpet without flattening the pile.

Jet spray techniques for printing carpets have been developed by a number of textile machinery companies. This technique relies on small jets of dye that are controlled by computer. Production speeds can be very fast (up to 15 to 20 meters per minute). Rollers, screens, and other equipment requirements are simplified. One of the most versatile of these machines is the *Millitron*® unit, a machine developed by the Milliken Company that uses thousands of tiny jets to apply color. Since neither rollers nor screens are used, the pile is not distorted, and exceptional pattern clarity is possible. The machine can switch from one pattern to another in less than 1 second, allowing the production of relatively short runs quite economically. (See Figure 23.14.)

References

Datye, K. V., and A. A. Vaida. 1984. *Chemical processing of synthetic fibers and blends.* New York: Wiley.

Haller, R. 1939. The technique of early cloth printing. *CIBA Review* 26 (October): 933.

Lewis, E. 1937. *Romance of textiles.* New York: Macmillan.

Review Questions

1. Describe the way that batik, tie and dye, and ikat printing are done, and explain why these are called "resist" printing techniques.

2. Describe screen printing, rotary screen printing, roller printing, and heat transfer printing. Listed below are descriptions of several different types of fabric. Which of these printing processes would be the most logical choice for making each of these fabrics? Explain your choice.
    - A multicolored fabric with very fine designs that sells large quantities of fabric year after year.
    - A fabric with an exceptionally large repeat that will be used in high-priced fabric for interiors.
    - A fabric whose relatively small repeat motif is a fad that will probably not be popular after this year.
    - A knitted polyester-cotton blend fabric for a retailer who wants to participate in Quick Response merchandising.

3. What are the unique aspects of the following types of printing?

    duplex printing   flock printing

    blotch printing   jet spray printing

    discharge printing   ombre printing

Recommended Readings

Carr, W. W. 1991. Printing textile fabrics with xerography. *Textile Chemist and Colorist* 23 (May): 33.

Doujak, R. 1994. Automation in the textile printing industry. *American Dyestuff Reporter* 83 (September): 76.

Fabrics that change color with temperature. *Apparel International* 19 (June): 15.

Fulmer, T. 1989. Printing. Where is it now? Where will it go? *America's Textiles International* 18 (December): 64.

Graham, L. 1989. Ink jet systems for dyeing and printing of textiles. *Textile Chemist and Colorist* 21 (June): 27.

Liquid crystals, red, hot, and blue. 1991. *The Economist* 319 (May 18): 92.

Shore, J. 1990. Textile Coloration: Part 2: Application by printing. *Textiles* 19 (1): 19.

Zimmer, R. 1994. Automating the textile printing industry. *Canadian Textile Journal* 111 (June): 12.

CHAPTER 24

THE CARE OF TEXTILE PRODUCTS

A ttention to the correct procedures for cleaning and maintaining textile products will extend the useful life of the product. Improper cleaning and storage can result in either severe damage to the fabric or an increased rate of wear over a period of time.

The accumulation of soil on fabrics is one of the factors that causes fabrics to deteriorate. Spilled food, for example, can make a fabric that is normally unappetizing to insects into an attractive meal for moths and carpet beetles. The "ground-in dirt" that television commercials decry can increase the abrasion of yarns as gritty soils rub against fibers, causing them to break. Soil removal is, therefore, one of the most important aspects of caring for fabrics if they are to be maintained in good condition.

Soil deposited on fabrics is made up of different materials. Some types of soil are soluble; other types are insoluble. Soluble dirt is made up of organic acids, mineral acids, alkaline substances, blood, starches, and sugars. All these substances dissolve in cool or warm water, and although they may sometimes require special stain-removal techniques, these soluble substances present no extraordinary problems in cleaning.

Water alone will remove soluble soil, but insoluble soils may be held onto the fabric by physical attraction or in films, greases, or oils. Such soil requires the use of some kind of cleaning aid.

Historical Development

Just when soap was developed is not clear. Soaplike materials dating from 2500 B.C. have been found in clay cylinders from the city of Babylon in the Near East, but whether this substance was used as a cleaning agent or as a dressing for the hair is not known. Other references from antiquity likewise provide no clear description of the uses of soap, although the Roman writer Pliny describes the process by which it was made. By the Middle Ages the craft of soapmaking was well enough developed that guilds or associations of soapmakers had been formed.

For many centuries the making of soap from natural materials was a major household task. Animal fats and lye, made by soaking wood ashes in water, were boiled together to make a strong soap. Commercial soapmaking coexisted with the home process. Over time the commercial processes gradually improved and eventually replaced the homemade product as chemists found better ways of isolating and manufacturing the components used in the soapmaking process.

Soap is a good cleaning agent, but it does not perform well in hard water, which is water with higher concentrations of minerals such as calcium and magnesium, which are usually dissolved in water from limestone rock. The minerals in the water combine with soap to form an insoluble gray curd, or scum. Once the soap has combined with these minerals, less soap is available for cleaning, and larger quantities of soap must be used. Also, the hard-water scum may be deposited on clothing, leaving it gray or dull looking.

An alternative cleaning agent to soap was developed during World War I in Germany when fats and oils normally used for making soap were in short supply. This substance, a synthetic detergent, had another advantage: it did not form a scum with hard-water minerals.

The term *detergent* can create some confusion. Cleaning agents are commonly known as detergents. Both soaps and synthetic detergents are, technically speaking, detergents, even though the term *detergent* is often used by the general public to refer only to synthetic detergents. For purposes of this discussion, *detergent* will be used to refer to synthetic detergents and to both soaps and detergents where those terms are interchangeable.

Although synthetic detergents were produced in the United States as early as the 1930s, it was only following World War II that their use increased dramatically. Today, synthetic detergents dominate the home laundry market, and only a few brands of laundry soap remain.

Soil Removal

Soil can be removed from fabrics by laundering or by dry cleaning. These processes can be carried out in the home or by professional cleaners. The principles used are the same in both instances, but the equipment and laundry or dry-cleaning products will vary.

Laundering

The process of laundering soiled fabrics consists of wetting the fabric and its soil, removing the soil from the fabric, and holding the soil in suspension so that it does not redeposit on the fabric during washing. Detergents increase the cleaning ability of water. The addition of detergent to water decreases the surface tension of water (molecular forces in the outer layer of water), thereby increasing its wetting power. When the wetting power of water is increased, textiles are penetrated more completely by water. A simple experiment will demonstrate this principle. Take a small piece of nylon fabric and float it on the surface of a small bowl of water. The surface tension of the water enables the nylon to float for a time, until it becomes wet throughout. Drop a few drops of liquid detergent into the water. The fabric will become wet immediately and sink.

The wet fabric is agitated by the motion of the washing machine or by hand scrubbing. The soil is broken into smaller particles, is surrounded (emulsified) by the detergent, and is then lifted off the fabric by the action of the detergent molecules. The detergent surrounding the soil particles prevents them from being redeposited on the fabric as the washing progresses. When fabrics are rinsed, the soil and detergent are rinsed away.

Soaps

Soap is made from fatty acids and alkali that react together to form the soap. Some degree of alkalinity is necessary for cleaning, and as the soap dissolves, the washing water becomes somewhat alkaline in reaction. Much soil is acid in chemical reaction and will tend to neutralize some of the alkalinity of the soap and decrease its effectiveness. Therefore, more heavily soiled items require more soap.

To ensure that adequate alkalinity is present for thorough washing, extra alkali is added to increase the effectiveness of the soap. Soaps with added alkali are known as *built* or *heavy-duty* soaps and are designed for general laundering. Less-alkaline soaps are also available for laundering more delicate fabrics. Because protein fibers are damaged by excessive alkali, only light-duty soaps should be used for washing wool, silk, and other delicate fabrics.

Non-soap Detergents

Synthetic detergent products are made from petroleum and natural fats and oils. Unlike soaps, synthetic detergents do not form hard-water scum but dissolve readily in both hard and soft water. Some detergents are made to maintain low suds levels, whereas others are made to produce more suds. Synthetic detergents are available in high-, medium-, and low-sudsing formulations. All suds levels clean equally well, but low-suds formulations are often necessary for optimum cleaning in front-loading washers, in which the laundry is carried up and around as the basket rotates. When the wet laundry reaches the top of the circle, it drops to the bottom, thereby providing the agitation necessary for releasing soil. High-suds detergents break the fall of the fabrics, thereby decreasing the washing action. Low-suds detergents provide the cleaning agent without interfering with the washing action.

Typically, non-soap synthetic detergents are formulated from the following materials: surfactants, builders, processing aids, agents to protect washer parts, antiredeposition agents, fluorescent whiteners, and perfumes.

1. *Surfactants.* Surfactants are organic chemicals, the active ingredient in synthetic detergents, that alter the properties of water and soil so that dirt can be removed. The surfactant molecule might be described as having a long "water-hating," or hydrophobic, body with a "water-loving," or hydrophilic, head. The action of the surfactant breaks up water droplets that surround soil particles, allowing water to penetrate. Groups of surfactant molecules (called *micelles*) surround the soil, with the hydrophobic section of the molecule

Figure 24.1

Diagram showing the action of a surfactant removing and suspending greasy soil.

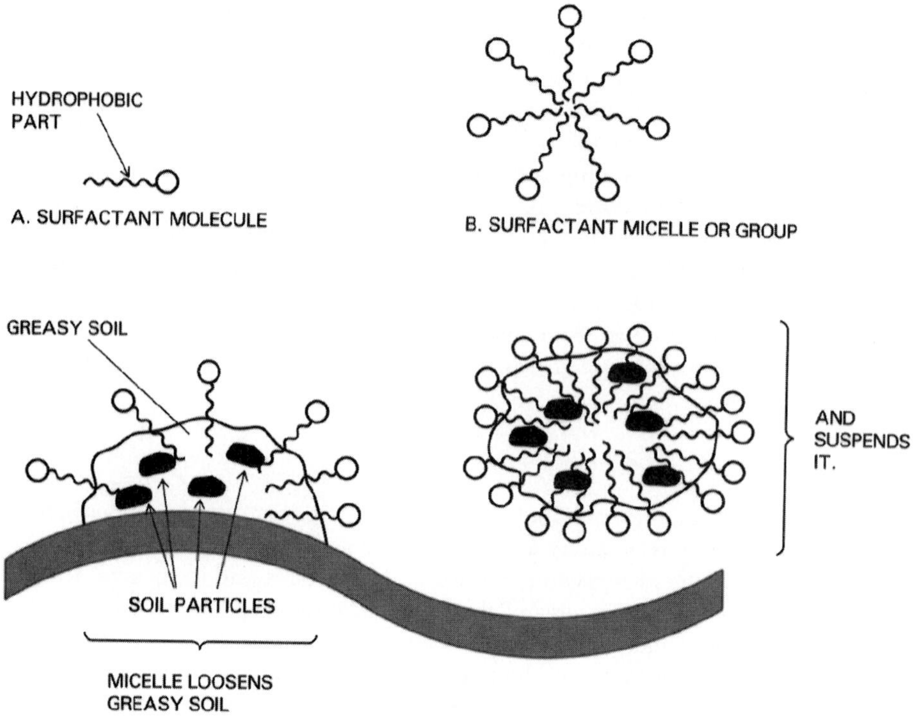

HYDROPHOBIC PART

A. SURFACTANT MOLECULE

B. SURFACTANT MICELLE OR GROUP

GREASY SOIL

AND SUSPENDS IT.

SOIL PARTICLES

MICELLE LOOSENS GREASY SOIL

attached to the soil and the water-loving head of the molecule oriented toward the water in which the particles become suspended (Figure 24.1). The most commonly used surfactants are linear alkyl benzene sulfonate (LAS), alcohol sulfates (AS), nonionic surfactants, and soap. Both LAS and AS surfactants and soap are anionic; that is, they generate negative electrostatic charges in water. Similar electric charges repel each other. Most fabrics also carry negative charges, so that the negative charge of the surfactant molecules surrounding the soil particles is effective in preventing the redeposition of soil on the fabrics being washed.

Nonionic surfactants do not carry electric charges as they dissolve. They are more effective in removing oily soil than are anionic surfactants. Soaps may also be used as a minor ingredient in detergent formulations because they help to break the foam produced by LAS-containing products. Soap is often used in controlled-suds products. Detergent manufacturers use one or more of these types of surfactants in their formulations. One of the popular detergent combinations is made up of LAS, soap, and nonionic surfactants.

2. *Builders.* Builders are substances that soften water and maintain alkalinity. Until recently, the majority of builders used in detergent formulations were phosphates, which are especially effective in counteracting water hardness. They also disperse and suspend dirt and maintain alkalinity, which is necessary to neutralize many soils that tend to be acid in chemical reaction.

Fears that phosphates may be contributing to water pollution have led some states and communities to restrict the use of phosphate-containing detergents. As a result, detergent manufacturers have developed a variety of nonphosphate or low-phosphate detergents that contain other builders. These nonphosphate builders include sodium silicate, sodium carbonate, sodium sulfate, and sodium citrate. Research has shown, however, that detergents containing these builders are not as effective in removing soil as are those with phosphates (Avery and Harabin 1975).

Some of these builders require high alkalinity to operate most efficiently and may irritate or harm the skin and/or mucous membranes. Such products must be labeled to warn consumers to use care in handling them.

3. *Processing aids.* Materials are added that maintain good powder properties in powdered detergents. Commonly used materials include sodium silicate (also cited previously as a builder), sodium sulfate, and small amounts of water.

4. *Agents to protect washing machine parts.* Silicates added to detergents help to prevent corrosion of the parts of the washer that are exposed to water and detergents.

5. *Antiredeposition agents.* Although anionic surfactants help to prevent the redeposition of soil, other agents are also added to the detergent to prevent redeposition. The most common chemical used for this purpose is sodium carboxymethyl cellulose.

6. *Fluorescent whiteners, or optical brighteners.* Fluorescent whiteners are additives that make white wash appear whiter and brighter. (See "Optical Brighteners" in chapter 20.)

7. *Perfumes.* Many detergents contain perfumes. These products give the laundered items a more pleasant odor.

8. *Other additives.* Enzymes, oxygen bleaches, blueing, and/or fabric softeners may be added to some detergents to create what the industry calls *multifunctional products.* Each of these additives can be purchased and used separately from the detergent by the consumer, as well.

The specific formulation of each synthetic detergent varies, of course, from one product to another. Detergent manufacturers have revised formulations to conform with restrictions on phosphates. Also, concern about the slow decomposition of some detergents in sewage treatment and in surface water has led to the use of biodegradable surfactants, which are readily decomposed after use.

Laundry detergents are produced in both liquid and powder form. Heavy-duty liquid detergents have shown remarkable growth in the last decade. One reason for the increase in these products is that they can be formulated more readily without phosphates than can powdered detergents.

Water Softeners or Conditioners

Synthetic detergents do not produce hard-water scum as soaps do, but it is necessary to use larger quantities of detergent in hard water than in soft water. (Soft water is free from these dissolved minerals.) Many families, therefore, find it helpful to decrease the hardness of water by some form of water conditioning. Hard water can be softened either by commercial softening systems installed in the home to soften all water used in the household or by the addition of powdered water softeners to the laundry. Powdered softeners are of two types: precipitating and nonprecipitating.

Precipitating water softeners combine with the minerals that cause water to become hard to form a compound that precipitates, or settles out of solution, into visible granules. These granules may be deposited on laundered items. Also, precipitating softeners must be added to wash water *before* the soap is added. They cannot dissolve soap scum once it has been formed. Super Washing Soda® is one example of a precipitating water softener.

Nonprecipitating water softeners keep hard-water minerals tied up in chemical combination and in solution so that neither soap scum nor a precipitate is formed. Furthermore, nonprecipitating softeners can dissolve soap scum formed before the softener was added to the water and can strip scum left in clothes from previous washings in hard water.

Minerals, such as iron or manganese, in water may stain fabrics. The addition of bleach to such water may cause the formation of colored salts that, when deposited on fabrics, cause discoloration. Nonprecipitating water softeners will prevent such staining by tying up the minerals. Calgon® is a nonprecipitating water softener.

Bleaches

Bleaches are often used along with soaps and synthetic detergents in laundering. It is important to remember that bleaches do not *clean* clothing. Detergents do the cleaning; bleaches are used to whiten fabrics and remove stains.

Bleaches oxidize the coloring matter in fabric, and some stains are removed by the oxidation of the coloring matter in them. Two basic types of bleaches are used in the home: chlorine bleaches and perborate bleaches.

Chlorine bleaches are the stronger of the two. They contain active chlorine to oxidize colored matter. But after the chlorine has oxidized all stains, color, and so on, it begins to oxidize susceptible fibers. For this reason, chlorine bleaches need to be used in correct concentrations, be dissolved thoroughly before application, and rinsed out thoroughly, or they may damage the fibers. Some dyes are damaged by chlorine bleach; therefore, it is rarely recommended that colored fabrics be bleached with chlorine bleach.

The following are the most frequent mistakes made in handling chlorine bleach.

- *Using too much bleach.* Follow directions on the package. Do not assume that if a little bleach is good, twice as much is better.
- *Pouring bleach directly onto clothing.* Bleach should be added to a full tub of water and agitated thoroughly before any laundry is added. Adding concentrated bleach to a washer full of clothing will result in concentrated bleach being poured over some garments, which may damage them. If bleach must be added to the wash at a later point, bleach should be diluted in one or more quarts of water before it is poured into the washer.
- *Bleaching items that should not be bleached.* Read care labels carefully. Some resins or fibers such as spandex will yellow on contact with chlorine bleach. Chlorine bleach damages fibers such as silk or wool or spandex.
- *Soaking heavily stained items in concentrated bleach solutions.* Exposure to concentrated bleach solutions may damage certain fibers and should be avoided. Items should not be soaked in even low concentrations of chlorine bleach for longer than 15 minutes.

Chlorine bleaches are sold in both dry and liquid forms under a variety of trade names. Clorox® and Purex® are trademarks of chlorine bleaches. It is important to rinse bleached fabrics carefully, or deterioration of the fibers can continue for as long as any bleach remains in the material.

Oxygen bleaches do not use chlorine for oxidation but use other chemicals such as sodium perborate, hydrogen peroxide, and potassium monopersulfate. They also do not whiten as efficiently in a short period of time. These bleaches will work best if used in hot water and in every laundering. Like chlorine bleaches, oxygen bleaches should be diluted before addition to the wash, as some colors may be sensitive to the bleaching action of these products. Some of the trade names of oxygen bleach include Clorox-2®, Snowy®, and Purex All Fabric Bleach®. Hydrogen peroxide is sold in drugstores as an antiseptic.

Pretreatment Products

Certain types of stains are especially hard to remove. Among these are protein-based stains such as body soils, blood, eggs, baby formula, grass stains, and chocolate. Special enzyme presoak products contain selected types of enzymes that may break down these soils to simpler forms that are then more readily and completely removed by the laundry soap or detergent. Fabrics are soaked from 30 minutes to overnight, depending on the instructions and the age and amount of the stain. Enzymes may be incorporated into the formulation of some multifunctional detergents.

Aerosol prewash soil and stain removers that contain perchlorethylene or other petroleum-based solvents are sold for use on synthetics and durable press fabrics. They help to remove greasy stains such as those made by lipstick, bacon fat, coffee with cream, and ballpoint pen. Instructions on the label generally recommend that they be applied to fabrics 5 minutes or longer before washing.

Fluorescent Whiteners, or Optical Brighteners

Most detergent formulations contain fluorescent whiteners. It is also possible to purchase fluorescent whiteners—referred to as optical brighteners—for use in the home. These agents do not attach themselves to different fibers to the same degree, so their effectiveness may vary from fiber to fiber. Also, chlorine bleach may destroy the active ingredients in fluorescent whiteners, so that the two products should never be added to the laundry at the same time.

Before optical brighteners for household use were developed, white laundry could only be treated with *blueing*. Blueing is a laundry product available in liquid or powder form that is added to the rinse cycle. It contains small quantities of blue dye that masks yellow color by reflecting blue-white light. In using blueing, one must follow directions carefully. Too great a concentration of the dye may give white laundry a bluish tint, instead of just cancelling out the yellow color.

Disinfectants

One of the purposes of laundering clothing and household items is to destroy bacteria. Ordinary laundering procedures using detergent and hot water will destroy many bacteria. Recent trends toward using cooler washing temperatures may have the effect of allowing more bacteria to survive, however, so that when there is illness or infection in a home, special care may be required to sanitize items being washed.

To be suitable for sanitizing laundry, a disinfectant should kill bacteria without injuring or discoloring fabrics. Furthermore, disinfectants should not leave a residue that is harmful to the user and they must be compatible with detergents. Four types of products meet these criteria:

1. *Liquid chlorine bleaches.* Labels should state that the bleach contains 5.25 percent of sodium hypochlorite.
2. *Quarternary disinfectants.* These are colorless and odorless compounds that are effective in hot, warm, or cold water. Such substances are available in drugstores, mass merchandisers, grocery stores, and from janitorial, hospital, or dairy supply houses.

3. *Pine oil disinfectants.* These products are effective in hot or warm water. They have a characteristic odor that does not remain after laundering. The label should state that the product contains at least 70 percent steam-distilled pine oil. Pine oil disinfectants are sold in supermarkets or grocery stores.

4. *Phenolic disinfectants.* Effective in warm or hot water, these products should be used according to directions on the package. Lysol® is the brand name of one of the better-known phenolic disinfectants.

Fabric Softeners

Fabric softeners deposit a waxy, lubricative substance on fibers that causes fabrics to feel softer. All fabric softeners are based on quarternary ammonium compounds. Although different chemical compounds are used, all have a long fatty chain that imparts the soft feel to the fabric. The softening effect is especially desirable for fabric with a napped or pile surface that may become stiffer and less soft after laundering, particularly if the fabrics are line dried rather than tumble dried. Towels, washable blankets, diapers, corduroy or other pile fabrics, and sweaters are often washed with fabric softeners.

In addition to making fabrics feel softer, fabric softeners cut down static electricity, make ironing easier, and improve the performance of wash-and-wear finishes, often making touch-up ironing unnecessary. At the same time, the continual use of fabric softeners causes a buildup of the softener on the fibers, thereby decreasing absorbency. On items where absorbency is an important function, such as towels or diapers, it is recommended that fabric softeners not be used in every wash but in alternate washings or periodically.

Fabric softeners are designed for addition to the wash, the rinse, or the drying cycle. Wash-added liquid fabric softeners should be added to the wash water *before* the detergent and the clothes are placed in the water to prevent fabric staining. These products can generally be used in the final rinse cycle as well.

Rinse-added fabric softeners cannot be used in the wash cycle, nor should they be used along with other laundry additives such as blueing or water softeners. These products and detergents may interfere or react adversely with the softener. They should be diluted, unless machine dispenser instructions state that this is not necessary, and they should not be poured directly onto fabrics as they may cause staining.

Dryer-added fabric softeners are added to a load of clothes in the dryer and are usually supplied in sheet form. Sheet-type softeners are impregnated into a nonwoven fabric or polyurethane foam sheet. The heat of the dryer and the tumbling action of the clothes cause the softener to be transferred to the clothes and spread evenly on the fabric surfaces.

Packages of fabric softeners provide specific instructions that should be followed carefully to achieve best results.

Starches

Starches are sizings that are added during home laundering. They help to restore body or stiffness to limp fabrics. Starches help to keep fabrics cleaner, as dirt tends to slide off the smooth finish produced by starching. Also, soil may become attached to the starching material rather than to the fiber, making the soil easier to remove.

Since vegetable starches were used originally for this purpose, the term *starch* was given to these products. Today, however, "starches" may be either vegetable or resinous compounds. Liquid or dry sizings are added in the rinse cycle of laundering. Aerosol

Fiber	Cycle Time	Water Temperature	Agitation and Spin Speed
Wool	1–3 min	110°–120°F	Slow
Cotton and linen	10–12 min	120°–140°F	Normal
Manufactured and durable press	5–7 min	110°–120°F	Slow

Table 24.1

Washing Machine Settings for Various Fibers

sprays are added at the time of ironing. Vegetable starches must be renewed after each washing. Resins penetrate the fiber more thoroughly and will last through several washings.

Laundry Equipment

Washing Machines. Except for hand-laundered items, most laundry in the home is done in washing machines. Washing machines may be of three types: automatic, semiautomatic, and wringer style. Many households use automatic dryers.

Each of these appliances differs in its construction, features, and operation. It is beyond the scope of this book to discuss the variety of types of laundry equipment in relation to the care of fabrics.

Although some fully automatic washers have programmed cycles that require only the selection of a suitable term, such as *permanent press,* it is more likely that the user will have to select water temperature, time duration for washing, and type of agitation. Most washers offer a low, moderate, or high water temperature; washing time durations of from 2 to 14 minutes; and either gentle or normal agitation. Washing machine instruction manuals give specific directions for selecting settings for varying types and loads of laundry. Of course, the user must select the detergent and other laundry additives such as bleach, water softener, fabric softener, and so on that are to be used in the wash.

Table 24.1 offers typical time, speed of agitation, and water temperature for various fiber groups.

The expansion of the use of wash-and-wear and durable press finishes has led to the manufacture of washers and dryers that have permanent press cycles. These cycles are designed to produce optimum performance from durable press finishes by using varying water temperatures in washing and rinsing, by offering decreased agitator speeds in extracting water, and by ending the drying cycle with a cool temperature to avoid heat-setting wrinkles into dried clothing. During the extraction of the water in the spin cycle, clothes are compressed against the basket walls. If the fabric is warm, the cooling that takes place will cause the fabrics to wrinkle, whereas the cool water cycles of the special durable press cycle provide better wrinkle resistance. If the clothes are to be dried in an automatic dryer, these wrinkles will be tumbled out of the fabric. If clothes are to be line dried, however, durable press items should be removed from the washer before the final spin cycle.

Laundry Procedures

Although the washer and dryer do the physical work of laundering, the selection of appropriate laundry procedures is essential for efficient cleaning. Sorting, selecting washing time and water temperature, pretreating spots and stains, and carefully selecting laundry products for use all require that decisions be made by the person doing the washing.

Laundry should be sorted carefully according to color, fiber type, degree of soil, and delicacy of construction. Items should be grouped together that require the same laundry products, water temperature, length of washing, and speed of agitation.

White items should be washed together. White permanent press and nylon fabrics are most prone to discoloration if washed with items of color and should be washed only with other whites. Colorfast items may be laundered together, even if the colors are not the same, but it is advisable to separate light and dark colors at least until it has been ascertained that the dark colors will not bleed. Those items that are not colorfast should be washed separately; in some cases they may have to be washed by hand.

Fabrics that produce lint, such as bath towels, chenille fabrics, terry items, and the like, should be washed separately from those that attract lint; that is, corduroy, synthetic fabrics, and durable press. It is especially important to separate light-colored lint-producing fabrics from dark-colored lint attractors, such as dark nylon underclothing or socks.

Loads should, as much as possible, be balanced with some small and some larger items. This will provide better washing action. However, lightweight manufactured fiber items should be dried separately from heavy cellulosic fabrics, such as towels, because the manufactured fiber items will dry first and then become overheated during the time required for the heavier, cotton fabrics to dry.

Heavy items such as blankets or bedspreads may have to be washed alone because of their size. When a heavy load is put into a washer, it should be arranged carefully so that the washer balance is maintained during spin cycles.

Heavily soiled items should not be washed with lightly soiled items, but alone. The lightly soiled items may pick up soil or discoloration from the wash water.

Before laundering, clothing should be checked carefully. Pockets should be emptied since coins or other items left in pockets can damage washers or dryers, and tissues left in pockets will produce lint that will be picked up by garments. Lint and dirt should be brushed out of pant cuffs. Zippers and hooks should be closed so that they do not catch onto other items and tear them. Pins, heavy ornaments, and buckles may also cause damage to fabrics and should be removed. Tears should be mended before laundering, as the agitation of washing and drying may cause them to be enlarged.

Some items may require pretreatment for optimum cleaning. Soil lines that are formed around collars and cuffs may be difficult to remove from synthetic and durable press fabrics. The area may be pretreated by dampening the area and then rubbing liquid detergent or a paste made of powdered detergent and water over the soiled area.

Stain Removal

Stains, which are specific substances spilled on a fabric as opposed to general soiling through use, should be treated as soon as possible. The longer a stain remains on an item, the harder it will be to remove.

In treating fabrics to remove stains, the first consideration must be the composition of the material that has been stained. Knowledge of fiber content may help to determine appropriate solvents. For example, attempting to remove a nail polish stain on an acetate fabric with nail polish remover that contains acetone would destroy the fabric. Once fiber content has been taken into consideration, then fabric structure must be evaluated. Rubbing hard on a stain on a pile fabric will flatten the pile. Rubbing may abrade the surface of a satin weave fabric.

Stain removal is easiest immediately after the fabrics have been subjected to staining. It is important to know the kind of material that caused the stain and the fiber of which the fabric is made. The selection of the method to use in removing the stain will be determined by the type of stain, and the type of stain remover to be used may be limited by the type of fabric.

Before any stain remover is used, the fabric should be tested to determine whether it is colorfast to the stain remover or whether it may have a finish that the stain remover will harm. Fabrics can be tested by sponging a small amount of stain remover onto a seam, hem, or other hidden part of the item. If a suitable stain remover cannot be found, the item should be taken to a professional dry cleaner for treatment.

Table 24.2 lists a wide variety of materials that may produce stains on fabrics and suggests appropriate treatments for fabrics that (1) are washable and (2) have fiber content and fabric structures that are compatible with the recommended treatment. Some stains cannot be removed. Extensive staining by hard-to-remove substances or stains on delicate and/or nonwashable fabrics are probably best removed by a professional dry cleaner who has a variety of spot- and stain-removing chemicals and an expert knowledge of stain removal. It is always helpful to the cleaner, however, if the customer points out the stain and identifies the staining substance.

Drying

Automatic dryers generally provide both time and temperature settings. Temperatures for drying may range from no heat to moderate and high temperatures. The drying time is determined by the size of the load and the weight of the fabrics being dried. Some dryers have an automatic sensor that turns off the dryer when the wash is dry, whereas others will continue to tumble for the length of time set on the dial, even after the laundry is dry.

Fabrics that have been laundered may be either line dried or dried in an automatic dryer. Some fabrics should not be dried in dryers, because the heat and action of the dryer may cause some shrinkage in heat-sensitive fabrics. Elastics made with natural rubber may lose their elasticity over a period of time if dried in a very hot dryer. Care labels should be consulted to ascertain whether fabrics should be placed in a dryer.

Heat-sensitive fabrics should be dried at low-heat or no-heat settings. Durable press and synthetic fabrics should be removed from the dryer immediately after completion of the drying cycle to prevent the setting of wrinkles. These fabrics should not be line dried.

Dryers in coin-operated laundromats often operate at much higher temperatures than do home units. Synthetics that dry quickly and are thermoplastic sometimes melt when they come in contact with the sides of the hot dryer drum.

As in washing, fabrics of similar colors should be dried together. It is possible for colors to run from one fabric to another if damp, noncolorfast fabrics are placed on top of other fabrics during drying.

Pressing

Although many synthetic and durable press fabrics will not require pressing, other items will need touch-up pressing before use. Linens and cottons require the highest temperature settings, synthetics the lowest. Even though irons have temperature

Table 24.2	Stain Removal Chart

Stain	Treatment
Adhesive tape, chewing gum, rubber cement	Apply ice or cold water to harden surface; scrape with a dull knife. Saturate with cleaning fluid. Rinse; then launder.
Baby formula	Soak in a product containing enzymes for at least 30 minutes (several hours for aged stains). Launder.
Beverages (coffee, tea, soft drinks, wine, alcoholic beverages)	Sponge or soak stain in cool water. Then pretreat with prewash stain remover, liquid laundry detergent, liquid detergent booster, or paste of granular laundry product and water. Launder using chlorine bleach, if safe for fabric, or an oxygen bleach. Older stains may respond to soaking in a product containing enzymes, then laundering.
Blood	If stain is fresh, soak in cold water. For dried stains, soak in warm water with a product containing enzymes. Launder. If stain remains, rewash using a bleach safe for fabric.
Brown or yellow discoloration from iron, rust, manganese	Use a rust remover recommended for fabrics; launder. Do not use a chlorine bleach to remove rust stains because it may intensify discoloration. For a rusty water problem, use a nonprecipitating water softener in both wash and rinse water. For severe problems, install an iron filter in the system.
Candle wax	Scrape off surface wax with a dull knife. Place stain between clean paper towels and press with a warm iron. Replace paper towels frequently to absorb more wax and to avoid transferring stains. Place stain face down on clean paper towels. Sponge remaining stain with cleaning fluid; blot with paper towels. Let dry. Launder. If any color remains, rewash using a chlorine bleach, if safe for fabric, or an oxygen bleach.
Chocolate	Prewash with a product containing enzymes in warm water or treat with a prewash stain remover. Launder. If stain remains, rewash using a bleach safe for fabric.
Collar, cuff soil	Pretreat with prewash stain remover, liquid laundry detergent, or paste of granular detergent and water. Launder.
Cosmetics	Pretreat with prewash stain remover, liquid laundry detergent, paste of granular detergent, or laundry additive and water or rub with bar soap. Launder.
Crayon	For a few spots, treat same as candle wax. For a whole load of clothes, wash with hot water using a laundry soap and 1 cup baking soda. If color remains, launder using chlorine bleach, if safe for fabric. Otherwise, soak in a product containing enzymes or an oxygen bleach using hottest water safe for fabric, then launder.
Dairy products (milk, cream, ice cream, yogurt, sour cream, cream soups)	Treat as for baby formula. Soak in a product containing enzymes. Launder.
Deodorants, antiperspirants	Pretreat with liquid laundry detergent. Launder. For heavy stains, pretreat with prewash stain remover. Allow to stand 5 to 10 minutes. Launder using an oxygen bleach.
Dye transfer	You can attempt restoration of white fabrics that have picked up color from other fabrics by using a packaged color remover, following label directions. Launder. If dye remains, launder again using a chlorine bleach, if safe for fabric. For colored fabrics and whites that cannot be chlorine bleached, soak in oxygen bleach. Launder. This type of stain can be prevented if proper sorting and laundering procedures are followed.
Egg	Treat as for baby formula. Soak in a product containing enzymes. Launder.
Fabric softener	Dampen the stain and rub with bar soap. Rinse out, then launder.
Fruit, juices	Wash with bleach safe for fabric.
Grass	Soak in a product containing enzymes. If stain persists, launder using chlorine bleach, if safe for fabric, or oxygen bleach.
Grease, oil (car grease, butter, animal fats, salad dressings, cooking oils, motor oils)	Pretreat with prewash stain remover, liquid laundry detergent, or liquid detergent booster. For heavy stains, place stain face down on clean paper towels. Apply cleaning fluid to back of stain. Replace paper towels under stain frequently. Let dry, rinse. Launder using hottest water safe for fabric.

(continued)

Table 24.2	(continued)

Stain	Treatment
Ink	Some inks in each of the following categories—ballpoint, felt tip, and liquid—may be impossible to remove. Laundering may set some types of ink. Try a pretreatment method using a prewash stain remover, denatured alcohol, or cleaning fluid.
	Use one of the following methods with denatured alcohol or cleaning fluid. First, sponge the area around the stain with the stain remover before applying it directly on the stain. Place stain face down on clean paper towels. Apply denatured alcohol or cleaning fluid to back of stain. Replace paper towels under the stain frequently. Rinse thoroughly. Launder.
	Another method is to place the stain over the mouth of a jar or glass and hold the fabric in a taut position. Drip the stain remover through the spot so that the ink will drop into the container as it is being removed. Rinse thoroughly. Launder.
Mildew	Badly mildewed fabrics may be damaged beyond repair. Launder stained items using chlorine bleach, if safe for fabric. Or soak in oxygen bleach and hot water; then launder.
Mud	When dry, brush off as much as possible. Pretreat with a paste of granular detergent and water, liquid laundry detergent, or a liquid detergent booster. Launder. For heavy stains, pretreat or presoak with a laundry detergent or a product containing enzymes. Launder.
Mustard	Pretreat with prewash stain remover. Launder using chlorine bleach, if safe for fabric.
Nail polish	May be impossible to remove. Try nail polish remover but do not use on acetate or triacetate fabrics. Place stain face down on clean paper towels. Apply nail polish remover to back of stain. Replace paper towels under stain frequently. Repeat until stain disappears, if it does. Rinse and launder.
Paint	**Water-based:** Rinse fabric in warm water while stains are still wet; then launder. Once paint is dry, it cannot be removed.
	Oil-based and varnish: Use the same solvent the label on the can advises for a thinner. If label is not available, use turpentine. Rinse. Pretreat with prewash stain remover, bar soap, or laundry detergent. Rinse and launder.
Perfume	Pretreat with prewash stain remover or liquid laundry detergent. Launder.
Perspiration	Use a prewash stain remover or rub with bar soap. If perspiration has changed the color of the fabric, apply ammonia to fresh stains, white vinegar to old stains and rinse. Launder using hottest water safe for fabric. Stubborn stains may respond to washing in a product containing enzymes or oxygen bleach in hottest water safe for fabric.
Pine resin	Sponge cleaning fluid into the stain; let dry. Mix liquid laundry detergent and ammonia; soak stain in the solution. Launder using liquid laundry detergent.
Scorch	Treat as for mildew. Launder using chlorine bleach, if safe for fabric. Or soak in oxygen bleach and hot water, then launder.
Shoe polish	**Liquid:** Pretreat with a paste of granular detergent and water; launder.
	Paste: Scrape residue from fabric with a dull knife. Pretreat with a prewash stain remover or cleaning fluid. Rinse. Rub detergent into dampened area. Launder using a chlorine bleach, if safe for fabric, or an oxygen bleach.
Tar	Scrape residue from fabric. Place stain face down on paper towels. Sponge with cleaning fluid. Replace paper towels frequently to absorb more tar and to avoid transferring stains. Launder in hottest water safe for fabric.
Tobacco	Dampen stain and rub with bar soap. Rinse. Soak in a product containing enzymes; then launder. If stain remains, launder again using chlorine bleach, if safe for fabric.
Typewriter correction fluid	Let stain dry thoroughly. Gently brush excess off with a clothes brush. Send to professional dry cleaner and mention the type of stain.
Urine, vomit, mucous, feces, or stool	Soak in a product containing enzymes. Launder using chlorine bleach, if safe for fabric, or use oxygen bleach.

Source: Reprinted courtesy of the Soap and Detergent Association.

settings for different fabric types, the iron temperature should be tested in an inconspicuous part of the item, as thermostats of irons vary in accuracy.

Fabrics are best pressed when they are slightly damp or with steam, as wrinkles are removed more easily. Dark-colored fabrics of all fibers, silks, acetates, and rayons should be ironed from the wrong side to prevent shine. When these fabrics require pressing on the right side, press over a press cloth, not directly on the fabric.

Wool fabrics should be pressed with steam or a dampened press cloth. Silk should be pressed with a dry press cloth. Fabrics with textured surface should be tested carefully to see if ironing will flatten the surface. Sometimes these fabrics can be pressed lightly on the wrong side over a folded terry towel or other soft surface. Corduroy can be pressed in this way, although it is better to use a special pressing board called a needle board. Velvets, velveteens, and plushes also require the use of a needle board. These fabrics may respond better to steaming (holding a steam iron or a "wrinkle remover" steamer several inches away), then hanging to dry to allow the wrinkles to hang out. The same effect may be achieved by hanging items in a bathroom that is warm and moist from a hot shower.

Commercial Laundering

Commercial laundering procedures are used by local dry-cleaning establishments to clean washable items such as men's shirts or household linens. Commercial laundering procedures are similar to those used in the home, except that the conditions under which laundry is done commercially are more controlled and wash loads are considerably larger than in the home laundry. These large wash loads are made up of items from a number of different customers, so that identification numbers or tags must be affixed to each item for identification purposes.

The first step in the commercial laundering process is to sort the fabrics. Items are separated accordingly to color, fiber content, and degree of soil. As many as twelve different classifications can be used.

Different laundries utilize different detergent formulations and procedures, but, in general, bleachable items are subjected to several sudsings with soap or detergent and added alkali at temperatures of 125° to 160°F, a chlorine bleaching at 160°F for 3 to 5 minutes, three or four rinses at different temperatures, each one lower than the last, an acid sour, and blueing. In the rinse, starch is added for those items for which customers have requested it.

The purpose of the acid sour is to neutralize the alkalinity of the water, to remove iron stains, to kill bacteria, and to destroy excess or unused bleach. Some typical sours are acetic acid, sodium bisulfite, sodium acid fluoride, and oxalic acid.

Light-colored fabrics are washed at lower temperatures than are white fabrics, generally, 100° to 120°F, and no chlorine bleach is used. Dark-colored fabrics are laundered at still lower temperatures, 90° to 100°F, as they are more likely to lose color or bleed at higher temperatures. They, too, are not bleached.

After the final rinse, fabrics are spun in an extractor to remove excess water. The extraction may be done by the same machine that washes the items, or it may be done by a separate piece of equipment. This step is comparable to the spin-dry cycle on home washers. After extraction the fabrics are dryer dried and, if the customer wishes, pressed. Different types of pressing equipment are used for various items. Flat pieces are ironed on a machine called a *flatwork* ironer. A smooth, heated iron plate provides the heat and pressure, while the fabrics travel across a rotating, padded roll.

Special equipment is made for ironing shirts, small pieces, and oversized items such as curtains.

Customers may send washable silk and wool garments to commercial laundries. These are handled in special machines and without the use of chlorine bleach. Neutral soaps and detergents are used without additional alkali, and the washing machine uses a gentle agitation. Three to five rinses are needed to remove all the soap and detergent, so that discoloration of the fabric does not take place. An acid sour is used. Extraction is done gently.

Dry Cleaning

The term *dry cleaning* derives from the use of special cleaning solvents that dry quickly. Washing of cloth has been the chief method of cleaning washable fabrics since before the beginning of recorded history. Dry cleaning is a relatively recent development, supposedly discovered in 1825 by a Frenchman, Jean Bapiste Jolly, who observed that a tablecloth over which the contents of a paraffin lamp were spilled lost its staining in the area of the spill. He recognized that he might be able to clean clothing using this solvent and established the first dry-cleaning business. Benzene replaced paraffin as the solvent fairly early, but the technique was still a far cry from present-day dry-cleaning processes. Originally, the entire garment was taken apart, and each piece was cleaned separately by dipping it into pans of benzene. The pieces were brushed on a scouring board, dipped again, dried in a warm oven, and ultimately reassembled.

For both economic and environmental reasons, used dry-cleaning solvents are not discarded; instead, they are recycled and reused. Solvents are purified, and accumulated soil is removed either by filtration or distillation. The continual use of dirty solvent will interfere with cleaning.

After cleaning, the garments are checked for spots or stains that have not been removed in the dry cleaning. Spotters are trained to handle different fabrics and stains as effectively as possible.

If dry cleaning and spotting have not been adequate to remove all soil, the garments may have to be wet cleaned. Wet cleaning is not laundering, but the treatment of fabrics with small amounts of water to remove soil.

Final touches are given to the clean garment in the finishing department. Buttons or trimmings that have been removed are replaced, garments are steamed or, if necessary, pressed, and minor repairs are made.

Storage of Textile Products

Between uses, textile items may be put away for either short or long periods of time. Some attention to the way in which clothing is stored may help to prolong the life of textile products.

Textile products will wear longer if given a chance to "rest" between uses. Rotating items in use, either clothing or household textiles, will provide this rest period. Storage practices may encourage this rotation. For example, towels or bed linens that have been laundered may be placed at the bottom of the stack of items, and the next item to be used taken from the top of the stack.

When table linens, bed linens, or other items are pressed, care should be taken to fold these items at different places. Continuous folding of fabrics, especially where sharp creases are pressed into the material, in the same place will cause the yarns to break or wear first in those spots.

Areas that show up as light spots on this photograph are holes created by moth larvae.

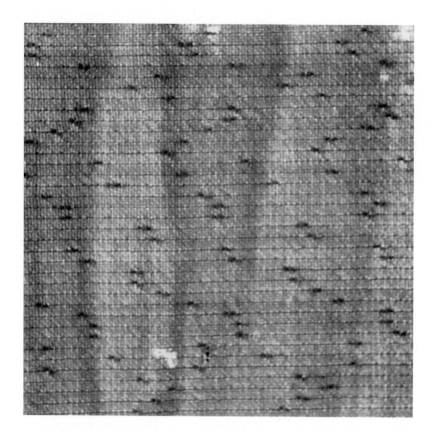

Fabrics that are to be put away for long-term storage should always be put away clean. Moths or other insects and fungi will more readily attack soiled fabrics. Furthermore, some spots or stains that are only slightly evident may be oxidized. Oxidized stains darken and are exceedingly difficult to remove. Fabrics should not be put away with pins left in them, as the pins may rust and cause stains to appear around the pinned area.

Fabrics that are subject to attack by insects and mildew should be stored carefully. Wool and animal hair fabrics can be mothproofed before storage or stored in tightly closed containers with moth repellents. (See Figure 24.2.)

Fabrics that are susceptible to mildew should be stored clean and dry, in a dry place. The fairly widespread use of central or room air conditioning has decreased humidity in many buildings. Closed closets can hold humidity, so that leaving doors slightly ajar or using ventilated doors will help to prevent humidity buildup in closed areas.

If fabrics that are normally starched are to be stored for a long period of time, it is best to store them without starching, as silverfish find the starch especially appetizing. If starch is required later, garments can be spray starched before use. If starched garments are stored, they should be put away in a closed container that insects cannot penetrate.

Historic Costumes and Textiles

Historic costumes and/or textiles may be collected by museums, historical societies, and individuals. Once acquired, these materials are generally stored and may be displayed periodically. The general storage principles outlined heretofore apply to historic materials, but given their age and fragility, additional cautions should be observed.

As in selection of any care procedure, the fiber from which the item is made must be considered. Historic fabrics are generally made from natural materials: cotton, linen, silk, or wool. The most important considerations in storing these materials is that they be stored away from light and in acid-free containers.

Ordinary paper contains acid residues that may cause deterioration of fabrics. Special acid-free boxes and tissue paper are manufactured. The names of several of the firms that sell these supplies are listed at the end of this chapter. Items should not be stored in plastic bags as these bags will deteriorate and release substances that may harm the fabrics, a phenomenon referred to as *off-gassing*. Ideally, temperature and humidity should be maintained at 70°F, 60 percent relative humidity.

As with other materials, it is best if historic fabrics are clean when stored; however, ordinary laundering and dry-cleaning processes may be too harsh for these materials. Some items made from cotton or linen can be laundered by hand if special precautions are taken. The bibliography at the end of this chapter includes several references in which specific instructions for laundering of historic textiles are given.

Wool and silk garments cannot be laundered. Nor should they be dry cleaned except by an expert in historic conservation who has been trained to handle these materials. To remove loose dust and soil silk and wool garments can be vacuumed, using a small hand vacuum cleaner. Items should be placed on a flat table for support. Synthetic netting should be placed between the item to be cleaned and the vacuum cleaner. Care must be taken to avoid damage to trimmings. See Consumer Box 24.1.

The names and addresses of organizations devoted to the study of historic textiles and costumes are listed at the end of this chapter, and a list of publications dealing with the care, preservation, and restoration of historic material is included in the bibliography in Appendix A.

Permanent-Care Labeling Requirements

Since July 1972 wearing apparel and fabrics sold by the yard must carry a permanently affixed label giving instructions for the care of the item. Current provisions of the rules are as follows. All textile wearing apparel and piece goods sold for making apparel are subject to the legislation except shoes, gloves, hats, and items not "used to cover and protect the body," such as belts, neckties, handkerchiefs, and suspenders. Nonwoven, one-time use garments are also excluded, as are manufacturers' fabric remnants up to 10 yards in length when the fiber content is not known and cannot easily be determined, and trim up to 5 inches wide. These provisions apply whether the items were manufactured in the United States or abroad.

Manufacturers are required to provide full care instructions about regular care or to provide warnings if a garment cannot be cleaned without harm. Care labels are attached to finished garments before they are sold. These labels must remain legible throughout the useful life of the garment. Piece goods information is to be provided on the end of each roll or bolt. Consumers, therefore, would need to make note of care procedures themselves when purchasing piece goods, as copies of instructions are not provided.

Labels must be placed so that they can be seen or easily found by consumers at the point of sale. If packaging obscures the label, additional information should appear on the outside of the package or on a hang tag fastened to the product.

CONSUMER BOX
24.1 Preserving Antique and Heirloom Textiles

Consumers may want to preserve such diverse items as a recently worn wedding dress, vintage clothing, or antique quilts and samplers. In handling textiles that you want to preserve, be sure you are working in a clean area, that your hands are clean, and that you are not wearing jewelry that will catch on delicate fabrics. Support fragile items so that no one place in the fabric must sustain the full weight of the fabric.

Do not allow newsprint, gummed tape, wood, or iron to remain in contact with objects during storage or display. If objects are to be displayed, use only acid-free backing materials, use no glue or adhesives, minimize exposure to light, rotate pieces, and display behind glass that filters out ultraviolet light.

Following are some common problems encountered in long-term preservation of both old and new textiles and the recommended means of preventing or solving those problems.

Problem	Solution
Loss of strength	Store away from the light, preferably in acid-free materials or wrapped in clean, undyed cotton fabrics. Weighted silks dating from the late nineteenth century up to the 1920s are likely to break apart. Nothing can be done to prevent this, nor can damaged fabrics be repaired.
Color changes	White silk and wool will usually yellow over time; this cannot be prevented. Acetate may be subject to fume fading. Store so that items are not exposed to atmospheric gases.
Development of stains during storage	Put items away clean so that spills that may not show at the time of last usage do not oxidize and appear later. To avoid rust spots, be sure no pins are left in items, and wrap metal zippers, hooks, snaps, and buttons so that they will not touch the fabric.
Damage from moths, carpet beetles	Put away clean. Store in closed container with moth repellent, or if odor from moth repellent is a problem, store for a week in an airtight container with moth insecticide, remove, put away, and monitor material for signs of insect activity.
Damage from mildew	Store only in dry, well-ventilated area. Do not wrap in plastic.
Development of cracks or breaks at folds	If possible, roll large items such as quilts or tablecloths around a cardboard tube or dowel covered with acid-free paper. Cover items with clean, undyed cotton fabric. If items must be folded, pad folds with acid-free tissue, and change the position of the folds periodically.
Yellowing of starched cottons and linens	Put items away unstarched. Starch also makes cotton and linen materials appetizing to silverfish.
Mysterious holes in vintage garments of the 1940s and 50s	Nitrocellulose plastics used in buttons can decompose and, if garments are stored where there is no air circulation, release nitric acid fumes that damage or discolor the fabric. If items are believed to have buttons of this type, remove before the item is stored.

Some types of products, however, need not include any care instructions. These are products sold to institutional buyers for commercial use, such as employee uniforms that are purchased by and cared for by a hospital, garments custom made from fabric provided by the customer, and items completely washable and sold at retail for $3.00 or less.

Some other products need not have permanently affixed labels but have to be provided with temporary labels. Totally reversible clothing without pockets and those granted exemptions because a label would harm their appearance or usefulness are cited in the rule, although special permission for items in the latter category must be obtained through petition. Products that may be washed, bleached, dried, ironed, or dry-cleaned by the harshest procedures available are also exempt, provided that the instruction "Wash or Dry Clean, Any Normal Method" appears on a temporary label that is conspicuous at the point of sale.

The directions to manufacturers as to the contents of the care label make the following stipulations. The label must have either a washing or dry-cleaning instruction. If a product can be both washed and dry-cleaned, it need carry only one of these instructions. If it can be neither washed nor dry-cleaned, the label must say "Do Not Wash—Do Not Dry Clean."

The rule includes a glossary of terms. It is recommended, but not required, that the terms in this glossary be used when applicable. Symbols may be used in addition to words, but symbols alone are not permitted.

If a garment is labeled as washable, the label must say whether the product should be washed by hand or machine, and if regular use of hot water will harm the product, a water temperature must be stated. For example, a label that says "Machine Wash, Cold" means that the consumer can machine wash the garment but only in cold water. A label that says "Machine Wash" means that any temperature ranging from cold to hot could be used. The word "wash" cannot be used alone but must stipulate whether the item should be machine or hand washed.

If all commercially available bleaches can be used on a regular basis, the label need not mention bleach. If chlorine bleach would harm the garment, but nonchlorine bleach would not, the label should say "Only Nonchlorine Bleach When Needed." If all commercially available bleaches would harm the product, the label should say "No Bleach" or "Do Not Bleach."

The appropriate drying method must be stipulated, and if regular use of high temperature would be harmful, the appropriate temperature setting must be given. "Machine Wash, Tumble Dry" would indicate that there are no restrictions of washing or drying temperatures.

Ironing information is to be given if ironing will be needed on a regular basis. As in washing and drying instructions, temperature should be stipulated unless a hot iron can be used without harm.

The rule also requires that consumers be warned against processes that they might be expected to use that would harm the product. For example, if ironing would be harmful to a garment that consumers might touch up occasionally, the label should read "Do Not Iron." If an item is not colorfast, it must be labeled "Wash Separately" or "Wash with Like Colors." It is not necessary to warn users about alternate procedures that may be harmful to the item. For example, if instructions say "Dry Flat," it is not required that labels also say "Do Not Tumble Dry."

For items labeled as dry-cleanable, other provisions apply. If all commercially available types of solvents can be used, the label need not mention any type of solvent. If one or more solvents would harm the product, a solvent that is safe to use

Garments with faulty care labels. (a) Garment with "Dry clean only" label has white surface dots that were not resistant to dry-cleaning solvent. The solvent caused them to dissolve and transfer to other portions of the garment. (b) Dry cleaning is recommended on care label; however, after the garment was dry-cleaned, one sleeve and one side of the front showed severe color loss. The manufacturer apparently used two different bolts of fabric in the one garment, and one bolt was colored with dye that was not fast to dry cleaning. It is the manufacturer's responsibility to ascertain that garments can be handled according to care labels. Reprinted by permission of International Fabricare Institute. Copyright by International Fabricare Institute; all rights reserved.

(a)

(b)

must be mentioned. If any part of the dry-cleaning process will harm the garment, the label must warn "Do not . . ." or "No . . ." or provide other wording that would clarify appropriate procedures. For example, "Professionally Dry Clean, No Steam" would indicate that no steam should be used in pressing or finishing the garment. If the words "Dry Clean" are used without the word "Professionally" in front of it, the item should be dry-cleanable by any machine process with no restric-

---

CONSUMER BOX
24.2

The Dress That Can't Be Cared For

This is the story of a white dress with blue sequins that has two distinct care labels. The story was originally reported in *Clothes Care Gazette,* November 1991.

These two care labels were attached to the same sequin dress.

DRY CLEAN ONLY
REMOVE SEQ TRIM

USE A PROFESSIONAL DRY CLEANER ONLY
INSTRUCT CLEANER TO USE SHORT CYCLES—5 MINUTES
INSTRUCT CLEANER TO USE PURE PERCHLORETHYLENE ONLY
INSTRUCT CLEANER TO USE MAXIMUM 120F IN DRYCLEANING PROCESS
INSTRUCT CLEANER NOT TO PRESS OR STEAM GARMENT
Do NOT allow perfume, deodorant, hair spray, or alcoholic beverages to come into contact with sequins.
  If garment should become dampened with perspiration or water:
  1. Do NOT place garment in airtight container or plastic bag.
  2. Dry garment in air. Do NOT use heat.
  3. Be certain garment is dry before dry cleaning.

The smaller care label recommends dry clean only, **remove sequin trim.** This is impossible. The many sequins on the article are actually sewn to it. It would be impossible for anyone to remove the sequins, clean the garment, and then reattach them. Obviously, this label was not intended for a garment of this type. Furthermore, the larger care label has other problems in that it recommends the dry cleaner use perchloroethylene only. Unfortunately, perchloroethylene dissolved the dye on the sequins almost immediately and this caused many of the blue sequins to turn white after cleaning. In addition to this, the instructions suggest the garment should be dried in the air, which is against all regulations that govern the professional dry cleaner using perchloroethylene.

In this case, the dry cleaner cleaned it in a short, two-minute cycle, which is in line with the care label, only to experience drastic loss of color on some of the blue sequins. Additional colorfastness tests indicated the sequin trim would be colorfast to a washing procedure, but the extensive finishing details on the article would not withstand a washing process. This garment is fabricated in such a way that it cannot be successfully dry cleaned or washed—certainly not according to the care instructions given on either label.

Source: Reprinted by permission of International Fabricare Institute. "The Dress That Can't Be Cared For," November 1991. Copyright © 1991 by IFI, all rights reserved.

---

tions on solvents, moisture content, heat, and steam. "Professionally Dry Clean" is used when the normal dry-cleaning process must be modified in some way. This term is not used alone but must be followed by a description of the modifications that are needed. For example "Professionally Dry Clean, Short Cycle, No Steam" would mean that any commercially available solvent could be used, the cleaning time should be reduced, and steam should not be used during pressing or finishing (FTC 1984).

The problems that can result from an improper care label are illustrated in Figure 24.3 and Consumer Box 24.2.

Textile Tests for the Evaluation of Dimensional Change

Consumers find that changes in the dimensions of fabrics often take place after laundering or dry cleaning. (See chapter 21 for a discussion of factors involved in shrinkage of textiles.) Sometimes these changes make products unusable. It is possible for manufacturers and textile researchers to perform tests that will ascertain whether textile fabrics will undergo dimensional change as a result of laundering or dry cleaning.

Directions for the preparation of samples for testing and the procedures for laundering or dry cleaning are set forth in test specifications published in the AATCC *Technical Manual.* The process requires the measurement of test samples before and after laundering or dry cleaning and the calculation of the percentage of change in both the lengthwise and crosswise direction of the fabric.

Further Sources of Information

Many organizations publish booklets or pamphlets that offer information to the consumer about the care of textile products. Soap and detergent manufacturers and consumer magazines frequently publish materials that instruct the consumer in the appropriate care techniques for textiles of all kinds.

Consumers who wish to obtain further information about textile cleaning, storage, and maintenance can often find current information on these subjects from the Department of Agriculture and from State Home Economics Extension Offices. Lists of publications of the U.S. Department of Agriculture can be obtained from the U.S. Government Printing Office, Washington, D.C. 20402. Most of these materials are published as "Home and Garden Bulletins." Lists of state extension publications are generally available from the land-grant college in each state.

Manufacturers of detergents and other laundry products also write and distribute a variety of informational materials for consumers and professionals. The Soap and Detergent Association holds symposia for its members and others at which new developments are examined. The proceedings of these meetings are published and can be obtained by those who are unable to attend meetings. The International Fabricare Institute, an organization that does research and supplies current information to dry-cleaning establishments, publishes newsletters and fact sheets about dry-cleaning practices and problems. These materials can be obtained by purchasing a membership in the institute for a reasonable fee.

References

Avery, C. E., and D. Harabin. 1975. *A comparison of phosphate and non-phosphate detergents.* Bulletin No. 415. Kingston, R.I.: Agricultural Experiment Station, Univ. of Rhode Island.

FTC. 1984. (March). *Writing a care label* [pamphlet]. Washington, D.C.: Bureau of Consumer Protection, Federal Trade Commission.

Review Questions

1. Describe the purpose of each of the following substances during laundering of soiled textiles, and explain how each substance accomplishes its purpose.

   detergents   fluorescent whiteners

   water softeners   fabric softeners

   bleaches

2. Explain why it is desirable to have a cool rinse as the final cycle in laundering durable press garments.
3. Make a list of do's and don'ts that you would give to consumers if you were assigned to advise them about laundering procedures.
4. Make a list of do's and don'ts that you would give to consumers if you were assigned to advise them about having clothing dry-cleaned.
5. Develop five generalizations about stain removal procedures that you can derive from Table 24.2.
6. Based on what you have learned about the properties of textile fibers and fabric constructions, develop care labels that meet permanent-care labeling requirements for each of the following imaginary textile products. Explain why you chose these care procedures.

   • Plain weave 100 percent cotton shirt dyed dark navy blue. The shirt has no special finishes.

   • White 100 percent silk chiffon blouse with white silk embroidered decoration.

   • Jersey knit sweater of 100 percent acrylic fiber.

Recommended Readings

Bevan, G. 1979. Mechanism of soiling of textiles. *Textiles* 8 (October): 69.

Drycleaning. 1994. *Textiles Magazine* 23 (2): 11.

Harvey, E. 1993. Handling antique items. *International Fabricare Institute Bulletin* (July).

Lloyd, J., and C. Adams. 1989. Domestic laundering of textiles. *Textiles* 18 (3): 72.

Lusk, C. B. 1975. The invisible danger of visible light. *Museum News* (April): 22.

Making your clothing last—a practical guide. 1994. *Clothes Care Gazette,* no. 86 (September): 1.

Oehlke, N. 1990. Care labels and you. In *ACPTC Proceedings,* ed. P. E. Horridge, 7. Monument, Colo.: Association of College Professors of Textiles and Clothing, Inc.

Soap and Detergent Association. *A handbook of industry terms.* 1987. New York: Soap and Detergent Association.

Store your wedding gowns carefully. 1994. *Clothes Care Gazette* no. 85 (August): 3.

What is drycleaning? *Clothes Care Gazette,* no. 89 (December): 1.

Sources of Storage Supplies for Historic Textiles

Conservation Materials Ltd., 1395 Greg St., Suite #110, Sparks, NV 89431

Conservation Resources International, 8000–H Forbes Place, Springfield, VA 22151

Talas, 213 West 35th Street, New York, NY 10001

University Products, P.O. Box 101, Holyoke, MA 01041

Organizations That Study Historic Costumes and Textiles

Costume Society of America, 55 Edgewater Drive, P.O. Box 75, Earleville, MD 21919

The Textile Conservation Group, c/o Department of Anthropology, American Museum of Natural History, Central Park West at 79th Street, New York, NY 10024–5192

Textile Society of America, c/o 4401 San Andreas Ave., Los Angeles, CA 90065

TEXTILES AND THE ENVIRONMENT, HEALTH, AND SAFETY

G rowing awareness of the relationship between individual, business, and industry practices and a healthy and safe environment for consumers and workers has led to concerns about the ecological impact of textile use, production, and processing. As a result, some consumers purchase products they believe are environmentally friendly, have changed their practices in caring for textile products, or engage in recycling. Other environmental, health, and safety problems may be less obvious to the general consumer but have important economic implications for the textile industry.

Legislation and Regulation

The generation of air, water, and soil pollution and health hazards for textile workers and consumers have led governmental bodies to enact laws and regulations that are intended to protect individuals and the environment. A number of those laws have a significant impact on textile and textile product manufacturing. Of particular importance to the textile industry are the Occupational Safety and Health Act (OSHA), which regulates the safety of the workplace, The Toxic Substances Control Act, which regulates the management of toxic substances within the workplace, and licensing requirements and pollution limits imposed by the United States Environmental Protection Agency (EPA) under the Clean Water and the Clean Air Acts. The former regulates discharge into waterways, and the later controls air emissions.

Discharge of materials into waterways is also controlled under the Safe Drinking Water Act.

The National Environmental Policy Act requires license applications for "environmentally dangerous activities" and requires environmental impact assessments. Under the Resource Conservation and Recovery Act and the Pollution Prevention Act, stress is placed on limiting the amount of material coming into the waste stream for disposal. The Pollution Prevention Act requires that businesses submit source reduction and recycling reports each year.

Many states have also enacted environmental legislation that affects textile industries. While these laws have improved the safety of textile production and have helped to protect the environment, they have also had an impact on industry productivity, profitability, and competitiveness with imported products from countries that do not have comparable environmental legislation. It should also be noted that although the textile industry contributes to environmental pollution, it is not on the list of major polluters targeted by the federal government.

Environmentally Friendly Products

Consumers with a strong commitment to protecting the environment are ecologically conscious shoppers. They look for products manufactured in ways that do not harm the environment and products that will save natural resources during or after use. The textile industry has responded by publicizing those products that are environmentally friendly. Examples include the new regenerated cellulosic fiber lyocell, organically grown cotton, naturally colored cotton, naturally dyed fabrics, and recycled textiles.

Organic cotton, which is grown without the use of pesticides, is increasing as a proportion of cotton production in the United States. Consumers pay a higher price for organic cotton, but cost should be reduced if demand increases.

Concerns about use of synthetic dyes have led to consumer interest in purchasing products dyed with natural dyes. Natural dyes from plants, insects, and minerals are being used in modern mills to color fabrics. The consistency of the dye lots is lower than with synthetic dye processes, and the fabrics are not as colorfast; however, the response of environmentally conscious consumers to the products has been very good.

It is not just the manufacture of textile products that affects the environment. Studies have shown that most of the environmental impact from textile products occurs during their use (Ecolabelling 1994). Energy and water are consumed in caring for textile products. Pollution may be produced by laundering and dry cleaning.

Because the lifetime of machines for washing and drying textile products is finite, their disposal also contributes to the stream of consumer waste. The Association of Home Appliance Manufacturers (AHAM) has established an Appliance Recycling Information Center that will encourage appliance recycling by conducting research, influencing public policy, educating consumers, and disseminating information. Recycling discarded appliances not only keeps these materials out of landfills but also serves as a source of metals, particularly steel. Four times as much energy is required to manufacture steel from virgin iron ore than to make the same steel from salvaged scrap metal.

Marketing to environmentally conscious consumers may result in *ecolabeling* of products. One such scheme is being proposed in Europe, where the European Union

(EU) will require labeling of textile products according to the environmental impact of their manufacture as well as their use and ultimate disposition.

Textiles and Pollution

Manufacturing

Textile production has always been a source of water pollution. Not only the manufactured fibers but also natural fibers create pollutants, as in the scouring of wool and in many of the dyeing and finishing operations. The concern with industrial pollution of air, soil, and water has focused attention on by-products of textile manufacture. Federal, state, and regional standards for air, water, and hazardous solid waste have been imposed on businesses, industries, and municipalities, and textile companies must comply with these regulations.

Air Pollution

Problems in relation to air pollution are generated during heat setting of fabrics and in curing of finished fabrics. Heat causes the vaporization of organic compounds used in such finishes as durable press or coating of fabrics. They are carried off as airborne gases. In piece dyeing, some dye materials are carried off in water vapor. A wide variety of processing steps involve chemical solvents that may vaporize. Where possible, companies attempt to prevent pollution and also save money by recovering and reusing chemical solvents.

Water Pollution

Water pollution can take place at almost any step of textile production, from preparation of the fiber through to the finishing of fabrics, posing a threat to fish and the ecological balance of streams. The dyeing and finishing of fabrics require a great deal of water, and the disposal of chemicals used in these processes presents serious problems for the manufacturer. These environmental concerns have led to the development of processes that use less water, such as foam and low-wet-pickup finishing and dyeing, and to dyebath reuse.

The legal requirements for meeting clean water standards imposed by local, state, or national governments have led the textile industry to look for means of waste disposal that do not pollute streams. Recycling of water or other processing materials (such as sizing), treating the water in special wastewater treatment facilities to render it safe or remove pollutants, and using biodegradable substances are techniques used by manufacturers to maintain clean water. Difficulties encountered in meeting clean water requirements have led some textile companies to discontinue the manufacture of some products, such as rayon (see chapter 7).

Solid Waste

Disposal of solid wastes from textile firms and from chemical companies associated with the textile industry is another difficulty. Incineration and burial, which have been used to eliminate wastes, both present problems. Burial may lead to the contamination of groundwater, to fires, or to the generation of noxious gases from the indiscriminate mixing of chemical substances. Incineration may produce air pollution or water pollution as a by-product of the incineration process. To be successful, both processes require careful monitoring and control.

Solid waste materials that require disposal are many and varied. Some waste products from fiber synthesis and spinning, finishing, and dyeing may be contaminated with toxic chemicals. Not only yarn and fabric scraps but also storage, packing, and shipping materials add to the solid waste stream.

Industry Programs

As a result of environmental regulations and concerns, industry groups have developed a number of programs to help companies comply with requirements. The American Textile Partnership (AMTEX) is a consortium made up of Cotton Inc., the Institute of Textile Technology, The Textile/Clothing Technology Corporation, Textile Research Institute, and the National Textile Center, which consists of Auburn University, Clemson University, Georgia Tech, and North Carolina State, together with an industry operating board and a number of Department of Energy laboratories across the country. This government-industry partnership, which is intended to enhance technology through research, has identified promoting environmental quality and waste minimization as one of its initiatives. Another will focus on energy. After AMTEX's first year of operation, its Textile Resource Conservation (TreC) project was already demonstrating advances in polyester/cotton recovery and recycling, and application of chemical finishes to textiles with minimal water use (AMTEX 1995).

The American Textile Manufacturers Institute (ATMI) launched its Encouraging Environmental Excellence (E3) campaign in 1992 to promote environmental awareness and preservation in the industry. Member companies pledge to adhere to a ten-point plan of action that includes performing environmental audits, developing spill prevention and control plans, conducting employee training in environmental practices, distributing recycling bins, and providing environmental expertise to cities and towns. Companies are working together to minimize waste in manufacturing processes and with suppliers to reduce the waste coming into plants.

Environmental awareness has become an important factor in manufacturing. Some apparel manufacturers and retailers help to support the efforts of manufacturers by purchasing fabrics from companies that emphasize waste reduction. According to David Mention, manager of process improvement at L. L. Bean, "When we rate our suppliers, environmental soundness is right there with quality goods, timely delivery, innovations, and the soundness of their business. . . ." (Maycumber 1994, 2).

Laundering and Dry Cleaning

The fear of water pollution from household wastes that contain large quantities of phosphates has led a number of states to restrict phosphate-containing detergents. Phosphates have been used in laundry detergents because they are very effective in enhancing detergent performance. (See chapter 24 for a discussion of the role of builders in laundry detergents.) Although phosphates pose no problem to human health, they are a problem in wastewater because they are plant nutrients that promote growth of algae and depletion of oxygen (eutrophication), thereby changing the ecosystems in rivers, lakes, and bays.

Detergent manufacturers are also working toward the production of a wide range of detergents that are more biodegradable; that is, substances that decompose more rapidly during sewage treatment. Like manufacturers of other products, they are packaging detergents and other laundry aids in recycled cardboard boxes and refillable bottles.

Dry cleaning can also be a source of pollution. There is environmental concern over the chlorinated hydrocarbons used in dry cleaning. Dry cleaners routinely recycle cleaning fluid so that its disposal will not be a problem.

Dry cleaners deliver clean clothing to customers on hangers inside plastic bags. Some dry cleaners give customers credit for returning hangers, generally from one to two cents for each hanger. They may collect the plastic bags for recycling. Some provide regular customers with reusable cloth bags for delivery and return of laundry.

The Landfill Problem

Much of the textile waste produced by manufacturers and consumers has been buried in landfills. Disposable nonwovens used in medical institutions present particular problems. Patient contact items must be separated and decontaminated before disposal. Disposable diapers have substantially increased the quantity of discarded textile products. Natural fibers are biodegradable and will eventually break down, but synthetics are quite resistant and are not so easily disposed of.

Disposable Diapers

The environmental controversies that surround disposable diapers provide an interesting overview of many of the difficulties that arise from the use of disposable items. Sales of disposable diapers grew rapidly during the 1970s and 1980s. Present estimates of the quantity of diapers to be disposed of range from 3.6 billion to more than 5 billion pounds of diapers a year. Environmentalists claim that disposable diapers are clogging landfills and that viruses and bacteria are leaching into groundwater. About two dozen states have either enacted or proposed legislation to discourage or tax use of disposables. The industry responds by noting that diapers make up less than 2 percent of total solid waste in municipal landfills and that there is no evidence of any cases of disease caused by diaper disposal. Industry spokespersons also note that care of cloth diapers, the alternative preferred by some environmentally minded consumers, consumes up to six times as much water as is used in the manufacture of disposables and that laundering cloth diapers creates nearly ten times as much water pollution as manufacturing disposables (Joseph 1990).

In the case of the disposable diaper controversy, both biodegradability and recycling are seen as ways to diminish the problem. Some manufacturers advertise that their products are biodegradable, although critics claim that in the airless environment of a landfill, *nothing* degrades. Some communities have developed methods for disposal of the wastes in the diapers and recycling of the fibers and plastic in the diapers.

Biodegradable Fibers

Some initial steps in the development of biodegradable fibers have been taken; others are sure to follow. Shimadu Corporation and Kanebo Ltd. of Japan have developed a biodegradable fiber called *Lactron*. Based on lactic acid, the fiber will completely decompose in the ground and in water in about a year. Although the product is still in the test production stage, two hundred T-shirts made from a blend of 65 percent cotton and 35 percent Lactron were presented to athletes representing Japan in the Asian Games in 1994 (*JTN* 1994). Researchers are seeking to produce biodegradable polymers from corn and other starch crops that can be used in agricultural products such as plant protectors, twine for tying hay, surgical sutures, and composting bags (*DataTextile* 1993).

Recycling

The EPA is currently emphasizing waste minimization and pollution prevention. As a result, the EPA sees recycling as a "last resort," stressing the need for industry and consumers to avoid making waste in the first place (Kalogerdis 1992). Even so, a considerable amount of excess material is generated, and with the closure of landfills and severe limitations on space for disposal of solid wastes, interest in textile recycling has grown. A number of states actively encourage recycling through tax credits to businesses that recycle or by giving preference in purchasing of recycled products by state-funded agencies.

Pre-consumer Waste

Both small and larger textile scraps are produced during the spinning of yarns, fabrication of cloth, and manufacture of garments. These items that have not yet been used by consumers are known as *pre-consumer waste.* The textile recycling industry purchases these materials and where possible reprocesses them. The Wool Products Labeling Act and its requirement that recycled wool be labeled as such shows clearly that, in some parts of the industry, the waste materials from manufacture have traditionally been reclaimed.

While reclamation of fiber waste from yarn production has been fairly widespread, reclamation of colored fibers and waste from previously woven or knitted goods made from a variety of different natural and manufactured fibers has been limited. Experimentation with improved techniques for reclaiming textile waste and utilization of the resulting yarns in outerwear, furnishing, and household textiles has had positive results, and Fehrer A. G., an Austrian textile machinery company, is now advertising the use of its DREF2 spinning machine for producing yarns from recycled textile waste (*Chemiefasern* 1985). Furthermore, customers who used to look with disfavor on products made from "reused" products are likely to be positively disposed toward "recycled" products.

Post-consumer Waste

In the textile recycling industry, items discarded after use are referred to as *post-consumer waste.* The recycling industry processes 2.5 billion pounds of post-consumer waste each year (about 10 pounds for every person in the United States). A substantial quantity of this used textile material is purchased from charitable organizations. The textile recycling firms include used clothing dealers and exporters, wiping rag producers, and fiber recyclers. Table 25.1 gives a breakdown of the ultimate destination of post-consumer textile waste.

Purchase of secondhand clothing is one form of recycling. Some apparel designers have shown that innovative clothing can be made from used blue jeans, neckties, socks, sports pennants, or woven fabrics with strips of used fabric as filling.

Textile waste from manufacturers of garments or other textile products is relatively easy to process, since the manufacturer can identify the textile fiber. In reclamation fibers must be sorted into different generic categories, and the identification

	Domestic	Exports	Total
Used clothing sales	—	35%	35%
Fiber for reprocessing	7%	26%	33%
Wiping cloth	25%	—	25%
Disposed of in landfill	7%	—	7%
Total	39%	61%	100%

Table 25.1

Ultimate Destination of Post-Consumer Textile Product Waste Processed by the Textile Recycling Industry

Source: Data provided by the Council for Textile Recycling, 1994.

Figure 25.1

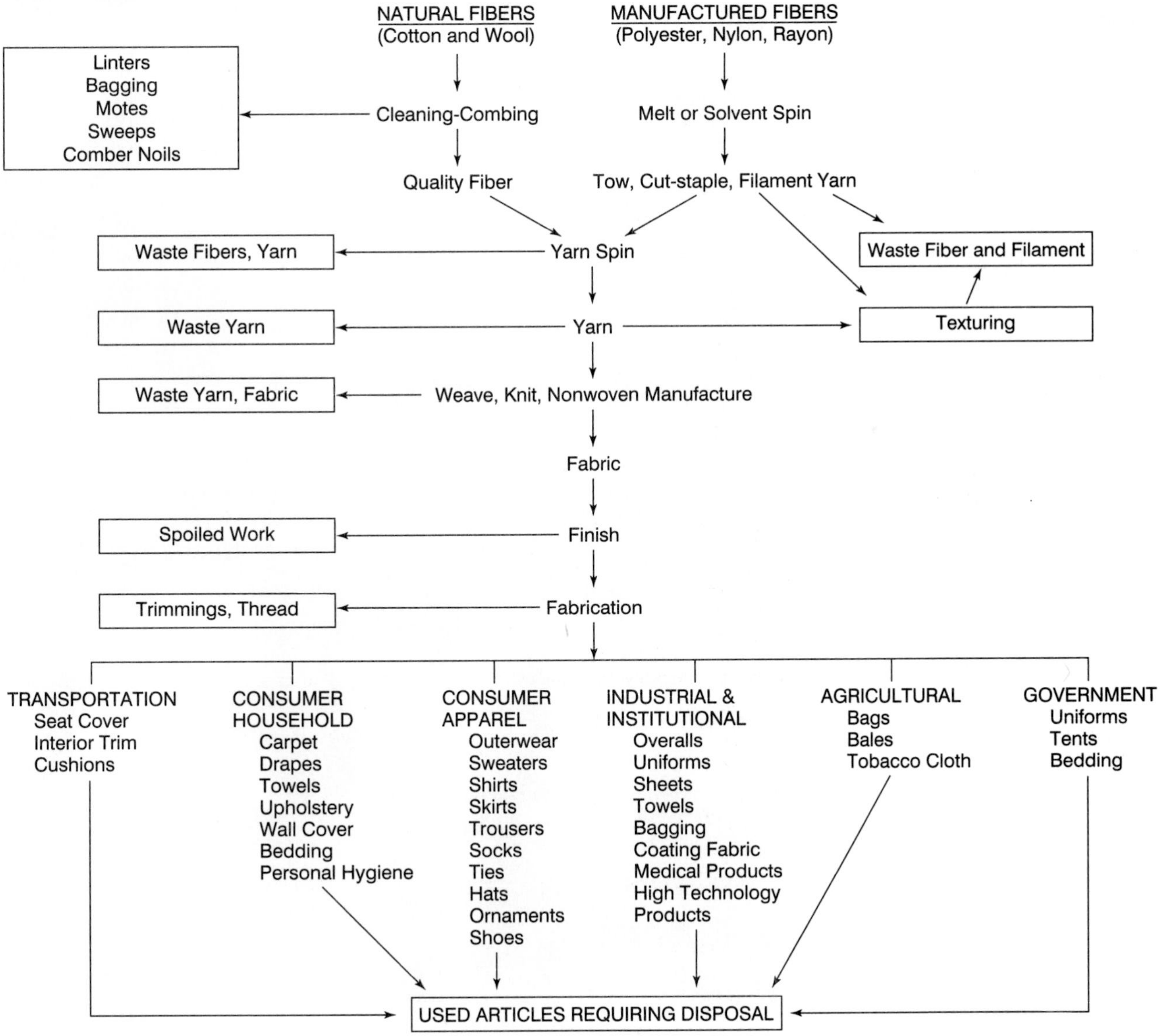

Typical flow of textile fibers in process and the resulting generation of waste at each step of production and consumption

of unknown manufactured fibers or blends is difficult. Chemical analysis for identification purposes may be necessary. Recycling textiles used and discarded by consumers is extremely difficult. Not only is fiber content unidentified, but the quality of fibers may also be quite uneven as a result of wear.

Natural fibers and rayon present relatively few problems of identification and recycling. Wool is recycled and is made into "new" fabrics. Cotton, linen, and rayon can be utilized in the production of paddings and fine rag paper battings.

The separation of blends into their component parts is more difficult. Often this is achieved by identifying the components of the blend and then dissolving out one of the fibers, leaving the other intact. Manufactured fibers can be reused in making flock, as industrial fillers in the manufacture of plastic, or in the regeneration of synthetic fibers. Some thermoplastic fibers can be recycled by melting and forming them

Figure 25.2

Hats, jackets, sweaters, and T-shirts are made from Fortrel® EcoSpun™ fiber, made of 100 percent recycled soda bottles. Photograph by Rod Walker; garments by American Global, Climb High, Demetre, Ganesha E. C. Design, Hat Attack, Medalist, Patagonia, and Tee Jays; courtesy of Wellman, Inc.

into nonfibrous materials such as polymer films or tubes. However, some thermoplastics, like acrylics, decompose during melting.

The plastics recycling industry is more advanced than is that for textiles. Recycled plastics are used in a number of products including reinforcement for asphalt. Compatibilizers are used to solve the problem of different polymers in the recycle mix. These substances can bond to two different polymeric materials, holding them together.

Special finishes that are applied to fabrics may create additional problems for recycling. Many of these finishes are virtually impossible to recycle, and they contaminate the fibers, making their recycling impossible too.

As the raw materials from which many textiles are made become more scarce, the importance of recycling textile products becomes increasingly important. It is imperative that priority be given to intensive research into ways to turn discarded textile products into usable raw materials. Figure 25.1 summarizes the flow of products in textile waste utilization.

CONSUMER BOX
25.1   Recycled Polyester

The environmental movement has spurred development of recycling processes for both industrial and consumer waste. This recycling can take one of two forms: waste can be reintroduced into the same production process to produce the same good, or a solid waste can be made into a completely different product. A significant advance in the second area has been the reprocessing of polyester products into polyester fibers. Companies in the United States are using two-liter soft drink bottles, as well as film and fiber waste from manufacturers, to make new polyester fibers.

Soft drink bottles are composed of the same polymer as polyester fibers: polyethylene terephthalate (PET). Several fiber producers have developed processes for collecting the used bottles, melting them, and extruding the PET as fibers. Soft drink bottles are collected from consumers and recyclers and crushed and compacted for shipping to recycling plants. Initial processing involves separation of the polyester bottles from other foreign materials such as aluminum caps, paper labels, and the rigid base cups used in some bottles. Clear and green bottles are separated, to give clean streams of each.

The clear bottles are processed into polyester fibers for use in sleeping bags, carpeting, pillows,

quilted jackets, and other products. Polyester waste from film and fiber producers is often added to the waste stream for fiber production. Producers may also add virgin polyester polymer to the melt before extrusion. At least one producer is molding packaging materials from a melt of recycled and virgin PET.

The green bottles can be reprocessed into green polyester fiber that is made into needle-punched nonwoven geotextiles for erosion control and other engineering applications. The black base cups that are used in two-liter bottles for stabilization are composed of polyethylene and must be separated from the PET before reprocessing. Although the base cups can also be reprocessed into packaging materials, separating them from the bottles increases the cost of reprocessing. Increasingly, soft drink bottles are made without the base cup, with a ridged bottom providing the necessary stability for the filled bottles.

Work on refining recycling processing continues, with an emphasis on increasing the quality of the recycled fibers. The slightly lower quality, which dictates the end uses, is due to the remelting and re-extrusion, as well as to impurities that may remain in the polymer melt. As the quality increases, recycled polyester will be used more in apparel as well as filling and furnishing materials.

Recycling of Plastics into Fibers

Probably the most successful of the recycling efforts for textiles has been the production of polyester fibers from plastic soft drink bottles. These bottles are blow-molded polyethylene terephthalate, the same polymer as fibers. They are melted and extruded as fibers. Fortrel® EcoSpun™ is a recycled polyester fiber produced by Wellman, used in a variety of knit products (Figure 25.2). Trevira II®, made by Hoechst Celanese from a blend of 50 percent recycled polyester and 50 percent nonrecycled polymer, has been made into T-shirts, baseball caps, tote bags, and cold weather performance fabrics.

Consumer Box 25.1 describes some of the uses of recycled polyester.

Health Hazards

Hazards for Textile Workers

Lung Disease

The deleterious effect of inhaling minute, invisible particles of grit or hard inorganic matter has been recognized for many years. The constant exposure of the lungs to these irritants is harmful and may eventually produce lung disease in many of the persons exposed.

This type of exposure has long been recognized as a hazard in the production of asbestos. Recently, two similar problem areas in textile processing have been given increased attention. Glass fibers are hard and fairly durable. Questions have been raised about whether the inhalation of fibers of glass may cause lung disease. To date, research into this question is continuing, and researchers are searching for evidence of a relationship between inhaling glass fiber and lung disease.

For many years it has been known that cotton industry workers may, after a period of exposure to cotton dust, develop byssinosis, or "brown lung" as it is called by the workers. Researchers had thought that the sand and other gritty particles present in bales of cotton might be responsible for the development of byssinosis. The most recent research, however, tends toward the conclusion that the cause of byssinosis is probably toxins from bacteria or fungi that are present in the leaf dust that is part of the raw cotton. The precise cause, however, is still not clear.

OSHA has established maximum allowable levels of cotton dust that may be present in the air of factories where cotton is being processed. In the United States the problem has been brought under control by the development of equipment and manufacturing operations that have substantially decreased worker exposure to cotton dust. Closed systems for processing raw cotton, improved air ventilation, and personal safety devices, rather like gas masks, are among the technologies that have been put into place. One researcher commented at a Cotton Dust Research Conference held in Manchester, England, in 1989 that it seems possible that the problem will be eliminated before researchers determine its real cause.

Chemicals

Some of the chemical substances with which textile workers come into contact are highly toxic. For the most part, companies have been able to identify these substances and to protect workers from contact with them.

From time to time, however, research findings attribute harm to materials that had never been identified as presenting any serious health problems. Vinyl chloride is such a chemical. An important ingredient in the production of polyvinyl chloride plastics, vinyl chloride is used in the production of plastic backings and coatings for fabrics. Evidence indicates that continued exposure to vinyl chloride monomers will produce cancer of the liver in some of the persons exposed. Unfortunately, this discovery has come too late to help those who have already been affected, but steps are now being taken to protect those workers who must handle this material.

Some dyestuffs have been proven to be harmful to workers. When evidence is found linking dyes to health hazards, their use may be discontinued. For example, some dyes with excellent colorfastness characteristics have been removed from use because of health hazards.

Formaldehyde is another chemical that is widely used in the textile industry. Research has indicated that high levels of formaldehyde are associated with nasal cancer in rats. Whether it is a carcinogen in humans has not been proven. Long-term studies of workers exposed to formaldehyde have been inconclusive. The American Cancer Institute is conducting additional studies that may yield more reliable data. The Consumer Product Safety Commission has concluded that consumers are not at risk because garments do not give off enough formaldehyde to affect wearers. Even so, investigations are continuing into the effect of the chemical on the skin.

The controversy about formaldehyde has centered on the workplace. About 1.5 million workers are estimated to be exposed to formaldehyde; about 970,000 of those work in the textile and apparel industries. Present allowable levels of formaldehyde in the workplace are 1 part per million (ppm). It is possible that further reductions may be mandated. Although a final resolution has yet to be made about the formaldehyde issue, formaldehyde levels in textile mills and apparel factories have been reduced considerably. Several finishing techniques that reduce the quantity of formaldehyde used or the amounts released into the atmosphere have been developed (see "Problems of Durable Press" in chapter 21).

As of May 1986, OSHA employee health protection rules required that information about hazardous chemical substances be communicated to employees by the employer. In summary, the requirements are:

- Hazard information must be conveyed to employees through appropriate labels on the products that they use.
- Safety data sheets provided to employees must identify hazard information.
- Affected industries must have a written hazards information communications program.
- Industries must establish and conduct employee chemical hazard training programs.

The specific means by which these requirements are met are not mandated, but both the producers of chemicals deemed hazardous and the industries using the chemicals must comply. The textile industry sectors that manufacture or process a wide variety of textile products are therefore affected.

Noise

Noise levels in textile manufacturing plants can be very high. Governmental standards regulate noise levels in the workplace. These standards were imposed because of the relationship between high noise levels and hearing loss. The standards limit noise based on the employees' length of exposure and also require periodic hearing tests for machine operators.

Textile manufacturers meet these standards in a number of ways. The problem is most acute in factories using older equipment, which operates at much higher sound levels than does newer equipment, which is engineered to satisfy noise-level regulations. Shuttleless looms, now rapidly replacing shuttle looms, are an example of a newer type of textile machinery that has made a significant contribution to reducing sound levels. Those who work in areas with high sound levels are required to wear ear protectors.

Hazards to Consumers

Hazards to consumers from textiles might be divided into dangers posed by flammable fabrics, fibers or finishing materials that may pose health risks, and individual sensitivity or allergy to certain types of textile products.

Flammability

Some textile products will ignite and burn, and individuals may suffer injury if garments, mattresses, bedding, or upholstery catch fire. Regulation of highly flammable fabrics was enacted as early as 1953. Additional products have been subject to regulation in the intervening years. See chapter 21 for full discussion of flammability.

Dangerous Substances

When textile products are shown to be dangerous to health, they are withdrawn from consumer products, as was the case with asbestos. Probably the best known instance of public concern with textile chemicals is the TRIS case. Federal law in effect since the 1970s has required that sleepwear for children (sizes 0 to 14) be made fire retardant. TRIS [chemically tris-(2,3-dibromopropyl) phosphate] was a chemical finish used to make some polyester, acetate, and triacetate children's sleepwear fabrics flame retardant. When TRIS was found to be an animal carcinogen, TRIS-treated garments were withdrawn from the market, and its use was prohibited. Much of the public failed to realize that not all sleepwear fabrics were being treated with this particular chemical, and many consumers rejected sleepwear of cotton and other fibers treated with safe substances.

The issue of safety has also been raised in regard to formaldehyde-finished products. Research indicates that consumers are not exposed to sufficient levels of formaldehyde from fabrics to pose health hazards.

The chemical 4-PCH (chemically known as 4-phenyl hexane) is used in carpet finishing and associated with "new carpet" odor. Reports of ill effects and death of laboratory mice exposed to carpeting subjected to heating resulted in speculation that

4-PCH might have been the cause. Further laboratory tests on mice indicated no adverse effects even at levels more than a thousand times higher than those that can be expected in new carpet installation (Tests 1993).

Dermatitis

Dermatological problems associated with textile use are sometimes reported by consumers. In some instances, skin irritation may result from continued contact with coarse wool fabrics or fabrics containing glass fiber. Some dyes, especially those used on nylon and polyester, and some chemical finishes have also been associated with consumer complaints. Individual consumers may be allergic to specific fibers, dyes, or finishing materials that do not cause problems for the general population.

Some consumers also report irritation or allergic reactions to laundry products. Laundry products most likely to be identified as the source of perceived dermatological problems are soaps and detergents, fabric softeners, and bleaches (Dallas et al. 1992).

Energy

The focus on energy use and conservation in the textile industry originated in the 1970s after the supply of petroleum was disrupted. Changes in petroleum supply or increased prices for petroleum products adversely affect the textile industry because petroleum and petroleum by-products are the single most important raw material used in the manufacture of most synthetics. Furthermore, a major cost in the production of fibers, yarns, fabrics, and finishing materials is the cost of the energy required for manufacturing.

As a result, the industry moved rapidly to find means of processing textiles that save energy. Dyeing and finishing are aspects of the manufacture of textiles that are especially energy intensive. Among the energy-saving innovations already adopted for use in dyeing and finishing are solar heating of water used in processing fabrics, reducing quantities of hot water required, recovering and reutilizing heat from processing, changing processes to permit use of lower temperatures, and adopting techniques that shorten time requirements (Olson 1977). Methods for reducing the wet pickup of fibers in dyeing and finishing are described in chapter 20.

Many consumers who are concerned about the environment believe that a return to the use of larger quantities of natural fibers will have a positive effect on the environment. The issue, however, is more complex than it appears. There are not enough natural fibers to supply the demands of consumers from all over the world. Furthermore, natural fibers also require energy for their production and processing, so that these fibers are not "energy free." Many fertilizers are made from petrochemicals, and tractors and other farm machinery are run on petroleum fuels.

The consumer must also think in terms of energy use for the care of textile products. Washing, drying, and ironing all require the expenditure of energy. The selection of fabrics that require shorter drying time or can be line dried, as well as those that can be washed in cooler water or do not require ironing, will have the end result of costing the consumer less money because less energy will be used in their care.

One study reported that fiber production accounted for less than 15 percent of the total energy required for production and manufacture of a garment, whereas care of the garment after purchase accounted for 55 to 80 percent (Van Winkle et al. 1978).

Home laundry equipment manufacturers are seeking to design more energy-efficient products. Under consideration is a change in washer design to emulate European-style machines that rotate around a horizontal rather than a vertical axis. These machines consume less water and energy than the vertical axis machines used in most washers produced in the United States.

An increased consumer emphasis on durability may also contribute to a reduction of energy needs. If textile items are used longer, they will have to be replaced less often, thereby reducing the amount of the raw materials needed. Longer use before disposal will also decrease the problem of disposal of used textiles. Fashion, however, is such an important aspect of the apparel industries that many items are discarded before they are outworn. Even another energy crisis would not be likely to remove fashion as a factor in clothing choice. Consumers may find it useful to identify certain of their purchases as "fashion" items in which durability may not be so important as it is in "classic" or other items that do not go out of style quickly.

Summary

Both industry and the public have obligations for the protection of the environment. Whereas at first glance industry would seem to be more responsible for pollution, a deeper examination of the issues leads inexorably to the conclusion that this is a shared responsibility. In the long run, the public must be willing to pay for the improvements in pollution control that industries make. Environmentally safe manufacturing of textiles is expensive. The cost of cleaner factories and mills will be paid for by increasing prices of the items that are marketed. At the same time, consumers must recognize that imported fabrics and apparel are often produced in countries that have little or no regulation of the workplace environment. Such goods compete with domestically produced fabrics into which the costs of cleaner factories and mills must be calculated. No one relishes increases in the cost of textiles, but the trade-off for lower prices would be to continue the deterioration of the environment that future generations will inherit.

References

AMTEX projected to help save $12 billion annually. 1995. *Textile Chemist and Colorist* 27 (April): 9.

Biodegradable polymers in agriculture studies. 1993. *DataTextile* 5 (October): 3.

Dallas, M. J., et al. 1992. Dermatological and other health problems attributed by consumers to contact with laundry products. *Home Economics Research Journal* 21 (September): 34.

Joseph, L. 1990. The bottom line on disposables. *New York Times Sunday Magazine*, 23 September, 26.

Kalogerdis, C. 1992. Recycling should be your last resort, says EPA. *Textile World* 142 (June): 73.

Olson, E. S. 1977. New dyeing and finishing equipment and processes which minimize energy requirements. *Textile Chemist and Colorist* 9 (February): 20.

Maycumber, S. G. 1994. Environmental issues rank up with QR when choosing vendors: L. L. Bean exec. *Daily News Record*, 26 April, 2.

Shimadzu and Kanebo develop biodegradable synthetic fiber. 1994. *JTN*, no. 480 (November): 14.

Tests show no ill effects from use of 4-PCH on carpets. 1993. *Textile Chemist and Colorist* 25 (March): 6.

Textile waste recycling—answer to a present-day challenge. 1985. *Chemiefasern/Textilindustrie* 35/87 (July/August): 498.

Van Winkle et al. 1978. Cotton versus polyester. *American Scientist* 66 (September-October): 280.

Review Questions

1. Identify five specific actions consumers can take in relation to textile products that would have a beneficial effect on the environment. Explain the impact of each action you have identified.

2. Pollution and/or generation of waste occurs in textile manufacturing at each of these stages: fiber production, yarn spinning, weaving and knitting, dyeing, finishing, apparel manufacture, distribution of products. For each stage:
   - identify the potential pollution and/or waste products
   - describe the problems that result
   - identify ways in which these problems might be overcome

3. What organization is charged with the responsibility of monitoring the workplace to ascertain whether conditions for workers are safe? What are some of the potential threats to the health and safety of textile employees?

4. Imagine that your employer required you to defend the idea that a shirt made from 100 percent cotton fabric would be more environmentally friendly than one made of 100 percent polyester. Develop a list of reasons to support this position. Now imagine that you were required to argue against this position. Develop a list of arguments supporting polyester.

Recommended Readings

Bockner, B. 1994. Pollution prevention: Key to survival for the dyestuff industry. *American Dyestuff Reporter* 83 (August): 29.

Dillard, B. 1994. A measure of success. *Bobbin* 35 (April): 70.

Ecolabelling. 1994. *Textile Horizons*, June, 17.

Glover, B., and L. Hill. 1993. Waste minimization in the dyehouse. *Textile Chemist and Colorist* 25 (June): 15.

Gross, P., and D. C. Braun. 1984. *Toxic and biomedical effects of fibers*. Park Ridge, N. J.: Noyes.

Grove, N. 1994. Recycling. *National Geographic* 185 (July): 93.

Gund, N. 1995. Environmental considerations for textile printing products. *Journal of the Society of Dyers and Colorists* 111 (1/2): 7.

Kron, P. 1992. Recycle—if you can. *Apparel Industry Magazine* 53 (September): 74.

Rudie, R. 1993. "Green" apparel grabs center stage. *Bobbin* 34 (August): 12.

———— 1994. How green is the future? *Bobbin* 35 (February): 16.

Ryland, R. 1993. Byssinosis—pathogenic mechanisms revisited. In *Proceedings of the Beltwide Cotton Production Conference,* 237.

Shimadzu and Kanebo develop biodegradable synthetic fiber. 1994. *JTN,* no. 480 (November): 14.

The go-betweens. 1994. *The Economist* 333 (October 1): 109.

The greening of the textile and clothing industry. 1994. *Textiles* 23 (Spring): 18.

Wallenberger, F. T., et al. 1980. The effect of fabric composition on energy demand in home laundering. *Textile Chemist and Colorist* 12 (July): 20.

FABRIC STRUCTURE: THE SUM OF ITS PARTS

Fiber, yarn, fabric structure, and finish each play a role in the way in which a given textile product will behave during its "use lifetime." This chapter seeks to explore the contributions of all the structural characteristics to special aspects of textile behavior. When finished, the authors hope that the reader will be able to view textiles as the sum of their various parts and to have a more complete understanding of the meaning of that equation.

Fabric Behavior

The sum total of fabric behavior is affected by fiber, yarn, fabric construction, and special finishes. Some of the aspects of fabric performance that are affected include durability, appearance, and comfort.

Durability Factors

Strength

Yarn strength is of primary importance in determining ultimate fabric strength. Yarn strength is due first to the inherent strength of the fibers in the yarn. Yarns of high-tenacity nylon fibers, for example, are stronger than those of regular nylon. In certain end uses fiber modulus is also a consideration. High initial resistance to force is important for many industrial fabrics such as seat belts, parachutes, and sailcloth.

Another significant factor in fabric strength is the yarn structure. Filament yarns are stronger than spun yarns because all of the fibers in a filament yarn are contributing to yarn strength. The yarn breaks when the fibers are ruptured. Spun yarns, however, are broken by breaking some fibers but also by overcoming the twist frictional force holding the fibers together. This takes less force than breaking all the fibers in a comparable filament yarn.

As twist is increased in spun yarns, the strength increases (up to a point) because the frictional force between fibers prevents slipping. Overtwisting, however, will decrease strength due to increased strain in the yarn. Coarser yarns can withstand tensile forces better than finer yarns and normally contribute more to fabric strength.

In addition to fiber and yarn strength, fabric strength is affected by the fabric construction. It is at this level that the difference between breaking strength and tearing strength becomes apparent. In testing breaking, or tensile strength, all the yarns share equally in the stress applied, but in tearing strength testing, a few yarns, at most, are subject to stress.

The important fabric variables affecting strength of woven fabrics are weave and fabric count. Fabric weaves with a high number of interlacings, such as plain weaves, can transfer the tensile stresses at the intersection points and therefore have higher breaking strength than satin weaves (all else being equal). On the other hand, in tightly woven plain weaves the yarns are bound in position, and they cannot move to group together to share the stress imposed in tearing. They therefore exhibit a lower tearing strength than twills, oxfords, or satins.

The effect of weave can be increased or offset by changing the fabric count of a woven fabric. A plain-weave fabric with a very low fabric count, such as cheesecloth, has a low breaking strength but a high tearing strength. The breaking strength is low because there are very few yarns to share the load applied. The yarns in this structure, however, can slide around easily and group together to share the load during tearing. Try to tear a piece of cheesecloth and the strength of this type of structure becomes apparent (Figure 26.1).

Strength of knitted fabrics is considered to be less important for durability than it is in woven goods. This is because knitted fabrics are easily stretched to accommodate changes of shape as a result of stresses imposed in wear and care.

Figure 26.1

A cheesecloth under a tearing load showing yarns bunching together at the point of load concentration. Reprinted by permission from Robert Merkel, *Textile Product Serviceability* (New York: Macmillan, 1991), 180. Copyright © 1991 by Prentice Hall.

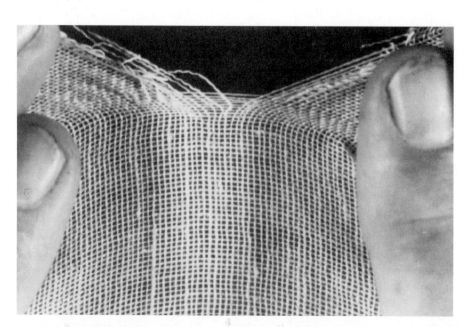

In nonwoven fabrics that do not contain yarns, the strength comes from fiber entanglement and adhesion, as well as inherent fiber strength. Fiber webs of coarser and higher strength fibers will be stronger than those made from finer, weaker fibers. The bonding of the fibers in the nonwoven structure also provides strength. Fabrics with a large number of bonding points will be stronger, and the strength will also depend on the strength of the individual bonds. Fiber webs with only fiber entanglement for adhesion, such as needle-punched nonwovens, derive their strength from the frictional forces between the entangled fibers.

A final feature that may affect fabric strength is finish. Durable press finishes in particular lower fiber strength. These finishes cross-link the cellulose chains in the fibers, inhibiting molecular movement that might absorb the stress. As a result, the fibers are weaker, and this loss in strength is translated to the yarns and fabric. Softeners decrease tensile strength of staple yarns by increasing fiber slippage but increase the tear strength of woven fabric by allowing yarns to bunch and accommodate tearing stresses.

Elongation and Recovery

The elongation and recovery of fabrics are important in determining their end use and performance. Fabrics that stretch and recover, such as most knits, are very comfortable and are appropriate for hosiery, swimwear, and other specific uses.

One way to obtain high elongation is to use elastomeric fibers such as spandex or rubber. These fibers stretch up to 5 times their length (500%) and then recover. Of the other generic fiber types, wool and rayon exhibit higher elongation but their recovery is also lower. Nylon and polyester have good recovery from tensile forces and are ideal choices for fabrics that must retain their shape.

Crimp added to yarns, as in textured yarns, and the natural crimp created in all fabrics when yarns interlace are also related to extensibility. When warp and filling yarns cross each other, they cannot continue to move in an absolutely straight line, but each set of yarns must bend over and under yarns in the other set. Each yarn, therefore, develops a wavy configuration. As the fabric is stretched, the crimp in the direction of the stretch is removed, permitting the fabric structure to reach its maximum extensibility. The greater the yarn crimp, the more extensible the fabric. Since warp yarns are under more tension during weaving, there is usually more crimp, and greater extensibility, in the filling direction. In unbalanced weaves, however, where there are many warp yarns interlacing with fewer filling yarns, the warp yarns will have more crimp. (See Figure 26.2.)

In comparison to knitted fabrics, woven fabrics are generally firmer and have less elongation. In knits the loops in the structure can be deformed horizontally or vertically, increasing the stretch in both directions. But as was noted earlier, variations in knitting techniques can increase or decrease extensibility of knitted fabrics. Double knit fabrics and warp knit fabrics are usually less extensible than single knit fabrics.

Abrasion Resistance

Resistance to abrasion is determined by the ability of a material to absorb the energy applied during abrasion. The difficulty in assessing the complex interrelationships of fiber, yarn, and fabric structures is especially well illustrated in the question of abrasion resistance. A number of textile properties affect the resistance of a fabric to abrasion, among them fiber toughness, yarn structure, yarn crimp, fabric construction, and finish.

Some fibers have better abrasion resistance than do others. Polyester and nylon, for example, are tougher than cotton or rayon. They can withstand more force and energy and have higher abrasion resistance. Carbon and glass fibers have high tenacity but low abrasion resistance.

Figure 26.2

As warp and filling yarns pass over and under each other, they develop crimp. Smaller warp yarns (shown in black) develop greater crimp as they pass over larger filling yarns (shown in white).

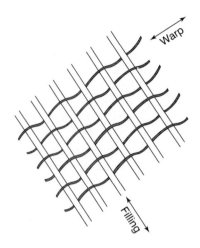

Yarn construction is also a factor. Loosely twisted yarns abrade more easily than do tightly twisted yarns, and in the loosely twisted yarns individual fibers are more likely to be plucked out of the fabric surface.

In woven fabric construction, the aspect of crimp distribution seems to be particularly important. The crown—the part of the yarn that protrudes above the surface of the fabric—receives the pressure of abrasion. The more crowns of the same height there are in a given area of cloth, the more evenly the wear will be distributed over the surface of the fabric, as shown in Figure 26.2. Prominently ribbed fabrics, such as faille or grosgrain, will tend to abrade easily because the crowns of the warp yarns are so exposed. Interrelationships of construction and yarn structure may be observed in a fabric like shantung, in which uneven, loosely twisted slubbed yarns present higher crowns that are unevenly spaced; this is an example of a fabric that has poor abrasion resistance.

Weave also enters into abrasion resistance. In knits and fabrics with floats, yarns and fibers are freer to move to absorb energy and are less consistently exposed to abradants. For this reason, twills and some tightly woven satin fabrics may show superior abrasion resistance.

Some nonwoven fabrics may show lower abrasion resistance if the fibers are not tightly held in the structure. Abrasion will pull fibers out, and the fabric will wear.

Finishes may have a negative impact on resistance to abrasion. Durable press and other resin finishes applied to cotton or rayon have this effect. To compensate, the cellulosic fibers may be blended with synthetic fibers such as polyester or nylon.

Effects of Light and Chemicals

As detailed in chapters 4 to 14, environmental conditions and certain chemicals can degrade textile fibers. Exposure to light and chemicals can affect the strength, elongation, and/or abrasion resistance of fabrics as the fiber degradation is translated to yarn and fabric performance properties. Knowing which fibers are susceptible to light and chemical degradation will enable selection of appropriately durable textile products for specific end uses.

Aesthetic Factors

Drape and Hand

Drape refers to the ability of fabric to form pleasing folds when bent under its own weight. Drape is related to bending and shearing behavior, which are in turn affected by yarn and fabric properties. Shearing is the deformation of a structure in which a rectangle becomes lozenge shaped. In woven fabrics this results from movement of yarns from what one might call a normal position in which they run horizontally and vertically and interlace at right angles to other positions in which the interlacing is deformed away from the 90 degree angle (Figure 26.3). Yarn and fabric structures that allow movement at the yarn intersections will increase shearing. Woven fabrics with smooth yarns, low fabric counts, and higher crimp will exhibit lower resistance to shearing.

Fabrics that shear easily will be softer and more drapable. To illustrate this principle, think about cutting a half-circle skirt from a fabric. Parts of the garment will lie along the straight grain (true warp or filling directions), but other parts will lie along other directions, some at a diagonal called the *bias*. In the bias direction, fabric is particularly subject to shear deformation. If the fabric is unable to shear, it remains stiff and will not mold or drape softly. A skirt made from a nonwoven fabric such as felt would have very little shearing and would appear stiff. Since the fibers are strongly bonded, and are not able to move at the crossover points, the structure cannot accommodate the shearing force. Instead, when a shearing force is applied, the fabric buckles, much as paper does.

In general, because of the ways in which yarns are combined, woven fabrics have higher shearability than do knitted fabrics, although knitted fabrics have good flexibility and are easily extended. Warp knits do not shear as easily as weft knits. Finishes that make yarns more rigid or that restrict yarns from moving freely in relation to one another will reduce shearing.

Figure 26.3

Shear deformation is the movement of yarns from a normal position (A) where yarns run horizontally and vertically to other position(s) (B) where interlacing is deformed to a less than ninety degree angle. Fabrics with low shearability (C) are not as soft and drapable as fabrics with high shearability (D).

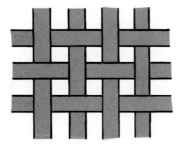

A. NORMAL STATE

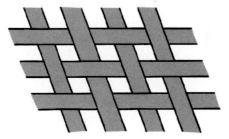

B. SHEARED

C. LOW SHEARABILITY

D. HIGH SHEARABILITY

These qualities must be taken into account by designers, although they may not be aware of the technical terminology used to describe the fabric properties. For example, a warp knit tricot fabric with low shearability would not be used to make a bias-cut garment in which the intention is to take advantage of high shearability. Instead, the designer would be likely to use a soft, gathered construction where the high flexibility of the fabric would work to good advantage, but where most of the draping would fall in the vertical direction of the fabric.

To form the graceful folds desirable in draping, fabrics also must have low resistance to bending. Lower fabric counts and fine yarns with flexible fibers will give fabrics the ability to bend easily and will contribute to draping. Fabrics such as satins that have long floats in the weave are more flexible, bending more easily and improving draping qualities.

Twist also affects the bending of yarns. Very tightly twisted yarns bend more easily because the fibers are oriented at a sharp angle to the yarn length. This behavior is apparent in crepe yarns, which are highly twisted. True crepe fabrics, those made from crepe yarns, have high drapability, while fabrics that have only a crepe weave or embossed crepe appearance will be less drapeable.

Fabric hand refers to the tactile sensations or impressions that arise when fabrics are touched, squeezed, rubbed, or otherwise handled (AATCC 1994). Hand is an important consideration in consumer selection and acceptance of apparel and apparel fabrics. Like drape and other properties, it is a complex phenomenon involving a number of different fabric characteristics. One important factor in the assessment of hand is the smoothness of the material. Filament yarns and fine combed spun yarns will feel smoother than textured or crepe yarns. In addition, a fabric that compresses easily and recovers from compression or squeezing will feel soft. This feeling is enhanced by resilient fibers and yarns with high loft that are not compact. Consider the difference in feel between a bulky wool sweater knit and a wool gabardine.

The shearing and bending behavior of fabrics affects hand as well as drape. Fabrics with low resistance to shearing and bending will feel softer than stiffer fabrics that do not shear easily. These properties also relate to the shaping of fabrics into garments. Fabrics that bend and shear easily can be shaped to fit the body and to form design lines.

A Japanese researcher, Dr. Sueo Kawabata, has developed a system, the Kawabata Evaluation System for Fabric (KES-F), to evaluate fabric hand (Kawabata 1980). This system takes into account the fabric mechanical properties that affect hand and relates objective measurement of these properties to subjective evaluation.

The subjective component of the system was supplied by a team of textile experts in Japan who evaluated a large number of apparel fabrics. The objective component was determined by a series of instruments designed by Kawabata. These instruments measure fabric responses to small deformations such as those that occur in ordinary wear or other use of textiles; that is, the forces applied are much less than those used in breaking or tearing strength tests.

The four instruments in the KES-F are:

1. *Tensile and Shear Tester.* Measures response to slight stretching and recovery from stretching, as well as resistance to shearing and recovery from shearing.
2. *Pure Bending Tester.* Measures resistance to bending and recovery from bending (Figure 26.4).

Figure 26.4

Kawabata Pure Bending Tester. Fabric is being bent between holding clamps.

3. *Surface Tester.* Contains a series of small piano wires, which are pulled over the fabric surface to measure friction, and a single U-shaped wire whose deviations from a straight plane indicate surface roughness.
4. *Compression Tester.* Measures resistance to compression and recovery from compression.

After obtaining subjective ratings of the fabrics, as well as objective measurements of tensile, shear, bending, surface, and compression properties, Kawabata correlated the two series of measurements. With this correlation, the objective measurements can be used to predict specific hand properties or a "total hand value" (THV). This hand value is used in Japan and other parts of the world in specifying fabric properties in apparel production.

Wrinkle Recovery

Different fibers have differing resiliency. When a manufacturer begins with a fiber that is resilient, the wrinkle recovery of the yarn into which it is made and the fabric into which that yarn is woven or knitted will be enhanced. When the fiber has poor wrinkle recovery, the opposite is true. A fabric of 100 percent polyester should wrinkle less than one of 100 percent cotton because polyester is much more resilient than cotton.

Yarn properties must also be considered. Yarn stiffness, or resistance to bending, is related to twist and size among other properties. When a crease forms in woven or knitted fabric, the yarns bend. The fibers in the outer side of the yarn are strained, while those on the inner side are compressed. In looser yarn structures, with lower twist, fibers are freer to move to relieve the stresses of bending. In more tightly twisted yarns the frictional forces within the yarn will tend to keep fibers from shifting position, and they will tend to return to their original configuration. As previously described, however, overtwisted yarns show reduced resistance to bending. The most flexible yarn of all should be one in which filaments are com-

Figure 26.5

Cotton cheesecloth (left) and cotton print cloth (right) after wrinkling.

bined with little or no twist. The least flexible yarns should be those in which the fibers are bonded together by an adhesive or fused by heat or chemical means. An excellent example of this principle can be seen after a heavily starched or sized fabric with a water-soluble sizing has been laundered. The fabric after laundering will be much softer and more flexible when the sizing that has held the fibers rigidly together has been removed.

Yarn count or size affects stiffness as well. Heavier yarns resist wrinkling more than finer count or size yarns. Yarn count can be increased by putting a larger number of fibers into a yarn or by using fibers of larger diameter. Very fine fibers, even in coarse yarns, however, will reduce resistance to bending.

Fabric structure affects the ability of yarns and fibers to move and must therefore be given close attention. In general, woven fabrics with few interlacings and knits wrinkle less than do other fabrics. This is because loosely constructed fabrics generally allow more fiber redistribution and motion. It follows, then, that plain weaves wrinkle more than twill or satin weaves, and fabrics with higher fabric counts also wrinkle more. Cheesecloth, with a very low fabric count, does not wrinkle as much as higher count plain weaves (Figure 26.5).

Another consideration in determining wrinkle recovery of fabrics is the application of special finishes. Durable press finishes, of course, will increase wrinkle recovery and can offset low recovery due to fiber, yarn, or fabric structure.

Dimensional Stability

Fiber content is a critical element in dimensional stability of yarns and fabrics. Fibers with high moisture regain will swell when wet. Thermoplastic fibers that have not been heat stabilized may be plasticized by heat and shrink when agitated in hot water. As noted before, however, special finishes can be given to fabrics to counteract these inherent properties.

In fabrics, dimensional stability problems are often related to unreleased stresses introduced in the manufacturing processes. This is particularly true when yarns or fabrics are elongated beyond their natural dimensions. When the fabric is then subjected to moisture, or heat in the case of thermoplastic fibers, the stresses within the fibers are relieved, and the fabric relaxes. Fabrics containing moisture-absorbent fibers often shrink in laundering because the fibers absorb a significant amount of water and swell. Accordingly, the yarn diameter increases, and the yarns in each direction must move closer together to accommodate the yarns in the opposite direction. This is a less strained position for the yarns and results in a permanent increase in crimp, especially in warp yarns that were woven under more tension than the filling yarns. This is why woven fabrics often shrink more in the warp direction. (See Figure 26.6.)

Shrinkage can also be affected by fabric count in woven fabrics. Generally, if there is room in the structure for the yarns to swell without moving closer together, then the fabric will be more dimensionally stable. If there is not much room between the yarns, they move closer together when the fibers swell. Therefore, fabrics with higher fabric counts will shrink more until they reach the point where they are forced together into a "jammed" construction.

Knitted fabrics, because of their greater extensibility, are more likely to lose their shape in laundering. The stresses applied in knitting distort the shapes of the loops rather than just stretching the yarns as in weaving. On relaxation, the loops broaden, shrinking the fabric length and increasing the width. As with woven fabrics, the tighter the structure, the higher the shrinkage until the structure becomes so tight that further shrinkage is not possible. Such fabrics may, however, buckle.

Covering Power

The terms *covering power* and *cover factor* refer to both the optical and geometric properties of fabrics. Optical covering power is the ability of the fabric to hide that which is placed under it.

Fiber characteristics affect the optical covering power. If the fibers used are translucent or transparent, the fabric will be more translucent or transparent. The same fiber may have greater opacity if it has been delustered and will reflect more light, rather than allowing light to pass through the fiber. Fiber cross-sectional shape and degree of crimp also affect the optical covering power.

Yarn structure and fabric construction will influence optical covering power. Smaller diameter yarns or smoother yarns will cover less well. An open-construction fabric will obviously cover less well than a densely constructed fabric. Sheer fabrics are often desired and can be achieved by fine yarns and/or low fabric counts. Differences in covering power can be seen among the three fabrics in Figure 26.7.

Fabric crimp is also related to covering power in woven fabrics. As yarns in one direction cross and exert pressure on the yarns in the opposite direction, these yarns may be flattened somewhat. Flatter yarns provide better cover.

Knitted fabrics tend to have lower cover than do woven fabrics, with weft knits having substantially more porous structures than warp knits, unless the fabric is deliberately made to have an open, lacy construction as in some Raschel knits. Use of thinner or thicker yarns can increase the cover of knitted fabrics.

Dyeing and finishing will also have an effect on cover. Darker colors tend to cover better than do lighter, for instance.

The geometric aspect of covering power is expressed as the cover factor, which is the ratio of fabric surface occupied by yarn to total fabric surface. A cover factor of 100 percent means that all the fabric surface is covered completely by yarn. It would require that the yarns be packed densely, with no open spaces between the yarns. Few fabrics can actually achieve such complete cover, as there is generally some space, however small, between the yarns even in the most closely constructed fabrics.

Figure 26.6

Effect of yarn swelling on fabric shrinkage. Cloth length represents the space between adjacent filling yarns, which decreases as fabric shrinks in the warp direction. A. Stretched fabric. B. Original dry state of fabric. C. Filling yarn swelling increases amplitude of warp yarn path; hatched area represents strain in warp yarn. D. Filling yarns move closer together to minimize strain. From H. F. Mark, N. S. Wooding, and S. M. Atlas, *Chemical Aftertreatment of Textiles* (New York: Wiley, 1971), 163. Copyright © 1971 by John Wiley & Sons, Inc. Reprinted by permission of John Wiley & Sons, Inc.

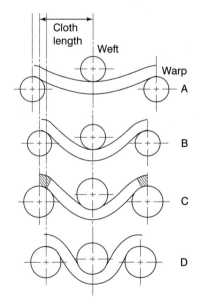

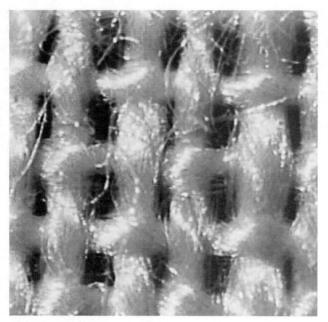

(a)

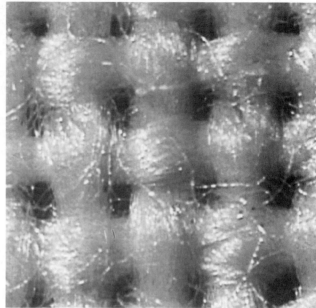

(b)

Figure 26.7

Effects of fabric construction and cover factor on air permeability. Fabric (a) has the highest permeability and lowest cover factor. Fabric (c) has the lowest permeability and highest cover factor. Photomicrographs of woven fabrics by Helen H. Epps, University of Georgia, Dept. of Textiles, Merchandising and Interiors. Reprinted by permission of the International Textile and Apparel Association.

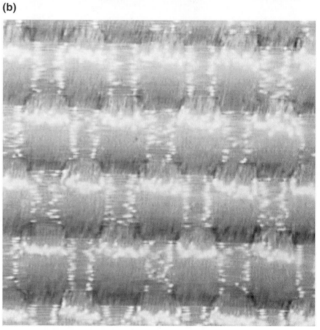

(c)

Comfort Factors

Heat Transfer

Heat transfer is the transfer of heat energy from a generating body to the surrounding atmosphere. Textile fabrics can provide resistance to heat transfer from a body, or in the case of some interior furnishings, from buildings. Their contributions to comfort are therefore important. Textile technologists have defined a unit for measurement of resistance due to clothing called the *clo,* it represents the insulation or resistance necessary to keep a resting man (producing heat at a standard rate) comfortable at 21°C and air movement of 0.1 meter/second. The clo value is analogous to the R-value used in evaluating home insulation.

An important consideration in providing resistance to heat transfer is the amount of trapped air contained within a textile structure. Since this so-called dead air is a poor thermal conductor, the more dead air within the structure, the more heat will be kept near the body.

Some fibers have physical characteristics that enhance this effect of air insulation. For example, wool is a good fiber for insulation because its natural crimp maintains a high volume of dead air. Likewise, manufactured fibers are often given a degree of crimp to increase their insulative value.

Yarn structure and its related property of fabric thickness are also extremely important in determining the thermal comfort of fabrics. A spun yarn or textured filament yarn will entrap more air than a flat filament yarn and will therefore offer more resistance to heat transfer. The degree of twist also affects thermal comfort, as the higher twist yarns have less air volume.

Fabric construction plays an important role in insulation. Knits usually will entrap more air than woven fabrics, although the tightness of the weave or knit is a factor as well. Pile or napped constructions are especially good for cold weather because the yarns or fibers perpendicular to the surface provide numerous spaces for dead air. This effect is maximized if such fabrics are worn with the napped or pile surface next to the body, or if they are covered with another layer.

As mentioned, fabric thickness is of primary importance and is usually considered to be the most important single variable in determining thermal comfort. However, there is a limit to how thick the fabric can be without adding too much weight. Multicomponent fabrics such as quilts are thick, but their inner layers of fibers or down have a high volume of air and therefore very little weight. This is why down comforters and jackets are so warm. The down feathers between the outer layers allow for a larger volume of dead air to serve as resistance to heat transfer. The glass fiber insulation in buildings is in a loose mat form for the same reason—to provide a significant volume of dead air space.

Moisture Vapor Transmission and Water Repellency

Another physical phenomenon that affects comfort is moisture transport, whether moisture vapor or liquid water. Moisture is produced by the body in the form of perspiration: either *insensible perspiration,* moisture that evaporates within the skin layers and is emitted as vapor; or *sensible perspiration,* liquid perspiration produced under hot or strenuous conditions. The contribution of textile fabrics to comfort depends on their ability to carry away moisture vapor or water. Fabrics that enhance the transport of vapor are said to *breathe.* This quality differs from permeability to air, which is discussed shortly.

Water vapor may be absorbed by fibers, transported through the fibers, and desorbed to the outside. This process depends on the inherent absorbency of the fibers or their affinity for water. Rayon and wool absorb moisture readily from the body, whereas polyester does not. Moisture vapor can also pass through air spaces between fibers, and yarns and looser structures will enhance this movement.

Transport of sensible perspiration through the capillary spaces in yarns, called *wicking,* is also a factor in comfort. Wicking depends on the wettability of fiber surfaces as well as yarn and fabric surfaces. Polypropylene fabrics, which are often recommended for sports activities, will not absorb water, but liquid perspiration will wick down the yarns quite effectively.

Most fibers are not naturally water repellent but must be given special treatments to render them water repellent. Dense cotton fabrics, by contrast, may provide better water repellency by virtue of the fact that they are hydrophilic. The fibers swell on exposure to water, jamming the construction and forming a barrier to keep out water. Gore-Tex® fabrics, described in chapter 21, overcome the trade-offs between moisture transport and water repellency. The microvoids in the fluorocarbon film layer allow the moisture vapor to escape but do not allow liquid water in.

Air Permeability

Air permeability is the ability of air to pass through a fabric. Obviously, where openings between yarns or between fibers within yarns are large, a good deal of air will pass through the fabric. Conversely, when compact yarns are packed tightly into fabrics, with little air space between them, the flow of air through the fabric is diminished. (See Figure 26.7.) It follows, then, that fabrics with compact, tightly twisted yarns will have lower permeability, as will fabrics with high fabric counts. To make garments that are warm enough for sports such as skiing in which moving air may cool the athlete, a fabric with low air permeability (such as closely woven nylon) may be combined with materials of low thermal conductivity (such as a polyester or acrylic fiberfill or a pile fabric) that trap air close to the body.

Some finishes for fabrics—such as ciréing of thermoplastic fabrics—decrease air permeability by causing fibers and yarns to fuse slightly. Fabrics may be coated with another material that closes up spaces in the fabric.

Softness

Those qualities that contribute to hand and softness have been discussed, but it should be noted that softness is a quality consumers generally associate with comfort. Factors relating to the sensorial comfort of fabrics are shown in Figure 26.8.

Cotton, noted for its comfort, is smooth and cool. Wool fibers, on the other hand, have scaly rather than smooth surfaces and might be irritating to some people. Fabrics made from microfibers have an exceptionally soft feel because the flexibility of the yarn is enhanced by finer fibers. This property of microfiber fabrics is being used in marketing these products, mainly in the high-end segment of the market.

Loosely twisted yarns and many novelty yarns have rougher surfaces that decrease the smoothness of fabrics. Filament yarns are generally smoother than spun yarns. Sheets made of filament silk yarns are softer and more luxurious than those of linen or cotton.

Finishes and dyes used on textile fabrics may cause allergies in those who are sensitive to these substances. In addition, residual traces of detergent after laundering may cause reactions, especially in infants.

Maintenance of Appearance

Consumers evaluate the useful lifetime of fabrics not only on the basis of mechanical performance such as adequate strength and durability or dimensional stability but also by the maintenance of an attractive appearance. Textile products that undergo

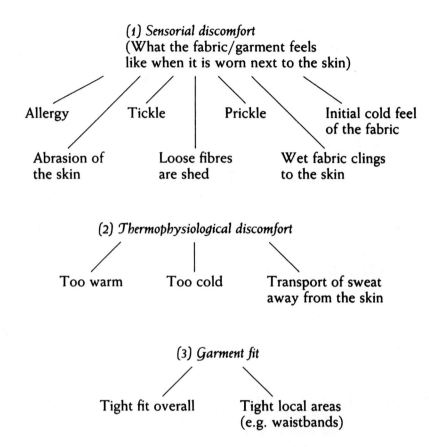

(1) Sensorial discomfort
(What the fabric/garment feels like when it is worn next to the skin)

- Allergy
- Tickle
- Prickle
- Initial cold feel of the fabric
- Abrasion of the skin
- Loose fibres are shed
- Wet fabric clings to the skin

(2) Thermophysiological discomfort

- Too warm
- Too cold
- Transport of sweat away from the skin

(3) Garment fit

- Tight fit overall
- Tight local areas (e.g. waistbands)

Figure 26.8

Factors that are related to physiological discomfort. Reproduced from *Textiles Magazine,* a publication of the Textile Institute, UK.

color changes or become unsightly from pilling may be discarded long before they have worn out.

Pilling is related to fiber content and yarn structure and is most likely to occur in fabrics made from synthetic fibers that have been spun into staple yarns. Natural fibers and rayon, which are usually weaker, are more likely to break off rather than to form pills. Textured filament synthetic yarns can provide the appearance of staple yarns without having short, loose fibers that form into pills.

Color change or loss may not be predictable, as it can result from use of dyes that are not colorfast (see chapter 22). Consumers can check to see if the manufacturer has provided a label that specifies that an item is colorfast. Use of strong bleaches in caring for colored garments or failure to follow care labels can also result in color change.

Summary

Fabrics are rarely used just as they come from the textile mill. They usually move along to a manufacturing process in which a textile product is constructed from the fabric. Textile fabrics must, therefore, be "processable." For apparel construction where many layers of fabric are cut at the same time, fabric layers should not slide or shift out of position and should have sufficient body that they can be cut into correctly shaped pieces. When pieces are sewn together, the fabric must feed through the sewing machine smoothly and without stretching. The sewing machine needle must be able to penetrate the fabric easily without puncturing the yarns. As is true for all other choices among textiles, predicting textile performance in processing requires that manufacturers, consumers, or craftspersons recognize that fiber content, yarn structure, fabric construction, and finish all contribute to the properties of the final fabric.

Sometimes there are trade-offs among the various components. For example, highly twisted yarns may decrease the strength of a fabric but increase its drapeability. These fabric components may also complement each other, making the product more than the sum of its parts. Nevertheless, in evaluating fabrics, the properties of the individual components of fiber, yarn, fabric, and finish should be considered.

In all cases, it is important to focus on the intended end use of the textile. In product development this end use is specified, and manufacturers select fabrics that meet the requirements. Where it is important to predict the performance of fabrics, the effects of all the structural characteristics should be taken into account.

Case Studies

This chapter and this book conclude with several case studies of textile products. Each case analysis of the requirements is combined with discussion of how the properties and characteristics of particular fibers, yarns, fabric structures, coloring processes, and finishes can meet these needs.

Putting It All
TOGETHER

F O R . . . *Sailcloth*

Fabrics for sailcloth have a number of different requirements in terms of strength, elongation, weight, flexibility, porosity, absorbency, and environmental resistance. Designing or selecting sailcloth fabric must balance the requirements for each of these properties while maintaining a reasonable cost.

Tensile Properties

The tensile properties important in sailcloth are high strength and low elongation. Sails must withstand the forces of the wind without stretching out of shape. This requires first of all a strong fabric with strong yarns. Sailcloths of polyester or nylon filament yarns have the requisite strength.

A further necessity for sailcloth is resistance to stretch or elongation. Fibers with higher modulus will have initial resistance to stretch, and for this reason, polyester is a better choice than nylon. The new gel-spun polyethylene fibers have high strength and modulus and were originally considered appropriate for sailcloth. The creep exhibited by textiles of these fibers, however, made them unacceptable in terms of elongation and recovery. Kevlar® aramid fibers have very desirable properties but because of their cost are mainly used only in racing sails in competition.

Because of the way they are used, sails are subjected to forces in all directions. Woven fabrics normally would have less stretch than knits, but even wovens with high strength and low elongation in the warp and filling directions would still stretch in the bias direction. If this happened, the sail would lose its aerodynamic efficiency. For this reason, many woven sailcloths are stabilized by laminating a polyester film to the fabric. Lamination decreases the elongation in all directions, preserving the shape of the sail. Most sailcloths used today are multicomponent laminated fabrics or have a resin finish applied to stabilize the structure.

Weight

Fabric weight is probably the second most important property for sailcloth. Lighter weight fabrics are desirable because less wind is needed to fill them during sailing and also because they are easier to handle and to store. For many years sailcloths were made of cotton or linen. These fibers made strong, sturdy fabrics with excellent resistance to elongation. They were, however, of heavier weight than most materials used today. Polyester and nylon fibers have lower specific gravities than the cellulosic fibers, making them better candidates for sailcloths.

Absorbency

Related to the concern with sailcloth weight is the absorbency of the materials used. Fibers with high absorbency will increase in weight and be less desirable. This was another problem with cotton and linen sails, which absorbed water and became even heavier. Better fibers for sailcloths are those with lower moisture regains. Although nylon has good strength and durability, its regain, while lower than that of cotton or linen, is still higher than polyester. Furthermore, nylon can lose some of its strength when wet.

Flexibility

Flexibility is a secondary consideration in sailcloths. It is important for ease of handling and for preservation. Sailcloths undergo wrinkling and bending when they are stored after use. If they are stiff, repeated bending could permanently crease, or even crack, the sails, making them unusable. Flexible fibers and yarns, and thinner laminates, minimize such damage.

Air Permeability

Sails should have very low air permeability to maintain different amounts of air pressure on each side of the sail. High fabric counts, lamination, and resin finishes decrease the porosity of the sailcloth and enhance its performance.

Light Resistance

Since sails are used out of doors, their resistance to environmental conditions, especially sunlight, is an important factor in their performance. The fiber and film used in the sail structure must have good resistance to ultraviolet light. Many of the fibers with other properties desired in sailcloth are degraded by sunlight. These fibers can, however, be treated with light stabilizers to increase their resistance.

Putting It All
TOGETHER

F O R . . . *Upholstery Fabrics*

When consumers purchase upholstered furniture, they frequently make a selection based on their response to the appearance of the upholstery fabric. Cost of furniture and durability of upholstery fabric generally are not related, and an expensive piece of furniture may be upholstered with a fabric that wears out in a relatively short time. The most important considerations in evaluating the durability of upholstery fabrics are its resistance to abrasion, its resistance to soil and stains, and colorfastness to light.

Abrasion

Fibers. Upholstered furniture is constantly subjected to abrasion as people sit on it. Almost any fiber or blend of fibers can be and is used to make upholstery fabric. Some fibers obviously have better abrasion resistance than others. See Table 2.2, page 40, for comparison of abrasion resistance of various types of fibers. In fabric structures where one set of yarns predominates on the surface, the abrasion resistance of the fibers that form that yarn would be a very important factor in durability. In many upholstery fabrics, however, yarn and fabric construction may compensate for lower fiber strength.

Yarns. Yarns with high twist and even diameter, resist abrasion better than those with low twist and/or uneven diameter. Yarns with loops, nubs, or slubs, often used because of their attractive texture, are especially subject to abrasive wear.

Fabrics. In closely woven fabrics with balanced weaves, wear is evenly distributed across the surface of the fabric. If fibers are strong and yarns have high twist and uniform diameter, these fabrics can be quite durable. In plain-weave fabrics with large ribs or cords, the raised rib or cord area has the potential for uneven wear.

Twill woven fabric structures are generally strong, durable, and resist abrasion. In satin-weave fabrics, the long floats may catch or snag. Furthermore, to capitalize on the attractive appearance of satin-weave fabrics, manufacturers often use acetate, silk, or nylon fibers in low-twist yarns that are not very durable.

In pile fabrics such as velvet or velveteen, abrasion resistance will depend on fiber choice and density of pile. Nylon velvet, for example, can be quite durable thanks to its excellent abrasion resistance and good resilience, whereas silk or rayon pile fabrics are more likely not only to abrade but also to remain flat and worn-looking after the pile has been flattened by sitting on it. Uncut pile fabrics tend to wear better, especially if yarns are tightly twisted and made from abrasion-resistant fibers.

Dobby and jacquard woven fabrics are frequently used in upholstery. Their resistance to abrasion is variable. Factors to assess include fiber content, tightness of twist of the yarns, presence of long floats or raised areas that may catch or wear unevenly, and denseness of the weave.

Soil and Stain Resistance

Fibers. Most stains on upholstered furniture are water or liquid borne. Hydrophobic fibers such as polypropylene, which is almost completely nonabsorbent, will resist staining best. It is important to note, however, that even though the upholstery fabric may not absorb moisture, the padding materials underneath may. Consumers should ascertain that there is a moisture-proof barrier between the upholstery fabric and the padding materials. When present, this barrier is often a nonwoven layer of nonabsorbent material such as polypropylene.

Upholstery fabrics made from fibers that do absorb moisture can have stain-resistant finishes applied to them. Customers should stipulate that these finishes be applied before purchase.

Colorfastness

Upholstery on furnishings that are placed close to windows may undergo color loss or color change after long exposure to sunlight. When fibers have been producer-colored, the color is locked into the fiber and cannot fade. Information about the types of dyestuffs or pigments used on fabrics is generally not available at the point of purchase. Consumers may be able to determine whether fabrics have been tested for colorfastness to various conditions by asking the retailer.

Overall Evaluation

In selecting the right upholstery fabrics, the purchaser must assess the uses to which the furniture will be put. A sofa for a family room where food and beverages will be served, where children will drag toys across the surface, and where cats and dogs will jump up and down must meet far different demands than a period reproduction chair in a formal living room that is rarely used. Careful evaluation of the expected functions and how fiber, yarn, and fabric construction will fulfill those functions can result in selecting upholstery fabrics that will satisfy the buyer's needs and expectations.

Putting It All TOGETHER

FOR . . . *Outdoor Clothing*

Vapor barriers . . . wicking . . . waterproof . . . breathable . . . down . . . microfibers . . . The serious jogger, hiker, backpacker, and cross-country skier is faced with a bewildering array of choices when selecting clothing for strenuous outdoor activities. Consumers need to make informed choices among the various types of fibers, yarns, and fabrics available, and these choices must be made in relation to specific recreational needs. Comfort and serviceability must be placed in the context of climatic factors such as temperature, humidity, and wind; levels of physical activity; and how to maintain desirable properties over time.

Most experienced outdoor recreationists recommend manipulating layers of clothing. This provides greater flexibility and allows easy adaptation as weather, temperature, and activity levels change.

Underlayers

Fabric close to the body quickly becomes wet with perspiration during physical activity. The moisture absorption properties of fibers are most important here. Also, garments must be easily laundered. Cotton readily absorbs moisture but dries slowly. In hot, dry conditions cotton is a comfortable underlayer, but in cool, damp climates it feels cold and wet.

Wool can absorb a good deal of moisture without feeling wet and is a good insulator, but it does not launder easily unless given special finishes. Some persons are allergic to wool, and it is often expensive. Manufactured fibers such as polyester or polypropylene are low in absorbency and also wick moisture away from the body. This allows it to evaporate more quickly, thereby maintaining a dry, more comfortable feeling in cold and damp conditions. Manufactured fibers are easily laundered.

Underlayers also need to be flexible and to fit closely, bending and stretching as the body moves. Weft knits, especially jersey knitted fabric structures, have the requisite elasticity.

Middle Layers

The function of the middle layer is usually insulation. In cold weather air trapped by fibers helps to conserve body heat. These fibers may be on the surface of a fabric such as a sweater knitted from woolen yarns (as opposed to smoother worsted yarns) or part of a pile fabric structure. Polyester and wool serve well as insulators because they are resilient and spring back. Once flattened and matted together, fibers no longer trap air, and insulating qualities decrease.

Many garments designed to provide good insulation use down or synthetic fiberfill held between two layers of woven fabric. Outer fabric layers must have a high yarn count, so the filling will not escape, and they need good tensile and tear strength. The high strength of nylon fibers, compact yarns, and tightly woven fabrics into which nylon can be made lead to its frequent use in such fabrics.

Another consideration may be the weight of garments. Goose and duck down fillings are warm and exceptionally light. (Goose and duck down can, by law, have up to 20 percent small feathers incorporated.) Synthetic fibers are also light. They are resilient, do not transmit heat, and can be textured to increase loft. Polyester is frequently used. Some fibers are hollow, trapping dead air not only between the fibers but also within the fibers.

Outermost Layers

The functions of the outermost layer could be divided as follows: (1) making direct contact with the physical environment, (2) serving as a windbreaker, and (3) keeping everything underneath dry.

The choice of fiber and construction of fabric are especially important for the first two functions. Tensile and tear strength are important for outer layers. Abrasion resistance is probably less important for jackets than for pants. High, balanced yarn count fabrics will usually be more resistant to abrasion. Fabrics made with smooth and slippery synthetic filament yarns are more likely to be damaged by catching on thorns or bushes than tightly woven cotton fabrics. High-count fabrics also serve well as windbreakers because they have fewer openings between yarn intersections for wind to pass through.

Completely waterproof outer layers, made by coating fabrics to block out moisture vapor, are useful for situations in which people are relatively inactive and when the weather is cool. For active persons waterproof, breathable fabrics (see page 393) are often preferable. In warmer weather and when water-repellent rather than waterproof garments are sufficient, garments made from microfibers may be comfortable for highly aerobic activities. Nylon and polyester fibers in either microfiber or regular deniers are often used in rain gear because they have good tensile strength, resiliency, low moisture absorbency, and are easy to care for.

Putting It All
TOGETHER

FOR ... *Automotive Textiles*

The average car uses about 50 square yards of textile fabrics. About 25 square yards are used for interior trim, and the remainder go into sound dampening, insulation, and hidden applications such as tires, filters, belts, hoses, and air bags (Smith 1994).

Although the ideal situation for purposes of eventual recycling would be to have all automotive textile materials made from the same kind of fiber, various parts of autos use different fibers because of specific performance requirements. Major fibers used in interiors are nylon, polyester, and nylon/polyester blends. Seat belts are most often polyester; airbags, nylon; and carpeting, nylon. For tire reinforcement, steel predominates, but substantial quantities of high-tenacity polyesters and nylons are also used, as well as smaller quantities of high-tenacity rayon.

Interior Fabrics

While aesthetic considerations are important in visible textile materials such as seat covers, carpets, and wall coverings, good performance is essential. Car interiors are subject to conditions, such as light exposure, high temperatures, and atmospheric gases, that can degrade fibers.

Fiber Choices. Both nylon and polyester perform well as upholstery fabrics and wall coverings. Both have excellent abrasion resistance (important in withstanding the sliding of individuals and objects on and off seats), good strength, and good crease resistance. Nylon is elastic, which allows fabrics to conform to the shape of seats for a smooth surface. It is somewhat less resistant to degradation from sunlight than polyester, but this problem can be overcome by applying ultraviolet light (UV) screening films, certain premetalized dyes, and anti-UV finishes on fibers.

Nylon is the fiber most often used for carpeting. It is preferred because of its abrasion resistance, strength, and resilience.

Colorfastness. Manufacturers can choose among solution-dyed fibers, yarn-dyed, and piece-dyed fabrics. Relatively little solution-dyed fabric is used, even though its colorfastness is superior. It is more expensive and requires a commitment to particular colors farther in advance than yarn or piece-dyed fabrics; however, industry sources do predict increased use of solution-dyed fabrics in the future (Fulmer 1993).

Piece-dyed fabrics, though the least costly, have the poorest colorfastness to light. Yarn-dyed fabrics perform well and are widely used. Colorfastness is increased if fabrics have been treated with ultraviolet stabilizers. Laboratory tests have shown no difference in performance between bright and delustered fibers but do indicate that as denier per filament decreases, lightfastness decreases.

Airbags

All automobiles and light trucks manufactured in the United States in 1999 and thereafter will be required to have both driver- and passenger-side airbags. Fabrics used in airbags must be capable of holding air when inflated and be strong enough to withstand impact without rupturing. Nylon is used because of its strength, toughness, and dimensional stability during storage. Although manufacturers are experimenting with the use of polyester, nylon is likely to continue as the predominant fiber due to its greater strength, especially for driver-side bags where performance standards are higher. Nylon bags also can be produced at relatively low cost.

To hold the air inside the bag, fabrics are coated either with neoprene or silicone. The European auto industry has moved to using more expensive uncoated fabrics made from airtight constructions, and the U.S. industry may also move in that direction in the future (Smith 1994).

Other Applications

The following areas of automobiles also use textile materials.

- *Seat cushions,* formerly made of urethane rubber foam, are now being made from polyester fiber, which is lighter, more comfortable, and recyclable.
- *Seat belts* must resist abrasion and have good strength. They are most often made of polyester.
- *Automotive hoses* must be strong and resistant to gasoline, oil, and other chemical substances. The most widely used fibers include polyester, rayon, and high performance fibers such as aramids.
- *Insulation* requires high-temperature resistance. Fibers in use include glass fiber, ceramic and silica fiber, aramid, molded temperature-resistant composites, and metalized fabrics.

Putting It All
TOGETHER
F O R ... *Swimwear Fabrics*

Bathing suits are a fairly specialized end use for fabrics; the fabrics chosen must satisfy both fashion and function. For most of the bathing suits worn today, important functional characteristics are stretch and recovery, colorfastness, absorbency, and environmental resistance.

Elongation and Recovery

The majority of bathing suits for women, and many for men, are tight fitting, with stretch required for getting the garments on and off. Fabrics are given the required stretch by knit construction and/or elastomeric fibers. Since knits have much higher elongation than woven or nonwoven fabrics, they are the preferred fabric construction for bathing suits that fit tightly to the body.

Fibers with lower modulus and high resilience will enhance the stretch and recovery properties of knits. Nylon and wool have low modulus and good recovery. Nylon is a good choice for swimwear because of these properties. Wool was used at one time, but its high absorbance, and consequent gain in weight, decreased its desirability for bathing suits. Polyester is not usually used because it has a higher modulus and therefore does not stretch as easily. Knitted fabrics of nylon blended with elastomeric fibers, such as spandex or rubber, will provide the highest amount of stretch. The elastic fibers also have very high recovery from stretch.

Colorfastness

Bathing suits are not only regularly worn outside in the sunshine, but they are also exposed to chlorine and other chemicals in swimming pools and salt water in oceans. Many fashion suits are made of bright-colored fabrics that should be colorfast to maintain the serviceability of the garments.

Lightfastness of dyed spandex is fair to good, while that of nylon dyed with acid dyes is good. Spandex normally makes up only a small percentage of the fiber content of swimwear fabrics and is often used in core-spun yarns wrapped with nylon. This helps to protect it from sunlight. Colorfastness of nylon and spandex exposed to pool and salt water is fairly good but will show some loss over time.

Environmental Resistance

Light, chlorine, and salt water can also degrade textile fibers. When this occurs, bathing suit fabrics may lose some of their recovery from stretch. Nylon and polyester are more resistant to ultraviolet light and chlorine than spandex. That is another reason why spandex is usually used in small percentages blended with nylon. The use of rubber as an elastomeric fiber in swimwear has decreased because of its susceptibility to degradation by light and other environmental conditions. Because resistance of nylon to degradation by light is higher for fibers that have not been delustered, brighter nylons are usually used in swimwear.

Absorbency

Since bathing suits are worn while swimming in water, the absorbency of the fabric is a consideration. If a material absorbs and retains a significant amount of water, the weight of the suit will increase, affecting its comfort and function. Synthetic fibers have low water regain and are more appropriate for bathing suits than the natural fibers that were used many years ago.

References

AATCC. 1994. *Evaluation Procedure 5* [technical manual]. Research Triangle Park, N.C.: AATCC.

Fulmer, T. D. 1993. Dyeing textiles for automotive interiors. *America's Textiles International* 23 (December): 88.

Kawabata, S. 1980. *The standardization and analysis of hand evaluation.* Osaka: The Textile Machinery Society of Japan.

Smith, W. C. 1994. Automotives: A major textile market. *Textile World* 144 (September): 68.

Review Questions

1. What are the contributions of each of the following to the strength of textile fabrics: fiber, yarn, fabric construction?
2. Distinguish between fiber crimp and yarn crimp. What is the effect of each on fabric elongation?
3. How is fabric construction related to abrasion resistance?

4. Define *shearing*. Describe how shearability would be important in a tablecloth and in a woman's dress.

5. What does the Kawabata Evaluation System for Fabric evaluate? How are these evaluations determined?

6. Identify the various ways that fiber, yarn, fabric structure, and finish are related to wrinkle recovery.

7. What are the factors that determine whether a textile product will be dimensionally stable?

8. What are some of the aspects of fabric structure that contribute to making a textile product comfortable to wear?

9. Develop a case study similar to those at the end of this chapter for one of the following products. Focus on fiber, yarn, fabric structure, coloration, and finishes. Do not be concerned about construction details of garments or household textiles.
   - Bed sheets.
   - Sleepwear for a newborn infant.
   - Man's dress shirt.
   - Blanket for winter in cold climate.
   - Socks to be worn under hiking books for summer hikes.

Recommended Readings

Abend, J. 1994. Fabric development takes the driver's seat. *Bobbin* 35 (May): 44.

Bresee, R. R., P. A. Annis, and M. M. Warnock. 1994. Comparing actual fabric wear with laboratory abrasion and laundering. *Textile Chemist and Colorist* 25 (January): 17–23.

Collier, B. J. 1991. Measurement of fabric drape and its relation to fabric mechanical properties and subjective evaluation. *Clothing and Textiles Research Journal* 10 (Fall): 46.

Epps, H. H., and M. K. Song. 1992. Thermal transmittance and air permeability of plain weave fabrics. *Clothing and Textiles Research Journal* 11 (Fall): 10.

Etters, J. N., and M. D. Hurwitz. 1985. The influence of surface texture on the colors of textile home furnishings. *America's Textiles* 14 (November): 56.

Gong, R. H., and S. K. Mukhopadhyay. 1993. Fabric objective measurement: A comparative study of fabric characteristics. *Journal of the Textile Institute* 84 (2): 192.

Hatch, K. L., et al. 1992. Skin response to fabric: A review of studies and assessment methods. *Clothing and Textiles Research Journal* 10 (Summer): 54.

Kothari, V. K., and S. K. Tandon. 1989. Shear behavior of woven fabrics. *Textile Research Journal* 59 (March): 142.

Moore, C. L. 1992. Factors that affect undesirable garment drape. *Journal of Home Economics* 84 (Fall): 31.

Smith, J. E. 1993. The comfort of clothing. *Textiles* 22 (1): 18.

Vatsala, R., and V. Subramiam. 1993. The integral evaluation of fabric performance. *Journal of the Textile Institute* 84 (3): 495.

Wada, O. 1992. Control of fiber form and yarn and fabric structure. *Journal of the Textile Institute* 83 (3): 322.

Weiner, M. 1993. Stretching the life cycle of performance fabrics. *Bobbin* 35 (October): 36.

BIBLIOGRAPHY

General References:
Texts and Encyclopedias

Beech, S. R. et al., eds. 1988. *Textile terms and definitions*, 8th edition. Manchester, England: Textile Institute.

Belck, N. 1990. *Textiles: Decision making for the consumer.* East Lansing: Michigan State Univ. Press.

Burnham, D. K. 1994. *Warp and weft: A textile terminology.* Toronto: Univ. of Toronto Press.

Cohen, A. 1982. *Beyond basic textiles.* New York: Fairchild.

Collchester, C. 1991. *The new textiles.* New York: Rizzoli.

Fritz, A., and J. Cant. 1988. *Consumer textiles.* New York: Oxford Univ. Press.

Gioello, D. 1982. *Understanding fabrics from fiber to finished cloth.* New York: Fairchild.

Goswami, B. C., et al. 1988. *Fibers, yarns, and fabrics: Properties and uses.* New York: Wiley.

Grayson, M., ed. 1984. *Encyclopedia of textiles, fibers, and nonwoven fabrics.* New York: Wiley-Interscience.

Hatch, K. L. 1993. *Textile science.* Minneapolis/St. Paul, Minn.: West.

Ishida, T. 1991. *An introduction to textile technology.* Osaka, Japan: Osaka Senken.

Jerde, J. 1992. *Encyclopedia of textiles.* New York: Facts on File.

Joseph, M. L. 1988. *Essentials of textiles.* Fort Worth, Tex.: Harcourt Brace.

———. 1988. *Introductory textile science.* Fort Worth, Tex.: Harcourt Brace.

Kadolph, S., et al. 1992. *Textiles.* New York: Macmillan.

Larsen, J. L., and J. Weeks. 1975. *Fabrics for interiors.* New York: Van Nostrand Reinhold.

Needles, J. L. 1986. *Textile fibers, dyes, finishes, and processes.* Park Ridge, N.J.: Noyes.

Neilson, K. 1991. *Textiles for today's interiors.* New York: Van Nostrand Reinhold.

Price, A., and A. C. Cohen. 1994. *J. J. Pizzuto's fabric science.* 6th ed. New York: Fairchild.

Tortora, P., and B. Merkel. 1996. *Fairchild's textile dictionary.* New York: Fairchild.

Yeager, J. 1987. *Textiles for residential and commercial interiors.* New York: HarperCollins.

Historic and Ethnic Textiles

Barber, E. W. 1991. *Prehistoric textiles.* Princeton, N.J.: Princeton Univ. Press.

———. 1994. *Women's work: The first twenty thousand years; women, cloth, and society in early times.* New York: W. W. Norton & Co.

Broudy, E. 1979. *The book of looms—a history of the handloom from ancient times to the present.* New York: Van Nostrand Reinhold.

Chen, W. 1992. *A history of the science and technology of textile traditions in China.* Rego Park, N.Y.: Science Press.

D'Harcourt, R. 1974. *Textiles of ancient Peru and their techniques.* Seattle: Univ. of Washington Press.

Gillow, J., and B. Nicholas. 1993. *Traditional Indian textiles.* New York: Thames and Hudson.

Harris, J., ed. 1993. *Textiles, 5000 years: An international history and illustrated survey.* New York: Harry N. Abrams.

Harvey, N. 1991. *Illustrated history of textiles.* New York: Random House.

Jorgensen, L. B. 1992. *North European textiles until AD 1000.* Philadelphia: Coronet Books.

King, R. R. 1985. *Textile identification, conservation, and preservation.* Park Ridge, N.J.: Noyes.

Landi, S. 1992. *The textile conservator's manual.* 2d ed. Newton, Mass.: Butterworth Heinemann.

Lebeau, C. 1994. *Fabrics.* New York: Crown.

Leene, J. E. 1992. *Textile conservation.* Washington, D.C.: Smithsonian Institution.

Montgomery, R. 1984. *Textiles in America.* Wilmington, Del.: Winterthur.

Nylander, J. C. 1990. *Fabrics for historic buildings.* Washington, D.C.: Preservation Press.

Pianzola, M., and J. Coffinet. 1974. *Tapestry.* New York: Van Nostrand Reinhold.

Rathbun, W. 1993. *Beyond the Tanabata Bridge: Traditional Japanese textiles.* New York: Thames and Hudson.

Sieber, R. 1972. *African textile and decorative arts.* New York: Museum of Modern Art.

Weiner, A., and J. Schneider, eds. 1989. *Cloth and human experience.* Washington, D.C.: Smithsonian Institution.

Wilson, K. 1979. *A history of textiles.* Boulder, Colo.: Westview Press.

Zeronian, S. H., and H. L. Needles. 1989. *Historic textile and paper materials.* Vol. II, *Conservation and characterization.* Washington, D.C.: American Chemical Society.

Textiles as an Art and Craft

Albers, A. 1965. *On weaving.* Middletown, Conn.: Wesleyan Univ. Press.

Brown, R. 1987. *Weaving, spinning, and dyeing book.* New York: Alfred A. Knopf.

Earnshaw, P. 1988. *A dictionary of lace.* New York: State Mutual Book Service.

———. 1989. *Threads of lace: From source to sink.* Guilford, England: Gorse.

Kliot, J., and K. Kliot, eds. 1989. *The art of netting.* Berkeley, Calif.: Lacis.

Meller, S., and J. Eiffers. 1991. *Textile designs: Two hundred years of European and American patterns for printed fabrics.* New York: Harry N. Abrams.

Palliser, B. 1984. *History of lace.* New York: Dover Books.

Regensteiner, E. 1986. *The art of weaving.* New York: Schiffer.

Ross, M. 1988. *Encyclopedia of handspinning.* Loveland, Colo.: Interweave Press.

Storey, J. 1992. *Thames and Hudson manual of dyes and fabrics.* New York: Thames and Hudson.

———. 1992. *Thames and Hudson manual of textile printing.* New York: Thames and Hudson.

Textile Care

American Association for Textile Technology. 1973. *The technology of home laundering.* Textile Monograph 108. New York: American Association for Textile Technology.

Dantaygi, S. 1983. *Fundamentals of textiles and their care.* New York: Apt Books.

Finch, K. 1977. *Caring for textiles.* New York: Watson-Guptill.

Mailand, H. F. 1980. *Consideration for the care of textiles and costumes: A handbook for the non-specialist.* Indianapolis: Indianapolis Museum.

Moss, A. J. E. 1961. *Textiles and fabrics: Their care and preservation.* New York: Chemical.

Soap and Detergents Association. 1989. *Detergents in depth.* Proceedings. New York: Soap and Detergents Association.

U.S. Department of Agriculture. 1973. *Soaps and detergents for home laundering.* Home and Garden Bulletin no. 139. Washington, D.C.: U.S. Department of Agriculture.

Textile Chemistry

Billmeyer, F. W. 1984. *Textbook of polymer science.* New York: Wiley.

Carter, M. E. 1971. *Essential fiber chemistry.* New York: Marcel Dekker.

Happey, F., ed. 1979. *Applied fibre science.* New York: Academic Press.

Hearle, J. W. S. 1982. *Polymers and their properties.* Vol. 1, *Fundamentals of structure and mechanics.* Chichester, England: Ellis Horwood.

Hiemenz, P. C. 1984. *Polymer chemistry—the basic concepts.* Brookfield Center, Conn.: Society of Plastics Engineers.

Kaufman, H. S., and J. J. Falcetta, eds. 1977. *Introduction to polymer science and technology.* Brookfield Center, Conn.: Society of Plastics Engineers.

Lewin, M., and E. Pearce. 1985. *Handbook of fiber science and technology: Fiber chemistry.* New York: Marcel Dekker.

Mark, J. E., et al. 1984. *Physical properties of polymers.* Washington, D.C.: American Chemical Society.

Miles, J. 1983. *Handbook of chemical specialties. Textile fiber processing, preparation, and bleaching.* New York: Wiley-Interscience.

Needles, H. L. 1981. *Handbook of textile fibers, dyes, and finishes.* New York: Garland STPM Press.

Seymour, R. B. 1981. *Polymer chemistry: An introduction.* New York: Marcel Dekker.

Trotman, E. R. 1984. *Dyeing and chemical technology of textile fibres.* New York: Wiley-Interscience.

Textile Construction (Technical Works)

AATCC. 1974. *Handbook of bonded and laminated fabrics.* Research Triangle Park, N.C.: American Association of Textile Chemists and Colorists.

Brackenburg, T. 1992. *Knitted clothing technology.* Cambridge, Mass.: Blackwell Scientific.

Chou, T-W., 1989. *Textile structural composites.* New York: Elsevier.

Emery, I. 1966. *The primary structures of fabrics.* Washington, D.C.: Textile Museum.

The future of high performance fabrics. 1990. St. Paul, Minn.: Industrial Fabrics.

Gioello, D. 1981. *Profiling fabrics: Properties, performance, and construction techniques.* New York: Fairchild.

Giroud, J-P. 1984. *Geotextiles and geomembranes: Definitions, properties, and design.* St. Paul, Minn.: Industrial Fabrics.

Goerner, D. 1986. *Woven structure and design. Part 1: Single cloth.* New York: State Mutual Book Service.

———. 1990. *Woven structure and design. Part 2: Compound structures.* New York: State Mutual Book Service.

Goswami, B. C., et al. 1977. *Textile yarns, technology, structure and applications.* New York: Wiley.

Greenwood, K. 1977. *Weaving, control of fabric structure.* Watford, England: Merrow.

Henshaw, D. E. 1981. *Worsted spinning.* Manchester, England: Textile Institute.

Holloway, L., ed. 1994. *Handbook of polymer composites for engineers.* Cambridge, England: Woodhead.

Klein, W. 1993. *New spinning systems.* Short Staple Spinning Series, vol. 5. Manchester, England: Textile Institute.

Marks, R., and T. C. Robinson. 1976. *Principles of weaving.* New York: State Mutual Book and Periodical Service.

Naik, K. 1993. *Woven fabric composites.* Lancaster, Pa.: Technomic.

Nield, R. 1975. *Open end spinning.* New York: State Mutual Book Service.

Omerod, A., and W. S. Sondheim. 1995. *Weaving: Technology and operations.* Manchester, England: Textile Institute.

Pierce, F. T., and J. R. Womersley. 1978. *Cloth geometry.* Manchester, England: Textile Institute.

Piller, B. 1973. *Bulked yarns: Production, processing, and applications.* Manchester, England: Textile Trade Press.

Reichman, C., ed. 1972. *Knitting encyclopedia.* New York: National Knitted Outerwear Association.

Schwartz, P., et al. 1982. *Fabric forming systems.* Park Ridge, N.J.: Noyes Data Corporation.

Slater, K. 1987. *Textile mechanics.* Shirley, England: Textile Institute.

Spencer, D. J. 1989. *Knitting technology.* Oxford, England: Pergamon.

Spinning into the future. 1989. Proceedings of the 1989 Yarn Conference. Manchester, England: Textile Institute.

Talavsek, O. 1981. *Shuttleless weaving machines.* New York: Elsevier.

Wilson, D. K. 1978. *Production of textured yarns by methods other than the false twist method.* New York: State Mutual Books.

———. 1978. *Production of textured yarns by the false twist technique.* New York: State Mutual Books.

Textile Dyeing, Printing, and Finishing (Technical Works)

AATCC. *Book of papers, Technical Conference.* Published annually. Research Triangle Park, N.C.: American Association of Textile Chemists and Colorists.

AATCC. 1981. *Dyeing primer.* Research Triangle Park, N.C.: American Association of Textile Chemists and Colorists.

AATCC. 1987. *Trends in dyeing and finishing: A global view.* Research Triangle Park, N.C.: American Association of Textile Chemists and Colorists.

AATCC. 1989. *Basics of dyeing and finishing.* Research Triangle Park, N.C.: American Association of Textile Chemists and Colorists.

AATCC. 1991. *Color measurement principles and the textile industry.* Symposium papers. Research Triangle Park, N.C.: American Association of Textile Chemists and Colorists.

Bogle, M. 1977. *Textile dyes, finishes, and auxiliaries.* New York: Garland.

Datye, D. V., and A. A. Vaidya. 1984. *Chemical processing of synthetic fibres and blends.* New York: Wiley-Interscience.

De Boos, A. G. 1990. *Finishing wool fabrics to improve their end-use performance.* Manchester, England: Textile Institute.

Kulkarni, S. V., et al. 1986. *Textile dyeing operations: Chemistry equipment, procedures, and environmental aspects.* Park Ridge, N.J.: Noyes.

Lewin, M., and S. B. Sello, eds. 1984. *Handbook of fiber science and technology.* Vol. I, *Fundamentals and preparation.* New York: Marcel Dekker.

———, eds. 1984. *Handbook of fiber science and technology.* Vol. II, *Functional finishes.* New York: Marcel Dekker.

Makinson, K. 1979. *Shrinkproofing of wool.* New York: Marcel Dekker.

Miles, L. W. C. 1982. *Textile printing.* 2d ed. Watford, England: Merrow.

Milner, A. 1992. *The Ashford book of dyeing.* London: Batsford.

Nettles, J. E. 1983. *Handbook of chemical specialties: Textile fiber processing, preparation, and bleaching.* New York: Wiley.

Olson, E. S. 1983. *Textile wet processes.* Vol. 1, *Preparation of fibers and fabrics.* Park Ridge, N.J.: Noyes Data Corporation.

Rivlin, J. 1993. *The dyeing of textile fibers: Theory and practice.* Philadelphia: Philadelphia College of Textiles and Science.

Sandberg, G. 1989. *Indigo textiles.* London: A & C Black.

Vigo, T. L. 1994. *Textile processing and properties: Preparation, dyeing, finishing, and performance.* New York: Elsevier.

Textile Fibers (Technical Works)

Arthur, J. C. 1984. *Polymers for fibers and elastomers.* Washington, D.C.: American Chemical Society.

Cook, J. G. 1984. *Handbook of textile fibers.* Vols. 1 and 2. Watford, England: Merrow, Technical Library.

Donnett, J. B., and R. C. Bansal. 1990. *Carbon fibers.* New York: Marcel Dekker.

Fibres: Technological solutions for textile problems. 1989. Papers from the Textile Institute's 1989 Fibre Science Group Conference. Manchester, England: Textile Institute.

Gohl, E. P. H., and L. D. Vilensky. 1981. *Textile science: An explanation of fibre properties.* London: Longman Group.

Hamby, D. S., ed. 1965–1966. *American cotton handbook.* 2 vols. New York: Wiley-Interscience.

Happey, F., ed. 1978–1979. *Applied fibre science.* Vols. 1 and 2. New York: Academic Press.

———. 1983. *Contemporary textile engineering.* New York: Academic Press.

Hearle, J., and D. Brunnschweiler. 1993. *Polyester.* Manchester, England: Textile Institute.

Hearle, J. W., ed. 1990. *High performance fibres, composites and engineering textile structure.* Manchester, England: Textile Institute.

Hearle, J. W. S., and R. H. Peters. 1963. *Fiber structures.* London: Butterworth.

Hongu, R., and G. Phillips. 1991. *New fibers.* Englewood Cliffs, N.J.: Prentice Hall.

Hunter, L. 1993. *Mohair: A review of properties, processing, and applications.* Manchester, England: CSIRO Division of Textile Technology, International Mohair Association, and Textile Institute.

Kaplan, D., et al., eds. 1994. *Silk polymers: Material science and technology.* Washington, D.C.: American Chemical Society.

Kroschwitz, J. 1990. *Fibers and textiles, a compendium.* New York: Wiley.

Lewin, M., and J. Preston. 1985. *Handbook of fiber science and technology.* Part A. New York: Marcel Dekker.

———. 1989. *Handbook of fiber science and technology.* Part B. New York: Marcel Dekker.

———. 1993. *High technology fibers.* Part A. New York: Marcel Dekker.

Mark, H. F., N. S. Wooding, and S. M. Atlas. 1971. *Chemical aftertreatment of textiles.* New York: Wiley.

Masson, J. C. 1995. *Acrylic fiber technology and applications.* New York: Marcel Dekker.

Militky, J., et al. 1991. *Modified polyester fibers.* New York: Elsevier.

Moncrieff, R. W. 1974. *Man-made fibres.* London: Newnes-Butterworth.

Morton, W. E., and J. W. S. Hearle. 1993. *Physical properties of textile fibres.* 3d ed. Manchester, England: Textile Institute.

Mukhopadhyay, S. K. 1993. *Advances in fibre science.* Manchester, England: Textile Institute.

Nakajima, T., ed. 1994. *Advanced fiber spinning technology.* Cambridge, England: Woodhead.

Plastics and Rubber Institute staff, eds. 1986. *Carbon fibers: Technology, uses, and prospects.* Park Ridge, N.J.: Noyes.

Postle, R., et al. 1988. *The mechanics of wool structures.* Chichester, England: Ellis Harwood.

Seymour, R. B., and R. S. Porter, eds. 1993. *Manmade fibers: Their origin and development.* London: Elsevier.

Von Bergen, W., ed. 1963, 1970. *Wool handbook.* Vols. 1 and 2. New York: Wiley-Interscience.

Warner, S. B. 1995. *Fiber science.* Englewood Cliffs, N.J.: Prentice Hall.

World directory of manufactured fiber producers. 1994–1995. Roseland, N.J.: Fiber Economics Bureau.

Yang, H. H. 1993. *Kevlar aramid fiber.* New York: Wiley-Interscience.

Ziabecki, A., and H. Kawai. 1991. *High speed fiber spinning.* New York: Wiley.

Textile Industry

Berkstresser, G. A. 1984. *Textile marketing management.* Park Ridge, N.J.: Noyes Data Corporation.

Berkstresser, G. A., and D. R. Buchanan. 1986. *Automation and robotics in the textile and apparel industries.* Park Ridge, N.J.: Noyes.

Cohen, A. 1988. *Marketing textiles: From fiber to retail.* New York: Fairchild.

Dickerson, K. 1995. *Textiles and apparel in the global economy.* 2d ed. Columbus, OH: Merrill/Prentice Hall.

Hunter, N. A. 1990. *Quick Response in apparel manufacturing.* Manchester, England: Textile Institute.

Toyne, B., et al. 1983. *The U.S. textile mill products industry.* Columbia: Univ. of South Carolina.

———. 1984. *The global textile institute.* Boston: George Allen and Unwin.

Textile Testing, Standards, and Legislation

AATCC. *Technical manual.* Published annually. Research Triangle Park, N.C.: American Association of Textile Chemists and Colorists.

ASTM. *Annual Book of ASTM Standards.* Philadelphia: American Society for Testing and Materials.

Booth, J. E. 1968. *Principles of textile testing.* London: Newnes-Butterworth.

Cassidy, C., and D. Bishop. 1994. *Characterization and evaluation of sensory and mechanical properties of fabrics.* Manchester, England: Textile Institute.

Hearle, J. W. S., et al. 1989. *Fibre failure and wear of materials.* Chichester, England: Ellis Horwood.

Mahall, K. 1993. *Quality assessment of textile damage detection by microscopy.* New York: Springer Verlag.

Merkel, R. S. 1991. *Textile product serviceability.* New York: Macmillan.

Perry, D. R., et al. 1985. *Identification of textile materials.* 7th ed. Manchester, England: Textile Institute.

Slater, K. 1993. *Physical testing and quality control.* New York: State Mutual Book Service.

———. 1994. *Chemical testing and analysis.* Manchester, England: Textile Institute.

Standards for safety tests for flame propagation of fabrics and films. 1993. Northbrook, Ill.: Underwriters Laboratories.

Weaver, J. W., ed. 1984. *Analytical methods for a textile laboratory.* 3d ed. Research Triangle Park, N.C.: American Association of Textile Chemists and Colorists.

Miscellaneous

Backer, S. 1976. *Textile fabric flammability.* Cambridge, Mass.: MIT Press.

Crown, F. 1973. *The fabric guide for people who sew.* New York: Grosset & Dunlap.

Fourt, N., and N. R. Hollies. 1970. *Clothing/comfort and function.* New York: Marcel Dekker.

Gross, P., and D. C. Braun. 1984. *Toxic and biomedical effects of fibers.* Park Ridge, N.J.: Noyes.

Slater, K. 1977. *Comfort properties of textiles.* Manchester, England: Textile Institute.

Periodicals

Abstract Alert, Institute of Textile Technology, Charlottesville, Va.

Ars Textrina, Winnepeg, Canada.

American Dyestuff Reporter, Secaucus, N.J.

America's Textiles International, Billian Publishers, Atlanta, Ga.

Canadian Textile Journal, Montreal, Quebec, Canada.

Clothing and Textiles Research Journal, International Textile and Apparel Association, Monument, Colo.

Cotton Digest International, Cotton Digest Col, Houston, Tex.

Daily News Record, Fairchild Publications, New York, N.Y.

Fiber Organon, Roseland, N.J.

Geo-technical Fabrics Report, Industrial Fabrics Association International, St. Paul, Minn.

Handwoven, Interweave Press, Loveland, Colo.

High Performance Textiles, Elsevier Publishers, New York, N.Y.

Home Textiles Today, Bowker Magazine Group, New York, N.Y.

Industrial Fabrics Product Review, Industrial Fabrics Association International, St. Paul, Minn.

International Fabricare Institute, Silver Springs, Md.

Journal of Coated Fabrics, Technomic Publishing Co., Lancaster, Pa.

Journal of Industrial Fabrics, RCM Enterprises, Wayzata, Minn.

Journal of the Textile Institute, Manchester, England.

JTN, Osaka, Japan.

Knitting Times, New York, N.Y.

Nonwoven World, Miller Freeman Inc., New York, N.Y.

Nonwovens Industry, Rodman Publishing Corp., Ramsey, N.J.

Shuttle, Spindle, and Dyepot, Handweaver's Guild, Bloomfield, Conn.

Textile Chemist and Colorist, American Association of Textile Chemists and Colorists, Research Triangle Park, N.C.

Textile Hi-Lights, American Textile Manufacturers Institute, Washington, D.C.

Textile History, Leeds, England.

Textile Horizons, London, England.

Textile Month, Reed Business Publishing Co., New York, N.Y.

Textile Museum Bulletin, Washington, D.C.

Textile Museum Journal, Washington, D.C.

Textile Outlook International, Economist Publications, London, England.

Textile Progress, Manchester, England

Textile Research Journal, Textile Research Institute, Princeton, N.J.

Textile Technology Digest, Institute of Textile Technology, Charlottesville, Va.

Textile World, Maclean Hunter Media, Atlanta, Ga.

Textiles Magazine, Textile Institute, Manchester, England.

Threads, Taunton Press, Inc., Newtown, Conn.

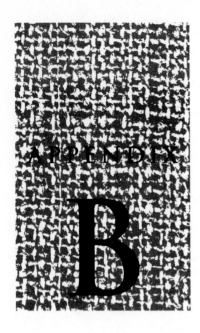

APPENDIX B

GLOSSARY

Abrasion* The wearing away of any part of a material by rubbing against another surface.

Absorption* A process in which one material (the absorbent) takes in or absorbs another (the absorbate) as the absorption of moisture by fibers.

Adsorption* A process in which the surface of a solid takes on or absorbs in an extremely thin layer molecules of gases, of dissolved substances, or of liquids with which it is in contact.

Amorphous areas (in the fiber structure) Areas within fibers in which long-chain molecules are arranged in a random, or unorganized, manner.

Appliqué Attaching, usually by sewing, small pieces of cloth or other materials to the surface of a larger textile.

Bandanna Indian textiles decorated by the tie-and-dye method.

Bast fibers Fibers found in the woody stem of plants.

Batik Indonesian technique of resist printing in which areas of fabric that are to resist the dye are covered with wax.

Batt A mass of fibers slightly matted together, often formed into a sheet or roll.

Bicomponent bigeneric fiber Bicomponent fiber consisting of two generically different fibers.

Bicomponent fiber* A fiber consisting of two polymers which are chemically different, physically different, or both.

Bigeneric fiber See *Bicomponent bigeneric fiber.*

Bleaching* The procedure, other than by scouring only, of improving the whiteness of a textile material by oxidation or reduction of the coloring matter.

Blended yarn* A single yarn spun from a blend or mixture of different fiber species.

Block printing The application of printed designs by pressing dye-covered blocks onto a fabric.

Bobbin lace Lace made with a number of threads, each fastened to a spool. The pattern to be followed is anchored to a pillow, so that this lace is also called *pillow lace.*

Byssinosis A lung disease to which cotton mill workers are subject; thought to be caused by toxins in the cotton dust.

Calendering The process of passing fabric between rollers with the application of heat and pressure.

Carbonized wool* A term descriptive of scoured wool processed to destroy cellulosic impurities by treating with a mineral acid or an acid salt, drying and baking, crushing, and dusting out the embrittled cellulosic matter followed by neutralization of the acidified wool.

Carding* The process of untangling and partially straightening fibers by passing them between two closely spaced surfaces that are moving at different speeds, and at least one of which is covered with sharp points, thus converting a tangled mass of fibers to a filmy web.

Casement cloth A term used to refer to a wide variety of curtain fabrics.

Ciré A shiny, lustrous surface effect achieved by applying a wax finish or by heat treatment of thermoplastic fibers.

Cohesiveness* The resistance to separation of fibers in contact with one another.

Colorfastness The ability of a textile material to retain its color during use and care.

Combing A process that follows carding that pulls fibers into more parallel alignment.

Courses* In knitted fabrics, the series of successive loops lying crosswise of a knitted fabric, that is, lying at right angles to a line passing through the open throat to the closed end of the loops.

Cover factor The ratio of fabric surface occupied by the yarns to the total fabric surface.

Covering power (optical) The ability of a fabric to hide that which is placed under it.

Crimp, fiber* The waviness of a fiber expressed as waves or crimps per unit length.

Crochet A technique of creating fabric by pulling one loop of yarn through another with a hook.

Crocking* A transfer of color from the surface of a colored fabric to an adjacent area of the same fabric or to another surface principally by rubbing action.

Cross-dye effect* Variation in dye pickup between yarns or fibers resulting from their inherent dye affinities.

Cross-linking The attachment of one long-chain molecule to another by chemical linkages.

Crystallinity (in fiber structure) Orderly, parallel arrangements of molecules within a fiber.

Cut The number of needles per inch in the bed of a circular filling knit machine.

Cystine linkages Chemical cross-linkages in the wool fiber.

Delustered fiber A manufactured fiber that has had its natural luster decreased by chemical or physical means.

Denier The weight of 9,000 meters of fiber or yarn expressed in grams.

Density, fiber* Mass per unit volume of the solid matter of which a fiber is composed, measured under specified conditions.

Detergent Any cleaning agent.

Dimensional stability The ability of a fiber or yarn to withstand shrinking or stretching.

Discharge printing The creation of design by applying a discharge material that removes color from treated areas of a dyed fabric.

Doupion silk A double strand of silk produced by two silkworms spinning a cocoon together. Also called *doupioni silk.*

Dry spinning The formation of manufactured textile fibers in which the polymer is dissolved in a solvent that is evaporated, leaving the filament to harden by drying in air.

Dull fiber See *delustered fiber.*

Durable finishes Those finishes that have good durability over a reasonably long period of use.

Durable press* Having the ability to retain substantially the initial shape, flat seams, pressed-in creases, and unwrinkled appearance during use and after laundering or dry cleaning. The use of the term "permanent press" as a substitute for "durable press" is undesirable.

Dyes Natural or synthetic substances that add color to materials by being absorbed therein.

Elasticity* That property of a material by virtue of which it tends to recover its original size and shape immediately after removal of the force causing deformation.

Elongation* The ratio of the extension of a material to the length of the material before stretching.

Embroidery The use of yarns applied to fabrics with a needle in a variety of decorative stitches.

Ends Warp yarns.

Fasciated yarns Yarns made from a bundle of parallel fibers wrapped with a surface wrapping of other fibers.

Felt, wool* A textile composed wholly of any one or combination of new or recycled wool fibers physically interlocked by the inherent felting properties of wool and produced by a suitable combination of mechanical work, chemical action, moisture and heat, but without weaving, knitting, stitching, thermal bonding, or adhesives.

Fiber dyeing See *Stock dyeing.*

Fibrillation The creation of fibers or yarns by drawing a polymer sheet in the lengthwise direction so as to cause the sheet to split into a network of fibers (that may be formed into yarns).

Filament* Continuous fiber of indefinite length.

Filature A factory in which silk fibers are processed.

Filet An embroidered net, also known as *lacis.*

Filling* Yarn running from selvage to selvage at right angles to the warp in a woven fabric.

Fineness* A relative measure of size, diameter, linear density, or mass per unit length expressed in a variety of units.

Flexibility* That property of a material by virtue of which it may be flexed or bowed repeatedly without undergoing rupture.

Flock* A material obtained by reducing textile fibers to fragments, as by cutting, tearing, or grinding, to give various degrees of comminution [powdering].

Fulling In the processing of wool or animal hair fabrics, treatment with moisture, heat, soap, and pressure that causes yarns to shrink, lie closer together, and give the fabric a more dense structure.

Garnetting A process for recovering fibers from yarn or fabric by use of a garnett, a machine similar to a carding machine, which pulls the structure apart.

Generic name Names assigned by the Federal Trade Commission to the various types of manufactured fibers according to the chemical composition of the fiber-forming substance.

Gigging Brushing up of loose fibers onto the surface of a fabric made from staple yarns; a synonym for *napping.*

Glass transition* The reversible change in an amorphous polymer or in amorphous regions of a partially crystalline polymer from (or to) a viscous or rubbery condition to (or from) a hard and relatively brittle one.

Graft polymers* A copolymer in which polymeric side chains have been attached to the main chain of a polymer of different structure.

Greige goods* Textile fabrics that have received no bleaching, dyeing, or finishing treatment after being produced by any textile process.

Hackling A step in the processing of flax fibers that is comparable to combing.

Heat setting The treatment of thermoplastic manufactured fibers or fabrics with heat to set the fibers or fabrics into a specific shape or form.

Heat transfer printing A system of textile printing in which dyes are applied to a paper base and are then transferred from the paper to a fabric under heat and pressure.

Heddle A cord or wire eyelet through which warp yarns are passed on a loom.

High wet modulus The quality in a fiber that gives that fiber very good stability when wet.

Hydrophilic Term used to describe materials that have an affinity for water (literally, "water-loving").

Hydrophobic Term used to describe materials that have no affinity for water (literally, "water-hating").

Ikat A form of resist printing in which sections of warp yarns are made to resist dyes; a type of warp print. Dye is applied to the warp yarns, and filling yarns are inserted. The resultant patterns have an indistinct, shimmering pattern.

Kemp hairs Coarse, straight hairs in a wool fleece that do not absorb dye readily.

Lacis See *Filet.*

Latch needle A needle used in knitting machines that has a latch that opens and closes to hold the yarn on the needle.

Linters* The short fibrous material adhering to the cotton seed after the spinnable lint has been removed by ginning and that is subsequently recovered from the seed by a process called "delinting."

Loft The ability of fibers to return to their original thickness after being flattened or compressed.

Luster* That property of a textile material by virtue of which the latter exhibits differences in intensity of light reflected from within a given area of material when the angles of illumination or viewing are changed.

Macramé A technique for creating fabric by knotting yarns together.

Malimo See *Stitch-through.*

Man-made fibers See *Manufactured fibers.*

Manufactured fibers Fibers created through technology either from natural materials or from chemicals.

Matrix fiber A bicomponent fiber in which one polymer is dispersed throughout another polymer. See *Bicomponent fiber.*

Melt spinning The formation of manufactured textile fibers in which the polymer is melted for extrusion and hardened by cooling.

Mercerization* The process of subjecting a vegetable fiber to the action of a fairly concentrated aqueous solution of a strong base so as to produce great swelling with resultant changes in fine structure, dimensions, morphology, and mechanical properties.

Micrometer (μm)* One millionth of a meter, 0.001 mm.

Micron A measurement that is 1/1000th of a millimeter or 0.000039 of an inch. See *Micrometer.*

Mildew A fungus that grows on some fibers under conditions of heat and dampness.

Moiré A ribbed cloth that has a wavy, watermarked pattern on the surface.

Moisture regain* The amount of moisture in a material determined under prescribed conditions and expressed as a percentage of the weight of the moisture-free specimen.

Monofilament yarn* A single filament; also a single filament that can function as a yarn in commercial textile operations; that is, it must be strong and flexible enough to be knitted, woven, or braided.

Monomer* A relatively simple compound that can react to form a polymer.

Mordant Substance used in dyeing that reacts with both the dyestuff and the fiber to form an insoluble compound, thereby fixing the color within and on the fiber.

Multifilament yarn Yarn made from two or more, usually more, filament fibers.

Nap The "fuzzy" raised fibers that have been brushed up on the surface of a fabric.

Needlepoint lace Lace made by embroidering over other threads held in a pattern across a sheet of parchment.

Needle punching Fabric formation technique in which fabric is formed by the entangling that results when a series of needles are punched through a batt of fiber.

Netting A technique of creating fabric by looping and knotting a continuous strand of thread into an open mesh.

Novelty yarns Yarns made to create interesting decorative effects.

Oleophilic Term used to describe materials that have an affinity for oil (literally, "oil-loving").

Open-end spinning machine* A textile machine for converting staple fiber into spun yarn by a continuous process in which the individual fibers or groups of fibers are caused to assemble at the open end of the forming yarn.

Orientation (of molecules within a fiber) Arrangement of polymers in a position parallel to the length of the fiber.

OSHA Occupational Safety and Health Act.

Permanent finish A finish that will last for the lifetime of the fabric.

Picks Filling yarns.

Piece dyeing Dyeing of woven or knitted fabrics as opposed to dyeing of fibers or yarns.

Pigment* An insoluble compounding material used to impart color.

Pile (in pile fabric)* The raised loops or tufts (cut loops) that form all or part of the surface.

Pillow lace See *Bobbin lace.*

Pills* Bunched or balls of tangled fibers that are held to the surface of a fabric by one or more fibers.

Pirns Small metal pins around which yarns are wrapped. These pins are then inserted in a shuttle that carries the yarns across the fabric during weaving. Also called *quills.*

Plissé A puckered effect achieved on cotton fabrics by shrinking some areas of the fabric with sodium hydroxide.

Ply yarns* Yarn formed by twisting together two or more single yarns in one operation.

Polymer* A macromolecular material formed by the chemical combination of monomers having either the same or different chemical composition.

Polymerization The formation of polymers.

Progressive shrinkage Shrinkage that continues after the first laundering and/or dry cleaning through successive cleanings.

Pure dye silk Silk with less than 10 percent of weighting (or less than 15 percent if it is black in color).

Quills See *Pirns.*

Regenerated fibers Fibers produced from natural materials that cannot be used for textiles in their original form but that can, through chemical treatment and processing, be made into textile fibers.

Relaxation shrinkage Shrinkage that takes place during initial laundering and/or dry cleaning as a result of the relaxation of tensions applied to yarns or fabrics during manufacture.

Residual shrinkage Shrinkage remaining in a fabric after it has been preshrunk. Residual shrinkage is generally expressed as a percentage.

Resilience* That property of a material by virtue of which it is able to do work against restraining forces during return from a deformed state.

Resist printing The achieving of designs by causing sections of fabric to resist dye.

Retting The process of decomposing the woody stem and gums surrounding bast fibers to remove the fiber.

Ring spinning Method of spinning yarns from staple fibers in which the twist is imparted to the fibers by the concurrent movement of a spindle and a metal ring that moves around the spindle.

Roller printing The application of printed designs to fabrics by the use of engraved rollers over which the fabrics pass.

Roving* A loose assemblage of fibers drawn or rubbed into a single strand, with very little twist. In spun yarn systems, the product of the stage, or stages, just before spinning.

Sanforization A trademarked compressive shrinkage control process.

Schreiner finish A finish that improves luster of fabrics that is produced by passing steel rollers engraved with fine lines over the cloth to flatten and smooth the surface.

Scouring* A wet process of cleaning by chemical or mechanical means, or both.

Screen printing The application of printed design to fabrics by the use of screen coated with resist materials that permit dye to penetrate through the screen only in selected areas.

Scrim An open-weave fabric that is often used as a backing material.

Seed hair fibers Those fibers that grow around the seeds of certain plants, such as cotton or kapok.

Sericin The gum that holds silk filaments together in a cocoon.

Sericulture The cultivation of the silkworm for the production of silk fiber.

Shed The passageway between the warp yarns through which the shuttle is thrown in weaving.

Shuttle The device that carries the yarn across the loom, through the shed, in weaving.

Shuttleless machine Weaving machine in which the yarn is carried across the fabric by some means other than a shuttle. These machines may utilize jets of water, air, metal rapiers, metal grippers, or mechanical action.

SI* The International System of Units (abbreviation for "le Système International d'Unités") as defined by the General Conference on Weights and Measures (CGPM); based on seven base units, two supplementary units, and derived units, which together form a coherent system.

Simple yarn Yarn with uniform size and regular surface.

Singeing Treatment of woven fabrics with heat or flame to remove surface fibers from fabric to produce a smooth finish.

Sizing* A generic term for compounds which, when applied to yarn or fabric, form a more or less continuous solid film around the yarn and individual fibers.

Sliver* A continuous strand of loosely assembled fibers that is approximately uniform in cross-sectional area and without twist.

Solution dyeing Addition of color pigment to the liquid solution of manufactured fibers before the fiber is formed.

Specification* A precise statement of a set of requirements to be satisfied by a material, product, system, or service, indicating, whenever appropriate, the procedure by means of which it may be determined whether the specified requirements have been met.

Specific gravity* The ratio of the mass of a unit volume of a material at a stated temperature to the mass of the same volume of distilled water at the same temperature.

Spindle A long, slender stick used in spinning to provide the necessary twist to fibers being formed into a yarn. Spindles may be hand devices or part of a spinning wheel.

Spring beard needle A needle used in knitting machines that holds yarns on the needle by means of a springlike action of the flexible hook.

Spunbonding A fabric formation technique in which extruded fiber filaments are randomly arranged and bonded together by heat or chemical means.

Spunlace A fabric formation technique in which a fiber web is formed by air entanglement.

Standard* A reference used as a basis for compensation or calibration; also a concept that has been established by authority, custom, or agreement to serve as a model or rule in the measurement of quantity or the establishment of a practice or a procedure.

Staple fibers Fibers of short, noncontinuous lengths.

Stitch-through A fabric formation technique in which fibers or yarns are held together by stitching through the materials.

Stock dyeing Dyeing of fibers before they are made into yarns or fabrics.

Striations Lengthwise markings on the surface of the manufactured fibers when seen through a microscope.

Sublimation printing See *Heat transfer printing*.

Surfactant Organic chemicals, the active ingredient in synthetic detergents, that alter the properties of water and soil so that dirt can be removed.

Tapa Cloth made from bark.

Tapestry Woven designs, created on a tapestry loom.

Temporary finishes Those finishes that are removed through use and cleaning and must be renewed to be effective.

Tenacity* The tensile stress when expressed as force per unit linear density of the unstrained specimen; for example, grams per tex or grams-force per denier.

Tensile strength A measure of strength of textile fabrics.

Tentering Drying of wet fabrics after finishing or dyeing on a frame on which fabrics are stretched taut and flat.

Tex* A unit for expressing linear density, equal to the mass in grams of 1 km of yarn, filament, fiber, or other textile strand.

Textured fibers Fibers that have had some alteration of their surface texture.

TFPIA Textile Fiber Products Identification Act.

Thermoplastic* A material that will repeatedly soften when heated and harden when cooled.

Thread Yarn made for the purpose of sewing together sections of garments or other items.

Tow* (1) In bast fibers, the short fibers removed by hackling; (2) in manufactured fibers, a twistless multifilament strand suitable for conversion into staple fibers or sliver or for direct spinning into yarn.

Trademark name A distinctive name registered with the U.S. Patent and Trademark Office by a manufacturer to identify such goods as made or sold by that firm. Registration of trademark is necessary in defending the legal right to exclusive use of the term.

Triaxial weave A type of weaving in which three sets of yarns are utilized, with two sets of yarns moving in a diagonal direction to the third, rather than at right angles.

Tussah silk Silk fiber from wild silkworms.

Union dyeing The dyeing to the same color of two different fibers with different affinities for dye.

Wale* In knitted fabrics, a column of loops in successive courses. The column is parallel with the loop axes; in woven fabrics, one of a series of raised portions or ribs lying warpwise in the fabric.

Warp* The yarn running lengthwise in a woven fabric.

Warp knit A hand- or machine-made knit in which the loops interlace vertically.

Warp print A print in which the design is printed on the warp yarns before the filling yarns are interlaced. See *Ikat*.

Weft The crosswise direction of a woven fabric; the filling.

Weft knit A knit in which the loops interlace horizontally rather than vertically.

Wet spinning The formation of manufactured textile fibers in which the fibers are hardened by extruding the fibers into a chemical bath.

Wicking* Transmission of a gas or liquid along the fibers of the textile due to pressure differential or capillary action.

Woolen yarns* Yarn spun from wool fibers which have been carded but not combed or gilled.

Worsted yarns* Yarn spun from wool fibers which have been carded, and either gilled or combed, or both.

Yarn dyeing The dyeing of yarns before they are woven or knitted into fabrics.

SUMMARY OF REGULATORY LEGISLATION APPLIED TO TEXTILES

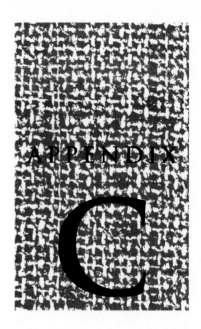

APPENDIX C

The following summarizes *briefly* the major pieces of legislation and/or regulations that apply to textile products. Fuller details are provided about each of these acts or rulings in the body of the text. Only those items of legislation that have an impact on consumers are included. Those that regulate the industry, such as OSHA, are not included.

Textile Fiber Products Identification Act

Passed 1960, Amended Subsequently

The TFPIA requires that each textile product carry a label listing the generic names of fibers from which it is made. These generic fiber categories are established by the Federal Trade Commission (FTC), which can add new generic categories as needed. At present there are twenty-one generic fiber categories for manufactured fibers, as well as the names for the natural fibers.

The listing of fibers is made in order of percentage by weight of fiber present in the product, with the largest amount listed first, the next largest second, and so on. Fiber quantities of less than 5 percent must be labeled as "other fiber" unless they serve a specific purpose in the product. Fibers that cannot be identified must be listed as "X percent of undetermined fiber content."

The law prohibits the use of misleading names that imply the presence of fiber not in the product. Labels must carry either the name, trademark, or registered identifica-

tion number of the manufacturer. All items covered under the law must be clearly and visibly labeled as to whether they are imported or produced in the United States. (For details, see chapter 2, pages 27–30.)

Wool Products Labeling Act

Passed 1939

This legislation regulates the labeling of sheep's wool and other animal hair fibers. The Wool Products Labeling Act requires that all wool products be labeled and the fibers, except for ornamentation, be identified as either new or recycled wool. The rules and regulations of the FTC established in relation to the act require that the terms *wool, new wool,* or *virgin wool* be applied only to wool that has never been used before. Recycled wool is either (1) wool that has never been used in any way by the ultimate consumer but has been spun into yarns or woven or knitted into cloth (these formed but unused pieces of yarns or fabrics are pulled apart and the fibers are reprocessed into fabrics) or (2) wool that has been used by consumers and is reclaimed by pulling the fabrics apart into fibers and spinning and weaving these fibers into other yarns and fabrics.

The law requires that the percentage of wool used in pile fabrics be identified as to the percentage of wool in the face and percentage of wool in the backing. The proportion of fiber used in face and backing must also be noted. Contents of padding, linings, or stuffings are designated separately from the face fabric of products, but must be listed with the same items noted. Items of wool must be clearly and visibly labeled as to whether they are imported or produced in the United States. (See chapter 5, pages 99–100.)

Fur Products Labeling Act

Passed 1951

This law requires that a fur product carries the true English name of the fur-bearing animal from which it comes and the name of the country of origin of the fur. (See chapter 5, page 13.)

Flammable Fabrics Act

Original Provisions Enacted in 1953

The original provisions of the act stated that wearing apparel (excluding hats, gloves, and footwear) and fabrics that are highly flammable may not be sold. Standards were established for testing to determine whether items were highly flammable. (See chapter 21, page 396, for discussion of the standard.)

Amendments to the Act, 1967

The scope of the act was broadened in 1967 to cover a wider range of clothing and interior furnishings. The act called for the establishment of standards for flammability for items covered by the act and banned from sale those carpets, mattresses, and items of children's sleepwear, sizes infant to 14, that do not meet the established standards. Some aspects of the standards have been revised periodically. (See chapter 21, page 397, for discussion of the standards.) Labels giving care instructions for children's sleepwear that is flame retardant must be placed so that they can be read at the point of purchase. These instructions must be permanently affixed to the garment. Some small carpets and one-of-a-kind carpets are exempt from the provisions of the act but must be labeled indicating that they do not meet the standard. The responsibility for administering and implementing the act was given to the Consumer Product Safety Commission. (See chapter 21 for full discussion of the legislation.)

Permanent-Care Labeling Ruling of the FTC

Established 1972

This ruling requires all wearing apparel and bolts of fabric sold by the yard to carry permanently affixed labels giving instructions for care. Exempt from the ruling are household textiles, retail items costing the consumer less than $3, footwear, head gear, and hand coverings, and all items that would be marred by affixing a label. The kind of information that must be provided is clearly specified. (See chapter 24 for complete description of provisions.)

FTC Ruling on the Weighting of Silk

Established 1938

No silk products containing more than 10 percent weighting except those colored black may carry a label saying that they are "silk" or "pure dye silk." Black silks can contain 15 percent of weighting. Fabrics not meeting these standards must be labeled as "weighted silk." (See chapter 5, pages 116–117.)

INDEX

517